Assessing & Guiding READING INSTRUCTION

Assessing & Guiding READING INSTRUCTION

Martha D. Collins
East Tennessee State University

Earl H. Cheek, Jr.
Louisiana State University and A&M College

The McGraw-Hill Companies, Inc.

New York St. Louis San Francisco Auckland Bogotá
Caracas Lisbon London Madrid Mexico Milan Montreal
New Delhi Paris San Juan Singapore Sydney Tokyo Toronto

McGraw-Hill Higher Education
A Division of The ***McGraw-Hill*** *Companies*

Assessing and Guiding **READING INSTRUCTION**

1 2 3 4 5 6 7 8 9 0 FGR FGR 9 0 9

ISBN 0-697-24140-8

Editor: Beth Kundert
Cover Design: Maggie Lytle
Printer/Binder: Quebecor Printing Fairfield

To Courtney and Collin, who have lived through three of the five editions.

In memory of our mothers, whose combined classroom experience exceeded seventy years of helping students communicate through writing, speaking, listening, and reading. We were two of those students.

To Courtney and Collin, who have lived through three of the five editions.

In memory of our mothers, whose combined classroom experience exceeded seventy years of helping students communicate through writing, speaking, listening, and reading. We were two of those students.

Contents

Assessing and Guiding Reading Instruction in Today's Classroom

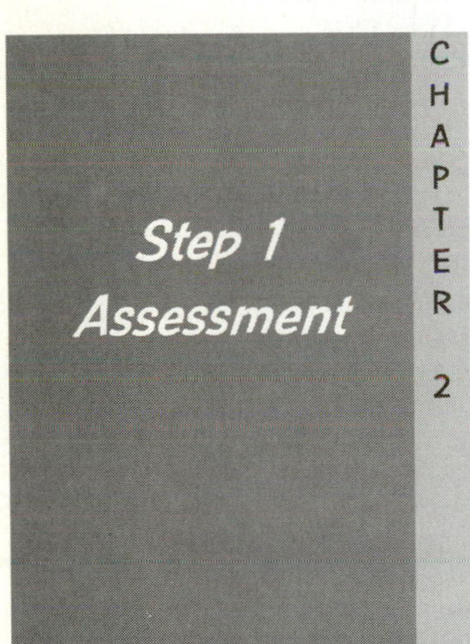

Informal Assessment Procedures

Formal Assessment Procedures

Step 2 Synthesizing Data

CHAPTER 4

Organizing Assessment Information

Step 3 Organizing the Classroom for Instruction

CHAPTER 5

Organizing for Effective Classroom Reading Instruction

Step 4 Guiding Reading Instruction

Chapter 6 Providing Appropriate Reading Instruction

Chapter 7 Emergent Literacy

Chapter 8 Word Identification

Chapter 9

Comprehension

Chapter 10

Study Skills and Strategies

Chapter 11

Personal Reading

Teaching Students with Special Needs

Step 5 Fitting the Parts Together

CHAPTER 13

Making It Work

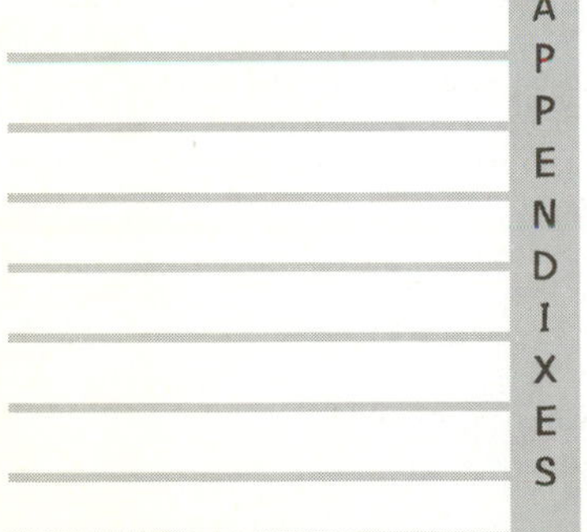

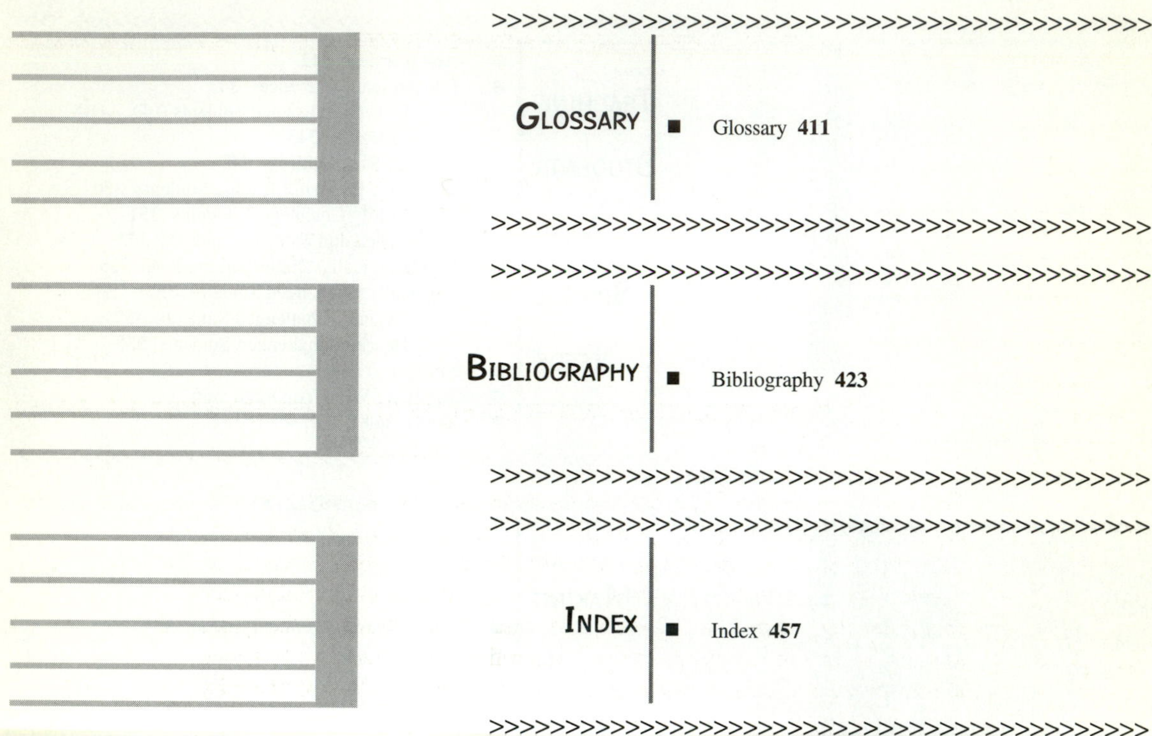

Glossary

Bibliography

Index

PREFACE

Through the years, reading instruction in elementary and secondary schools has changed significantly. The five editions of this text reflect these changes, with the first edition providing classroom teachers with information on developing a systematic procedure for assessing reading skill performance and providing appropriate prescriptive instruction. Through the years research in reading has presented new information about reading instruction, the importance of early learning in reading development, and the necessity for developing a positive attitude toward reading as a learning process. Likewise, students have changed. The first edition of this text in 1980 did not address the needs of teachers who were providing instruction to students who had significant skills in technology, who held the controls of a Nintendo game as comfortably as others had held soft toys in days past. With the wealth of new information and the changing student population in today's schools, each revised edition has incorporated new research to assist classroom teachers as they seek to incorporate these ideas into their world of practice.

In this edition, we emphasize student assessment rather than the more clinical concept of diagnosis. Likewise, the concept of guiding instruction, as opposed to prescribing instruction, is presented. With students today we know that few prescriptions can be generalized to instruct them. At best, we can identify ways to guide their learning and must remain cognizant of the need to continuously assess and adjust our strategies for instruction. We realize that teachers continue to be faced with the basal versus whole-language dilemma within the school system and in dealing with parents. As authors, we do not take a strong stand for either type of material. Rather, we promote the idea that in whole-language instruction skills must continue to be developed and that in basal instruction good literature must be included. Teachers should use an eclectic approach that works best for them and with individual learners. Our philosophy is that the answer to successful reading instruction does not reside in an either-or approach. Effective teachers must develop sound philosophies as they understand reading as a language process. Using this understanding, they can assess students in their classrooms through dialogue, observations, and formal and informal procedures to determine their strengths and needs in reading. These needs then help teachers to design the appropriate instructional activities for reading development.

The first chapter of this book addresses reading as a language process and establishes the basic conceptual framework for the text. The remainder of the book is organized around five steps that should be followed to provide effective reading instruction:

1. Assessment, or knowing about the student (Chapters 2 and 3)
2. Synthesizing data, or organizing what you know about the student (Chapter 4)
3. Organizing for instruction, or getting things together to teach (Chapter 5)
4. Guiding appropriate instruction, or teaching students based on their needs (Chapters 6–12)
5. Fitting the parts together, or reviewing what you're doing and making adjustments (Chapter 13)

Each chapter opens with a list of questions, which suggest its objectives, an introductory scenario, and vocabulary relevant to the chapter. All vocabulary words are defined within the chapter and in the glossary. The chapters close with a summary, exercises for applying the information in a classroom, and notes to sources. The appendixes include a list of reading skills, a list of informal reading inventories, a sample interest and attitude inventory, a sample observation checklist, a select bibliography of children's books, information on the construction of an informal reading inventory, and a sample interpretive report.

The fifth edition of this book addresses the importance of assessing and guiding reading through language literacy development. When we approach reading instruction as a part of the language process, we make language development and writing to reading the foundation of instruction. Each chapter gives an up-to-date survey of research related to the chapter topic. The many changes in each edition of this text are a result of our professional growth, experiences, and input of our students, colleagues, and their students. For this we are most appreciative, and we continue to invite comments as you use the current edition.

Special thanks is extended to Beth Kaufman, who assisted in the transition of this text from Brown & Benchmark to McGraw-Hill, and Linda Hensley, graduate assistant, who provided significant assistance in making these transitions. Because of you, there is a fifth edition.

Martha D. Collins
East Tennessee State University

Earl H. Cheek, Jr.
Louisiana State University
and A & M College

TORPEDO RUN!
CAROLINA
CAROLINA

CHAPTER 1

Assessing and Guiding Reading Instruction in Today's Classroom

The teachers at Twin Lakes School are concerned that the reading instruction being provided in their school is not meeting the individual needs of many students. Twin Lakes has a typical elementary school population with a mix of Caucasian, African American, Asian, Hispanic, and Native American students from many backgrounds that reflect a variety of multicultural experiences and perspectives. Some of the students arrive at kindergarten already reading, while others have had little exposure to books. Some students have had a range of experiences, including using computers in their homes, while others have had little more than sand lots for play. In addition to the ethnic diversity and different backgrounds of experience, students bring to the classroom a variety of special needs that must be accommodated.

The reading program at Twin Lakes was discussed in a meeting of the team chairpersons, and they decided to invite the principal to the next meeting to talk over the current program as well as alternatives for improving it. Between the meetings, the teachers met with other teachers, reviewed their professional literature, and conferred with some outside consultants. The one suggestion that continually surfaced as a concept worthy of further consideration was the need for immediate and continuous assessment of each student's strengths and weaknesses and for appropriate reading instruction to address those needs. As the crucial topic of assessment and providing appropriate instruction to each student was discussed in the meeting with the principal, the entire faculty soon realized that each of them had a different perception of assessment and how to provide appropriate reading instruction to each student. As these faculty discussions continued, a number of questions were developed for further exploration as teachers considered improving their school reading program by becoming more aware of the need to continuously assess their students' progress in order to provide appropriate instruction.

These questions, which arise in the mind of any teacher who is considering the importance of assessment in providing appropriate instruction, are addressed in this chapter. They should be reviewed and discussed before exploring the remainder of the book, which elaborates on the specific steps involved in providing appropriate reading instruction.

- How does reading relate to language?
- What is assessment?
- How does assessment relate to providing appropriate reading instruction to students?
- Who is involved in an effective reading program?
- What role do parents play in an effective reading program?
- How does the effective teacher establish an environment to facilitate reading development in the classroom?

Vocabulary to Know

- **Appropriate instruction**
- **Assessment**
- **Basals**
- **Comprehension**
- **Concepts**
- **Continuous assessment**
- **Effective instruction**
- **Individualized instruction**
- **Reading/language process**
- **Scope and sequence**
- **Study skills**
- **Teacher effectiveness**

READING AS A LANGUAGE PROCESS

Much research in reading focuses on the theory that reading is a process. Reading is defined as a process used to associate meaning with printed symbols in order to understand ideas conveyed by the writer. It is a process that requires the use of complex thought procedures to interpret printed symbols as meaningful units and comprehend them as thought units in order to understand a printed message. However, realizing that reading is a process does not tell teachers how to meet the variety of needs in today's classroom. Careful analysis of theory and research can provide information for developing sound instructional practices. To summarize the research at this time the following conclusions may be drawn:

- Reading is part of the language process.
- Diversity in student needs affects learning and requires continuous assessment.
- Appropriate instruction is necessary for cognitive development.

Reading instruction must interface with the language process, it must recognize that each student is different and that each student requires appropriate instruction geared to his or her background, strengths, and needs. To meet this challenge, teachers need to assess the levels of performance of each student, individual interests and attitudes toward reading, and provide appropriate instruction to accommodate the range of needs within a classroom setting.

The complexity of reading instruction intensifies when we consider the theoretical models of the reading process proposed by many researchers. These various theories and models of reading instruction range from Gray's taxonomic model to the linguistic models of Chomsky, Goodman, and Ruddell to Rosenblatt's transactional model.[1] While all of these models have had an impact on reading instruction, as Singer has suggested, a series of models is probably necessary to explain and predict reading performance.[2]

Realizing the diversity in today's classroom, teachers must note the existence of different models and approaches to reading instruction along with how these variations relate to their students. For example, in developing a better understanding of the reading process, researchers have given much attention to linguists, psycholinguists, and sociolinguists. Goodman's idea that reading is an interaction between thought and language whose major goal is meaning has led teachers to realize that a reader may not recognize every graphic cue. Indeed, errors in decoding can affect meaning; the good reader corrects these errors when they interfere with comprehension.[3] Errors that are dialectical and that do not interfere with understanding may not be corrected. Goodman suggests that a divergent dialect itself is not an obstacle in learning to read; the problem for the divergent-dialectic speaker is the rejection of the dialect by teachers.[4] An example of putting this theory into practice is the movement in Oakland, California, to treat the dialect of some African American students as a second language. Thus, their reading instruction is being approached from the perspective of a second-language learner.

The concept of reading as a language process has been further developed by other linguists, such as Frank Smith, who claim that the reader's past experiences, expectations about meaning, and word recognition strategies all come into play as the reader formulates meaning from the printed page. Thus, Smith believes that it is impossible to learn the sound of a word by building up from the sounds of letters. "Reading does not easily lend itself to compartmentalization," Smith states.[5] This statement summarizes a major emphasis of the linguist's concept of the reading process.

On the other hand, there are traditional views of the reading process, such as that of William S. Gray. Gray suggests that reading is a four-step process that includes the following:

1. *Word Perception.* The reader perceives the printed word.
2. *Comprehension.* The reader understands the meaning of the word as used in the context.
3. *Reaction.* The reader reacts to the idea presented by the writer based on the reader's feelings and past experiences.
4. *Integration.* The reader integrates the new ideas gained from reading into his or her personal perspective and applies the ideas to daily activities.[6]

Reading is a language process.

Photo courtesy of Edward B. Lasher.

Gray's view of the reading process describes the philosophy found in many skill-centered reading programs. This approach to reading instruction is described as a "bottom-up" process of instruction, meaning that reading begins with the printed symbol and moves to a level of understanding. As this process for reading instruction has been used through the years, teachers have noted that compartmentalized instruction is not the natural way students learn to read. The process is not appropriate for many students, especially the language-different student whose language and experiences are varied.

The reading process, however, involves much more than the development of skills to facilitate the perception or identification of words and understanding. Readers derive meaning from print based on their past experiences, language, and purpose in reading. Thus, the importance of language understanding and background experiences as aids in comprehension must be recognized. Writers transmit ideas and feelings using their backgrounds of experiences and their unique language style. To obtain meaning from these written words readers must call upon their own individual experiences and understanding of language. The extent to which the reader has the background knowledge to relate to the meaning that the writer is presenting determines the degree to which understanding will occur, and understanding is the most essential aspect of reading. Because student experiences are so varied, instructional adjustments must accommodate the learner.

Since language and experiences have come to be recognized as crucial to reading success, the "top-down" and interactive models of reading have become more accepted. Proponents of the top-down model such as Goodman and Ruddell suggest that reading is based on what the reader brings to the printed page. Reading is hypothesis testing that verifies the appropriateness of decoded words and meaning provided by text. The reader begins with an idea about the printed information and monitors her understanding.[7]

On a continuum between the bottom-up and top-down models of reading is the interactive model. Rummelhart's work has suggested that the reader and the text must work in concert to obtain meaning from print.[8] The reader combines his past experiences with new information from the text to gain an understanding of the printed page. While these varying models may seem more theoretical than practical, they are indeed very important in planning reading instruction. Literature-based reading programs tend to reflect the interactive model and build on the experiences of the student. The traditional basal program tends to be categorized as a bottom-up model, which builds from lower-level to higher-level skills. Some categorize the use of language experience as an example of top-down instruction.

While none of these approaches always fits neatly into one category, teachers need to note the global differences in philosophies as they study this text, think of implementing strategies in their classes, and consider their philosophical views about reading. The issue of the "best" philosophy for reading instruction is well summarized from a research perspective by Stanovich:

> Research on the reading process has been undertaken from a variety of perspectives. Too often progress in understanding reading is impeded when researchers working from different perspectives adopt a strong assumption of paradigm incompatibility: that a gain for one perspective is a loss for another. These *paradigm wars* in reading research mirror those that have taken place within the general educational research community during the last decade. It is argued that this assumption of paradigm incompatibility is false, and that progress toward a comprehensive understanding of the reading process would be hastened if we declared an end to the paradigm wars in the reading field and if investigators from all perspectives agreed to peaceful coexistence.[9]

In the discussion of the reading process, language is frequently mentioned as a significant factor in reading development. Reading research, classroom practices, and, indeed, the 1992 National Assessment of Educational Progress promote reading as a language process.[10] Speaking, writing, and listening are interrelated partners in the development of language literacy. As appropriate reading instruction is planned, the relationship of language to reading must be viewed as an integrated process.

Assessing and Guiding Instruction

The concept of assessing and guiding reading instruction has been implemented in classrooms for years. Programs range from testing and teaching isolated skills to placing students into different basal reading books to implementing a literature-based program using a vast array of trade books. With the increasing demands society is placing on schools to better prepare students to take their places in an increasingly more global economy, it is critical that the individual strengths and weaknesses of each student are identified through various assessment procedures and that instruction is based on this assessment.

Assessment involves observation of students' language behaviors when speaking, reading, listening, and writing; review of written work; and discussions with students and other teachers, supplemented as needed with appropriate informal and formal evaluation procedures. Appropriate instruction means that students are taught based on their interests and needs. This includes excellent readers with special needs to be further developed in language, whether it be vocabulary extension or expressing ideas in writing, as well as less able readers with many reading difficulties. Implementing the concepts inherent in assessing and guiding reading instruction requires faculty and administrative commitment in addition to an understanding of the reading process. In conjunction with this leadership, the following specific considerations are crucial.

- ***A scope and sequence of reading skills and knowledge expectations in listening, speaking, and writing***. Familiarity with a hierarchy of skills, known as a scope and sequence, is important for teachers wishing to create an effective reading program. While there is no one correct hierarchy in reading and students should not just progress through the skills list, teachers should be knowledgeable about the reading skills in order to incorporate skill development into the instructional program where appropriate. Likewise, teachers need to be knowledgeable about expectations of students in other areas of language development so that appropriate instruction can be planned. Knowing what the students are expected to learn in reading, writing, speaking, and listening encourages the integration of the areas for more effective instruction.
- ***Learning more about the student***. Assessment information, checklists of behavior, and information from others provide a profile of each student. However, this profile may be affected by mitigating factors such as home environment, stress, siblings, and comfort in the school environment. Teachers need to learn about each student to discover other important pieces of information.
- ***Procedures to facilitate continuous assessment of each student***. Obtaining useful assessment information from a variety of sources is another essential component of an effective instructional program. The teacher does not need to spend a great deal of time testing individual students, but plans must be developed to determine the various sources of information that will be monitored for each student. Chapters 2 and 3 present procedures for obtaining appropriate assessment, that is, through portfolios, observations, and tests.
- ***Providing appropriate instruction***. In an effective reading program, instruction is based on individual needs, although the instruction may be conducted one-on-one, in a small group, or in a class setting. Appropriate and effective instruction requires carefully planned teaching activities using a variety of strategies and materials to develop the language skills identified as important for each student.

Planning and organization are crucial elements in providing appropriate instruction. Chapter 5 gives specific ideas for organization. Chapters 6 through 12 contain suggestions for providing appropriate instruction. The concept of assessing and guiding instruction is based on meeting students' needs. Instruction must be carefully planned to fully utilize both student and teacher time.

- ***Procedures to monitor student progress***. As teachers learn more about students, the information they obtain should be recorded and maintained in some systematic manner. In some school systems, reading skill development is recorded using skill checklists. However, because reading development is more than skill development, other information is also monitored. What about interests in reading, writing, spelling, and speaking? Strengths or deficiencies in these areas are related to success in reading and are noted in the development of language literacy. Although making these records requires teacher time, they are essential components of the reading program that aid in guiding instruction, conferring with parents, and evaluating progress. Chapters 4 and 5 provide ideas on how record keeping can be managed by the classroom teacher.

The need for providing individualized reading instruction is obvious when one thinks of the diversity in a typical elementary classroom. Teachers and parents note that no two students in the classroom are exactly alike in their reading development. The teacher may locate six students reading near the same level, but each of these students has a different background of experiences along with specific needs and interests that must be met through appropriate instruction. As suggested earlier, the reading process is not a simple process but consists of many interrelated components that are integrated by the reader. Thus, readers react to print in different ways based on their abilities and experiences. When teachers understand that the process of reading is not an exact, step-by-step procedure followed in the same way by all students, they can better appreciate differences in learning. They will also realize that traditional organizational plans using one set of materials cannot be successful in teaching all students to read. The complex nature of reading as a language process itself shows the need for the concept of assessing and guiding reading instruction as a major part of literacy development. Figure 1.1 provides a model for assessing students' needs and providing appropriate instruction.

We can better illustrate the concept of assessing and providing appropriate reading instruction to students by examining two very different classrooms at Twin Lakes School.

Mr. Johnson has thirty-one students in the classroom. He has reviewed their records and has achievement test data on each one. At the beginning of the school year, Mr. Johnson organizes his class into three reading groups, and each group moves through the designated basal reader in a step-by-step procedure. The test at the end of each unit in the basal reader is given before going on to the next unit. Few changes are made in the three groups.

Figure 1.1 Model for Assessing and Guiding Reading Instruction

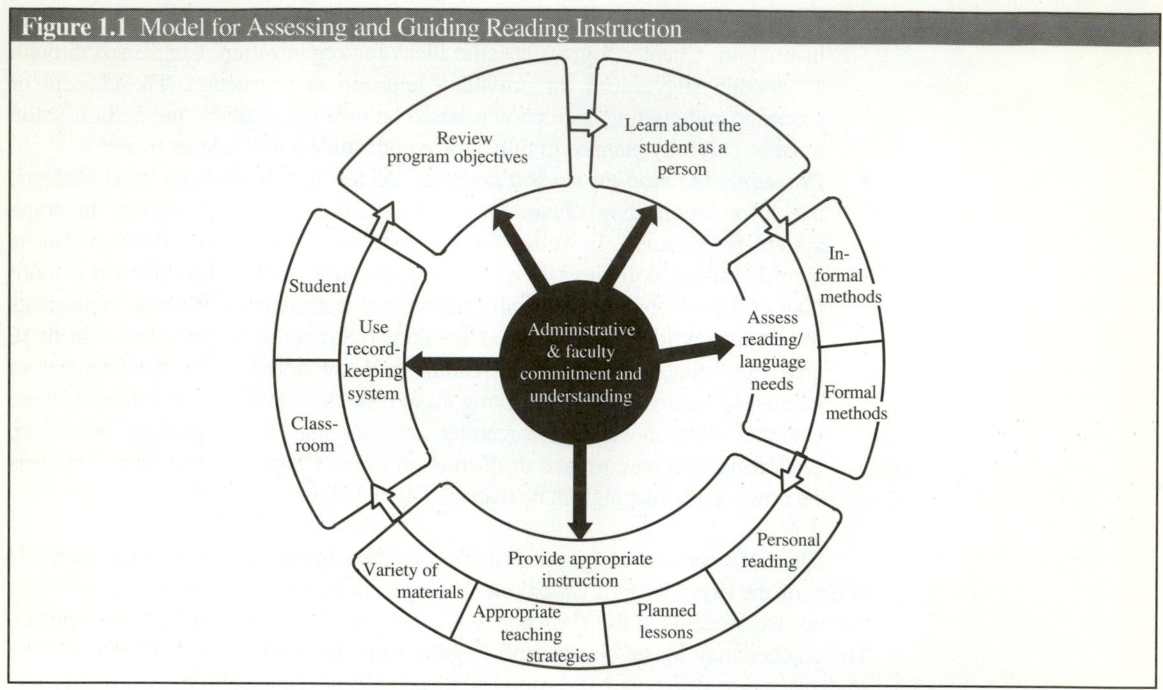

The teacher's manuals for the basal readers are the major teaching tools used by Mr. Johnson. He follows these guidebooks very closely and has never really considered the scope and sequence of reading skills to be developed in his classroom. To assist in managing his classroom, Mr. Johnson provides seatwork for the students to do during the reading class when they are not in the reading group. This seatwork consists of worksheets, randomly selected cards from a kit, board work, and workbook pages. In Mr. Johnson's class, most of the responsibility is on the teacher to provide for all of the student's activities.

Ms. Perez also has thirty-one students in her class. These students are organized into five basic groups, but they work in different skill and interest groups and individually, as necessary, to achieve predetermined objectives. The five reading groups are quite flexible; their composition changes as needs are assessed. Ms. Perez uses various assessment procedures, such as informal reading inventories, observation, worksheets, criterion-referenced tests, audiotapes of a student's reading, various checklists, journals, shared reading activities, and many other assessment procedures to evaluate the progress of each student. Before school opened, Ms. Perez met with other faculty members to determine the scope and sequence of skills being followed in the school. She felt that this was very important information, as she does not always follow the teacher's manuals for the basal series, and typically relies quite heavily on trade books to provide appropriate instruction to each student.

On one particular day, Ms. Perez was working with three students conducting a shared reading activity using a trade book that allowed them to read and express their ideas regarding a recent fire at a neighborhood store. In fact, Ms. Perez uses various approaches such as language experience and individualized reading, along with the basal and trade books, to better meet the students' needs. She provides direct instruction in reading for every student each day, either in groups or in a one-to-one situation.

As Ms. Perez works with one group or student, however, others in the class are involved in activities designed to develop their individual skills. For example, several students were involved in free reading and preparing for individual conferences with the teacher. Four students were at the listening center working on the skills of following oral directions and locating details in the selection. Other students were in the skills center working with activities designed to strengthen their dictionary skills. Two students were working together using various activities to improve their sight word vocabulary. Five students were involved with miscellaneous tasks including seatwork, manipulative games, and writing—all of which related to their specific, assessed needs.

In this classroom, a variety of materials and approaches are used in order to provide appropriate instruction. Ms. Perez feels that the additional time required to plan for such instruction is well spent. She feels that her students are more involved with their learning, since they know why they are expected to do the various assignments, and can become more self-directed during the school day.

The second classroom is quite different from the first one. The atmosphere is more student centered and the rate of learning is faster in Ms. Perez's class. Students are taught as individuals whose reading needs have been identified and for whom appropriate instruction is provided.

STAFF RESPONSIBILITIES FOR READING INSTRUCTION

The school reading program has traditionally required the involvement of all members of the school staff. Implementing an effective program necessitates greater communication among the faculty and a great deal of planning. It requires the involvement of support staff, such as the librarian; the guidance counselor; the school reading teacher; teachers of music, art, and physical education; and teachers in exceptional education. The school principal is the instructional leader in the school. The atmosphere of the school, cooperation among the faculty, the involvement of parents, and the general philosophy of the school depend to a great extent on the involvement of the principal. The focus of this section is on the various responsibilities of the teacher and on how other staff can support the teacher in assessing and providing appropriate instruction to students.

The teacher in the self-contained classroom has responsibility for a group of students who remain in the same classroom with that teacher for the entire school day. In this role, the teacher instructs all students in this classroom in all the subjects they will encounter for an entire school year. A teacher in a self-contained classroom must be an expert in many areas of instruction. This arrangement has definite advantages, especially for reading instruction. Plans for the integration of reading instruction with writing and speaking are easier to develop. Social studies and science become more than separate content areas as the teacher has the opportunity to integrate appropriate strategies for reading expository as well as narrative materials. An example of this is the thematic unit.

As teachers learn more about reading instruction, they realize that appropriate reading instruction relates to all students in all areas of the curriculum. Thus, a more systematic approach to evaluating reading/language learning is crucial for the self-contained classroom teacher. Teachers soon realize that systematic assessment involves the use of appropriate assessment procedures to evaluate the student's progress.

Teacher Responsibilities

The departmentalized classroom teacher has the responsibility for teaching a specific content area or areas to several classes of students during the school day. This teacher is responsible for teaching one or more subjects, such as social studies, science, or math, to all students in a particular grade level (or levels). Departmentalized classroom teachers are usually trained to teach a specific content area and may not fully understand their responsibility to integrate reading, writing, listening, and speaking into their content instruction. However, a content teacher teaches the application of language and literacy skills to content information to facilitate learning. The following sections describe specific difficulties teachers may encounter in teaching language skills, especially reading, in the content classroom.

Readiness for Learning

Readiness for learning is an important variable. Departmentalized teachers need to review information on child growth and development and then spend some time in a primary classroom to fully appreciate the concept of readiness for learning. First-grade teachers face a new group of squirming students each year. A few of these students already read, some will be ready to read in a few weeks or months, and others will require a year or more of early literacy work to develop language competencies before they are ready to read. The mental age of students in a typical first-grade class on the first day of school may range from three to eight years of age; thus, their individual needs must be met. At the end of the first grade, the range has probably increased, with the second-grade teacher finding a range of mental ages from about four to ten. Some students still may not be ready to begin formal reading instruction at the end of the first, second, or third grade. However, social and emotional factors do not permit these students to be held in the first grade for several years. Some students, therefore, reach the middle grades unable to read, write, or speak as they should; they enter school without the necessary prereading behaviors for academic learning and never catch up. Content teachers must realize how far their students advanced during the primary grades and help them continue to progress.

Individualized Instruction Is Essential for Learning in the Classroom

Teachers at both the elementary and middle-school levels not only have students who approach school with varying levels of readiness for learning, but these students have many different backgrounds, interests, and opportunities for the application of school information in their environments. This diversity affects their level of performance and their response to the learning environment. Instruction must be adjusted to meet these individual needs. While each student need not receive one-on-one instruction, small-group instruction along with large-group instruction and some one-to-one instruction is essential for meeting the many individual needs in all classrooms. If the individual learning needs of students are not met each year, students slowly fall further and further behind until they become so frustrated that no learning occurs. Teachers often find that students who cannot perform in the classroom cope with school by appearing not to care about learning. This is characteristic of students who have been frustrated to the point of rebelling or withdrawing from the situation. Content teachers face the challenge of attempting to motivate these students to learn again, sometimes about subjects that seem to have little relevancy to their lives.

Departmentalized content teachers also have students who are good readers and writers. These students are accepted as good students, and their success is enjoyed by all until the student becomes bored because of a lack of challenges and loses interest in school. Individualized instruction with these successful students allows them to participate in group activities that are more challenging and decreases the likelihood of problems. Meeting individual student needs is essential in motivating such students to learn in the classroom.

Content Reading Is Different from Reading a Trade Book or Basal

Changing from the narrative-type readers used in the elementary grades to the expository texts used in the upper elementary and middle-school levels can be difficult for many students. This transition begins in about the third or fourth grade and presents problems for both good and poor readers. Students in classes using a variety of materials for reading instruction, whose teachers use literature and thematic teaching to integrate content instruction and reading instruction, have less difficulty with this transition. Difficulties arise from the different format of textbooks, the application of reading and writing skills, the vocabulary load, and the many concepts presented.

Content materials also require the application of higher-level reading skills. In some reading classes, more emphasis is placed on literal comprehension skills, primarily recall of information, than on interpretive and critical reading skills.[11] However, in content material, the student uses the higher-level comprehension skills to understand what is being read. Comprehension and study skills at the inferential, interpretive, and application levels are emphasized in content materials. Unless great care is taken in using these materials, the stress on higher-level skills can create frustration and lead to a decrease in students' performance as well as a corresponding decline in their self-concept.

Coping with compact presentation is another challenge encountered by students studying content materials. Students may have difficulty understanding a selection because many new concepts and facts are presented in a very brief span of time, as compared with the typical narrative story found in many reading materials, which presents a few concepts or ideas. In addition, encountering a mass of unrelated facts in content reading poses further problems for students. Although the trend in content reading instruction is to teach students how to learn, rather than simply expect them to absorb new information, students are often faced with a barrage of unrelated facts from all content areas, whereas in basal readers they encounter a more limited number of concepts to be synthesized. This places severe stress on less able readers, who have difficulty learning even the limited information presented in the reading materials. For the student to function and progress at a satisfactory level, the content teacher must emphasize the learning process rather than the importance of learning facts.

Another major problem students encounter when reading content materials is understanding the many new words introduced. The vocabulary load suddenly becomes much greater as more new words are introduced over a shorter span of time. This is especially true in the beginning sections of content materials, where new vocabulary seems to fill every page. Again, in reading materials, the student may be accustomed to having fewer new words introduced and devoting time to discuss them. Although content teachers sometimes introduce new vocabulary in class, they may require students to become familiar with the words on their own. Teachers cannot assume that students will select the appropriate vocabulary necessary for learning; guidance from content teachers is needed when new vocabulary is being introduced.

Closely related to understanding new words is the problem of introducing technical and specialized vocabulary in each of the content areas. Many of these words may be familiar to the students, but the appropriate or precise meaning may not be clear and may need attention if students are to comprehend the material. While all teachers help students develop their vocabulary, each content teacher is responsible for the development and clarification of the specialized and technical vocabulary appropriate to the particular subject area.

Specialized vocabulary is vocabulary that changes in meaning from one content area to another. For example, the word mass refers to the quantity of some material in science but has a different meaning to a religious ceremony in literature. As a result of these various definitions, students need to be taught the special meaning of this word in its particular context. Technical vocabulary is vocabulary that is essential to the understanding of a specific subject or field. Since it relates to only one field, technical vocabulary is usually critical to the understanding of concepts in that field. An example of a technical vocabulary word is gene. For students to comprehend the concept of genetics, they must first understand the meaning of this word. A student's comprehension of content materials depends on understanding the meaning of content-specific words.

Comprehending the numerous concepts presented is another difficulty in reading content materials. So many new concepts are introduced in a short span of time that students often experience frustration. Content teachers must understand the need to adjust instruction so that students with reading problems and limited experiences have the opportunity to learn the concepts being introduced. Unless they grasp the introductory concepts, students may become totally lost as the year progresses, because many concepts within the content areas build on one another. The less able reader needs more time and adjusted instruction in order to fully understand the basic concepts being introduced. Without these basic concepts, such students have little chance for success in the content areas and are sometimes regarded as nonlearners. At this point, frustration mounts and the self-image becomes more negative, increasing the likelihood that these students will become dysfunctional readers.

Reading in a variety of sources may cause difficulty for students who previously worked with only one book at a time. At the upper levels in the content areas, students are encouraged to supplement their textbook reading with information from outside sources, and they are expected to use many sources in their quest for information on specific topics. They often have to switch from one type of material to another and may be unfamiliar with the use and format of these other resources. In addition, some types of materials are inherently more difficult to read, so less able readers may be unable to use them. Poor readers cannot be expected to work with some types of sources as efficiently as good readers.

The readability level of the content material itself often causes the less able and average reader great difficulty. In the content areas, only one book is usually available for each grade level; and these texts are frequently two or more grade levels higher in readability than they purport to be.[12] Thus, content teachers need to locate various texts and library books on different reading levels (See Figure 1.2).

Students need to understand that all content learning is similar. For example, although each content area has its own technical and specialized vocabulary, the methods for learning this vocabulary are the same. In a similar fashion, inferential comprehension is the same in all content areas; the same method of inference used in learning one subject can also be used in learning another. Content teachers working together to stress the similarity of learning methods in all content areas will benefit the students and offset many inconveniences experienced by the teachers.

The integration of reading and language instruction with the content areas greatly assists all students in understanding content materials. Many departmentalized content teachers integrate these areas into their total instructional program, realizing the importance of integrated learning experiences. Noting which language or reading skills are needed to read the content materials allows teachers to adjust their instruction to meet the individual needs of each student. The less able readers then have a reasonable chance for success, while the better readers will be challenged in their learning experiences.

Figure 1.2 Factors Contributing to the Difficulty of Content Reading

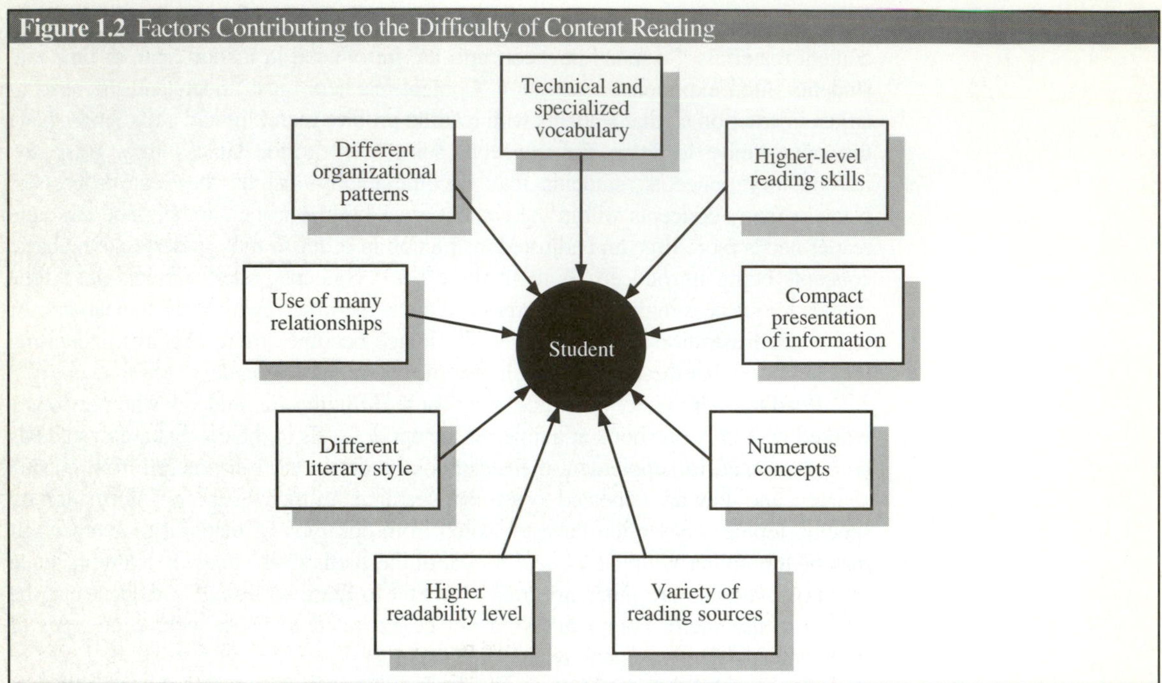

Responsibilities of Other Staff

Self-contained and departmentalized teachers are primarily responsible for the direct instruction of students in their classes. However, this instructional process is facilitated as others on the school faculty become part of this process. As suggested earlier, the principal is the key to a successful reading program. The principal forms the foundation for a successful reading program by understanding the reading process and the concepts of providing appropriate and effective instruction, providing necessary staff time for planning, locating materials for instruction, supporting the faculty as they face the initial frustrations of change, and helping parents and students understand the changes occurring in the reading program. An enthusiastic principal with a positive attitude toward the program evokes a positive response from teachers, students, and parents.

The school media specialist or librarian also has an essential role in an effective reading program. Media specialists have at their disposal an extensive collection of reading materials that are essential to motivate students to read and that add to the instructional program. Sharing these materials with the students through book reviews, storytelling, creative dramatics, and displays makes them aware of the wealth of information found in books. The media specialist reinforces the development of reading by helping the students to apply their knowledge in reading as they read for enjoyment and to locate information for their various classes.

The role of the school reading teacher varies, depending on the job description provided for the position. In some schools this person is a resource teacher who works in the classroom helping teachers to meet their students' reading needs. In this capacity, the reading teacher helps the classroom teacher to develop assessment skills, such as observation and informal testing, and also provides ideas for appropriate and effective reading instruction. In other schools, this person may have the role of a special reading teacher who works only with the less able readers. In this capacity, the reading teacher must coordinate instruction with the classroom teacher. The reading teacher always works with the classroom teacher in assessing and providing appropriate instruction regardless of the specific role of the reading teacher.

Music, art, and physical education teachers are also members of the reading program team. These persons work with the classroom teacher to identify students with specific reading deficiencies and assist with providing appropriate instruction in their related areas. For example, the music program can be a great help to the student with poor auditory skills by providing instruction in the identification of various instruments by their sounds. The art teacher can design instruction to help younger students develop their tactile senses and visual perception. The physical education teacher can work with the classroom teacher to design specific exercises to develop in young students the necessary motor skills, such as eye-hand coordination. With older students, the physical education teacher can often recommend books, activities, or assignments and elicit a more positive response than the classroom teacher. Together with the classroom teacher, these special-area teachers can develop student interests that enhance reading.

Teachers in exceptional education may have self-contained classes of students at either extreme of the mental ability scale, or they may serve as resource teachers to students included in regular classes. The exceptional education teacher may provide assistance in the reading program by helping the classroom teacher assess specific needs but can assist more significantly in planning appropriate instruction. Students with handicaps such as hearing and vision impairments need additional teaching assistance to develop their reading abilities. The exceptional education teacher, like the reading instructor, must continuously coordinate with the classroom teacher to provide the most appropriate instruction for these learners.

Guidance counselors at all levels have a major responsibility in the reading program. While they do not necessarily deal with direct instruction in the classroom, they can support the teacher in providing reading instruction. The responsibilities of counselors include helping students develop a positive attitude toward school and reading, helping individual students develop a positive self-concept, helping the teacher investigate personal problems that may be impeding learning, promoting communication among the faculty, and aiding in parent-teacher conferences to communicate the student's strengths and weaknesses as identified in the program.

To provide appropriate instruction for all students, teachers may find that the services of noninstructional school personnel are necessary. The school nurse can help with students suspected of having physical problems that are health related, such as poor nutrition or diseases. The nurse can also help diagnose vision and hearing problems that so frequently affect learning. The physical well-being of the student is certainly a major concern since poor health often hinders learning.

The school psychologist provides assistance in evaluating students suspected of having learning problems. Referrals to the school psychologist can bring assistance through observation of behaviors, testing, and recommendations for changes in the instructional program.

As these descriptions suggest, everyone in the school is involved in an effective reading program. Teamwork is essential. The entire staff continuously shares their observations and collaborates in designing all areas of the curriculum to enhance students' learning. The leadership of the principal and collaboration of the faculty are all parts of a complex puzzle that, when put together, will create a program that produces students who can read and who enjoy reading (see Figure 1.3).

PARENTAL INVOLVEMENT IN READING AND LANGUAGE DEVELOPMENT

Parents are an essential element in language development and likewise in an effective reading program. Parental involvement in learning is the topic of many articles and texts, which all emphasize its importance, and one that will be discussed repeatedly throughout this book. Educators tend to identify parental contributions as activities or duties that parents perform in the school, such as serving as volunteers or classroom aides and attending parent-teacher organization meetings. While these are important activities, parental involvement in the language process begins before students come to school and continues with many activities outside the school environment. Parents are the child's first teachers. Not only are they role models for their child, but parents establish the home literacy environment, an environment that supports or discourages literacy learning.

The literary-rich home is "reader friendly" with books for children throughout the house. The children visit the library on a regular basis and are aware of the many different forms of print in their environment, such as the telephone book, catalogs, newspapers, cookbooks, and their own mail, including the abundance of advertisements and other junk mail received each day. Writing is encouraged and modeled as lists are made, bills paid, and letters mailed to friends. Children in the literacy-rich home assist in sending birthday invitations, making cards, and writing thank-you notes for gifts (using pictures, invented spelling, or the computer). They have a variety of writing tools: paper in all shapes and colors along with crayons, pencils, pens, markers, and paints. Reading and writing are viewed as important forms of communication with others.

In the literary-rich home, children are read to on a regular basis and allowed to experiment with language through conversation, asking questions, doing pretend reading with pictures and story memory; they also write using invented spelling and pictures. As parents encourage children to play with language, children become free to use a variety of means to communicate and realize the benefits of communication with others. Developing a positive attitude about language is very important in preparing children for school. However, parental involvement in language learning must continue after the child is in school. Parents can encourage reading and writing activities in their children by sharing information with them about reading and writing in their adult world.

Figure 1.3 Roles in Assessing and Guiding Reading Instruction

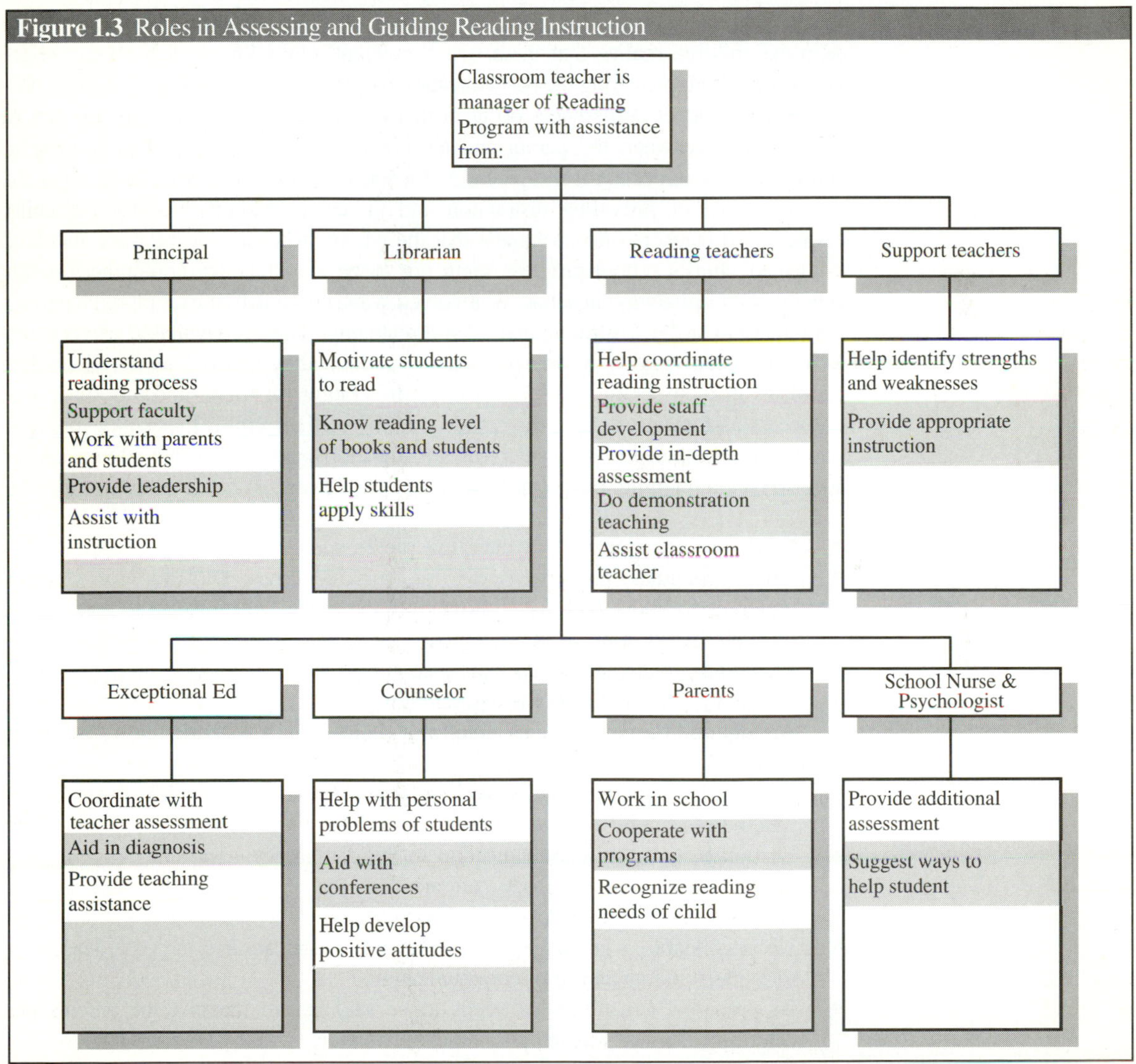

Parents are also involved with school activities. A parent may serve as a school volunteer or a guest resource person, visit the class to share a story with children on a periodic basis, attend an open house, or work on a school committee. Parents and teachers must communicate through conferences, phone conversations, and notes; the more face-to-face discussions the better. Teachers get to know the parents while parents gain a new understanding of their child. Communication between parents and teachers needs to be honest, open, and frequent to avoid misunderstandings and to help the children realize that these two significant adults know each other and are concerned about providing the best educational opportunities for them.

Parent-teacher conferences occur in many ways. At the beginning of the school year, contact between the parent and teacher is needed. A phone call or note of introduction is important if the parent and teacher are unable to meet to discuss the common goal of providing instruction and guidance that are best for the child. Experienced teachers often comment that the parents who need to be more involved with their child's school progress seem not to be available for conferences, while other parents are always at school or involved with school activities. For some parents conferences can be frustrating and even threatening. These unavailable parents may know that their child is having problems in school; they themselves may have had problems in their school years; school was frustrating for them, and this frustration reappears as they hear about the "inadequacies" of their child. Especially for these parents, teachers need to consider ways to develop parent-teacher conferences that focus on team building. Berger provides a few basic tips:

- Send notes to parents asking their time preferences.
- Offer schedules for conferences at varying times allowing for parental preferences. Phone calls as a follow-up to the invitation can serve to confirm the time, clarify questions, and welcome parents.
- Provide a private and comfortable meeting place that is away from the children, and post a note on the door to avoid interruptions.
- Arrange the furniture so that tables and chairs do not separate the teacher from the parent.
- Have samples of the child's work so that references to specific strengths and weaknesses can be discussed.
- Encourage two-way communication in the conference—warmth, an attitude of caring, smiling, and empathy are needed; the ability to listen and respond develops a sense of respect.
- Understandable language is essential. Education jargon leads to misunderstanding and stops communication.
- Be prepared. Practice what needs to be said before meeting the parents and determine the best way to present the information.
- Organize the information to make efficient use of parent and teacher time.[13]

Parental involvement is an essential part of an effective program. Teachers need opportunities to share their knowledge of the child with parents, while parents provide related information from a different perspective. This type of communication is an essential component that serves as the basis for a successful reading program.

SCHOOL AND CLASS ENVIRONMENT FOR EFFECTIVE READING INSTRUCTION

Teachers, like children, approach tasks positively or negatively depending on the environment, or school climate. Positive school climates encourage risk taking, while negative environments foster the status quo or doubtful behavior in learning and attitudes for students and teachers. Language literacy, especially reading, requires risk taking with printed words in a safe environment. This environment presents opportunities for literacy development if activities are functional, relevant, and meaningful for individuals and relate to their own social purposes and goals.[14] As Shirley Brice Heath so wonderfully describes in *Ways with Words*, as children learn to use language, they exhibit many differences, in differences in acquiring the formal structure of language, and they need much more than parent-child interaction to learn to use language.[15] Language socialization in the home and school requires appropriate environments to develop positive feelings about speaking, listening, reading, and writing. Teachers help parents understand the importance of environment for learning in the home and have a major responsibility in establishing the school environment. But what is the appropriate school environment for effective reading instruction?

From the wealth of research with at-risk and disadvantaged learners, many beliefs about appropriate instructional procedures have changed. These changed beliefs have significantly affected the classroom environment as philosophies and instructional activities have been adjusted. The first report by the Study of Academic Instruction for Disadvantaged Students suggests the following alternatives for improving conventional practice.

- An emphasis on the knowledge students bring to school.
- Explicit teaching of how to function in the "culture" of the school.
- Early emphasis on appropriate "higher order" tasks.
- Extensive opportunities to learn and apply skills in context.
- A combination of teacher-directed and learner-directed instruction.
- Variation in classroom management approaches depending on the kind of academic work being done.
- Some use of grouping arrangements that mix ability levels.
- More flexibility in grouping arrangements.[16]

Environmentally speaking, this translates into a classroom that is rich, stimulating, and interactive with purposeful print and language activities. Teachers encourage learning in a natural, noncompetitive, risk-taking setting. The literate classroom environment has a physical arrangement that encourages student dialogue, an instructional curriculum consisting of literacy activities rich with quality literature and writing opportunities, and an organizational arrangement that facilitates meeting individual student needs.[17]

Effective reading instruction exists within this type of environment. Assessment through ongoing observation, dialogue, and evaluation with students provides the basis for effective instruction using appropriate literacy activities and grouping students to learn from one another and the teacher. Meeting the variety of learning needs helps create an environment that facilitates diversity and encourages relevancy for learning. Language literacy thrives as students experience enjoyment and success in the world of print.

THE EFFECTIVE TEACHER

Program characteristics, parental involvement, positive classroom environments, and an appropriate philosophy for effective reading instruction are all part of a high-quality language literacy curriculum. However, the crucial element of the instructional program is the effective teacher. While much research over the years has worked to identify the most significant role of the classroom teacher, researchers in the last decade have focused on identifying the main characteristics of the effective teacher. Duffy and Roehler suggest that the effective teacher is an instructional decision maker who demonstrates the following characteristics:

- Effective teachers think in terms of what students must learn, rather than the tasks to be completed.
- They view reading broadly rather than as a series of skills or a discrete subject.
- These teachers understand the motivational aspect of learning to read—liking to read is as important as learning to read.
- Effective teachers emphasize cognitive processing and awareness, rather than rote memory and accurate answers.
- These effective teachers are not dependent on basal texts, viewing them as tools rather than as an instructional imperative.
- They recognize the teacher's guide as initial suggestions for tasks and activities to be expanded and explained—as teachers they must show students *how* to do a task and apply a concept appropriately.
- Effective teachers understand the complexity of reading instruction and do not look for a panacea. "The answer" for solving the complexities of reading instruction, classrooms, and students and teachers is as evasive as gold at the end of the rainbow.
- In the classrooms of effective teachers, change is always occurring. As their professional knowledge grows, they are continuously thinking, changing, modifying, and innovating—ways to improve are always experimentations.[18]

Related to the characteristics of the effective teacher proposed by Duffy and Roehler are the findings of Guzzetti and Marzano, which indicate that the teacher's beliefs and perceptions about themselves, students, and teaching in general are as important as their instructional practices. These beliefs are manifested in three areas that appear to be strongly related to student achievement: (a) high expectations on the part of the teachers toward the success of their students, (b) a belief in the basics, and (c) dissatisfaction with the status quo, which translate into constructive behavior as teachers alleviate dissatisfaction by implementing new and more effective instructional programs.[19]

Other factors that appear to assume major roles in providing effective reading instruction are organization, time on task, engagement, peer interactions, and type of instruction. Organizational ability is a trait that is highly regarded by both students and peers. Teachers who are well organized are not only highly regarded by their students but also appear to be more effective teachers than disorganized teachers.[20] Perhaps the primary characteristics exhibited by organized teachers are the ability to plan effectively and being well prepared to teach the lesson.[21]

One of the variables that consistently has a direct impact on effective instruction is time on task. Rosenshine and Berliner found that students who spend more time on tasks directly related to the teacher's objective will learn more of the content of a lesson than those spending less time on the content presented in the lesson.[22] Clearly, both research and personal experience indicate that more time spent on a task results in higher student achievement. Thus, it is important for teachers to plan instructional activities to facilitate on-task behavior. Student engagement in literacy acquisition has been emphasized in a number of studies of effective teaching. Guthrie suggests that teachers must provide an environment that promotes student engagement and motivates students to want to read and become more involved in the learning process.[23] Another advocate of student engagement is Cambourne, who believes that this occurs when learners are convinced that they can perform the demonstrations they are observing, that they have a purpose pertinent to their lives, and that they can attempt to emulate these demonstrations without risk of physical or psychological injury if they are unsuccessful.[24]

Another important factor to consider in providing effective instruction is peer interaction. Research indicates that students are aware of their ability in the reading class in relation to other students. Rosenholtz believes that interaction is directly related to the student's perceived ability in the reading class.[25] Students who perceive themselves as good readers will interact more, while those students who perceive themselves as poor readers will interact less. This status characteristic is a process that students use to make decisions about how bright other students are in relation to themselves. In addition, Cohen found that group work is affected in a similar manner.[26] Group members who perceived other group members as better readers were less likely to participate in group work. For these reasons, a variety of language activities are needed using flexible grouping procedures.

These research findings are particularly important to teachers of reading since student interaction is an important aspect of an effective program. Without sufficient student participation in the reading process, it is difficult to determine a student's progress or to provide instruction appropriate to that student's needs. Students with lower self-concepts are encouraged to interact more in class through literature and language activities that emphasize oral abilities, dramatization, artwork, and discussion. Success in these activities improves the student's perceived status in the reading class, thus ensuring a more successful transition to reading print.

A final factor of considerable importance in the examination of effective teaching is the type of instruction provided in reading classes. One model of teaching reading that has gained support is the direct instruction model.[27] Direct instruction is predicated on the mastery of skills keyed to specific objectives. It features such principles as immediate feedback, a structured learning environment, and repetition and reinforcement. Direct instruction has gained widespread popularity in recent years because of its apparent success in teaching students basic reading skills. Others believe that the direct instruction model focuses too much on skill development and should be tempered by more holistic approaches emphasizing language development and social interaction. This lack of a consensus may be confusing to teachers; however, it is safe to assume that a teaching model emphasizing the more effective aspects of direct instruction and the holistic approaches will result in positive student gains in reading.

The effective teacher of reading understands the nature of reading and views reading as a language process. Effective teachers are knowledgeable and use their knowledge to be decision makers as they exercise control in the learning environment. They expect their students to be successful and provide opportunities for students to see their success as they enjoy experimenting with language. These teachers help students learn what reading is all about and how it works in relation to their world. Effective teachers are dedicated to knowing the needs of their students and providing appropriate instructional activities to expand their strengths as they overcome their weaknesses. Teacher's guides and tests do not dictate the curriculum for the effective teacher; the needs and motivation of the students are the challenges of these knowledgeable teachers.

There has been considerable discussion in recent years regarding the future of reading instruction and the possibilities for change in our school systems to increase the likelihood that real learning will occur. During this period of debate, innumerable suggestions and recommendations have been made, but one of the more logical positions has been formulated by Richard Allington. Allington suggests that we might begin by reemphasizing the importance of the classroom teacher and classroom lessons in developing literacy in all children.[28] We should consider reorganizing the school day and week to bring our schools more in line with current lifestyles. Another step in this process would involve replacing the broad curriculum of today with a deep curriculum that develops greater levels of integrated understanding of far fewer topics. A fourth step would be to replenish the classroom and the classroom teacher by providing more materials and equipment for instruction and supporting professional development activities for all teachers. The final step, which is particularly important, would reformulate the way students' learning is evaluated. There would be less emphasis on standardized test results and more emphasis on alternative methods of evaluation such as portfolios, student self-evaluation, and student-teacher collaborative evaluations.

We believe that a reexamination of the state of reading instruction is long overdue. It is now time to make some critical decisions for the sake of our children and our schools. We invite you, whether a beginning or experienced teacher, to learn to put student needs first in your instructional program.

SUMMARY

Speaking, listening, reading, and writing are integrated parts of the language learning process. This process begins with young children and parents as literacy emerges; talking, listening, reading together, and experimenting with writing are essential in the developmental process. Parents are the first teachers.

As children enter school, their backgrounds of experience and home learning environment are the most important predictors of success in academic activities. While parents must stay involved in the learning process, the teacher becomes another significant model in providing an appropriate learning environment and effective instruction. The effective teacher is a good classroom manager and a knowledgeable decision maker. This teacher recognizes the strengths and weaknesses of each student to facilitate positive cognitive social and emotional growth opportunities. This teacher also has a philosophy about reading instruction that underlies the learning experiences provided and accommodates the needs of the students. Providing appropriate and effective reading instruction is the overriding aim. Effective reading instruction requires administrative and faculty commitment and understanding of the learning process. Specifically, providing appropriate and effective instruction in reading means that the individual strengths and weaknesses of each student are identified through various assessment procedures and then instruction is based on that assessment. Elements of an effective instructional program include:

- Familiarity with reading skills and knowledge expectations in listening, speaking, and writing to guide teachers as they plan for students.
- Procedures to facilitate continuous assessment of each student using informal and formal assessment strategies.
- Use of a variety of materials and teaching techniques to meet individual student needs and encourage the use of the reading/language process for enjoyment and learning.
- Planned lesson procedures to make maximum use of student and teacher time as the individual needs of students are met in the instructional program.
- Methods for keeping records on each student such as checklists, portfolios, and files.

Each faculty member is involved in the implementation of an effective reading program. Additionally, the administration provides the leadership and helps parents better understand the program. An effective reading program requires teamwork to develop better readers who are able to function in a complex society.

Applying What You Read

1. The principal in your school has asked that you lead a discussion on the involvement of the faculty in an effective reading program. Outline your ideas.
2. Some teachers in your school use basal materials, while others promote the concept of whole-language instruction in their reading program. How does your instruction relate to these philosophies?
3. Compare the reading program in the elementary or middle school that you attended or last observed with the effective reading program described in this chapter.
4. In your present or future role as a content teacher, reading specialist, or administrator, how do you see the reading/language process relating to content instruction?
5. Select several basal readers and compare them with content textbooks used in your school.
6. Continuous assessment is a crucial component of an effective reading program. What is continuous assessment? Why is it so important? Is continuous assessment actively pursued in your classroom or school? How?

NOTES

1. William S. Gray, "Reading and Physiology and Psychology of Reading," *Encyclopedia of Educational Research*; edited by E. W. Harris; Noam Chomsky, *Language and Mind*; Kenneth S. Goodman, "Behind the Eye: What Happens in Reading," in *Theoretical Models and Processes in Reading*, 2nd ed., edited by Harry Singer and Robert Ruddell; Robert B. Ruddell, *Reading-Language Instruction: Innovative Practices*; Louise M. Rosenblatt, "Towards a Transactional Theory of Reading," *Journal of Reading Behavior*.
2. Harry Singer, "Theoretical Models of Reading," *Journal of Communications*.
3. Goodman, "Behind the Eye," p. 5.
4. Kenneth S. Goodman and Catherine Buck, "Dialect Barriers to Comprehension Revisited," *The Reading Teacher*.
5. Frank Smith, *Understanding Reading: A Psycholinguistic Analysis of Reading and Learning to Read*, p. 8.
6. William S. Gray, *On Their Own in Reading*, pp. 35–37.
7. Kenneth S. Goodman, "Unity in Reading," *Theoretical Models and Processes of Reading*, 3rd ed., edited by Harry Singer and Robert Ruddell.
8. David Rummelhart, *Toward an Interactive Model of Reading*.
9. Keith E. Stanovich, "A Call for an End to the Paradigm Wars in Reading Research," *Journal of Reading Behavior*.
10. Robert Rothman, "NEAP Board Adopts Blueprint for 1992 Reading Test," *Education Week*.
11. Frank Guszak, "Teacher Questioning and Reading," *The Reading Teacher*.
12. Barbara K. Clarke, *A Study of the Relationship between Eighth Grade Students' Reading Ability and Their Social Studies and Science Textbooks*.
13. Eugenia H. Berger, *Parents as Partners in Education*, 3rd ed.
14. Bambi B. Schieffelin and Marilyn Cochran-Smith, "Learning to Read Culturally: Literacy Before Schooling," in *Awakening Literacy*, edited by H. Goelman, A. A. Oberg, and F. Smith.
15. Shirley Brice Heath, *Ways with Words*.
16. Michael S. Knapp and Brenda J. Turnbull, "Better Schooling for the Children of Poverty: Alternatives to Conventional Wisdom," *Study of Academic Instruction for Disadvantaged Students*, Vol. 1.
17. Jeanne B. DeGrella, "Creating a Literate Classroom Environment," *Resources in Education*.

18. G. G. Duffy and L. R. Roehler, *Improving Classroom Reading Instruction: A Decision-Making Approach*, 2nd ed.
19. Barbara J. Guzzetti and Robert J. Mazano, "Correlates of Effective Reading Instruction," *The Reading Teacher*.
20. M. Trika Smith-Burke, "Classroom Practices and Classroom Interaction during Reading Instruction: What's Going On," *The Dynamics of Language Learning*, edited by James R. Squire.
21. Donald J. Leu, Jr., and Charles K. Kinzer, *Effective Reading Instruction in the Elementary Grades.*
22. Barak V. Rosenshine and David C. Berliner, "Academic Engaged Time," *British Journal of Teacher Education*.
23. John T. Guthrie, "Educational Contexts for Engagement in Literacy," *The Reading Teacher*.
24. Brian Cambourne, "Toward Educationally Relevant Theory of Literacy Learning: Twenty Years of Inquiry," *The Reading Teacher*.
25. S. J. Rosenholtz, "Modifying a Status-Organizing Process of the Traditional Classroom," in *Pure and Applied Studies in Expectation States Theory*, edited by J. Berger and M. Zelditch, Jr.
26. Elizabeth G. Cohen, "Expectation States and Interracial Interaction in School Settings," in *Annual Review of Sociology*, edited by R. H. Turner and J. F. Short.
27. Fran Lehr, "Direct Instruction in Reading," *The Reading Teacher*, James F. Baumann, "Teaching Third-Grade Students to Comprehend Anaphoric Relationships: The Application of a Direct Instruction Model," *Reading Research Quarterly*.
28. Richard L. Allington, "The Schools We Have. The Schools We Need," *The Reading Teacher*.

STEP 1 ASSESSMENT

Step 1 of an effective reading program is to become acquainted with the many informal and formal assessment procedures that teachers can use as they plan reading instruction strategies in their classes. The teachers at Twin Lakes School know that they must use assessment procedures to determine the interests, backgrounds, and attitudes of their students toward reading. This basic knowledge is the beginning point for determining other appropriate assessment techniques to learn about their students strengths and needs in reading. With the emphasis placed on reading tests in today's educational society, classroom teachers may not be aware of the vast array of additional procedures available for learning about students' reading behaviors. A review of the information in Chapters 2 and 3 helped the Twin Lakes faculty to examine their school's reading program.

CHAPTER 2

Informal Assessment Procedures

Experience at many grade levels has suggested to Mr. Turner that informal assessment procedures are the best tools to determine student proficiency in reading. He has learned about many of the procedures through various preservice classes but needs to update his knowledge about these informal assessments including nonstandardized, commercially available informal tests and naturalistic assessments developed by the teacher using classroom reading materials that are closely related to the instructional program. Mr. Turner knows that informal procedures are simple to administer, inexpensive, and as accurate as many standardized tests for meeting the instructional planning needs of the teacher. As reading instruction has become more language based, integrating reading and writing processes with literature and placing less emphasis on testing and teaching isolated skills, teachers have questioned the use of standardized reading skills tests. Questions have been raised about reading tests, and many classroom teachers now make greater use of informal assessment procedures as they plan reading instruction.

Because classroom teachers are realizing the valuable information that can be obtained about their students as they teach, more attention is being given to informal classroom assessment. Some of the common questions asked by classroom teachers regarding informal assessment are discussed in this chapter.

- Why are informal measures so important?
- What are the different informal assessment procedures?
- What is an informal reading inventory (IRI) and how is it used?
- How can informal procedures be used to greater advantage in the classroom?
- How does informal assessment fit with the use of a literature-based reading program?
- What does a teacher look for when using observation as a technique for informal assessment?

- What informal assessment procedures can a content teacher use to assess reading?
- What informal procedures are useful in assessing comprehension difficulties?
- How is word identification assessed using informal procedures?
- What is authentic assessment?

Vocabulary to Know

- **Attitude inventory**
- **Authentic assessment**
- **Cloze procedure**
- **Comprehension**
- **Content reading inventory**
- **Criterion-referenced tests**
- **Critical reading**
- **Frustration level**
- **Graded basal series**
- **Hesitations**
- **Independent level**
- **Informal assessment**
- **Informal reading inventory (IRI)**
- **Insertions**
- **Instructional level**
- **Interest inventory**
- **Interpretive comprehension**
- **Literal comprehension**
- **Literature-based reading**
- **Miscues**
- **Mispronunciations**
- **Naturalistic assessment**
- **Objective-based tests**
- **Observations**
- **Omissions**
- **Portfolios**
- **Prior knowledge**
- **Readability**
- **Repetitions**
- **Substitutions**
- **Word identification inventories**

AN OVERVIEW

Informal assessment procedures are nonstandardized techniques used by teachers to determine their students' strengths and weaknesses in reading. Areas measured include (a) prereading, which includes oral language and auditory and visual perception skills; (b) decoding or word identification, more specifically, knowledge of sight words, dictionary skills, and phonic, contextual, and structural analysis skills; (c) context processing or comprehension, including literal, interpretive, and critical reading; (d) study skills, such as reference skills and using parts of a book; and (e) personal reading, which involves the application of the other areas via reading for information and enjoyment.

Informal assessment is also the most appropriate procedure for use in measuring student performance in language, writing, and listening to determine how reading proficiency relates to learning in these areas. Language development is demonstrated through oral language, listening, writing, and comprehension performance. Writing skills relate not only to language development but also to word identification, comprehension, and study skills such as organization of information. Informal assessment procedures allow the teacher to interrelate classroom performance in all areas of language by monitoring behaviors such as oral reading, discussion, writing, following directions, and general attitude toward reading. Whether using a language-based, skill-based, or combination approach in the classroom, the teacher should know the skills involved in reading. An extensive listing of the specific skills in each of the reading areas is provided in Appendix A.

Informal assessment data should go beyond academic performance information. Awareness of the students' prior knowledge and experiences is important in understanding reading and language proficiency. Physical, intellectual, and emotional factors, along with students' interests and attitudes toward reading, are significant factors in understanding reading performance. Because various facets of the students' reading behaviors need to be seen in the context of daily reading experiences, informal assessment procedures are preferred, especially for initial assessment information. Using a variety of informal procedures, teachers can easily observe and evaluate behaviors during instruction to obtain data that more accurately reflect the students' strengths and weaknesses in reading. Informal procedures yield a great deal of qualitative data, whereas formal assessment tests provide quantitative information. Informal procedures encourage teacher interpretation of responses, allowing greater flexibility in scoring responses. Harlin and Lipa suggest that informal measures are better predictors of reading performance with young children than formal assessment methods.[1] Hoffman concurs by stating that standardized measures often do not reveal the real knowledge possessed by an adult or child.[2]

With the diversity of informal procedures for reading/language assessment used by classroom teachers and the flexibility encouraged in designing and interpreting the procedures, different informal techniques are created each day. However, the basic informal strategies are presented in this chapter. Teachers can combine these, redesign them, and create new procedures as they informally assess their students. The more common techniques include observation; informal instruments such as attitude and interest inventories, informal reading inventories, word recognition inventories, criterion-referenced and objective-based tests, the cloze procedure, content reading inventories; and authentic assessments obtained through writing samples, learning centers, and classroom activities (see Figure 2.1). These informal instruments are usually developed by the individual classroom teacher. Regardless of the procedure, informal assessment strategies can provide essential information for:

- Grouping students for reading/language instruction.
- Determining students' strengths and weaknesses in reading as related to the school curriculum.
- Selecting teaching techniques and resources appropriate to the students' reading levels, needs, and interests.
- Monitoring students' reading development.
- Providing specific information to parents.
- Determining how a student interacts with print and the language process.

Figure 2.1 Informal Assessment Procedures

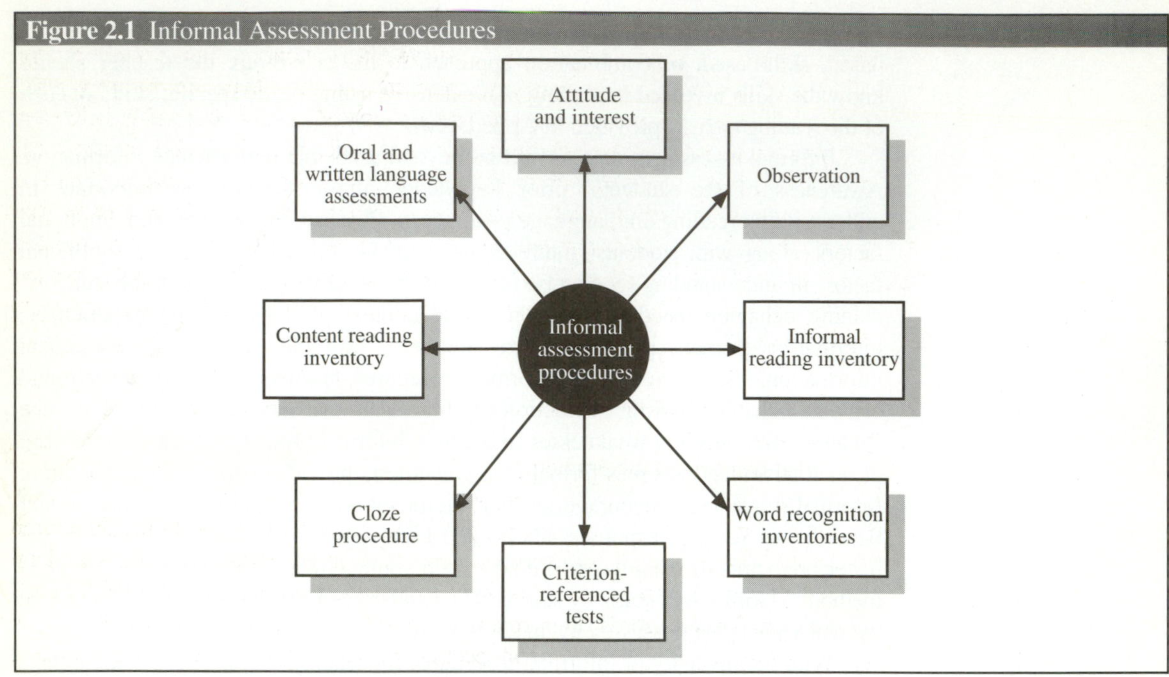

Informal assessment procedures provide excellent sources of information about students' ability to read and use language. To maximize the information that can be learned from this data, teachers must be good listeners, observers, and interpreters.

INFORMAL ASSESSMENT PROCEDURES

Observation

Teacher observation is one of the most important methods of informal evaluation, especially given that reading is a language process. Used alone or in conjunction with other informal procedures, observation of students in work and play situations allows the teacher to note their traits and attitudes while involved with print and nonprint activities. Changes in behavior are clues to the astute teacher that progress is occurring or problems loom on the horizon. Teachers have many opportunities during the school day to observe the reading and language patterns of students. Observations of silent reading as well as oral reading of both textbooks and fiction, computer screen reading and workbook activities, writing, and discussions all provide valuable information to the teacher interested in learning more about students' reading behaviors. Depending on the type of reading they are doing, students change their reading styles and act differently.

Further observation of students working in reading groups as compared with reading or writing alone is helpful for the teacher in developing an assessment profile. Although characteristics such as overaggressiveness in play, hyperactivity, propensity to distractions, or passiveness in class participation are easily observable behaviors that signify reading problems, there are many less noticeable signals. For example, the student who looks long and hard to find an appropriate book for leisure reading and frequently says he doesn't really have time to read or one who selects a book way beyond her reading level both have a problem with reading. The student who finishes first but doesn't participate in discussions may be frustrated with materials that are too difficult or bored with the repetition of information she already knows. Important questions remain:

- What is the specific problem?
- What is the cause?
- What will correct the problem?

More structured observations are needed to address these questions. Structured observation takes one of two forms: a checklist or anecdotal records. Anecdotal records are detailed notes concerning individual students with dates recorded for each observation. These records often reveal consistent patterns of behavior that may be significant for instruction. Anecdotal records are most helpful in observing a student with a severe reading disability. Some teachers keep an anecdotal record-card box or notebook to note significant events for individual students each day. Such information is of great value in parent conferences and referrals for further evaluations. Having factual records of observations, along with dates and times, provides teachers with a handy reminder guide.

Anecdotal records require the teacher to carefully note the behavior and reactions of the student during a specified time. The most difficult problem for an observer using the anecdotal record is to keep fact separate from opinion. Only actual facts or events are to be recorded; no interpretations or opinions are added until all observations for the student are complete (see Figure 2.2).

Checklists allow teachers to record concise information on a large number of students. A checklist is a versatile instrument of one or more pages listing specific reading/language behaviors about which the teacher desires student performance data. The checklist does not lend itself to in-depth observations of students over a long period of time; this is the function of the anecdotal record.

To guide classroom observation, checklist record forms need to follow consistent criteria: (a) items should address a specific behavior that can be observed, (b) space should be included for additional observations and comments, and (c) a limited number of specific items should be used so that the checklist is not too lengthy. Teachers must be familiar with the items to be evaluated on the observational checklist. Some of the standard items include the following:

- Understands facts in materials read.
- Is fluent in oral reading.
- Participates in classroom discussion.
- Enjoys reading assigned material.
- Enjoys reading self-selected material.
- Demonstrates ability to recognize new words.
- Uses variety in oral vocabulary.

Checklist observations take place during a scheduled reading time or at any time the student is reading. The teacher informally observes designated students for a few minutes during the selected time over a period of days to note the designated information. Specific steps should be followed in using an observation checklist.

1. Design a checklist that meets the needs of your classroom.
2. Make copies of the checklist to provide one per student to be observed.
3. Become familiar with the checklist to ease its use during observation time.
4. Schedule short periods of time to observe the student while reading.
5. Select one or two specific areas on the checklist, then observe the student to note strengths and weaknesses in these areas.
6. Note the results of your observations.
7. Select other areas to be observed at different times.

Figure 2.2 Sample Anecdotal Record

Joe Smith

9-28 *Joe played in the game area during free reading time. He had a fight with Sam about one of the games.*

10-2 *Joe looked at books during free reading time. He could not tell me what he read.*

10-5 *During the reading group Joe pronounced all the words correctly but he could not answer any of the comprehension questions.*

10-8 *Joe refused to come to the reading group and spent the time sleeping on his desk.*

Observation checklists are developed by the classroom teacher. Possible items to be included on such a checklist are listed in Appendix D. Items must be limited to facilitate ease of use.

Perhaps the most difficult phase of the observation process is interpreting the results. It is one thing to record a student's actions and statements during the day but quite another to identify the underlying reasons for the behavior observed. An example of behavior that may be very difficult to interpret would be consistent emotional reactions recorded during the observation period. Use a cautious approach when assessing the reasons for such an emotional upheaval, and discuss your ideas with another knowledgeable person.

Observations of reading and writing activities provide the teacher with many new insights into a child's difficulties, learning patterns, and avoidance strategies.[3] To further the use of observations of language behavior through more informal procedures, Goodman suggests using a naturalistic assessment procedure called "kid watching." Kid watching involves (a) observing, (b) interacting, (c) documenting, and (d) interpreting. Observation is done while interacting with the students; documentation and interpretation are done following an anecdotal record format.[4] Using this less structured procedure allows the teacher to use checklists and anecdotal records for documentation of the results of their authentic assessment. Before drawing any conclusions or making decisions based on observation, note the frequency with which the problem seemed to appear and the consistency of the problem from day to day. Remember that observation checklists involve less subjective evaluation than anecdotal records; thus, it may be helpful to use one to support or reject the findings of the other. Observation should be viewed as a beneficial part of all areas of assessment; however, teachers must be very aware of their students and cautious in interpreting the information gained from observing them.

Observation is only one of many tools needed to assess behaviors during the reading process; it provides general information that can be used to direct further investigation. Observation is an authentic assessment procedure used by teachers as they monitor reading and language development and adjust instruction as they see learning occur in the classroom. Remember, students are always changing and growing, necessitating that up-to-date observations be used to direct teaching and conferencing rather than six-month-old notes. Teachers should continuously note the reading behaviors of all students, focusing on a few students at one time for more in-depth review. Using information gleaned from observations can guide the teacher, to sources of additional information. The teacher must, however, be cautious of drawing conclusions based on limited information; the values of teachers can easily affect evaluations of a student. Stick to the facts, and form opinions cautiously. With the influx of formal tests, state assessments, achievement tests, standardized tests, and end-of-book tests, teachers must continue to trust their intuitions and observe students as they interact with print and one another in the classroom environment. This form of authentic assessment is the beginning of providing appropriate instruction to each student.

Attitude and Interest Inventories

Research studies consistently link reading interest and attitude with reading success.[5] According to Turner and Paris, choice is a particularly powerful motivator. Allowing students to choose tasks and texts of high interest to them motivates them to expend more effort in understanding the material.[6] Athey cites evidence that "tends to support the view that good readers are likely to be more intellectually oriented, and to exhibit higher aspirations and drive for achievement, and show more curiosity, and more positive attitudes toward school in general and reading in particular.[7] Attitude and interest toward reading create feelings, both positive and negative, that become habitual. As Smith suggests, "the emotional response to reading . . . is the primary reason most readers read, and probably the primary reason most nonreaders do not read."[8] Consequently, teachers need to be familiar with a variety of procedures to assess students' interests and attitudes toward reading. The observation techniques previously discussed are quite helpful. However, other procedures compatible with observation may also be used with individuals or groups. This section reviews these various procedures, beginning with teacher-generated inventories and moving to student-generated narrative responses to language and reading. A sample interest and attitude instrument is found in Appendix C.

Inventories

One of the more common ways to determine students' reading attitudes and interests is the inventory. Interest inventories are effective tools for determining areas in which students exhibit specific interests. Some inventories use questions or incomplete sentences, while others use a rating scale that allows the student to indicate the degree or extent of feelings about an idea. A Likert scale rating of 1 through 5 may be used with older students, while younger students may respond by marking a smiling or frowning face. McKenna and Kear developed a rating scale for teachers in grades 1 through 6 to measure attitude using Garfield poses.[9] A sample of this instrument is provided in Figure 2.3. More recently, Henk and Melnick developed an instrument to measure how intermediate-level students perceive themselves as readers. This instrument is known as the Reader Self-Perception Scale (RSPS).[10]

The interest and attitude inventory is easy to develop and use since the only criterion is that questions be designed to explore the interests of the student. The teacher can determine the types of questions to be asked, put them into a questionnaire format, and administer the inventory individually or in groups. After administering the inventory, the teacher interprets the results and uses the information gained to structure the students' learning activities around their interests in an effort to improve attitude toward reading.

Figure 2.3 Elementary Reading Attitude Survey

ELEMENTARY READING ATTITUDE SURVEY

School ____________ Grade ____ Name ________________

1. How do you feel when you read a book on a rainy Saturday?

Jim Davis

2. How do you feel when you read a book in school during free time?

3. How do you feel about reading for fun at home?

4. How do you feel about getting a book for a present?

Autobiography

Another way to learn more about a student is through a reading autobiography. This autobiography can be formulated orally or in writing, depending on the student's age and skill. Disabled readers who dislike writing usually prefer to use the oral autobiography or to record their message on a tape recorder. The procedure may be developed in various formats, ranging from a checklist to a series of open-ended questions that the student uses as the basis of a narrative response. A checklist of descriptors can be easily written and quickly administered; the students mark the words or phrases that best describe them as a reader. This format, however, does not allow students to express their feelings because it presents preselected ideas. More meaningful information may be obtained using focused questions and asking students to write about their feelings toward reading, as in the following:

- How would you feel at the end of your birthday party if all your gifts were books?
- Describe your idea of a great day at the library.
- How do you feel when you have to read?
- What do you think when your teacher says it's time for reading?
- What is your favorite subject in school? Why?
- What is your least favorite subject in school? Why?
- When did you read your first book? How did you feel?
- What do you like most (or least) about reading?

Using a few stimulating questions that are not to be answered directly, students can then give a developmental history of their reading experiences. This gives the teacher a more in-depth look at individual students, their attitudes toward other students in the class, their feelings about themselves in relation to their peers, their sentiments about reading, and perhaps even their reactions to the teacher. The teacher also gains information about the various forms of spelling and grammar used, vocabulary development, sentence structure, organizational pattern, and overall skill in written expression. With older students, the reading autobiography allows students to gain insight into their reading strengths or weaknesses and put them into perspective. With this self-evaluation and teacher guidance, personal goals for reading are set, and steps are taken for further development.

Book Title Rating

Another effective method of determining interests is to provide students with book titles and ask that they rate the titles according to their interest. Individual students can evaluate a series of titles according to personal likes and dislikes. From this rating, the teacher determines the areas of interest for each student.

Discussions and Interviews

Group discussions or one-on-one interviews encourage free expression of frustration or success with reading and language activities. Interaction provides poor readers with an opportunity to verbalize their feelings and allows students to learn how others deal with the printed word, how they decode words, how they use clues to determine the appropriate meanings of an unfamiliar word, or how they locate answers to specific questions. Through discussion, the teacher has an opportunity to study how the students' thought processes work and find ways of adjusting instruction to better meet individual needs.

Class discussions may be initiated using student responses to questions about the reading material or they may emerge as students discover how peers locate or remember information. This strategy helps students realize that people learn in different ways and that they are not alone with problems in reading, that all students experience successes and failures.

Individual student interviews with the teacher provide the frustrated, hostile reader with a private period of time to express feelings and begin to set short-term goals for success. This short period of time with a teacher or other adult provides students who may want or need individual attention with the opportunity to express their feelings verbally and may prevent hostile actions that could lead them to be labeled as behaviorally disordered, emotionally disturbed, or juvenile delinquent.

A classroom atmosphere conducive to expression of true feelings is essential if interviews or discussions are to be used to determine students' interests and attitudes toward reading. Close teacher-student relations and a feeling of trust contribute to this openness.

Reviews and Journals

Teachers and students need to write each day about special happenings. These writings might focus on a positive reaction to a story the teacher reads to the class, a book checked out of the library, the frustration of being asked to read from the social studies book, or the teacher's observation of an improved attitude of a group of students. Students who write brief reviews of their reading also provide teachers with an opportunity to see what kinds of materials they enjoy. This activity should in no way be construed as a "book report," which many students regard as a major turn-off to reading.[11] These written or oral reviews are for the purpose of gaining an understanding of the student's interest. Young readers may be encouraged to "sell" a book to a friend after reading it. In order to sell the book, the student tells enough of the story to interest the friend in reading it. The teacher learns much about a student's interest by keeping a record of the books being "sold."

Another means of eliciting student response to books is to establish a graffiti board. Cover a bulletin board with heavy paper, and encourage students to write book titles and their reactions to those titles to help others select books for leisure reading. Again, teachers can determine students' interests by observing their response to various books.

Personal journals encourage students to write about daily activities. Frequently, such activities include events of the day that were particularly pleasant or frustrating. For the astute teacher, journal entries offer important messages that suggest interests and feelings about reading that can be addressed through related learning activities in the classroom. The student who writes of his excitement after finishing *Charlotte's Web* might be invited to share the story with peers or develop a science project on spiders. Likewise, the student who enters the same line in her journal each day saying "I hate to write" needs to be given other options of self-expression to develop a more positive feeling about her skills in writing.

Free writing is yet another way of learning about the reading interests and attitudes of students. Teacher creativity is the only limit when using written language as an assessment tool in this area. For example, free writing letters to authors or characters, expressing feelings through verse, or sending notes can be used to assess written communication skills.

Information gained from inventories, autobiographies, discussions, interviews, reviews, and journals provide the teacher with information about students' likes, dislikes, and attitudes and possibly even some insight into the students' values, peer interactions, and self-concepts. With this type of information, a word of caution is needed regarding the interpretation of these instruments. The results of any of these instruments need periodic review; quickly changing interests and peer pressure greatly affect reading, both positively or negatively. Students develop more diverse interests, have more experiences, encounter changes in their peer group, and are influenced by various teachers and adults. Thus, current assessment information is critical when using data related to interests and attitudes. Moreover, student responses cannot always be taken at face value. For example, poor readers frequently respond positively to the question, "Do you like to read?" This response may spring from a desire to not offend the teacher, to create a favorable impression, or to hide guilty feelings about poor reading skills.

Teacher awareness of student interests and attitudes about reading is of great value in providing appropriate learning activities to overcome reading problems or prevent their development. Teachers cannot generalize about the interests and attitudes of students towards reading; all first graders do not come to school eager to learn to read, just as all sixth-grade boys do not enjoy books about sports. Know your students and try to use this personal knowledge of their feelings as your guide in creating an atmosphere conducive to good instruction.

Informal Reading Inventory

One of the most informative assessment procedures is the Informal Reading Inventory (IRI). An IRI is a compilation of graded reading selections arranged in sequential order from easiest to most difficult with comprehension questions to accompany each selection. The selections used may be passages from a graded basal reading series, graded passages from miscellaneous materials, graded passages written by the teacher, or one of many published inventories. Many school districts have developed their own IRIs, and most publishing companies provide an IRI to accompany their basal series. Appendix B contains a listing of published IRIs.

An IRI is administered individually, enabling the teacher to determine the student's specific word identification and comprehension strengths and weaknesses, while observing both oral and silent reading habits. This instrument is also helpful to the teacher in analyzing the processes the student uses to deal with print (see Figure 2.4).

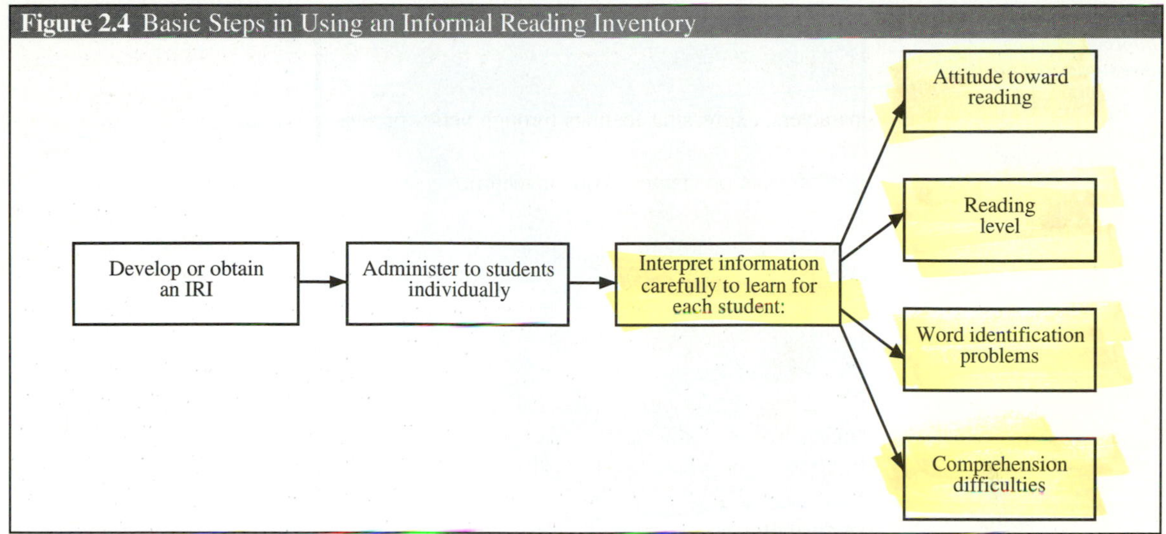

Figure 2.4 Basic Steps in Using an Informal Reading Inventory

The IRI is frequently used during the beginning weeks of school to assess more carefully those students for whom the teacher needs more specific information. The instrument is also used to assess new students and to continuously monitor the progress of all students as their reading proficiency develops.

Since many published IRIs are available, teachers must be aware of their advantages and disadvantages. Jongsma and Jongsma found that these instruments varied in the content, style, and length of the passages, and that readability estimates were used as the primary means to gauge passage validity and levels. Differences in directions to the examiner were noted, as well as differences in what constituted an error in oral reading. Factual recall questions were the dominant type of comprehension assessments. Additionally, they found no data on any of the 11 tests evaluated to validate the correspondence between reading levels established through informal reading inventory testing and classroom performance.[12]

Other evaluations of commercial IRIs suggest that there is a reasonable amount of agreement between IRIs constructed by teachers using teaching materials and some commercial IRIs.[13] In evaluations of commercial IRIs, the questions of reliability and validity are always raised; there are more questions in this area than answers, although Helgren-Lempesis and Mangrum found that these instruments were "by no means as unreliable as some critics have suggested."[14]

Published inventories offer the teacher complete word lists, passages, and questions in a ready-to-use format. Most inventories provide multiple passages at each level to assess oral and silent reading and to determine a listening level. Although there are many IRIs available for teacher use, these instruments can be developed by the teacher. Appendix G describes the construction of an IRI. Information on how to administer and interpret an IRI in the classroom is provided in the following sections.

The many published Informal Reading Inventories require careful teacher review.

Photo courtesy of Edward B. Lasher.

Administration of an IRI

One of the practical aspects of the IRI, if designed properly, is that it can be easily and quickly administered by the classroom teacher. To begin, the teacher needs appropriate passages for the student, a response sheet for recording and summarizing information, and the teacher copies of the passages, which include the comprehension questions and on which the teacher can mark word identification errors. The teacher is now ready to administer an IRI to determine the individual's independent, instructional, and frustration levels in reading as well as strengths and weaknesses in comprehension.

Specific criteria for each of the levels of reading have been debated for many years, but the question of which criteria are most accurate remains unresolved. The most commonly used criteria are those provided by Emmett Betts in 1957. Further research regarding the criteria was done by William Powell. Studies by Pikulski, Hays, and Ekwall present evidence that supports retaining the traditional Betts criteria.[15] Johns and Magliari suggest rethinking the use of Betts' criteria for primary students.[16] The teacher needs to be aware of divergent opinions on this matter and be consistent in the use of selected criteria. When using a published IRI, note the criteria used in determining reading levels. The specific criteria given by both Powell and Betts for each of these levels are found in Table 2.1. The levels are defined as follows:

- ***Independent level***. This is the level at which students read for recreational purposes. The material is easy enough to read quickly with maximum comprehension of the information.
- ***Instructional level***. This is the level at which instruction in reading is provided. The student can read the material but has some difficulty with the recognition of words and comprehension to the extent specified in the criteria.
- ***Frustration level***. At this level, the student has extreme difficulty in pronouncing words and comprehending the material. This is the level at which the student should *not* be reading for instructional purposes and certainly not for leisure.

Table 2.1 Criteria Used in Scoring Informal Reading Inventories

Powell Differentiated Criteria

Book Level (1–2)	*Word Pronunciation*	*Comprehension*
Independent	94% or more	81% or more
Instructional	87% or more	55%–80%
Frustration	86% or less	54% or less
Book Level (3–5)	*Word Pronunciation*	*Comprehension*
Independent	96% or more	86% or more
Instructional	92% or more	60%–85%
Frustration	91% or less	59% or less
Book Level (6+)	*Word Pronunciation*	*Comprehension*
Independent	97% or more	91% or more
Instructional	94% or more	65%–90%
Frustration	93% or less	64% or less

Betts Criteria

Level	*Word Pronunciation*	*Comprehension*
Independent	99% or more	90% or more
Instructional	95% or more	75% or more
Frustration	90% or less	50% or less

Source: William R. Powell, "Measuring Reading Performance" ERIC, November 1978, ED 155 589; Emmett A. Betts, *Foundations of Reading Instruction* (New York: American Book Company, 1957) p. 449. Copyright © 1957, American Book Company.

Researchers and practitioners generally agree on the following steps in the administration of an IRI.

1. Rapport is established with the student through a discussion of what the student is to do and is enhanced by developing readiness for reading each of the selections. During this time the student's prior knowledge of the topic is activated.
2. The teacher uses a word list to ascertain the student's word identification level. If the Dolch Basic Sight Word List is used, the following criteria assist in determining the grade placement.[17]

Dolch Words Known	Equivalent Reader Levels
0–75	Preprimer
76–120	Primer
121–170	First reader
171–210	Second reader or above
Above 210	Third reader or above

If the teacher has developed a graded word list from other lists, the grade placement is determined using the general criterion that the student should miss no more than one of every five words. This is the student's instructional level on the word list portion of the IRI. With this information or other knowledge of the student's readiness, the teacher proceeds with the IRI reading selections.

The word list measures instantaneous recognition of words (sight vocabulary) and word analysis ability. A word is first shown rapidly in a timed presentation of approximately three seconds to determine if the student can recognize the word by sight. If a correct response is given, the teacher moves to the next word. If the response is incorrect, the word is presented again for the student to further examine. This presentation is not timed and no clues are provided by the teacher, allowing the student to use word analysis skills to pronounce the word. The teacher records the pronunciations of the word from the timed presentation as well as the untimed exposure. A marking system such as the following can be used:

✓	= correct response
_	= no response
?	= don't know
ē ′ ver ′ rē	= pronunciation of sounds or word units

3. The teacher chooses a selection approximately two grade levels below the student's estimated instructional level. Readiness for reading the selection is developed by introducing the selection and giving the student a purpose for reading the material.
4. The student reads the paragraph orally. The teacher marks the oral reading errors on the response sheet as the student reads. The following marking procedure is suggested.

   Words pronounced by the teacher = *p* over the word

   Mispronunciation = *mp* over the word with the word written above as mispronounced (Mark only mispronunciations that affect the meaning of the selection.)

Substitution = ——— through the word with new word written above (Substitutions do not affect meaning.)

Omission = ⬭ Circle the words or punctuation omitted

Hesitation = / between words on which hesitation of more than 5 seconds occurs

Repetition = ︶︶︶︶︶ over the word

Insertion = ^ with word written in

A sample marked paragraph and highlighted examples are shown in Figures 2.5 and 2.6. Another way of noting word identification errors is through the use of a miscue analysis. The general types of miscues proposed by Goodman and Burke are substitutions, omissions, insertions, reversals, and repetitions.[18]

Figure 2.5 Sample Marked Selection

The swimming pool was ^very pretty ~~beautiful~~. The sun was *shining on* ~~reflecting off~~ the blue water. People were swimming and splashing (around). Hours passed quickly and (soon) the pool was empty of people. Lights were turned on and the pool looked different. No longer was the sun (shining) on the water. Now *mp (distant)* / *mp (sounds)* the reflections were from the lights underwater. Still, the pool was ^very pretty ~~beautiful~~.

✓ 1. What was this paragraph about?
(a swimming pool)

✓ 2. How do you think the pool looked during the day?
(beautiful with the sun reflecting off the water and people playing around the pool)

x *not very many people swimming* 3. What made the pool look different at night?
(the sun was not shining and the lights under the water were turned on)

x *when it's hot* 4. When did the people enjoy the pool?
(during the day)

x *he liked pools* 5. Why do you think the writer thought the pool was beautiful?
(because of the sunlight shining on the water and then the lights reflecting under the water)

Figure 2.6 Word Identification Types and Coding System

Word pronounced by the teacher: Write p over the word.

Now the reflections were from the lights underwater. (p over "underwater")

Mispronunciations: Write the incorrect word over the correct word in the text with mp written over the correct word in the text.

Lights were turned on and the pool looked different. (mp (distant) over "different")

Substitution of a word: Write the incorrect word over the correct word in the text with a line through the correct word in the text.

The swimming pool was ~~beautiful~~. (pretty over "beautiful")

Omission of a word or phrase: Circle the omitted words.

People were swimming and splashing (around).

Hesitation: Put a / between words on which there is a pause of more than 5 seconds.

Now the / reflections were from the lights underwater.

Repetition: Put a wavy line over the word or phrase.

No longer was the sun shining on the water. (wavy line over "water")

Insertion of a word: Use a caret and write the word above.

Still, the pool was ^ beautiful. (very above the caret)

5. The teacher asks comprehension questions following oral reading, and indicates correct and incorrect responses on the sheet. For this comprehension check, the student does not refer back to the selection but rather answers from what is remembered. When a response is incomplete, the teacher may probe for more information by questioning further, asking the student to give more information or to explain what was meant by the response. Responses to these questions are recorded as follows:

   ✓ = correct response
   x = incorrect response
   Q = further questioning needed
   ? = don't know

6. The teacher counts and records the words pronounced for the student, the mispronunciations, substitutions, omissions, insertions, and repetitions. Using the

criteria for word identification as outlined in Table 2.1, the teacher determines whether the passage is on the student's independent, instructional, or frustration level.

7. Another passage is used for silent reading. The teacher introduces the passage and gives the student a purpose for reading.
8. The student reads the passages silently, while the teacher records the words the student asks about while reading.
9. The teacher asks the comprehension questions following the silent reading and indicates on the response sheet the correct and incorrect answers.
10. The teacher counts and records the words asked by the student, and the satisfactory or unsatisfactory responses are indicated. Once again using the criteria for comprehension in Table 2.1, the teacher determines whether the student's comprehension of the material indicates the independent, instructional, or frustration level. If the errors on either the word identification portion of the oral reading or the comprehension section of the silent reading indicate the frustration level, an easier passage should be selected. If the passage is at the student's instructional level, the teacher moves to the next higher level and attempts to ascertain the student's frustration level. Few errors in both areas, as outlined in the criteria, indicate the student's independent reading level. The teacher then moves to more difficult passages in an effort to determine the student's instructional and frustration levels. Several levels may be skipped if the material seems extremely easy for the student.
11. Using alternate passages, read selections to the student to determine a listening comprehension level. The teacher may begin with the passage at the student's grade level or the passage one level higher than the instructional reading level passage. The selection is read to the student, and questions are asked to determine the information recalled. The student's listening comprehension level is the highest passage at which 80% or better is achieved on the comprehension questions. Passages of increasing difficulty are read until the student achieves less than 80% comprehension. When the student falls below this level, the assessment is discontinued. This listening comprehension level indicates to the teacher what can be expected of the student when specific word identification or comprehension difficulties are overcome.

Interpretation of an IRI

Through the experience of administering IRIs and observing students' reading habits, the teacher gathers a great deal of assessment information about each student. The following discussion introduces the significant factors to note when administering the IRI and provides suggestions for interpretation. As the teachers become more familiar with the IRI, their observational and interpretive skills will improve greatly.

General Observations When interpreting the errors made in oral reading, the teacher should consider these points:

- Dialectical or regional pronunciations are not counted as errors. This type of mispronunciation does not affect comprehension, although the teacher may wish to note the pronunciation.
- Young students often hesitate while reading orally. The teacher may wish to mark these hesitations but not count them as errors. Fluency in reading comes with practice, which the young reader has not had.
- Repetitions are noted, but the teacher may elect not to count them as errors. This is a habit that can be corrected. Repetitions slow the rate of reading but usually do not indicate a lack of comprehension. Rereading is a comprehension-monitoring strategy.
- Substitutions, omissions, and insertions are marked and counted as errors; however, teachers must also note whether these changes hinder comprehension. Errors that could fit the context of the sentence and do not affect comprehension are less severe than those that have no relationship to the sentence. For example, compare the following student readings:

    car *got* *around* *home* ʘ
    1. The ~~cat~~ ~~ran~~ ^ under the ~~house.~~

    kitten *went* *porch* ʘ
    2. The ~~cat~~ ~~ran~~ under the ~~house.~~

  While both sentences have many errors, those in the first sentence are more serious because of their effect on comprehension.

Word Identification Errors noted in the identification of words on the word list and in the oral reading section of the IRI reveal significant information about the student's word identification skills. Teachers need to note that few persons read orally without making errors or miscues. The most significant word identification errors are those that affect meaning. Gillet and Temple distinguish these errors through a tabulation made by calculating a *gross* oral reading accuracy score and a *net* oral reading accuracy score.[19] The gross score reflects the total of all word identification errors, or those that affect meaning as well as those that do not affect meaning. The net score is the total of only those errors that affect the meaning of the passage. The net score is used to determine reading levels "if the teacher tolerates a number of miscues or if the material is to be read silently."

Responses to note for possible interpretation of word identification strategies include the following:

- Does the student make more word identification errors on the word list or in oral reading? Fewer errors during oral reading indicate that context clues are being used. However, numerous errors on the word list and during oral reading suggest that the student is lacking in word analysis strategies, including contextual analysis.
- Does the student attempt to pronounce words that he is not sure of or ask that they be pronounced? Failure to attempt to pronounce a word indicates that the

student has poor word analysis skills and does not know how to divide words to determine their correct pronunciation.

- Does the student frequently hesitate prior to pronouncing a word? This indicates that the student is analyzing the word because of uncertainty. Word analysis is an essential skill in proper decoding of words; however, if this is a frequent occurrence, the student may become a very slow reader and have poor comprehension. Easier materials and assistance in developing a basic sight vocabulary are needed to overcome the problem.
- Does the student often repeat a word several times before going on to the next? Students use this as a way to gain time when they do not know the next word. Note how the word following the repetition is pronounced. Usually the student who uses this technique is unsure and needs to be encouraged to move on more quickly. Activities that encourage the student to pronounce each word in a sentence only once may be used to overcome the problem.
- Does the student mispronounce the words? This may indicate one of several different problems. Sometimes the student calls the word another word that differs by only one letter or sound. This is an indication that the student is not looking at the entire word or using context clues as a word identification technique. Note whether the errors seem to be with the initial, medial, or final sounds; then assist the student in looking at the entire word as it is read. In other cases, the student calls the word an entirely different word, unrelated in meaning and with only a vague resemblance in sounds. This is an indication that the student is not using context clues or knowledge of sounds. This requires help in all aspects of word identification and comprehension monitoring.
- Does the student more frequently miss basic sight words for which most phonic generalizations do not apply or miss words that can be easily analyzed? Many students have great difficulty in recognizing the basic sight words and confuse them with one another. If this error is noted, one way of assisting the student is by using activities that require identification of words in context. If, on the other hand, the student consistently misses words that can be analyzed by using either phonetic analysis, structural analysis, or a combination, then the teacher should note the strategy used and expand this knowledge to use multiple strategies.
- Does the student make consistent insertions or omissions? Students who make these errors and do not correct themselves are not attending to the context of the information. Because of their errors, these students usually have difficulty in comprehending the material. If omissions are the problem, the teacher must determine whether the student knows the word and is just skipping it or if the word is skipped because it is not known. These are two entirely different problems. The student who continuously inserts words may do so in an effort to keep words flowing when a specific word is not known. Students who consistently either insert or omit words should be carefully screened to determine whether a vision problem is contributing to the errors.

Comprehension Often the student who has difficulty with word identification will also have difficulty with comprehension. However, some students have little difficulty in recognizing the words but are unable to process the information for comprehension. When interpreting the data reflecting comprehension, the teacher must determine whether comprehension errors are occurring because the student does not recognize the words or because the material is not understood. Lack of understanding may be the result of poor language development, limited background experiences, or difficulty in processing the information.

Research related to comprehension questions on the IRI suggests that main idea questions should be used cautiously because "student's performance is just as likely to be a reflection of ill suited passages as of the student's inability to comprehend main ideas."[20] Further study of vocabulary questions on IRIs points out that "the vast majority of vocabulary questions did not function properly . . . because they had an unacceptable level of passage independence."[21] Keeping these cautions in mind, however, much evaluation of comprehension-processing strategies can be determined through careful interpretation:

- Does the student not understand the material because of word identification errors? If this is the problem, the student should be able to respond to questions about materials in which no word identification errors occurred. If easier materials seem to improve comprehension significantly, the student may be diagnosed as having word identification difficulties that contribute to the comprehension problems. Correcting the word identification problem should improve the comprehension skills. If the student makes few errors in word identification but continues to have difficulty comprehending the material, then further assessment is needed to determine the cause(s) of the comprehension errors.
- Does the student respond better to questions measuring literal, interpretive, or critical reading skills? If the teacher has appropriately labeled each question according to the area and skills being measured, a rapid review of the errors may indicate a pattern. With this information, the teacher can provide appropriate instruction.
- Is there a difference in the comprehension levels when reading orally versus silently? Some readers need to hear themselves say the words in order to comprehend; this is especially true with younger readers and students whose reading experiences have been primarily oral. For these students, silent reading involves mumbling or voicing the words in a soft manner. As students get older, their silent reading comprehension level usually becomes higher than their oral reading comprehension level because silent reading is emphasized more as students leave the primary grades.
- Is there a difference in the listening comprehension level and the instructional reading level? If these levels are the same, the student may be reading as well as possible at this time; however, a discrepancy in these levels indicates to the

teacher that corrective help with the identified reading problems will help the student achieve at this potential level (listening comprehension level). A few students may have a listening comprehension level that is below their instructional reading level. This type of discrepancy suggests several things: (a) the student may have a hearing acuity problem; (b) the student may not have the prior knowledge to understand the concepts presented in the listening passage; (c) the student may not be an auditory learner; or (d) the leveling of the passages may be inaccurate, causing an inaccurate estimate of the instructional level or listening level.

While most IRIs use a format in which questions follow the passage, recent research suggests that teachers should allow students to retell the story prior to questioning. Retellings provide an opportunity for the student to relate the facts of the story as well as tell how she understands the interactions of the various components of the passage. The experiences and prior knowledge of the reader become more evident to the teacher along with the strategies used by the student to understand the author.[22] Thus, using retellings as another measure of comprehension adds to the assessment data available from the IRI.

IRIs have become a part of the age of computer technology and will likely be more available in reading software in the future. The *Computer-Based Reading Assessment Instrument* is one IRI in microcomputer format.[23] It is based on John's *Computer-Based Graded Word Lists*.[24] Further use of the computer can be made through the *Computer-Assisted Reading Achievement*, which interprets general information about students, IRI results, and offers an assessment.[25] While all of these instruments are new in the area of reading assessment, Henk proposes that the reading assessments of the future must become more precise; to achieve this end, one possibility for incorporating our knowledge into a highly diversified assessment instrument is through the use of computers.[26] With their vast storage capacity, computer programs could offer an enormous set of diverse reading materials reflecting narrative and expository text, which could be selected by the teacher. These selections would take into account the prior knowledge and interests of the student, and present both considerate or inconsiderate text as well as differing paragraph structures and types of verbal illustrations. A hard copy of the passages could be provided for students to use. Certainly, the IRIs of the future must reflect the changes suggested by our research today. Computerized IRIs are one more tool for putting research into practice.

Informal reading inventories are valuable assessment instruments that furnish information about the strengths and weaknesses of each student. By following the guidelines outlined in this section, the teacher can determine students' independent, instructional, and frustration reading levels as well as listening comprehension levels. However, these levels only represent a small portion of the information that can be gleaned from an IRI. Through careful analysis and interpretation the teacher can note the types of word identification errors made by students, the impact of these errors on meaning, the relationship of prior knowledge to comprehension, as well as many characteristics of the students' language and strategies used in reading.

Word Identification Inventories

Teachers develop word identification inventories based on their students' needs. Specific directions for developing inventories using word lists are provided in Appendix G. This section presents information on the various word lists that teachers can use in devising a word identification inventory.

Many word lists are available for developing a word identification inventory. One of the more widely used word lists is the Dolch Basic Sight Word List, developed in 1941 from three lists in wide use at that time: (a) a list published by the Child Study Committee of the International Kindergarten Union, (b) the first 500 words from the Gates list, and (c) the Wheeler and Howell list.[27] The Dolch list consists of 220 basic sight words comprising those words occurring most frequently in basal readers on the first-, second-, and third-grade levels. This list is still used by classroom teachers and reading specialists. The relevancy of the Dolch list has been studied by Johnson and Hillerich.[28] Johnson's study suggests that the Dolch list has become outdated compared with the Kucera-Francis word list. Hillerich, however, in reviewing 14 different studies, arrived at the following conclusions:

1. The recentness of a list is no assurance of its importance.
2. The language base of the word count is more important than the date it was compiled.
3. The structure words in our language tend to remain constant, although the language is continually changing.
4. The Dolch list does not seem particularly outmoded.

A more recent but similar word list is the Fry New Instant Word List, revised in 1980 (see Table 2.2). This list consists of the 300 most frequently used words in the English language, with students needing to recognize these words instantly in order to achieve fluency in reading, writing, or spelling. Interestingly, the first 10 words make up about 24% of all written material; the first 100 words make up about 50%, and the first 300 words make up about 65% of all the words written in English.[29]

As teachers use more literature-based materials in reading instruction, the word list of high-frequency words used in children's literature levels K through 3 is helpful in forming word identification inventories. Examining 400 books for beginning readers, Eeds developed a list of 227 high-frequency words for use in teaching beginning reading through literature books rather than basals.[30] This list of "bookwords" is presented in Table 2.3. Eeds does not recommend presenting these words in isolation; rather the list gives teachers a sense of the types of words occurring most frequently in literature books. Again, high-frequency words appear in all contexts: magazines, newspapers, textbooks, and children's books.

Table 2.2 Fry's List of "Instant Words"

First Hundred Words (approximately first grade)				Second Hundred Words (approximately second grade)				Third Hundred Words (approximately third grade)			
Group 1a	*Group 1b*	*Group 1c*	*Group 1d*	*Group 2a*	*Group 2b*	*Group 2c*	*Group 2d*	*Group 3a*	*Group 3b*	*Group 3c*	*Group 3d*
the	he	go	who	saw	big	may	fan	ask	hat	off	fire
a	I	see	an	home	where	let	five	small	car	sister	ten
is	they	then	their	soon	am	use	read	yellow	write	happy	order
you	one	us	she	stand	ball	these	over	show	try	once	part
to	good	no	new	box	morning	right	such	goes	myself	didn't	early
and	me	him	said	upon	live	present	way	clean	longer	set	fat
we	about	by	did	first	four	tell	to	buy	those	round	third
that	had	was	boy	came	last	next	shall	thank	hold	dress	same
in	if	come	three	girl	color	please	own	sleep	full	tell	love
not	some	get	down	house	away	leave	most	letter	carry	wash	hear
for	up	or	work	find	red	hand	sure	jump	eight	start	yesterday
at	her	two	put	because	friend	more	thing	help	sing	always	eyes
with	do	man	were	made	pretty	why	only	fly	warm	anything	door
it	when	little	before	could	eat	better	near	don't	sit	around	clothes
on	so	has	just	book	want	under	than	fast	dog	close	through
can	my	them	long	look	year	while	open	cold	ride	walk	o'clock
will	very	how	here	mother	white	should	kind	today	hot	money	second
are	all	like	other	run	got	never	must	does	grow	turn	water
of	would	our	old	school	play	each	high	face	cut	might	town
this	any	what	take	people	found	best	far	green	seven	hard	took
your	been	know	cat	night	left	another	both	every	woman	along	pair
as	out	make	again	into	men	seem	end	brown	funny	bed	now
but	there	which	give	say	bring	tree	also	coat	yes	fine	keep
be	from	much	after	think	wish	name	until	six	ate	sat	head
have	day	his	many	back	black	dear	call	gave	stop	hope	food

Source: Edward Fry, "A New Instant Word List," *The Reading Teacher*, *34* (December 1990), 286–288. Reprinted with permission of Edward Fry and the International Reading Association.

Other valuable published word lists include *Kucera-Francis Corpus,* by Henry Kucera and W. Nelson Francis; *Basic Elementary Reading Vocabularies* by Albert Harris and Milton Jacobson; *A Revised Core Vocabulary: A Basic Vocabulary for Grades 1–8, An Advanced Vocabulary for Grades 9–13* by Standford Taylor, Helen Frackenpohl, and Catherine White; *Word Frequency Book* by John B. Carroll, Peter Davies, and Barry Richman; "Sight Words for Beginning Readers" by Wayne Otto and Robert Chester; and *The Ginn Word Book for Teachers* by Dale Johnson, Alden Moe, with James Baumann.[31] These and other word lists may be used to develop word identification inventories.

Table 2.3 Bookwords

the	look	love	new	tell	door
and	some	walk	know	sleep	us
a	day	came	help	made	should
I	at	were	grand	first	room
to	have	ask	boy	say	pull
said	your	back	take	took	great
you	mother	now	eat	dad	gave
he	come	friend	body	found	does
it	not	cry	school	lady	car
in	like	oh	house	soon	ball
was	then	Mr.	morning	ran	sat
she	get	bed	yes	dear	stay
for	when	an	after	man	each
that	thing	very	never	better	ever
is	do	where	or	through	until
his	too	play	self	stop	shout
but	did	let	try	still	mama
they	could	long	has	fast	use
my	good	here	always	next	turn
of	this	how	over	only	thought
on	don't	make	again	am	papa
me	little	big	side	began	lot
all	if	from	thank	head	blue
be	just	put	why	keep	bath
go	baby	read	who	teacher	mean
can	way	them	saw	sure	sit
with	there	as	mom	says	together
one	every	Miss	kid	ride	best
her	went	any	give	pet	brother
what	father	right	around	hurry	feel
we	had	nice	by	hand	floor
him	see	other	Mrs.	hard	wait
no	dog	well	off	push	tomorrow
so	home	old	sister	our	surprise
out	down	night	find	their	shop
up	got	may	fun	watch	run
are	would	about	more	because	own
will	time	think	while		

Source: Eeds, Maryann, "Bookwords: Using a Beginning Word List of High Frequency Words from Children's Literature K–3," *The Reading Teacher*, *38* (January 1985), 420. Reprinted with permission of Maryann Eeds and the International Reading Association.

Formal word identification inventories are available to assist teachers who do not wish to develop their own lists. One of the more commonly used lists is the Slosson

Oral Reading Test (SORT), which is discussed in Chapter 3.[32] Another formal instrument that has an oral reading section designed as a word identification inventory is the Wide Range Achievement Test (WRAT); this can be used for ages 5 through adult and can provide a grade equivalent score.[33]

Word identification can be evaluated informally through a variety of other activities used continuously in the classroom. Activities such as workbook pages, games, and writing assignments provide additional insight into word identification difficulties. Informal assessments of word identification strategies are an integral part of any reading program, especially at the elementary school level. Another interesting technique than can be used in assessing decoding abilities is the Names Test, which was developed by Cunningham[34] and then revised by Duffelmeyer, Kruse, Merkley, and Fyfe.[35] As teachers assess ability through observation and occasional informal appraisal, appropriate instructional adjustments are made to develop necessary word identification strategies.

Word lists assist the classroom teacher in the identification of sight word deficiencies. In addition, they give the teacher insight into techniques used by students to decode words. Teacher notes indicate whether students have difficulty with initial, medial, or final sounds or if they do not use strategies in analyzing words; such information is essential for appropriate instruction. Word identification inventories assess only one area of reading. They do not measure comprehension; thus, the scores cannot be used to provide a reading level for the student.

Criterion-Referenced and Objective-Based Tests

Criterion-referenced and objective-based tests are designed to measure what a learner knows or can do relative to a specific objective. The criterion-referenced test is based on objectives that contain the specific conditions, outcomes, and criteria that are expected for satisfactory completion of the task. The objective-based test is also based on specific objectives, but no predetermined criteria for achievement are provided. This lack of specific criteria is the technical difference between criterion-referenced and objective-based tests.

These tests, in contrast to norm-referenced, or standardized, tests, do not compare one student's performance with that of another. Students are evaluated on their individual ability to perform the specific skills being measured; their performance is not compared to established norms on a group of related test items. Thus, the criterion-referenced or objective-based test is becoming more popular as an assessment tool in local and state testing programs.

To evaluate the benefits of criterion-referenced reading instruments more easily, consider how they contrast to norm-referenced (standardized) instruments, as outlined by Otto.[36]

1. Standardized tests have a low degree of overlap with the objectives of instruction at any given time and place. The overlap for criterion-referenced measures is absolute because the objectives are the referents.

2. Norm-referenced tests are not very useful as aids in planning instruction because of the low overlap just mentioned. Criterion-referenced measures can be used directly to assess the strengths and weaknesses of individuals with regard to instructional objectives.
3. Again, because of their nonspecificity, norm-referenced tests often require skills or aptitudes that may be influenced only to a limited extent by experiences in the classroom. This cannot be so for criterion-referenced measures because the referent for each test is also the referent for instruction.
4. Standardized tests do not indicate the extent to which individuals or groups of students have mastered the spectrum of instructional objectives. Again, there is no such problem with criterion-referenced measures because they focus on the spectrum of instructional objectives in a given situation. Table 2.4 provides a further contrast of the two types of tests.

Table 2.4 Comparison of Norm-Referenced and Criterion-Referenced Tests

Point of Comparison	Norm-Referenced	Criterion-Referenced
Purpose	Determines a student's grade-level achievement.	Determines extent to which student objectives are being achieved.
Testing procedures	Each student takes a complete test.	Items may be randomly assigned as purposes dictate.
Achievement standard	Comparison with other students of the same age.	Performance of the individual in regard to the objective.
Reporting of results	Grade-level achievement norms for individuals or groups.	Percentage score on the number of items correct for specific objective.
Implications for teaching	Teaching for the test constrains classroom activity and invalidates the test.	Teaching for the objectives is desirable and expected if the objectives have been carefully formulated.

The primary advantage of criterion-referenced tests is that they directly evaluate the performance of individuals with regard to specified instructional objectives. There are, however, some limitations inherent in criterion-referenced tests. Otto describes such problems as the following:

1. Objectives involving hard-to-measure qualities, such as appreciation or attitudes, may be slighted.
2. Objectives involving the retention and transfer of what is learned may become secondary to the one-time demonstration of mastery of stated objectives.
3. Specifying the universe of tasks (determining critical instructional objectives) to be dealt with is of extreme importance. Good tests will do nothing to overcome the problem of bad objectives. Note that the problem here is no different from norm-referenced testing.

4. Determining proficiency standards can be troublesome. Perfect or near-perfect performance should be required if (a) the criterion objectives call for mastery, (b) the skill is important for future learning, and (c) items are of the objective type and guessing is likely. Less demanding performance may be adequate if any of the three conditions do not prevail.[37]

Instead of attempting to choose between either norm- or criterion-referenced instruments, teachers should use them to complement each other, choosing the most appropriate instrument for a particular purpose and testing situation. Teachers interested in knowing how students are performing in relation to national standards should use a standardized or norm-referenced test. Teachers who want to know about a student's performance on a specific skill will find a criterion-referenced or objective-based test to be helpful.

Criterion-referenced tests are being used frequently in schools that are focused on reading skill assessment. In addition, statewide testing programs use objective-based tests to determine student performance on specific minimum objectives or standards. As a result, these tests have become readily available to teachers. Many current basal reading programs contain criterion-referenced tests to aid in classroom assessment. These tests are based on the scope and sequence of skills for the series and are used as part of the assessment to evaluate skills taught in the basal.

Cloze Procedure

The cloze procedure is a versatile, informal instrument for use in determining a student's reading level, use of context while reading, and knowledge of vocabulary. Developed by W. L. Taylor in 1953, the cloze procedure was initially used as a tool for measuring readability.[38] Further research has suggested that the cloze procedure can also be used as an alternative to the Informal Reading Inventory for determining reading levels.[39]

Some research involving a qualitative analysis of the cloze suggests that this procedure is an invalid test of reading comprehension because it measures a set of thinking processes related to both reading and writing. Ashby-Davis suggests that cloze probably favors students who are not only good readers but also good writers. While the scores of such students are inflated in terms of reading comprehension, the scores of good, average, or poor readers are underestimated when they are deficient in writing skills, particularly in those skills needed to complete cloze test.[40] However, Jonz and McKenna and Layton reported the cloze to have a high level of validity and reliability and concurrent validity, and DeSanti concurred that the scoring procedure used in the cloze was a valid measure for use with a variety of passages and grade levels.[41] With continuing research indicating that the cloze procedure is effective, this instrument offers another informal procedure to aid in classroom assessment.

A cloze test can be developed without special training in test construction. To develop and administer a cloze test, gather reading selections from textbooks, basal readers, or any other material that is appropriate and unfamiliar to the students, and follow these steps:

1. Select a passage of approximately 250 to 300 words on a level at which the student is or should be reading.
2. Check the readability level of the passage using a readability formula as outlined in Chapter 5.
3. Retype the passage. Beginning with the second sentence, delete every fifth word. Replace each deleted word with a line, making sure that each line is of the same length. Place a number under each line to aid scoring and student response. Do not delete words from the first or last sentence. There should be approximately 50 blank spaces in the selection.
4. Make copies of the test for students to complete.
5. Direct the students to fill in the blanks with the words they think best complete the sentence.
6. Score the papers by counting as correct only those responses that exactly match the original selection. Using a percentage score of correct responses, determine the student's reading level:

   58%–100% correct = independent level
   44%–57% correct = instructional level
   0%–43% correct = frustration level[42]

Teachers find the cloze technique quite useful for learning more about their students' reading levels and skills in reading incomplete text. To use the cloze procedure, passages at several different reading levels need to be assembled into a booklet for students to work through as an assignment. The objective of using this procedure is to gain an estimate of the level of material the student can satisfactorily read and to gain more assessment information through alternative interpretation of responses. As a method of evaluating comprehension, the teacher evaluates each word used in the responses. If the student fills in the blanks with totally irrelevant words, the material is probably not understood. On the other hand, if the student completes the blanks with meaning-appropriate words that fit the context but are more frequently used words rather than the technical or multisyllabic word used in the text, the teacher has information indicating a limited student vocabulary.

More assessment information can be gathered by examining the types of words substituted in the blanks and the use of other words in the sentence to assist in figuring out the omitted words. Students unable to use these context clues need instructional assistance with this reading strategy.

Activities using a modified cloze format also provide diagnostic information. To determine the extent of the student's vocabulary, students may be asked to list as many words as they can think of to complete each blank. Students with limited vocabularies will encounter difficulty in completing the assignment, indicating to the teacher their need for further vocabulary study.

Another activity using a modified cloze format provides choices of visually similar or meaning-similar words for each blank, requiring the student to use context, vocabulary knowledge, and decoding strategies to determine the correct response. Teachers may also design passages that omit all adjectives or other parts of speech, allowing students to create their own selections. Activities with a modified cloze format not only provide the teacher with varying types of information but also provide students with experience in using the cloze format and context clues. This experience is important in comprehension development, especially when taking standardized tests that measure comprehension using a modified cloze format.

The value of the cloze procedure, like an IRI, depends on teacher analysis, with information regarding reading levels being of secondary importance. The cloze procedure is a good assessment tool for use in content classes at all levels. It can be administered to groups of students, thereby minimizing the loss of teaching time in assessment and maximizing the amount of information gained from the instrument. A sample close test is provided in Figure 2.7.

Content Reading Inventory

A content reading inventory (CRI) is a procedure used by content teachers to assess the specific reading skills necessary to learn the concepts in a content area lesson. The teacher must first identify the concepts or content to be taught during a particular period of time. Using these concepts, the teacher then identifies the reading skills needed to learn the content. The CRI can be developed when these two aspects, concepts and reading skills, are identified, as in the following example:

Concept Generalizations

- Determine the location of Pearl Harbor.
- Understand the meaning of the quote "I shall return."
- Understand the significance of the Battle of the Coral Sea.
- Understand the term "unconditional surrender."
- Realize the impact of the use of the atomic bomb on Hiroshima and Nagasaki.

Reading Skills

- Using the atlas
- Interpretation
- Cause-effect relationships
- Main idea
- Word meanings
- Prefixes
- Drawing conclusions
- Anticipating outcomes
- Evaluation

Figure 2.7 Sample Cloze Selection

What factors affect local climate?

Mountains affect the local climate in a region. They change the movement ________ (1) air masses. Mountains also ________ (2) patterns of precipitation. The ________ (3) shows air being forced ________ (4) over a mountain. As ________ (5) rising air cools, water ________ (6) in the air condenses ________ (7) forms clouds. Rain or ________ (8) falls on the side ________ (9) the mountain where the ________ (10) is rising. By the ________ (11) the air reaches the ________ (12) of the mountain, it ________ (13) lost most of its ________ (14). So the air that ________ (15) down the other side ________ (16) the mountain is dry. ________ (17) bodies of water affect ________ (18) climate of nearby land. ________ (19) near water often have ________ (20) rain or snow than ________ (21) far from water. Places ________ (22) large bodies of water ________ (23) have smaller differences between ________ (24) summer and winter temperatures ________ (25) do places far from ________ (26). Water heats and cools ________ (27) slowly than does land. ________ (28) the water is cooler ________ (29) nearby land, the air ________ (30) the land is cooled. ________ (31) the water is warmer ________ (32) nearby land, the air ________ (33) the land is warmed.

________ (34) prevailing winds over an ________ (35) affect climate. Regions where ________ (36) prevailing winds ________ (37) from over the oceans ________ (38) a lot of precipitation.

________ (39) affects climate. Altitude is ________ (40) distance above sea level. ________ (41) high altitudes the air ________ (42) tends to be lower ________ (43) at low altitudes. The ________ (44) tree and the mountain ________ (45) are both near the ________ (46). Yet the top of ________ (47) mountain, which is almost ________ (48) km (about 3.5 mi) ________ (49) sea level, is covered ________ (50) snow. What does this tell you about the temperature at the top of the mountain?

Source: Mallinson, G. G. et al., *Science Horizons* (Morristown, New Jersey: Silver Burdett & Ginn, 1991). Reprinted with permission of Silver Burdett & Ginn, Morristown, New Jersey.

For each of the identified reading skills, three to five questions are generated using the content materials at an appropriate reading level for the students. The student uses the materials to answer the questions in the next section.

Sample Questions for Content Reading Inventory

I. Vocabulary Development
   A. *Word meaning*. Directions: Turn to page 30. Write a brief definition of the term *unconditional surrender*.
   B. *Prefixes*. Directions: Turn to page 30. Now that you have defined the term *unconditional surrender*, what does the prefix *un* mean?

II. Comprehension
   A. *Author's purpose*. Directions: Turn to page 25. What does MacArthur mean when he says, "I shall return"?
   B. *Cause-effect relationships*. Directions: Turn to page 28. What is the significance of the Battle of the Coral Sea?
   C. *Evaluation*. Directions: Turn to page 31. How important was the decision to use the atomic bomb on Hiroshima and Nagasaki?
   D. *Anticipating outcomes*. Directions: Turn to page 32. How has this decision to use the atomic bomb in World War II affected present-day relationships between countries?

III. Reference Skills
   A. *Using the atlas*. Directions: Turn to the map on page 35. Locate the Pearl Harbor naval base.

Thus, the student is asked to read specified materials and provide written responses to the questions prior to beginning the unit. With information gathered about each student's knowledge of necessary reading skills, the teacher can determine alternative teaching procedures to help each student develop better skills and learn the content material more easily.

One of the advantages of the CRI is that it can be administered several times during the year, using different material each time. Because it is important to ascertain students' progress throughout the year and because the CRI is a group test, it has obvious advantages over other informal and standardized instruments, especially for the content teacher. Using this instrument, the teacher can assess the progress students have made in learning to apply reading skills in content reading. An important point to remember is that not all students are reading at the same level; therefore, materials at various levels are needed to assess the skills. For example, in middle school the grade-level textbook is used for those reading at or above level, a textbook from a slightly lower level for those who are two or three years below grade level, and an elementary textbook for those greatly below level. Unless this differentiation is made, the teacher will be unable to determine whether the student cannot apply the skill or just cannot read the material.

The CRI provides teachers with an informal method for determining the extent to which their students are applying their knowledge of reading to their content materials. This inventory evaluates strategies used as students are reading to learn, as compared with many other informal procedures that measure how well students are learning to read. The CRI has a place in every classroom that students are asked to read informational materials.

Authentic Assessment

Reading is a language process used to interpret printed symbols. This interpretation occurs as a student interacts with print in books, newspapers, brochures, advertisements, and the environment. One of the major advantages in using authentic assessment is that teachers are encouraged to look, listen, and interpret as students interact with print in a natural way, that is, while reading their social studies text or reviewing information to use in a group presentation. This authentic assessment facilitates process assessment, which is an examination of the influences of reading, writing, listening, and speaking on each other. Process assessment requires that reading be viewed as a part of the language process. Assessment and instruction are so closely related that they are basically indistinguishable. To assess the reading/language process, the teacher must understand how reading, writing, listening, and speaking are interrelated as well as understand the components of each process separately.

Language and reading instruction have become more integrated during the last 15 years, and assessment using authentic reading experiences to gain information is a significant new direction in the assessment of reading. In particular, the recent emphasis on using trade books or authentic children's literature as part of a literature-based approach to reading instruction has necessitated the use of a more authentic approach to assessment. According to Cheek, Flippo, and Lindsey, authentic assessment is the use of appropriate assessment techniques to learn more about students' reading capabilities in fair and nonjudgmental ways representative of the actual reading activities that students encounter in their classrooms.[43]

Language-based teachers evaluate students throughout their instruction against specific objectives that support the goal of producing a child who can read and loves to read. These teachers are continuously using informal procedures to evaluate the language process so they can provide appropriate activities that capture students' interests, improve their attitudes, encourage their learning, and allow them to explore the unknown. Although all of the previously discussed informal assessment procedures can provide information about students' oral and written language skills, there are other informal strategies that focus directly on reading as a language process. Teachers using a language approach to reading instruction realize that "learning is too complex and assessment too imperfect to rely on any single index of achievement."[44] They use many forms with many different labels such as observation, or "kid watching," checklists, written records, objective- or performance-based assessments, portfolios, and holistic assessment procedures. The following sections present additional informal assessment procedures that focus on language assessment.

Think-Alouds

Comprehension monitoring is the purpose of using the think-aloud. This procedure requires readers to provide verbal self-reports about their thinking process to obtain information about how they construct meaning from text. Using prior knowledge of the text information, the student uses his schema to develop a hypothesis of what the text will say and then reads to test the hypothesis. Responding to one hypothesis leads to the development of another, and reading becomes an interactive process between the text information and the background knowledge of the reader. Ideally, readers process text in this manner, allowing new information to affect their existing knowledge and enhancing their schema or storage of information. However, poor comprehenders rely only on the text for information and seem to forget that they may have relevant prior knowledge. Poor comprehenders may also rely exclusively on their background knowledge and allow new information to have little impact on what they already believe. These students develop an understanding according to their own definitions, learning little from the author.

The think-aloud procedure is a form of verbal reporting that requires the student to read short selections and talk to the teacher one-on-one about what comes to mind as she is reading. The teacher provides vague probes such as "Is there anything else?" or "Can you tell me more?" The information is tape-recorded; nonverbal actions such as signs of frustrations or puzzled looks are recorded in teacher notes. By listening to what the student says she is thinking during reading, the teacher can analyze the student's comprehension strategies. Table 2.5 provides a summary of the procedures for administering and scoring a comprehension think aloud.

From analysis of think-aloud assessments, Wade categorizes comprehenders as follows:

- The good comprehender, who constructs meaning and monitors comprehension while interacting with text
- The nonrisktaker, who tries to remember what the text says but never goes beyond the text to hypothesize
- The nonintegrator, who uses text clues and prior knowledge and continuously forms new hypotheses but never relates previous hypotheses to the information presented
- The schema imposer, who holds on to an initial hypotheses regardless of the information presented
- The storyteller, who draws more on prior knowledge than on information presented.[45]

The think-aloud procedure allows the teacher to assess the comprehension process through personal dialogue with the student. Knowing how students think as they read greatly assists the teacher in providing appropriate instructional guidance to expand comprehension.

Table 2.5 Procedure for Administering and Scoring a Comprehension Think-Aloud

A. Preparing the text

Choose a short passage (expository or narrative) written to meet the following criteria:

1. The text should be from 80 to 200 words in length, depending on the reader's age and reading ability.
2. The text should be new to the reader, but on a topic that is familiar to him or her. (Determine whether the reader has relevant background knowledge by means of an interview or questionnaire administered at a session prior to this assessment.)
3. The text should be at the reader's instructional level, which can be determined by use of an informal reading inventory. Passages at this level are most likely to be somewhat challenging while not overwhelming readers with word identification problems.
4. The topic sentence should appear last, and the passage should be untitled. Altering the text in this way will elicit information about the reader's strategies for making sense of the passage and inferring topic.
5. The text should be divided into segments of one to four sentences each.

B. Administering the think aloud procedure

1. Tell the reader that he or she will be reading a story in short segments of one or more sentences.
2. Tell the reader that after reading each section, he or she will be asked to tell what the story is about.
3. Have the student read a segment aloud. After each segment is read, ask the reader to tell what is happening, followed by nondirective probe questions as necessary. The questions should encourage the reader to generate hypotheses (what do you think this is about?) and to describe what he or she based the hypotheses on (what clues in the story helped you?).
4. Continue the procedure until the entire passage is read. Then ask the reader to retell the entire passage in his or her own words. (The reader may reread the story first.)
5. The examiner might also ask the reader to find the most important sentence(s) in the passage.
6. The session should be tape-recorded and transcribed. The examiner should also record observations of the child's behaviors.

C. Analyzing results

Ask the following questions when analyzing the transcript:

1. Does the reader generate hypotheses?
2. Does he support hypotheses with information from the passage?
3. What information from the text does the reader use?
4. Does he/she relate material in the text to background knowledge or previous experience?
5. Does the reader integrate new information with the schema he/she has already activated?
6. What does the reader do if there is information that conflicts with the schema he/she has generated?
7. At what point does the reader recognize what the story is about?
8. How does the reader deal with unfamiliar words?
9. What kinds of integration strategies does the reader use (e.g., visualization)?
10. How confident is the reader of his hypotheses?
11. What other observations can be made about the reader's behavior, strategies, etc.?

Source: Suzanne E. Wade, "Using Think Alouds to Access Comprehension," *The Reading Teacher 43* (March 1990): 445.

Portfolio Assessment

As teachers have attempted to evaluate the oral and written language development of their students through the years, they have used samples of the student's work over a period of time. The idea of collecting one's best work in various areas into a portfolio has long been useful for artists, designers, and other professionals needing to show their products. This concept is now being applied in education (in elementary through university programs) as teachers organize a variety of samples of a student's work to evaluate learning. Valencia suggests that a portfolio approach to reading assessment is well founded intuitively, theoretically, and pragmatically. She summarizes with four guiding principles:

1. Authenticity is basic to sound assessment, and portfolios are comprised of authentic tasks, texts, and contexts experienced by the student.
2. Assessment is an ongoing, continuous process that must reflect development. A portfolio is formed from a collection of the best work of a student over a period of time.
3. Reading is a multifaceted process requiring assessment via a variety of means that reflect the cognitive processes, attitudinal interaction with print, and literacy activities reflecting the reading/language process.
4. Students and teachers must be active participants in the assessment process which encourages collaboration and reflection by both participants.[46]

Portfolios are another approach to obtaining diagnostic information about a student's performance in reading and language. The contents of a portfolio depend on the ideas of the teacher and student; however, the information could be organized in an expandable file folder and include (a) samples of the student's work selected by the teacher or the student, (b) the teacher's observational notes, (c) periodic self-evaluations done by the student, and (d) progress notes of the student and teacher.[47] There are several types of portfolios that are available to the teacher. One of these is the teaching (working) portfolio that Farr and Tone believe should be the central focus for reading assessment.[48] It contains items selected to show reflection, thought, and effort.

A second type of portfolio, suggested by Tierney, Carter, and Desai, is the showcase portfolio, which represents the student's best work and is intended for display and sharing with others.[49] For the most part, students decide which items should be included in this portfolio. Cheek, Flippo, and Lindsey suggest the use of a teacher observational portfolio, in which the teacher keeps checklists, notes about student's behavior, parent or family progress reports, notes received from parents about their child's reading progress or problems, and any other pertinent information related to a student's progress in reading.[50] Other types of portfolios are also in use. Milone reports on the successful use of computerized portfolios in a number of school districts,[51] and Hoffman suggests a family portfolio to evaluate family literacy programs.[52]

There have been numerous attempts to quantify the evaluation of portfolios through the use of rubrics (criteria developed to evaluate the performance of students on various tasks or activities) and anchor papers (model criteria for evaluating students' works). Some of these efforts have been more successful than others. Successful implementation of portfolio assessment in a schoolwide setting requires collaboration among teachers and the belief that this type of assessment is effective.

It is important to remember that the primary purpose of portfolios is to indicate a student's progress or growth over a period of time. This fact can empower individual teachers to implement their own form of portfolio assessment in order to serve the best interests of their students. As a culminating activity for the school year, Hiebert and Schultz suggest a "portfolio evening," where students invite their parents to school to share with them their portfolios.[53]

Portfolio assessment is a hot topic in literacy assessment among practitioners and researchers. Irwin-DeVitis offers suggestions that lead to growth, collaboration, and learning about students through the use of portfolios and cautions against its use as a quick fix in authentic assessment.[54] Portfolios are but another way to learn more about students, using their work over time to determine progress and needs in reading development.

MISCELLANEOUS SOURCES

Teachers sometimes overlook many sources from which they can informally obtain assessment information without ever testing a student. These sources include the daily work of the student such as workbook pages, learning center activities, and instructional games. Additionally, the teacher can use information from parent conferences and discussions with the students' other teachers to develop an effective reading program. These miscellaneous sources of data exist in every school and are necessary to provide thorough assessment in reading.

Daily classroom activities are used to assess progress in language and specific skill development and to note strengths and weaknesses as well as feelings toward tasks. Observant classroom teachers make notes regarding individual student errors. Errors such as difficulty with specific word identification skills or responding to literal comprehension questions are noted so that appropriate instruction can be provided. Workbook pages can be used to confirm teacher observations made in a reading group or to alert the teacher to particular difficulties. Workbook exercises can serve as excellent criterion-referenced tests for the teacher who has identified specific tasks to be taught in the reading class.

Learning centers are also used as informal assessment resources. As students participate in activities at learning centers, teachers can use observation and student feedback to gather information about strengths and weaknesses in reading and language use. For example, a learning center devoted to the study of contractions allows the teacher to determine which students have no understanding of contractions, which can understand simple contractions, and which use contractions in their oral and written communication.

Instructional games, whether purchased or teacher made, provide the same types of information as learning centers. Teachers may group students to work as teams with specific games and ask them to report any difficulties encountered with the activity. Using these miscellaneous assessment procedures assists the classroom teacher in several ways:

1. Less teaching time is spent in administering paper and pencil tests.
2. More assessment data are continuously being used to assist in providing appropriate instruction.
3. Students are not continuously facing testing situations and developing a careless attitude toward tests.
4. Evaluation is an integral part of the instructional program.

In addition to these sources of data, remember that students' parents provide excellent information that aids in assessment. Brief conversations with parents give answers to questions such as

- Does the student spend any time reading at home?
- Do the parents read at home or do they read to the student?
- What is the family's attitude toward reading?
- How does the mother or father feel about the student's performance in school?
- What kind of family life does the student have?
- Are there reading materials in the home?

Parents are valuable sources of information. They can assist by answering these general types of questions; for students with severe reading difficulties, parents can provide information about possible physical or emotional difficulties that may be contributing to a reading problem. In an effective reading program, everyone and everything is used to assist in supplying the appropriate instruction to the individual student.

Tips on Informal Testing

Teachers rely to a great extent on informal testing procedures in order to provide appropriate instruction. Experience is one of the best teachers when it comes to using the various informal assessment tools and interpreting data. However, the following suggestions may help the teacher who is just beginning to use informal assessment procedures in the classroom.

- ***Make testing situations as informal as possible***. Much information can be obtained by using observational techniques and analysis of classroom work.
- ***Check the readability levels of all materials used in informal testing***. Unless the teacher knows the approximate level of the materials, the level at which the student succeeds or fails cannot be determined.
- ***Various instruments should be used in informally assessing reading difficulties***. No one instrument can provide all the needed data.

- ***Limit the testing time according to an individual student's interest and attention span.***
- ***Verify data from one instrument by using other observations or another form or procedure for testing a given area.*** Do not draw conclusions based on limited information from one observation or test.
- ***Ask for assistance from fellow teachers.*** Consult with others as you review the assessment information on individual students. It is quite likely that another person can assist you in obtaining more information informally.

PHYSICAL FACTORS

The previous sections of this chapter have focused primarily on the assessment of cognitive performance in reading with some information related to the affective areas. However, to properly assess and guide effective learning activities, teachers must be aware of the many physical factors that may hinder learning. Physical problems are formally diagnosed by a medical doctor, but the initial observation and informal assessment is frequently noted by the classroom teacher. The physical factors commonly related to reading difficulties fall into three categories: (a) visual and auditory acuity, (b) alcohol and drugs, and (c) nutrition.

Visual and Auditory Acuity

Physical factors such as poor auditory and visual acuity account for many difficulties that affect reading. The teacher who suspects a reading problem should first determine whether the problem is in part caused by a physical factor that can be corrected. Common signs of vision and hearing problems include the following:

Indicators of Visual Acuity Problems

- Headache in forehead or temples
- Rubbing eyes frequently
- Tilting head
- Holding book too close to face
- Losing place in reading
- Blinking excessively
- Frequent errors in copying
- Evident tension during visual work
- Squinting or covering one eye
- Nausea or dizziness
- Reddened eyes
- Poor sitting position
- Excessive head movement when reading
- Avoiding close visual work
- Frequent sties or encrusted eyelids
- Blurring of print while reading
- Excessive tearing
- Evident fatigue and distress while reading

Indicators of Auditory Acuity Problems

- Monotonous voice pitch
- Cupping hand behind ear
- Turning ear toward speaker
- Misunderstanding directions frequently
- Requesting speaker to repeat statements
- Generally inattentive
- Poor pronunciation abnormal to age
- Turning tape player or radio to unusually loud volume
- Difficulty in auditory discrimination tasks
- Hearing ringing or buzzing sounds in ear
- Blank expression
- Strained posture in listening
- Excessive amounts of wax in ears

Alcohol and Drugs

As society changes, so do schools. Alcohol and drug use has skyrocketed, contributing to several school-related problems: (a) children whose mother was a substance abuser during pregnancy, (b) children born with alcohol or drug addiction due to use by the mother, and (c) children directly using alcohol and drugs. Chronic substance abuse of the mother during pregnancy results in several types of abnormalities that affect learning. Central nervous system development is maximal during the first three months of pregnancy, and protein starvation (which occurs with substance abuse) during this period is devastating for future intellectual development. If brain tissue does not receive proper nourishment at this time, repair cannot be achieved later. Thus, children will likely have lower intelligence or a learning disability. Techniques for teaching these students are discussed in Chapter 12.

Schools are seeing more children who were born with a substance abuse addiction. These children, while no longer addicted, have mental, physical, and emotional problems caused by the addiction. Students who were crack cocaine babies show severe mood swings, short attention spans, difficulty in processing information, and delayed mental and physical development, as well as other symptoms. Research is lacking as to the best ways to teach these children, but, as part of the diagnostic process, the teacher must attempt to determine the cause of these behaviors and be assured that the problem is indeed birth-related rather than current.

Substance abuse with alcohol and drugs seems to begin at earlier ages each year. Drugs are available to many young children, making it necessary for teachers to be aware of the symptoms of drug use:

- Mood swings from lethargic to silly highs
- Inattentiveness in group and individual situations
- Social disruptions in class
- Keeps distance from acquaintances; tends to work alone

- Poor nutrition and sleep habits
- Regularly late or sick
- Dilated pupils
- Does not keep promises
- Looks for sources of money
- Seems depressed

While all of these symptoms may not be observed, teachers should seek assistance if several symptoms appear or if there is an overall change in a student's behavior. The first person to contact is the school counselor, who should be able to do the necessary follow-up to obtain assistance for the student.

Nutrition

The effect of nutrition on learning was once described briefly by saying that the hungry child cannot concentrate on learning. While this is an accurate statement, the impact of nutrition on learning is an area of intense investigation. Children need food, and they need food on a regular basis—breakfast, lunch, snacks, dinner. However, the types of food provided have a significant effect on learning, an effect that varies from student to student. Basically, we know that diets high in sugar products tend to decrease attention spans. Some students become hyperactive, or unable to control their physical movement and focus on learning tasks.

Some learning deficiencies can be traced to food allergies ranging from flour to red meat. In assessment, teachers need to be aware of changing behaviors in students and determine if these behaviors are related to a need for food or to types of food eaten. Students with low blood sugar levels may blank out when in need of food, while students with an allergy to flour may zoom around the room after a lunch of pasta and bread.

SUMMARY

Because of the growing importance of the teacher in assessment, informal assessment measures are becoming the basis for instructional planning. Using informal assessment procedures, the teacher can learn a great deal about each student in the class.

Informal assessment procedures in reading focus on how students process information as they read as well as their specific knowledge of reading skills. Observation is a valuable assessment tool. Using the two observational techniques of anecdotal records and checklists, teachers can obtain much information about the reading behaviors of students.

Other informal instruments include attitude and interest inventories, the informal reading inventory, word identification inventories, criterion-referenced and objective-based tests, the cloze procedure, and the content reading inventory. Procedures for developing, administering, and interpreting these instruments were discussed.

Informal strategies for assessing oral and written language include think-alouds and portfolios as well as miscellaneous classroom activities such as games and learning centers. When using informal assessment strategies, the teacher must continuously assess, using many sources of information to more adequately identify the student's reading behaviors when interacting with language in different situations.

Although the primary focus of this chapter was on the informal assessment of cognitive and affective behaviors related to reading, the last portion of the chapter reminded the teacher of the importance of physical factors in determining the instructional needs of a student. Visual and auditory acuity problems are responsible for many difficulties that affect reading. Two other important physical factors that affect reading performance are alcohol and drug use and nutrition.

Applying What You Read

1. Administer an informal reading inventory to five students and identify their areas of strengths and weaknesses. Then spend time observing these same five students to determine what additional information you can glean from observation.
2. Using a checklist, observe several students and record your observations. From this data, determine what other informal assessment procedures may be needed to more specifically assess their reading needs.
3. Develop your own interest inventory. Administer this inventory to several poor readers and several good readers. Compare the results.
4. Determine several specific objectives for your reading program. Develop objective-based assessment procedures to measure the objectives.
5. Make a list of sources of informal assessment data currently available in your classroom. How are you using this information? What other information do you need?
6. Identify three ways that writing is used daily in the elementary classroom. How can assessment information be obtained in each of these situations?
7. Portfolios may sound like an interesting concept to incorporate into your informal assessment procedures. How would you initiate the development of portfolios, and how would you maintain the information during the year? How would you introduce this information to parents?

NOTES

1. Rebecca Harlin and Sally Lipa, "Emergent Literacy: A Comparison of Formal and Informal Assessment Methods," *Reading Horizons.*
2. J. Lorraine Hoffman, "The Family Portfolio: Using Authentic Assessment in Family Literacy Programs," *The Reading Teacher.*
3. Courtney B. Cazden, " Contexts for Literacy: In the Mind and in the Classroom," *Journal of Reading Behavior.*
4. Yetta M. Goodman, "Kid Watching: An Alternative to Testing," *National Elementary School Principal.*
5. Herbert J. Walberg and Shiow-Ling Tsai, "Correlates of Reading Achievement and Attitude: A National Assessment Study," *Journal of Educational Research*; M. Cecil Smith, "A Longitudinal Investigation of Reading Attitude Development from Childhood to Adulthood," *Journal of Educational Research.*
6. Julianne Turner and Scott G. Paris, "How Literacy Tasks Influence Children's Motivation for Literacy," *The Reading Teachers.*

7. Irene Athey, "Reading Research in the Affective Domain," in *Theoretical Models and Processes of Reading,* 2nd ed., edited by Harry Singer and Robert Ruddell.
8. Frank Smith, *Understanding Reading: A Psycholinguistic Analysis of Reading and Learning to Read,* 4th ed.
9. Michael C. McKenna and Dennis J. Kear, "Measuring Attitude toward Reading: A New Tool for Teachers," *The Reading Teacher.*
10. William A. Henk and Steven A. Melnick, "The Reader Self-Perception (RSPS): A New Tool for Measuring How Children Feel about Themselves as Readers," *The Reading Teacher.*
11. Charles Bruckerhoff, "What Do Students Say about Reading Instruction?" *The Clearing House.*
12. Kathleen S. Jongsma and Eugene A. Jongsma, "Test Review: Commercial Informal Reading Inventories," *The Reading Teacher.*
13. John J. Pikulski and Timothy Shanahan, eds., "Informal Reading Inventories: A Critical Analysis," *Approaches to the Informal Evaluation of Reading*; Page Bristow, John Pikulski, and Peter Pelosi, "A Comparison of Five Estimates of Instructional Level," *The Reading Teacher.*
14. Valerie A. Helgren-Lempesis and Charles T. Mangrum II, "An Analysis of Alternate-Form Reliability of Three Commercially-Prepared Informal Reading Inventories," *Reading Research Quarterly.*
15. Eldon E. Ekwall, "Informal Reading Inventories: The Instructional Level," *The Reading Teacher;* Eldon E. Ekwall, "Should Repetitions Be Counted as Errors?" *The Reading Teacher;* Warren S. Hays, *Criteria for the Instructional Level of Reading;* John Pikulski, "Informal Reading Inventories," *The Reading Teacher.*
16. Jerry L. Johns and Anne Marie Magliari, "Informal Reading Inventories: Are the Betts Criteria the Best Criteria?" *Reading Improvement.*
17. Maud McBroom, Julia Sparrow, and Catherine Eckstein, *Scale for Determining a Child's Reader Level.*
18. Yetta M. Goodman and Carolyn L. Burke, *Reading Miscue Inventory.*
19. Jean Wallace Gillet and Charles Temple, *Understanding Reading Problems: Assessment and Instruction.*
20. Frederick A. Duffelmeyer and Barbara Blakelly Duffelmeyer, "Are IRI Passages Suitable for Assessing Main Idea Comprehension?" *The Reading Teacher.*
21. Frederick A. Duffelmeyer, Susan S. Robinson, and Susan E. Squire, "Vocabulary Questions on Informal Reading Inventories," *The Reading Teacher.*
22. James R. Kalmbach, "Getting at the Point of Retellings," *Journal of Reading;* Karen D. Wood, "Free Associational Assessment: An Alternative to Traditional Testing," *Journal of Reading.*
23. Jay S. Blanchard, *Computer-Based Reading Assessment Instrument.*
24. Jerry L. Johns, *Computer-Based Graded Word Lists.*
25. Michael C. McKenna, *Computer-Assisted Reading Achievement.*
26. William A. Henk, "Reading Assessments of the Future: Toward Precision Diagnosis," *The Reading Teacher.*
27. Child Study Committee on the International Kindergarten Union, *A Study of the Vocabulary of Children before Entering First Grade*; Arthur I. Gates, *A Reading Vocabulary for the Primary Grades*; H. E. Wheeler and Emma A. Howell, "A First Grade Vocabulary Study," *Elementary School Journal.*
28. Dale D. Johnson, "The Dolch List Re-Examined," *The Reading Teacher*; Robert L. Hillerich, "Word Lists: Getting It All Together," *The Reading Teacher.*
29. Edward Fry, "A New Instant Word List," *The Reading Teacher.*
30. Maryann Eeds, "Bookwords: Using a Beginning Word List of High Frequency Words from Children's Literature K–3," *The Reading Teacher.*
31. Henry Kucera and W. Nelson Francis, *Computational Analysis for Present-Day American English*; Albert J. Harris and Milton D. Jacobson, *Basic Elementary Reading Vocabularies*; Stanford E. Taylor, Helen Frackenpohl, and Catherine White, *A Revised Core Vocabulary: A Basic Vocabulary for Grades 1–8, An Advanced Vocabulary for Grades 9–13*; John B. Carroll, Peter Davies, and Barry Richman, *Word Frequency Book;* Wayne Otto and Robert Chester, "Sight Words for Beginning

Readers," *Journal of Educational Research;* Dale D. Johnson, Alden Moe, with James Bauman, *The Ginn Word Book for Teachers.*

32. Richard L. Slosson, *Slosson Oral Reading Test.*
33. J. F. Jastak, S. W. Bijou, and S. R. Jastak, *Wide Range Achievement Test.*
34. Patricia M. Cunningham, "The Names Test: A Quick Assessment of Decoding Ability," *The Reading Teacher.*
35. Frederick A. Duffelmeyer, Ann E. Kruse, Donna J. Merkley, and Stephen A. Fyfe, "Further Validation and Enhancement of the Names Test," *The Reading Teacher.*
36. Wayne Otto, "Evaluating Instruments for Assessing Needs and Growth in Reading," in *Assessment Problems in Reading*, edited by W. H. MacGinitie, p. 17–18.
37. Otto, "Evaluating Instruments," p. 18.
38. Wilson L. Taylor, "Cloze Procedure: A New Tool for Measuring Readability," *Journalism Quarterly.*
39. Eugene R. Jongsma, *The Cloze Procedure: A Survey of the Research.*
40. Claire Ashby-Davis, "Cloze and Comprehension: A Qualitative Analysis and Critique," *Journal of Reading.*
41. John Jonz, "Another Turn in the Conversation: What Does Cloze Measure?" *TESOL Quarterly;* Michael C. McKenna and Kent Layton, "Concurrent Validity of Cloze as a Measure of Intersentential Comprehension," *Journal of Educational Psychology*; Roger J. DeSanti, "Concurrent and Predictive Validity of a Semantically and Syntactically Sensitive Cloze Scoring System," *Reading Research and Instruction.*
42. John Bormuth, " The Cloze Readability Procedure," *Elementary English.*
43. Earl H. Cheek, Jr., Rona F. Flippo, and Jimmy D. Lindsey, *Reading for Success in Elementary School*, p. 411.
44. Sheila W. Valencia, "Alternative Assessment: Separating the Wheat from the Chaff," *The Reading Teacher.*
45. Suzanne E. Wade, "Using Think-Alouds to Assess Comprehension," *The Reading Teacher.*
46. Sheila W. Valencia, "A Portfolio Approach to Classroom Reading Assessment: The Whys, Whats, and Hows," *The Reading Teacher.*
47. Valencia, "A Portfolio Approach," p. 339.
48. Roger Farr and Bruce Tone, *Portfolio and Performance Assessment*, pp. 1–19.
49. R. J. Tierney, M. A. Carter, and L. E. Desai, *Portfolio Assessment in the Reading-Writing Classroom.*
50. Earl H. Cheek, Jr., Rona F. Flippo, and Jimmy D. Lindsey, *Reading for Success in Elementary Schools*, p. 415.
51. Michael M. Milone, Jr., "Electronic Portfolios: Who's Doing Them and How? *Technology and Learning.*
52. J. Lorraine Hoffman, "The Family Portfolio: Using Authentic Assessment in Family Literacy Programs," *The Reading Teacher.*
53. E. Hiebert and L. Schultz, "The Power of Portfolios," *Educational Leadership.*
54. Linda Irwin-DeVitis, "Literacy Portfolios: The Myth and the Reality," in *Literacy Assessment for Today's Schools*, edited by Martha D. Collins and Barbara G. Moss.

CHAPTER 3

Formal Assessment Procedures

Following a study of the various informal assessment strategies, Mr. Turner and the teachers at Twin Lakes School turned their attention to learning more about the formal assessment procedures that can be used to guide their reading instruction. The teachers defined formal assessment procedures as those instruments that are administered using specific guidelines and that provide norms to compare a student's scores with those of other students at the same age or grade level. The teachers at Twin Lakes School are most familiar with the formal testing procedures associated with administering group achievement tests and their state test. They realize that these tests are not designed to yield the in-depth assessment that can be obtained from other specific reading tests. The teachers used the information in this chapter to familiarize themselves with other formal procedures that may be used in conjunction with the informal procedures presented in Chapter 2.

Mr. Turner, Ms. Brooks, and Ms. Self have suggested that they should use formal procedures to further explore students' reading problems in order to provide more appropriate reading instruction. They realize that some formal assessment instruments are administered to groups of students, while others must be administered individually. Most of the formal tests are relatively simple to administer. The teacher needs only to review the materials and administer the instrument several times under the supervision of a trained person prior to using it in the classroom.

This chapter reviews a variety of formal assessment procedures, including oral reading tests, diagnostic reading tests, auditory discrimination tests, intelligence tests, and survey reading tests. The following specific questions regarding these tests are addressed in the chapter.

- What are formal assessment procedures?
- Why are formal procedures important in assessing reading?
- What types of formal procedures are available to evaluate reading difficulties?
- What are some differences between individually administered and group-administered formal procedures?

- How does the teacher select appropriate tests for use with particular students?
- What are the various individually administered formal instruments?
- How do they compare?
- What are the various group-administered formal assessment instruments?
- How do they compare?
- How are the different tests administered?

Vocabulary to Know

- **Formal assessment procedures**
- **Group achievement tests**
- **Group-administered formal tests**
- **Group assessment tests**
- **Group survey tests**
- **Individual assessment reading tests**
- **Individual auditory discrimination tests**
- **Individual intelligence tests**
- **Individual oral reading tests**
- **Individually administered formal tests**

AN OVERVIEW

Formal assessment procedures are the standardized techniques used by teachers and reading specialists to learn more about students' strengths and weaknesses in reading. However, as Bussis and Chittenden suggest, "although research of the past 30 years has fundamentally reshaped conceptions of language and language learning, these changes have yet to find expression in reading tests."[1] Likewise, Squire and Valencia and Pearson say that while our research in reading reflects the importance of reading as a process, emphasizing cognitive processing, our assessment in the classroom continues at the skills level.[2] This contrast between research findings and current classroom practice is described further in Table 3.1. Current literature is filled with descriptions of how reading is a holistic process in which prior knowledge and language understanding are essential to comprehension. However, the formal tests in today's market represent a more traditional view of reading as a skills-oriented procedure; they provide data on students' strengths and weaknesses in specific areas, especially word identification and general comprehension. This chapter presents information on formal assessment instruments currently available to teachers. Some of the newer instruments incorporate current research, while others continue to reflect a traditional view of reading. In viewing formal assessment at this time, it must be said that reading educators are at a crossroads.

One of the major premises of our text is that formal assessment procedures can be used to supplement informal procedures. Informal procedures, as outlined in Chapter 2, allow more latitude in the testing situation; they are not bound by the standardized procedures required of formal tests. Teacher use of formal tests should be limited to selected tests that can provide more information on a specific problem area identified through informal procedures. Thus, large amounts of teacher and student time are not necessary for formal assessment; formal tests should be administered only as needed.

Table 3.1 Reflections on Current Research Versus Current Practices in Assessing Reading

New views of the reading process tell us that . . .	Yet when we assess reading comprehension, we . . .
Prior knowledge is an important determinant of reading comprehension.	Mask any relationship between prior knowledge and reading comprehension by using lots of short passages on lots of topics.
A complete story or text has structural and topical integrity.	Use short texts that seldom approximate the structural and topical integrity of an authentic text.
Inference is an essential part of the process of comprehending units as small as sentences.	Rely on literal comprehension test items.
The diversity in prior knowledge across individuals as well as the varied causal relations in human experiences invite many possible inferences to fit a text or question.	Use multiple choice items with only one correct answer, even when many of the responses might, under certain conditions, be plausible.
The ability to vary reading strategies to fit the text and the situation is one hallmark of an expert reader.	Seldom assess how and when students vary the strategies they use during normal reading, studying, or when the going gets tough.
The ability to synthesize information from various parts of the text and different texts is a hallmark of an expert reader.	Rarely go beyond finding the main idea of a paragraph or passage.
The ability to ask good questions of text, as well as to answer them, is a hallmark of an expert reader.	Seldom ask students to create or select questions about a selection they may have just read.
All aspects of a reader's experience, including habits that arise from school and home, influence reading comprehension.	Rarely view information on reading habits and attitudes as being important information about performance.
Reading involves the orchestration of many skills that complement one another in a variety of ways.	Use tests that fragment reading into isolated skills and report performance on each.
Skilled readers are fluent; their word identification is sufficiently automatic to allow most cognitive resources to be used for comprehension.	Rarely consider fluency as an index of skilled reading.
Learning from text involves the restructuring, application, and flexible use of knowledge in new situations.	Often ask readers to respond to the text's declarative knowledge rather than to apply it to near and far transfer tasks.

Sheila Valencia and P. David Pearson, "Reading Assessment: Time for a Change," *The Reading Teacher 40* (April 1987): 731. Reprinted with permission of Sheila Valencia and P. David Pearson and the International Reading Association.

Formal assessment procedures, like informal assessment procedures, have both advantages and disadvantages. The chief disadvantages are finding the time needed to administer the instruments, in the case of testing individuals and acquiring a sufficient number of copies of a test when using them with groups. To deal with the first problem, teachers may use group tests whenever possible and request the assistance of the reading teacher if numerous individual tests are needed. In the second case, they can select initially only one or two formal tests that seem to best meet the general needs of students and then build a test file in the school over several years.

The advantages of formal assessment procedures definitely outnumber the disadvantages. Although the time factor for individual testing may be viewed as a disadvantage, the one-on-one testing situation is an advantage in itself because the teacher learns more about the student. Additionally, formal procedures provide the teacher with a more complete profile of the student, as well as a means of comparing the student with others of a similar age. Although a diagnosis is not based on this comparative data, these data assist in communicating with parents.

The tests presented in this chapter are classified as group or individual tests and further subdivided by type. The tests classified as individual formal assessment procedures are administered to only one student at a time. These are more time-consuming and require increased proficiency and experience on the part of the examiner to interpret the information. However, they yield much valuable information and assist in determining students' strengths and weaknesses more accurately.

Group-administered formal tests can be used to test large or small groups of students. However, these tests may not yield as much information on the individual student, and the teacher does not obtain the helpful personal information that is gained in an individual testing situation. This lack of specific information, combined with the time involved in scoring and interpreting test results, may dissuade teachers from using group tests.

Because of the various factors involved in implementing effective reading instruction, a concern of the classroom teacher is when to use these formal tools. Practically speaking, using group tests is probably a more realistic objective than using individual tests. Group tests are relatively easy to administer since the time involved is minimal and an entire class can be tested at one time. The teacher's schedule can be adjusted for several hours to accommodate this type of testing.

Individual formal instruments are time-consuming to administer because students must be tested on a one-to-one basis. These instruments require time as well as more specialized training for administration, scoring, and interpretation. Thus, they are best used as supplements to informal measures and formal group measures. However, individual formal instruments play an important role in providing an in-depth assessment of a small number of students in the classroom.

Because of the constraints associated with individual formal instruments, a classroom teacher's testing time may be more wisely spent using group tests in conjunction with the informal procedures already discussed in Chapter 2. Nevertheless, in particular instances such as the case of a severely disabled reader, the teacher might use one or two well-chosen, individually administered instruments. The teacher needs a working knowledge of these instruments to better understand reports from the reading specialist or to request further testing from other outside sources. Regardless of the pros and cons of using formal assessment procedures, teachers must be familiar with them in order to provide more effective reading instruction in their classes. To assist the teacher in selecting appropriate formal assessment procedures, the tests discussed in this chapter are summarized in Table 3.2 (group tests) and Table 3.3 (individual tests; see page 80). Using these tables as references, teachers can select the testing instruments that best meet their needs at a given time. A further resource for selecting tests is provided by Mavrogenes, Hanson, and Winkley.[3] Reviews for many standardized tests are found in the *Mental Measurements Yearbook.*

GROUP TEST PROCEDURES

Group-administered tests come in several types and are used for various purposes; what they have in common is that they can be administered in a group situation. The various types include survey reading tests, assessment reading tests, and achievement tests (see Table 3.2). Each type has a specific purpose that is different from the others. The use of each depends on the testing conditions and information desired.

Table 3.2 Formal Group Tests

Test	Appropriate Levels	Subtest Scores
Survey Tests		
Boehm Test of Basic Concepts, Revised	Grades K–2	Total score of concept knowledge
Gates-MacGinitie Reading Tests	Grades K–12	Vocabulary, comprehension, total
Diagnostic Reading Tests		
MAT6 Reading Diagnostic Tests	Grades K.5–9.9	Varies with form—visual discrimination, auditory discrimination, sight vocabulary, reading comprehension, rate of comprehension
Stanford Diagnostic Reading Test	Grades 1.5–13.0	Varies with form—phonetic analysis, vocabulary, comprehension, and scanning
Test of Reading Comprehension	Ages 7.0 to 7.11	General reading comprehension core, general vocabulary, syntactic similarities, paragraph reading, sentence sequencing
Achievement Tests		
California Achievement Test	Grades K–12	Reading, spelling, language, mathematics, reference skills
Comprehensive Test of Basic Skills	Grades 0.1–13.6	Reading, language, arithmetic, study skills
Metropolitan Achievement Test	Grades K–12.9	Reading, comprehension, language, mathematics, science, social studies
Stanford Achievement Test	Grades 1.5–9	Reading comprehension, language, mathematics, science, social science, auditory skills
Peabody Individual Achievement Test	Grades K–12	General information, reading recognition, reading comprehension, written expression, mathematics, spelling

Table 3.3 Formal Individual Tests

Test	Appropriate Levels	Subtest Scores
Oral Reading		
Gray Oral Reading Test, Revised	Grades 1–12	Oral reading quotient, passage score, comprehension score
Slosson Oral Reading Test, Revised	Grades 1–8 and high school	Reading level
Diagnostic Reading		
Diagnostic Reading Scales	Grades 1–6	Independent, instruction, frustration levels, eight phonic tests
Durrell Analysis of Reading Difficulty	Grades 1–6	Oral reading, silent reading, listening, flash words, word analysis, spelling, handwriting, visual memory, hearing sounds
Formal Reading Inventory	Grades 1–12	Standard scores, percentile ranks
Test of Early Reading Ability, 2nd ed.	Ages 3.0 to 9.11	Total score
Tests of Language Development, 2nd ed.	Ages 4.0 to 12.11	Twelve tests of oral language concepts
Test of Written Language, 2nd ed.	Ages 7.0 to 17.11	Nine subtests of written language concepts
Intelligence		
Peabody Picture Vocabulary Test, Revised	Ages 2.6 to 18	I.Q., mental age
Slosson Intelligence Test, Revised	Ages 4 and above	I.Q., mental age
Test of Nonverbal Intelligence	Ages 5 to adult	I.Q., mental age
Emergent Literacy		
An Observational Survey of Early Literacy Achievement	K–1	Oral reading, letter identification, concepts about print, sight word recognition, writing vocabulary, hearing and recording sounds in words

Survey Reading Tests

Survey reading tests are used to determine reading levels in three areas: vocabulary, comprehension, and rate of reading. The primary reason for their popularity is the ease with which they can be administered by classroom teachers. The manuals for these instruments are usually quite clear and concise in describing the appropriate manner for administering, scoring, and interpreting the data. There are other reasons for their popularity as well. Survey reading tests can be administered and scored in a relatively short period of time, especially when compared with individually administered tests. They are standardized, using national norms, and some, such as the Gates-MacGinitie Reading Tests, provide local norms. In most instances, these instruments are carefully constructed by persons with expertise in test construction and in the area of reading.

Survey reading tests also have disadvantages. One disadvantage is that the information obtained lacks depth. For example, only two or, at the most, three scores are obtained from these instruments. The scores are in the general areas of vocabulary, comprehension, and rate of reading. The results are reported in grade equivalents, stanines, or percentiles, or perhaps all three. One suggestion for turning this disadvantage into an advantage is to analyze each item in the instrument so that more detailed information about a student can be obtained. However, such an analysis is quite time-consuming, and there are other instruments that provide the same data in less time.

Another disadvantage of survey reading tests is that the scores obtained are frequently inflated, representing the students' frustration levels; the scores do not indicate the students' instructional or independent levels. However, if scores represent the most accurate information available, use them as a starting point for assessment in conjunction with an informal reading inventory.

By considering the advantages and disadvantages of survey reading tests, teachers can determine whether such instruments would be beneficial in their classrooms. The primary purpose of a survey reading test is to serve as a screening device. Thus, the most appropriate way to use this instrument in a classroom situation is to administer it to the entire class, determine grade-equivalent scores for each student, make an item analysis to obtain more assessment information, set up initial groups using the results of this instrument and any other available information, and then begin to administer other assessment instruments to students about whom more in-depth information is desired. Used in this manner, the survey reading test can provide helpful information. Survey reading tests are frequently used in special reading programs in which general data are needed to measure the progress of all enrolled in the program. Two of the most widely used survey reading tests are the *Boehm Test of Basic Concepts* and the *Gates-MacGinitie Reading Tests.*

Boehm Test of Basic Concepts, Revised (Boehm-R) and Boehm-Preschool

Ann E. Boehm
The Psychological Corporation, San Antonio, Texas, 1986
Grades preschool–2

The Boehm-R is designed to measure children's mastery of basic concepts considered important for following teachers' verbal instructions and for success during the first years of school. Because language knowledge is so essential for success in reading, teachers may want to use this test, which can be administered to small groups or individuals, to determine the concept knowledge of young students. Students who do not understand these basic concepts will experience difficulty in early reading.

Forms C and D of the test measure the same 50 concepts with 26 additional concepts measured at the applications level for grades 1 and 2.[4] Information from this test can be used by kindergarten and primary-level teachers to provide appropriate instruction based on items answered incorrectly on the test. The *Boehm Resource Guide for Basic Concept Teaching* may be used as a guide for teaching these basic concepts.

The Boehm-Preschool version is a downward extension of the Boehm-R. It measures a child's understanding of the basic relational concepts necessary for achievement in the beginning school years. It is individually administered and is most appropriate for use with three- to five-year-old children and older children with identified language difficulties.

Gates-MacGinitie Reading Tests, 3rd edition

Walter H. MacGinitie and Ruth K. MacGinitie
The Riverside Publishing Company, Chicago, Illinois, 1989
Grades K–12

The Gates-MacGinitie Reading Tests are among the better-known group survey reading test batteries. This instrument was developed in 1965 by Arthur Gates and Walter MacGinitie; however, it was primarily a revision of the *Gates Primary Reading Tests,* the *Gates Advanced Primary Reading Tests,* and the *Gates Reading Survey.*

The 1989 battery uses a booklet format, which facilitates test administration and hand scoring. One of the main advantages of this instrument is that a classroom teacher can administer the instrument one day, hand-score the booklets, and have the grade equivalents, stanines, or percentiles available for use the next day. All items are in multiple-choice format.

Another useful feature of the third edition is that the test materials are new and relate to the current experiential patterns of students. This edition was field-tested with students of various socioeconomic and racial backgrounds to develop items that decrease cultural bias in the instrument. As a result, new national norms were developed. Out-of-level norms are also available.

The *Gates-MacGinitie Reading Tests* consist of nine tests for grades K through 12. A new level, PRE (prereading), has been added for kindergarten and the beginning of the first grade. This test is untimed and measures literacy concepts, reading instruction relational concepts, oral language concepts, and letters and letter-sound correspondences. Level R, also untimed, is designed for use with first graders and assesses knowledge of initial consonants and consonant clusters, final consonants and consonant clusters, vowels, and use of context.

Interesting comprehension passages that correspond in difficulty and suitability to the specified grade level are provided for levels 1 through 10–12. Each level includes two tests: a vocabulary test and a comprehension test.

The third edition uses scoring keys or self-scoring answer sheets, which enable the teacher to score the booklets much faster. Another useful service provided by the publisher is the machine-scored profile sheet, which not only reports the testing data but also includes a brief evaluation of the student. For school systems using the Riverside Scoring Service this is an added advantage. *Gates-MacGinitie Reading Tests* have two forms at each level except for levels PRE, R, and 1. Each level, with the exception of PRE and R, provides three scores: vocabulary, comprehension, and total reading score. The levels are divided as follows:

- Level PRE: grades K–1.1
- Level R: grades 1.0–1.9
- Level 1: grades 1.5–1.9
- Level 2: grades 2
- Level 3: grades 3
- Level 4: grades 4
- Level 5/6: grades 5–6
- Level 7/9: grades 7–9
- Level 10/12: grades 10–12[5]

The teacher's manual includes information on raw scores, standard scores, grade equivalents, percentile ranks in grade, NCE scores, and stanines. This test is widely used as a screening device in reading, and has proven to be a valuable instrument for use with groups of students.

Diagnostic Reading Tests

Group diagnostic reading tests are used quite extensively in school systems throughout the country. They have a valuable role in assisting teachers to gather more in-depth information about their students in minimal time. Their popularity is further enhanced by the fact that they are easy to administer.

Detailed manuals and the provision of norms further enhance the ease of administration. The manuals that accompany group diagnostic reading instruments are easy to understand and facilitate the successful administration, scoring, and interpretation of the tests. For example, the manual that accompanies the *Stanford Diagnostic Reading Test* is extremely thorough and quite detailed. The time required for administering these instruments is relatively brief compared with that required for individually administered instruments. A classroom teacher's time is so valuable that speed is imperative in considering appropriate instruments. Of equal importance are the norms provided. Diagnostic reading instruments are standardized using national norms. Therefore, they allow school systems to compare their school population with others.

The primary advantage of the group diagnostic reading test is that a great deal of information is obtained during a relatively brief period of time. In contrast to group survey reading tests, which yield only vocabulary, comprehension, and rate-of-reading scores, group diagnostic reading tests furnish more in-depth information. They provide several subtest scores that aid in ascertaining areas of strengths and weaknesses. The *Stanford Diagnostic Reading Test* yields scores in several areas, including structural analysis, auditory discrimination, auditory vocabulary, and literal and inferential comprehension. The basic difference between the two types of instruments, other than subtest information, is the time and expense involved. Usually, group survey reading tests require less time than group diagnostic reading tests and are less expensive.

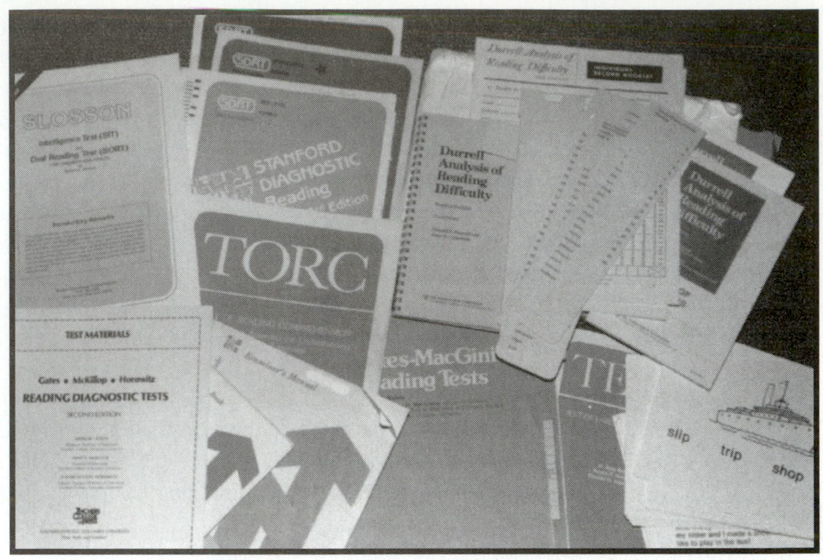

Formal reading tests are used to provide specific evaluation data on individuals and groups.

Photo courtesy of Edward B. Lasher.

The primary disadvantage of group diagnostic tests is the lack of teacher-student interaction during testing. While these tests are being taken, teachers can obtain evaluative data by observing individual students. Such individual observation and interaction, of course, is not possible when tests are group administered. Other limitations of the various tests are explored in the following pages. Teachers should note, however, that the primary objective of the group diagnostic reading test is to provide as much in-depth information in as short a period of time as possible.

Metropolitan Achievement Tests, 6th edition (MAT6), Reading Diagnostic Tests

Roger C. Farr, George A. Prescott, Irving H. Balow, and Thomas P. Hogan
The Psychological Corporation, San Antonio, Texas, 1986
Grades K.5–9.9

The MAT6 Reading Diagnostic Tests are designed to provide classroom teachers with detailed, criterion-referenced, prescriptive information needed to assess student strengths and weaknesses in reading. The levels of the tests include primer (grades K.5–1.9), primary 1 (grades 1.5–2.9), primary 2 (grades 2.5–3.9), elementary (grades 3.5–4.9), intermediate (grades 5.0–6.9), and advanced 1 (grades 7.0–9.9). Each level of the instrument contains tests that reflect the curriculum generally taught at that level.

- *Primer:* visual discrimination, letter recognition, auditory discrimination, sight vocabulary, phoneme-grapheme—consonants, vocabulary in context, and reading comprehension

- *Primary 1:* auditory discrimination, sight vocabulary, phoneme-grapheme—consonants, phoneme-grapheme—vowels, vocabulary in context, word part clues, and reading comprehension
- *Primary 2:* sight vocabulary, phoneme-grapheme—consonants, phoneme-grapheme—vowels, vocabulary in context, word part clues, and reading comprehension
- *Elementary:* phoneme-grapheme—consonants, phoneme-grapheme—vowels, vocabulary in context, word part clues, rate of comprehension, and reading comprehension
- *Intermediate:* phoneme-grapheme—consonants, phoneme-grapheme—vowels, vocabulary in context, word part clues, rate of comprehension, skimming and scanning, and reading comprehension
- *Advanced 1*: vocabulary in context, rate of comprehension, skimming and scanning, and reading comprehension

The information provided by this group diagnostic test includes the student's overall reading achievement, an estimate of the student's instructional reading level, and information regarding performance on each of the objectives assessed. The reading comprehension subtest measures literal and inferential comprehension as well as critical analysis. The primer level has only one form (L), while the primary 1 through advanced 1 levels have two forms (L and M).

The instructional reading level (IRL) is derived from silent reading passages on the reading comprehension test. From this information, the teacher is provided with a report listing the students' scores and suggested instructional groupings. Each passage on the reading comprehension test also has a purpose-setting question to assist the reader in activating prior knowledge about the given topic. The detailed teacher's manual provides criterion-referenced information, teaching suggestions, a table noting the importance of the various reading skills, and tables that provide a full range of derived scores, including scaled scores, percentile ranks, stanines, grade equivalents, and normal curve equivalents. Norms are also provided for national and local school populations.[6]

The MAT6 is a welcome addition as a group assessment reading instrument. Classroom teachers, especially those employed in school systems using the Metropolitan Achievement Tests, should find it very useful.

Stanford Diagnostic Reading Test, 4th edition (SDRT4)

Bjorn Karlsen and Eric F. Gardner
The Psychological Corporation, San Antonio, Texas, 1995
Grades 1.5–13.0

The SDRT4 is one of the more widely used group assessment reading tests. The latest edition of the SDRT4 has six levels, with one form at each of the first three levels and two alternate and equivalent forms at each of the three upper levels. The six levels are red (grades 1.5–2.5), orange (grades 2.5–3.5), green (grades 3.5–4.5), purple (grades 4.5–6.5), brown (grades 6.5–8.9), and blue (grades 9.0–13.0). The areas assessed on each level are as follows:

- *Red, orange, and green levels*: phonetic analysis, vocabulary, and comprehension
- *Purple, brown, and blue levels*: vocabulary, comprehension, and scanning

Within the comprehension section of each level, three different types of texts are used in an effort to more adequately assess each student's strengths and weaknesses. These include recreational texts such as fiction, textual material such as nonfictional literature and textbooks, and functional texts such as directions, rules, advertisements, and labels.

In addition to the various standardized levels, there are three optional informal assessment instruments that are scored and interpreted by the classroom teacher: (a) a Reading Strategies Survey, designed to examine which reading strategies students use in a variety of reading situations; (b) a Reading Questionnaire, developed to examine students' attitudes toward reading, reading interests, and familiarity with concepts found in the comprehension subtest; and finally, (c) Story Retelling, which allows teachers to evaluate comprehension in a story retelling setting.

The primary purpose of the SDRT4 is to assist in evaluating reading strengths and weaknesses. Scores are reported in stanines, percentile ranks, scaled scores, and grade equivalents.

One of the strengths of the SDRT4 is the excellent manual. The section on interpreting the data is one of its best features. Other strengths of the SDRT4 include teacher time for administration and interpretation, the use of silent reading as well as interactive formats such as story retelling, and ideas for instruction. It can be administered in less than two hours and generates a great deal of useful information. Like other group diagnostic tests, the SDRT4 does not require the classroom teacher to be a testing specialist in order to administer and interpret it. The directions in the manual are quite clear and specific as to proper administration, and the interpretive section of the manual is excellent.

This test is obviously well suited for use by the classroom teacher and is an excellent group diagnostic tool for obtaining initial evaluative information.

Test of Reading Comprehension, 3rd edition (TORC3)

Virginia L. Brown, Donald D. Hammill, and J. Lee Wiederholt
Pro-Ed, Austin, Texas, 1994 (May also be purchased through The Psychological Corporation) Ages 7–0 to 17–11

Using references addressing the psycholinguistic and cognitive components of reading, the authors of TORC3 have developed a diagnostic test that measures general reading comprehension and specialized reading comprehension for various content areas. The four subtests that form the general reading comprehension core are general vocabulary, syntactic similarities, paragraph reading, and an optional subtest of sentence sequencing. These subtests are relatively free from the influences of specific content area vocabulary. Four diagnostic supplements provide additional information about the students' comprehension abilities in dealing with content area vocabularies (mathematics, social studies, and science) and in reading directions for schoolwork.

The TORC3 is a silent reading test with no time limits. The format of each subtest varies to fit the area being assessed.

- ***General Vocabulary***. This subtest consists of 25 items, with each item consisting of three stimulus words that are related in some way. The student is asked to select two words from the set of four provided that are related to the three stimulus words.
- ***Syntactic Similarities***. This subtest consists of 20 items, with five sentences for each item. The student chooses two of the sentences that have the same or nearly the same meaning.
- ***Paragraph Reading***. Six paragraphs are followed by five multiple-choice questions for each paragraph. Each set of questions uses the same format: (1) best title, (2) story details, (3) inference, (4) negative inference, and (5) story details. This format allows the teacher to determine if a pattern exists in the errors.
- ***Sentence Sequencing***. This optional subtest has 10 items consisting of five randomly ordered sentences. The student must place the sentences in order to develop a meaningful paragraph.
- ***Mathematics Vocabulary, Social Studies Vocabulary, and Science Vocabulary***. There are 25 items used on each of these three subtests to measure the student's understanding of sets of vocabulary items related to the various content areas. Using a format like that in general vocabulary, the student selects the appropriate words that form a relationship with the given stimulus words. The subtests are scored separately by content area.
- ***Reading the Directions of Schoolwork***. This is another optional subtest designed for younger and remedial readers to determine their comprehension of written directions encountered in schoolwork. These 25 items require that the item be read and the directions carried out on the answer sheet.

The manual that accompanies TORC3 provides careful directions for administration, information on interpreting the results, an answer key, and normative tables including percentile ranks and standard scores. Additionally, the test materials include a summary and profile sheet that can be used to review diagnostic data on an individual student.

This norm-referenced test of reading comprehension is relatively easy to administer and is comparable to other group diagnostic reading tests in the amount of time required for administration (one to three hours). Given the amount of new knowledge available regarding comprehension in the last 10 years and the doubts expressed in the research about the formats of traditional reading comprehension tests, the TORC3 represents a good beginning in adjusting both content and format. Teachers wanting more information on the comprehension abilities of their students may find this a helpful instrument.

Achievement Tests

Achievement tests are designed to measure student knowledge in various broad areas of the curriculum, the extent to which specific information has been acquired, or the extent to which certain skills have been mastered. These tests are intended to determine whether instruction in the broad areas of the curriculum has been effective.

Achievement tests are rigidly standardized, using norms developed from a large sampling of the appropriate school-age population. They are group-administered instruments that survey several curriculum areas taught in the schools. The information elicited is similar to that obtained from survey reading tests in that it does not provide in-depth evaluative information. By their very nature, achievement tests are not designed to be assessment instruments. They provide information that is general rather than specific. Scores are reported in grade equivalents, stanines, or percentiles.

The majority of achievement tests basically measure the same curriculum areas: language, mathematics, reading, science, and social studies. School systems are anxious to determine how effective their instruction is and to test as many areas of instruction as possible; achievement tests are often the least expensive means of obtaining this general information. Thus, they account for a large percentage of the standardized instruments used in the school systems.

Widely Used Tests

Five of the more widely used achievement tests and their subtest areas are described below.

California Achievement Tests, 5th edition

- CTB/McGraw-Hill, Monterey, California, 1992
  Grades K–12
  This test measures reading, spelling, language, mathematics, and study skills. Science and social studies are included at level 12 and above; there are optional end-of-course tests in many areas.

Comprehensive Test of Basic Skills, 4th edition

- CTB/McGraw-Hill, Monterey, California, 1989
  Grades K–12

This test measures reading, language, mathematics, reference skills, science, social studies, and spelling.

Metropolitan Achievement Test, 7th edition

- The Psychological Corporation, San Antonio, Texas, 1992
  Grades K–12
  This test measures reading, mathematics, language, science, and social studies through the survey battery and reading, mathematics, and language through diagnostic batteries.

Stanford Achievement Test, 9th edition

- The Psychological Corporation, San Antonio, Texas, 1996
  Grades K–13
  This test measures reading, language, mathematics, and listening. Science and social studies are measured for grade 3 and above. There is an optional writing test.

Peabody Individual Achievement Test, Revised (PIAT-R)

- American Guidance Service, Circle Pines, Minnesota, 1990
  Grades K–12
  This test measures general information, reading recognition, reading comprehension, written expression, mathematics, and spelling.

Strengths and Weaknesses

All types of instruments have strengths and limitations, and achievement tests are no exception.

Strengths

- School systems receive information covering a wide range of curriculum areas.
- Classroom teachers can easily administer these tests. Strict norming procedures are followed.
- Data assists in evaluating students' progress over a period of time.
- Some tests provide criterion-referenced test data on specific reading areas.

Limitations

- Lack of depth in information necessitates an item analysis to evaluate specific data.
- Scores received are on the students' frustration level.
- Improper administration procedures, such as massing large groups of students together in the cafeteria or auditorium, may occur; these circumstances often result in fallacious data.
- Tests require the use of silent reading skills, thus results in many instances reflect a reading problem rather than knowledge of the material being tested.

- Test results are not promptly returned to classroom teachers.
- Local norms may not be available.

With proper use under appropriate conditions, and with a recognition of their strengths and limitations, achievement tests, as broad group-survey instruments can be useful to school districts in evaluating their total curriculum. If the criterion-referenced or diagnostic test data is available and requested by the school district, achievement tests can also provide some individual assessment data on students' strengths and weaknesses in specific areas.

INDIVIDUAL TEST PROCEDURES

Individually administered instruments include oral reading tests, diagnostic reading tests, intelligence tests, and emergent literacy tests (see Table 3.3). Here we discuss instruments that are likely to be most useful to the classroom teacher. Some instruments, omitted here because they are not used frequently, may still be outstanding assessment tools.

Oral Reading Tests

In the 19th century, oral reading was the most important aspect of reading. Proper enunciation and pronunciation of words were the mark of an educated person. Students were taught to read through oral activities such as round-robin oral reading and choral reading. It was assumed that a person with good oral skills likewise possessed good silent reading skills. This assumed correlation between oral and silent reading went virtually unchallenged for many years.

More recently, questions about the use of oral reading tests have surfaced. Researchers have noted that the relationship between oral and silent reading is not great enough to use one type of instrument to predict success in the other.[7] Thus, when teachers want diagnostic data on oral reading performance, they must use an oral reading test. However, as these instruments are used, teachers need to consider Goodman's comment about oral reading when administering and interpreting such a test: There are periods in the development of reading competence when oral reading becomes very awkward. Readers who have recently become rapid, relatively effective silent readers seem to be distracted and disrupted by the necessity of encoding oral output while they are decoding meaning. Ironically, then, "poor" oral reading performance may reflect a high degree of reading competence rather than a lack of such competence.[8]

In the early 1900s, the ideas of Parker and Huey began to influence reading instruction.[9] Huey noted that reading in daily life was done silently, while students were taught oral reading at school. Parker considered oral reading, like speech, to be a means of expression, while silent reading was a matter of attending to the printed material. These comments prompted research comparing oral and silent reading. The results suggested the superiority of silent over oral reading and led to changes in testing procedures. Some felt so strongly about the importance of silent reading that they urged that oral reading not be taught.[10] The debate has continued; most teachers now realize that both oral and silent reading must be taught and that oral reading is an excellent means of diagnosing a student's word difficulties in context.

In administering oral reading tests, the teacher asks the student to read aloud and then marks the errors made, carefully noting such difficulties as mispronunciations, omissions, repetitions, substitutions, unknown words, and sometimes hesitations. Comprehension questions are asked to measure the student's understanding of material when reading orally. With this information, the teacher can assist in correcting many reading difficulties. Each oral reading test has its own marking and scoring procedures, which the instructor should review. The marking system is usually similar to that presented in the discussion of informal reading inventories in Chapter 2.

Two useful oral reading tests are the Gray Oral Reading Test and the Slosson Oral Reading Test.

Gray Oral Reading Test, 3rd edition (GORT-3)

Revised by J. Lee Wiederholt and Brian R. Bryant
Created by William S. Gray; edited by Helen M. Robinson
Pro-Ed, Austin, Texas, 1992
Also sold by The Psychological Corporation, San Antonio, Texas
Grades 1–12

The original *Gray Oral Reading Test* was a major revision of the *Standardized Oral Reading Paragraphs* first published by William S. Gray in 1915. GORT-3 is the third edition, which reflects minimal changes from GORT-R. GORT-R was a major revision based on current research and theoretical ideas. The principal purposes of this test are to assess oral reading speed and accuracy and to assist in assessing oral reading miscues and comprehension. This revised test has two equivalent forms, each containing 13 increasingly difficult passages.

The GORT-R has new normative, reliability, and validity data based on new passages designed with careful attention to story structure and content, comprehension questions in a multiple-choice format, and modifications in the scoring criteria. Time in seconds (rate) and oral reading errors (deviations from print) are combined to give an overall passage score (see Figure 3.1). Any deviations from print or miscues are counted as errors, but, of course, normal speech variations are acceptable. Five types of miscues that are classified for further assessment include meaning similarity, function similarity, graphic-phonemic similarity, multiple sources, and self-correction. The passage score is combined with the comprehension score to provide an oral reading quotient, which is the primary score for interpreting oral reading performance on the GORT-R. Grade-equivalent scores are not provided.

Figure 3.1 Summary Sheet Results for Gray Oral Reading Test

Summary of GORT-3 Test Results

Section I. Identifying Information

	Year	Month	Day
Date tested	____	____	____
Date of birth	____	____	____
Chronological age	____	____	____

School ________ Grade ____

Examiner's name ________

Examiner's title ________

Section II. Record of GORT-3 Scores

PRETEST: ____ POSTTEST: ____

Story	Rate	Accuracy	Passage Score	Comp. Score
1				
2				
3				
4				
5				
6				
7				
8				
9				
10				
11				
12				
13				
Raw Score				
Grade Equiv				
%ile				
Std. Score				

Sum of Std. Scores ____

%ile ____

Oral Reading Quotient (ORQ) ____

Section III. Record of the Test Scores

	Test Name	Test Date	GORT-3 Equiv.
1.			
2.			
3.			
4.			
5.			

Section IV. Profile of Scores

Std. Score	GORT-3 Scores: Rate	Accuracy	Passage Score	Comp. Score	ORQ	Other Scores: 1	2	3	4	5	Quotient
20	•	•	•	•	•	•	•	•	•	•	150
19	•	•	•	•	•	•	•	•	•	•	145
18	•	•	•	•	•	•	•	•	•	•	140
17	•	•	•	•	•	•	•	•	•	•	135
16	•	•	•	•	•	•	•	•	•	•	130
15	•	•	•	•	•	•	•	•	•	•	125
14	•	•	•	•	•	•	•	•	•	•	120
13	•	•	•	•	•	•	•	•	•	•	115
12	•	•	•	•	•	•	•	•	•	•	110
11	•	•	•	•	•	•	•	•	•	•	105
10	•	•	•	•	•	•	•	•	•	•	100
9	•	•	•	•	•	•	•	•	•	•	95
8	•	•	•	•	•	•	•	•	•	•	90
7	•	•	•	•	•	•	•	•	•	•	85
6	•	•	•	•	•	•	•	•	•	•	80
5	•	•	•	•	•	•	•	•	•	•	75
4	•	•	•	•	•	•	•	•	•	•	70
3	•	•	•	•	•	•	•	•	•	•	65
2	•	•	•	•	•	•	•	•	•	•	60
1	•	•	•	•	•	•	•	•	•	•	55

In revising the passages, the authors gave considerable attention to text structure and content rather than just to readability levels as determined by a readability formula. The content reflects more general reading types of passages compared with content-related passages. The complexity of the sentence structure, logical connections between sentences and clauses, and the density of words and other related factors were considered in fashioning the text structure. This attention to content and text structure rather than to readability levels resulted in passages that do not make a smooth progression from level to level when readability formulas are applied, raising questions from one reviewer. Radencich suggests that "the lack of a smooth progression from grade to grade in the readabilities . . . combined with low alternate form reliabilities . . . indicate that it cannot be used with confidence for documenting progress nor for research which requires alternate forms."[11] However, for individual assessment of oral reading strengths and weaknesses, this test seems to be adequate.

The change in comprehension questions represents another major revision in the GORT-R. The multiple-choice questions are literal, inferential, critical, and affective. The vocabulary used in the questions is carefully controlled and the questions are passage-dependent.[12]

The scores provided on this instrument give only general information; teacher interpretation of miscues and other oral reading behaviors provide the necessary assessment data. Assistance with this interpretation is available in the examiner's manual along with detailed information on test administration and scoring, and data on the development of the test.

Slosson Oral Reading Test, Revised (SORT-R)

Richard L. Slosson
Revised by Charles L. Nicholson
Slosson Educational Publications, Inc., East Aurora, New York, 1990
Grades 1–8 and high school

The *Slosson Oral Reading Test, Revised*, "is based on the ability to pronounce words at different levels of difficulty. The words have been taken from standardized school readers and the reading level obtained from testing median or standardized school achievement."[13]

This oral reading test consists of 10 lists of 20 words each and measures only word pronunciation in isolation. It makes no attempt to ascertain comprehension of oral reading. The test is not timed, except that hesitation on a word for more than five seconds counts as an error. The test should take from three to five minutes to administer. The student's raw score, the total number of words correct, can be converted to a reading level using the tables provided.

If the teacher selects the SORT as an assessment tool, it should be viewed as a test of word identification techniques rather than as an oral reading test. Thus, the teacher should note the mispronunciations made by the student as well as the types of word analysis skills employed in attempting an unknown word. Information obtained from this test depends on the teacher's knowledge and skill in observing and interpreting student responses.

Diagnostic Reading Tests

Standardized diagnostic reading tests are designed to provide in-depth analysis of reading difficulties. The individual diagnostic reading tests discussed in this section provide the most thorough assessment of reading problems. These tests are used with students who exhibit more severe reading difficulties on informal or group tests or for whom the teacher desires more detailed information.

The individual standardized diagnostic tests are time-consuming to use with a large number of students; however, the teacher can use these instruments with selected students as needed. These tests have various subtests, which assist the teacher in identifying individual reading problems.

In this section, six individual diagnostic reading tests are discussed. There are many more such tests; however, those selected are most commonly used in schools.

Diagnostic Reading Scales (DRS)

George D. Spache
CTB/McGraw-Hill, Inc., Monterey, California, 1981
Grades 1–6 and disabled readers in grades 7–12

The Diagnostic Reading Scales consist of a series of tests designed to analyze oral and silent reading skills as well as auditory comprehension. The testing materials include an examiner's manual, an examiner's record book, and a student reading book; the examiners record book is expendable. This test was revised in 1981. The purpose of this revision was to update, expand, and facilitate use of the test. The major thrust of the revision centered around reassigning grade levels to the reading selections. The new level assignments were based on analyses of revised readability formulas and results from the national study for the revision of the DRS.[14]

Additionally, the word analysis and phonics tests were revised and expanded to present nonsense words instead of isolated letters and their sounds. The manual for the examiner was revised and a cassette provided to aid in training in the use of the DRS. A 1982 technical report provides data from studies of the earlier editions as well as the 1981 edition. The test book contains three word recognition lists, two sets of 11 graded reading passages, and 12 supplementary word analysis and phonics tests. The word recognition lists form the first part of the test battery. These lists have three basic purposes:

- To function as a pretest, indicating the entry level for testing in the reading selections.
- To reveal the student's methods of decoding words in isolation.
- To evaluate the student's sight word vocabulary.

Using the level from the word recognition list, the teacher selects a passage to be read orally. The passages range in difficulty from a grade placement of 1.4 to 2.5.

There are two passages at each level. The student's oral reading performance is evaluated according to word recognition and comprehension errors. The specific number of errors allowed is indicated for each paragraph. As the student reads, the teacher marks the following errors: omissions, additions, substitutions or mispronunciations, repetitions (two or more words), and reversals.

Hesitations and self-corrections are not counted as errors, and words are not pronounced for the student. When the student fails either in word recognition or comprehension, the oral reading should stop. Spache considers the instructional level a measure of oral reading and comprehension; it is usually one level below the point of failure in the oral reading selections.

The main caution concerning the DRS is that it uses the terms "instructional" and "independent" in a way that is different from their customary use in the informal reading inventory. Teachers need to be cognizant of the difference in terminology and avoid comparing results for those levels with those for like-named levels in other instruments. It might be better to think of the DRS levels as "oral reading level" and "silent reading level" to avoid confusion.

Once the instructional level (or oral reading level) is determined, the student's independent level (or silent reading level) is ascertained by means of silent reading. Spache contends that "the majority of children can read silently with adequate comprehension at levels above the instruction level."[15] Thus, the student reads silently until more than the allowed number of comprehension questions are missed. The independent level is the final level at which the student shows the minimal level of comprehension.

In the *Spache Diagnostic Reading Scales*, the reading passages are also used to determine the student's "potential level," or the level at which the student can listen and respond satisfactorily to questions. The potential level is determined by reading the next passage above the independent level to the student and then asking questions. The potential level is the last level at which the student gives the appropriate number of correct responses.

Following the use of the reading passages, the twelve supplementary word analysis and phonics tests are administered. The content of these tests are as follows:

1. Initial consonants
2. Final consonants
3. Consonant digraphs
4. Consonant blends
5. Initial consonant substitution
6. Initial consonant sounds recognized auditorily
7. Auditory discriminations
8. Short and long vowel sounds
9. Vowels with *r*
10. Vowel diphthongs and digraphs

11. Common syllables or phonograms
12. Blending

The revised edition of the Diagnostic Reading Scales was reviewed by Lipa, who questioned the "advantage in using the DRS in preference to other published IRIs now available." She specifically criticized the length and complexity of the examiner's manual, the releveling of passages in the revised edition, the interest level of the passages, and the factual nature of some questions.[16] Questions regarding the reliability and validity of the test were addressed by Spache in the DRS technical bulletin.[17]

The DRS is useful for the classroom teacher or the reading clinician at the elementary and middle-school levels. The detailed information provided can be used with data from other instruments to obtain an in-depth profile of the reader.

Durrell Analysis of Reading Difficulty, 3rd edition

Donald D. Durrell and Jane H. Catterson
The Psychological Corporation, San Antonio, Texas, 1980
Grades 1–6

The *Durrell Analysis of Reading Difficulty* is a series of tests and situations that allow various aspects of a student's reading to be observed. It consists of a manual of directions, a booklet of reading paragraphs, a tachistoscope, various cards for use with the tachistoscope, and an individual record blank. Approximately 30 to 45 minutes of testing time are necessary to administer this test, which is composed of the following subtests:

1. Eight oral reading paragraphs with comprehension questions are provided. The student reads at least three selections. The teacher should find the "basal paragraph" or paragraph in which no more than one error is made. The "upper level" is found when seven or more errors are made in a single paragraph or when the student takes more than two minutes to read the paragraph. During the oral reading, the teacher marks omissions, mispronunciations, repetitions, words pronounced for the student, insertions, punctuation marks ignored, and hesitations. Each paragraph is timed. Following the oral reading of each paragraph, comprehension questions are asked. The checklist of errors is marked at the completion of this section. Three kinds of data are collected on these passages: oral reading errors, comprehension, and time for reading. The time element is the most important factor in scoring.
2. The silent reading subtest uses a second set of eight paragraphs. The student is timed as the designated paragraph is read silently. When the paragraph has been completed, the student is asked to tell everything remembered about the story. Following this unaided recall, the teacher asks questions to assist the student in remembering more about the story. The grade norms are based on time and memory scores.

3. The listening comprehension subtest consists of nine paragraphs. The teacher begins reading the paragraph appropriate for the student's grade or chronological age. After listening to the material read, the student responds to comprehension questions. The listening comprehension level is determined when no more than one question in eight is missed.
4. The tachistoscope is used on the word recognition and word analysis subtests. Lists of words are printed on strips of cardboard. A word is flashed for the student to recognize; if the word is missed, it is shown again with time provided for word analysis. The teacher must carefully note the student's responses during the flash and the analysis. The test is stopped when seven successive errors are made in each area. All or part of these tests may be administered as necessary to learn more about the performance of the student.
5. A listening vocabulary subtest is provided to furnish a second index of reading capacity, using the same words that appeared in the word recognition and word analysis subtests. The scores obtained on the listening vocabulary subtest are compared with the scores on the word recognition and word analysis subtests.
6. Sounds in isolation is a subtest designed to require students to produce the sounds of isolated letters, letter groups, and word parts. Included in the word parts are affixes.
7. Other subtests include spelling, phonic spelling of words, visual memory of words (primary and intermediate), and identifying sounds in words. An additional subtest included to aid in diagnosing the kindergarten-age student is the prereading phonics abilities subtest, which measures knowledge of letter names, ability to write letters, knowledge of letter sounds, and skill in matching written and spoken words.

This test provides numerous checklists to assist in deriving maximum information from each subtest. These checklists, used in conjunction with the profile chart on the front of the test booklet, will provide much assessment data on the student. The main criticism of the earlier edition of this test, as well as this edition, is its lack of information on reliability and validity. Nevertheless, the test has proven over the years to be an excellent source of diagnostic information on poor readers. Teachers should, however, be aware of the lack of technical information on this test and should consult such reviews as Schell and Jennings[18] before deciding to use the entire instrument.

Formal Reading Inventory

J. Lee Wiederholt
Pro-Ed, Austin, Texas, 1985
Grades 1–12

The *Formal Reading Inventory* is designed to provide data on silent reading comprehension as well as oral reading miscues. This test was developed in response to concerns about the lack of normative data, as well as reliability and validity information, for informal reading inventories. Four forms (A, B, C, D), each consisting of 13 stories with five comprehension questions per story, make up the basic components of the test. Form A can be used for diagnosing silent reading and form B for oral reading. Forms C and D can be used in the same way or for reassessments. The student record form is used to record answers to the questions and to summarize other information about the student. Teacher worksheets are used to code oral reading miscues of five types: meaning similarity, function similarity, graphic-phonemic similarity, multiple sources, and self-corrections. This miscue analysis provides detailed assessment data. The examiner's manual gives background information on the test, test administration and scoring procedures, and suggestions for interpreting the results.

Scores obtained on this test include standard scores and percentile ranks; no information is provided relating to grade equivalents or independent, instruction, and frustration reading levels.[19] Thus, this test provides assessment information via teacher interpretation and analysis of errors rather than through separate types of scores. The Formal Reading Inventory shares some of the same weaknesses as the Gray Oral Reading Test, Revised.[20] However, this test is a step forward because it offers normative data along with reliability and validity information.

The Test of Early Reading Ability, 2nd edition (TERA)

D. Kim Reid, Wayne P. Hresko, and Donald D. Hammill
Pro-Ed, Austin, Texas, 1989
Ages 3.0 to 9.11

TERA is designed to identify children who are significantly behind their peers in the development of reading, suggest instructional practices for overcoming their difficulty, and document their progress. Thus, the young students with whom this instrument is used must be able to understand the directions for the items, provide some type of response for these items, and have some facility with the English language. Children who have limited exposure to the sociocultural experiences in the United States will be penalized on this test.

The three areas specifically measured on this test are construction of meaning in print, knowledge of the alphabet and its functions, and knowledge of the conventions of written language. The measurement of these areas provides one test score to reflect the child's level of reading development; there are no subtest scores.

Items relating to construction of meaning are of three types: (a) awareness of print in environmental contexts (identifying signs, logos, and words frequently found in context; selecting words that go with other words: story retellings; anticipation of written language; and a cloze task), (b) knowledge of relations among vocabulary items (letter naming and alphabet recitation, oral reading, and proofreading), and (c) awareness of print in connected discourse (book handling and response to other print conventions).

A total of 50 items are used to measure these three areas and to provide three kinds of normative scores: reading quotients, percentiles, and reading ages. No grade equivalents are given.[21]

The examiner's manual provides directions for administering and scoring the test as well as suggestions for analyzing the results. To facilitate appropriate reading instruction, an item profile is offered to assist the teacher in obtaining an idea of the child's functioning across the three areas and to provide guidance in determining what further assessment may be needed.

Tests of Language Development, 2nd edition (TOLD2)

Phyllis L. Newcomer and Donald D. Hammill
Pro-Ed, Austin, Texas, 1988
Ages 4.0 to 12.11

TOLD2 is designed to identify children who have language disorders and isolate the particular types of disorders they have. This instrument is especially adept at analyzing language problems relating to semantics, syntax, and phonology.

The *Tests of Language Development* are divided into primary and intermediate sections. The primary section has seven subtests that measure different components of spoken language. Picture Vocabulary assesses the understanding of words from a semantics perspective, while Oral Vocabulary assesses defining words, also from a semantics perspective. The third, fourth, and fifth subtests—Grammatic Understanding, Sentence Imitation, and Grammatic Completion—assess understanding sentence structures, generating proper sentences, and using acceptable morphological forms from a syntax perspective respectively. Word Discrimination is the sixth subtest and assesses noticing sound differences from a phonology perspective. The seventh subtest is word articulation, which assesses saying words correctly, also from a phonology perspective.

The intermediate section of TOLD2 has six subtests that evaluate components of spoken language: Sentence Combining, which assesses constructing sentences from a syntax perspective; Vocabulary, which assesses understanding word relationships from a semantics perspective; Word Ordering, which assesses constructing sentences from a syntax perspective; General, which assesses knowledge of abstract relationships from a semantics perspective; Grammatic Comprehension, which assesses recognizing grammatical sentences from a syntax perspective; and finally, Malapropisms, which measures ability to correct ridiculous sentences from a semantics perspective.

The examiner's manual provides directions for administering and scoring the test as well as other pertinent information that helps facilitate appropriate reading instruction.

Test of Written Language, 3rd edition (TOWL3)

Donald D. Hammill and Stephen C. Larsen
Pro-Ed, Austin, Texas, 1996
Ages 7.0 to 17.11

TOWL3, designed to assess various aspects of written language, uses both essay analysis (spontaneous) and traditional test (contrived) formats. This instrument has two alternative equivalent forms and is intended for use with individuals or small groups.

The subtests that use an essay or spontaneous format are as follows:

- *Thematic Maturity*—examines the number of content elements that are included in the student's story.
- *Contextual Vocabulary*—assesses the number of nonduplicated long words used in the student's story.
- *Syntactic Maturity*—is designed to identify the number of words in the story that are used in grammatically and syntactically correct sentences.
- *Contextual Spelling*—the number of words in the story that are spelled correctly.
- *Contextual Style*—the number of different capitalization and punctuation rules that are used by the student in composing an essay.

Those subtests using a traditional or contrived test format include the following:

- *Vocabulary Sentences*—Students write sentences that show knowledge of stimulus words.
- *Style and Spelling*—Dictated sentences are written by the student and checked out for proper spelling, capitalization, and punctuation
- *Logical Sentences*—Students correct sentences that contain common illogicalities.
- *Sentence Combining*—Students combine the ideas expressed in simple sentences to write compound or complex sentences.

The examiner's manual provides directions for administering and scoring the test. It also has a section that provides suggestions for assessing written language informally and suggests ideas for teachers to use in improving their students' writing capabilities.

Intelligence Tests

The use of intelligence tests to aid in reading assessment or predict reading success is both supported and discredited in the research. However, the general conclusion is that group intelligence tests are more a measure of reading ability than intelligence. Individual intelligence tests seem to be better indicators of potential. In fact, an IQ test is not an essential measure in assessing a reading problem and usually provides little information beyond that gained by observation or by administering an individual reading test.

Should the teacher believe that an intelligence measure is needed to provide more necessary information, and if individual IQ test data are not available, he can choose from three individual intelligence measures that can be administered by teachers.

Peabody Picture Vocabulary Test, Revised (PPVT-R)

Lloyd M. Dunn and Leota M. Dunn
American Guidance Service, Inc., Circle Pines, Minnesota, 1981
Ages 2.6 to adult

The PPVT-R is designed to provide an estimate of a student's verbal intelligence by assessing hearing vocabulary. This is done using 150 sets of four pictures; the student selects the named picture for each set. The kit includes a spiral-bound book containing the pictures, a manual, and individual test record booklets. There are two forms, A and B, which are included in one kit. The test requires about 10 to 15 minutes for administration and provides an IQ, a percentile score, and a PPVT score. Teachers should recognize that studies of this instrument show that it provides varying information depending on the assessed population,[22] and that this test is strictly a measure of intelligence based on the student's vocabulary knowledge. Because vocabulary and language knowledge are so important to success in reading, this test is better used as a predictor of reading success than of intelligence.

Slosson Intelligence Test, Revised (SIT-R)

Richard L. Slosson
Revised by Charles L. Nicholson and Terry L. Hibpshman
Slosson Educational Publications, Inc., East Aurora, New York, 1991
Ages preschool to adult

The SIT-R provides a verbal measure of mental age, which is indicated by the raw score. Validity, reliability, and relevance to reading success are the points often questioned about this intelligence test. The Slosson was developed to emulate the Stanford-Binet. Many items were adapted from the Stanford-Binet (form L–M) and this test is used to provide criterion validity for the SIT-R. The test is individually administered using verbal questions that call for short or moderate-length answers. The manual suggests that the test can be administered in 10 to 20 minutes, but the experience of the authors is that about 15 to 30 minutes are necessary.

This test was developed as a short screening instrument for teachers and others without extensive training in test administration. Armstrong and Mooney found that the results were equally valid when the test was given by a teacher or a test administrator.[23]

The SIT-R, like all other verbal measures of intelligence, penalizes the student with limited experiences in language. Thus, the classroom teacher must exercise caution. A number of changes were made in the 1990 edition of the SIT, but it remains very similar in content to the other editions. This edition contains sections on validity, independent sampling, and other research findings, as well as an extended bibliography. Moreover, an item analysis can be purchased as a supplement to aid in screening for strengths and weaknesses in various areas.

Test of Nonverbal Intelligence, 2nd edition (TONI2)

Linda Brown, Rita J. Sherbenou, and Susan K. Johnsen
Slosson Educational Publishers, East Aurora, NY, 1990
Also available from American Guidance Service, Circle Pines, MN
Age 5 to adult

The TONI2 is a language-free measure of intelligence, aptitude, and reasoning. Administration of the test requires no reading, writing, speaking, or listening on the part of the test subject. Because of its nonverbal format, the TONI2 can be used to evaluate the aptitude of individuals who have traditionally been difficult to evaluate. This test is well suited for subjects who have speech and language disabilities, who are deaf or hearing impaired, who do not speak English, or who are learning disabled.

There are two equivalent forms of the test. Test items include a variety of problem-solving tasks that increase in complexity and difficulty. Each item shows a set of figures in which one or more components is missing. The subject must examine the differences and similarities among figures, identify one or more problem-solving rules that define the relationship among these elements, and then select a correct response.

The TONI2 yields a quotient that is a standard score with a mean of 100 and a standard deviation of 15. Percentile ranks can also be computed. The test requires 10 to 15 minutes to administer and can be given to individuals or small groups of up to five.

Emergent Literacy Tests

Early literacy tests are designed to assess the literacy abilities of children in the early stages of language development, particularly from age 4 to 6. The following instrument is currently one of the more widely used tests for gathering information on current literacy development and ascertaining future literacy potential.

An Observational Survey of Early Literacy Achievement

Marie M. Clay
Heinemann, 1993
Grades K–1

This survey provides six measures of emergent literacy skills. The interpretation of the test information places an emphasis on the strategies that a student uses in reading and writing. Although stanines are reported, this survey is most appropriate when used to compare a child's performance over a period of time. Observational tasks focus on the following:

- Use of running records to determine text difficulty (easy, instructional, and hard)
- Letter identification

- Concepts about print
- Word lists (for sight word recognition)
- Writing vocabulary (of the words a child knows)
- Hearing and recording sounds in words

SUMMARY

This chapter presented an overview of various formal assessment procedures available for use by the classroom teacher. Some of the instruments discussed require special training while others do not. However, classroom teachers willing to devote a minimum amount of time to the study of these tests can administer and interpret the instruments described.

Diagnostic procedures fall into two broad categories: group and individual testing procedures. The three main types of group-administered tests are: survey reading tests, diagnostic reading tests, and achievement tests. The four types of individually administered tests that are most commonly used by teachers are oral reading tests, diagnostic reading tests, intelligence tests, and emergent literacy tests.

Each of these instrument has strengths and limitations. As teachers become more knowledgeable about formal assessment, they will find that these instruments in certain cases can be of use in assessing student needs in reading.

Applying What You Read

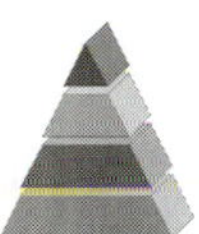

1. What type of instrument would be better suited for screening a fourth-grade class for specific word identification and comprehension skills? Why?
2. Your school is selecting some formal assessment tools to use in the reading program. What individual tests would you recommend? Why? What group tests would you recommend? Why?
3. A second-grade student in your classroom has a reading problem and exhibits difficulties with sight words, auditory and visual perception, and word identification. What type of formal diagnostic instrument could you use with this student? What specific tests would you recommend? Why?
4. Identify a battery (two or three tests) of formal tests that you would like to have available in your classroom. Tell why you selected each.

NOTES

1. Anne M. Bussis and Edward A. Chittenden, "Research Currents: What the Reading Tests Neglect," *Language Arts*.
2. James R. Squire, "Introduction: A Special Issue on the State of Assessment in Reading," *The Reading Teacher*. Sheila Valencia and P. David Pearson, "Reading Assessment: Time for a Change," *The Reading Teacher*.
3. Nancy A. Mavrogenes, Earl F. Hanson, and Carol K. Winkley, "A Guide to Tests of Factors That Inhibit Learning to Read," *The Reading Teacher*.
4. Ann E. Boehm, *Examiner's Manual: Boehm Test of Basic Concepts-Revised.*
5. Walter H. MacGinitie and Ruth K. MacGinitie, *Gates-MacGinitie Reading Tests: Teacher's Manuals*.
6. Roger C. Farr, George A. Prescott, Irving H. Balow, and Thomas P. Hogan, *MAT6 Reading Diagnostic Tests: Teacher's Manual*.

7. Connie Juel and B. Holmes, "Oral and Silent Reading of Sentences," *Reading Research Quarterly*.
8. Kenneth S. Goodman, "Behind the Eye: What Happens in Reading," in *Theoretical Models and Processes in Reading*, 2nd ed., edited by Harry Singer and Robert Ruddell.
9. Francis W. Parker, *Talks on Pedagogies*; Edmund B. Huey, *The Psychology and Pedagogy of Reading*.
10. Nila Banton Smith, *American Reading Instruction*, 3rd ed., pp. 158–164.
11. Marguerite C. Radencich, "Test Review: Gray Oral Reading Test-Revised and Formal Reading Inventory," *Journal of Reading*.
12. J. Lee Wiederholte and Brian R. Bryant, *Manual: Gray Oral Reading Tests*, 3rd ed.
13. Richard L. Slosson, *Slosson Oral Reading Test*, p. 1.
14. George D. Spache, *Diagnostic Reading Scales: Examiner's Manual*, p. 10.
15. George D. Spache, *Diagnostic Reading Scales: Examiner's Manual*, p. 18.
16. Sally Lipa, "Test Review: Assessment Reading Scales," *The Reading Teacher*.
17. George D. Spache, *Diagnostic Reading Scales: Technical Bulletin*.
18. Leo M. Schell and Robert E. Jennings, "Test Review: Durrell Analysis of Reading Difficulty," *The Reading Teacher*.
19. J. Lee Wiederholte, *Formal Reading Inventory*.
20. Marguerite C. Radencich, "Test Review: Gray Oral Reading Test Revised and Formal Reading Inventory," *Journal of Reading*.
21. D. Kim Reid, Wayne P. Hresko, and Donald D. Hammill, *Manual: The Tests of Early Reading Ability*.
22. Spache, *Diagnosing and Correcting Reading Disabilities*, p. 88; Eldon E. Ekwall, *Diagnosis and Remediation of the Disabled Reader*, p. 177; John Pikulski, "The Validity of Three Brief Measures of Intelligence for Disabled Readers," *Journal of Educational Research*.
23. Robert J. Armstrong and Robert F. Mooney, "The Slosson Intelligence Test: Implications for Reading Specialists," *The Reading Teacher*.

STEP 2

SYNTHESIZING DATA

The teachers at Twin Lakes School have gathered a wealth of assessment information about their students as they have worked with the various informal and formal assessment procedures. Problem: What do they do with the information? Step 2 is a key link in using assessment information for providing appropriate instruction. The principal, Ms. Gresso, realizes that much time can be wasted if the assessment data is not properly organized, interpreted, and summarized. She encourages the faculty to carefully investigate ways to obtain maximum information from the data on each student and to organize the information into a usable format. Chapter 4 provides suggestions to address these needs.

CHAPTER 4

Organizing Assessment Information

Knowing the amount and variety of information that they have collected on the students in their elementary and middle grades at Twin Lakes School, the teachers realize that synthesizing data from the assessment information gathered on each student is an essential step in providing effective instruction. Ms. Knight reminds everyone that this initial information is but the beginning as the students are continuously assessed, informally and formally, during the school year providing even larger amount of data. She underscores that the information gained is little more than a series of test scores, observational information, and miscellaneous data gathered about each student without some systematic way of organizing the material. For information to have any significance to the teacher, students, parents, or others involved in the program, the teachers must synthesize the data. To accomplish this, Ms. Knight suggested that the teachers identify a series of tasks to be carried out including organizing the data, analyzing and interpreting it, providing recommendations for instruction, and summarizing the findings (see Figure 4.1).

The completion of these four tasks is essential if the assessment information obtained is to have a meaningful impact on the teaching process. Synthesizing the data to form a meaningful whole enables the teacher to provide the most effective techniques and materials for each student. It allows other school personnel to better understand the reasons for using specific procedures in dealing with the reading development of individual students.

During the period when the assessment information is obtained, the teacher gains valuable insights into the student's personality, attitude, value system, peer relationships, and, perhaps to some extent, cultural and environmental factors that affect a student's performance in reading. These affective aspects of assessment are extremely important in the synthesizing process, and are as relevant as the cognitive information obtained through informal and formal testing procedures. Both cognitive and affective determiners go hand in hand in providing the most effective instruction for students. As teachers consider these determiners, they should ask themselves these questions:

- What procedures should be used in synthesizing data?
- How are data organized for teacher use?
- What are the interrelationships between analysis and interpretation of assessment information?
- Why are these interrelationships so vital to the process of assessment and the provision of effective instruction?
- How are assessment data analyzed and interpreted?
- How does the teacher effectively summarize assessment information to enhance the instructional process?
- How can the assessment information be organized for daily classroom use?
- What do the various terms used on the test instruments, such as raw score, stanine, and grade equivalent, mean to the teacher?

Figure 4.1 Four Basic Tasks in Synthesizing Diagnostic Data for Appropriate Instruction

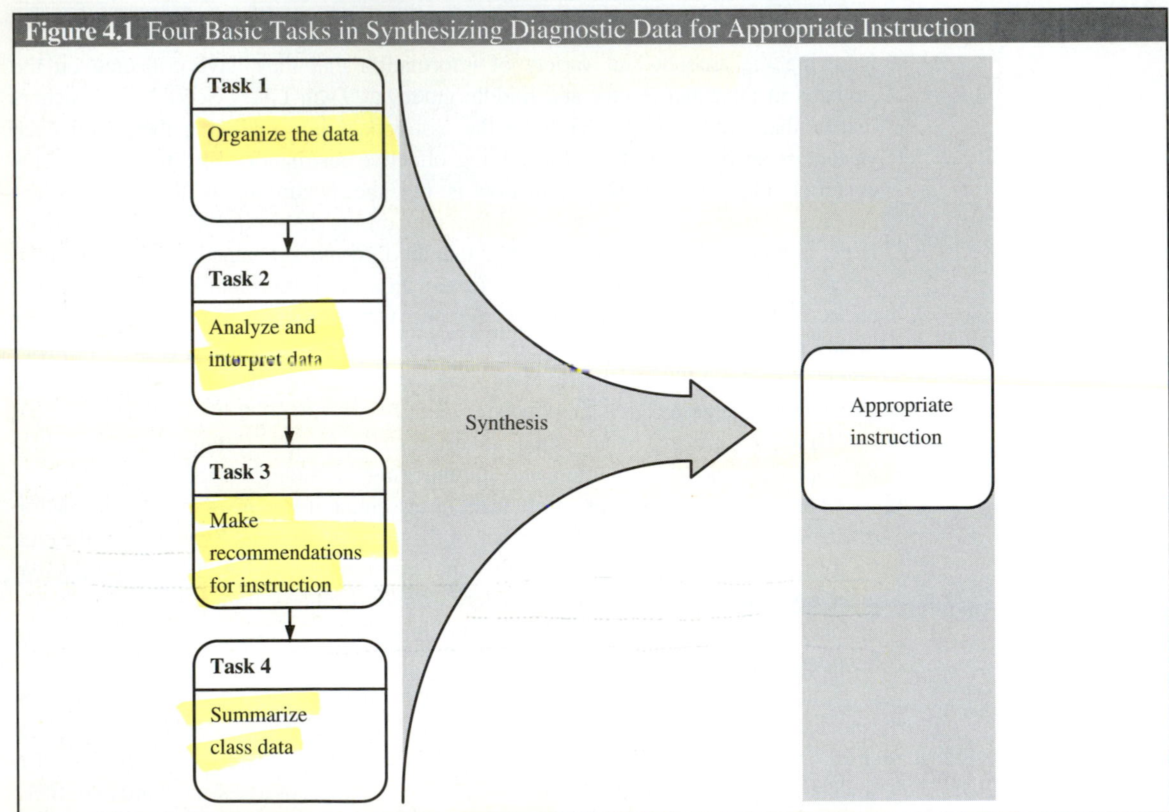

Vocabulary to Know

- **Analysis**
- **Correlation**
- **Data**
- **Grade equivalent**
- **Grade level**
- **Grade placement**
- **Interpretation**
- **Mean**
- **Median**
- **Normal curve**
- **Percentile**
- **Range**
- **Raw score**
- **Reliability**
- **Standard score**
- **Stanine**
- **Summarizing**
- **Validity**

KNOWING WHAT WE HAVE

After the assessment information has been gathered, it is essential for teachers to determine what they have and to organize this data in a way that will enhance its usefulness. This information should be recorded in a logical sequence so that the teacher can refer to it as needed. An important aspect of assessment is to have data that is both accessible and useful. This enables the teacher to provide a more appropriate learning environment for students.

Knowing what we have in terms of assessment information about students requires organization, which, in turn, enhances instruction and is indispensable in synthesizing data. Data can be organized in many ways; as teachers become more accustomed to gathering and interpreting assessment information, they will develop and refine their own ideas for organizing this information. The following suggestions may be helpful in organizing assessment data.

Keeping a folder for each student will help make the information readily available for the teacher's use. The folder may contain tests, observations, and other pertinent data useful for effective instruction. Remember that the information should be objective and factual. Personal opinions concerning the student's behavior or home life should not be recorded in a student's folder, which is open for review by many people.

As data are collected, the teacher may wish to consider the organizational plan used by the authors (see Figure 4.2). The steps in this plan are gathering basic information about the student, learning about her background, identifying assessment information, interpreting the data, and listing recommendations for appropriate instruction.

The first step is to record basic information such as the student's name, chronological age, and the dates during which assessment information was obtained. Another important item is the student's grade level. Although this step may seem elementary, it is crucial that this basic information be reported correctly since many test norms use this information. The teacher may record this basic information on the front of the student folder or on a separate sheet of paper inside the folder. For students with severe reading problems, the teacher would include any formal case reports as part of this introductory information.

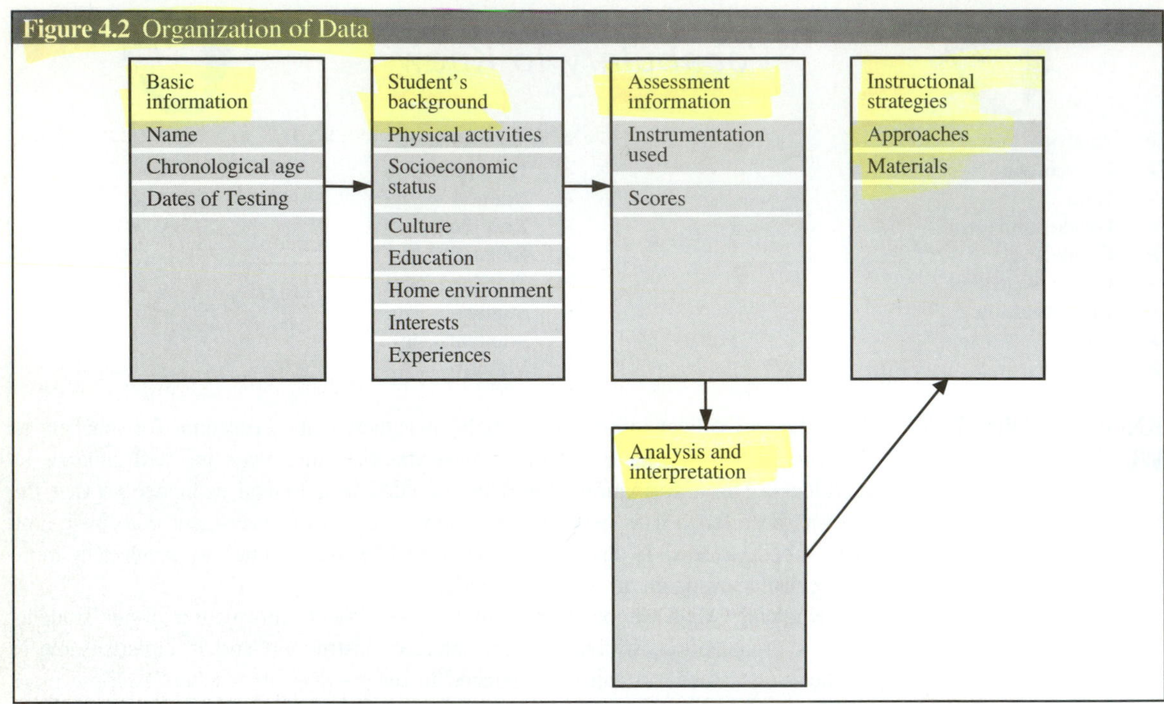

In the second step, the student's background is explored. Many factors affect a student's reading ability—variables such as physical condition, cultural and socioeconomic background, educational factors, the home environment, interests, experiential background, and prior knowledge. Knowing about all of these is useful in developing an appropriate instructional program for the student. Indeed, these factors can greatly influence the student's educational progress. The authors have seen many students with adequate reading skills and cognitive abilities who theoretically should have been able to read but could not because of a number of other factors that adversely affected them. Foremost among these are unstable homes, poor experiential backgrounds, lack of prior knowledge, cultural differences, and language differences.

Unfortunately, there are so many background factors that can adversely affect a student's ability to read that the teacher often experiences great difficulty in dealing with them. Learning to read is not always contingent on the improvement of oral language abilities, learning phonetic and structural analysis skills, and improving comprehension; many outside forces heavily influence reading progress. For this reason, it is imperative that as much background information as possible be available to the teacher. This not only allows teachers to be better informed about their students but further enhances the prospect for success in improving the student's reading capabilities. To organize this data, the teacher may find it useful to list significant information about the student as obtained from parent conferences or from the student. Possible leading questions that might be asked include the following:

Parents

- Were there any difficulties with the pregnancy, the birth process, or development of the child?
- How many children are in the family?
- How does this child get along with others in the family? Father? Mother? Siblings?
- Have you noticed that your child has difficulty with reading?
- When did you first notice the difficulty?
- What kind of activities does the family enjoy together?
- How much reading does each of the family members engage in during the week?
- What is the longest trip that your child has taken?
- Do you take your child with you when you go shopping, visiting, or on trips?
- How does your child feel about school? About reading?

Student

- Do you like to read? What types of material?
- Do you have your own books at home? What is your favorite book?
- Do your parents read to you? When?
- What is your favorite activity after school?
- What do you like to do best with your father? Mother? Brother(s)? Sister(s)?
- Have you been to the zoo? To the grocery store? On trips to other states?

In addition, the teacher may wish to use parent information sheets and interest inventories such as those in Appendix C to gather more information regarding the student's background. This information should be listed on the inside of the student's folder or on a separate sheet kept in the folder. The teacher should remember that the purpose of this information is to assist in better assessing the student's reading needs and providing appropriate instruction.

The third step in organizing data is identifying the assessment information. The teacher should list on a summary page the instruments used and their scores. Other informal information obtained from portfolios, journals, observation checklists, interest and attitude surveys, criterion-referenced tests, and notes on daily work should also be listed. The teacher should arrange or formulate the information so that data are readily accessible and easy to use. This step is essential for the task of analyzing and interpreting the data.

The fourth step in organizing the data is determining appropriate instructional strategies for the student. After the data have been interpreted to discover the student's strengths and weaknesses and the background information analyzed, the teacher is ready to recommend the instructional strategies to be used in teaching. This can be accomplished by using either a list format or a narrative format for enumerating materials and approaches for teaching. A list format saves time and is easy to refer to. The teacher should list the appropriate approaches, methods, and strategies for each student and the materials to be used. It is important to remember that instructional plans can and do change.

Knowing what we have in the way of assessment data and effectively organizing these data into a usable format is an essential first step in the process of synthesizing and using assessment information. Data that are both accessible and useful enhance the instructional process and enable teachers to more effectively use the facilities and materials available to them.

USING WHAT WE KNOW

After the data have been organized and we know what we have, the next step in synthesizing assessment information is to analyze and interpret this information. Analysis is crucial to the process of determining a student's strengths and weaknesses and involves the objective evaluation of the assessment information that has been gathered. For example, a primary student might exhibit difficulties in directionality and left-to-right sequencing in his daily journal recordings. An examination of the journal by the teacher would indicate problems in these areas and the necessity for providing appropriate instruction without adversely affecting the student's interest in this journal-writing activity.

An example of analysis using a formal testing instrument might involve the inferential comprehension subtest of the *Stanford Assessment Reading Test*, red level. An analysis of this subtest reveals a third stanine score, which is slightly below average. On further analyzing this score, the teacher realizes that the student had great difficulty in activating his schema as he responded to many of the questions. In other words, the student has little or no prior knowledge or depth of experience to enable him to answer the questions satisfactorily.

Another example of analyzing data might involve the results obtained from an informal reading inventory such as the *Classroom Reading Inventory*. Suppose a third-grade student's performance yields an instructional reading level of low 2 (lower second grade). An analysis of these data indicates that this student's actual classroom reading level (instructional level) is below that of the student's grade placement level. This information alerts the teacher to a potential problem in this student's instructional program. Thus, objective analysis involves evaluating the types of errors made by the student without interpreting the consequences of these errors.

Analysis of the scores taken from test data enables the teacher to look at the individual phases of the total picture so that essential questions about particular problems can be raised and answered. Looking at a total score is not likely to reveal the information needed for providing an appropriate instructional program. For example, two students might score at a low third-year level on an informal reading inventory; however, a closer analysis of the data indicates that one student shows strengths in word identification skills, while the other is stronger in comprehension.

Portfolios require teachers and students to conference frequently as progress is monitored.

Photo courtesy of Edward B. Lasher.

By analyzing the individual test scores, a teacher can gain a better understanding of the student's strengths and weaknesses. Does the student exhibit strengths in sight vocabulary, literal comprehension, and word identification skills? Does the student experience difficulty in the area of inferential comprehension? Does the student show an interest in certain reading materials but not others? These are the types of questions that can be answered when assessing reading difficulties. Without looking at all the individual components, it is difficult for the teacher to arrive at an adequate understanding of the student's capabilities. Thus, analysis of the test data is of major importance in determining why a particular student does or does not experience difficulty in reading.

For many students data analysis can be made rather briefly; in other cases an in-depth interpretation of a student's strengths and weaknesses may be desirable. Since the teacher's time is so valuable, doing an in-depth evaluation of each student is not realistic. For most students, a brief but thorough examination of the data should suffice for developing an appropriate instructional plan. The teacher may wish to briefly summarize the data on a half-page for each student, and refer to it as needed. Figure 4.3 gives an example of one way to briefly analyze the data for an individual student.

Interpretation is a necessary adjunct to analysis of the data. In this procedure, the strengths and weaknesses revealed in the data are further evaluated to ascertain the underlying causes for poor test results. Adequate interpretation is essential in instructional planning.

Figure 4.3 Brief Analysis of Data

Name: Joe Hunter Grade: 3

Interests: Racing cars, motorcycles, and machine guns
Likes to make things with tools
Likes to watch television

Sucher-Allred Reading Placement Inventory
- Satisfactory comprehension; poor sequencing skills
- Poor phrasing—ignores punctuation
- Omits word endings
- Weak in medial sounds
  - Independent level: Primer
  - Instructional level: 2^2
  - Frustration level: 3^1

Stanford Diagnostic Reading Test–Red Level
- Difficulty in auditory discrimination
- Poor vocabulary
- Unsure when tested using a cloze format
  - Auditory Discrimination:
    - Stanine 4-Grade equivalent 1.9
  - Phonetic Analysis:
    - Stanine 6-Grade equivalent 3.2
  - Auditory Vocabulary:
    - Stanine 5-Grade equivalent 2.6
  - Word Reading:
    - Stanine 5-Grade equivalent 2.8
  - Reading Comprehension:
    - Stanine 5-Grade equivalent 3.1
  - Total Comprehension:
    - Stanine 5-Grade equivalent 2.6

When interpreting test data, certain patterns in performance on the various tests are normally observable, and these can be used to develop a complete assessment that can serve as a basis for appropriate instruction. It is important to note that when assessment information is obtained from a variety of sources, specific patterns of strengths and weaknesses for individual students become more evident and identifiable.

Many difficulties can arise when interpreting a student's reading problems. These difficulties may be manifested in various reading skills, behavior patterns, and attitudinal tendencies that influence classroom reading performance. Other primary areas that provide positive or negative influences on reading performance are language factors, prior knowledge, experiential factors, socioeconomic factors, environmental factors, and physical conditions.

When interpreting assessment information, the teacher should consider *all* data together as well as any other aspect that could be affecting the student's reading performance. For example, a student is observed experiencing difficulty in recognizing certain vocabulary while working in a shared reading group and has also scored below level on the informal reading inventory in word identification. However, the student's performance on the comprehension subtest of the *Stanford Assessment Reading Test* and the reading passages of the *Classroom Reading Inventory*, while also below level, is considerably better. Although these data yield somewhat conflicting results, the teacher is aware of other primary factors affecting the student's reading performance. These factors include a limited experiential background and language base, which have resulted in a lack of prior knowledge, thus preventing the student from activating the schemas needed to appropriately decode certain vocabulary. Thus, the teacher correctly concludes that the student is compensating for deficiencies in schemas through the efficient use of contextual analysis and interactive comprehension strategies. The teacher's primary responsibility in this situation is to assist in strengthening the student's experiential background and language base in order to expand the student's schemas. When analyzing information derived from formal, informal, and authentic procedures, it is critical to consider other influential factors such as:

- Print awareness
- Prior knowledge and experiential background
- Language acquisition, both oral and written
- Cognitive ability
- Sociocultural factors
- Interest and motivation
- Physical factors including visual, auditory, and motor
- Home environment
- Maturation
- Ability to interact with text materials

A sample analysis and interpretation of the reading capabilities of a student in a typical classroom setting is shown in Figure 4.4. A more in-depth case report is presented in Appendix E. Both of these students are in normal classroom settings, and their teachers have summarized the assessment information according to the steps outlined in Figure 4.2. The teachers have followed the case report format presented on page 110.

Figure 4.4 Interpretive Report

I. **STUDENT DATA**

Student's name:	John Baxter
Date of birth:	October 16, 19_
Sex:	Male
Chronological age:	Ten Years
School:	Oaks Elementary
School district:	Washington County
Grade:	3.2
Examiner:	Debbie Smith
Dates tested:	October 30, 19_ November 1, 19_ November 6, 19_ November 7, 19_

II. **BACKGROUND INFORMATION**

Family History

John is a 10-year-old male who lives with his mother and siblings in Baker. John is one of three children and was the third born. He has an older sister, Alice, age 12 and an older brother, Sam, age 11. John's parents are divorced. His father completed his education through the tenth grade and his mother through the twelfth. His mother works as a teacher's assistant.

Social History

John is a friendly, quiet child with a rather serious demeanor. He enjoys playing football with his brother and going to the mall with his mother. John does see his father and likes to go bowling with him. John has been on vacations to the beach in Florida. He has been to the circus, the zoo, a museum, and a farm but has never been on an airplane.

Educational History

Currently, John attends Oaks Elementary, a neighborhood school. He was retained in first grade and again in second grade. John is presently in third grade. His grades for the first nine weeks of this year were as follows: F in reading, D in language, C in spelling, C in mathematics, C in science, and B in social studies. John received an A in both conduct and work habits. Recently, however, he has become discouraged and doesn't try. He also does not complete homework assignments. A review of John's most recent *California Achievement Test* scores revealed total stanines of 2 in reading, 2 in language, and 2 in math.

Physical Factors

John exhibited no apparent physical problems during any of the testing procedures.

General Behavior during Testing

John seemed to enjoy being tested. He maintained a relaxed and friendly attitude throughout all procedures.

. . . *continued*

Figure 4.4 Interpretive Report

III. **ASSESSMENT**

Test Data

Test administered:	Classroom Reading Inventory
Test date:	October 31, 19_
Word recognition:	2
Independent level:	Primer
Instructional level:	1
Frustration level:	L2
Listening capacity:	H3

Analysis and Interpretation of Data

The Elementary Interest Inventory

In the first section of the inventory, Home Relationships, John indicated that he gets along well with his sister and brother. They enjoy playing football together. John helps out at home by taking out the trash. In his spare time he enjoys playing outside.

In the Personal Life area of the Elementary Interest Inventory, John indicated that he is happy when he gets to go places with his father. He worries most about his mother working late and leaving him home alone. John stated that he wants to be a professional football player when he grows up.

In the third section of the Elementary Interest Inventory concerning reading, John stated that he enjoys reading and thinks it is fun and important. He indicated that he has lots of books at home, but he had a difficult time naming any of them.

When questioned about school, John revealed that he likes school. His favorite subject is math and his least favorite is language. He said that he does not enjoy copying from the language book. John likes the fact that lots of his friends are in his room. He acknowledged that he gets in trouble at school for not having done his homework, but he then contradicted himself by saying that he does his homework in the living room every day after school.

John indicated in the Peer Relationship section of the Elementary Interest Inventory that he has a best friend who is nice to him. John would rather play with a friend than be alone but wishes that his friends were nicer.

The Interest section of the Elementary Interest Inventory revealed that John most enjoys playing sports outdoors. His favorite indoor activity is playing with his car collection. He enjoys making things and would like to make his own car. He admires his mom the most and wishes he could spend more time with her.

John added no further information about himself in the Unaided Question section of the Elementary Interest Inventory.

Classroom Reading Inventory

On the word recognition subtest, John achieved a grade equivalent of 2. John made one error on the primer list. He read "horse" for "house." On the grade 1 list John made three errors. He read "ladder" for "letter'', "foot" for "feet" and did not attempt "learn". Finally, on list 2, John had five errors. He read "mouse" for "mice," "farm" for "free," "sleep" for "asleep," and he did not attempt "beautiful" and "branch." These errors are evidence of difficulty with vowel sounds and structural analysis.

John's independent reading level as indicated by the Oral Reading section of the Classroom Reading Inventory was at the primer level. He had one comprehension error.

John attained an instructional level of grade 1 on the Classroom Reading Inventory. He made two word recognition errors at this level. The errors consisted of one mispronunciation and one substitution. John missed one comprehension question.

The frustration level for John was determined to be at a grade level of 2. There was a marked increase of word recognition errors, with a total of 10, and 3 comprehension errors. John's listening capacity was determined to be at level 3.

. . . *continued*

Figure 4.4 Interpretive Report

Synthesis

Overall analysis of the data indicates that John is functioning well below level for his current grade placement and chronological age. On all tests, John exhibited weaknesses with basic vocabulary recognition and word identification. He has no apparent method for decoding unfamiliar words and therefore seems reluctant to attempt decoding. John's instructional program should include approaches that would provide him with strategies for analyzing words and improving his word identification skills.

John's comprehension ability is somewhat stronger. When he reads material that is not too difficult, his comprehension is good. With more difficult reading material, John's numerous word-identification errors severely impede his comprehension.

IV. INSTRUCTIONAL PLAN

Because of John's severe limitations in reading, combined with his chronological age and grade placement, extensive instruction with the basal should be limited. An eclectic approach utilizing a variety of methods would be most appropriate for John. A literature-based approach to expand John's experiential background combined with a multisensory approach would be beneficial.

The literature-based approach of providing John with experiences he has never had and then using his own words to discuss and write about the experience would be meaningful and relevant for him. As an integral part of this approach, John should then be encouraged to write more. Through these activities, John's reading, writing, speaking, and listening skills should be enhanced.

The multisensory approach would incorporate words John wants to learn and those words, in turn, would be used for writing stories. By following the VAK (visual-auditory-kinesthetic) procedure, John's senses of hearing, vision, touch, and muscle movement would be stimulated in learning those new words.

John should receive direct instruction in word identification techniques. Following basic procedures such as discussing a particular skill (e.g., contractions), explaining and modeling its use to determine an unknown word, and then providing opportunities to develop the skill through games and other activities would help John develop independent decoding strategies. John should be provided with ample opportunity to apply these skills in the context of meaningful reading selections.

To increase his comprehension skills, John should be provided with activities that encourage him to draw conclusions, predict outcomes, and identify main ideas. This should be accomplished in the context of John's own reading. The use of predictive trade books should be particularly effective.

John apparently lacks motivation for reading. His personal reading skills should be expanded and developed by providing him with various types of reading material specifically related to his abilities and interests. Art and writing activities should be used as a means for self-expression with John.

Because of John's lack of motivation and low self-esteem, one-to-one or small-group instruction should be employed whenever possible. Individual counseling might also be recommended. John's previous retention and lack of success have, no doubt, contributed greatly to his current problems. His instruction should be designed and paced in such a manner that allows John to experience success on a frequent and continuous basis.

For the first student, a minimal number of tests were administered. The analysis and interpretation for this student can serve as a guide for classroom teachers who are not writing detailed reports on each of their students. The second student (see Appendix E) receives reading instruction as a member of a special reading pullout program in addition to the reading instruction provided by the classroom teacher.

Since more in-depth assessment information is helpful in providing an appropriate instructional program for this student, a more extensive case report is presented. Both reports have an instructional planning component to demonstrate the application of the analysis and interpretation of information to the classroom instructional program.

The following outline of a case report can serve as a guide when preparing reports. In this outline, note that four primary areas are suggested for inclusion in a case report: student data, background information about the student, assessment, and instructional planning.

Case Report Outline

I. Student Data
   Student's name: __________
   Date of birth: __________
   Chronological age: ___________School: __________
   School district: _____ Grade level: __________
   Parents: _________ Home phone: __________
   Address: ___________________
   Examiner: ___________________
   Dates tested: ___________________

II. Background Information
   Family, birth, and development history
   Social history
   Educational history
   Physical factors (vision, hearing, other)
   General behavior during testing

III. Assessment
   Test data (instruments administered and scores)
   Analysis and interpretation of data (Each instrument should be analyzed and interpreted.)
   Synthesis (Data from various instruments should be briefly summarized, focusing on the student's strengths and weaknesses.)

IV. Instructional Plan
   Approaches
   Methods
   Techniques
   Materials (published and teacher made)

The following tips can assist the teacher in writing both regular and in-depth reports.

1. *Follow an organized procedure for presenting the information.* The teacher may wish to use the steps outlined in this chapter or some other plan that provides the necessary information. It is much easier to organize information when a basic outline or planned procedure is followed.
2. *Give specific data first, including the name of the test, date administered, and scores.* This basic information is essential for future reference and communicating with others. Be sure to check the information carefully when it is transferred from the primary source.
3. *Provide a brief analysis and interpretation of the data using only the information obtained from the assessment information.* Teachers must carefully study the test scores, the correct and incorrect answers of the items, as well as the actions of the student, and interrelate this information to properly assess strengths and weaknesses in reading.
4. *Prepare a summary list of the information, giving both the reading strengths and weaknesses of the student.* Assessment information is more usable when it is succinctly presented. Thus, significant findings from the analysis and interpretation of the discussion should be listed for easy reference.
5. *List specific recommendations for instruction to help improve the student's reading.* Using the assessment data, the teacher must give specific suggestions for providing appropriate instruction. These suggestions should be listed for ease of use.
6. *Communicate the ideas so that other teachers as well as parents will understand the information.* This is a professional report that should be beneficial not only to the classroom teacher but also to others who are interested in the student's reading progress. Keep the information objective and present it in a positive manner. Reports such as these may stay in the student's folder for many years.

RECOMMENDATIONS FOR USING DATA

After organizing, analyzing, and interpreting the assessment information, the teacher is ready to recommend specific instructional strategies. These are discussed in Chapters 6 through 12. Since these recommendations or plans are based on the strengths and weaknesses revealed in the assessment data, it is essential that the teacher use them to the greatest advantage. For reading instruction to be successful, appropriate recommendations must be based on adequate assessment.

SUMMARIZING INFORMATION FOR CLASSROOM USE

The primary purpose of this chapter is to further develop the teacher's abilities to organize, analyze, and interpret assessment information. However, the assessment information gathered, analyzed, and interpreted for each student is almost totally useless without summarizing it for classroom use. Information that is not summarized will not be used. Thus, the teacher's final task is to concisely combine the data on all students in the class so that the information is readily accessible for daily use. To be used effectively for instructional planning, assessment information must be available in a format that is clear and easy to use, allowing the teacher to quickly review the strengths and weaknesses of each student, along with relevant information such as interests and instructional level.

Assessment information should be used to develop various grouping situations as well as to individualize instruction. Because these groups are very flexible, the teacher should have the data available to shift students to appropriate activities during the school day. The authors have used different formats for organizing the information. One example is the chart shown in Figure 4.5.

Some school systems or individual schools may computerize the information and furnish a classroom summary sheet to each teacher. This type of summary saves teacher time but necessitates continuous updating.

Still another effective way of gathering and summarizing data is through the use of portfolios. Portfolios are a way of collecting assessment information each day from the students. This includes such information as stories, journals, daily reading and writing activities, and other material generated by the students. This information can be kept in brown envelopes, expandable folders, or any other collection device deemed appropriate by the teacher. This material can be examined periodically by the teacher to determine the progress of each student.

MEASUREMENT TERMS DEFINED

As teachers review assessment information and analyze and interpret data, they should be familiar with the terminology used in test materials. The following terms are frequently used in assessment data.

- *Correlation.* The degree of relationship between two variables expressed by the coefficient of correlation, which extends along a scale from 1.00 through 00.00 to –1.00. A coefficient of 1.00 denotes a perfect positive relationship, a coefficient of 00.00 denotes no relationship, and a coefficient of –1.00 denotes a perfect negative relationship.
- *Grade equivalent.* A derived score converted from the raw score on a standardized test, usually expressed in terms of a grade level divided into tenths. The grade equivalents in sixth grade, for example, range from 6.0 to 6.9, with 6.9 indicating six years, nine months, or the end of the sixth grade. Remember that this score represents the student's frustration level, or level at which he should not be taught, and should be viewed with caution. Figure 4.6 summarizes the position of the International Reading Association on the use of grade equivalents.
- *Grade level.* The actual grade in which the student is enrolled.

Figure 4.5 Skills Chart

	Word Analysis							Comprehension				
	Short vowel sounds	Long vowel sounds	Variant vowel sounds	Variant consonant sounds	Basic sight words	Compound words	Contextual analysis	Details	Main idea	Sequence	Conclusions	Cause/ Effect
Sally					✓	✓				✓		✓
Sally											✓	✓
Pam	✓		✓		✓	✓	✓		✓	✓	✓	✓
Sally												
Jane										✓		✓
Sally					✓		✓	✓	✓	✓		✓

✓ = skill deficiency

- *Grade placement.* The level at which the student is placed for instruction. A student in the fourth grade with a low second-grade reading level may have a grade placement of 2.3 at the fourth-grade level. This term may also be used on some tests as a synonym for "grade equivalent."
- *Mean.* The average of a set of numbers derived by taking the sum of the set of measurements and dividing it by the number of measurements in the set.
- *Median.* The central number in a set. Equal numbers of scores fall above and below the median number in a set.
- *Normal curve.* Same as the bell curve. It has more scores at the mean or median and a decreasing number in equal proportions to the left and right of the center (see Figure 4.7).
- *Percentile.* The percentage score that rates the student relative to the percentage of others in a group who are below the score. A student at the 47th percentile has done better on the test than 47 percent of the other people taking the test. Percentile scores may be reported in *quartiles* and *deciles,* in which the distribution of scores is divided into four and ten classes, respectively. A 50th percentile would fall in the second quartile and the fifth decile. Percentiles, quartiles, and deciles cannot be averaged, added together, subtracted, or treated arithmetically in any manner.
- *Range.* The distance between the largest and smallest numbers in a set, calculated by subtracting the smallest score from the largest score. For example, if the scores on a test were 10, 8, 15, 22, 36, and 20, the range, calculated by subtracting 8 from 36, would be 28.

Figure 4.5 Skills Chart

	Comprehension						Study Skills						
	Fact/ Opinion	Predicting outcomes	Follow directions	Abbre-viations	Mood/ emotional reactions	Relevant/ Irrelevant informa-tion	Dictionary	Title page	Table of Contents	Maps, etc.	Specialized vocabulary	Card catalog	Outline
Sally	✓	✓			✓		✓		✓	✓	✓	✓	✓
Sally	✓	✓									✓	✓	✓
Pam	✓			✓			✓	✓	✓	✓	✓	✓	✓
Sally	✓				✓		✓			✓			✓
Jane	✓			✓							✓	✓	
Sally	✓	✓							✓		✓	✓	✓

✓ = skill deficiency

Figure 4.6 Misuse of Grade Equivalents

WHEREAS, standardized, norm-referenced tests can provide information useful to teachers, students, and parents, if the results of such tests are used properly, and

WHEREAS, proper use of any standardized test depends on a thorough understanding of the test's purpose, the way it was developed, and any limitations it has, and

WHEREAS, failure to fully understand these factors can lead to serious misuse of test results, and

WHEREAS, one of the most serious misuses of tests is the reliance on a grade equivalent as an indicator of absolute performance when a grade equivalent should be interpreted as an indicator of a test-taker's performance in relation to the performance of other test-takers used to norm the test, and

WHEREAS, in reading education, the misuse of grade equivalents has led to such mistaken assumptions as (1) a grade equivalent of 5.0 on a reading test means that the test-taker will be able to read fifth grade material, and (2) a grade equivalent of 10.0 by a fourth grade student means that student reads like a tenth grader even though the test may include only sixth grade material as its top level of difficulty, and

WHEREAS, the misuse of grade equivalent promotes misunderstanding of a student's reading ability and leads to underreliance on other norm-referenced scores which are much less susceptible to misinterpretation and misunderstanding, be it

RESOLVED, that the International Reading Association strongly advocates that those who administer standardized reading tests abandon the practice of using grade equivalents to report performance of either individuals or groups of test-takers and be it further

RESOLVED, that the president or executive director of the Association write to test publishers urging them to eliminate grade equivalents from their tests.

Resolution passed by the Delegates Assembly of the International Reading Association, April 1981.

Figure 4.7 Various Types of Standard Score Scales in Relation to Percentiles and the Normal Curve

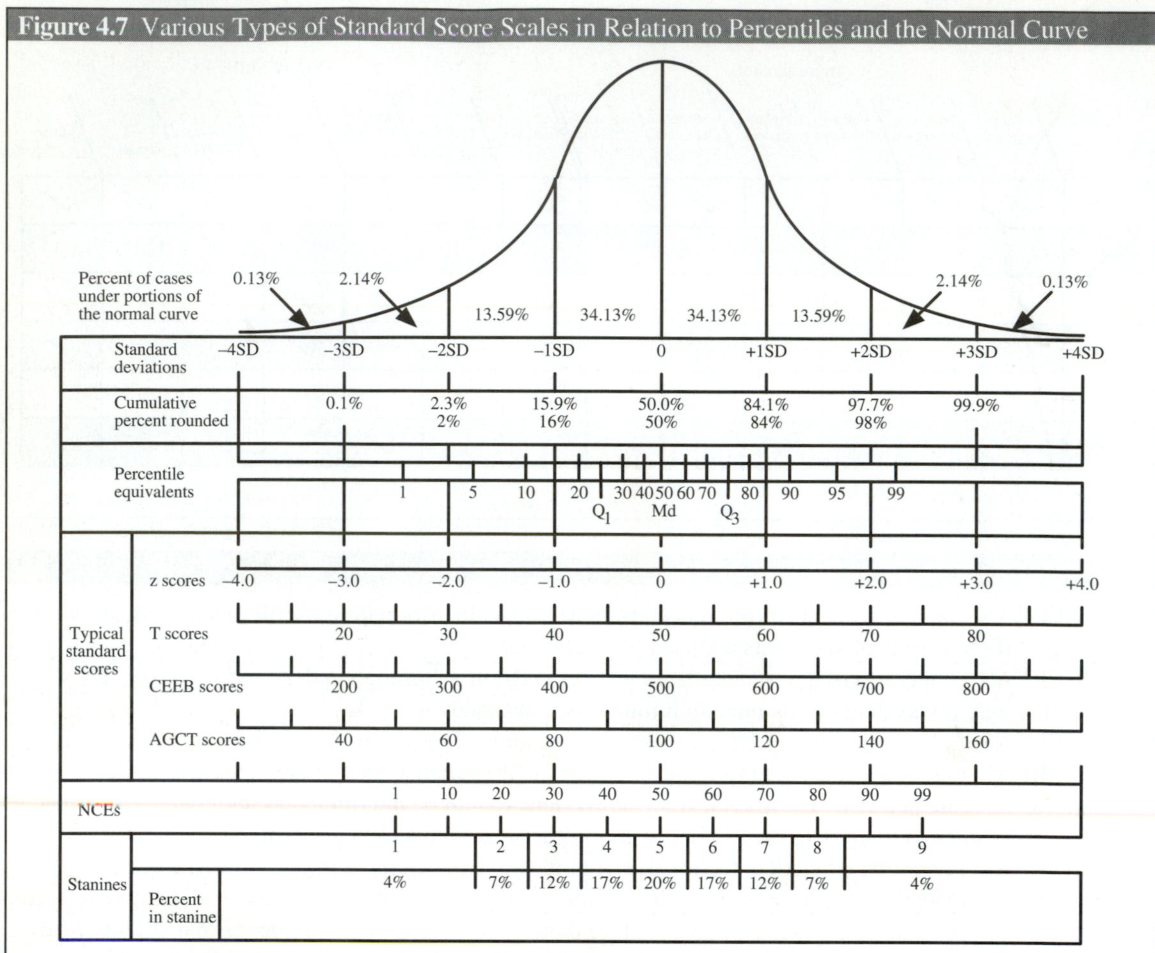

- *Raw score.* An untreated test score usually obtained by counting the number of items correct. The raw score is used to determine the other scores, such as grade equivalent and percentile.
- *Reliability.* The consistency with which a test agrees with itself or produces similar scores when readministered over a period of time by the same individual.

- *Standard deviation.* A term used to describe the deviations of scores from the mean that varies with the range in a set of scores. Thus, the greater the range in scores, the larger the standard deviation can be.
- *Standard score.* A raw score expressed in some form of standard deviation units. These scores can be dealt with arithmetically and are easier to interpret than raw scores. Various types of standard scores include z scores, T scores, CEEB scores, and stanines.
- *Stanines. A* nine-point scale that is another form of a standard score with a mean of 5 and a standard deviation of about 2. The nine stanines fit along the base of the normal curve with stanines 1, 2, and 3 considered below average, stanines 4, 5, and 6 average, and stanines 7, 8, and 9 above average.
- *Validity.* The extent to which a test measures what it is designed to measure. *A* test may be reliable but not valid, in that it does not measure what it purports to measure.

To visualize these various terms in relation to the normal curve, the teacher should carefully study Figure 4.6. In selecting as well as interpreting tests, teachers should note the types of data provided as well as the reliability and validity of the instruments.

SUMMARY

Synthesizing assessment information is an important aspect of the instructional process. For assessment information to be used effectively, it must be clear and well organized. This can be achieved more readily by using specific guidelines for synthesizing data. The data must be organized, analyzed, and interpreted before recommendations for instruction can be developed. From this individual assessment information for each student teachers should create a usable classroom summary for daily use in managing instruction.

Perhaps the key to the successful implementation of appropriate reading instruction is the analysis and interpretation of the assessment information, since this leads directly to the recommendations for instruction. It is primarily the responsibility of the classroom teacher to detect the strengths and weaknesses of each student. Once this objective is achieved, the teacher will be able to effectively implement an appropriate instructional program for the student.

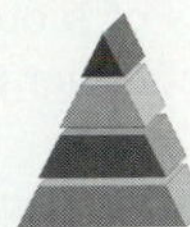

Applying What You Read

1. In your classroom, you have administered a group reading test and an individual test to the five lowest students. How would you summarize the data from these tests for your daily use?
2. As a middle-school teacher, you have two students for whom you need to write in-depth reports regarding their performance. Outline the information that should be included in the report.
3. How would you, as an elementary or middle-school teacher, summarize and use assessment information in your classroom?

STEP 3

ORGANIZING THE CLASSROOM FOR INSTRUCTION

Assessment information is most effectively used for guiding instruction in reading when the classroom is properly organized and managed. Experienced teachers recognize that the organization step is crucial to the success of their instruction. Therefore, they carefully consider the ways in which their classes are organized and arranged in order to meet the assessed needs of the students. Chapter 5 shares research findings about classroom organization along with related experiences of the authors and other teachers.

Organizing for Effective Classroom Reading Instruction

Ms. Self knows that the logical organization of materials, curriculum, and students is an essential and challenging aspect of effective instruction. Without an organizational framework, teachers run the risk of omitting needed information, neglecting certain students, or misusing instructional materials. Additionally, a great deal of effort may be expended only to result in lower-quality instruction. Ms. Self's goal of effective teaching is possible only if procedures, student information, materials of instruction, knowledge to be acquired, and means of delivering content are organized within the larger frameworks of the school year and the physical facility in which she provides instruction. Careful orchestration of these components requires long-term planning that is regularly supplemented by review and revision to the original plan. By establishing an instructional framework, she can assess progress routinely by simply comparing where the students are with where they need to be. Effective organizational techniques develop as experience in teaching and using materials accumulates. Ms. Self began familiarizing herself with a few key materials and strategies ten years ago as a beginning teacher; this gave her both confidence and energy to learn more. Effective experienced teachers at the elementary and middle-school levels continually find ways to better organize their classrooms since student needs, materials, and curricula are ever changing with each passing year. As you peruse this chapter, consider the following questions that Ms. Self has used to continue to focus on ways to more effectively organize her instructional program.

- What is the role of the effective teacher?
- How does an effective teacher manage the classroom for reading instruction?
- What are the various procedures for grouping?
- How do effective teachers plan and make decisions that provide positive learning experiences in a nurturing environment?
- How is the furniture arranged in the classroom to facilitate effective instruction?
- What role do curricular considerations play in organizing and managing the effective classroom?

- How important is concept-based instruction?
- Why does the selection of instructional materials exert such a major influence on effective organization and management of the classroom?

Vocabulary to Know

- **Achievement groups**
- **Concept-based instruction**
- **Concept density**
- **Cooperative learning**
- **Direct instruction**
- **Effective teaching**
- **Heterogeneous**
- **Homogeneous**
- **Indirect instruction**
- **Integrated instruction**
- **Interest groups**
- **Management**
- **Peer groups**
- **Readability**
- **Skills groups**

AN OVERVIEW

On entering Ms. Self's third-grade classroom, one immediately notices how busy everyone seems to be. Some students are in the reading area intently using reference books and making notes as they read. Looking over their shoulders, an observer learns that they are investigating the impact of human encroachment on wildlife populations. Others are at their desks, talking with partners about questions for interviewing peers to determine their knowledge of endangered species. Ms. Self is meeting with a small group that is drafting a play based on a book the class is reading, *A Place for Owls*, a nonfiction story about the perils and triumphs of rehabilitating wild owls.[1] Two students are at the computer designing a cover for a recycling book they have written and illustrated for a kindergarten class down the hall.

The activity and apparent interest in tasks somehow matches the physical environment in the classroom. The reading area is placed in the center of the room with carpeted areas on each side intended for small-group meetings. The teacher's desk and instructional materials are arranged on a side wall near the windows, and students are using selected materials from this area as well. From the ceiling hang various environment-related art projects, seasonal displays, and a few old bones gathered by Ms. Self's grandfather. The front of the room clearly belongs to students: student-designed bulletin boards frame the erasable board; boxes, tubs, and baskets of materials are stacked on shelves; and students' tables are placed nearby. Computers are situated near the teacher's desk because Ms. Self uses them on a regular basis, just like her students. The room has a comfortable feeling that is enhanced by the smooth flow between individual activities involving numerous materials.

At 10:30, Ms. Self moves to the center of the room, waits for the hum of activity to subside, then quietly directs students to prepare for recess. Without further comment, students replace books, return to their seats, tidy their tables, and visit quietly or read until asked to form a line. The students seem to be able to anticipate what comes next and automatically respond to the teacher's physical location in the room as well as to verbal prompts from the teacher and from one another. How has Ms. Self accomplished such a smooth operation? What skills does she possess that facilitate such cooperation among students and between students and the teacher? Ms. Self has developed a facilitative teaching style that allows her class to remain on task and attentive to her direction, thereby enhancing her instructional efforts.

Take a few moments to consider characteristics that you believe make Ms. Self an effective teacher; jot down the characteristics in list form. Although it may only take a few seconds to create the list, the task of ranking each item by importance can be a different matter. Educators have wrestled with the task of identifying the exact characteristics of effective teaching for years. Certain characteristics, however, frequently occur on many people's lists. Effective teachers of reading view themselves as creators of a classroom community and they accomplish this by orchestrating classroom life, assuming a variety of roles, valuing diversity, using an explicit teaching model, encouraging students to pursue their own interests, and viewing language literacy instruction as a team effort involving parents, students, and teachers.[2]

EFFECTIVE TEACHING

Effective teaching of language literacy has changed in recent years because skills are viewed differently than they were in the 1970s and early 1980s. Once structured primarily by commercial products (basal series), reading instruction involved the introduction of isolated skills with controlled opportunities to apply those skills by reading brief, uninteresting selections and completing several workbook pages.[3] In this environment, educators viewed skills as a means to an end. Success meant effective application of skills in order to understand text. With increased access to literature, teachers began to build their own lessons or units, selecting the skills to be included in the literature study from the basal scope and sequence charts.[4] Basal publishers noticed this trend and began to include longer excerpts from existing literature to replace boring, shorter pieces with limited vocabulary. Although supplementary materials have changed little, effective teachers use these materials sparingly;[5] instead, they depend on their intuition, the literature selection, and knowledge of their students to guide their instructional decisions. By encouraging skill application in meaningful integrated reading and writing activities, teachers are more likely to produce life-long readers and writers. Such meaningful activities are considered to be "authentic" in that they give students opportunities to interact with the world in a real way. Examples include writing to businesses or politicians for information, creating a class newspaper about environmental issues and sharing it with the community, studying other countries in which literature selections are set, and relating events in stories to real-life events. In this way, students are learning to use strategies in a personalized way that will facilitate greater interest and success in reading. The result is that students use language literacy skills as tools for exploring and understanding their roles in a global society.

Integrated instruction involves the simultaneous implementation of reading, writing, expressive and receptive language, studying, researching, and content strategies in the classroom. Expanding students' schemata calling upon their experiences and prior knowledge, and developing their interests are all part of integrated instruction. This is crucial to the total effort to make learning more of a naturalistic process that is spontaneous and real to students.

Reutzel and Cooter suggest that the classroom environment and daily routine must encourage reading as a primary activity and integrate reading with other language modes such as writing, speaking, and listening.[6] Students should be encouraged to write, respond, discuss, and become thoroughly involved with books, not to complete worksheets in social isolation. It is further essential that teachers communicate the importance of reading by reading for their own purposes and reading *with* the students in order to set a positive example. Teachers also need to provide opportunities for demonstrating reading strategies, for sharing in the reading process, and for evaluating individual reading progress.

Acheson and Gall identify six major areas for evaluating effective teaching:

1. Teaching of academic knowledge and skills
2. Development of student attitudes and motivation to learn
3. Responding to intellectual, cultural, and gender differences among students
4. Classroom management
5. Planning and decision making
6. Implementation of curriculum change[7]

Each of these areas is discussed in greater detail in the following sections. In contemplating each individual point, remember that effectiveness is a result of combining skills across areas. If any one area is neglected, the others will surely suffer.

Effectiveness in the teaching of academic knowledge and skills is most often measured by achievement test scores. Unfortunately, this practice does not provide an in-depth picture of what effective teachers actually *do*, nor does it provide results that square with generally accepted notions of what constitutes students' success. Current theorists are searching for ways to better define and evaluate success, as well as teacher behaviors conducive to success. Even though scores may indicate effectiveness in one area, one must be careful not to assume that a certain teaching method works equally well in all contexts. For example, a method that is successful in math instruction may not be equally successful in teaching reading. Because one cannot depend on even expert use of instructional methods to be consistent across curricula, several measures should be considered in evaluating effectiveness of the teaching method being utilized. Rosenshine and Furst identify nine characteristics of teachers whose students demonstrated consistent, cross-curricular gains in academic achievement:

1. Clarity in directions, expectation, and procedures
2. Variety in methods, evaluation, content, and materials
3. Enthusiasm toward students and toward content
4. Businesslike approach to academic and management tasks
5. Encouragement during instruction and avoidance of harsh criticism
6. Offering students ample opportunities to participate in instruction by using indirect teaching
7. Emphasis on achievement test content without restriction of other information
8. Use of overviews of content to be presented and summaries of content previously covered
9. Use of higher-level questions as well as lower-level questions[8]

Although all teachers are expected to acquire and refine each characteristic on entering the profession, few teachers exhibit expert use in all of these areas. Indeed, most teachers, like Ms. Self, strive throughout their careers to become effective in each area.

Use of time in teaching is obviously an important issue in planning and delivering appropriate instruction. In studies of time and learning outcomes, Borg found that increasing allocated time for instruction results in greater student success.[9] Similarly, students who spend a greater amount of time on task show more improvement than do students who spend less time on task. One way to improve students' time on task is to increase the amount of substantive interaction with students. This can be accomplished by engaging students in conversation, assisting them in problem solving, reviewing prior knowledge or requisite skills, teaming with other students, or perhaps varying the approach, materials, or strategies used to teach.

The ability to effectively teach knowledge and skills is clearly based on abundant knowledge of students' abilities, the content to be presented, and a trusting relationship between students and teachers. By establishing such an environment, teachers become more effective in meeting the primary goal of instruction, the development of productive citizens who use language literacy skills in their work, personal, and social lives.

CLASSROOM MANAGEMENT

Management refers to the flow of classroom activities; it includes the rationale, procedures, and expectations that get tasks accomplished during the school day. Everston, who studied the results of effective classroom management, identifies four key teaching practices:

1. *Careful analysis of procedures to be used in learning and record keeping*. Are procedures logical? Are they helping students to accomplish learning goals? Do they facilitate orderly flow of classroom activities?
2. *Conveyance of procedures to all participants using simple language*. Do students and parents understand why they are asked to work in a certain way?

Are the procedures easily followed? In what ways has the teacher conveyed procedures (parent meetings, notes home, class announcements, posting of procedures)?

3. *Systematic teaching of rules throughout the school year.* Do students recognize the stability of rules? Do students and parents understand the need for rules? Are students complying with the rules?
4. *Expectations for compliance with procedures in addition to continuous monitoring of student behavior.* How often does the teacher have to correct students? What reaction do students have when corrected? How do students know they are expected to comply with procedures and rules? How does the teacher know that procedures and rules are working? How are behaviors documented?[10]

If a teacher does not provide a realistic rationale for procedures and rules, students may fail to understand the need to comply. Teachers should carefully reflect on why certain things need to be done as well as why certain steps need to be followed. Without compliance, much instructional time is lost, which can never be reclaimed. Doyle conducted a comprehensive study of classroom management to isolate those aspects of classroom instruction requiring clearly stated procedures.[11] They include the following:

- Location, type, and use of materials
- Starting and ending of each day
- Completing and handing in assignments and late work
- Acceptable noise and movement within the room
- Suitable "free-time" independent activities
- Leaving the room during class
- Asking for assistance
- Handling of misbehavior
- Appointing students to or volunteering for assisting roles
- Consumption of food

In these areas individual teacher preferences and school policy should be considered in developing classroom guidelines. Student involvement is encouraged when setting up classroom guidelines on consequences for misbehavior.

In the Phi Delta Kappa poll of teachers' attitudes toward public schools, 50% of the teachers surveyed reported that discipline problems in today's schools are "very serious" or "fairly serious." In addition, 43% of teachers who leave the profession blame discipline problems for their departure.[12] Perhaps one of the most difficult aspects for novice teachers, classroom discipline need not be the undoing of one's career or sanity. The current "me-centered" mind-set of students, when combined with unparalleled materialistic goals requiring fast-paced work schedules for both parents (or double jobs for single parents), often results in delayed responses to problems in school. This situation places new demands on classroom teachers, who must not only teach but must identify misbehavior, rectify problematic situations, and often convey a moral lesson to the troubled student. Regardless of society's wishes for in-home moral instruction, misbehavior displayed by some students demands decisive and clear correction, remediation, and review of long-term effects of misbehavior within the classroom setting so that the offending behavior will not be repeated.

Current models for managing misbehavior emphasize teacher personality, the needs of the student population, and administrative style as important factors to consider when designing a policy for handling discipline problems. In many schools, there is a school-wide policy used by all teachers.

However, in reviewing the professional literature on behavior management, one finds an abundance of research dating from the mid-1970s to the mid-1980s. Experts explain that little has changed in the field since that time. With correct implementation, what worked then is still applicable today.[13] Several models that teachers need to be familiar with include the following:

- *Teacher effectiveness training* (TET) focuses on ownership of problems and suggests use of active listening and *I*-messages to convey one's feelings about behavior.[14] The emphasis of TET is on effective communication between students and teachers.
- *Dreikurs's goals of misbehavior* address causes for misbehavior including needing attention, attempting to gain power, seeking revenge, and displaying inadequacy.[15] Identification of the child's goal is tied to teacher feelings about behavior.
- *Glasser's reality therapy* encourages building self-esteem so that students feel success and have the desire to keep learning.[16] The theory involves eight steps ending with "Never give up!"

Teachers and students who genuinely enjoy one another have much happier and productive learning experiences. Tauber makes several suggestions for creating better classroom relations:

- Seal it with a handshake
- Correct in private
- Overprepare
- Don't ask why
- Be calm and businesslike
- Don't hold a grudge
- Don't take things personally
- Assign responsibility
- Act, don't react

- Maintain eye contact
- Be friendly as opposed to being a friend
- Don't abuse legitimate teacher power
- Surprise them![17]

In taking a closer look at Ms. Self's third-grade room, one sees the care that has been taken in providing an enriching visual landscape for learners. Not only is student work prominently displayed but students have been given the task of deciding how and where to showcase their peers' work. Ms. Self has added centerpieces to each table: a reproduction of Rodin's statue *The Kiss*, a galvanized bucket full of tree branches from different species growing in her yard, a large basket of seashells asking to be picked up and turned over and over by small hands, a few engine parts from an old car. Students spend free time examining the centerpieces with magnifying glasses, and the centerpieces are often the inspiration for creative writing assignments. The appearance of Ms. Self's classroom changes continually, but the busy feeling and interesting landscape remain constant. It is a lively environment that stimulates thought, imagination, and reading. Even so, there are quiet places to which students can escape, to do their work free from distraction. Ms. Self has included these areas because she knows that students have different learning styles.

The physical environment in which students learn must be organized in a way that creates visibility for instructional displays, accessibility for materials and spaces, and low distractibility instruction. Figure 5.1 illustrates possible arrangements that allow for whole-class and group activities, access to materials and peers, and areas for independent work. For a classroom to become "community property" shared by students and teacher, students need free access to all parts of the room, so they have the ability to make some decisions about what to do, how to do it, and when.

In classrooms that are well managed, students are obviously free to interact with one another. In these classrooms, the students and teacher share frequent eye contact, as do students within the class. Students can trust the teacher and one another to proceed in a predictable manner. This does not mean that lapses in classroom protocol do not occur. They do, but they are the exception rather than the rule.

Teachers must consider students' wishes in displaying work because writing and art are often personal reflections of the individual writer or artist. Students who feel comfortable when working with the teacher will also trust the teacher to use discretion in sharing their work. As with adults' art and writing, teachers should ask students' permission before displaying individual or group accomplishments. It is also appropriate to display all phases of a project, to show visitors how things are accomplished in the classroom.

A well-managed classroom is extremely important in fostering success and a positive attitude toward reading. The goal is classroom management to develop students who enjoy reading, respect the learning community, and develop a love for learning throughout their lives.

Figure 5.1 Sample Floor Plan for a Classroom

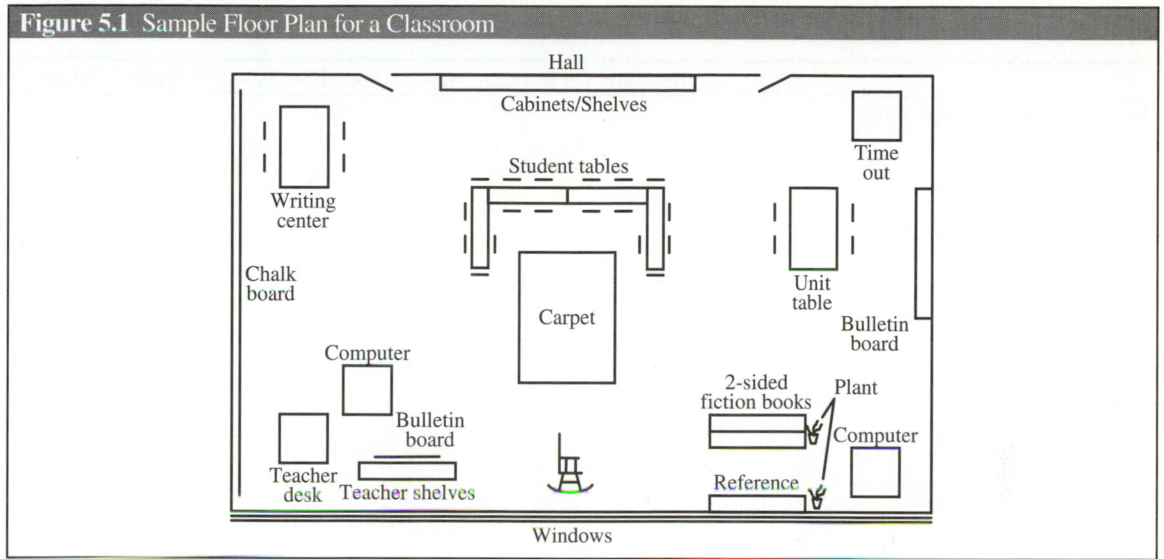

PLANNING AND DECISION MAKING

Bailey reports that teachers who had fond memories of reading and writing as children *and* who continued to read and write for personal reasons were better planners than were those who had negative memories and little time for reading and writing in their adult lives.[18] There is a complex relationship between teaching and learning, and the constant need to make instructional decisions is the basis for most of the complexity. When a teacher uses school assessment data to create an instructional plan, she is anticipating student reaction and performance. The degree of confidence one feels in making instructional decisions depends on the confidence one has in the assessment information. If the instructional plan is implemented and is successful, the teacher is then free to plan for another day. If, however, the lesson is not successful, the teacher must make an immediate decision about what to do next. The teacher has learned about the student by teaching the student and adjusts instruction accordingly. This never-ending chain of events is frequently seen in classrooms of effective teachers.

To effectively deliver curricula, teachers must first plan. At the start of the year, the teacher makes a yearly plan. This yearly plan sets the goals for the year. From that, quarterly and then perhaps unit plans are developed that lead toward accomplishing these goals. Weekly plans come next, and daily plans are the final result. Figure 5.2 is an example of a teacher's yearly organizational plan showing what topics will be covered in each quarter under each content area.

Figure 5.2 Yearly Plans (topics taught in each quarter)

	Reading	Language Arts	Social Studies	Science	Math
Reading and Language Arts					
Folktales	1	1	1		
Biography	2	2	2	2	2
Newspaper	3–4	3–4			
Poetry	3	3			3
Social Studies					
Cities and towns	1		1		
Maps			2		2
State history	3–4	3–4	3–4	3	4
Science					
Scientific methods				1	1
Weather	2		3–4	2	2
The water cycle		3	1	3–4	3–4
Plants	3		3–4	2	
Math					
Set theory					1
Multiple-digit addition and subtraction			3		2
Fractions				2	2
Geometry	3	3	4	4	3

Some school districts have specific forms on which to record plans, and others leave the format of the plan up to the individual teacher. Quarterly plans begin to describe how major concepts will be addressed. Weekly plans are even more descriptive, including materials, procedures, and student processes or products. An example of a weekly lesson plan is given in Figure 5.3.

As teachers gain experience, they no longer feel the need to write a detailed lesson plan for each lesson they teach. They are able to anticipate student reaction, time requirements, and methods that work best with the current class. The beginning teacher is well served by the thought processes involved in mapping out a detailed lesson plan. Repeated successful lesson planning is what leads to the confidence implied in more experienced teachers' scaled-down lesson plans. Over time, changes in daily plans will affect weekly plans, then perhaps the unit or monthly plans. In turn, the yearly plan may be affected as well. As previously mentioned, in order to implement the plans, specific classroom procedures must be clearly identified and shared, using simple language, with students, parents, administrators, and assisting teachers.

The lesson plan in Figure 5.3, designed for intermediate students, incorporates each step in each model. It is an example of how one teacher might go about delivering content over a five-day period using a combination of direct and indirect teaching. The lesson is multidisciplinary, using science content to develop language arts skills and social studies concepts.

By integrating subject areas in such an environmental lesson, the teacher is effectively leading students to explore relationships that exist between human activity, natural events, and wildlife and also between reading and writing. This type of teaching also offers ample opportunities for informal assessment, as described in Chapter 2. Regardless of the teaching model one chooses, effective teaching requires assessment of what is known, modeling of new information, checking to see whether information is understood, extension of content to new learning situations, and evaluation of progress. In each step, the teacher is a crucial key to the quality of the learning experience and usefulness of what has been learned.

CURRICULA CONSIDERATIONS

The curriculum in a given subject is an organized hierarchy of what is to be taught, when, and to what degree of proficiency. Like weekly, monthly, and yearly plans, curricula also change over time. Think of curricula as living creatures, responsive to the needs and abilities of students, the availability of materials, the capabilities of teachers, and learning goals dictated by society. To effectively deliver curricula, teachers must recognize this fact and become attuned to subtle changes.

There are several stages represented in a teacher's attempts to adapt or change curricula (see Figure 5.4). First, teachers acquire basic information about curricula, such as content to be delivered, methods and materials used in delivery, and evaluation of learning. Once these basics have been acquired, the teacher moves on to preparation for first use of curricula. This involves observing and interviewing other teachers about how they implement methods and use materials, reading more extensively about the content, and collecting related information about resources. Next comes "mechanical delivery," in which the teacher attempts to use the new methods and materials in an effective manner. As the teacher becomes more comfortable with the content, he incorporates his own ideas, methods, and materials. During the last stage of curriculum development the teacher modifies curricula extensively, striving to deliver more understanding and knowledge to students. These steps take time, years perhaps, to refine. Even experienced teachers feel the need to reacquaint themselves with content they are expected to teach, sometimes finding that it has been altered slowly. The best way to avoid surprises is to review state curriculum guides and new editions of texts thoroughly during the first part of the planning process each year.

Figure 5.3 A Weekly Lesson Plan

Title of Lesson: The Mighty American Kestrel, North America's Smallest Falcon

I. Objectives: At the end of the lesson, students will be able to
   A. Identify the range of the American kestrel and describe its natural habitat (science).
   B. Discuss the relationships that exist between current environmental issues and the survival of the American kestrel (social studies).
   C. Write an editorial about conservation (language arts).

II. Materials
   A. National Audubon Society, *Hawks up Close* (Carrboro, NC: National Science Network, 1992.)
   B. C. Henderson, *Woodworking for Wildlife* (St. Paul, MN: Minnesota Department of Natural Resources, 1992.)
   C. C. Sutton and P. Sutton, *How to Spot Eagles and Hawks* (Shelburne, VT: Chapters Publishing, Ltd., 1996.)
   D. K. Chubb, *The Avian Ark* (Minneapolis, MN: Hungry Mind Press, 1995.)
   E. G. Holroyd, I. Shukser, D. Keith, and L. Hunt, *Prairie Raptors* (Alberta, Canada: Minister of Environment Canadian Wildlife Service, 1995.)
   F. W. Clark and B. Wheeler, *Peterson's Field Guide to Hawks* (Boston: Houghton Mifflin, 1987.)
   G. B. Wheeler and W. Clark, *A Photographic Guide to North American Raptors* (San Diego, CA: Academic Press/Harcourt Brace and Company, 1995.)
   H. Newspapers and/or popular magazines (editorial pages)
   I. Writing supplies
   J. Word-processing software
   K. World map/globe

III. Requisite Skills
   A. Fact versus opinion
   B. Use of reference texts
   C. Process writing
   D. Word-processing software
   E. Cooperative learning roles

IV. Procedure
   A. Day 1 (Introduction)
      1. Begin the lesson by displaying photographs of different raptors, focusing on the American kestrel.
      2. Create a discussion web, focusing on what students know about the American kestrel from prior experiences or from the photos.
      3. Ask students to work in small groups to brainstorm questions they have about the bird and its importance to a healthy environment.
      4. As a whole class, compile a list of approximately 10 of the most important questions to be answered (range, identification, habitat, prey base, behavior, and environmental impact should be addressed). Provide each student with a copy of the discussion web and the list of questions.
   B. Day 2
      1. Review the discussion web and list of questions from Day l.
      2. Introduce and watch the video about raptors.
      3. Model the process of answering one of the questions and completing the form.
      4. Students are then to choose another question for which they will assist in locating the answer and completing the form. Assign or let students choose partners (four in each group), and distribute the remainder of the questions evenly among groups. Review the roles that different members assume in cooperative learning; leader, note–taker, time keeper, runner, materials manager, or other roles appropriate for the students' abilities. Call attention to the location of reference books, maps/globe, and other materials that might be used to find answers to questions. As implied in the form, students are to first predict what answers might be, collect information from available resources, then draw conclusions about the collected facts.

. . . Continued

Figure 5.3 A Weekly Lesson Plan

C. Day 3
   1. Continue answering questions, checking to see that all members are contributing and that reference materials are being used properly.
   2. As a class, listen to each group present answers to their chosen questions. As they are presented, write answers on the master list created on Day 2, and then display the information in the classroom.
   3. Through discussion, use environmental editorials from the local newspaper or popular magazines to identify persuasive techniques. Begin by reading an editorial to students, verbally responding as the author intended. Distinguish facts from opinions presented by the author, recording each; then discuss the strengths of the argument in light of known facts.
   4. Together, read three additional editorials, and create a discussion web of concerns raised in previous reading, discussion, and viewing. Topics might include encroachment, habitat destruction, use of pesticides or herbicides, fluctuations in prey base, automobile strikes, shootings, trappings, ingestion of lead shot, electrocution, building strikes, theft or sale of skin or feathers, and limited support for the U.S. Department of Natural Resources (DNR).

D. Day 4
   1. Through discussion, review the web created on Day 3.
   2. Working in pairs, small groups, or alone, students are to draft an editorial focusing on an area of conservation. Encourage continued use of reference materials and published editorials during the drafting phase.

E. Day 5
   1. Continue the editorial writing, following the steps of process writing: prewriting (completed on Day 3), drafting (started on Day 4), revising and editing, and publishing or sharing. During the revising-editing stage, students are to exchange papers with others in order to gain and offer peer feedback.
   2. Print two final copies of each editorial, and assemble two identical class books, one to be placed in the class and the other in the school library.

V. Evaluation

A. Objective 1—Identify the range of the American kestrel and describe its natural habitat. The cooperative learning forms and list of questions and answers should reflect that this information was collected from reference materials. Participation in discussions will also provide evidence of this knowledge.

B. Objective 2—Discuss the relationships that exist between current environmental issues and the survival of the American kestrel. The discussion web will reveal how well students were able to identify issues, and their cooperative learning forms will provide evidence that students understand the basic needs of the American kestrel. The editorials students write will demonstrate how well they were able to link environmental concerns with the birds' needs.

C. Objective 3—Write an editorial on conservation. The editorial is to be evaluated on the validity and quality of arguments presented; organization, grammar, spelling, punctuation, and appropriate use of software may also be evaluated.

VI. Follow-up

A. Mail editorials to local newspapers or popular magazines for publication consideration.

B. Invite a DNR representative to visit the class for a debate or discussion regarding conservation.

C. Create a collage about raptors, habitats, prey, and threats to their survival; display in the school library or entrance.

D. Write a class newspaper designed to educate a chosen group about the role of raptors and issues that concern their welfare.

E. Write or call local and state politicians, and request a statement on their views and actions regarding conservation.

F. Read *The Egyptian Cinderella* by S. Climo (1989.)

G. Visit websites on the Internet to learn more. A place to start is Soarin' Hawk Raptor Rehabilitation (http://www.sfc.edu/sknight).

Figure 5.4 Cycle of Curriculum Development

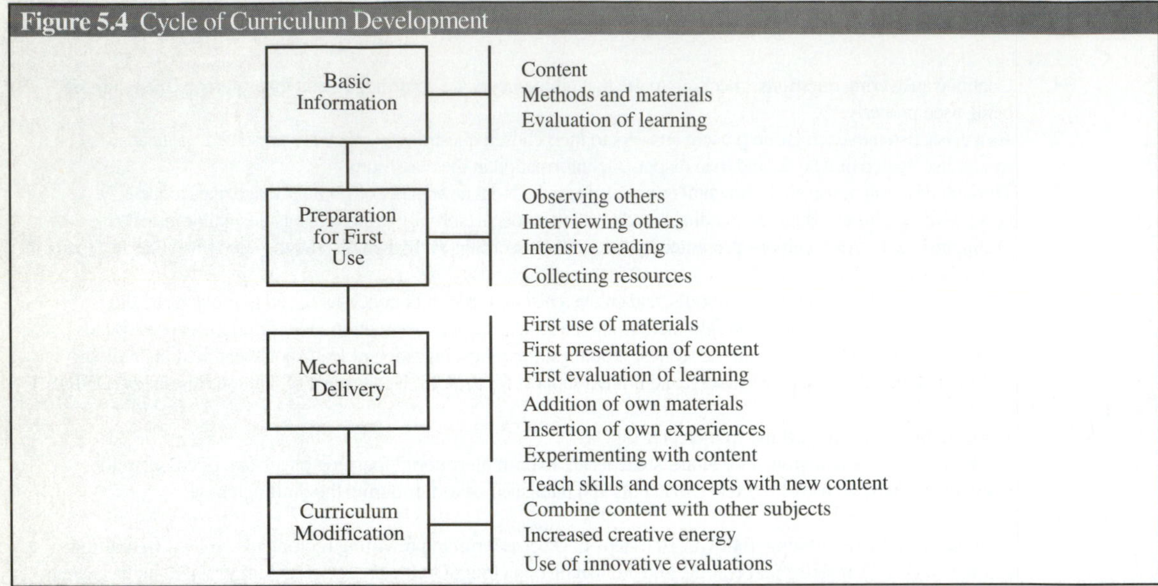

How does the teacher match student abilities with teaching methods, content, materials, and assessment? One of the most important aspects of instruction is matching student abilities to the content to be presented. As seen in Figure 5.5, the effects of not matching abilities and content can be devastating. When a mismatch occurs, students may demonstrate behaviors that are inappropriate. This behavior, often reflecting an attempt to solve a perceived but unnamed problem, typically involves withdrawal from classroom activities or acting out in some way, such as clowning, refusing to complete assigned work, or being inattentive to class activities. When students lack the background experiences that would help them recognize the real problem, they may use inappropriate techniques, such as repeatedly asking for directions, copying from peers, pretending to lose completed work, blaming others for incomplete work, or refusing to begin assigned work. To further compound the issue, some teachers do not recognize the mismatch themselves because of lack of planning, inexperience, insufficient or incorrect assessment data, poorly selected materials, or severe distraction from the real problem due to the inappropriate behavior of students. To prevent problems with inappropriate instruction, teachers should:

1. Collect formal and informal assessment data available in cumulative folders, from previous teachers and from parents and students.
2. Form general groups representing the range of abilities in the class.
3. Identify trends or patterns in the data that have been collected.
4. Use teacher-made forms to summarize and record accumulated data.
5. Determine the need for reassessment or additional assessments by examining information on the forms.

6. Update assessment information as additional assessments are done.
7. Confirm conclusions using a variety of assessments.

The initial step in ensuring an appropriate match between student abilities and content to be presented is collecting formal and informal assessment data. As indicated in Chapter 3, the formal assessments most commonly utilized by classroom teachers to identify broad ability levels are diagnostic tests and achievement tests. Scores on these tests are usually found in students' cumulative folders or on a class printout provided by the principal or guidance counselor. While such scores offer little guidance for daily instruction, they do suggest broad groupings that could be made based on achievement or skills. At the same time, these scores give a general sense of how a student is functioning in relation to other students in the class.

Figure 5.5 Matching Student Abilities, Methods, and Content

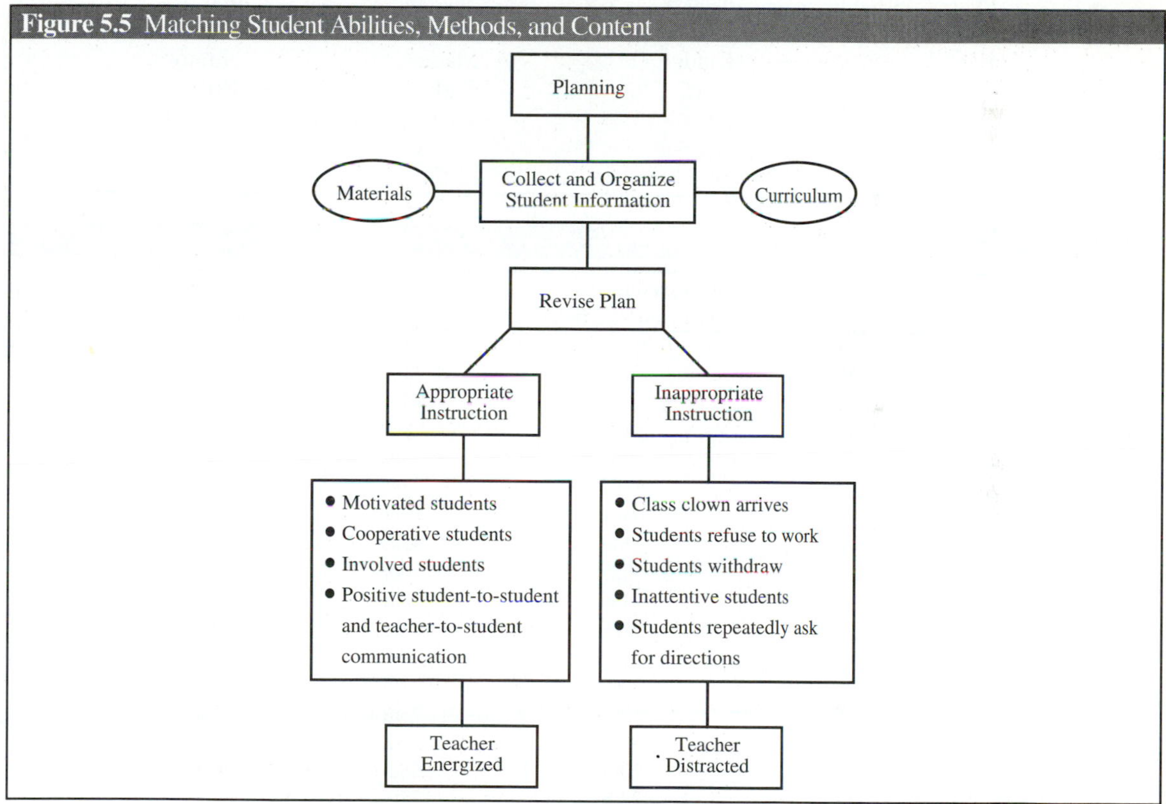

For example, consider the list of percentile scores on the subtests of two formal assessments for a class of fifth-grade students presented in Figure 5.6. Notice that there can be a wide range of abilities in a single class. On first viewing scores such as these, a teacher might feel uncertain about how to use them to direct students'

learning; however, one can take charge of the situation by grouping the scores into ranges. Students can be tentatively assigned to one of three groups: above level, on level, and below level. This is done by dividing the total range of percentiles (99) roughly into thirds (1–39, 40–69, and 70–99), and then assigning students to one of the broad groups based on the majority of their reading scores. The next step is to observe students for a few days or weeks and plan more specific assessments so that students' individual abilities can be more accurately pinpointed. The general groups formed from formal assessments usually do not stand as the primary instructional groups in the class; instead, they serve as a starting point. Using the class scores from Figure 5.6, the student listings for each reading group would be as follows:

Above Average	Average	Below Average
Mandy	Samuel	Joe
Randy	Joshua	Rachel
Cindy	Maria	Jimmy
April	Carl	Roger
Al	Julia	Amelia
Kristen	Gwen	
Marshall		

Figure 5.6 Standardized Test Percentile Scores for One Class

	Stanford Diagnostic Reading Test		California Achievement Test	
	Comprehension	Auditory Vocabulary	Reading	Mathematics
April	61st	87th	75th	23rd
Joe	25th	14th	34th	76th
Mandy	92nd	91st	89th	87th
Samuel	50th	53rd	88th	60th
Randy	47th	89th	78th	80th
Joshua	71st	56th	61st	73rd
Cindy	90th	94th	89th	98th
Rachel	46th	32nd	45th	73rd
Maria	62nd	58th	50th	66th
Jimmy	32nd	41st	60th	71st
Carl	56th	59th	71st	45th
Julia	49th	61st	41st	67th
Al	98th	99th	97th	97th
Roger	22nd	18th	23rd	32nd
Amelia	41st	39th	50th	51st
Kristen	87th	70th	68th	66th
Marshall	81st	77th	77th	82nd
Gwen	66th	67th	64th	65th

In forming these groups, only the reading scores (comprehension, auditory vocabulary, and reading) were considered. In cases when scores seem to contradict one another, the two scores that most agree are used to make the decision about group placement. It is important to remember that while subtests of formal assessments do measure different aspects of reading, it is common for scores in multiple areas of reading to be similar for children who have no learning problems in reading. Scores on subtests taken by students who have diagnosed reading difficulties are usually low, a phenomenon known as "the Matthew effect."[19] The "bargaining" with similar scores is seen in Randy's scores. The 89th percentile in auditory vocabulary and the 78th percentile in reading suggest that the 47th percentile in comprehension may be inaccurate. The same is true of Samuel's scores, in that the comprehension (50th percentile) and the auditory vocabulary score (53rd percentile) do not support the reading score (88th percentile). Placing students in general groups based on formal test scores helps to set the stage for informal assessments and, ultimately, confirmation of students' assumed abilities. It is for this reason that many teachers use formal assessment scores to group students loosely at the start of the year.

Once a general determination is made regarding groups, teachers can begin to supplement formal records with additional data. Usually, supplementary information is gained through informal assessment. As noted in Chapter 2, informal assessments used for group placement may include checklists, surveys, inventories, scales, observations, anecdotal records, journals, basal materials, and teacher-made assessments. By recording assessment data, teachers can more clearly understand overall student abilities (see Figure 5.7 for a sample teacher-made form). Teachers should experiment with various ways of organizing assessment data.

The information in Figure 5.7 could be used with an intermediate-level class (third, fourth, and fifth grades), although a primary-level form (kindergarten, first, and second grades) would likely include more individually administered tests. In addition, primary-level formal assessments would include achievement test scores less frequently, although the format for recording other types of formal assessments could remain the same. For informal assessments, primary teachers may depend more on checklists for documenting observed behavior (see Appendix D). Assessment data can be stored in file cabinets, in individual folders, in a single folder, in binders, in file boxes (using preprinted cards instead of paper), or in portable files.

To ensure a good match between instruction and students' needs, teachers must determine when to reassess or when to use a new type of assessment. If a teacher has doubts about how students will receive a topic or lesson, it is prudent to collect additional student information before completing the planning and collection of materials and before actually teaching the lesson. For example, if a teacher learns from the beginning-of-year interest inventories that a student greatly dislikes reading in school, it might be wise to follow up with a more specific assessment about topics that interest the student. Another example of the need for additional assessments might be a new student to the class. In this case, formal assessment scores are often the most immediate or only information a teacher has available. A quick cloze test, an interest inventory, a writing sample, and a listening test may fill in the gaps well enough to allow the teacher to proceed with some degree of confidence until more information arrives or until she gets to know the student.

Figure 5.7 Sample Teacher-Made Form for Recording Assessment Data

Example 1: Intermediate

Student ________________________ Date of Birth __________

I. Formal Assessments

A. *Stanford Diagnostic Reading Test*[a]

Subtests:	Percentiles:	Subtests:	Percentiles:
Auditory Vocabulary	______	Phonetic Analysis	______
Structural Analysis	______	Comprehension	______

B. *California Achievement Test*[b]

Subtests:	Percentiles:	Subtests:	Percentiles:
Reading	______	Spelling	______
Language	______	Mathematics	______
Reference Skills	______		

II. Informal Assessments

A. Interest Inventory Summary

1. School ______________________________
2. Home ______________________________
3. Social ______________________________
4. Life Experiences______________________________

B. *Scales for Measuring Attitude Toward Reading*[c]

1. Recreational score ______ (circle one): positive neutral negative
2. Academic score ______ (circle one): positive neutral negative

C. Developmental Stage in Spelling

___ prephonemic ___ early phonemic ___ letter name ___ transitional ___ correct

D. Writing Sample

	Above	Average	Below
Handwriting	______	______	______
Grammar	______	______	______
Sentence Structure	______	______	______
Punctuation	______	______	______
Organization	______	______	______
Following Directions	______	______	______

E. Observation

Date ______ Notes ________________________

Date ______ Notes ________________________

Date ______ Notes ________________________

[a] Karlsen & Gardner, 1984

[b] 1987

[c] McKenna & Kear, 1990

Having completed the preceeding steps, the teacher plans a course of instruction that best meets students' needs. It is important that the teacher continuously use observation to further confirm assumptions about placement, since it is possible for many variables to affect any testing situation. Only by close monitoring of student progress can a teacher be sure that instruction is appropriate and progress is occurring.

GROUPING FOR INSTRUCTION

In elementary schools, grouping is the most frequently used instructional management procedure. Grouping allows the classroom teacher considerable flexibility in implementing the instructional program, permitting the teacher to devote more time to individuals than would ordinarily be possible in a whole-class type of format. Grouping also facilitates better adaptation of materials and resources to individual needs.

Recent research has contributed much information about the issues related to grouping. Grouping is supported in all studies. Grouping allows the teacher or another adult to spend more time working with students, which seems to be the critical component in improving achievement. Kean, Summers, Ravietz, and Farber found that achievement was improved when students were taught via small-group and whole-group class combinations as compared to students who received individual instruction only, small-group instruction only, or whole-class instruction only.[20] Related to this conclusion are the findings of a beginning-teacher evaluation study, which suggests that students working with a teacher or another adult were usually engaged about 84% of the time, while those students working alone were on task only 70% of the time.[21] Rosenshine and Stevens, summarizing the research in this area note that, "three general instructional procedures have frequently been correlated with reading achievement: teacher-directed instruction, instruction in groups, and academic emphasis."[22]

Various types of grouping procedures are used in schools and classrooms. Procedures differ from classroom to classroom, and especially from the elementary to the middle-school levels. The two main types of grouping often debated are homogeneous and heterogeneous.

Homogeneous grouping puts students together in a class based on their ability or achievement levels. For example, Ms. Brooks has the top group of fifth graders this year, that is, all of the students reading at the fifth grade or higher, while Ms. Cox has the middle group and Ms. Day has the low group. On the other hand, heterogeneous grouping mixes students of different ability or achievement levels in each class. Usually through random or alphabetical assignments, Ms. Brooks, Ms. Cox, and Ms. Day would each get some of the top group, middle group, and low group of readers. While many teachers argue that a homogeneous grouping arrangement is easier and that they can do a better job of meeting needs when the students are not so diverse, this argument is not supported by research. Kulik and Kulik concluded from a review of studies on homogeneous grouping that homogeneous or ability grouping is often beneficial for high-ability students but not for low-ability students.[23] This finding is supported by Persell, who, in a review of studies of ability grouping, concluded that a slight improvement in achievement occurred for the high-ability groups, but that gain was negated by the substantial losses of the middle- and low-ability groups.[24]

Homogeneous grouping is used more at the upper levels when students are grouped by ability or assigned to tracks. At the elementary level, more heterogeneous grouping patterns are usually found. One of the greatest misconceptions is that homogeneous grouping alleviates the need for smaller groups within the individual classroom. Whether a classroom is homogeneously or heterogeneously grouped according to the school management design, further grouping within the classroom is essential. Few classrooms contain thirty students whose performance is exactly the same and who need exactly the same instruction.

Intraclass Formats

The population of a classroom may be grouped in two ways: intraclass and interclass. In an intraclass format, students are grouped *within* the class in various ways for instructional purposes. Intraclass groups include achievement groups, skills groups, interest groups, cross-age or peer groups, and collaborative or cooperative-learning groups (see Figure 5.8).

Figure 5.8 Intraclass Grouping Formats

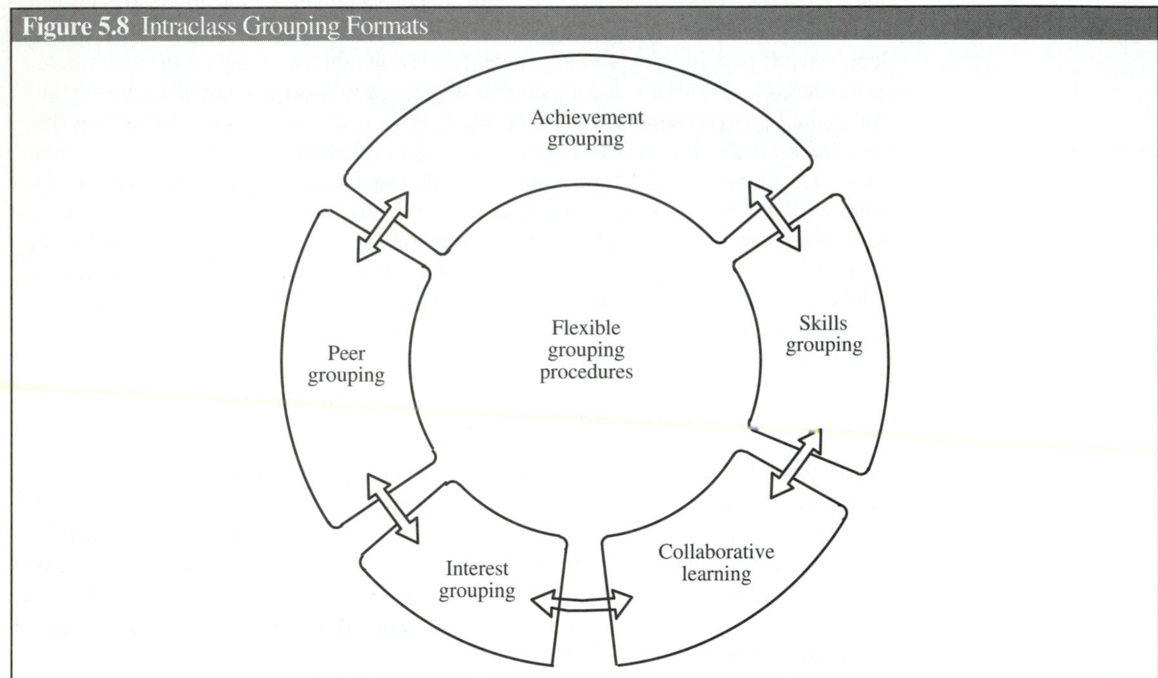

Achievement Grouping

The most widely used grouping technique in traditional reading instruction is achievement grouping. In this technique, a classroom of students is divided into several groups based on their level of achievement. Those performing at the highest level are grouped together and those performing at the lowest level are grouped together, with one or more groups organized between the highest and the lowest levels. A rather common practice is for the classroom teacher to form three reading groups. While three achievement groups may serve the students and teacher well initially, as soon as management procedures permit, these should be expanded to perhaps as many as five. Remember, that in a typical fifth-grade classroom that is heterogeneously grouped, reading levels may range from low-first to ninth-grade level. Therefore, more than three achievement groups are needed to accommodate this wide variation in levels.

Since achievement grouping is the most widely used grouping procedure, teachers should be flexible when placing students in groups. Through continuous evaluation of the student, try to avoid a situation in which the student is labeled a poor reader and not given an opportunity to improve his position in the classroom. Teachers should allow students to move from one group to another as their performance dictates. Research indicates that students frequently are not moved into other achievement groups during the school year.[25] Once placed in a certain reading group, they usually remain there. This is unfortunate, as students' learning rates change during the school year, and all students within a group do not progress at the same rate.

In addition, caution should be exercised in determining what instruments are used to place students in achievement groups. Many times achievement tests do not accurately reflect the student's knowledge or skill. Thus, using these tests as a basis for grouping is very dangerous. If used for grouping purposes, achievement test results should be considered in conjunction with teacher observations and other individualized measures. No one instrument alone can serve as the basis for grouping students. However, instructional grouping based only on teacher judgment tends to create greater socioeconomic segregation than grouping based on test scores alone.[26]

Teachers also seem to praise lower-ability groups more than the higher-achievement groups, although the students read on a lower level and answer more questions incorrectly.[27] Moreover, in teaching achievement groups, instructors tend to treat the group as a teaching unit, rather than consider individual student needs. Low-level groups generally receive highly structured instruction in decoding and basic comprehension skills, while the top group enjoys more flexibility in procedures and assignments, as well as instruction in the more sophisticated comprehension skills.[28]

Obviously, there are differences in the instruction provided to various ability groups. Hiebert and Peterson, Wilkinson, and Hallinan summarized many research studies that addressed reading instruction for low- and high-ability groups as follows:

1. Decoding tasks were the focus of instruction for students in the low-ability group, while high-ability groups were involved with meaning-related activities.
2. Silent reading was the predominant means of reading for the good readers, whereas poor readers spent the majority of their time reading orally. Errors made by poor readers were corrected using graphophonic cues. When cues were recommended to good readers, which was less frequently than to poor readers, they were syntactic and semantic cues.

Teachers work with individual students, and the class as a whole to provide effective instruction.

Photo courtesy of Larry Smith.

3. Low-ability groups were less attentive to instructional activities and spent more time off task for administrative and disciplinary reasons than students in high-ability groups.
4. Low-ability students were less popular with their peers, had a poorer self-concept, and more negative feelings toward reading and their reading groups than did the high-ability groups.[29]

To alleviate some of the negative feelings of students in low-ability groups, Peterson, Wilkinson, and Hallinan suggest that teachers should be more flexible in moving students to different groups, attempt to provide good instruction to all groups, use alternative grouping procedures to encourage low-ability students to interact more with others, avoid labeling groups, and be aware of the long-range impact of grouping on the educational and emotional development of students.[30] Thus, teachers must consider other grouping patterns in addition to achievement groups in managing reading instruction.

Skills Grouping

A second grouping technique is based on reading skills. Skills grouping places students into groups for instruction in a specific skill. It is entirely possible that a student's skills placement will be different from his achievement placement. For example, a student may be in the high reading group but have difficulty with a reading skill that others in the group seem to have learned. This student would work in a skill group that may be composed of students from several other achievement groups who also have difficulty with this skill.

Although research on the pros and cons of skill-group instruction has not been conducted, studies that deal with grouping in general recommend that grouping formats other than ability grouping be used to provide flexibility in the classroom and to allow students in the various ability groups to interact. Those who are opposed to skills instruction in reading would, of course, also oppose this type of grouping. However, because skills and strategies for using these skills form the content to be developed in reading, skill groups are vital in an effective reading program. Crucial to the success of using such groups are the procedures used to develop and reinforce the skills. Students in skill groups need to first receive direct instruction from the teacher, who demonstrates the process for using the skills to enhance reading. Once students show that they have an understanding of the skill, the teacher moves them into the application of the skill in various reading situations in conjunction with other skills already known. Various strategies including study techniques, think-aloud processes, reciprocal questioning, and study guides are incorporated into this instructional process. Instruction in skill groups is not aimed only at passing a test on an isolated skill but rather focuses on the understanding and application of skills in the total reading process.

When one or more students exhibit difficulty in using a specific skill, corrective instruction is needed from the teacher either through skill grouping or one-on-one instruction. This type of grouping usually lasts for a short period of time, since the primary purpose is to strengthen a skill. When the skill is learned, the student leaves the skill group and moves to another, as needed.

Interest Grouping

Another type of grouping that has been used rather successfully is interest grouping. This allows students who have similar interests to work together to explore their interests in greater depth. A positive aspect of this type of grouping is that students from all achievement levels are intermingled, which provides for considerable interaction without regard to reading level. Used interchangeably with achievement and skill grouping, this type of instructional grouping has proven to be highly effective, since it motivates students to learn and work together. One of the weaknesses of achievement grouping is the lack of opportunity for students from different levels to interact and discuss subjects of importance to them. Interest grouping provides this opportunity, thus overcoming one of the reasons students become disenchanted with learning to read. In addition, interest grouping helps to make reading enjoyable and interesting as students are encouraged to read materials related to their unique interests. Therefore, interest grouping can help motivate students who generally are not enthusiastic about reading materials assigned to them. The use of interest grouping also allows students from deprived backgrounds to learn by interacting with their peers from more diversified experiential backgrounds. Learning about other students' experiences helps to improve the oral language development of the poorer readers and, in turn, improves their reading. Interest grouping is a useful procedure that teachers should use continuously in their classes, because the social behaviors practiced in groups can improve students' opportunities in later life.[31] Social development and reading groups are related.

By allowing students to read materials of special interest to them, comprehension is enhanced. Asher found that when students indicated a high interest in a passage, their comprehension was greater than when they had a low interest in the material.[32] Why does this happen? Interest in a topic suggests more knowledge about the topic, and thus the student has a better developed schema. Furthermore, interest in a topic means that the students have a greater attention span and become more involved in learning. Anderson, Hiebert, Scott, and Wilkinsen have suggested that students can read at a higher level, as compared to the level at which they typically read, when interacting with materials on topics of special interest.[33] For all these reasons, interest grouping is a viable option for the teacher who is concerned about the reading development of individual students. The procedures outlined in Chapter 2 can help teachers determine student interests; use this information as an aid in personalizing reading instruction.

Peer Grouping

A fourth type of grouping, which has proven very helpful in elementary and middle-school classrooms, is the concept of student or peer tutoring. In peer tutoring one student in a class helps another student who needs assistance in a particular area. Teachers may use this grouping procedure to allow a student who needs to practice oral reading to do so with another student rather than with the teacher or an entire group. Another way of using peer tutoring is to ask a student who has learned a skill or has strength in one area to help a student who is not as proficient. In peer tutoring, the tutor usually progresses as much as, if not more than, the person being tutored. Although the tutor may already "know" the skill, through tutoring that student achieves a higher level of understanding. This type of grouping is referred to as cross-age tutoring when an older student works with a younger student in an effort to improve the reading skills of the latter. In many cases the older students also improve their reading skills, especially if they are poor readers.[34] Labbo and Teale conducted a study using lower-achievement fifth graders to tutor kindergarten children.[35] In this study the fifth graders prepared and read storybooks to kindergarten students. Both the quantitative data and qualitative results gathered suggest that a cross-age reading program is a promising way of helping poor readers in the upper elementary grades to improve their reading.

An example of a successful cross-age tutoring program is the one implemented by Morrice and Simmons, in which older and younger students became "reading buddies."[36] In this program, fifth graders and primary grade students collaborated in a whole-language, cross-age program developed around activities using big books, special holidays, and outdoor science. An added advantage of this program is that students who would not ordinarily read books they consider childish read them so that they can help the younger student. Thus, in peer tutoring everyone seems to benefit: the student, the tutor, and the teacher.

In experiences with peer tutoring, the authors have found this to be an effective way to motivate the poor reader. The procedure has an overall positive effect on reading; students also exhibit increased interest in learning to read and have a more positive attitude toward themselves. Furthermore, students doing the tutoring likewise develop a more positive self-image and show greater interest in their schoolwork. In the classroom an atmosphere of helping and caring for one another develops.

One way the authors have used peer tutoring is with 15-year-old nonreaders tutoring kindergarten and first graders in an adjoining school. The older students, all boys, had an extra incentive for reading "easy" materials; they had to learn to read them in order to provide the story hour for the younger classes. On one occasion the boys had to learn to read "The Three Bears" because of a request from a little kindergarten girl. They felt they could not let her down, but they also felt they could not learn to read the story with only a two-day notice. So they decided to tell the story via a play and only learned to read certain parts. They drew straws for the Goldilocks part, put on wigs and costumes, and created a smash hit with these younger students. Needless to say, they had a very proud teacher!

Collaborative Learning

Collaborative, or cooperative, learning utilizes group dynamics within a classroom setting by emphasizing shared learning experiences to reach a common goal or to solve a common problem. In this setting, students of varied abilities, interests, and experiences are grouped together and given the responsibility for completing a particular task. It is incumbent on the students in a particular group to organize the work, guide each other, and complete individual assignments to reach their common goal.

Proponents of collaborative learning believe that these small-group configurations not only increase interest among students but also promote critical thinking. For example, Johnson and Johnson found that cooperative teams achieved at higher levels of thought and retained information longer than students working individually.[37]

Another proponent of cooperative learning, Robert Slavin, cites a number of advantages to students:

1. Students are more highly motivated to learn with greater intrinsic motivation.
2. More academic improvement in both tutor and tutee is demonstrated.
3. An increase in the student's self-esteem is evident.
4. Students develop more positive perceptions about the intentions of others.
5. Negative competition among students decreases.
6. Students accept differences among themselves more readily.
7. Dependence upon the teacher is decreased significantly.
8. Higher achievement-test scores result.[38]

There are many ways to implement collaborative learning in the classroom. Bromley, for example, suggests using a "buddy journal," which is a diary that a pair of students keep together in which they write back and forth to each other.[39] The journal serves three basic functions for students; it sets a purpose for communication (sharing an idea in writing), provides an opportunity to compose a message, and elicits feedback from a peer, who answers with a response in the journal.

Keegan and Shrake implemented literature study groups in their classrooms as a way to foster collaboration and as an alternative to ability grouping.[40] These groups are comprised of seven or eight students who sit in a circle around a tape recorder; one member begins the discussion by reading a thought-provoking quotation. This initiates a brief period of sharing ideas using their books for reference. Next, students read the pages they have assigned themselves. Then, in their literature logs, which are read by the teacher, they react to their stories and to the preceding group discussion using a friendly letter format. This creates a situation in which the student and teacher can pursue a dialogue about literature.

There is growing evidence to indicate that collaborative learning is an effective way to teach in an integrated instructional environment. We believe that this type of grouping encourages more cooperation among students, heightens interest, results in better learning, and offers an effective alternative to achievement grouping.

Cooperative learning carries specific responsibilities for students. One role is that of group leader, the student who directs discussions, delegates tasks, and speaks for the group. Another role is secretary. In this role, a student takes notes, creates an outline of tasks, or documents in some other way the group's progress. A third role is runner or materials manager, who asks the teacher or other groups questions, gathers materials, or collects other types of information on behalf of the group. Some teachers include the role of time-keeper, the only person in the group who has authority to direct the leader to proceed, adhering to the given time frame. Figure 5.9 illustrates how these roles interact to enable the team to complete a task.

Figure 5.9 Cooperative Learning Roles

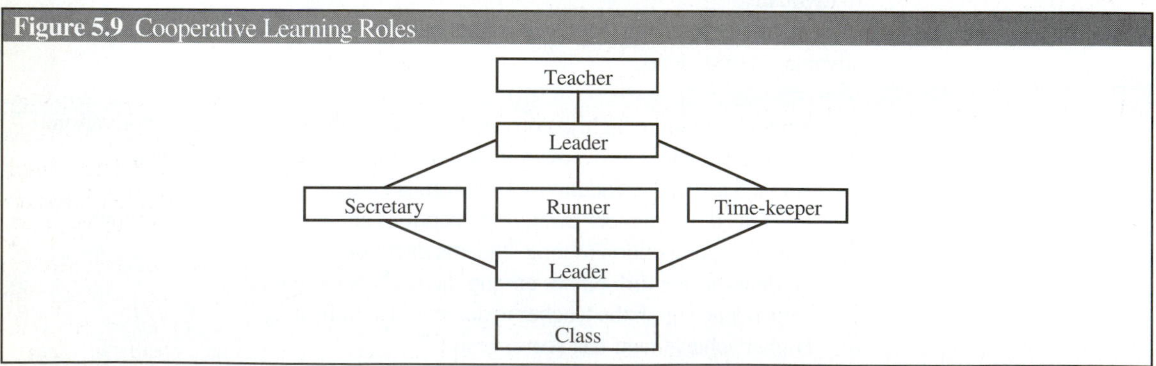

Although there are no specific criteria for each role, the teacher and students are best served in reaching a consensus about what each will involve and then prominently displaying those expectations in the classroom. Roles may be assigned by the teacher or students, but all students should experience each role on occasion. The ideal size for a cooperative learning group is four, although groups ranging in size from three to six are usually able to complete tasks. Membership in cooperative learning groups, like all other types of groups, is most effective when it is flexible. By changing partners regularly, students learn to work with more personalities and with students of differing abilities.

As with any new strategy, teachers must describe the process carefully, and might conduct a simulation exercise. With the first implementation of cooperative learning, most teachers ask, "What do I do to keep everyone on task?" The answer will vary, but some suggestions follow:

1. Provide verbal and written descriptions of the task to be completed.
2. Review the major steps involved before groups begin work.
3. Monitor membership if students group themselves. Some groups may need more attention than others.
4. Provide a structured way for groups to document their progress.
5. End each cooperative learning session with a whole class wrap-up, giving every group a chance to speak.

The various procedures for intraclass grouping discussed in the preceding pages will be of assistance to teachers in organizing their classroom learning environments. The teacher serves as manager of the instructional program and must use a variety of intraclass grouping procedures to provide the most appropriate instruction for each student. A student might be involved in all five types of groups during one day.

Needless to say, no instructional plan yet devised can compensate for a poorly organized classroom setting or ineffective teaching. Effective reading instruction can only be implemented by means of careful planning, good management, and good organizational techniques.

Interclass Formats

Interclass or cross-class grouping is the second major grouping procedure. With this type of grouping, students from several classes are integrated in common reading classrooms according to their achievement levels. In other words, parallel scheduling among classes is used to facilitate reading instruction. The purpose of interclass grouping is to permit teachers involved to develop homogeneous instructional units. Several groups are formed, as determined by the reading levels of the students involved, then each teacher works with a specific group. This type of grouping may be limited to one grade level or may cross several grade levels. For example, all the students in the fifth grade could be divided into groups according to their reading levels. Then each fifth-grade teacher would work with a particular group during the time designated for reading. Crossing grade levels would involve grouping students from several grade levels into groups according to their reading levels, regardless of age or maturity. Teachers would then work with these mixed-age students for specific purposes.

In many schools with primary grades, multi-age classes have been formed to facilitate students learning from one another. The success of these classes has caused the expansion of the concept to upper levels, with groups composed of 8- and 9-year olds, or 9- and 10-year-olds, and even 10-, 11-, and 12-year-olds. Different formats are used depending on the purpose of instruction, available facilities, and student needs. Within these classes, many of the intraclass grouping procedures can be effectively employed.

Regardless of the grouping format used in the school, intraclass or interclass, obtaining and using assessment information is a major responsibility of the classroom teacher. This information is essential for deciding how to group students to provide the most appropriate instruction. The teacher is responsible for evaluating, organizing, synthesizing, and updating assessment data. Because a student's learning is not constant, adjustments in grouping assignments must be made during the year. These adjustments require that classroom teachers use continuous assessment as a basis for change. This point is stressed because the tendency in the elementary and middle-school grades is to make an initial grouping assignment, allow a routine to set in, and forget to reevaluate the student's group placement. For many students, this has meant that they remain in the same achievement group for their entire elementary school life!

PLANNING FOR CONCEPT-BASED INSTRUCTION

An effective language-based program of reading instruction can be achieved by building on the strengths of basal materials. Teachers can adapt and expand the suggested basal materials and supplement them with appropriate trade books. The predominance and general acceptance of basal materials combined with the need to adapt instruction for students' specific needs strongly supports language-based strategies based on basal materials.

Language-based instruction, commonly called whole-language instruction, can make use of the basal text and trade books or basals alone or trade books alone. Instructional materials are selected for their interest to the student and the way in which the material can be used.

Likewise, skills instruction has a place in language-based reading instruction. Isolated skill instruction is inappropriate, however, necessary skills must be taught as students learn concepts. For example, learning to outline information for a report on *The Hunchback of Notre Dame* requires students to understand main ideas and details and how these skills are interrelated. As they learn these skills, they are learning how to interpret and use text. Thus, reading skills are developed continuously through content area study, trade books, and direct instruction during a designated time. To develop skills in a meaningful content-learning situation, appropriate concepts are first identified and necessary reading skills noted.

The integration of commercial materials (basals) with language-based methods requires careful planning. Skills and concepts to be covered can be identified by analyzing curriculum guides and scope and sequence charts. The next step is determining how to merge materials and methods for the most effective instruction. Assessment and student-teacher interaction provide guidance about which instructional strategies will best facilitate development in multiple areas.

Six steps are involved in planning and delivering concept-based instruction:

1. Identify concepts and associated reading skills to be taught.
2. Compare teacher-made lists with scope and sequence charts provided by basal series in all subjects, narrowing and combining where possible. As seen in Figure 5.10, creating a matrix is one way to gain an overall idea of how and when skills will be presented in various content areas. The first activity, investigating a topic of interest, includes a wide variety of skills that could be addressed in multiple areas. By concentrating instruction in the area of reading, the teacher streamlines the instructional process and identifies ample opportunities to reinforce primary instruction through other subjects.
3. Identify and group vocabulary to be addressed.
4. Plan and implement lessons using an organized student-centered format.
5. Evaluate instruction regularly through holistic measures of student performance.
6. Revise plans as necessary for future use.[41]

The cycle of steps is summarized in Figure 5.11. Further discussion of each step follows.

1. Identify a text that addresses concepts in both language arts and in content areas. Plan weekly lessons, referring to matches identified in scope and sequence charts, curriculum guides, experiences with previous classes, and information gained from student assessments.
2. On a large chart, record subjects separately, listing major concepts and subconcepts. Then begin narrowing, combining, deleting, and inserting information where needed. In some cases, concepts or subconcepts may overlap in one or more subjects. For example, concepts related to reading graphs, use of specialized reference materials and organization of information are often included in the scope and sequence charts in mathematics, social studies, science, reading, and language arts texts.
3. List appropriate vocabulary necessary for understanding the text and applying concepts and reading skills, sorting vocabulary where possible. Vocabulary should be introduced in context during the introductory stage of the unit or lesson,[42] and terms should appear frequently throughout the study, providing students with many opportunities to read and use terms in varying contexts.

Figure 5.10 Activities and Skills across Subjects: Reference Skills Used in "The Mighty American Kestrel" Lesson

	Skills									
Activities	A	B	C	D	E	F	G	H	I	J
Independent research of a topic of interest:	–	1	1	1	1	1	1	1	1	–
American kestrel	–	–	2	–	2	–	2	2	–	–
	–	–	3	–	3	3	–	3	3	3
	–	–	–	–	4	–	–	4	–	4
	–	–	–	–	–	–	–	–	5	5
Read/discuss newspaper and/or magazine editorials	1	1	–	1	1	1	1	1	–	1
concerning conservation	–	–	–	–	2	–	2	2	–	2
	–	–	–	–	3	3	–	3	–	3
	–	–	–	–	–	–	–	–	–	–
Study/report physical environment	–	–	1	–	–	–	–	–	–	–
	–	–	2	–	2	2	2	2	–	2
	–	–	–	–	3	3	3	3	–	3
	–	–	–	–	4	4	4	4	–	4
	–	–	–	–	–	–	–	–	5	–
Produce class newspaper	1	1	–	1	1	1	1	1	–	1
	–	–	–	2	2	2	2	–	–	–
	–	–	–	3	3	–	–	–	–	–
	–	–	–	4	4	4	–	–	4	–
	–	–	–	–	–	–	–	5	5	5
Design multiple displays of data	–	–	–	1	1	1	1	1	1	1
	–	–	–	–	2	2	2	2	–	–
	–	–	–	–	3	3	3	–	–	–
	–	–	–	–	4	4	4	–	4	–
	–	–	–	–	5	5	5	5	5	–

Notes

1 = Reading
2 = Social studies
3 = Science
4 = Math
5 = Writing

A = Table of Contents
B = Index
C = Encyclopedia
D = Card catalog
E = Charts/tables
F = Diagrams
G = Maps
H = Evaluates information/sources
I = Outlines
J = Draws conclusions

4. Plan units based on identified concepts, student needs, and expressed interests. The most important materials to teach a unit, are likely to be trade books. Regardless of the unit of study, one can usually locate fiction to supplement content area concepts. Incorporating these texts with nonfiction provides a balance for students and for teachers. It also facilitates creative-writing activities related to the topic of study.
5. Assess comprehension and vocabulary development continuously using informal assessments. Results of assessments, recorded on group or class checklists or on individual student summaries, can be used to modify instruction for those in need of alternate learning experiences. Of the possible informal assessment techniques, observation is perhaps the most informative for documenting student progress. As students work independently or in groups, the effective teacher moves throughout the room, recording pertinent information in writing or making mental notes. Aspects of student progress that can be monitored through observation include social interaction, physical state, frustration, boredom, and enthusiasm.
6. The most crucial part of planning is the revision process. In this step, teachers must examine their students' progress and adjust their instruction to meet the needs of each student. It is this step that requires the teacher to effectively integrate all aspects of language-based reading instruction regardless of philosophical orientation. The most effective reading program is always the one that meets the needs of the students.

Figure 5.11 Steps for Developing Concept Units

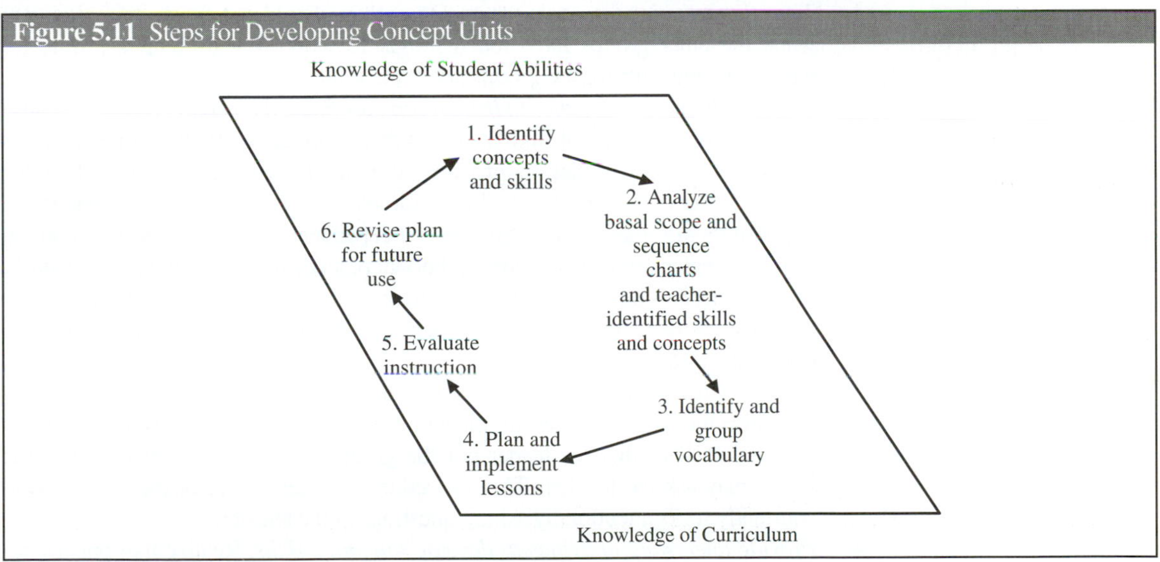

Classroom teachers vary in their approach to reading instruction. Many feel comfortable in a literature-based classroom teaching related concepts using various works in literature. Many other teachers prefer a more traditional approach to reading instruction, in which the content class is organized into various reading groups. Both organizational approaches are acceptable as long as the needs of the students are met through interesting and appropriate instruction. School districts and individual schools may have a preference on how the classroom should be organized.

ORGANIZING THE TRADITIONAL READING LESSON

One of the more critical aspects of grouping is the manner in which groups are organized. Since the type of groups generally used has been discussed, let us now examine ways to develop these groups in the traditional classroom. Because many classroom teachers in a traditional class frequently have a three-group instructional format, the sample design will use three groups.

Table 5.1 shows a basic format for implementing an instructional program in reading in the elementary and middle-school grades. This design uses three groups and a directed reading activity format; the design can easily be expanded and adapted for use with more than three groups. The three groups are achievement groups, but other grouping patterns can be used as needed within the design. The time variable may be adjusted by the teacher to reflect hours actually spent in reading and language arts. This plan will be used for several days, since an entire reading lesson for three groups cannot be completed in the limited time provided for reading instruction each day. The following guidelines will help teachers implement a design like the one presented in Table 5.1.

1. *Time the activities for each group.* One group should not finish its assignment while the other groups have much longer to work. Try to keep the time for various assignments for the groups about the same.
2. *Provide alternatives for the students when they finish their assignments.* Because it is impossible to have all students finish their work at exactly the same time, it is necessary for the teacher to provide activities to engage students when the assigned work is completed. For example, a reading center provides an opportunity for the student to enjoy independent reading activities, and an activities center can give students additional practice in developing reading skills. Students need to be aware of their alternatives as they finish assignments so that they will not need to interrupt the teacher's work with another group or disturb others in the class.
3. *Appoint a leader for each group.* If students have questions as they work, they can direct them to the leader; in this way they will not disturb the other groups or the teacher. If neither the leader nor the group can answer a question, then the leader may ask the teacher. This procedure also helps control the student who constantly seeks attention by asking questions of the teacher.
4. *Provide interesting activities to develop language skills.* Realize that paper-and-pencil tasks become very boring to students; thus, manipulative activities are essential. In addition, games and learning centers can furnish other activities

when students finish their assignments. In far too many classrooms students are expected to spend their time doing worksheets and copying from the board. This is a waste of student time (and paper) and leads to boredom, frustration, and disruptive behavior.

5. *Spend some time on total-class activities.* At the beginning of each school day or each class, take a few minutes for a total-class activity. This may include listening to an audiotape or story, singing a song, or playing a game. Social skills, as well as language skills, are developed through such activities. During this time, the teacher may give group assignments, making certain that students understand what they are to do as well as what they can do when they finish assignments. Depending on the students' age level and attention span, the teacher will need to bring the class together as a total group every 10 to 30 minutes for a brief break. Otherwise, students become confused as they move from area to area and tend to lose interest in their work.
6. *Provide activities that are appropriate to the student's level and needs.* Do not provide the same listening activity or skills activities to several groups. In Table 5.1, the activity categories are the same for each group, but the specific activities for each group must be designed to meet individual levels and needs. Although it takes time to develop learning centers, games, and activities, this is necessary for maximum learning to occur.

Grouping procedures can also be useful for teaching reading in the content areas. More effective instruction can take place in the content areas if some attention is given to individual students through grouping. The role of the content teacher has changed from that of a conveyor of information to one of facilitating instruction and attending more to the individual needs of students. Necessity has dictated this change because of the increased problems that students have had in coping with content material. Thus, content teachers at the elementary and middle-school levels may find it beneficial to incorporate reading instruction in their classes.

Figure 5.12 presents the basic design for implementing reading instruction in the content areas. Three groups are used, and various activities are incorporated. This format can be easily expanded for use with more than three groups. Since some activities require more time than others, the content specialist should determine the average amount of time that the activities will require in order to establish a framework for presenting them. This design follows the directed reading activity format and the SQ3R procedure for reading the material.

Content teachers can also benefit from the organizational suggestions previously discussed. By adjusting instruction to the reading levels and interest of the students, content teachers will find that students gain more information about the subject area and show more interest in the classroom. Thus, organizing and managing the classroom becomes an easier task.

Table 5.1 Organizational Format for Reading Instruction

Time*	Group 1	Group 2	Group 3**
—to—	*Review/apply previously learned skills.* As a group, individualized into smaller skill groups or using peer tutoring, these students are provided activities in which they apply skills or strategies taught in earlier lessons. Students from the other groups may be included as necessary.	*Language development.* Writing, listening, or other language activities are done by the group or individualized according to the needs or interests of the students. Students from the other groups may be included as appropriate.	*Readiness and skill development* (*teacher*). Introduce the new concepts to develop background knowledge and provide direct instruction for the skills needed for what is to be read. May include students from Groups 1 and 2.
—to—	*Language development*	*Readiness and skill development* (*teacher*)	*Skill application.* Through various activities, the students apply the newly introduced skills.
—to—	*Readiness and skill development* (*teacher*)	*Skill application*	*Language development*
—to—	*Skill application*	*Personal reading.* A specific time is provided for students to read books of their choice. Activities such as dioramas, designing book jackets, letters to the author, etc., are included to encourage the sharing of information.	*Review and introduce material* (*teacher*). Concepts, vocabulary, and skills (new and previously taught) needed to read the material are reviewed and a purpose for reading is established.
—to—	*Personal reading*	*Review and introduce material* (*teacher*)	*Silent reading.* Using the purpose(s) established, the students read all or a portion of the material silently. Suggest that they read it at least twice.
—to—	*Review and introduce material* (*teacher*)	*Silent reading*	*Read along.* Because this group needs many opportunities to review reading materials, they are allowed to work together to interact about the material. This can be done by peer grouping of partners to read aloud to each other, reading into a tape recorder, or discussing what they have read using teacher-generated questions.

* Times vary but generally range from 10 to 20 minutes per time block.
** Group 3 is considered the low-achievement group in this class; thus, the teacher begins with this group.

Table 5.1 Organizational Format for Reading Instruction

Time*	Group 1	Group 2	Group 3**
—to—	*Silent reading*	*Read along*	*Guided reading (teacher).* Based on silent readings and other interactions with the materials, the teacher discusses the information with the students via questions, retellings. and oral reading of selected parts. This serves as a way of obtaining ongoing diagnostic data.
—to—	*Student guided reading.* Via teacher-designed activities, the students review the information read to assess their comprehension and to clarify points. Questions and discussions are used well here.	*Guided reading* (*teacher*)	*Follow-up.* Activities to extend the concepts presented are included at this time via various art, music, creative dramatics, or other language activities. Teachers can also use this time to reteach information that the students do not seem to understand. This can be done via skill groups, peer groups or achievement groups as appropriate to the situation.
—to—	*Guided reading (teacher)*	*Follow-up*	*Follow-up.* Because these students so frequently spend their follow-up time doing more skill work, two periods of time are included so that they will have an opportunity to be involved with some fun extension activities.
—to—	*Follow-up*	*Follow-up*	*Readiness and skill development (teacher).* New material.
—to—	*Language development*	*Readiness and skill development (teacher).* New material.	*Skill application*

The procedure for the direct reading lesson is followed again with new material.

SELECTING INSTRUCTIONAL MATERIAL

Text selection in the classroom is a complex task because the teacher must consider the physical appearance of the item, print size, page organization, illustrations, concept density, vocabulary, and readability. To determine readability, or the grade level for which the text is written, one can use the Fry readability graph (see Figure 5.13).[43] Some texts, particularly content area texts, have high concept density due to the visual presentation of information, the presence of technical and specialized vocabulary, and the number of ideas presented.

Figure 5.12 Organizational Format for Incorporating Reading Instruction and Grouping in the Content Class

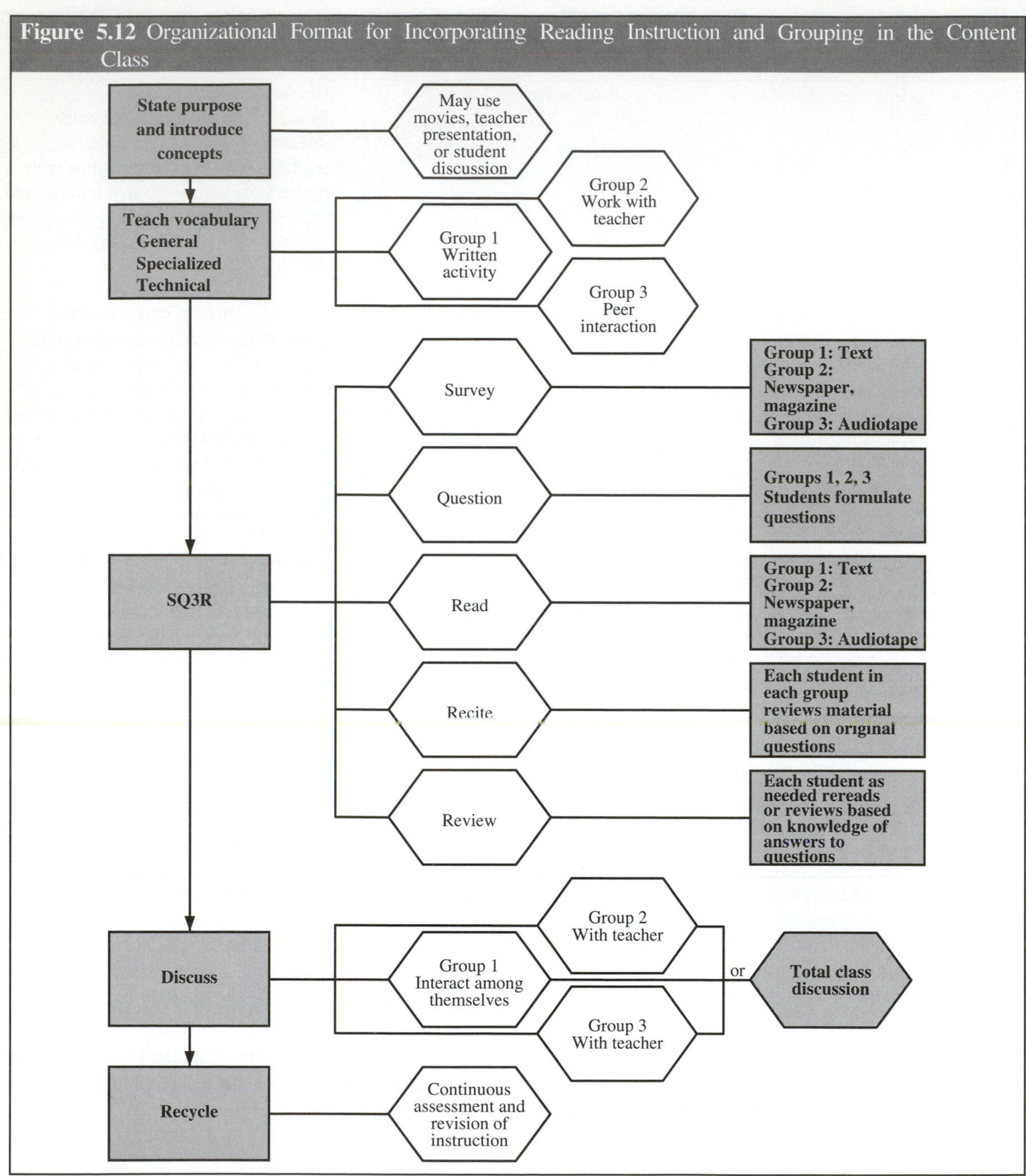

Figure 5.13 The Fry Readability Graph

GRAPH FOR ESTIMATING READABILITY—EXTENDED
by Edward Fry, Rutgers University Reading Center, New Brunswick, NJ 08904
Average number of syllables per 100 words

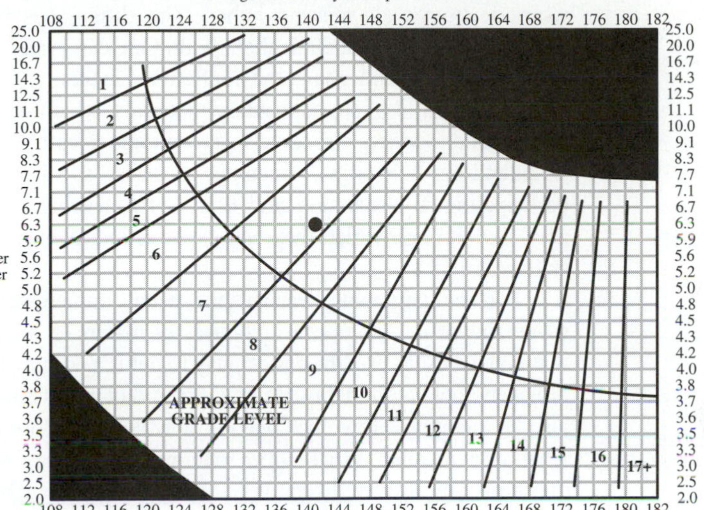

DIRECTIONS: Randomly select 3 one hundred word passages from a book or an article. Plot average number of syllables and average number of sentences per 100 words on graph to determine the grade level of the material. Choose more passages per book if great variability is observed and conclude that the book has uneven readability. Few books will fall in gray area but when they do grade level scores are invalid.

Count proper nouns, numerals and initializations as words. Count a syllable for each symbol. For example, "1945" is 1 word and 4 syllables and "IRA" is 1 word and 3 syllables.

EXAMPLE:

	SYLLABLES	SENTENCES
1st Hundred Words	124	6.6
2nd Hundred Words	141	5.5
3rd Hundred Words	158	6.8
AVERAGE	141	6.3

READABILITY 7th GRADE (see dot plotted on graph)

Consider a fourth-grade level nonfiction text about the Civil War. The book would probably include a discussion of differing opinions about slavery, the conflicts in some states over secession from the Union, the differences between a rural agricultural economy and an industrial one, the horrors of war, and rebuilding a nation torn apart by differences. To impart these concepts, the author would probably include many proper names, terms related to the political process, dates, and military, industrial, and agricultural terms. Taken one at a time these ideas are complex, but a text about the Civil War would also need to describe relationships among these elements. Now, compare this sort of text to a fictional account of how one family endured the Civil War. Students would be better able to understand unfamiliar concepts by seeing how they affect one family's life. Their own knowledge of day-to-day family life would allow students to empathize with characters who were hungry or worried about their missing father. The differences between the two texts are a compelling reason to include them both. One can easily see that a fictional text would assist students to understand the nonfiction account.

The unit file of supplementary materials, which grows from year to year as new information is added, can serve as a resource for both teacher and students. As a result of attending field trips, listening to guest speakers, reading trade books, and participating in discussion and drama, the teacher can assist students to develop networks through which they can explore, internalize, and apply knowledge to new studies.

For the beginning teacher one point immediately becomes clear: there are mountains of information, warehouses of materials, and endless opinions about what material is best to use, the easiest way to get it, and how to adapt it once acquired. The prevalence of high-quality materials in today's classroom is encouraging, but it can also be daunting. How does one know which ones to try? How does one learn about what is available? Where does one get the money to buy the materials? These questions are answered relatively quickly once a teacher is placed in a school and classroom.

The most common resources for learning about commercial materials are as follows:

1. Teacher magazines and professional journals are published regularly, offering a wide variety of practical ideas and thought-provoking theoretical discussions.
2. Professional conferences provide demonstrations of new methods and materials, and also offer teachers a way to advance professionally.
3. Peer observations and peer interviews offer opportunities to learn about classroom management in the real world.
4. Catalogs advertising materials keep teachers apprised of the newest books, games, kits, equipment, software, and hardware.

Several teacher magazines supply ready-made activities: lesson plans, classroom decorations, seasonal activities, and organization ideas, to name a few. Teacher magazines also include a wide variety of advertisements that describe products currently on the market. Typically, such advertisements are accompanied by an address to which one may write for additional information or a phone number for interested callers. Teacher magazines are particularly useful to new teachers and to those who feel they need an occasional boost in their instructional programs. The ideas in these magazines are normally based on scholarly research and writing found in professional journals. The differences between these two types of resources are significant: Professional journals are published by scholarly societies and focus on theoretical foundations and tests of those theories in the classroom, while teacher magazines are commercially published and focus on classroom applications of tested theories. Both resources offer the teacher a valuable view of current instructional theory, and both belong on every teacher's professional reading stack. A list of teacher magazines and scholarly journals that can be located at most university libraries, school or district media centers, and curriculum labs follows.

Teacher Magazines

- *The Mailbox*, Box 51676, Boulder, CO 80323
- *Instructor*, Box 53895, Boulder, CO 80323
- *Writing Teacher*, Box 794137, San Antonio, TX 78279
- *Teaching K–8*, Box 50408, Boulder, CO 80322
- *The Horn Book*, Park Square Building, 31 Saint James Avenue, Boston, MA 02116
- *Booklinks*, Box 1347, Elmhurst, IL 60126
- *The New Advocate*, 480 Washington Street, Norwood, MA 02068
- *CBC Features*, The Children's Book Council, Inc., 350 Scotland Road, Orange, NJ 07050

Professional Journals

Published by the International Reading Association, 800 Barksdale Road, PO Box 8139, Neward, DE 19711:

- *The Reading Teacher*
- *Journal of Adolescent and Adult Literacy*

Published by the National Council of Teachers of English, 1111 Kenyon Road, Urbana, IL 61801:

- *Language Arts*
- *Primary Voices K–6*
- *Voices from the Middle*

Another option for learning about materials and methods is attending professional conferences. Held annually, conferences offer teachers opportunities to network with colleagues from various geographic areas, to socialize, to preview new materials on exhibit, and to attend short sessions on new teaching strategies and longer workshops for intensive exploration of ideas and strategies. Designed to rejuvenate as well as inform, conferences are invigorating experiences for all who attend. Teachers who attend conferences and learn about new teaching methods often serve as trainers to teachers who were not in attendance.

Peer observations and peer interviews are another resource for learning about materials and methods. As with professional conferences, school districts usually offer a limited number of professional leave days for such activities, especially for new teachers. Teachers may survey principals and peers to learn about effective teachers of particular subjects, those who are using specific materials in a novel way, those who have designed creative classrooms, and teachers who are well organized.

Catalogs of teaching materials are also a good resource for learning about new materials of instruction. There are many well-established companies that rely on ideas from in-service teachers for product development. The media center is usually the place to find numerous catalogs. Teachers are another source, and of course the principal receives many catalogs featuring products for every subject area.

One thing that teachers quickly learn is that they can make many of the materials they see in magazines and other classrooms, thus saving funds for other items. Students are delighted to see the creative skills of their teacher, and they appreciate the fact that the material was made just for them. To make sturdy materials with common items, one need go no further than a sewing box, the paper closet, and that cluttered desk drawer in the kitchen. Here are some rules of thumb for making classroom materials:

1. *Use everyday materials.* Chances are the teacher will have to replace parts of teacher-made items that are used by students. Using easy-to-find items makes this task less time-consuming.
2. *Use durable materials.* Even when laminated, construction paper is not very strong. Use cardboard, tagboard, wood, permanent markers or paint, heavy fabric, and other materials that can take a beating.
3. *Use colorful materials.* Everyone enjoys using colorful materials. Given a choice, few children would pick up a plain manila folder or an unmarked box when interesting colors, patterns, and textures are nearby. Paints, chalk, markers, fabric, construction paper, tissue paper, cellophane, wallpaper, gift wrap, contact paper, and student art can all be used to package learning activities. Some teachers make one or two game boards or generic packets that can be used for several activities. Making sets of cards or figures focusing on different skills or concepts allows activities to be used for different levels and subjects.
4. *Incorporate animals, fantasy, and playful characters (tied to literature).* Activities that contain a familiar element are usually popular. For example, a game can feature a character in a book the class is reading, a country under study, imaginative figures, children's artwork, TV characters, video-game characters, or pets.
5. *Write simple directions.* So that students can feel a sense of independence, activities should include directions for using the activity. When written in simple language, perhaps accompanied by illustrations, students are more likely to experience success without having to involve others.
6. *Make activities self-checking.* Providing students with a way to evaluate their progress helps them become more independent and saves the teacher from interruptions when working with other students. Options for making a game self-

checking include having the answers written on a card or folder, listening to an audiotape, placing a stencil over work, or providing an answer box that is within easy reach.

ACTIVATING THE PLAN

Another visit to Ms. Self's classroom allows us to see how the ideas in this chapter have been implemented. Like most teachers, Ms. Self thinks about her instructional program even when school is out of session. During the last weeks before school begins, she begins thumbing through materials catalogs, listing those items she would like to acquire and how they could supplement existing materials. She creates a wish list for her principal, including notes about how others might take advantage of the same materials. In finalizing the list, Ms. Self takes another look at her goals and objectives. She confirms her assumption that materials would be helpful and, at the same time, thinks about new ways to combine and personalize the content for her students. She enjoys weaving her own experiences and personality into her program, and she has noticed that students enjoy it as well. Ms. Self has learned that personalizing instruction enhances the sense of community she strives to build in the classroom early in the year.

As the first day of school grows closer, Ms. Self begins to review students' cumulative files. She forms loose ability groups using test scores, report card grades, and comments recorded by colleagues. She learns that her class is mostly boys and that the girls have formed unusually close social ties. Realizing that they may have become dependent on one another, Ms. Self plans activities allowing the girls to work cooperatively and ones that involve both boys and girls. She hopes to extend the girls' sense of community to the larger group by acknowledging the bonds previously formed. Ms. Self also learns that she will have two inclusion students: a Down's syndrome girl and a hearing-impaired boy. She places them close to her desk in case they need closer monitoring. In this way she can check on them without being obvious, thus providing an increased sense of independence. Noting questions or concerns to be investigated further, she plans assessments to be given early in the year. Results of these assessments will provide direction for other types of grouping, too. Group membership will surely be revised since pencil and paper alone cannot provide a true portrait of three-dimensional individuals.

At last the first day of school arrives. Ms. Self has created a friendly atmosphere conducive to group and individual work. She has devoted parts of the classroom to students' exclusive use: a bulletin board, shelf space, and a cabinet. They quickly determine how these areas will be used, obviously pleased to have their own space beyond the confines of their desks. Tonight Ms. Self will take writing samples home for a quick review. On the drive home, she will think about each student and how he or she fared in the new classroom. She continues such reflection throughout the next few months.

Continually Ms. Self finds herself thinking about that neat video on whales, a guest speaker who would fit well into her unit on the environment, the way her friend at work keeps track of process writing, what to say at the opening of a parent meeting, and where she left those catalogs. Such is the stuff of the rewarding life of a teacher.

SUMMARY

Organizing for effective teaching includes classroom management, planning and decision making, planning for concept instruction, and materials identification and selection. Effective teachers provide integrated language-based instruction that meets the needs of each student, motivates students, and facilitates positive attitudes about learning. They also value diversity, make good classroom management decisions, plan extensively, and develop an understanding of an integrated curriculum and how it can be adapted for their classroom. All of these characteristics result in appropriate instruction for learners and positive experiences for teachers.

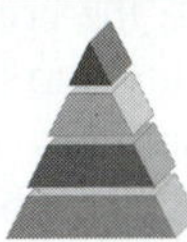

Applying What You Read

1. You have just been assigned to teach a class that was formed after the school year started. The principal has informed you that your new class will be held on the school stage for three months while a classroom is being prepared. Draw a map of the arrangement of furniture, supplies, and students. List ways in which you could create a sense of community in the temporary setting.
2. If you could only have 20 materials of instruction for reading, what would your list include? Why did you include each item? Rank the items in order of importance.
3. One of your ability groups is not progressing as well as the others. List behaviors that would make you question a student's placement in this group. What type of assessment could you use to confirm your suspicions?
4. One of your ability groups is not progressing as well as the others. List student's behaviors that make you question their group placement. What type of assessment could you use to confirm your suspicions?

NOTES

1. K. McKeever, *A Place for Owls.*
2. G. Tompkins, *Literacy for the Twenty-First Century: A Balanced Approach.*
3. T. Shannon, *Broken Promises: Reading Instruction in Twentieth-Century America.*
4. D. Strickland, "Reinventing Our Literacy Programs: Books, Basics, and Balance," *The Reading Teacher.*
5. E. Noll and Kenneth Goodman, "Using a Howitzer to Kill a Butterfly," *The New Advocate.*
6. D. Ray Reutzel and R. B. Cooter, Jr., "Organizing for Effective Instruction: The Reading Workshop," *The Reading Teacher.*
7. K. Acheson and M. Gall, *Techniques in the Clinical Supervision of Teachers: Preservice and Inservice Applications.*
8. Comments made by R. Rosenshine and Furst in Acheson and Gall, *Techniques in the Clinical Supervision of Teachers: Preservice and Inservice Applications.*
9. W. Borg, "Time and School Learning," in *Time to Learn*, edited by C. Denham and A. Lieberman.
10. C. Evertson, "Managing Classrooms: A Framework for Teachers," in *Talks to Teachers*, edited by D. Berliner and B. Rosenshine.
11. W. Doyle, "Classroom Organization and Management," in *Handbook of Research on Teaching*, edited by M. Wittrock.
12. S. Elam, "The Second Gallup/Phi Delta Kappa Poll of Teachers' Attitudes toward the Public Schools," *Phi Delta Kappa.*

13. R. Tauber, *Classroom Management from a–z.*
14. T. Gordon, *Teacher Effectiveness Training.*
15. R. Dreikurs, B. Grunwald, and F. Pepper, *Maintaining Sanity in the Classroom: Illustrating Reading Techniques*.
16. W. Glasser, *Control Theory in the Classroom.*
17. R. Tauber, *Classroom Management from a–z.*
18. Comments by M. H. Bailey in Tompkins, *Literary for the Twenty-First Century: A Balanced Approach.*
19. K. Stanovich, "Are We Overselling Literacy?" in *Understanding Reading Problems: Assessment and Instruction*, edited by J. Gillet and C. Temple, p. 90.
20. M. Kean, A. Summers, M. Ravietz, and I. Farber, *What Works in Reading*, p. 9.
21. C. W. Fisher, N. N. Filby, R. Marliave, L. S. Cahen, M. M. Dishaw, J. E. Moore, and D. C. Berliner, *Teaching Behaviors, Academic Learning Time, and Student Achievement.*
22. Barak Rosenshine and Robert Stevens, "Classroom Instruction in Reading," *Handbook of Reading Research*, edited by P. David Pearson, p. 758.
23. C. C. Kulik and J. A. Kulik, "Effects of Ability Grouping on Secondary School Students: A Meta-Analysis of Evaluation Findings," *American Educational Research Journal.*
24. C. Persell, *Education and Inequality: The Roots and Results of Stratification in American Schools.*
25. Linda L. Brown and Rita J. Sherbenou, "A Comparison of Teacher Perceptions of Student Reading Ability, Reading Performance, and Classroom Behavior," *The Reading Teacher;* Chris Moacdieh, "Grouping of Reading in the Primary Grades: Evidence on the Revisionist Argument," paper presented at the Annual Meeting of the American Educational Research Association, Los Angeles, California; John J. Pikulski and Irwin S. Kiroch, "Organization for Instruction," *Teaching Reading in Compensatory Classes*, edited by Robert C. Calfee and Priscilla A. Drum.
26. Emil J. Haller and Sharon A. Davis, "Does Socioeconomic Status Bias the Assignment of Elementary School Students to Reading Groups?" *American Educational Research Journal.*
27. Jeanne Martin and Carolyn M. Evertson, *Teachers' Interactions with Reading Groups of Differing Ability Levels.*
28. Linda Grant and James Rothenberg, *Charting Educational Futures: Interaction Patterns in First and Second Grade Reading Groups*; Paula R. Stern and Richard J. Shavelson, "The Relationship between Teachers' Grouping Decisions and Instructional Behavior: An Ethnographic Study of Reading Instruction," paper presented at the Annual Meeting of the American Educational Research Association, Los Angeles, California.
29. E. H. Hiebert, "An Examination of Ability Grouping for Reading Instruction," *Reading Research Quarterly*; P. Peterson, L. Wilkinson, and M. Hallinan, *The Social Context of Instruction: Group Organization and Group Processes.*
30. P. Peterson, L. Wilkinson, and M. Hallinan, *The Social Context of Instruction.*
31. Linda Grant and James Rothenberg, *Charting Educational Futures.*
32. S. Asher, "Topic Interest and Children's Reading Comprehension," in *Theoretical Issues in Reading Comprehension,* edited by R. Spiro, B. Bruce, and W. Brewer.
33. R. C. Anderson, E. H. Hiebert, J. A. Scott, and I. A. Wilkinsen, *Becoming a Nation of Readers.*
34. Jack Cassidy, "Cross-Age Tutoring and the Sacrosanct Reading Period," *Reading Horizons*; Hal Dreyer, "RX for Pupil Tutoring Programs," *The Reading Teacher*; Joan L. Fogarty and Margaret C. Wang, "An Investigation of the Cross-Age Peer Tutoring Process: Some Implications for Instructional Design and Motivation," *The Elementary School Journal.*
35. Linda D. Labbo and William H. Teale, "Cross-Age Reading: A Strategy for Helping Poor Readers," *The Reading Teacher*.
36. Connie Morrice and Maureen Simmons, "Beyond Reading Buddies: A Whole Language Cross-Age Program," *The Reading Teacher*.
37. Roger T. Johnson and David W. Johnson, "Action Research: Cooperative Learning in the Science Classroom," *Science and Children*.
38. Robert Slavin, *Cooperative Learning*.

39. Karen D'Angelo Bromley, "Buddy Journals Make the Reading-Writing Connection," *The Reading Teacher*.
40. Suzi Keegan and Karen Shrake, "Literature Study Groups: An Alternative to Ability Grouping," *The Reading Teacher*.
41. E. Cheek, Jr., and M. Collins, *Reading Instruction through Content Teaching*.
42. Cheek and Collins, *Reading Instruction through Content Teaching*.
43. E. Fry, "Fry's Readability Graph: Clarifications, Validity, and Extension to Level 17," *Journal of Reading*.

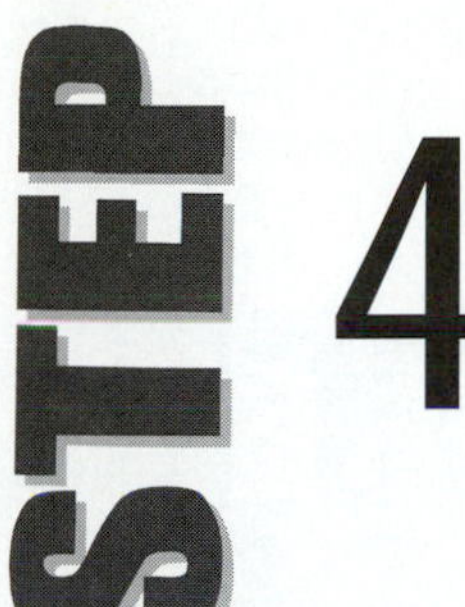

STEP 4 GUIDING READING INSTRUCTION

Teachers at Twin Lakes School realize that high-quality instruction is the key component in a successful reading program. Using informal and formal assessment data and daily evaluations along with their skill in organizing and managing reading instruction, Ms. Morgan and Ms. Floyd, as team leaders at the different grade levels, have focused their attention on providing appropriate reading instruction that meets the needs of individual students. Chapters 6 through 11 are designed to help teachers guide reading instruction for each student. In these chapters, instructional techniques and strategies are offered to assist in the teaching and learning process.

TORNADO
DRILL

CHAPTER 6

Providing Appropriate Reading Instruction

Ms. Floyd at the primary level, Ms. Knight at the elementary level, and Ms. Morgan at the middle-school level are the team leaders in a program to help teachers at Twin Lakes School recognize that the teacher is the instructional leader in the classroom. As instructional leaders, classroom teachers have the tremendous responsibility not only of identifying the reading strengths and needs of each student but also of providing appropriate instruction to meet each student's needs. The teachers at Twin Lakes believe that instruction based on the assessed needs of each student is essential to providing effective reading instruction. This chapter provides an overview of appropriate practices for day-to-day use in the classroom. The team leaders have proposed some basic principles of reading instruction, identified various approaches to teaching reading, and offered ideas on developing instructional programs for individuals and groups. More specifically, Chapter 6 addresses the following questions.

- How can appropriate reading instruction be provided?
- What are some basic guidelines for the teacher to follow in providing effective reading instruction?
- How does reading instruction differ in self-contained and departmentalized classrooms?
- What does the teacher need to consider before beginning reading instruction?
- What are the various reading approaches used to guide instruction?
- How do assessment data relate to providing effective instruction?
- How does the teacher develop an effective reading plan?
- When does a teacher plan for effective reading instruction?

Vocabulary to Know

- **Appropriate instruction**
- **Approaches**
- **Basal reader approach**
- **Computer-assisted instruction**
- **Direct instruction**
- **Directed learning activity**
- **Directed reading activity**
- **Eclectic approach**
- **Indirect instruction**
- **Individualized reading approach**
- **Language-based instruction**
- **Language experience approach**
- **Literature-based reading**
- **Multisensory approach**

AN OVERVIEW

When planning reading instruction, assessment data directs the instructional program for each student. We define appropriate reading instruction as teaching what you know the student needs rather than being unduly influenced by the textbook publishing companies. This is one way of thinking about teaching reading. However, as long as teachers follow a consistent plan, whether from the school or a publishing company, they will provide continuity in learning experiences and development from level to level.

When providing reading instruction, teachers are the decision makers and facilitators of the learning process. Knowing the needs of the students, they plan appropriate lessons to capture students' interests and develop reading abilities using appropriate materials and strategies. Basic instructional guidelines, which give teachers direction in implementing appropriate instruction in the classroom, are discussed in this chapter. A few of those guidelines are summarized here and in Figure 6.1.

- ***Effective teaching can be implemented in many ways; there is no one best way.*** Each teacher determines the best way to put various teaching ideas into effect in the classroom. Just as each student is unique, so is each teacher's style of teaching, classroom arrangement, and confidence in providing reading instruction. Teachers use ideas from this and other texts, from other teachers, from past experiences, and from various other sources, adapting them to their classrooms. The element that must always exist in effective instruction is that it be based on the students' assessed needs.
- ***Varied approaches and techniques must be used in providing instruction for a specific reading problem.*** Many approaches for teaching reading have been identified, and the research on these approaches is voluminous. However, as was found in the First-Grade Studies, there is no one best approach to teaching reading.[1] Likewise, no one technique is always successful in dealing with assessed reading problems. Each student is unique in her learning style, reading habits, background experiences, and self-expectations. Thus, a guide that tells a teacher what to do with each student cannot be provided; only suggestions can be made. The teacher must, through careful thought and in some cases trial and error, determine what works best with different students.

- ***Instruction should be consistent.*** Teachers using basal readers as their primary reading material have a scope and sequence of reading skills that gives structure to their instructional program. Teachers using a language-based approach do not have a hierarchy of skills directly associated with their materials, but they may find such a skills continuum in their local or state testing programs. Skills instruction must not be equated with good reading instruction; mastery of skills is not the goal of reading, nor is it the best description of a good reader. However, teachers must refer to some developmental sequence of reading and language skills in order to plan appropriate instruction and track how well students are learning.
- ***Instruction must be based on continuous assessment.*** The assessment made by the classroom teacher serves as a guide for identifying students' reading needs. For teaching to be truly effective, they must reevaluate and assess their students continually. This ongoing assessment is done through observation of the students' performance on assigned tasks, other informal procedures, and possibly some formal assessment tests. Regardless of how the information is obtained, the classroom teacher regularly assesses changes in reading performance to provide instruction based on the current needs of the student.
- ***Instruction should be flexible.*** Using their initial assessment information, teachers might begin instruction in an identified area of need, only to discover that the actual need is a lower-level skill or that the student has developed beyond what is being taught. Facilitative teachers make changes in the instruction they are providing. This may mean moving the student to another group for instruction or offering some individual instruction for a period of time. Flexibility is an essential element in guiding instruction.
- ***Effective teaching requires that all school personnel work together as a team.*** The entire school staff must work together not only in the continual assessment of students but also in guiding instruction. For example, the librarian may help develop personal reading by encouraging students to read books at their independent reading levels. She may also aid in the teaching of study strategies by helping the teacher develop specific library and reference skills as necessary. Content teachers can identify the reading skills necessary for learning content materials and help develop strategies for teaching these skills. Reading or language arts teachers should share with the content teachers all assessment data available to facilitate prescriptive reading instruction in all classes.

  The principal and guidance counselor facilitate reading instruction by locating materials and teaching ideas to help meet special student needs. Additionally, they provide much positive reinforcement to students as they improve in reading and to teachers as they strive to improve learning opportunities.

  For reading instruction to have the greatest impact, school faculty recognize that reading is essential in all schoolwork, that each student improves according to assessed needs, and that each teacher has a responsibility to help students improve. When the principal and school faculty understand their roles in the school reading program and work together for the benefit of the student, a reading program functions at its best.

- ***Effective teaching helps students to apply their knowledge of reading strategies to a wide range of printed materials.*** When developing reading strategies as well as when teaching their application, the teacher provides direct instruction and uses materials to reinforce and review. Reading strategies are not developed by "plugging" students into materials, but rather by explanation from the teacher, with reinforcement as needed, using various activities or materials. When students demonstrate a basic understanding of the reading process, teachers then show them how "school" reading is an integral part of their daily life experiences.
- ***Effective reading programs are designed to foster a positive self-image and enjoyment of reading as well as to develop the reading process.*** Reading instruction that meets identified needs and is on the appropriate level for the student not only enhances the development of reading but also helps students to have a more positive attitude toward themselves as a result of their success in learning. A basic knowledge of the language process and a good self-concept provide an excellent foundation for the enjoyment of reading. Thus, teachers should remember that the end product of the school reading program is a student who can read, who enjoys reading as a leisure-time activity as well as reading for informational purposes.

Figure 6.1 Basic Principles of Effective Reading Instruction

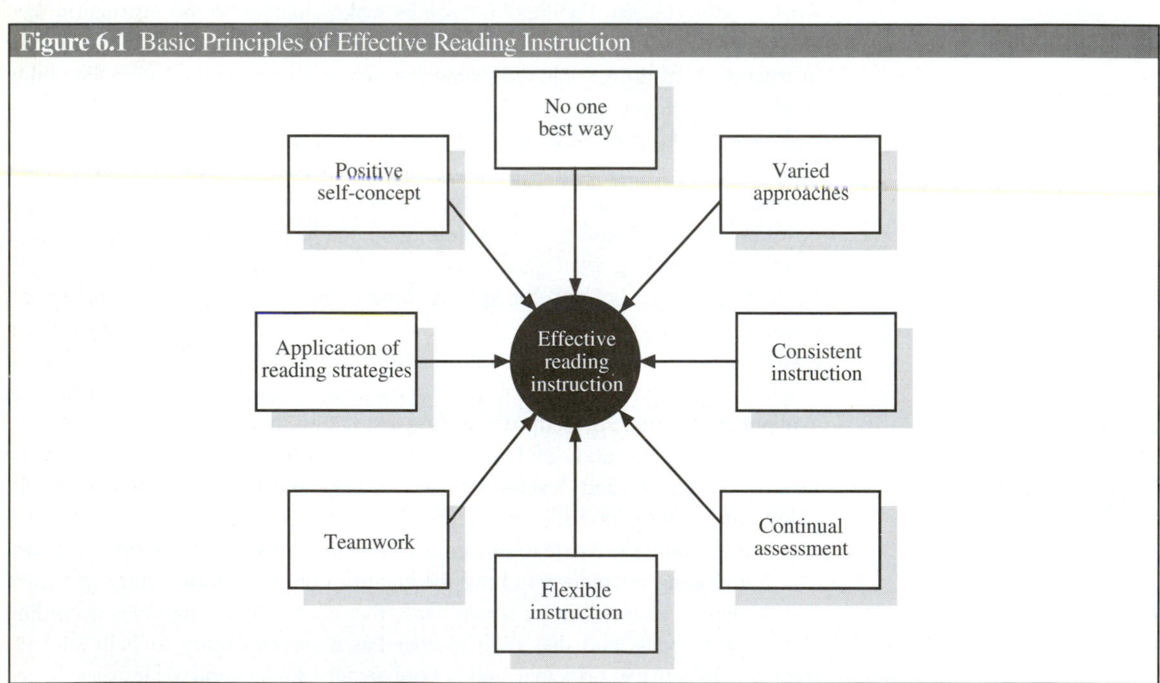

Using assessment data, classroom teachers can work together to develop a class profile of strengths and weaknesses in reading/language development and determine how to best meet individual student needs.

These basic principles provide general direction for implementing effective reading instruction. Teachers must interpret and apply them according to their individual teaching style and classroom needs.

APPROACHES TO EFFECTIVE READING INSTRUCTION

To provide effective reading instruction, the assessed needs, interests, and learning styles of the students must be considered. Thus, teachers need to be familiar with various approaches that may be used to provide appropriate instruction.

Many approaches have been presented by different writers; for some the term "methods" is synonymous with "approaches." Burns and Roe identify the major approaches as the basal reader approach, the language experience approach, the individualized reading approach, linguistic approaches, intensive phonics approaches, changed alphabet approaches, systems approaches, and eclectic approaches.[2] Fry discusses various methods of teaching reading, including the basal reader, reading systems, individualized reading, programmed instruction, different alphabetic approaches, audiovisual reading materials, a language experience approach, and a kinesthetic approach.[3] Other authors, including Vacca, Vacca, and Gove and Miller and McKenna,[4] offer slightly different lists of approaches for teaching reading.

As teachers read current professional materials, attend professional meetings, and talk about reading instruction in their classes, they will discover that two basic approaches are prominent. In the elementary and middle-school classrooms of the 1990s, teachers tend to use a basal reader approach or a language-based approach to reading instruction. While these approaches do not exist in complete isolation and are certainly not mutually exclusive, the current literature may lead one to think of these as the only two approaches to reading. To appropriately represent the trends and to provide information needed by the teacher to best meet individual student needs, these two major approaches are discussed first. Two secondary approaches are then presented; these secondary approaches can be used to modify the two primary approaches to meet student needs. Finally, an eclectic approach is discussed in which teachers combine elements from other approaches to devise the best method for meeting individual student needs.

Primary Approaches to Reading

When selecting the appropriate reading approach to use with students, teachers should consider several factors. These factors include (a) the teacher's philosophy and definition of reading and language instruction, (b) the characteristics of the students' cognitive and linguistic abilities, prior knowledge, experiential background, and sociocultural background), and (c) school and classroom environmental conditions (e.g., class size, equipment, materials).[5] Although the majority of school districts in this country use basal readers, many of which are eclectic in nature, literature- or language-based instruction is becoming very popular and is influencing the use of basal readers. Jagger[6] believes that several important themes regarding the essential role of language in learning to read have emerged in recent years. These themes are based on the following essential concepts which are inherent in language development.

1. *Language learning is a self-generated, creative process.* Children learn language without direct instruction. They learn it in a variety of ways (e.g., through experience or by listening to others), and they experiment with and practice their language in situations where language is purposeful.
2. *Language learning is holistic.* The language components of function, form, and meaning are learned simultaneously. Children acquire new and more complex forms and functions for language when they have a need for new and more complex meanings. Through this process they learn that the forms used to express meaning and intention may vary according to purpose and context.
3. *Language learning is social and collaborative.* Language is acquired by children in meaningful interactions with others who provide models. These individuals also support children's language learning by responding to what children are trying to say and do, rather than to form.
4. *Language learning is functional and integrative.* Children do not learn language first and then learn how to use it second. Language acquisition and communication are simultaneous functions. Both stimulate children's ability to use language to think and learn.
5. *Language learning is variable.* Because language learning is inherently variable, the meanings, forms, and functions of children's language depend on children's personal, social, and cultural experiences.

Although the selection of appropriate approaches to meet the needs of students is essential to effective reading instruction, developing and expanding the language base of students is one of the most important responsibilities of the teacher. The development of language as a communication skill is necessary for students to effectively interact with print. Not only do students need to have good language capabilities, but they need to be aware of the relationship between language and reading. This awareness enables them to more clearly understand the connections among language, reading, and writing. Thus, it is essential that language development permeate the overall reading instructional program without regard to the approach or approaches selected to meet an individual student's needs. In addition to concentrating on language development, teachers must also help children use language for a variety of purposes. The new International Reading Association/National Council of Teachers of English (IRA/NCTE) standards recommend a focus on four purposes of language use: (a) obtaining and communicating information, (b) literary response and expression, (c) learning and reflection, and (d) problem and application.[7]

However, as teachers consider approaches to develop language while involved in reading instruction, they should keep in mind that the significant element is instruction. Durkin suggests this definition of instruction: "Instruction refers to what someone or something does or says that has the potential to teach one or more individuals what they do not know, do not understand, or cannot do."[8] This definition of instruction suggests the importance of success, in that learning occurs, and pertinence, in that the something that is learned is important to know. Durkin further suggests that in order for appropriate instruction to occur, three elements need to exist: objectives, instruction, and application. As we discuss various approaches to effective instruction (see Figure 6.2), the elements of objectives, purpose for instructing and application, or use of what is learned will be incorporated.

Figure 6.2 Approaches to Reading Instruction

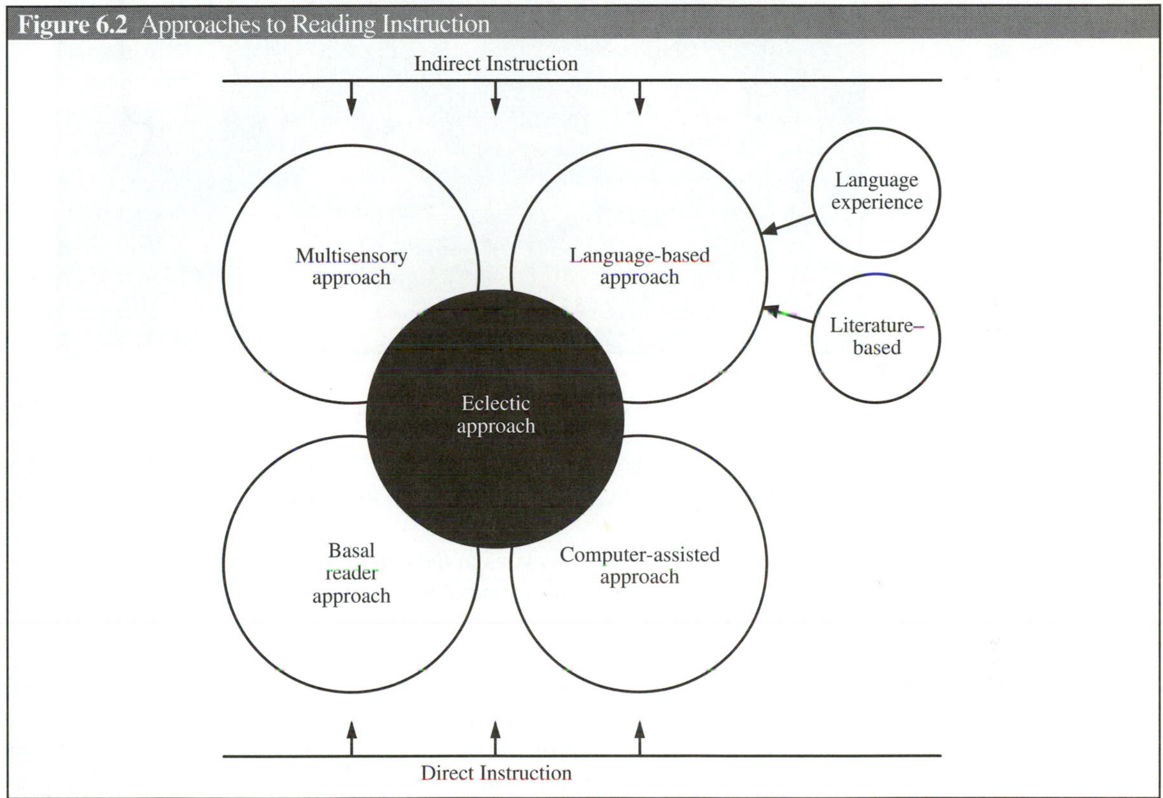

Basal Reader Approach

In previous editions of this book, the authors have not discussed the basal approach in a separate category but have incorporated basal materials as a part of the eclectic approach to reading. However, in the current research on approaches to reading instruction two basic methods—the basal reader approach and the language-based approach—are discussed. While all instruction in reading does not fit neatly into these two categories, it is appropriate to consider the use of basal materials as an approach to reading that emphasizes the sequential development of reading skills. As discussions of basal versus language-based approaches cause changes to occur in the classroom, teachers are finding that they can

Students work in groups based on needs and interests.

Photo courtesy of Larry Smith.

1. Use the basal reader and workbook to develop the reading skills as outlined in the teacher's manual.
2. Use the developmental continuum of skills from the basal to plan instruction using the basal and various other materials to implement an eclectic approach to reading instruction.
3. Use the basal materials as extras in the class while library books and children's literature become the primary sources for reading experiences.

Teachers using basal materials in the first two ways consider themselves to be using a traditional basal approach in that their instruction is skill driven from the developmental continuum of skills in the basal. Teachers using basal materials in the third way are using a more language-based approach, but they may feel compelled by parents, principal, or peers to allow students to read the basal. Although many current basal series are language oriented and use the story content of children's literature books, a variety of characters, and less rigidly controlled vocabulary, and although basal manuals encourage teachers to incorporate writing activities and language experiences into their teaching plans, basals have a skills continuum as their foundation. (These differences are discussed more extensively by McCarthey and Hoffman and by Reutzel and Larson.)[9] This skills continuum is a series of individual skills taught through the basal lessons and often reflects the testing programs of the school district or state. Thus, the use of basal materials for teaching reading is frequently encouraged, directly or subtly, to ensure better test scores on skills-oriented local and state tests.

As an example of this skills or test emphasis, one of the authors had an interesting personal experience when moving to a new area. In searching for a school district that had a good primary-level reading program for a language-fluent, ready-to-read, learning-is-fun five-year-old, several schools were identified with one teacher singled out as being one of the best kindergarten teachers. Upon further investigation, the author learned that this teacher used a language-based approach that resulted in good readers who had positive self-concepts and a love for reading. After moving into this school area and learning that the teacher was a neighbor, the author got to know her much better and had the opportunity to work in her classroom. All reports were accurate. However, one day as her teaching was being praised this teacher lamented, "I'm not sure my children are learning their reading skills well enough to go into some of the first grades so I'm giving them the kindergarten end-of-the-book basal test this week." As would be expected, the students did very well on the test. Nevertheless, this teacher who had 20 years of experience in providing developmentally appropriate language instruction to kindergarten students, who was recognized by her peers in the school system as being the best, and whose students consistently became good readers, had doubts about how well her children would do on a skills-based test. Clearly, teachers feel pressure to ensure that their students will do well on state and other skills-based tests. Thus, the basal will continue to be a major influence on reading instruction.

Another advantage of the basal approach is that it encourages continuity for students as they progress through the grades and as they transfer to other schools using the same basal series. Continuity in skill development is important in a program using a skills approach. Without the continuity provided by a continuum of skills, there is a risk that teachers will over-emphasize some skills and overlook other significant skills. In addition to providing continuity, the basal reader is accompanied by a teacher's manual that provides directions to the teacher for instructing the students in reading a story and developing the necessary skills. This lesson plan follows a guided or directed reading format that uses teacher-directed and student-directed activities. Teachers and administrators frequently feel more comfortable relying on planned lessons from the publishing company since they believe that the lessons are developed by reading specialists who know what needs to be taught.

The basal approach may also be a favored material because of the availability of related activities that reinforce the lesson. Workbooks, charts, skills sheets, computer programs, and manipulatives are available to supplement the basal reader, thereby freeing the teacher of the added responsibility of locating extra materials. This time-saving element is especially attractive to teachers with large classes.

Many teachers, administrators, and parents believe that the basal approach is the best alternative for providing good reading instruction in the elementary grades. For some teachers, this is the appropriate approach because it supports their philosophical belief about reading instruction, relates to their experiences, and provides them with the necessary plans and materials to implement this philosophy in the classroom.

Students develop an understanding of reading as a language process as they read the books they write.

Photo courtesy of Edward B. Lasher.

However, when guiding instruction, teachers who use the basal approach should remember that effective instruction means addressing the individual reading needs of the student. Thus, they may need to make instructional changes to better meet student needs. As teachers get to know their students, they identify those who have developed the necessary skills to function independently with minimum skill instruction from the teacher, those who have minimum skill knowledge but need a better language foundation before learning skills, and those who need to continue to develop reading skills in a structured manner. The instructional needs of all these groups of students may not be met through the exclusive use of a basal approach. A basal approach may serve to meet some of these varied instructional needs, but incorporating other approaches through the year will be necessary to maximize the learning potential of all students.

One final factor should be considered when evaluating the basal approach. Some students need a structured program that follows the same lesson format each day and allows them to see how many pages they have read during a specified time. Other students are totally bored with this approach and need more variety is lesson format and materials. Knowing the reading needs and interests of each student is important, but understanding individual learning styles is equally important in motivating students to read. For these reasons, teachers must be flexible in their teaching approach, adapting the approach to their philosophical belief about reading instruction. There is no one best approach for teaching reading. Teacher style, student needs, and learning environment are the crucial elements.

Language-Based Approach

"Whole language," "literature-based language experience," and "whole-literacy instruction" are all terms used to describe instruction that connects reading and writing and uses literature. Bergeron suggests that whole language describes any approach or program supportive of literature-based or integrated instruction.[10] Inconsistencies in the literature as to what this instructional strategy includes have caused confusion in classroom implementation. Bergeron, in a review of the literature, found whole language referred to as an approach, a belief, a method, a philosophy, an orientation, a theory, a theoretical orientation, a program, a curriculum, a perspective on education, and an attitude of mind.[11] Many teachers would say that they use a whole-language approach in their instruction. However, because definitions of whole language vary and because the approach grew out of early research on oral and written language development, here we will refer to this concept of teaching reading as the language-based approach. For the purposes of this discussion, the language-based approach is defined as instructional procedures that facilitate a naturalistic development of oral and written language skills used in speaking, listening, reading, and writing.

How does a teacher implement a language-based approach? According to Bergeron, the concept of whole language "includes the use of real literature and writing in the context of meaningful, functional, and cooperative experiences in order to develop in students motivation and interest in the process of learning."[12] Ridley, in comparing whole language to text-based reading, suggests that "whole language teaching incorporates authentic materials such as newspapers, literature, notes, recipes, student's books, and other writing, and ... is learner-centered as students choose topics, audiences, purpose, and books and they manage their own time with whole language activities ... as varied as the teachers who implement them."[13] Added to these descriptions of whole-language instruction are Hiebert and Colt's three patterns of incorporating literature-based reading instruction into the classroom:

- Pattern 1: teacher-selected literature in teacher-led groups
- Pattern 2: teacher- and student-selected literature in teacher and student-led small groups
- Pattern 3: student-selected literature read independently.[14]

Through a combination of these three patterns, they suggest, children will develop as thoughtful, proficient readers.

Two approaches previously considered individually as different ways of teaching reading are now part of the language-based approach. The language experience approach and the individualized reading approach are often discussed when teachers talk about implementing a whole-language or language-based approach in their classes.

The language experience approach is defined by Hall as "a method in which instruction is built upon the use of reading materials created by writing down children's spoken language."[15] Van Allen has provided another definition that presents the students' concept of the language experience approach:

- What I can think about, I can talk about.
- What I can say, I can write—or someone can write for me.
- What I can write, I can read.
- I can read what I can write and what other people can write for me to read.[16]

These definitions reflect the importance of using the students' language as the basis for the development of reading materials. The language experience approach integrates all areas in order to strengthen the communication skills of reading, speaking, writing, and listening for each student.

The basic idea of developing story or experience charts has been used in schools since the early 1900s. However, through the work of Van Allen, Stauffer, and Hall, this approach has become better understood and accepted for teaching reading to students of any age, preschool through adult.[17] The rationale for this approach is that by using the student's own oral language as dictated, reading can be a successful experience.

When using the language experience approach in the classroom, the teacher can follow these steps:

- Use the approach with an individual student, a small group, or a large group, depending on the purpose of the lesson.
- Discuss some experience that is common to the group or that seems important to the individual student, using a stimulus such as a field trip, an object, or a picture.
- Prepare the students for telling a story by having them summarize ideas from the discussion or give a title to the ideas discussed.
- Allow each student to contribute to the story by sharing ideas about the experience.
- Write each sentence on the board or a chart.
- Read each idea after it is written, sweeping your hand under each line to emphasize left-to-right progression.
- Read the story together (teacher and students) when it is complete.
- Discuss the story, pointing out capital letters, names, ideas, and so on.
- Make copies of the story; students can copy it by hand individually or the teacher can duplicate it.
- Reread the story on subsequent days and develop skills using the vocabulary and ideas in the story.

This last step is extremely important in the development of reading skills, yet it is often overlooked when using the language experience approach. Skill development may deal with word parts, letter sounds, capitalization and punctuation, word endings or any other skills needed by the student. Word cards with new vocabulary words may be developed to aid in other reading and writing experiences.

Language experience, as a strategy or approach, has advantages and limitations that must be recognized. These are summarized in Table 6.1.

Table 6.1 Language Experience Approach

Advantages	Limitations
The students' language is the basis for the reading material.	The approach is unstructured; thus, there is no sequential development of skills.
Several learning modalities are used: auditory in dictating the story, visual in seeing the words, and kinesthetic in copying or writing the story.	The teacher must assume major responsibility in using this approach as there are no prepared materials.
Students are motivated to read because the information is interesting to them.	The lack of repetition of vocabulary and control may be troublesome for some students.
Self-concept is enhanced as the student realizes that others think his ideas are important.	Like any other approach, the overuse of this format may become boring to the student.
Older students with poor reading skills are interested in the content of the material.	The development of the charts is time-consuming for the teacher.
Concepts such as left-to-right orientation, capitalization and punctuation, and word boundaries can be easily taught.	
Oral language skills, which are especially beneficial to the student from an educationally deficient environment, are developed.	

An individualized reading approach, as discussed in earlier literature, closely resembles the literature-based approach discussed in more current literature. This approach is based on Olson's philosophy of child development, which promotes the ideas of seeking, self-selection, and pacing.[18]

This concept was also used by Veatch to describe her own views about reading.[19] Veatch revisits this topic and many of her other views about reading in a more recent article.[20] To implement this approach in the classroom, the teacher should follow these steps:

- Know the reading levels and interests of the students with whom this approach will be used. These can be determined using procedures discussed in Chapter 2.
- Obtain library books and other materials of interest for the students to read. A large number of books that represent a variety of topics and reading levels is needed. The teacher must select the books very carefully, keeping in mind that different literary forms should be represented.
- The readability levels of the books should be determined either by using a readability formula or a library source such as the *Children's Catalog*.[21] The books should be organized by level to aid students in locating material that they can read.
- The student should select a book that he wants to read. The student should not be limited to books at his readability level; interest in a book goes a long way toward motivating a student to read. However, the student should be allowed to

read several pages before selecting a book to determine whether the book is too difficult and whether it is interesting.

- When the book is selected, the student should realize that he is expected to read the entire book and then sign up for a conference with the teacher to discuss the story. However, if help is needed while reading, the teacher should give assistance. During silent reading, the student may list words not recognized or understood.
- After completing the story, the student should notify the teacher that he is ready for a conference. During the conference, which may last from 5 to 20 minutes, the teacher should ask questions about the story, listen to the student read a short passage in order to diagnose word identification difficulties, provide some individual skill instruction, and summarize the results of the discussion. The conference requires that the teacher be very familiar with the stories read in the classroom and also with the reading continuum used in the school.

Literature-based reading can be used with an entire class of students or an individual student. It is not necessarily designed to supplement the basal readers, although it may be used with some students while others use the basal reader or to add variety to reading instruction. The following narrative describes the experience of one of the authors with literature-based reading. Initially this approach was used because there were no other materials available in an overcrowded elementary school. The parents insisted that the students have books, and most of the students hated reading.

> On the first day of school I was met by 37 second graders who were not ready for school to begin. With no basal readers, kits, or any instructional material, I had decided to use the language experience approach with a few students and children's books from the library with most of the class.
>
> My first task was to determine the reading levels of the students, which I soon discovered ranged from preprimer to sixth grade. With this information I went to the library to check out books for the students who were reading from a low second-grade level to sixth-grade level. There, I met my first obstacle, the librarian, who allowed me to keep books for only two weeks. As a first-year teacher, I continued to smile, took my books to the room, checked the readability levels, put a piece of colored tape on each to denote the level, and arranged them on the shelf.
>
> The students were directed to select books from those at their level. They were allowed to read those below their level during extra time and those above their level with permission.
>
> To ensure continuity of skill development because of local testing procedures and raised eyebrows from the third-grade teachers, I used the skills continuum for the basal series being used in most of the classes in the school. A large chart containing the students' names and the skills was made, laminated, and taped on my desk. Using observations and other informal procedures, I determined skill strengths and weaknesses and used the chart as my guide for grouping and conference discussions.
>
> As the students read their books, they kept a word bank of unknown words. When they finished a book, they placed a name card in a box on my desk to notify

> me of their need for a conference. They proceeded to another book until they were called for a conference.
>
> During the conference, we discussed words that were difficult, and I asked comprehension questions based on the needs of the student. Following the conference, I placed a note in my notebook that summarized our discussions. The student was given a gummed label with the title of the book just completed to put on his individual reading record poster, which decorated the wall.
>
> Each day the students worked in small groups to develop skills that needed to be strengthened. Many centers, games, and activities were used to reinforce this group work.
>
> Every two weeks, the class and I loaded our little red wagon, dressed in favorite character costumes, paraded the books to the library, and checked out a new group of books. This procedure continued for the entire school year. The result: a group of students who enjoyed reading!

In retrospect, the question arises as to how the author managed this hectic schedule over a long period of time. The response is that when students are excited about reading and are improving, the teacher is rewarded, and energy seems to come from unknown sources.

Another response to the management of literature-based reading in the classroom in that each child does not have to read a different book at all times. McGee and Tompkins conclude that one result of literature-based instruction is that quite often teachers are more likely to use a greater variety of different approaches and activities in a classroom rather than fewer.[22] Hiebert and Colt note that in addition to allowing students to individually select all literature, teachers can select the literature for groups of students to read and lead discussions with the groups, or teachers and students can jointly select the literature, which is discussed in both teacher- and student-led small groups.[23] Implementation of literature-based reading allows for teacher flexibility; the key is that the students are reading a variety of quality children's literature and developing an enjoyment of reading as they become mature readers. The advantages and limitations of literature-based reading are summarized in Table 6.2.

To implement a language-based approach in an elementary classroom, the teacher needs an understanding of children, child development, and language development. An understanding of children and child development helps the teacher to determine appropriate learning experiences in accord with the interests and behaviors of the student. Attention span, personality traits, and peer interactions are important factors in planning. Teachers also need an understanding of language development. They need to know that oral and written language develop as young children develop their listening and psychomotor skills. In addition to understanding these student behaviors, teachers need a knowledge of the writing process, children's literature, and classroom organization. A language-based approach does not use a text and teacher's manual; the instructions for implementing such an approach are based on the teacher's knowledge of content and children, creativity, and a willingness to take risks in providing students with appropriate instruction.

Table 6.2 Literature-Based Reading

Advantages	Limitations
Flexibility and freedom in grouping and adjusting instruction.	Time-consuming for the teacher, in that much planning, diagnosis, record keeping, and knowledge of the reading process is essential.
The teacher has regular interaction with the student on an individual basis.	Schools may not have enough library books to loan for an extended period of time.
Students read materials that meet their interests.	Teachers must be knowledgeable of children's literature in order to have effective conferences.
Students read in a manner that resembles real-life reading situations.	Vocabulary is not controlled.
Students build a more positive self-concept, as success in reading comes from working at the appropriate level.	Poor readers have difficulty attending to a book on their own.
Students are exposed to a variety of children's books.	Easy books for students with a limited vocabulary are difficult to locate.

Bergeron has further suggested "that many of the components of traditional reading instruction, such as ability grouping, controlled texts, or isolated exercises, no longer are consistent with the whole language concept. When one begins to contrast the overall concept of whole language with those approaches that have come to be defined in the construct of traditionalism, a conflict between whole language and tradition may be inevitable."[24] However, Farr has suggested that while some aspects of the traditional and whole-language approaches are incompatible, such as separate skills instruction and the lack of freedom of choice for teachers who are required to use teachers' manuals, other issues such as the use of quality literature and writing activities coincide with whole language.[25]

Teachers implementing an effective instructional program recognize that meeting the instructional needs of students requires the use of appropriate elements of a traditional basal approach and a language-based approach along with other approaches and techniques. For example, consider the inner-city youngster who comes to school with poor oral school language, a distrust of authority figures, and a low self-concept. Such a student is not likely to be successful if placed in a program using only a traditional basal text, with stories that have little relation to the child's background of experiences and that contain words she doesn't recognize. This child needs a language-based program that involves her in speaking and listening activities to expand her language and develop a feeling of success with teachers and peers. On the other hand, a child from a middle-class home, with many school-related experiences and a positive self-concept, who can read but with difficulty may profit from a more structured basal approach that develops the lacking skills to move the student from average to above-average reading performance.

Proponents of the basal approach say that the language-based approach lacks structure for practical implementation in the classroom. Proponents of the language-based approach retort that the basal approach is too structured and takes the fun out of learning and the creativity out of teaching. Both of these approaches offer different learning experiences for students. Teachers must follow their philosophical beliefs to determine the best approach for their teaching style and be willing to incorporate other approaches that benefit the student's instructional program.

In addition to the two primary approaches used in elementary schools today, other approaches exist, and teachers need an understanding of these different approaches in order to meet the variety of student needs in their classes. For students with severe reading problems, teachers may use a multisensory approach. All school districts are becoming involved with computers, and teachers need to recognize the computer-assisted approach as another means of teaching and motivating students to read and write. These two secondary methods can enrich the basal and language-based approaches.

Multisensory Approach

The multisensory approach involves the sense of touch and muscle movement along with the senses of vision and hearing. Most students learn to read using the basic receptive senses of the eyes and ears. Some learn better through the visual mode than the auditory mode, or vice versa, but these are considered the primary senses necessary for reading. However, some students must have other stimulation in order to learn words in reading. For these individuals, the multisensory approach works well. If the classroom teacher recognizes that this approach is necessary, there are several methods that may be used:

- Kinesthetic (VAKT)
- Visual-auditory-kinesthetic (VAK)
- Neurological impress

The kinesthetic method was developed by Grace Fernald as a way of teaching nonreaders.[26] This method, also known as the Fernald or visual-auditory-kinesthetic-tactile (VAKT) method, follows four basic stages in teaching words to the nonreader (see Figure 6.3). The teacher begins with words the student wants to learn, then proceeds to build a story with the words when the student is ready. Words are taught using the following stages:

1. *Tracing*. The word is written for the student. The student traces the word and says each part of the word as it is traced. This is repeated until the student can trace the word from memory. The student then writes the word, saying each part as it is written.
2. *Writing without tracing*. When the student seems familiar with the word, he looks at the word and writes it from memory without tracing.

3. *Recognition in print*. The student looks at a word, is told the word, pronounces it, and writes it from memory.
4. *Word analysis*. The student is taught to look for familiar parts of a word and to try to identify new words from the known parts.

This method is designed for use with the student who is experiencing great difficulty in reading.

Figure 6.3 Stages in Using the Fernald Method (VAKT)

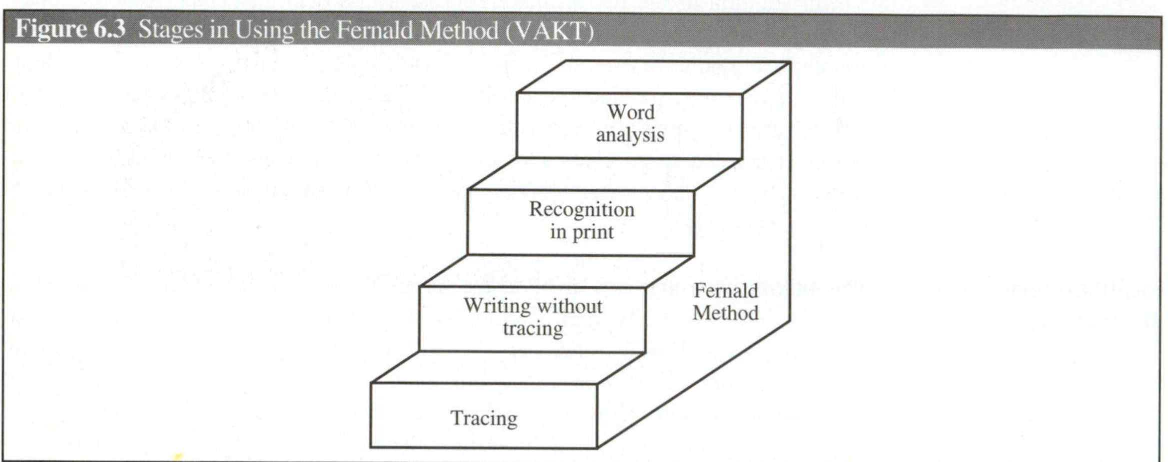

A similar method is the VAK, or visual-auditory-kinesthetic, method. This method, also developed by Fernald, is a modified VAKT procedure in which Stage 1 has been altered. The major change is that the student pronounces the entire word rather than the word parts as she writes. Like the VAKT, this method should be used with students who experience difficulty in learning through other approaches.

Neurological impress is another method designed to assist the student with reading problems. In this method, the teacher reads a selection and points to the words, while the student reads along, pronouncing as many words as possible. This method has been adapted for group instruction through the use of earphones and tape-recorded stories; as the student listens, she looks at the words in the story. As suggested by Harris and Sipay, this method seems to have more promise as a supplementary procedure since "the teacher can neither control nor observe where the child's eyes are focused, and the child may or may not be looking at the right word, on the right line, as he hears the spoken word."[27]

The methods included within the multisensory approach are used primarily with students having difficulty in reading. However, this approach may be used on occasion to assist any student in remembering troublesome sounds, syllables, or words.

Using technology to reinforce language is exciting!

Photo courtesy of Larry Smith.

Computer-Assisted Approach

Technology is a current trend in today's elementary and middle-school classrooms, many of which feature closed-captioned television for poor readers, and telecommunication systems. While all of these options can enhance reading instruction, the most widely available technological option is computer-assisted instruction, which can be used with either a basal reader approach or a language-based approach.

There are four basic options for using the computer-assisted approach:

1. Basic skills software, sometimes referred to as electronic ditto sheets, the first type of programs made available for assisting reading instruction.
2. Word-processing programs, designed to encourage students to write by easing the writing process through assistance in rewriting, checking spelling, and analyzing grammar.
3. Student-directed, open-ended software that encourages the student to think and make decisions as they work through the program.
4. Telecommunication systems provide information resources on a vast range of topics and allow interaction between the medium and the user.

Teachers using a basal reader approach usually have access to several types of computer software that accompany the series. This software may include a computer-management system that helps the teacher with record keeping by administering objective-based tests on the computer and recording student performance. This helps with instructional planning, but it is not an example of computer-assisted instruction. However, basal-related software that allows students to practice skills previously taught by the teacher *is* computer-assisted instruction. While these skill programs have been criticized by some as irrelevant time-fillers or slicker versions of workbooks,[28]

Wepner found that at-risk eighth graders dealt well with this drill-and-practice software as long as the content was relevant to their interests and level.[29]

Because of the abundance of this type of software (due to the ease of developing such programs) and because of questions about its usefulness for some students, teachers should identify student needs and plans for instruction prior to selecting programs for follow-up use. Remember, for some students, the best skills software is a significant improvement over traditional paper-and-pencil worksheets, while for others, computer drill-and-practice has no more impact than traditional procedures. Teachers must judge both the students and the software carefully before selecting such materials for use as part of a computer-assisted instructional approach.

Word-processing programs are also abundant in schools. While popular programs such as *Microsoft Word* and *Claris Works* are available for adult and student use, many word-processing programs are designed specifically to make the writing process easier for students. The features of these programs such as spell checking, grammar analysis, rewriting using the delete key, and moving text make writing easier for students and help them learn that writing is indeed a process and that the purpose of writing is to communicate meaning to a reader. Some programs, such as *Language Experience Recorder Plus* (LER+), use a speech-synthesized word processor with primary print that speaks what students record.[30] *Magic Slate* is another word-processing program with a fill-in feature to create clozelike stories for use with primary-level students.[31] *The Children's Writing and Publishing Center* allows students to insert graphics into their writing.[32] *Success with Writing* models the writing process by moving the student through the stages of writing: prewriting, arranging, composing, and evaluating/editing.[33] There are but a few of the word-processing programs available for use with computer-assisted instruction. To implement this approach in the classroom, teachers will need word-processing software to encourage the natural linkage between reading and writing and the development of writing using a process approach.

As teachers become more involved in using a language-based approach in their classes, they need to be aware of the many types of programs available that allow students to interact with language, literature, and writing as they enjoy learning. Software such as *The Semantic Mapper* and *The Literacy Mapper* facilitate the use of prior knowledge an students brainstorm their related experiences and develop printed copies of maps.[34] *The Comprehension Connection* provides on-screen assistance with each selection to encourage students to monitor their comprehension and implement metacognitive strategies as they read.[35] *Super Story Tree* is a program with the multimedia capability of using graphics, fonts, sound, and music to create interactive branching stories that allow students to develop or retell stories according to their own ideas.[36] *Success with Reading* is a literature-based software package that allows students to monitor their comprehension through the use of a cloze procedure.[37] Programs such as *Create with Garfield* allow students to develop their own comic strip ideas, combining word processing and comprehension to present their ideas.[38]

Extending these student-directed software packages, telecommunication systems such as the Internet are using computers to transfer information from one place to another. These systems provide teachers with up-to-date professional information and allow students to have access to resource information without spending days thumbing through the library. Developing a database for organizing, saving, and accessing information is an aid to reading and a tool needed in daily life in the 21st century.[39]

Hypertext programs are being developed to allow students to create their own scenarios as they interact with pictures or print. While this form of computer-assisted instruction is in its beginning stages, in many schools these programs facilitate student thinking as they explore various relationships and sequences of activities through their choices on the screen. *Amanda Stories* are short, animated, wordless stories about the adventures of a camel and a cat whose journeys are charted by the reader as choices are made on the computer screen.[40] *The Manhole* and *Cosmic Osmo* are similar programs that use text, graphics, speech, and sound effects to allow students to explore the universe.[41] Hypertext programs offer students the opportunity to control their own learning by investigating information in a nonsequential or nontraditional manner.[42] The *Living Books* are interactive CD-ROM storybooks that allow young learners to listen to and read along with a particular story, interact with the illustrations, switch between languages, and receive on-line help in pronouncing and defining selected words in thc text.[43] However, because the use of hypertext and hypermedia requires hardware resources beyond that available to many classroom teachers (i.e., large random access memories, hard-disk drives, compact-disc capabilities, and high-resolution color monitors), teachers may not consider this a viable option at this time when implementing a computer-assisted approach in the classroom. As technology advances, there are many opportunities for students to interact with computer text through the Internet. Students now have on-line access to libraries, museums, and experts throughout the world.[44]

Computer-assisted instruction is another approach available to the classroom teacher when implementing effective reading instruction. Computers are already in many schools and are sometimes available for the asking from computer companies or foundations willing to assist in getting technology into the classroom. Teachers are encouraged to use this approach as they work on cognitive and affective learning areas with their students.

Eclectic Approach

Teachers have long recognized that there is no one best way of teaching reading. If there were, this section of the book would be much shorter and there would be far fewer reading materials on the market. A combination of approaches to instruction is essential since students vary in their needs and learning styles. Thus, the eclectic approach, which combines the desirable aspects of other approaches to meeting student needs, is the approach most frequently used in an effective reading program. Many educators have recently been calling for a "balanced" reading philosophy, one that integrates language-based approaches with explicit instruction in graphophonic and comprehension strategies.[45]

Basal materials represent a structured type of eclectic approach. These materials have changed significantly in the last decade and now use various strategies for developing the skills. For example, the story selections more closely reflect the children's literature used in literature-based teaching. The controlled vocabulary and the limited number of story characters have disappeared. Language-based philosophies have had a definite impact on basal materials. Incorporated in most teacher guides, which accompany the basal materials, are suggestions for using language experience, ideas for furthering reading through literature-based instruction, techniques for using the multisensory approach to teach letters and words, and specific activities for word identification and comprehension skill development. The basal reader is no longer designed to function as a self-contained unit but rather provides a structured guide in the use of various approaches to teach reading. Unfortunately, the basal is often misused, and these ideas are not incorporated into the lessons; instead, the student may be limited to the reader and a workbook. When used in this manner, the basal is not considered to be a part of an eclectic approach.

When teachers use an eclectic approach, it is important to match the appropriate approach to the student's needs. For example, overemphasizing isolated skills with an above-average reader may impede the student's progress in such areas as reading rate, comprehension, and interest.

To teach reading effectively, teachers must be familiar with and use a variety of approaches. Thus, the strength of the eclectic approach is that students' needs can be met more thoroughly. The drawback is that this approach requires careful planning and coordination on the part of the teacher and an assortment of materials for the students. The teacher who provides appropriate instruction will overcome these two limitations by taking time to plan and locate materials, either from other places or by making them. The First-Grade Studies and the follow-up research leave no room for doubt that teachers must use the eclectic approach in order to meet the reading need of all students.[46]

TEACHING FOR STUDENT NEEDS

Regardless of which approach is used to provide reading instruction, certain elements are essential in the teaching process. All teachers need to be sure that assessment data is summarized for each student and organized into a usable format. This information indicates the students' interests, strengths and weaknesses in reading, and instructional reading level. The teacher can then use the student's interests and strengths to work on his areas of weakness. For example, the teacher might have a student who is interested in baseball, has a collection of baseball cards, and remembers all the details from each card along with the card's value to a card collector. Yet the student cannot organize ideas in the social studies lesson on the Industrial Revolution. The teacher can help this student in several ways by building on his interest. The teacher might use the concept of trading baseball cards to illustrate the economic development of a country during the Industrial Revolution, or, more concretely the teacher might present information on each phase of the Industrial Revolution in a card format and allow the student to complete the information on each card as he reads. The Industrial Revolution will, of course, not be as exciting to a baseball lover as baseball cards, but using a strategy that allows the student to apply a familiar technique for organizing information to a new subject will enhance his comprehension.

Teachers using a skills continuum as part of their instructional approach need to relate assessment data to the skills continuum to determine starting points for instruction. In both the basal approach and language-based approach, students develop skills in word identification, comprehension, and study skills and have many opportunities to apply them. Extreme skill deficiency in any of these areas is a signal to the teacher that direct instruction is needed in a small group or on an individual basis. More specific information on providing appropriate instruction in the areas of emergent literacy, word identification, comprehension, study strategies, and personal reading is provided in Chapters 7 through 11.

The content teacher in a departmentalized situation implements reading instruction in several ways. Instruction may be needed in reading strategies the students do not yet know but must use in order to learn content information. In addition, the content reading teacher can assist in both cognitive and affective reading development by using literature to supplement the content lessons. Not only does literature present similar information in a different manner, it shows students that reading in social studies or science can be enjoyable as well as informative. Content teachers need to use the agreement data of the reading and language arts teachers along with their own information to develop a class profile of reading needs and interests. This profile serves as a valuable resource to use in planning units of study in the content classroom.

Providing instruction in the self-contained or content classroom using any approach requires planning for direct and indirect instruction. Direct instruction is when the "teachers assume a highly structured, active, and dominant role in which teacher talk is relied upon to ensure that students interpret the work in the intended way and achieve the desired outcome."[47] Creating process and content outcomes requires the use of direct instruction. Indirect instruction depends more on a structured environment than on teacher talk. Students discover outcomes through activities that shape the student's interpretations.[48]

Although these two types of instruction may seem to be at opposite ends of the spectrum, they are often used in tandem to communicate information to the learner. For example, in a lesson in which the teacher wants to teach students how to interpret a story, she may guide them through the story by directly or deductively teaching the parts and showing how to interpret each part. She may then allow for more indirect instruction as the students practice this strategy using other works of literature and then report their interpretations to the teacher. The directed reading activity and directed learning activity outlined in the following sections reflect the use of direct instruction followed by indirect instruction.

Teachers using a language-based approach may use more indirect instruction followed by direct instruction as needed. For example, as students select their books in a literature-based reading class, they may be guided to select only fairy tales. After reading and discussing their books, the teacher will guide the students to identify the characteristics of fairy tales and possibly to write their own brief fairy tale using these characteristics. The teacher provides direct instruction only when necessary, and the lesson is planned so that students do more discovery or inductive learning. All lessons need some direct and some indirect instruction. How this instruction is implemented depends on the goals of the teacher, the reading levels of the students, and the information to be conveyed.

Directed Reading Activity

To facilitate direct instruction in both self-contained and departmentalized classrooms, the teacher needs to follow a plan. The most commonly used design in reading instruction is the directed, or guided, reading activity (see Figure 6.4). The DRA procedure has been followed for many years by elementary teachers using the basal reader. However, any classroom teacher can use this procedure with or without the basal.

Figure 6.4 Steps in a Directed Reading Activity

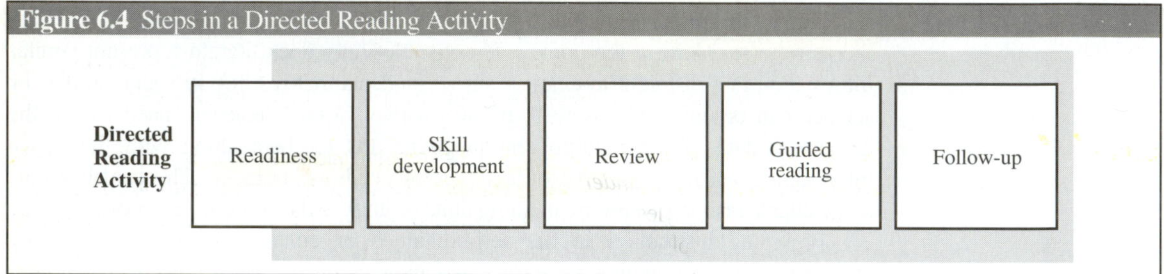

The five basic steps in the DRA should be followed in all reading lessons.

1. *Readiness.* Establish readiness for reading by introducing the topic and the skills needed to read the material. Teach vocabulary words as well as the concepts needed to understand the material by relating the new information to the student's prior knowledge.
2. *Skill Development.* Using the assessment information, provide students with instruction to develop the skills necessary to understand the material. This may be done individually or in small groups.
3. *Review.* The vocabulary, concepts, and skills necessary to be successful should be reviewed. At this time, the teacher gives the student a purpose for reading the material and asks for silent reading.
4. *Guided Reading*. With a purpose for reading clearly stated, the student begins to read the designated material (e.g., basal reader, newspaper, library book, experience story) silently. Following silent reading, ask comprehension questions that relate to the purpose given for reading and to the identified comprehension skill needs of the individual students. For example, the student who has difficulty

with distinguishing fact and opinion would be asked questions relating to this skill while reviewing information from the reading during the skill development portion of the lesson. Then, during the comprehension check after silent reading, the student may be asked to read portions of the story orally to locate specific information or for some other definite purpose.

5. *Follow-Up.* Do additional follow-up after the guided reading to work on skill deficiencies, extend knowledge on a given topic, and allow students to apply the information learned from reading to some activity. This follow-up session will vary from lesson to lesson and from student to student. It may be used to motivate some students to read; for others it may be a time for further skill development. The follow-up session is a valuable time for providing additional prescriptive instruction.

Directed Learning Activity

The departmentalized content teacher can use an adapted DRA to provide reading instruction in the content areas. The authors refer to this plan as the directed learning activity (DLA). This technique is for students using material written at their instructional reading level. The procedure is designed for use with small groups or a whole class. The following steps present ideas on providing reading instruction in the content areas. Step 4 of this plan incorporates the directed learning activity.

Step 1

Determine the concepts to be stressed in content material and teach the reading strategies needed to understand concepts. To meet individual student needs and various learning styles, the content teacher must select the key concepts to be taught rather than rely solely on the textbook. Thus, for a given topic, the content specialist identifies the specific concepts students need to learn. This way of looking at content material is important. First, with the wealth of knowledge, facts, and materials available today, it is impossible for one textbook to provide all the information students need. Thus, the teacher identifies key concepts and assists students in learning how to use materials to increase their knowledge. Second, no one textbook suits the reading level of every student in a classroom. Therefore, the content teacher must use a variety of materials to provide students with printed information they can read. If the content specialist is teaching concepts beyond those addressed in the textbook, then many materials can be used.

Step 2

Identify the reading strategies or skills necessary for understanding content materials. After the concepts have been identified, the content specialist selects the reading strategies that are essential to understanding those concepts. Usually four to six reading skills will be identified. Content teachers may wish to refer to the list of skills in Appendix A to make a list of all the reading skills that relate to their content area. At a later time, the content specialist will select appropriate skills from this list to help students understand particular concepts in the material, as in the following example.

Social studies concept	Freedom of speech is an essential part of a democracy.
Related reading skills	Vocabulary development Generalizations Cause-effect Contrast-comparison Relationships

Once teachers have identified this information, their instructional program will begin to take shape.

Step 3

Assess student strengths and weaknesses in reading strategies and skills. Several procedures may be used to assess strengths and weaknesses. One widely used procedure, the content reading inventory, is presented in Chapter 2.

Using the identified concepts and reading skills as well as the assessment data on the students, the content specialist may use a file folder or sheet of paper to develop a class chart such as the one shown in Figure 6.5. This will assist in organizing the information and aid in providing appropriate instruction.

Step 4

Outline teaching strategies for developing needed concepts and reading strategies. At this point, the teacher puts together materials that meet the students' assessed needs to teach the concepts necessary for learning the content. Using the DLA format as a guide, the lesson would proceed as follows:

1. *Introduce the concepts and vocabulary.* The content teacher introduces the concepts to be studied. This may be done directly, using questions or a movie, or in a more indirect manner based on previous classes. Regardless of the procedure used, the concepts to be studied for a unit or designated period of time need to be carefully introduced. Because the entire class is probably studying the same concepts, this would be a total-class activity.

   When introducing the concepts and materials to be studied, the content specialist also teaches the vocabulary necessary for reading the materials. This includes general vocabulary as well as the specialized and technical words. Teachers should realize that although a student may be able to pronounce a word, its special meaning within the content area may cause difficulty. The responsibility for teaching vocabulary rests with each content teacher. With various reading abilities in the classroom and various materials in use, it may be necessary to teach vocabulary development skills in small groups. Some of the groups can use written activities, while others can work with the content teacher or discuss the terminology with each other.

Figure 6.5 Assessment Chart for Content Teachers

Student name	Skill 1	Skill 2	Skill 3	Skill 4	Skill 5																		
Ginger	X			X																			
Lance	X	X	X	X	X																		
Kristy			X																				
Wendy		X	X		X																		
Joe	X																						
Harry					X																		
Carmen																							

X denotes need for additional instruction in the skill.

Here are some examples of written vocabulary activities for content learning.

Science
Give the antonym for each word.

- exhale ______
- ventricle ______

Social Studies
Fill in the missing word.

- A body of advisors of a head of state is a(n) _____ .
- Refusal to trade with another country is a(n) _____ .
- The title of the highest ranking official of the United States residing in another country is a(n) _____ .

2. *Teach or review reading skills.* This phase of the instructional process is concerned with identifying relevant reading skills as well as demonstrating the appropriate application of these reading skills. Although content teachers are not

reading specialists, they can help students adapt previously learned skills to content materials as well as learn how to apply new skills to these materials.

3. *Outline the purposes for study.* Students are more willing to accept some of the requirements made in content areas if they are given specific purposes for studying. Teachers usually receive negative responses when they give students a chapter to read with no specific reason for studying it. In addition, students need to know how studying this material relates to their present or future lives. Having a purpose helps students relate to the material and motivates them to study it.
4. *Read and study the material.* By this point, students have been introduced to key concepts, taught the vocabulary, and given a purpose for reading. Now the teacher is ready to ask them to read the material. At this point the content specialist may help the student use SQ3R or another appropriate study technique. The teacher must remember that students are to read only the material directly related to the concepts introduced. This may or may not be an entire section of the text or other source. The teacher should also remember to use materials that are appropriate to the students' varied reading levels. This may mean using other instructional tools, such as films, tapes, newspapers, magazines, records, and so forth. Thus, all students will not finish at the same time. This will allow the content specialist to begin the next step at different times by working with small groups.
5. *Discuss the information learned.* As the students complete their reading assignments, the content specialist begins discussions relating to the concepts being studied. These may be stimulated by written questions. As the discussions unfold, the content teacher must keep in mind the specific reading skills that need to be developed with various students. This information is obtained from the assessment instruments discussed in Chapters 2 and 3 and recorded in a format such as the chart in Figure 6.5. Some sample written activities that could be used to promote discussion and develop appropriate learning skills are given below.

   Social Studies (details)
   Read the following passage and then answer the following questions. (Insert short passage on "The Gettysburg Address.")
   - Who wrote "The Gettysburg Address"?
   - Where was the address delivered?
   - When was the address delivered?

   Mathematics (following directions)
   Give the students directions for factoring polynomials carefully and slowly. Then have them write the directions in their own words, step by step.

6. *Follow up the lesson.* After small-group and total-class discussions of the concepts, some follow-up activities should be used to reinforce the content.

These activities may be in the form of other outside readings, reports, special skill development, or art activities. The content specialist can provide additional assistance in developing reading skills at this time.

Step 5

Repeat steps 1, 2, 3, and 4. It is essential that assessment be a continuous part of teaching. If students are to understand content material, content teachers must assume responsibility of teaching reading skills. Teaching students at the appropriate level does not end in the primary grades. If content teachers want students to learn the content presented, they must take students as they are and develop their reading as needed. The procedure for carrying out a directed learning activity is summarized in Figure 6.6.

Figure 6.6 Procedures for Guided Reading Instruction in the Content Area Classroom

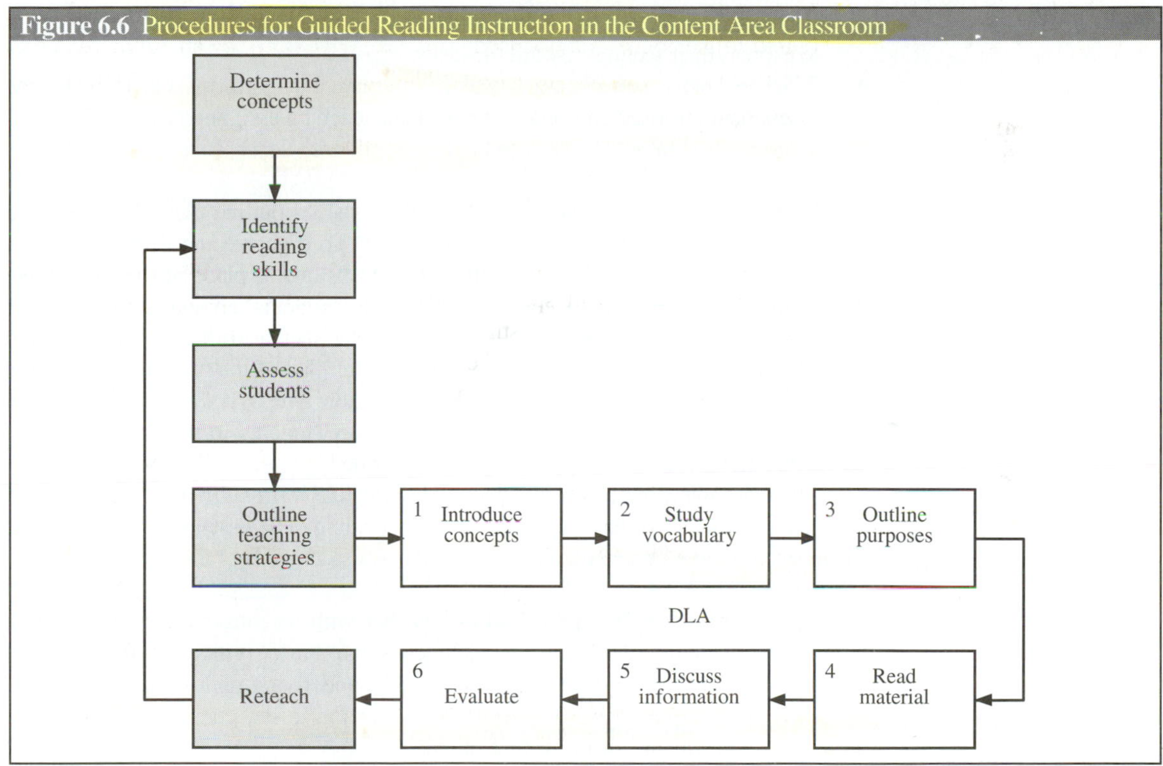

This chapter has addressed the basic issues involved in providing appropriate instruction and the different approaches that should be used in effective teaching. The next specific task confronting the teacher is that of developing a plan for instruction. Teachers should remember that, in effective instruction, each student has an assignment based on his or her assessed needs. This instructional plan may be written for the student each day or only outlined, but it must be designed with the individual in mind.

As teachers plan for instruction, these ideas need to be kept in mind.

- Each plan should guarantee success. Tasks that are performed while working with the teacher should be at the student's instructional reading level, while tasks to be performed alone should be at the independent reading level.
- In instruction, the teacher should provide direct instruction before asking the student to work alone or with a group. Individual work is done to reinforce the ideas taught by the teacher.
- Effective instruction allows the students opportunities for decision making. This includes the selection of a learning task from several choices and the opportunity to express their feelings toward the tasks.
- Teachers must continuously analyze a student's performance to gain the assessment information needed to reevaluate teaching assignments.
- Directions given on all tasks need to be specific and clearly stated.

To provide effective instruction, the teacher should outline plans for the entire class and write individual plans for each student. To organize the instruction for a class, the teacher should have an outline of all tasks taking place at the same time. This planning procedure helps the teacher to group students, arrange students in the different learning centers, and plan for other variables such as different noise levels in the room. In addition, the teacher can use this master plan of instruction to record the students' daily activities and plan for future instruction. The overall plan is outlined in the teacher's lesson plan booklet and used to direct students in their various tasks. Evaluation notes are added as observations are made.

There are many approaches to providing effective instruction and many ways of organizing students so that they learn to enjoy reading. The essential element is that the instruction provided be planned to meet the assessed needs of the students.

SUMMARY

This chapter has provided the classroom teacher with an introduction to providing appropriate reading instruction. It includes some basic principles for effective instruction to serve as guides for the teacher. The underlying philosophy is that there is no one best way to provide appropriate instruction in the classroom; the teacher must make adjustments for individual situations.

To present additional instructional ideas, five approaches to reading instruction were discussed. These included the basal approach, language-based approach, multisensory approach, computer-assisted approach, and eclectic approach. Each approach has advantages and limitations, which should be considered when determining the best techniques to use with each student.

Because teachers in self-contained classrooms and departmentalized classrooms must approach reading instruction with a slightly different emphasis, directed teaching procedures were outlined for each type of situation. The directed reading activity format is more appropriate for self-contained classroom teachers, while an adaptation of this procedure, the directed learning activity, allows departmentalized content teachers to integrate reading instruction in the content areas. Moreover, some specific techniques were offered to assist teachers in planning for reading instruction.

Applying What You Read

1. In your preservice training program you had two reading courses. One professor presented information as though reading skills were the major component of reading instruction. The other professor discounted reading skills as unnecessary parts of the reading process and presented strategies for involving students in literature and writing activities. Now, with your first teaching assignment in a low-income neighborhood, where seven of your third graders speak English as a second language and where the principal and teachers are talking about the new basal program, what will you do? How will you determine the best approaches for your students?
2. The principal in your school has asked that every teacher use a variety of approaches to provide effective instruction. To make sure that an effort is made in this direction, each teacher is asked to describe the three most common approaches used in his classroom. What three approaches would you identify? Why?
3. A friend of yours teaches sixth-grade social studies. The students need help in reading, so the faculty is adopting a philosophy of integrating reading instruction throughout the school. Your friend does not understand how reading instruction can fit into the social studies class. How could you explain?

NOTES

1. Guy L. Bond and Robert Dykstra, *Final Report, Project No. X-001.*
2. Paul C. Burns and Betty D. Roe, *Teaching Reading in Today's Elementary Schools.*
3. Edward B. Fry, *Elementary Reading Instruction,* pp. 134–227.
4. JoAnne L. Vacca, Richard T. Vacca, and Mary K. Gove, *Reading and Learning to Read,* pp. 234–372; John W. Miller and Michael McKenna, *Teaching Reading in the Elementary Classroom,* pp. 373–404.
5. Earl H. Cheek, Rona F. Flippo, and Jimmy D. Lindsey, *Reading for Success in Elementary Schools,* p. 441.
6. Angela Jagger, "On Observing the Language Learner: Introduction and Overview," in *Observing the Language Learner,* edited by Angela Jagger and M. Trika Smith-Burke, pp. 1–7.
7. *Standards for the English Language Arts.*
8. Dolores Durkin, "Dolores Durkin Speaks on Instruction," *The Reading Teacher*, p. 472.
9. Sarah J. McCarthey and James V. Hoffman, "The New Basals: How Are They Different?" *The Reading Teacher*; D. Ray Reutzel and Nycole S. Larson, "Look What They've Done to Real Children's Books in the New Basal Readers!" *Language Arts.*
10. Bette S. Bergeron, "What Does the Term 'Whole Language' Mean? Constructing a Definition from the Literature," *Journal of Reading Behavior.*
11. Peter B. Mosenthal, "The Whole Language Approach: Teachers between a Rock and a Hard Place," *The Reading Teacher*; P. J. Farris and D. Kacmarski, "Whole Language, a Closer Look," *Contemporary Education;* E. Hajek, "Whole Language: Sensible Answers to the Old Problems,"

Momentum; Maria Brountas, "Whole Language Really Works," *Teaching K–8*; J. C. Richards, J. P. Gipe, and B. Thompson, "Teachers' Beliefs about Good Reading Instruction," *Reading Psychology*; D. R. Reutzel and P. M. Hollingsworth, "Whole Language and the Practitioner," *Academic Therapy*; C. Edlesky, K. Draper, and K. Smith, "Hookin' 'Em in at the Start of School in a 'Whole Language' Classroom," *Anthropology and Education Quarterly*; Helen B. Slaughter, "Indirect and Direct Instruction in a Whole Language Classroom," *The Reading Teacher*; Mersereau, M. Glover, and M. Cherland, "Dancing on the Edge," *Language Arts*; D. J. Watson, "Defining and Describing Whole Language," *The Elementary School Journal*; S. J. Rich, "Restoring Power to Teachers: The Impact of 'Whole Language'," *Language Arts*.

12. Bergeron, "What Does the Term 'Whole Language' Mean?", p. 319.
13. Lia Ridley, "Enacting Change in Elementary School Programs: Implementing a Whole Language Perspective," *The Reading Teacher*.
14. Elfrieda H. Hiebert and Jacalyn Colt, "Patterns of Literature-Based Reading Instruction," *The Reading Teacher*.
15. Mary Anne Hall, *The Language Experience Approach to Teaching Reading,* 2nd ed., 1–2.
16. Roach Van Allen, "The Language Experience Approach," in *Perspectives on Elementary Reading*, edited by Robert Karlin, p. 158.
17. Roach Van Allen, *Language Experiences in Communication*; Russell G. Stauffer, *The Language-Experience Approach to the Teaching of Reading*; Mary Anne Hall, *Teaching Reading as a Language Experience.*
18. Willard C. Olson, *Child Development.*
19. Jeanette Veatch, *Individualizing Your Reading Program.*
20. Jeanette Veatch, "From the Vantage of Retirement," *The Reading Teacher,* pp. 510–516.
21. Rachel Fidell and Estelle A. Fidell, eds., *Children's Catalog.*
22. Lea M. McGee and Gail E. Tompkins, "Literature-Based Reading Instruction: What's Guiding the Instruction?" *Language Arts*.
23. Hiebert and Colt, "Patterns," pp. 14–20.
24. Bergeron, "What Does the Term 'Whole Language' Mean?", p. 320.
25. Roger Farr, "Trends: A Place for Basal Readers under the Whole Language Umbrella," *Educational Leadership*.
26. Grace M. Fernald, *Remedial Techniques in Basic School Subjects.*
27. Albert J. Harris and Edward R. Sipay, *How to Increase Reading Ability,* 6th ed., p. 403.
28. C. Doyle, "Creative Applications of Computer Assisted Reading and Writing Instruction," *Journal of Reading*; J. Hancock, "Learning with Databases," *Journal of Reading*.
29. Shelly B. Wepner, "Holistic Computer Applications in Literature-Based Classrooms," *The Reading Teacher*.
30. George E. Mason, *Language Experience Recorder Plus.*
31. *Magic Slate*, (Sunburst Communications).
32. *The Children's Writing and Publishing Center* (The Learning Company).
33. *Success with Writing* (Scholastic).
34. Gloria Kuchinskas and M. C. Radenchich. *The Semantic Mapper* and *The Literacy Mapper*.
35. David Reinking, *The Comprehension Connection.*
36. G. Brackett, *Super Story Tree.*
37. M. Balsam and C. Hammer, *Success with Reading.*
38. *Create with Garfield* (Developmental Learning Materials).
39. Robert J. Rickelman and William A. Henk, "Telecommunications in the Reading Classroom," *The Reading Teacher*, pp. 418–419.
40. *Amanda Stories* (Voyager Company).
41. *The Manhole* and *Cosmic Osmo* (Activation).
42. Jay S. Blanchard and Claire J. Rottenberg, "Hypertext and Hypermedia: Discovering and Creating Meaningful Learning Environments," *The Reading Teacher.*

43. Linda Lundgren, Diane Lapp, and James Flood, "Strategies for Gaining Access to the Information Superhighway: Off the Side Street and on to the Main Road," *The Reading Teacher*.
44. Rich Thome, "The Fourth R is Research," *Electronic Learning*.
45. Reggie Routman, *Literacy at the Crossroads: Crucial Talk about Reading, Writing, and Other Teaching Dilemmas;* Dorothy Strickland, "In Search of Balance: Restructuring Our Literacy Programs," *Reading Today*, Richard Vacca, "The Reading Wars: Who Will Be the Winners? Who Will Be the Losers?" *Reading Today*.
46. This research can be found in the following issues of *The Reading Teacher* May 1966, October 1966, May 1967, October 1967, January 1969, and March 1969.
47. Gerald G. Duffy and Laura R. Roehler, *Improving Classroom Reading Instruction,* 2nd ed., p. 76.
48. Ibid.

Caps for Sale
My favorite cap

CHAPTER 7

Emergent Literacy

Ms. Hoffman and Ms. Dossier, who know young children and are aware of their cognitive development, recognize that the wealth of information in emergent literacy carries an important message: the foundation for reading is established during the preschool years as literacy emerges through language and writing development. Home and school environments rich in oral language, print materials, and writing activities create a literate environment in which necessary early learning occurs.

The teachers at Twin Lakes decide that the conversations between adults and children as they explore topics of interest, drawing and writing, listening and responding to literature, and awareness of environmental print are such important components in preparing children for school reading experiences that they will form special parent groups for further study. This chapter presents information about each of the language areas of literacy development and discusses the impact of this learning on reading. Ideas for assessing and developing emergent literacy are presented to assist preschool and elementary teachers in understanding the developmental nature of the reading process and the integral role that language plays in this development. The chapter is organized to address the following questions.

- What is emergent literacy?
- Why is emergent literacy so important in reading development?
- Why has the terminology changed from "prereading" to "emergent" literacy?
- What does research tell us about this area?
- How can the teacher assess emergent literacy development?
- What ideas can be used to develop emergent literacy or to provide assistance to the student who is identified to have problems in this area?

Vocabulary to Know

- **Auditory discrimination**
- **Auditory memory**
- **Book handling**
- **Book sharing**
- **Dictation**
- **Emergent literacy**
- **Environment**
- **Environmental print**
- **Invented spelling**
- **Language development**
- **Listening comprehension**
- **Oral language**
- **Phonemic awareness**
- **Prereading skills**
- **Retelling**
- **Visual comprehension**
- **Visual discrimination**
- **Visual memory**
- **Visual-motor skills**
- **Word boundaries**
- **Writing**

THE IMPORTANCE OF EMERGENT LITERACY

Emergent literacy is a relatively new way of viewing the language processes of young children. Educators previously believed that language development in the early years was based on listening and speaking and that later development at age five or six focused on developing the necessary prereading skills associated with reading and writing. Research in the last decade has confirmed that the conditions that aid in the development of first language learning are the same conditions that promote literacy development. Teale and Sulzby suggest that the new research in emergent literacy has unique dimensions.

1. The age range studies have been extended to include children 14 months and younger.
2. Literacy is no longer regarded as simply a cognitive skill but as a complex activity with social, linguistic, and psychological aspects.
3. Since literacy learning is multidimensional and tied to the child's natural surroundings, it is studied in both home and school environments.
4. Researchers are now studying literacy learning from the child's point of view.[1]

In an extensive review of the literature, Mason and Allen found that certain specific communication patterns and practices, parent and child interactions, parent and child literacy activities, societal and parental expectations, linguistic contexts, story literacy concepts, home reading patterns, language interactions, and meaningful literacy events contribute to the acquisition of reading concepts.[2] They further concluded that

Reading to young children is the best language development/reading readiness activity provided by parents.

Photo courtesy of Edward B. Lasher.

1. Social and linguistic contexts for learning play a profound role in the development of early literacy.
2. Phonological awareness and story understanding are the primary components around which literacy concepts revolve. These are acquired through informal as well as formal home and school activities.
3. Literacy goals, both personal and public, affect learning.
4. Children with parents who assist in the development of literacy at home come to school prepared for reading instruction.
5. Experiences that emphasize phonological awareness, knowledge of print and speech relations, and story reading contribute to future reading success.

Thus, the acquisition of print appears to be a developmental process that begins at birth and continues into the school-age years. The foundation for successful reading must clearly be laid during a child's preschool developmental stage.

Our views of what happens in learning with young children as reading prerequisites are developed has shifted from a focus on cognitive skills to a focus on communication as it relates to the language process. As Strickland and Morrow suggest

> We now have new understandings about the origins of literacy development. Reading and writing start much earlier than we had suspected. The toddler's insistence on having "the ducky book" and no other, the two-year-old's uncanny ability to recognize all the sugar-laden cereals in the supermarket, and the three-year-old's persistence in writing her own shopping list are now valued as evidence of ongoing literacy development.[3]

Oral language, reading, and writing develop concurrently in young children. Children in literacy-rich environments learn as they observe, play, have dialogue with adults and peers, and receive encouragement. This is not cognitive instruction; experience is the teacher. Emergent literacy, then, is the natural development of the language process in young children. The concurrent development of oral language, reading, and writing lay a foundation for formal reading instruction in school. This perspective on learning to read and write focuses on the active use of language and print in a rich environment as compared with the notion of prereading skills or reading readiness, which suggests that children are not ready to read until a certain age or until discrete subskills are taught.

Teachers of young children assess emergent literacy behaviors and then plan the learning environment to develop and expand the student's understanding of print. Observation of students as they use reading and writing materials, write messages, keep logs or records in the classroom, and share their books and writings provide teachers with important assessment information.[4] Teachers need to know if young students understand the functions of reading and writing, if they have developed a sense of story structure and know how to comprehend a story, and if they can make attempts at reading and writing in their own way before beginning conventional reading and writing.[5] Roney suggests that the major concepts inherent in the early reading process are print awareness, language development, story structure, and the usefulness of reading.[6]

Print Awareness

A basic concept that influences reading is print awareness. An essential aspect of this concept is the child's awareness of how print functions. Clay suggests that children must understand numerous concepts about print that include, but are not limited to, the following:

1. Books have a specific orientation with an identifiable front and back, and pages have an identifiable top and bottom.
2. Print is important since it, not the pictures, is to be read.
3. The ability to identify the 26 letters of the English alphabet, both lower- and uppercase, is essential to successful reading.
4. Directionality is essential for successful reading. For example, print on the left page is read before print on the right page, and the print on each page is read from left to right and from top to bottom.
5. Linearity is important. Students must understand that letters in a word and words in a sentence are ordered from left to right, and that, by changing the order, you alter the meaning.
6. Recognition of a word as a cluster of letters surrounded by space is necessary for word identification.
7. An awareness of the basic elements of capitalization and punctuation is important.[7]

Books help children unlock mysteries of the world and their language.

Photo courtesy of Edward B. Lasher.

Print awareness begins as children scribble to communicate a message and read the McDonald's sign when they see the golden arches. This aspect of emergent literacy usually begins by the age of two and develops naturally according to the stimulation provided in the home environment.[8] Children whose home environment provides limited opportunities to experiment with books, paper, markers, pencils, and environmental print will be less ready to interact with print in the school environment.

Understanding the interrelatedness of the reading and writing processes is important in providing literacy development experiences for young children. Parents need to be educated to understand this relationship. As important and more basic to the development of print awareness is the parents' understanding of the school's theory of literacy. As Fitzgerald, Spiegel, and Cunningham reported, low-literacy parents tend to view language learning from a skills perspective while high-literacy parents view language learning from a cultural practice perspective.[9] This difference in perspective may cause problems when trying to sell a language-based philosophy to parents who believe in skill-based learning or skill-based learning to parents who believe in language-based learning. However, experiences in print awareness need to begin with all children in the home environment at an early age to allow literacy learning to emerge.

Language Development

An extension of the concept of print awareness is that children must become aware of the relationship between oral language and print very early in their development. As Roney notes, the simple act of recognizing that speech can be translated into print, and print into spoken language, enables children to begin to understand the symbol system of our language.[10]

Children have many experiences with both oral and written language as they progress through the various developmental stages. They are exposed to many types of communication devices such as television, radio, print media, traffic signs, and billboards. Parents and others have read stories to children with varied themes and topics. Children are exposed to written language in familiar situations, and in the process of learning to read and write they learn about its purposes, the processes by which others read and write, and the specific visual features that characterize print.[11]

Students who come from educationally deficient environments are often lacking in the area of oral language. Oral language is vitally important in the reading process in that language must be spoken first before it can be understood on the printed page. Much more will be said about oral language development in a later section of this chapter. It is sufficient to say here that oral language skills have a tremendous effect on reading; thus, the prime objective of many preschool programs is to develop oral language skills.

Halliday identifies seven functions evident in the language of young children:

1. *Instrumental*. Children use language to satisfy personal needs and to get things done.
2. *Regulatory*. Children use language to control the behavior of others.
3. *Personal*. Children use language to tell about themselves.
4. *Interactional*. Children use language to get along with others.
5. *Heuristic*. Children use language to find out about things, to learn things.
6. *Imaginative*. Children use language to pretend, to make believe.
7. *Informative*. Children use language to communicate something for the information of others.[12]

For children to become effective readers and understand the relationship between spoken and written language, it is essential to expose them to a wide variety of printed materials. Children are then more able to develop a sense of print and language awareness that will enhance their potential for success as readers.

Story Structure

Another type of early experience that affects a child's potential success as a reader is story structure. When initially interacting with print, children with a variety of story experiences are aware of the type of story that they are reading. They are able to recognize stories as being nursery rhymes, animal stories, or how-to books. However, children with limited story experiences are more likely to have a narrow sense of a story's structure. These children tend to have more difficulty interacting with various types of literature. Developing a sense of story structure, which involves learning under what circumstances various characters, settings, and linguistic idiosyncrasies can appear in various types of literature, enables children to become more successful readers.[13]

As young children become involved with books and story structure, the essential element is understanding. Listening comprehension is often measured by the student's skill in answering questions about what has been read. However, recent research suggests that story retellings can help determine the listener's (or reader's) understanding of the information. Sulzby suggests that in retelling stories children use different sources for the message, beginning with pictures and moving toward print as the child develops greater familiarity with the story and the language process (see Figure 7.1). This concept of story reading is based on the presence of a storylike unit or structure with some indication of past, present, and future.[14]

Figure 7.1 Storybook Reading by Emergent Readers

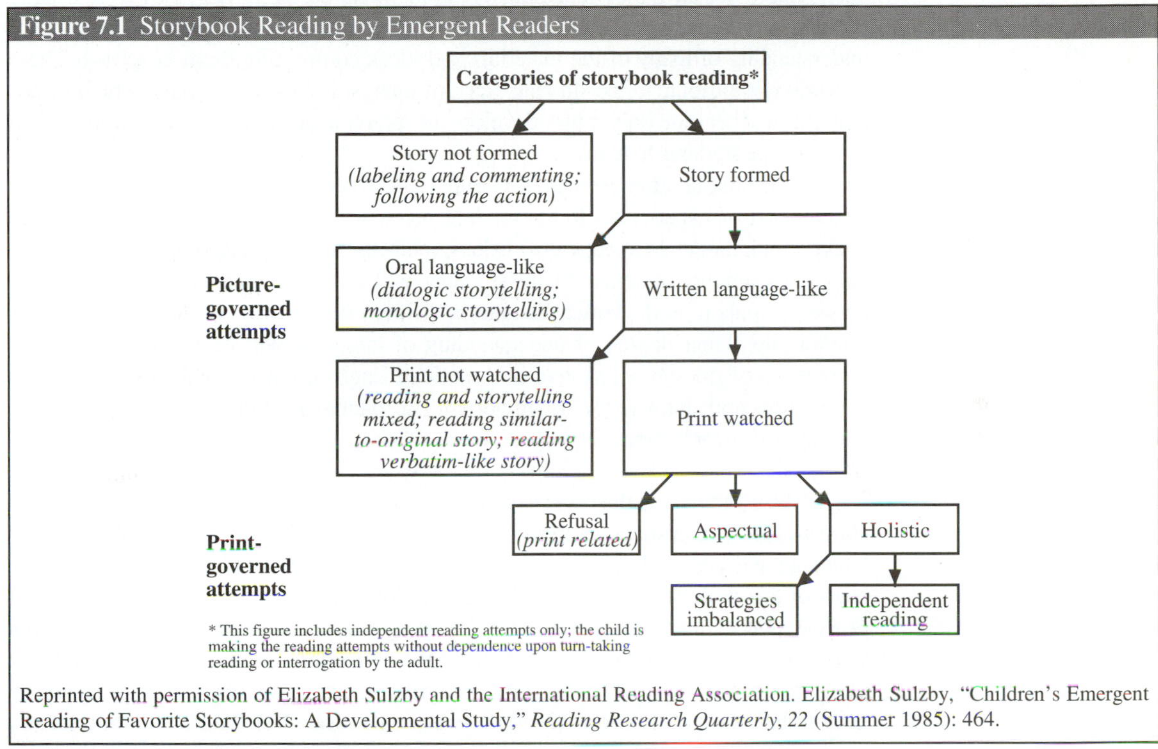

Reprinted with permission of Elizabeth Sulzby and the International Reading Association. Elizabeth Sulzby, "Children's Emergent Reading of Favorite Storybooks: A Developmental Study," *Reading Research Quarterly*, *22* (Summer 1985): 464.

Reading Usefulness

Roney believes that one of the most important aspects of learning to read is discovering that reading is both enjoyable and immediately useful.[15] Unless children's interest can be maintained, it will be more difficult for them to derive enjoyment or benefit from their reading activities. Failure to find enjoyment in reading during the child's early print experience may result in a negative attitude toward reading, which could impede the child's development as a successful reader. Children experiencing enjoyment and pleasure from reading activities, however, are more likely to continue developing into lifelong readers.

Relevancy of reading to the environment in the home and at school is extremely important in learning to read. Students from environmental conditions that are conducive to learning to read are more likely to experience success than students from less favorable environments. Some specific aspects that contribute to a positive environment include social and cultural awareness, experiential background, prior knowledge, oral language development, and interest in reading.

Students from homes in which reading is not important often enter school with little expertise in school literacy areas. These students may have had few experiences with books, newspapers, magazines, or other types of printed material. They have not been read to nor have they seen others read in the home. Moreover, they have usually not had any experiences outside their immediate culture, a condition that limits their understanding of many of the materials and ideas confronting them in school. These conditions contribute to the students' lack of interest in learning to read, which means that the teacher not only must develop the prerequisite knowledge but must also motivate the students to learn.

In teaching children to read, it is important to remember that each child brings a different set of experiences to the reading process. Such differences as sociocultural background, parental expectations, values, interests, and language tend to create wide disparities among students. Many students will clearly understand the connection between spoken and written language, while others will be unaware of this relationship. Their degree of understanding of language will be manifested in their knowledge of the symbol system of American English. Understanding these gaps in experience and knowledge is important in planning appropriate and effective instruction for each child.

DEVELOPING EMERGENT LITERACY

Linguistic awareness is the critical area that is developed as literacy emerges in young children. This linguistic awareness evolves as children experiment with all aspects of language and accumulate information about tasks such as reading and writing. The basis of this understanding is oral language. However, emergent literacy is a natural process that cannot be separated into language compartments. Research in recent years consistently emphasizes that listening, speaking, reading, and writing are integrated rather than separated in learning about language. However, teachers do need to be aware of performance in these separate areas. For this reason, this section is organized to provide ideas for classroom use that involve integrated language instruction as well as ideas that address the areas for language development separately.

Specific subskills described in discussions of prereading are developed in a language-based program through daily activities as children learn about language or through designated skill activities in a skills-based program. As discussed earlier, skills-based programs follow a specific continuum of skills, while language-based (or emergent literacy) programs, develop skills through learning activities that enhance language development. To implement an emergent literacy program, the teacher must design activities to use skills that the students know and to develop new skills. The three major areas of language development in the emergent literacy curriculum are oral language, reading, and writing (see Figure 7.2). In the following sections related subskills are included so that the suggestions can be used in either a skill- or language-based program for young children.

Figure 7.2 Language Areas in Emergent Literacy

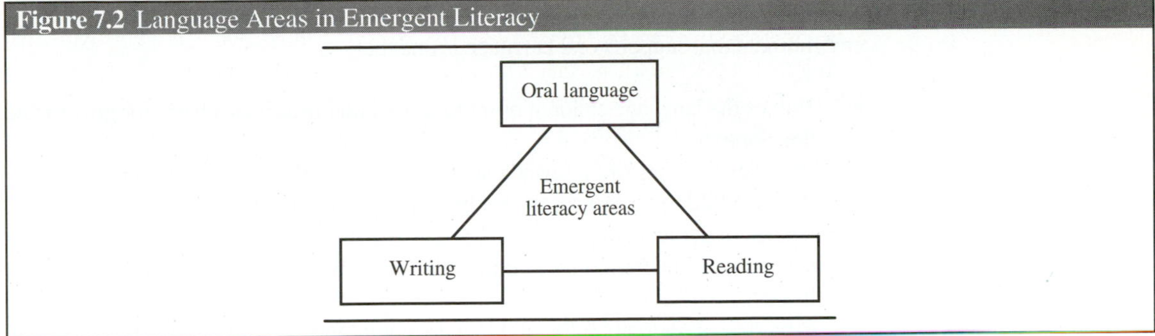

Oral Language

Oral language is a critical area in the development of early reading and writing. Students learn language by listening and speaking and interpret this knowledge through reading and writing. Understanding language enables the child to use scribbles to represent words or to read pictures in books. Early studies by Loban and Strickland indicate that reading can be influenced either adversely or positively by the language of the reader.[16] Students with good oral language skills tend to have advantages in reading over those with poor oral language skills because of the content of the materials and the language patterns used.

The culture from which the student comes is another important consideration in developing oral language. As Britton explains, students from a particular culture and dialect group learn to speak not only the language of that group but also learn to think and organize their ideas in accordance with the views of their closest contacts.[17] A serious error teachers sometimes make is attempting to change a student's language without understanding their culture and dialect. Teachers need to develop an understanding of students' backgrounds and cultures in order to encourage them to extend their learning and expand their language.[18]

Another essential component of language is syntactic ability. Chomsky examined the relationship between students' knowledge of complex syntactic structures and the amount of reading done by them as well as the amount of material read aloud to them. She found that students who were read to and who read more on their own had a much better knowledge of complex structures than students who heard and read fewer books.[19]

It is essential that teachers provide an atmosphere that is conducive to the development of oral language skills. An environment of acceptance and respect will encourage students to share their experiences with the teacher and with other students. As students share their various experiences, the teacher will have an opportunity to learn more about their modes of learning, language development, and the sociocultural factors that affect their learning in a positive or negative manner.

Teachers and parents need to provide activities such as creative dramatics, group discussions, child and adult conversations, storytelling and retelling, group recitations of poems and chants, and shared reading experiences to help children become effective language users. Strickland and Morrow further suggest that the classroom environment that supports oral language is one that

- Values the language children bring to school and uses it as a basis for growth and development.
- Provides a variety of first-hand experiences within the child's environment.
- Allows children to express themselves in a variety of ways.
- Values individual uniqueness.
- Encourages children to focus on events and materials that have meaning in their lives.
- Provides opportunities for children to communicate with a variety of people, including peers and adults.
- Recognizes and values the natural desire to communicate.
- Provides opportunities to express what they know and what they feel.
- Allows experimentation with language.[20]

While these suggestions are designed for classroom teachers, the first teachers who assist with oral language development are parents, and they, too, need to be aware of their role and ways they can encourage the development of oral language. Oral language is an integral part of the reading-writing process. Because of this important relationship between oral language and the printed word, teachers and parents must consider carefully the ways oral language development is encouraged in the child's environments.

Reading

Prereading and reading readiness have been discussed as major areas of cognitive development with young children for many years. What must a child know in order to read? When should a child begin to read? How do you teach a child to read? These questions have been asked and answered in a variety of ways. In learning the answers to these questions, much has been learned about language, the language process, and the relationships among listening, speaking, reading, and writing.

Reading develops as children learn to interpret messages provided through pictures in books, symbols on signs, and labels in their environment; it develops as they ride down the road or help with grocery shopping, as they read favorite books, and as they respond to nursery rhymes and stories read by others. Crafton suggests that big books and predictable books provide good opportunities for students to develop concepts about print as well as prediction and comprehension strategies.[21] Reading begins before the child picks up a book and decodes the symbols exactly as printed. These early reading activities have been referred to as "prereading" or "reading readiness" activities. Regardless of the label, children who engage in these activities are using oral language along with a visual and auditory awareness of language.

Visual awareness for the reading process involves understanding of directionality, being able to discriminate symbols, and remembering symbols, both letters and pictures. Directionality, sometimes considered a visual-motor skill, involves the mastery of left-to-right progression and top-to-bottom orientation. Children develop an understanding of directionality as they have experiences with print and see letters and words read to them. Directionality is also involved as students learn to recognize and form letters, especially commonly confused letters such as *b* and *d*; *p*, *q* and *g*; *m* and *w*; and *n* and *u*. While students sometimes reverse letters and words as they read, more frequently this occurs as they write. These confusions are more of a maturation problem than a reading problem, although parents and teachers often become anxious and may rush to assume there is a reading problem. The authors' experiences suggest that immature children are more likely to have this reversal problem and that, as they mature, the problem takes care of itself unless there is a learning disability or unless someone has made the issue a problem. An anxious parent once called to ask one of the authors how she might have her child evaluated for dyslexia. The author asked why the mother was concerned and was told that the child reversed letters, could not remember words when told, was hyperactive, and could not write letters on the line. While these are some characteristics of a learning disability, the real problem was uncovered when the parent was asked the age of the child. The mother responded, "Matt will be five in three months." Reversals are common in children up to the age of eight.

Understanding the left-to-right and top-to-bottom progression of print is a basic concept in learning to read and is necessary for independent reading to occur. Students develop this understanding as they see printed versions of their language experience stories being read to them or as the reader follows the line of print with her hand using a left-to-right sweeping motion while reading. The same development occurs in learning to read from the top of the page to the bottom. An example of student confusion about this concept occurred in a second-grade class as a bright little girl wrote her spelling words. Half the words were written perfectly from left to right while the other half were written perfectly but from right to left. The child was asked why she wrote the words differently. Her quick response was "The teacher told me to." When she was asked to repeat the teacher's instructions, she said, "The teacher said to start writing at the red line on the side of your paper and write toward the middle, so I started at this red line (she indicated the one on the left side of the notebook paper) and wrote my words. When I did the next side, I started at the other red line (she indicated the one on the right side of the paper) and did just like the teacher said." What a complex task to write words and letters backwards just to follow the directions of the teacher! An appropriate strategy for addressing this problem was quickly provided.

Successful readers also learn to distinguish letters and words. With practice this discrimination leads to memory of the symbols, which facilitates reading. For example, children learn to recognize the difference in the letter *a* and the letter *o* and combinations of letters such as *cat* and *dog* as they are beginning the reading process. There is no question of the importance of knowing how to visually discriminate and remember symbols; however, research has questioned the relationship of exercises using pictures to the visual discrimination of symbols.[22] Durkin and Ollila suggest that the most appropriate instructional procedures for direct instruction in visual discrimination involve the use of letters and words rather than pictures, shapes, and numerals.[23] Again, this discrimination skill usually develops as students are exposed to print and language without the use of specific workbook activities.

Visual memory of letters and words develops as students learn to discriminate symbols. In addition to recognizing letters, students start to know the basic sight words such as *the*, *what*, *come*, *and*, *with*. Learning to recognize the unique features of letters and words enables students to identify them quickly as they read. From a summary of the research, Adams suggests that "the speed with which they can name individual letters both strongly predicts success for prereaders and is strongly related to reading achievement among beginning readers."[24] She further explains that speed and accuracy in naming letters not only indicates the prereader's familiarity with letter identities but increases confidence and provides a basis for learning about letter sounds.

Reading pictures and words in the environment helps young children realize that symbols communicate a message. This reading of environmental print is one way for children to develop an understanding of what they see. However, recognizing that golden arches indicate a nearby McDonald's or that Tony the Tiger identifies a box of cereal is not enough; the letters in words and their associated sounds need to be pointed out to children. Adults need to go beyond the basic identification of visual symbols by helping children interpret letters in environmental print. Teachers can label items in the classroom, display daily messages or directions in the room, and identify topics of discussion using cards with words on them to communicate to young children that oral and written language are related. In these ways environmental print can be used to develop a visual comprehension of information. Allowing a young child to locate his name from several cards and use another card to "sign in" each morning helps the child learn to visually recognize his name and connect this reading process to writing using scribbles and letters as he develops.

Just as visual processing of information is important in emergent literacy, auditory processing is also essential. As children develop an awareness of oral language and talking, they initially use one word to communicate an idea and soon put words together to form phrases and sentences. Regardless of the number of words spoken, the child is using words to convey, not a sound or syllable, but a meaningful message. Children begin to develop the concept of individual words as words are pointed out to them when they are interacting with print. Words become a series of squiggly marks with a space in front and a space at the end. Visual and auditory processing of language occur together. As children hear and see words, they develop the concept of isolated words and can then begin to associate letters and sounds within the word. Every primary-level teacher has had the experience of being asked how to spell "onceuponatime" by the young writer beginning his own fairy tale. Auditorily the student has comprehended that one word is used to begin a story, and when the teacher begins to spell four separate words, the child is surprised.

Just as children learn to discriminate one letter from another visually, they also learn to discriminate letters auditorily. Research investigations into just how children should be taught to identify letters and learn sounds suggest that letters and sounds are best learned together.[25] Adams states that functional understanding of the alphabetic principle depends equally on knowledge of letters and on explicit awareness of phonemes because of the close association between them.[26] Thus, as we teach auditory discrimination of sounds it is important to teach visual discrimination of letters to assist students in associating the sounds and symbols of their language. Developing this phonemic awareness of language is important to a child's success in learning to read. Richgels, Poremba, and McGee state that phonemic awareness is reflected in a child's conscious use of phonemes, which are the sound units that speakers and listeners subconsciously combine and contrast to produce and understand words in spoken language. A young student must be consciously aware of phonemes to isolate sounds in words during invented spelling or to use the sound-symbol relationships to identify words and recognize word patterns.[27] In her analysis of research, Adams suggests that students possess phonemic awareness as evidenced through their speech production and understanding or oral language; however, this functional knowledge is not the same as the conscious knowledge needed to understand the phonological process.[28] As literacy emerges, teachers develop phonemic awareness of language by helping students associate sounds and letters in their oral and written language. However, an intensive phonics program is not needed for young children to develop phonemic awareness.

One technique available to teachers for assessing phonemic awareness in young children is the Yopp-Singer Test of Phoneme Segmentation, which could provide useful information to teachers in determining their students' basic knowledge level.[29] Indeed, if children are to learn letter-sound associations in a way they can continue to develop in later years, schools need programs rich in experiences that provide linguistic awareness, such as story reading; songs; nursery rhymes; oral language activities including discussions, free play in structured situations, and dramatizations; and language games encouraging both oral and written expression. Another valuable resource for developing phonemic awareness is read-aloud books. Yopp has compiled an annotated bibliography of read-aloud books specifically for this purpose, which includes selection criteria and instructions for using the books.[30] Developing phonemic awareness assists the students as they encounter words and later instruction in associating sounds and symbols.

All students will not learn to recognize or discriminate sounds at the ages of four, five, or six. Children who have not been involved with language activities in the home environment will not be ready for this phase of emergent literacy. Some children, particularly little boys, have difficulty with high-frequency sounds (/f/, /v/, /d/, /p/, /t/, /g/, /k/, /sh/, and /th/), because of auditory acuity problems caused by ear infections or delays in the formation of their middle or inner ear structure.[31]

The most important activity that parents and caretakers of young children can engage in with children from birth to school age is reading to those children. Repeatedly, researchers have concluded that the single most important activity for developing the skills and knowledge needed for success in reading is reading aloud to children.[32] In addition to learning concepts about print and sounds as discussed earlier, children learn about story structure and develop an understanding of the meaningful messages conveyed through stories and poems. Auditory or listening comprehension expands vocabulary and develops oral language as parents encourage comments and have dialogue with the child as the story is read.[33]

In a study of literacy events in home environments lacking emphasis on literacy, Teale found that events categorized as "storybook time" occupied, on the average, less than two minutes per day, with many children having no storybook reading time at all.[34] As Adams suggests, if these children continue this pattern throughout their preschool years, they will have received about 60 hours of storybook reading compared with about 1,000 hours of storybook reading for the child in a literacy-rich home environment.[35] The differences in the language awareness and listening comprehension performances of these two groups of children will be miles apart when they enter school. However, children who begin school understanding comparatively little about the vocabulary and syntax of written stories can gain this knowledge through encounters with books at school. Purcell-Gates, McIntyre, and Freppon found that differing kindergarten and first-grade programs can affect the extent of this knowledge. When compared with students in skills-based programs, students in meaning-based classrooms (with increased levels of storybook reading, book discussions, and opportunities to explore books and to write) demonstrated significantly greater growth in their knowledge of written language and more extensive breadth of knowledge of written linguistic features. Children who begin school behind in the acquisition of language can acquire it at school, particularly in classrooms that provide frequent opportunities to listen to stories and to respond in various ways.[36]

The wealth of children's literature in libraries, schools, and some homes must be put in the hands of all parents if literacy is to emerge for all young children. In a study of reading interests of 3-year-old children, Collins found that definite preferences in story content exist based on gender as well as socioeconomic level (see Table 7.1).[37] This difference in reading preferences should be considered when stories are read to young children. As children's language becomes better developed, their reading interests tend to veer away from pattern books toward books with greater content. Girls prefer storybooks about people or animals, real or fictional, while boys lean toward informational books about trucks, dinosaurs, or animals. The less well developed the child's language, the more he or she enjoyed pattern books, including nursery rhymes and repetitious verses. Initial data from a follow-up study with 5-year-olds suggests that middle-income girls develop a preference for pattern books as they try to read the book independently or with an adult reader (parents reported that these girls enjoyed pattern books prior to the age of 3), and middle-income 5-year-old boys have a preference for storybooks and informational books.[38] This change in reading interests appears to reflect the development of language literacy with age, oral language development, literacy experiences, and an environment leading to reading.

Table 7.1 Comparison of Reading Interests of 3-Year-Olds from Two Socioeconomic Levels

	Male	Female
Middle-income	Informational books Pattern books	Storybooks
Lower-income	Pattern books	Pattern books Storybooks

To understand information obtained by listening, students should have some command over the key components of the language, namely, phonology (sound structure), syntax (sentence structure), semantics (word meaning and the relationships among meanings), and text structure (conventions for conveying events and assertions within a text). Various researchers have found that the lack of facility in any one of these components leads to either reduced comprehension or increased processing time. Thus, a good listener orchestrates all of these components simultaneously.[39]

In a summary of literature related to teaching listening comprehension, Pearson and Fielding concluded that

1. Listening training in the same skills typically taught in reading comprehension curricula tends to improve listening comprehension.
2. Listening comprehension is enhanced by various kinds of active verbal responses on the part of students during and after listening.
3. Listening to literature tends to improve listening comprehension.
4. Certain types of instruction primarily directed toward other areas of language arts may also improve listening comprehension.
5. Direct teaching of listening strategies seems to help students become more conscious of their listening habits.[40]

For many years, auditory comprehension has been identified as an indicator of potential reading ability. In a review of studies that compared reading and listening comprehension at various levels, Sticht et al. found that in the elementary grades (1 through 6), almost all of the comparisons favor the listening comprehension mode. However, in grades 7 through 12, the proportion of studies showing an advantage to reading comprehension increases.[41] Although this summary suggests that, in the elementary grades, students can rely on their already well developed listening comprehension abilities to assist their less well developed reading abilities, Schell cautions against using a listening comprehension level to determine the reading potential of students in grades 1 through 3. In a review of the research, he found that students were overreferred for help in reading when listening comprehension was used as an indicator of potential.[42] Nevertheless, students are often able to attend more critically to material read to them than to material they read silently. It is not uncommon for students to be able to comprehend oral passages on a higher readability level than their silent reading level. This interesting correlation between listening and reading has resulted in the investigation of this phenomena over a period of several years.

Numerous studies have examined the relationship between listening and reading. Ross found that good listeners rated higher than poor listeners on intelligence, reading, socioeconomic status, and achievement, but not on an auditory acuity test.[43] This study indicates that auding (listening) requires a finer degree of discrimination than acuity.

Deutsch et al. found that children from lower socioeconomic backgrounds were at a distinct disadvantage in learning to read because their language patterns interfered with the comprehension of both oral and written materials.[44] In a related study, Clark and Richards found a significant deficiency in auditory discrimination in economically disadvantaged preschool students.[45]

Parents of young children are usually intensely interested in the reading performance of their child. Many investigations have been conducted to determine what factors in the home environments contribute to success in reading. McGee and Richgels[46] summarize this research by highlighting six factors that support literacy learning:

1. Availability and variety of reading and writing materials appropriate to the age and interests of the children[47]
2. Parents who are readers and writers[48]
3. A daily routine for storybook reading and use of writing as a part of the daily activities[49]
4. Discussions between children and parents as stories are read and talk about written language when they write together[50]
5. A feeling of responsibility toward literacy development[51]
6. A sensitivity to children's interests and experiences when reading and sharing books as well as acceptance of the level of the child's performance[52]

In a study of parents' perceptions of factors affecting the reading development of intellectually superior accelerated readers and intellectually superior nonreaders of preschool-age, Burns and Collins found that all parents were involved in literacy development activities with their children. However, mothers of accelerated readers provided more opportunities for their children to discuss, recall, and interact with information from stories or story-related materials than mothers of nonreaders. Mothers of accelerated readers also provided more opportunities in the home environment to interact directly with pictures, letters, sounds, words, sentences, and book-related concepts than mothers of nonreaders. There were no differences in the number of opportunities to interact with words in the context of signs, newspapers, magazines, labels, and television or in the number of opportunities to scribble, draw, form shapes, form letters, copy words, spell words, and write messages.[53]

While the length and detail of this section may suggest that reading is the most important aspect of emergent literacy, a review of the information clearly indicates that oral language and writing are integral parts of this process.

Writing

As one mother tried to explain to her young daughter that writing under the special message from Bill Martin in her *Brown Bear, Brown Bear* book was not a good idea because it messed up her favorite book, the child responded, "He put his name in it 'cause he wrote the book; I put my name in it 'cause I read the book." Who can argue with this logic? As Donald Graves suggests, when a young child marks with chalk, pens, or crayons, "The child's marks say 'I am.' "[54]

As literacy emerges, children express their developing language through writing and reading activities. Writing has been viewed for many years as a process that begins after reading, although current research shows that emphasis on writing activities in early reading programs results in special gains in early reading achievement.[55] Young children experiment with writing (just as they experiment with reading) using lines and marks to communicate a message. Maria Montessori promoted the idea of write first, read later,[56] and current studies of children who read early support her theory that many children write before reading.[57]

With young children writing begins with lines and scribbles. They progress to making drawings and then letter-like forms, reproduce well-known word units, use invented spelling, and finally begin to use conventional spelling (see Figures 7.3 and 7.4). Writing, like other areas of language, emerges in varying continuums depending on the child's background, experiences, and needs. For example, the 2-year-old makes marks on a paper to experiment with what a marker does on paper (or walls, sheets, clothes, arms). He is not trying to communicate a message; however, as he observes others using a pen to write a message, his purpose for using the marker changes. The lines become more than marks; they are interpreted by the young writer to carry a specific message.

Writing with scribbles progresses as children write, as they paint or play with clay, and builds to making stories or journals.

Photos courtesy of Edward B. Lasher.

Figure 7.3 Sean Demonstrates an Excellent Understanding of the Reading and Writing Processes at the End of Kindergarten As He Writes, "I Liked the Cat Story and *Wacky Wednesday*."

The inclusion of writing as part of the reading process in young learners represents a significant change in thinking in the last 10 years. Earlier discussions of prereading or early literacy development did not discuss writing. Indeed, writing was viewed as a way of communicating a message after the student learns to read and spell. With a wealth of new information supporting what primary teachers and parents have long believed, writing development is now part of all discussions of emergent literacy. As children begin to associate sounds and symbols, they begin to use this knowledge to write, using invented spelling to communicate their ideas. An extensive discussion of invented spelling can be found in Routman and Maxim's article, "Invented Spelling: What It Is and What It Isn't."[58] Chomsky summarizes the common features of invented spelling as follows:

- Children incorporate whole letter names into their spellings: *yl* (while), *thaq* (thank you), *ppl* (people).
- Long vowels generally speak for themselves: *bot* (boat), *agre* (angry).
- Short vowels sound like the correct spelling or are omitted altogether: *bad* (bed), *luks* (looks).
- Letters such as *i* and *r* tend to lose adjacent vowels: *grl* (girl), *tir* (tire).
- The letters *n* and *m* before stop consonants often go unrepresented: *wot* (won't), *plat* (plant).[59]

Figure 7.4 Ronnie Is also Completing Kindergarten and Is Using His Understanding of Invented Spelling to Write, "I Like the Books You Read to Us."

Teachers sometimes have concerns about the impact of invented spelling on correct spelling. Clarke found that in classes encouraging invented spelling, the students wrote longer stories, had greater success in spelling regularly spelled words and words on a standardized spelling test, and performed better when reading regularly spelled nonsense words and when reading lists of high-frequency irregular and lower-frequency regular words.[60] With the greater use of computers in classrooms, students need to be allowed to experiment with writing using the word processor. Letter recognition and discrimination are enhanced as sounds and symbols are associated to communicate a meaningful message.

Encouraging young children to write to communicate a message is the important part of the writing process in emergent literacy. Spelling, spacing, penmanship, and punctuation are mechanical skills that can and will be developed once children learn the real purpose for writing—to convey meaning.

PROVIDING APPROPRIATE INSTRUCTION IN EMERGENT LITERACY

As classroom teachers plan ways to encourage literacy, they need to adopt assessment procedures that are appropriate for young students. Observation is the best evaluation technique for noting what children know; however, teachers must know the relevant behaviors to observe and keep specific records of their findings. Procedures for evaluating emerging literacy are outlined in Table 7.2.

Table 7.2 Assessment Procedures for Evaluating Emergent Literacy Areas

Oral Language	Observation checklist
	Peabody Picture Vocabulary Test
	Test of Early Language Development–2
	Test of Early Reading Ability–2
	Test of Language Development–2
	Criterion and objective-based tests
Reading	Observation checklist
	Criterion and objective-based tests
	Test of Early Reading Ability–2
	Informal reading inventory
	Gates–MacGinitie, Prereading
	Observational Survey of Early Literacy Achievement
Writing	Observation checklist
	Test of Early Written Language
	Test of Written Language–2

Teachers of young children realize the importance of language development as the foundation of the reading and writing processes. Few children enter kindergarten or first grade at the same reading level because of differences in environment and experience. Strickland and Morrow suggest ideas for teachers to use daily to develop language and literacy (see Figure 7.5). Additional ideas are given in Table 7.3. Although these activities are separated into the three categories—oral language, reading, and writing—they reflect the integrated nature of the language process. Many of the reading activities require oral language and writing, while the writing activities require the use of oral language or reading. Thus, these activities can be used to aid in the development of several areas of language development.

Table 7.3 Instructional Techniques for Emergent Literacy Development

Area	Instructional Technique
Oral language	Ask students to say a specified number of words to describe an object or picture.
	Using a topic of interest, develop word walls containing as many words as the students can think about the topic. Add to this each day.
	Following a field trip, film, or story, ask students to use appropriate words to tell about their experience.
	Using various objects, ask students to point to them according to a specified color, shape, size, etc.
	Ask students to show or tell where objects are located when hearing such prepositions as *over*, *under*, *in*, *out*, etc.
	Label objects, pictures, or artwork in the room and have students dictate a sentence or phrase about their work.
	Ask students to dictate stories about pictures from newspapers or magazines.
	Ask students to tell about their favorite pet using complete sentences.
	Invite students to give the recipe for making their favorite food.
	Ask students to tell the sequence involved in making a garden, getting dressed to come to school, or in going on a field trip.
	Read a story and ask students to retell the story in proper order or with necessary characters.
	Let students work in small groups to discuss their favorite foods, TV programs, pets, etc.
	With an assigned topic, ask each student to contribute at least one related idea about the topic.
Reading	Have students string colored beads directionally from left to right in a given pattern.
	Give students cards containing their names written with sand and ask them to trace their name with their finger.
	Give students a letter and ask them to select from a set of letters, one that is exactly like the given letter; then select one that is different.
	Give students an alphabet board containing lower-case letters and a set of cards containing the upper-case letters to be matched.
	Give each student several cards containing names of students in the room. One card should have the student's own name to be selected by recognition.
	Show a picture of an event and list words that represent things that the students identify in the picture.
	Have students draw a picture of their home in as much detail as possible. Then ask them to dictate a story that describes to the class what their picture shows.
	Give students a series of photographs of an event and ask them to arrange the photographs in the correct sequence. Once properly arranged, ask them to dictate a story telling about the pictures.
	Play a tape of an automobile horn, a fog horn, and a boat horn. Then ask students to identify the sounds they heard.
	Using three paper bags, put rocks in one, sand in another, and coins in the last one. Allow students to shake the bags, describe what they hear, and dictate a story about these different sounds.
	Give students a series of two letters such as /b/ and /s/. Ask the students to clap or raise their hands when the two sounds are the same.
	Say several pairs of words, some with the same sounds and some different. Ask students to clap when the words sound the same and stand when they are different.
	Read students a story containing rhyming words. After reading a short portion of the story, ask them to supply the rhyming word as you read using a modified cloze passage.
	Play a game with students in which directions are given such as "Stand up and shake your foot." As the task is performed, give additional directions making each longer and more complex.
	Give students a specific sound. Then say several words containing the specific sound and ask students to clap when the sound is heard in each word.
	Give students two words with the same beginning sound. Ask them to give the sound with which both words begin.
	Say two words with different ending sounds (e.g., *can*, *pop*). Ask students to repeat the ending sounds.

. . . continued

Table 7.3 Instructional Techniques for Emergent Literacy Development

	Show pictures of several animals. Say two words and ask students to select the picture that begins with the same sound as the two given words.
	Tell a story about the beach using descriptive words such as *sifting sand*, *fat fish*, etc. Ask students to name the pairs of words that begin with the same sound.
	Show a picture of an object. Ask students to name as many objects as possible that begin or end with the same sound.
	Say several simple words with medial sounds such as fat and big. Ask each student to say at least one word with the same medial sounds as the examples.
	Give students two words with the same medial sound (*sit*, *trip*). Ask each student to say at least one word with the same medial sound as the examples.
	Read a sentence that has the last word deleted. Ask students to say the missing word that rhymes with another word in the sentence. For example: "The ham was better than ______ ."
	Give the students a word. Ask them to make up a sentence in which the last word rhymes with another word in the sentence. For example: "The big cat ate a *rat*."
	Ask a student to give a simple direction to another student and see that the direction is correctly followed. Then ask the second student to give a different direction to another student. Follow this procedure letting everyone experiment with giving directions.
	Describe an object and ask students to tell what it is and to find a picture of the object.
	Have a student describe an object. Ask the students to attempt to determine what the object is from the student's description. When the task is completed, have each student draw a picture of the object.
	Read a story to the students and ask them to retell their favorite part of the story.
	After reading a short story, ask students to draw a picture of how the main character looks in their minds.
	Have a student tell a story containing four events. Ask the other students to illustrate in order the four events that were described.
	Tell a story using pictures depicting the sequence of events. Place the pictures on a table in random order and ask the students to put them in the correct order.
	Read a portion of a predictable story and ask the students to predict what will happen next, telling why they think as they do.
	After reading a short sentence using descriptive language, ask students to illustrate their impression of the sentence.
	Read a short story that is emotionally descriptive. Ask students to tell how the characters felt in the story.
	Read a story and ask the students to tell why the story ended as it did.
	After hearing a story, ask students to illustrate the conclusion.
	Read part of a story and ask students to tell or illustrate how they think the story should end.
Writing	Give students a basket containing various colors and shapes of paper along with markers, crayons, and pencils. Ask them to select their favorite and write their favorite letter of the alphabet on it.
	Put a small pad of paper in the housekeeping center to encourage students to make shopping lists or take messages from the phone.
	In the writing center put labeled mailboxes for each child. Using the writing materials and envelopes in the center, encourage students to correspond with each other using pictures and invented spelling and putting the message in the appropriate mailbox.
	After making popcorn or some other food, ask the students to work in teams to list the steps followed or tell how the food was prepared.
	Encourage students to use the word processor and type or copy words or ideas that they wish to share with others.
	Use a graphic software package on the computer and help students develop their own invitations or announcements.
	Help students write the letters of the alphabet and draw pictures of objects that begin with the designated letter.
	Invite the students to write a thank-you note to a visitor to the class.
	Make booklets of dictated stories about a field experience or some exciting adventure of the week.

Figure 7.5 Daily Language and Literacy Opportunities

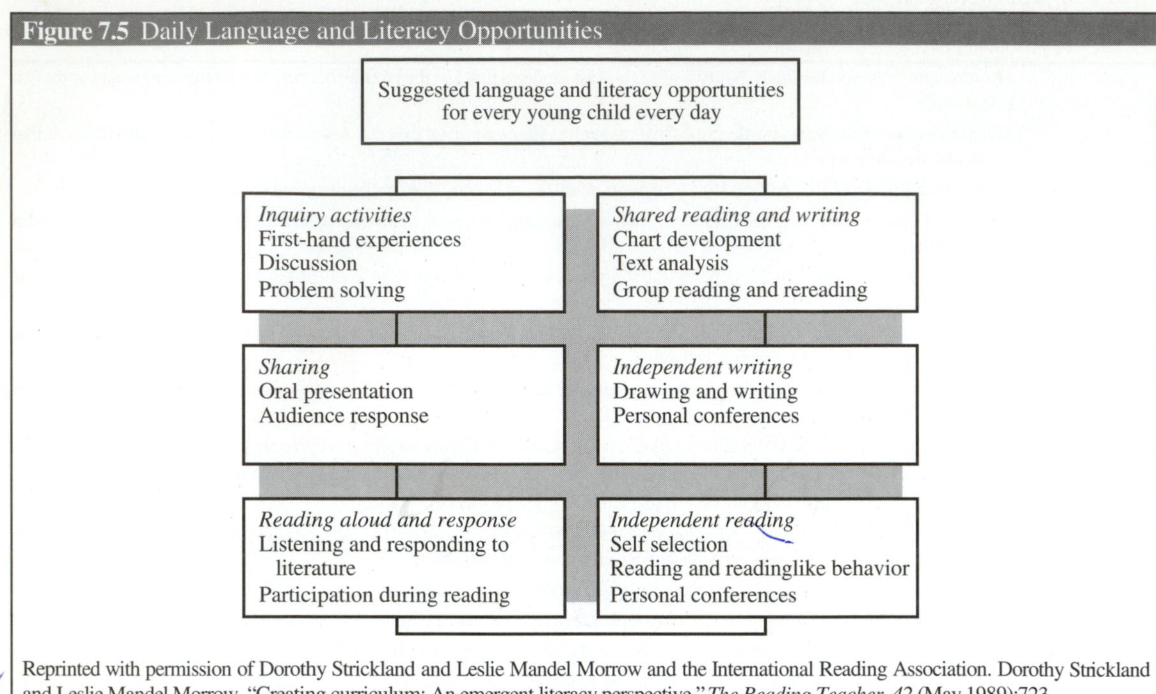

 Dorothy Strickland and Leslie Mandel Morrow, "Creating curriculum: An emergent literacy perspective," *The Reading Teacher*, *42* (May 1989):723.

SUMMARY

Emergent literacy is the foundation for developing the language skills necessary for success in reading and writing. The research and discussions presented in this chapter reiterate this idea in many different ways. The research summaries provided in the discussion of the three categories of literacy development—oral language, reading, and writing—emphasize the need for parents and teachers to assist in providing the necessary language experiences in an interrelated manner.

Language development is affected by the child's home and school environments. Parents are the first teachers who stimulate language and begin literacy development through exposure to print materials. When children enter school, their learning in this new environment is significantly affected by the experiences provided in the home environment.

The assessment information from the previous chapters was related directly to the emergent literacy areas through a chart indicating the most appropriate specific assessment procedures. Appropriate reading activities for emergent literacy were also described.

Applying What You Read

1. You are asked to talk with the kindergarten and first-grade teachers at a local elementary school about the concept of emergent literacy. What would you tell them? Why do we discuss emergent literacy now, rather than prereading skills, when evaluating young children?
2. Design a program for evaluating the language development skills of children entering your first-grade class. Be specific as to the behaviors that you would evaluate.
3. You have been hired as a kindergarten teacher in an inner-city school. How would you begin to determine the needs of your students? In what areas of emergent literacy would you suspect their development would be the weakest? Why?
4. Teachers in your school read to the students and encourage the students to discuss the stories and other daily activities. However, they do not see how writing fits into the scenario of emergent literacy. How would you explain this relationship?
5. Half of the kindergarten and first-grade teachers in your school have "thrown away the basals" and decided to implement a language-based program (using trade books). All of the second-grade teachers use a basal and do not wish to use anything else. How could this situation be resolved in the best interest of the students? Consider that a child could experience two different philosophies in the first two years of school.

NOTES

1. William Teale and Elizabeth Sulzby, *Emergent Literacy: Writing and Reading*.
2. Jana M. Mason and J. Allen, "A Review of Emergent Literacy with Implications for Research and Practice in Reading," in *Review of Research in Education*, edited by E. Z. Rothkopf, pp. 3–47.
3. Dorothy S. Strickland and Lesley Mandel Morrow, "New Perspectives on Young Children Learning to Read and Write," *The Reading Teacher*.
4. Dorothy S. Strickland and Lesley Mandel Morrow, "Assessment and Early Literacy," *The Reading Teacher*.
5. William Teale, Elfrieda Hiebert, and Edward Chittenden, "Assessing Young Children's Literacy Development," *The Reading Teacher*.
6. R. Craig Roney, "Background Experience Is the Foundation of Success in Learning to Read," *The Reading Teacher*.
7. Marie Clay, *The Early Detection of Reading Difficulties: An Assessment Survey*.
8. L. A. Kaster, N. L. Roser, and J. V. Hoffman, "Understandings of the Forms and Functions of Written Language: Insights from Children and Parents," in *Research in Literacy: Merging Perspectives*, edited by J. E. Readence and R. S. Baldwin pp. 85–92; Marilyn M. Manning and Gary L. Manning, "Early Readers and Nonreaders from Low Socioeconomic Environments: What Their Parents Report," *The Reading Teacher*; Lesley Mandel Morrow, "Home and School Correlates of Early Interest in Literature," *Journal of Educational Research*.
9. Jill Fitzgerald, Dixie Lee Spiegel, and James W. Cunningham, "The Relationship Between Parental Literacy Level and Perceptions of Emergent Literacy," *Journal of Reading Behavior*.
10. Roney, "Background Experience Is the Foundation."
11. Anne H. Dyson, "N Spell My Grandmama: Fostering Early Thinking about Print," *The Reading Teacher*.
12. M. A. K. Halliday, *Learning How to Mean: Exploration in the Development of Language*, pp. 19–21.
13. Roney, "Background Experience Is the Foundation."
14. Elizabeth Sulzby, "Children's Emergent Reading of Favorite Storybooks: A Developmental Study," *Reading Research Quarterly*.
15. Roney, "Background Experience Is the Foundation."
16. Walter Loban, *The Language of Elementary School Children*; Dorothy Strickland, "Black Is Beautiful vs. White Is Right," *Elementary English*.

17. J. Britton, *Language and Learning*.
18. Kenneth Goodman, "Let's Dump the Up-Tight Model in English," *Elementary School Journal*.
19. Carol Chomsky, *The Acquisition of Syntax in Children from 5 to 10*.
20. Dorothy S. Strickland and Lesley Mandel Morrow, "Reading, Writing, and Oral Language," *The Reading Teacher*.
21. Linda K. Crafton, *Standards in Practice: Grades K–2*.
22. Thomas C. Barrett, "The Relationship between the Measures of Pre-Reading Visual Discrimination and First-Grade Achievement: A Review of the Literature," *Reading Research Quarterly*; Albert J. Harris, "Practical Applications of Reading Research," *The Reading Teacher*; Robert E. Liebert and John K. Sherk, "Three Frostig Visual Perception Sub-Tests and Specific Reading Tasks for Kindergarten, First, and Second Grade Children," *The Reading Teacher*; Arthur V. Olson and Clifford I. Johnson, "Structure and Predictive Validity of the Frostig Developmental Test of Visual Perception in Grades One and Three," *Journal of Special Education*; Edward Paradis, "The Appropriateness of Visual Discrimination Exercise in Reading Readiness Materials," *Journal of Educational Research*.
23. Dolores Durkin, *Teaching Them to Read*, 3rd ed., pp. 181–82; Lloyd Ollila, "Reading: Preparing the Child," in *Reading: Foundations and Instructional Strategies*, edited by Posel Lamb and Richard Arnold.
24. Marilyn Jager Adams, *Beginning to Read: Thinking and Learning about Print*, p. 43.
25. D. C. Ohnmacht, "The Effects of Letter Knowledge on Achievement in Reading in the First Grade," in *Reading Research Revisited*, edited by L. M. Gentile, M. L. Kamil, and J. S. Blanchard, pp. 141–42.
26. Adams, *Beginning to Read*, p. 54.
27. Donald J. Richgels, Karla J. Poremba, and Lea M. McGee, "Kindergarteners Talk about Print: Phonemic Awareness in Meaningful Contexts," *The Reading Teacher*.
28. Adams, *Beginning to Read*, p. 54.
29. Hallie Kay Yopp, "A Test for Assessing Phonemic Awareness in Young Children," *The Reading Teacher*.
30. Hallie Kay Yopp, "Read-Aloud Books for Developing Phonemic Awareness," *The Reading Teacher*.
31. Henry P. Smith and Emerald V. Dechant, *Psychology in Teaching Reading*.
32. Richard C. Anderson, Elfrieda H. Hiebert, Judith A. Scott, and Ian A. G. Wilkinson, *Becoming a Nation of Readers*; Carol Chomsky, "Stages in Language Development and Reading Exposure," *Harvard Educational Review*; Dolores Durkin, *Children Who Read Early: Two Longitudinal Studies*.
33. Lesley Mandel Morrow, *Literacy Development in the Early Years*; G. J. Whitehurst, F. Falco, C. J. Lonigan, J. E. Fischal, B. D. DeBaryshe, M. C. Valdez-Manchaca, and M. Caulfield, "Accelerating Language Development through Picturebook Reading," *Developmental Psychology*.
34. William H. Teale, "Home Background and Young Children's Literacy Development," in *Emergent Literacy: Writing and Reading*, edited by W. H. Teale and E. Sulzby.
35. Adams, *Beginning to Read*, p. 47.
36. Victoria Purcell-Gates, Ellen McIntyre, and Penny A Freppon, "Learning Written Storybook Language in School: A Comparison of Low-SES Children in Skills-Based and Whole Language Classrooms," *American Educational Research Journal*.
37. Martha D. Collins, "How Do Three-Year-Olds Select Favorite Books?" Paper presented at College Reading Association, Philadelphia, PA, October 1989.
38. Martha D. Collins, "Reading Interests of Five-Year-Olds: Effects of Language Development," in progress.
39. P. David Pearson and Linda Fielding, "Research Update: Listening Comprehension," *Language Arts*.
40. Ibid.
41. Tom G. Sticht, I. J. Beck, R. N. Hanke, G. M. Kleiman, and J. H. James, *Auding and Reading: A Developmental Model*.
42. Leo M. Schell, "The Validity of the Potential Level Via Listening Comprehension: A Cautionary Note," *Reading Psychology*.
43. Ramon Ross, "A Look at Listeners," *Elementary School Journal*.

44. Martin Deutsch et al., *Communication of Information in the Elementary School Classroom.*
45. Ann D. Clark and Charlotte J. Richards, "Auditory Discrimination among Economically Disadvantaged and Nondisadvantaged Preschool Children," *Exceptional Children.*
46. Lea M. McGee and Donald J. Richgels, *Learning How to Mean: Exploration in the Development of Language*, pp. 70–82.
47. Lesley M. Morrow, "Home and School Correlates of Early Interest in Literature," *Journal of Educational Research;* William H. Teale, "Positive Environments for Learning to Read: What Studies of Early Readers Tell Us," *Language Arts*; Denny Taylor, *Family Literacy*.
48. Lesley Mandel Morrow, "Relationships between Literature Programs, Library Corner Designs, and Children's Use of Literature," *Journal of Educational Research*; J. A. Schickedanz and M. Sullivan, "Mom, What Does U-F-F Spell?" *Language Arts*; M. Clark, *Young Fluent Readers*.
49. Durkin, *Children Who Read Early*; Schickedanz and Sullivan, "Mom, What Does U-F-F Spell?"; Shirley B. Heath, *Ways with Words: Language, Life, and Work in Communities and Classrooms*; Shirley B. Heath and C. Thomas, "The Achievement of Preschool Literacy for Mother and Child," in *Awakening to Literacy*, edited by H. Goelman, A. A. Oberg, and F. Smith, pp. 51–72; H. J. Leichter, "Families as Environments for Literacy," *Awakening to Literacy*, edited by H. Goelman, A. A. Oberg, and F. Smith, pp. 38–50.
50. David B. Yaden, Jr., and Lea M. McGee, "Reading as a Meaning Seeking Activity: What Children's Questions Reveal," in *Thirty-Third Yearbook of the National Reading Conference,* edited by Jerry Niles, pp. 101–109; R. Gundlach, J. B. McLane, F. M. Scott, and G. D. McNamee, "The Social Foundations of Children's Early Writing Development," in *Advances in Writing Research: Vol. 1 Children's Early Writing Development,* edited by M. Farr, pp. 1–58.
51. N. E. Dunn, "Children's Achievement at School-Entry as a Function of Mothers' and Fathers' Teaching Sets," *Elementary School Journal*; Marcia Baghban, *Our Daughter Learns to Read and Write: A Case Study from Birth to Three*; C. E. Snow, "Literacy and Language: Relationships During the Preschool Years," *Harvard Educational Review*; J. C. Harste, C. I. Burke, and V. A. Woodward, *Children, Their Language and World: Initial Encounters with Print.*
52. A. Ninio, "Picture Book Reading in Mother Infant Dyads Belonging to Two Subgroups in Israel," *Child Development*; E. Hiebert and C. Adams, "Fathers' and Mothers' Perceptions of Their Preschool Children's Emergent Literacy," *Journal of Experimental Child Psychology*.
53. Jeanne M. Burns and Martha D. Collins, "Parents' Perceptions of Factors Affecting the Reading Development of Intellectually Superior Accelerated Readers and Intellectually Superior Nonreaders," *Reading Research and Instruction*.
54. Donald H. Graves, *Writing: Teachers and Children at Work.*
55. Robert D. Aukerman, *Approaches to Beginning Reading*, 2nd ed.; M. A. Evans and T. H. Carr, "Cognitive Abilities, Conditions of Learning, and the Early Development of Reading Skill," *Reading Research Quarterly*.
56. Maria Montessori, *The Secret of Childhood.*
57. Durkin, *Children Who Read Early,* p. 137.
58. Reggie Routman and Donna Maxim, "Invented Spelling: What It Is and What It Isn't," *School Talk.*
59. Carol Chomsky, "Approaching Reading through Invented Spelling," in *Theory and Practice of Early Reading*, edited by L. B. Resnick and P. A. Weaver, pp. 43–65.
60. L. K. Clarke, "Invented Versus Traditional Spelling in First Graders' Writing: Effects on Learning to Spell and Read," *Research in the Teaching of English*.

CHAPTER 8

Word Identification

Word analysis, decoding, word identification, word processing, word recognition. As Mr. Langwell thinks about his years in teaching, he realizes that all of these terms refer to a set of skills used to determine how a set of printed symbols is pronounced to form a word to which a meaning can be associated. Researchers and practitioners in reading and language literacy use these different terms to communicate a category of skills that include sight word knowledge, phonic analysis, contextual analysis, and structural analysis.

At Twin Lakes School, word identification receives considerable attention in the classroom and, as in other communities, this skill area is the most controversial among the public. Teachers and parent too often associate good reading with good word identification. Thus, much classroom time is given to the development of word identification skills, with little time remaining for the other reading areas, such as comprehension and study skills. This concerns many teachers at Twin Lakes because teachers at the upper grades see many students who are good word callers, but who have little understanding of what they read or how to apply their reading skills in their content studies.

Just last year at Twin Lakes School there was a public controversy regarding word identification that centered on whether students should be taught to read through the use of phonics or the look-say, or sight, approach Teachers spend much time helping parents understand that learning to recognize words is not a matter of learning one set of skills over another, but involves learning to use all of the word identification skills, as appropriate.

Because of the importance of this area and the widespread lack of understanding of the various word identification skills, the teachers at Twin Lakes School asked Ms. Gross to lead a faculty team to address the following questions, which are discussed in Chapter 8.

- What are the word identification skills?
- What does research say about the development of word identification?

- How does the teacher assist students in learning to use the various word identification strategies?
- What are some basic principles for teaching this area?
- Which assessment instruments are most appropriate for use in this area?
- What activities can be used in developing word identification skills?

Vocabulary to Know

- **Accent**
- **Affix**
- **Analytic phonics**
- **Automaticity**
- **Compound words**
- **Consonant cluster**
- **Consonants**
- **Context clue**
- **Contextual analysis**
- **Contractions**
- **Inflectional ending**
- **Phoneme-grapheme correspondences**
- **Phonic analysis**
- **Picture clue**
- **Prefix**
- **Sight words**
- **Structural analysis**
- **Suffix**
- **Syllables**
- **Synthetic phonics**
- **Variant patterns**
- **Vowels**
- **Word identification**

WORD IDENTIFICATION AND READING

Students enter school with a speaking and listening vocabulary that is as extensive as their background experiences and that exceeds their reading vocabulary. To develop a reading vocabulary, students must be taught to recognize printed words. Thus, teachers in the primary grades help students to acquire the strategies necessary to identify words, while teachers at higher levels extend and reinforce the application of these strategies.

Before beginning a discussion of the four areas of word identification, a broader issue needs to be considered: whether word identification should be developed via a whole-language process or through the teaching of word identification skills. Without question, young children develop an awareness of print through their experiences. For example, trips to the grocery store develop an awareness of labels, which leads to the identification of words such as *peanut butter*. As children listen to nursery rhymes and stories, they memorize the order of the words, the sounds, and the unique features of a word, and start to recognize words in print. Reading this "talk written down" goes further as parents and teachers write down the words and sentences spoken by young children and encourage them to read "their story." This whole-language approach to decoding words is recommended by proponents of naturalistic reading who say that reading will occur as children are exposed to print in meaningful situations. Goodman and Goodman and Jana Mason suggest that awareness of print in the environment is the first stage children pass through when developing written language abilities.[1]

Children who seem to read naturally prior to entering school have been studied to determine how they develop their decoding process. A number of studies[2] found that these accelerated young readers had been given some instruction to develop letter, sound, and word concepts and encouraged to respond during story-reading episodes. Thus, some word identification instruction appears to help these natural readers to focus on the necessary features of print. Beginning reading instruction cannot be viewed as either a whole-language process or strictly skills instruction. Parents and teachers must begin with the child's language and relate new words to known language. Word identification instruction in the areas of sight word vocabulary, phonic analysis, structural analysis, and contextual analysis is not going to leave the school curriculum, nor should it. However, teachers must provide appropriate instruction in these areas using the child's language as a basis, and realize that some readers develop their own system of decoding while others need more structured instruction.

In developing word identification skills, teachers assist students in learning a variety of techniques so they are prepared to decode unknown words (see Figure 8.1). Students must develop a sight word knowledge consisting of the words they see most frequently in their reading. Readers of all ages continuously expand their sight word knowledge as words are added to their reading vocabulary. However, initially students begin with a limited sight vocabulary consisting of words that cannot be decoded by any other procedure except memory. Another procedure that students are taught to use in recognizing words is phonics. Phonics knowledge involves learning to associate specific phonemes, or sounds, with the appropriate graphemes, or symbols. Phonic analysis is one procedure for recognizing unknown words, but this is not the only strategy needed for adequate word identification. Structural analysis skills are taught as another way of decoding unknown words. These strategies help the students to look at word parts such as syllables, affixes, contractions, and compound words to determine the correct pronunciation. Contextual analysis skills use the meaning of the phrase, sentence, or passage in conjunction with the other word identification skills to decode the unknown word. Using all of these strategies, students are able to recognize the many words they see in reading material.

Learning to identify the many words in the English language is complicated by many factors. One major factor is the language itself. Because our language is composed of so many other languages and dialects, students often encounter difficulties understanding the irregularities of English. This problem looms larger for the student in a program that teaches phonic analysis as the primary word identification strategy. Thus, word identification instruction should provide a variety of strategies to help students decode words in the English language.

Figure 8.1 Word Identification Skill Areas

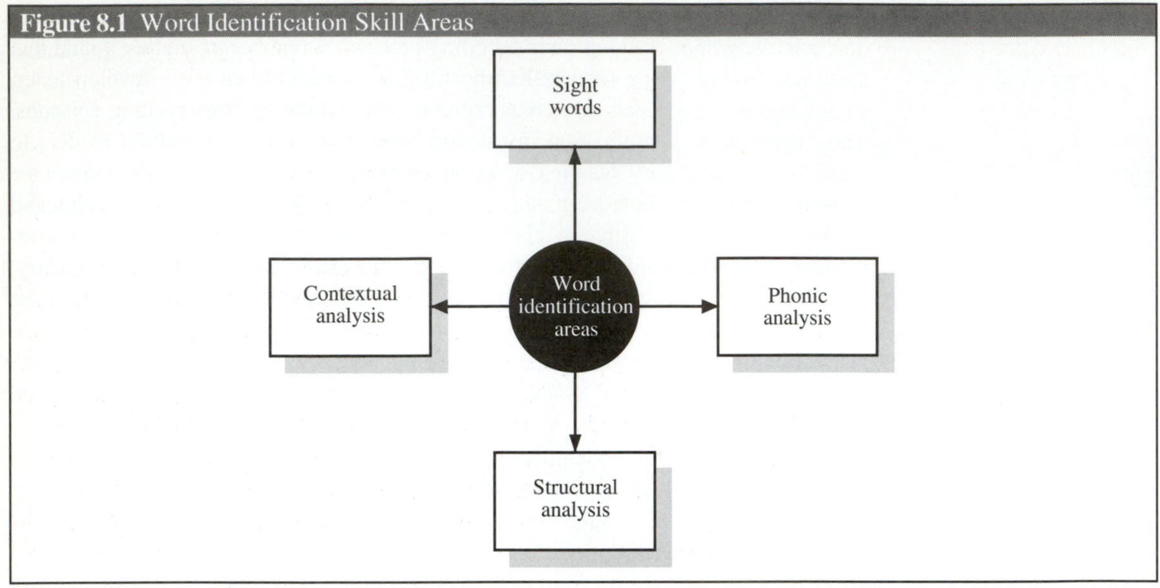

There are many factors that affect reading development, including intelligence, environment, and maturation. These factors need to be considered as the teacher provides instruction in the word identification skills. Intelligence, or the mental age of the student, has an impact on readiness for beginning to learn the various word identification skills. Parents and teachers realize that reaching the chronological age of 6 does not automatically indicate that the student is ready for instruction in the word identification strategies taught in reading.

Readiness for learning the word identification skills is also affected by environmental factors. As discussed in the previous chapter, many prereading skills are developed before formal reading instruction is begun. These are frequently started in the home, but when students do not develop some skills in auditory and visual discrimination prior to entering school, this instruction is provided in school. Many students who enter school with these deficiencies seem to have difficulty overcoming them and learning the various word identification skills. The difficulty stems from a home environment that has not stimulated language or provided experiences that motivate learning and interest in reading. This factor is further complicated when teachers do not consider the impact of environment on language development and fail to expand language as words are taught.

Maturation is another factor affecting the development of word identification skills. In addition to physical and emotional maturation, maturation in terms of speech or language development also plays an influential role in this process. Students who are unable to pronounce a sound, or who cannot auditorially distinguish certain sounds in the language, often have immature speech patterns. This immaturity in speech may make learning phonics difficult; thus, the teacher emphasizes other word identification strategies, such as sight vocabulary, while developing the speech skills.

Another element to be considered in providing effective instruction in this area is the learning style of the student. Most students learn equally well through the visual or auditory modes. For this reason, students are taught to use a variety of word identification skills to unlock words. However, some students have perception, or discrimination, problems that create difficulty in using either the visual or auditory mode in learning. These are not acuity difficulties but perception problems that cannot be physically corrected. Teachers must note these difficulties and adjust instruction accordingly. Students with strength in the visual mode and weakness in the auditory mode experience more success in learning words by sight, or the look-say method. Conversely, students with strength in the auditory mode and weakness in the visual mode can learn to sound out words using phonics. To assist these students in learning words, teachers may need to use the VAKT method discussed in Chapter 6.

Developing word identification skills is a complex process often complicated by the factors of maturation, learning styles, environment, and intelligence. Teachers who consider these factors to be important in learning to identify words have begun appropriate teaching. The following sections present a more in-depth discussion of the word identification areas along with a summary of research findings that affect reading instruction.

Sight Word Knowledge

Using sight word knowledge to identify words is a common method for teaching beginning reading. The look-say method is based on the premise that the student is taught to recognize words by sight rather than through an analytic process such as phonics or structural analysis. However, as a procedure for word identification, sight word knowledge means remembering words that occur most frequently in reading and are not easily analyzed through other procedures.

Teachers usually associate sight word knowledge with the Dolch Basic Sight Word List, the Fry New Instant Word List, or the word lists that accompany the basal series. These lists are composed of high-frequency words that should be identified quickly in order not to slow the reading rate and interfere with comprehension. Sight words are taught as whole units. Later, these words may be analyzed in parts (using analytic phonics) to help students recognize other words with similar components.

Teachers often find that students have difficulty remembering the more abstract words included on many sight word lists. In a study regarding the learning of words that were high in visual imagery as compared to words low in visual imagery (abstract words), Hargis and Gickling found that high-imagery words were easier to learn than low-imagery words and were remembered longer. Studies by Jorm and by Kolker and Terwilliger had similar results, indicating that both good and poor readers' memory of words is enhanced by word imagery.[3] Classroom teachers experience more difficulty in teaching these low-imagery words, such as *was* and *the*, than they do the high-imagery words, such as *cat*, or *mother,* and nouns that can be visualized.

Word identification strategies are developed individually, in groups, or with the total class as needed.

Photo courtesy of Edward B. Lasher.

Teachers also realize that words with similar shapes and sounds seem more difficult for the students to remember. McNeil and Keislar found that students had greater difficulty identifying test words that were similar in letter configuration.[4] Thus, teachers should provide much variety and repetition in helping students learn low-imagery words that are similar in sound and shape. The most common groups include words such as *who*, *what*, *where*, *was*, *when*, *were*, *the*, *this*, *them*, *then*, *that*, *there*, *these*, and *those*.

To assist in learning these essential but difficult words, teachers use many different strategies. King and Muehl found that the appropriate methods for teaching sight words varied with the similarity of the words.[5] Cues such as pictures were helpful in remembering similar words. The use of auditory or visual cues provided faster learning of the similar words but had little impact on learning words that were not similar.

Many research studies suggest that sight words should be taught in the context of other words.[6] This idea, however, is refuted by Singer, Samuels, and Spiroff, who conclude that "efficiency in learning to associate responses to graphic stimuli is significantly greater when the word is presented in isolation than when presented in sentence context or in association with a picture, or both."[7]

As teachers, the authors have found that students tend to remember the more abstract words better when they are presented in the context of a sentence. This technique of learning sight words combines sight word recognition with contextual analysis and places the word in the context of normal reading. This seems to be a more realistic way of learning sight words. In practice activities with these sight words, flash cards should include context clues such as phrases or sentences with the word underlined for emphasis. *Was* and *saw* look less similar in "I saw your dog yesterday."

When introducing new sight vocabulary, teacher-student discussions help the student focus on the word, assist in clarifying misconceptions of meaning, and tend to improve memory of the word. Using an inductive procedure to introduce a new word involves providing a sentence with the new word underlined. Students then provide their pronunciations and definitions of the word and the teacher can raise questions to clarify their understanding, leading to an appropriate response. This procedure focuses attention on the word and aids the students in expanding their vocabulary.

Further research regarding sight word learning has investigated the correlation of the interest of the words with the speed of learning. Harris concluded that kindergarten children from low socioeconomic backgrounds learned high-interest words and words not of high interest equally well. However, Braun found significant differences favoring interest-loading of words for both boys and girls.[8]

In developing knowledge of sight words, teachers may wish to consider the results of a study by Lahey and Drabman.[9] Using token reinforcement consisting of verbal feedback and tokens that could be exchanged for pennies, they found that the no-token subjects took about twice as long to learn the words as did the token group. This technique could be adapted to help students learn the more difficult sight words. In a study of the use of games to reinforce sight vocabulary, Dickerson found that games serve as better reinforcements than worksheets, and that those games involving the most movement were more effective than the more passive games.[10] Using these various procedures to teach and reinforce sight vocabulary will enhance word identification.

Teachers realize that most words become a part of a student's sight vocabulary as students become more experienced readers. Initially, sight word learning involves primarily the Dolch Basic Sight Word List or a similar list, along with words from the students' environment; however, other words are continually added. Although there has been some debate during the last 15 years as to whether the Dolch Basic Sight Word List is useful as a valid core list,[11] Johns, Edmond, and Mavrogenes have found that this list still accounts for more than 55% of the words used in materials written for students in grades 3 through 9.[12]

Though the research seems inconclusive as to exactly how sight words should be taught, teachers need to consider these findings in relation to individual student needs and develop instructional procedures accordingly. Students need good visual discrimination skills in order to see likenesses and differences in the sight words. Moreover, it is helpful if the student knows the names of the letters, so that specific letter differences in words can be discussed.

Much practice is necessary to remember sight words. How much practice is needed for students to achieve "automaticity?" It varies from student to student and from word to word.[13]

In beginning reading instruction, teachers sometimes encourage students to focus on words by noting clues that distinguish the words. One such procedure involves noting word shape or configuration to call attention to unique features and to aid in distinguishing between two confusing words. This crutch may be useful for some troublesome words; however, it should not be regarded as a primary strategy for teaching sight words. Similarly, colors have been used as clues for helping students note the difference in long and short vowel sounds (i.e., red for the long vowel sound and blue for the short vowel sound). This is not a good technique because students tend to rely on the color clues, and when they see the words in print without the colors, there is no transfer of learning.

Many follow-up games and activities are needed to reinforce the initial teaching activity. (Specific ideas are provided later in the chapter.) Other word identification strategies such as phonic, structural, and contextual analysis are necessary in expanding sight vocabulary. The best strategy for expanding and reinforcing sight vocabulary is practice: read, Read, READ. As Durkin suggests, "a sizable sight vocabulary is one of the most important instructional outcomes in the beginning years."[14]

Phonic Analysis

Phonics is the association of phonemes or sounds with graphemes or symbols. Since the publication of *Why Johnny Can't Read* and *Learning to Read: The Great Debate*, both teachers and the public have renewed their interest in phonics instruction.[15] Prior to this, instruction in the word identification skills had turned from phonics to the look-say, or sight, method. The basic issue in the debate over the teaching of word identification was not whether to teach phonics, but rather whether beginning reading should be taught through the use of synthetic or analytic phonics. As discussed in Chapter 6, analytic phonics begins by teaching an entire word and then teaching the sounds within the word. Synthetic phonics is taught by presenting the isolated sounds in the word and blending them to form the entire word.

The findings of Chall's research indicated that a mode-emphasis method using intensive synthetic phonics produced better results than the teaching of analytic phonics, and similar findings were reported by Bond and Dykstra in First-Grade Studies.[16] However, further follow-up research by Dykstra showed that by the second grade the students taught through a synthetic method were not superior in reading comprehension.[17]

Becoming a Nation of Readers, a report from the Commission on Reading, lead to another wave of interest in phonics. The two recommendations regarding phonics instruction were the only recommendations made about word identification instruction.

- Teachers of beginning reading should present well-designed phonics instruction.
- Reading primers should be interesting and comprehensive and give children opportunities to apply phonics.[18]

Many interpreted the report as suggesting a return to structured phonics instruction and the exclusion of other word identification skills. The authors warn against such a literal interpretation of the recommendations of this report and strongly urge teachers to use a variety of techniques for identifying words. For an in-depth examination of phonics instruction, teachers may wish to read a recent article in which Beck and Juel discuss the role of decoding in learning to read.[19]

Regardless of the method used for teaching phonics, the teacher must be cognizant of the research regarding what should be taught. Although basal materials and phonics texts present some organization of phonics skills, there is no one best sequence or hierarchy.

Each reading text or basal reading series has its own philosophy about phonics instruction. An analytic approach is used in some materials while others emphasize synthetic phonics. Some present phonics instruction as a part of the readiness or preprimer materials while other materials do not introduce phonics until the first reader. There is also a discrepancy as to how much is introduced at each level and whether consonants or vowels (long or short) are presented first. In considering the development of phonics skills, Boyd found that the most rapid growth in phonics was at the second and third grades, while development at the higher grades was slower.[20] Thus, some sequence for teaching phonic analysis must be followed during the first two or three years of school to provide continuity.

Cunningham's review of recent brain research suggests that the brain functions not as a rule applier but as a pattern detector. She recommends "rime" as the pattern most helpful for decoding one-syllable words. The following list of 37 rimes account for almost 500 primary words.[21]

ack	ap	est	ing	ot
ail	ash	ice	ink	uck
ain	at	ick	ip	ug
ake	ate	ide	it	ump
ale	aw	ight	ock	unk
ame	ay	ill	oke	
an	eat	in	op	
ank	ell	ine	ore	

Routman and Butler also suggest that the use of onset rimes can aid children in recognizing words.[22] The "onset" is the part of the syllable that precedes the vowel and is always a consonant, consonant blend, or consonant digraph. The "rime" is the rest of the unit. Onsets and rimes help students read and write because they are easier to learn than individual vowel sounds. Phonic patterns remain stable and word families are easily used for reading and writing. Gunning suggests a similar strategy for teaching phonics through word building.[23] In this variation, the teacher and the students build a series of words by starting with the core of a word pattern and adding onsets to rimes. For example, *at* (adding *s*) becomes *sat*. *S* is the onset and *at* is the rime, or pattern.

Students at the upper levels not only learn phonics at a slower rate but also seem to lose some phonics skills that were previously learned. Plattor and Woestehoff found that performance on tests of skills such as letter sounds and rhyming word knowledge seemed to decrease as students advanced from grade 3 to 6, yet reading performance remained good.[24] This finding has significant implications for reading programs and state testing programs. Students at the upper levels may reveal deficiencies in the phonics skills because they have already internalized them into their reading practices and have no use for the isolated skills. A need for additional instruction is not always indicated.

In teaching analytic phonics, rules or generalizations are presented to assist the student. Clymer identified some 45 generalizations that were presented in reading materials. He found only 18 of them to be useful according to the specified criteria. Further research concerning these generalizations by Emans and Bailey each drew similar conclusions.[25] In a replication of Clymer's study using more recent reading materials, Collins suggests that the generalizations in Table 8.1 are appropriate.[26] Spache identified 121 different phonics rules in the literature and found that the following rules meet the usefulness criteria at least 75% of the time.

- *Vowels*. When *y* is the final letter in a word, it usually has a vowel sound. When there is one *e* in a word that ends in a consonant, the *e* usually has a short sound.
- *Vowel digraphs*. In these double-vowel combinations—*oa*, *ay*, *ai*, *ee*—the first vowel is usually long and the second silent.
- *Vowel with r*. The *r* gives the preceding vowel a sound that is neither long nor short (true also for vowel with *l* or *w*).
- *Consonants*. When *c* and *h* are next to each other, they form only one sound. *Ch* is usually pronounced as in *kitchen*, *catch*, and *chair*, not as *sh*. When the letter c is followed by *o* or *a*, the sound of *k* is likely to be heard. When *c* is followed by *e* or *i*, the sound of *s* is likely to be heard. When two of the same consonants are side by side, only one is heard.[27]

The usefulness of teaching specific rules has been further researched. Hillerich found that students taught vowel rules showed no superiority in word recognition and were, in fact, inferior in reading comprehension when compared with students who had been taught first to discriminate short and long vowel sounds. Harris, Serwer and Gold suggest a negative correlation between the time devoted to instruction in phonics and the performance in comprehension. In addition, the second- and fifth-grade students in Glass and Burton's study made practically no use of phonics rules in decoding unfamiliar words; yet the teaching of these rules continues to be a major portion of the reading instruction in many schools.[28]

As reading educators have analyzed the findings of research in phonics, they have realized the importance of the work of the linguists. Although many of the phonics generalizations seem to be relatively useless in decoding the English language, Hanna and Moore found English to be 86.9 percent phonetic.[29] Linguists approach the teaching of decoding through the association of letter patterns with sound patterns. Individual sounds are not analyzed as in traditional phonics. Additionally, linguists are concerned with the language process involved in decoding words, rather than just the sound and pronunciation of words. Decoding, as defined by the linguist, includes finding meaning.

Table 8.1 Generalizations Taught in Basal Reading Materials in Grades 1 through 6 (% utility)

Generalization	% utility
Vowels	
A vowel between two consonants in a word produces a short sound. The pattern CVC and CVCC produce the short V sound.	50
Two or more consonants between vowels suggests that the first vowel represents the short sound.	95
One vowel sound can be represented by many spellings.	100
An *e* at the end of a word, and the only vowel in the word, represents the long *e* sound.	86
In words with two or more syllables that end with letter *y*, the *y* usually stands for the long *e* sound.	93
Two vowel letters can stand for one vowel sound.	77
If the letter *a* stands for the long vowel sound, the letter *e* at the end of the word is a marker to indicate that in these words the letter *a* stands for the long vowel sound.	99
The letters *ai* and *ay* also represent the long *a* sound.	83
When *o* is followed by a *w*, the *o* and the *w* together sometimes stand for the sound you hear in *flow* and *how*.	99
The two letters *o* and *a* together stand for a single vowel sound.	100
The two vowel letters *ea* usually stand for the sound of short *e*.	77
The two vowel letters *oo* represent one sound in the middle or end of a word.	99
The letter *r* following a vowel letter changes the vowel sound represented by that letter.	93
Unstressed vowels usually have the schwa sound.	100
Consonants	
Two letters in the English language can represent one sound.	100
The *ch* spelling for the sound *ch* may occur at the beginning, middle, or end but *tch* comes generally at the end of the word and the *t* in the middle of the word.	
ch for *ch*—beginning, middle, end	99
tch for *ch*—end	82
t for *ch*—middle	88
The letter *c* can represent two sounds. The sound of *s* as in celery and *k* as in *came*.	98
The letter *g* is followed by *e*, *i*, or *y* usually stands for the sound heard in *gem*. When *g* is followed by *a*, *o*, or *u* it usually stands for the sound heard in *game*.	
g followed by *e, i*, or *y*	84
g followed by *a, o*, or *u*	90
The letter *qu* represents the sound heard in *quite*.	94
A consonant cluster is two or more consonant letters commonly blended.	95
Digraphs consist of two letters that represent one sound.	91
The *c* spelling and the *k* spelling for *ck* may appear at the beginning, middle, or end of a word, while the *ck* may appear at the middle or end.	
c/k for *ck*—beginning, middle, end	100
ck for *ck*—middle, end	100
Syllabication	
The number of vowel sounds in a word represent the number of syllables found in that word.	100
A word with a vowel followed by two consonant letters and another vowel letter, the syllables are usually divided between the two consonants.	86
A word has a vowel followed by a single consonant letter and another vowel letter is usually divided after the first vowel letter. The first vowel letter represents the long sound.	65
When the second syllable of a word ends in *le*, the word is divided between the vowel and the consonant preceding the *le*.	33

Martha D. Collins, "Evaluating Basals: Do They Teach Phonics Generalizations?" in *Evaluation in Reading-Learning-Teaching-Administering, Sixth Yearbook of the American Reading Forum.* Muncie, IN: Ball State University Press, 1986.

Research by linguists regarding the teaching of phoneme-grapheme correspondences is extensive. Bloomfield and Barnhart suggest that the beginning reader should be given material designed for teaching the orthographic-phonic regularities of English and that irregular relationships should be introduced later.[30] Contrary to this belief, Levin and Watson and Joanna P. Williams have suggested that multiple phoneme-grapheme correspondences should be introduced early in reading instruction in order to develop a more useful problem-solving approach to reading.[31]

Research in the areas of phonics and linguistics is quite extensive. As linguists and reading specialists work together, the vast amount of knowledge regarding the teaching of sound-symbol relationships is being translated into classroom practice. With renewed emphasis on phonics instruction, textbook publishers and researchers have incorporated the ideas of linguists into materials to help the beginning reader develop more successful word identification skills.

Regardless of approach, phonics, like all other reading skills, should be taught directly through teacher demonstration of how the strategy is used. Specifically, as teachers introduce new vocabulary words, a system of decoding should be taught. Show how the vowel sounds are analyzed, the ways the consonants and vowels work together to represent various sounds, and how phonic analysis is used with other word identification skills to decode a new word. The learning of phonics should be a realistic process, developed through the application of appropriate principles as needed to decode words.

Structural Analysis

Structural analysis relies on the use of word elements or parts to recognize unknown words. Skills such as syllabication, using prefixes and suffixes, and recognizing contractions and compound words are included in this area. Structural analysis differs from phonic analysis in that larger meaningful units, or morphemes, are dealt with by critically examining the structure of the word.

As in other areas of word identification, the research is inconclusive. The skill area that has received the most attention is syllabication. In the studies done by Clymer,[32] Emans,[33] and Bailey,[34] eight generalizations were identified that related to syllabication. Six of these met the criteria of 75% usefulness:

- In most two-syllable words, the first syllable is accented.
- If *a*, *in*, *re*, *ex*, *de*, or *be* is the first syllable in a word, it is usually unaccented.
- In most two-syllable words that end in a consonant followed by *y*, the first syllable is accented.
- If the last syllable of a word ends in *le*, the consonant preceding the *le* usually begins the last syllable.
- When the first vowel element in a word is followed by *th*, *ch*, or *sh*, these symbols are not broken when the word is divided into syllables and may go with either the first or second syllable.
- When the last syllable is the sound *r*, it is unaccented.

In a review of current basal reading materials, Collins found the following principles of syllabication to exist in at least three of the five series reviewed.

- The number of vowel sounds in the word represent the number of syllables found in that word.
- When the second syllable of a word ends in *le*, the two syllables are divided between the vowel and the consonant preceding the *le*. (Clymer found 97% utility.)
- When a word has a vowel followed by a single consonant letter and another vowel letter, divide the word after the first vowel letter. (Clymer found 44% utility.)
- When a word has a vowel followed by two consonants and another vowel, the syllables are usually divided between the two consonants. (Clymer found 72% utility.)[35]

Syllabication seems to be a skill that is better used after the student can pronounce the word, rather than as an aid in pronunciation.[36] Courtney reinforces this belief as he notes that syllabication principles are of decreasing value above the elementary grades because of the increase in exceptions.[37] Canney and Schreiner found that intensive instruction in syllabication did not improve the word attack or reading comprehension skills of second graders, although the students could verbalize and apply the syllabication principles being taught.[38]

A study by Marzano et al. raises additional questions regarding the use of syllabication as a word recognition device.[39] Comparing gains in syllabication and comprehension in middle-school students, the authors found little correlation.

Harris and Sipay believe that syllabication knowledge can provide students with some guidelines for dividing polysyllabic words into units that can be analyzed phonetically.[40] Gleitman and Rozin advocate the use of the syllable as a unit for initial acquisition in reading, although this idea is not supported by researchers such as Goodman.[41]

In considering syllabication, one must also address the use of accents. Winkley studied the various accent generalizations and identified seven general conclusions that apply to multisyllabic words.[42] Harris and Sipay identify only two accent generalizations as important for teaching:

- The first syllable in a two-syllable word is usually accented.
- Affixes are usually not accented.

They further suggest that the good reader primarily uses trial and error in determining the appropriate syllable to accent.[43]

In research regarding other structural analysis skills, Spache questions the teaching of isolated prefixes, suffixes, and roots because these units vary within the context of the word, and students seem to use these analytic skills infrequently.[44] Thus, it is suggested that these elements be taught primarily as visual units or letter clusters.

Schell and McFeely reviewed the various areas of structural analysis and caution teachers that these skills must be taught in a realistic reading situation, rather than as isolated or independent rules.[45]

The instructional sequence of structural analysis skills in reading materials is organized in many different ways. One possible sequence is (a) inflectional endings, (b) compound words, (c) prefixes, (d) suffixes, and (e) contractions. Of course, within each of these categories subcomponents are outlined to move from the most frequently used word parts to the least frequent ones at higher grade levels. Using such an organization of the structural analysis skills provides some assurance that all areas will be addressed. However, teachers should make sure that words containing the components being taught are included in the reading material. Teacher's manuals that accompany reading materials frequently present structural analysis lessons as isolated features and do not allow the student to apply structural analysis skills to the text material read for that lesson. These skills can assist students in decoding some unfamiliar words but will be useful only to the extent that they are taught through application in context.

Contextual Analysis

Contextual analysis is defined by Spache as the ability "to determine word recognition and word meaning by the position or function of a word in a familiar sentence pattern."[46] This is the one area of word identification about which there is no debate. Emans identifies four uses of context clues in word recognition:

1. To help children remember words that they may have forgotten.
2. To use with other word-recognition skills such as phonics and structural analysis to check the accuracy of words.
3. To assist in the rapid recognition of words by anticipating from other words.
4. To aid in the correct pronunciation of words with multiple meanings and pronunciations.[47]

While other word identification skills seem to become less useful as the reader matures, contextual analysis skills become more valuable. Spache concludes that adult readers use letter sounds or word structure very little and rely on contextual analysis as their main tool for understanding strange words.[48] Goodman found that while first-grade students used context to some extent to recognize words, third graders greatly increased their use of this skill.[49]

The idea of using context clues to aid in word identification begins with young children as they use picture clues to gain meaning from their picture books. Later, they use the picture clues to assist in determining words. As students move into materials with more words and fewer picture clues, they look for other means of figuring out unknown words not in their sight vocabulary. Schwartz and Stanovich found that better readers tend to automatically look at other words in the sentence for assistance while poorer readers are more likely to look at individual sounds to analyze the word.[50] Similarly, Juel investigated the extent to which good, average, and poor readers in second and third grade identify words of varying difficulty using a text-driven method (decoding or sight recognition) and a concept-driven method (context clues). She found that good readers are predominately text driven, while poor readers are concept driven, and average readers fluctuate.[51]

Most research regarding context clues relates to the classification of the various types of clues. The most generally accepted classification is that of Ames, who has identified fourteen types of clues:

1. Language experience or familiar expression
2. Modifying phrases or clauses
3. Definition or description
4. Words connected in a series
5. Comparison or contrast clues
6. Synonym clues
7. Tone, setting, and mood clues
8. Referral clues
9. Association clues
10. Main idea and supporting detail pattern
11. Question-answer pattern in paragraph
12. Preposition clues
13. Nonrestrictive clauses or appositive phrases
14. Cause-effect pattern of sentence or paragraph[52]

Using Ames's classification scheme, Rankin and Overholzer attempted to rank the clues from easiest to most difficult. Their findings suggest the order of difficulty as numbered above is 4, 2, 1, 14, 9, 8, 6, 3, 12, 11, 5, 10, 13, with words connected in a series being the easiest clue and nonrestrictive clauses of appositives the most difficult.[53]

Contextual analysis clues most frequently used as word identification aids include titles or themes of a passage, syntactic clues, semantic clues, or a combination of these clues used with phonic and structural analysis clues. Syntactic clues are used by noting the function of the unknown word in a sentence. For example, in the sentence

Courtney accidentally _____ on Clem's tail,

the unknown word tells what Courtney did to Clem's tail. Possible words that could be determined from the syntax are *fell*, *stepped*, and *pulled*. By combining this syntactic clue with a phonic clue, the correct word can be pronounced.

Courtney accidentally s_____ on Clem's tail.

By combining clues, the student decides that *stepped* is a reasonable choice that fits the suggested pronunciation of the word and meaning of the sentence.

When students ignore syntax in reading, they miscall words and use inappropriate words that make no sense in the sentence. Comprehension is adversely affected by these errors. To improve the use of syntactic clues, teachers may use modified cloze sentences, like the following, for instructional and reinforcement exercises.

Erin has a _____ white cat named Snowball.
large wild furry ugly

Through class discussions, students can identify various options for completing the sentence, with the teacher showing them how to select words that fit the structure and make sense in the context of the sentence.

Semantic clues relate more directly to meaning and often function in conjunction with syntactic clues. Syntactic clues are found in the arrangement of words in the sentence, while semantic clues depend on other words in the sentence or adjoining sentences to assist in determining the meaning of the unknown word. For example, in the sentence given above the unknown word is easier to determine if a second sentence is read.

Erin has a _____ white cat named Snowball. This cat is small but she feels like silk.

Teaching context clues may seem complex, but these skills must be taught if students are expected to use them. Emans and Fisher suggest some simple ways of beginning to develop use of context clues: (a) giving no clue except the context, (b) giving the beginning letter, (c) giving the length of the word, (d) providing the beginning and ending letters, (e) giving a four-word choice, and (f) giving all the consonants in the word.[54]

In reviewing the research in these various areas of word identification, it is evident that students must be provided with a background in using all the different word identification strategies.

PROVIDING APPROPRIATE INSTRUCTION IN WORD IDENTIFICATION

Because word identification is so necessary in the development of comprehension, personal reading, and study skills, reading instruction must address this skill. To assist in this process, Table 8.2 reviews the assessment procedures that are appropriate for evaluating specific strengths and weaknesses in the various word identification areas.

Among informal assessment procedures, the informal reading inventory, observation checklist, and criterion-referenced tests are proper tools for use in all areas of word identification assessment. In addition to these informal procedures and the formal assessment tools listed in Table 8.2, the teacher may wish to add other instruments. The procedures included here are discussed in Chapters 2 and 3.

Table 8.2 Techniques for Evaluating Word Identification

Skill Areas	Procedures
Sight Vocabulary	*Botel Reading Inventory* (word recognition test) Criterion-referenced test *Diagnostic Reading Scales* (word recognition lists) *Durrel Analysis* of *Reading Difficulty* (word recognition) *Gates-McKillop-Horowitz Reading Diagnostic Tests* (words flashed, untimed) *Gray Oral Reading Test* Informal Reading Inventory Observation checklist *Reading Miscue Inventory* *Slosson Oral Reading Test* *Stanford Diagnostic Reading Test,* Red Level (word recognition) *Woodcock Reading Mastery Tests* (word identification) Word Recognition Inventory
Phonic Analysis	*Botel Reading Inventory* (phonemic inventory test) Criterion-referenced test *Diagnostic Reading Scales* *Durrell Analysis of Reading Difficulty* (word analysis, sounds of letters, hearing sounds in words, phonic spelling of words) *Gates-McKillop-Horowitz Reading Diagnostic Tests* (oral reading test, knowledge of word parts) *Gray Oral Reading Test* Informal Reading Inventory Observation checklist *Reading Miscue Inventory* *Sipay Word Analysis Tests* (Tests 1–15) *Stanford Diagnostic Reading Test* (phonetic analysis) *Woodcock Reading Mastery Tests* (word attack test)
Structural Analysis	*Botel Reading Inventory* (phonemic inventory test: syllabication) Criterion-referenced test *Gates-McKillop-Horowitz Reading Diagnostic Tests* (oral reading test, syllabication test) *Gray Oral Reading Test* Informal Reading Inventory Observation checklist *Reading Miscue Inventory* *Sipay Word Analysis Tests* (test 16: contractions) *Stanford Diagnostic Reading Test,* Green, Brown, Blue Levels (structural analysis)
Contextual Analysis	Cloze procedure test Criterion-referenced test *Gray Oral Reading Test* Informal Reading Inventory Observation checklist *Reading Miscue Inventory*

In using informal reading inventories, *Gray Oral Reading Test,* and *Reading Miscue Inventory* to assess word identification errors, teachers should note that there are no specific scores in the various word identification areas. Teachers must use their knowledge of the skills and observe the types of errors made in oral reading.

Using the assessment data, the teacher then provides instruction in the areas of need. In providing appropriate instruction, direct instruction is imperative. The teacher spends time modeling the skill and working with the students prior to assigning activities that use the skill. This procedure is especially important in developing word identification skills. Since students tend to be taught these skills in isolation, they are unable to use them in reading materials; they do not understand how to transfer skill knowledge from the worksheet to a written selection. This problem can be dealt with by following a carefully planned instructional procedure (see Figure 8.2):

1. *Discuss the skill with students, explaining how it is used in determining an unknown word.* For example, in teaching contractions, explain that shortened word forms are used in reading just as in speaking. Use a conversation with the students to note the contractions.
2. *Show students how to use the skill in decoding words.* Using the contractions from the conversation, the teacher could write the abbreviated form of the word and the two complete words to show how to recognize the contraction.
3. *Provide opportunities for students to develop the skill.* Games, learning centers, and various group activities are ways to provide practice in developing the skill.
4. *Arrange occasions for students to use the skill in the context of a reading selection.* The teacher may need to remind students of the appropriate skill to use in the situation; however, the skill is not mastered until students have it at their command for application when needed.

Figure 8.2 Steps in Teaching Word Identification Skills

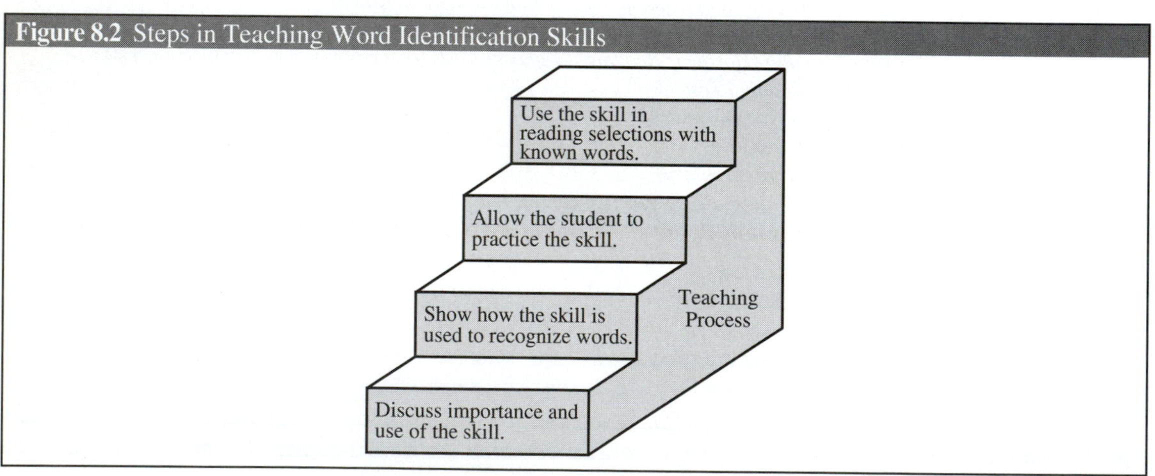

Singer identified 10 principles for teaching word identification, which should also be kept in mind when planning instruction.

1. Proceed from the familiar to the unfamiliar.
2. Help the student become independent in using word identification skills.
3. Teach a variety of ways to identify words.
4. Provide instruction in analyzing new words and much repetition to learn the skill.
5. Use interesting ways to practice learning new words.
6. Use variety in the drill exercises.
7. Let the students know as they make progress.
8. Maximize the probability of success in each lesson.
9. Coordinate instruction among teachers when working with the same student.
10. Follow a sequence of skills in developing word identification skills.[55]

Zutell has developed a technique that applies basic concepts from a language-based learning approach to word study.[56] The Directed Spelling Thinking Activity (DSTA) is designed to involve students in learning vocabulary through the use of problem-solving strategies. The steps in this technique are

1. Pretesting for prediction and sorting
2. Assisted word sorting
3. Word hunting
4. Cooperative and individual word sorting
5. Practice activities
6. Measuring and recording student success

As teachers work with students in using the various word identification strategies, the focus needs to be on using appropriate strategies as the situation dictates. One possible procedure for teaching students to use the various word identification strategies is described below.

1. Look at the word to see if it is a part of your sight vocabulary.
2. If not, look at the first letter or letters to see if this phonic analysis along with the use of context trigger a pronunciation.
3. Think about the type of word that would complete this sentence. Is it the name of something? Is it a describing word? Is it an action word? Think of words which fit this category and begin with this sound.
4. Look at the vowel. How many vowels are in the word? In a short word, one vowel at the beginning of a word or between two consonants usually represents a short vowel sound. One vowel at the end of a word usually represents the long sound. When two vowels are together, try the long sound of the first vowel. If

that doesn't sound right, then try the short sound. (Teach students to use the generalizations that are most frequently correct.)

5. Consider the ending sound. Blend the beginning sound, vowel sound(s), and ending sound to see if a sensible word is produced.
6. If not, try the other sound of the vowel. Again blend the sound to see if the new attempt makes sense in the context.
7. While the above steps usually work well with short words, multisyllabic words require the use of other strategies. Identify the base word using the above procedures to decode it appropriately. Then look at the prefix, suffix, or inflectional ending. Pronounce the base word plus the affix.
8. If these steps don't result in an appropriate pronunciation, skip the word and continue to read for the meaning. If you are reading aloud, ask the teacher for assistance. Remember: Meaning is the important aspect of reading. Every word does not have to be pronounced exactly as long as the reader understands the message the writer is trying to convey.

Table 8.3 gives specific suggestions for developing the different word identification skills. These activities can aid the teacher in providing reinforcement as appropriate instruction is provided for specific word identification skill needs.

The assessment procedures and activities included in the preceding tables can also assist the classroom teacher in providing instruction in word identification. Teachers must remember that students need to know a variety of techniques in order to analyze unfamiliar words in reading. There is no one best way of analyzing words; there is only a best way for analyzing an individual word in a specific situation.

SUMMARY

This chapter has presented many ideas on developing word identification. There are four major word identification areas: sight word knowledge, phonic analysis, structural analysis, and contextual analysis. Within each of these areas, there are specific skills to be developed to aid students in recognizing words.

Much research has been conducted to determine which word identification skill is most important in reading and which techniques are the most valuable in teaching the skills. This chapter presented many of the research findings, which indicate that no single word identification skill can function alone. Knowing various strategies, the students can select the appropriate one to use in a particular situation. Likewise, a variety of techniques may be used to help students learn the word identification skills.

The tables included in this chapter present a summary of the assessment procedures that are most appropriate for the specific word identification skills and suggestions for reinforcing these skills. As with all skill areas in reading, the teacher first assesses areas of need in word identification and then provides appropriate instruction for each student.

Table 8.3 Word Identification Skills

Skill	Instructional Techniques
Sight Vocabulary	
Identify familiar words.	Label familiar objects in the room such as chair, table, desk; then ask students to identify the familiar word in a sentence. Give students cards containing familiar words and let them hold up the cards when an object or action is shown by another student.
Identify basic sight words in context.	Use a tape recorder or machine such as a Language Master with cards containing the sight words and ask the student to record the words. The pronunciation can be checked with another tape or the instruction channel of the Language Master. Give students a flannel board with cards containing the sight words in a sentence. Let a student put a card on the board and another student pronounce the word and use it in another sentence.
Phonic Analysis	
Reproduce from memory upper- and lower-case letter symbols.	Select one student to be the "letter caller." Ask this student to call the letter and the others to write the designated letter on their individual slates (made from cardboard sprayed with black enamel) or paper. Write the upper- or lower-case letter form on the board and ask students to write the form not given by the teacher.
Associate concept of consonants with appropriate letters.	Tape *A B C* letter strips to the floor and ask a student to toss a bean bag on a consonant. Place each letter of the alphabet in upper- and lower-case form on individual squares of paper. Ask students to place all of the consonants in a jar.
Associate concept of vowels with appropriate letters.	Ask designated students to hold up individual letter cards. When the letter card contains a vowel the group stands up. Play a card game similar to Old Maid using cards containing vowels. One card should contain a consonant. The student left with this card is the "Vowel Villain."
Associate sounds and symbols for initial, medial, and final consonant sounds.	Pronounce a word and ask students to write the letter or another word containing the designated sound in a given position. Use unfamiliar or nonsense words and ask students to pronounce a part of the word or the entire word. This may be done as a game with points given for each correct response.
Recognize sounds and symbols of variant consonant patterns.	Give students small cards containing the variant consonant patterns. Have them group patterns that represent the same sounds and label the patterns with the sound. Pronounce a word containing a designated sound represented by a variant consonant pattern such as sign /n/. Ask the students to name other words containing this variant pattern or other variant patterns representing the /n/ such as know.
Associate sounds and symbols for initial, medial, and final long and short vowel patterns.	Use words containing a certain vowel sound. Ask students to identify the vowel and vowel sound prior to pronouncing the word. Then give an unfamiliar or nonsense word containing the same sound and ask students to pronounce the word. Give students three word cards and a clue, such as "The word I am thinking of has a long *a* sound." Then ask a student to select the word or words that fit the clue. That student may then give a clue to the next student.

. . . *Continued*

Table 8.3 Word Identification Skills

Recognize sounds and symbols of variant vowel patterns.	Play a game whereby a vowel sound is given and students identify words containing the vowel sound spelled in different ways. Ask students to hold cards representing the various vowel sounds. Give other students word cards containing words with variant vowel patterns. The student matches the word with the appropriate vowel card.
Blend sounds to form words.	Begin with words containing two sounds. Give two students big cards with the appropriate letters. Ask the others to pronounce the letter sounds. As the two students move closer together, the letters are blended more closely until the word is formed. Pronounce the sounds that must be blended to form a word and write them on the board as they are pronounced. The student must blend these sounds to form the word. For example. /c/ + /a/ + /t/ to form cat.
Substitute initial, medial, and final sounds to form new words.	Give students a word such as *sit* and ask them to substitute designated letters in certain positions to form new words. This can be done by using letter cards and changing the letter as directed. Using a word wheel or tachistoscope, change parts of the word by turning the wheel or sliding the tachistoscope card. As the new word is pronounced points may be given.
Structural Analysis	
Recognize compound words.	Select sets of words, some that form compound words and some that do not. Give the words to the students written as compound words, showing them how to look at the two known words to determine the unknown word. When the words are pronounced, ask students to identify the real compound words. Give students sections of the newspaper and marking pens. Ask them to circle each compound word that they find. The student with the most compound words wins the "Compound Detective Award of the Day."
Recognize contractions and original word forms.	Read the students a story containing contractions. Each time they hear a contraction they may stand or hold up a word card containing the two words forming the contraction. Use a game board in which each square contains a contraction. When the student lands on the square, the two words that form the contraction must be given.
Analyze affixes.	Give students selections containing words with prefixes or suffixes. Ask them to identify the affix that has been added. Then write several of the sentences, using the words without the affix. Discuss how the meaning is changed. Use sentences containing words whose meaning can be changed by adding prefixes or suffixes. After the student reads the sentence, ask that the meaning be changed by adding a suffix or prefix.
Recognize inflectional endings.	Give students sentences in which the inflectional endings are omitted. Ask them to add the endings and tell why they are needed. Distribute magazines or newspapers and ask students to cut out or mark words with inflectional endings.
Divide unknown words into syllables.	Write several unknown words on the board from a textbook or other reading material. Ask the students to identify the number of vowel sounds in each word. Then ask them to use the list of syllabication generalizations to divide the word into syllables. Divide the group into teams and let them select words for one another.

Applying What You Read

1. You are teaching in the upper elementary grades. Through assessment test data, you find a group of students in your class who have very limited structural analysis skills. What would you do? Design a program for them.
2. There are several parents in your school who believe that phonics instruction is the answer to all reading problems. How would you explain the importance of the various word identification strategies to them?
3. Three students in your second-grade class have very poor phonics skills. They also have difficulty with the auditory discrimination skills. What would you do about teaching the phonics skills to these students? What about the other word identification skills?
4. As a first-grade teacher, you have five students who are having difficulty with their sight vocabulary. They can learn the nouns and the more concrete words, but abstract words such as *the, and,* and *what* give them great difficulty. What ideas could be used in developing an appropriate program for these students?
5. Contextual analysis requires the use of the meaning of other words in the passage. As a sixth-grade teacher, you have some students who have poor comprehension skills and do not use context clues at all when they read. How could you help them learn to use context clues? How do you think this skill will affect their comprehension development?

NOTES

1. Yetta M. Goodman and Kenneth S. Goodman, "Spelling Ability of a Self Taught Reader," *The Elementary School Journal;* Jana M. Mason, "Preschoolers Concept of Reading," *The Reading Teacher.*
2. Dolores Durkin, "An Earlier Start in Reading?" *The Elementary School Journal;* G. Plessas and C. R. Oakes, "Prereading Experiences of Selected Early Readers," *The Reading Teacher;* L. Price, "How Thirty-Seven Gifted Children Learned to Read," *The Reading Teacher;* Jeanne M. Burns, "A Study of Experiences Provided in the Home Environment Associated with Accelerated Reading Abilities as Reported by Parents of Intellectually Superior Preschoolers," Ph.D. dissertation.
3. Charles H. Hargis and Edward F. Gickling, "The Function of Imagery in Word Recognition Development," *The Reading Teacher;* Anthony F. Jorm, "Effect of Word Imagery on Reading Performance as a Function of Reading Ability," *Journal of Educational Psychology;* Brenda Kolker and Paul N. Terwilliger, "Sight Vocabulary Learning of First and Second Graders," *Reading World.*
4. J. D. McNeil and E. R. Keislar, "Value of the Oral Response in Beginning Reading: An Experimental Study Using Programmed Instruction," *British Journal of Educational Psychology.*
5. Ethel M. King and Siegmar Muehl, "Different Sensory Cues as Aids in Beginning Reading," *The Reading Teacher.*
6. Kenneth S. Goodman, "A Linguistic Study of Cues and Miscues in Reading," *Elementary English;* Martha Dallmann, Roger L. Rouch, Lynette Chang, and John J. DeBoer, *The Teaching of Reading,* 4th ed; Martha Wood and Mavis Brown, "Beginning Readers' Recognition of Taught Words in Various Contextual Settings," in *Reading Research: Studies and Applications,* edited by Michael L. Kamil and Alden J. Moe, pp. 55–61; Richard L. Allington and Anne McGill-Franzen, "Word Identification Errors in Isolation and In Context: Apples vs. Oranges," *The Reading Teacher;* M. J. Adams and A. W. F. Huggins, "The Growth of Children's Sight Vocabulary: A Quick Test with Educational and Theoretical Implications," *Reading Research Quarterly;* J. Hudson and J. Haworth, "Dimensions of Word Recognition," *Reading.*
7. Harry Singer, S. Jay Samuels, and Jean Spiroff, "The Effect of Pictures and Contextual Conditions on Learning Responses to Printed Words," *Reading Research Quarterly.*
8. Larry A. Harris, "Interest and the Initial Acquisition of Words," *The Reading Teacher;* Carl Braun, "Interest-loading and Modality Effects on Textual Response Acquisition," *Reading Research Quarterly.*

9. Benjamin Lahey and Ronald Drabman, "Facilitation of the Acquisition and Retention of Sight-Word Vocabulary Through Token Reinforcement," *Journal of Applied Behavior Analysis.*
10. Dolores Pawley Dickerson, "A Study of Use of Games to Reinforce Sight Vocabulary," *The Reading Teacher.*
11. John N. Mangieri and Michael S. Kahn, "Is the Dolch List of 220 Basic Sight Words Irrelevant?" *The "Reading Teacher;* Dale D. Johnson, Richard J. Smith, and Kenneth L. Jensen, "Primary Children's Recognition of High-Frequency Words," *The Elementary School Journal.*
12. Jerry L. Johns, Rose M. Edmond, and Nancy A. Mavrogenes, "The Dolch Basic Sight Vocabulary: A Replication and Validation Study," *The Elementary School Journal.*
13. S. Jay Samuels, "Automatic Decoding and Reading Comprehension," *Language Arts.*
14. Dolores Durkin, *Teaching Young Children to Read*, 4th ed., p. 168.
15. Rudolf Flesch, *Why Johnny Can't Read and What You Can Do About It;* Jeanne Chall, *Learning to Read: The Great Debate.*
16. Jeanne Chall, *Learning to Read: The Great Debate*; Guy L. Bond and Robert Dykstra, "The Cooperative Research Program in First Grade Reading Instruction," *Reading Research Quarterly.*
17. Robert Dykstra, "Summary of the Second Phase of the Cooperative Research Program in Primary Reading Instruction," *Reading Research Quarterly.*
18. Richard C. Anderson, Elfrieda H. Hiebert, Judith A. Scott, Ian A. G. Wilkinson, and Members of the Commission on Reading, *Becoming a Nation of Readers: The Report of the Commission on Reading,* p. 118.
19. Isabel Beck and Connie Juel, "The Role of Decoding in Learning To Read," *American Educator.*
20. R. D. Boyd, "Growth of Phonic Skills in Reading," in *Clinical Studies in Reading III,* edited by Helen M. Robinson.
21. Patricia M. Cunningham, "Reasonable Rimes," *The Reading Teacher.*
22. Reggie Routman and Andrea Butler, "Phonics Fuss: Facts, Fiction, Phonemes, and Fun," *School Talk.*
23. Thomas G. Gunning, "Word Building: A Strategic Approach to The Teaching of Phonics," *The Reading Teacher.*
24. Emma E. Plattor and Ellsworth S. Woestehoff, "Specific Reading Disabilities of Disadvantaged Children," in *Reading Difficulties: Diagnosis, Correction and Remediation,* edited by William Durr.
25. Theodore Clymer, "The Utility of Phonic Generalizations in the Primary Grades," *The Reading Teacher;* Robert Emans, "The Usefulness of Phonic Generalizations above the Primary Grades," *The Reading Teacher;* Mildred H. Bailey, "The Utility of Phonic Generalizations in Grades One through Six," *The Reading Teacher.*
26. Martha D. Collins, "Evaluating Basals: Do They Teach Phonics Generalizations?" in *Evaluation Reading-Learning-Teaching-Administering,* edited by Donavan Lumpkin, Mary Harshberger, and Peggy Ransom.
27. George D. Spache, *Diagnosing and Correcting Reading Disabilities,* p. 219.
28. Robert L. Hillerich, "The Truth About Vowels," in *Insights into Why and How to Read,* edited by Robert Williams, pp. 63–68; Robert L. Hillerich, "Vowel Generalizations and First Grade Reading Achievement," *Elementary School Journal;* Albert J. Harris, Blanche Serwer, and Laurence Gold, "Comparing Approaches in First Grade Teaching with Disadvantaged Children Extended into Second Grade," *The Reading Teacher;* Gerald G. Glass and Elizabeth H. Burton, "How Do They Decode? Verbalizations and Observed Behaviors of Successful Decoders," *The Reading Teacher.*
29. Paul R. Hanna and James T. Moore, "Spelling: From Spoken Word to Written Symbol," *Elementary School Journal.*
30. Leonard Bloomfield and Clarence Barnhart, *Let's Read: A Linguistic Approach.*
31. Harry Levin and J. Watson, "The Learning of Variable Grapheme-to-Phoneme Correspondences: Variations in the Initial Consonant Position," A *Basic Research Program on Reading;* Joanna P. Williams, "Successive vs. Concurrent Presentation of Multiple Grapheme-Phoneme Correspondences," *Journal of Educational Psychology.*
32. Clymer, "The Utility of Phonic Generalizations in the Primary Grade."
33. Emans, "The Usefulness of Phonic Generalizations Above the Primary Grades."
34. Bailey, "The Utility of Phonic Generalizations in Grades One Through Six."

35. Collins, "Evaluating Basals: Do They Teach Phonics Generalizations?"
36. Ruth F. Waugh and K. W. Howell, "Teaching Modern Syllabication," *The Reading Teacher;* Ronald Wardhaugh, "Syl-lab-i-ca-tion." *Elementary English;* L. V. Ruck, "Some Questions about the Teaching of Syllabication Rules," *The Reading Teacher.*
37. Brother Leonard Courtney, "Methods and Materials for Teaching Word Perception in Grades 10–14," in *Sequential Development of Reading Abilities,* edited by Helen M. Robinson.
38. George Canney and Robert Schreiner, "A Study of the Effectiveness of Selected Syllabication Rules and Phonogram Patterns for Word Attack," *Reading Research Quarterly.*
39. Robert J. Marzano, Norma Case, Anne DeBooy, and Kathy Prochoruk, "Are Syllabication and Reading Ability Related?" *Journal of Reading*
40. Albert J. Harris and Edward R. Sipay, *How to Increase Reading Ability,* 6th ed., p. 377.
41. Lila R. Gleitman and Paul Rozin, "Teaching Reading by Use of Syllabary," *Reading Research Quarterly;* Kenneth S. Goodman, "The 13th Easy Way to Make Learning to Read Difficult: A Reaction to Gleitman and Rozin," *Reading Research Quarterly.*
42. Carol Winkley, "Which Accent Generalizations Are Worth Teaching?" *The Reading Teacher.*
43. Harris and Sipay, *How to Increase Reading Ability,* p. 379.
44. Spache, *Diagnosing and Correcting Reading Disabilities,* p. 223.
45. Leo M. Schell, "Teaching Structural Analysis," *The Reading Teacher;* Donald C. McFeely, "Syllabication Usefulness in a Basal and Social Studies Vocabulary," *The Reading Teacher.*
46. Spache, *Diagnosing and Correcting Reading Disabilities,* p. 402.
47. Robert Emans, "Use or Context Clues," in *Reading and Realism,* edited by J. Allen Figurel, pp. 76–82.
48. Spache, *Diagnosing and Correcting Reading Disabilities,* p. 404.
49. Kenneth S. Goodman, "A Linguistic Study of Cues and Miscues in Reading," *Elementary English.*
50. R. M. Schwartz and Keith E. Stanovich, "Flexibility in the Use of Graphic and Contextual Information by Good and Poor Readers," *Journal of Reading Behavior.*
51. Connie Juel, "Comparison of Word Identification Strategies with Varying Context, Word Type, and Reader Skill," *Reading Research Quarterly.*
52. W. S. Ames, "The Development of a Classification Schema of Contextual Aids," *Reading Research Quarterly.*
53. Earl F. Rankin and Betsy M. Overholzer, "Reaction of Intermediate Grade Children to Contextual Clues," *Journal of Reading Behavior.*
54. Robert Emans and Gladys Mary Fisher, "Teaching the Use of Context Clues," *Elementary English.*
55. Harry Singer, "Teaching Word Recognition Skills," in *Teaching Word Recognition Skills,* edited by Mildred A. Dawson, pp. 2–14.
56. Jerry Zutell, "The Directed Spelling Thinking Activity (DSTA): Providing an Effective Balance in Word Study Instruction," *The Reading Teacher.*

CHAPTER 9

Comprehension

Teachers at Twin Lakes School realize that comprehension is the critical aspect of reading instruction. Ms. Bevins has attempted to keep the faculty aware of the current research in reading comprehension. Although Twin Lakes School has a skills hierarchy and teachers attempt to teach comprehension skills appropriately from beginning reading through high school, these teachers are beginning to wonder what the research implications are for their instructional practices.

This chapter presents an overview of the current research on comprehension instruction. The chapter assists teachers in using their knowledge of comprehension skills as well as the research to provide the most effective instruction to improve students' comprehension. Many materials and testing programs in reading continue to identify individual comprehension skills. Thus, a comprehensive list of these skills is provided, together with ideas to assist classroom teachers in providing instruction to reinforce the skills as necessary and meet individual students' needs. Additionally, several strategies based on current information on comprehension instruction are presented. Also included are suggestions for using appropriate assessment techniques discussed in previous chapters. The following questions are answered in this chapter:

- What factors influence the development of comprehension?
- How do the various taxonomies of learning theory relate to comprehension?
- What does research tell us about this area?
- What is comprehension?
- How can comprehension be assessed by the teacher?
- What are some ideas that may be used in providing effective instruction in comprehension?
- How is comprehension developed through appropriate reading instruction?

Vocabulary to Know

- Acronyms
- Advance organizer
- Cause-and-effect relationships
- Cognitive development
- Comparisons
- Comprehension
- Contrasts
- Critical skills
- Discourse analysis
- Figurative language
- Interactive model
- Interpretive skills
- Literal skills
- Miscomprehension
- Organization patterns
- Questioning
- Reciprocal questioning
- Reciprocal teaching
- Relevant and irrelevant information
- Schema
- Semantic mapping
- Signal words
- Story grammar
- Story structure
- Structured overview
- Synthesis
- Taxonomy
- Text structure

FACTORS THAT INFLUENCE COMPREHENSION

The importance of comprehension in learning to read is seldom questioned. True reading is comprehending or understanding the printed word. Reading does not stop after a word has been analyzed and pronounced; the process has only begun. Pronunciation is influenced by the context of the word. As the meaning of a word is understood in relation to the other words or ideas, connected discourse occurs, allowing for communication between the writer and the reader. Because the primary purpose of reading is the communication of ideas to the reader, students must have the skills or strategies that will enable them to receive information from the printed page.

Unfortunately, some programs place so much emphasis on the development of word identification skills, especially phonetic analysis, that decoding the word has become paramount in the reading process. As a result, a student is able to pronounce words in isolation, but when the word is placed in context, the same student will have difficulty pronouncing the word and will not know its meaning. Likewise, many reading programs have placed an emphasis on the "mastery" of individual comprehension skills. The result has been students who can pass tests on individual skills, such as cause-and-effect relationships, main idea, and fact versus opinion, but who cannot put these skills together and apply them to understand what they read.

The concept of comprehension is somewhat difficult to understand because we cannot observe the ongoing neurological processes. While we know that comprehension occurs, it is also necessary to understand how it occurs, and in some cases, why it occurs. In contrast to word identification, which is more easily monitored, the secrets of comprehension are more mysterious and difficult to unlock. Why do some students exhibit more strength in comprehension than others? This is a question that has troubled teachers for quite some time. Obviously, there are many answers to this question, and yet, even with these answers, teachers are aware that a few students still do not comprehend well in spite of their best efforts. When examining this complex question, a closer look at students exhibiting weaknesses in comprehension is warranted. There are probably one or more factors interacting to create this difficulty.

Comprehension factors have been studied by various writers. Durkin identifies seven basic factors that affect ability in comprehension: oral language, intelligence, features of the material read, motivation, interest, familiarity with the content being read, and relevant correspondence between the dialect of the reader and that of the author.[1] Harris and Smith identify six factors they believe are the primary determinants of reading comprehension: background experience, language abilities, thinking abilities, affection (including such areas as interests, motivation, attitudes, beliefs, and feelings), reading purposes, and text.[2]

In addition to these factors, some of the factors that influence prereading, outlined in Chapter 7, also apply to the area of comprehension, namely, intelligence and environment. The environmental factors can be further subdivided into sociocultural awareness, background of experiences, oral language, and interests in reading.

Because of the numerous influences on the comprehension process, definite agreement cannot be reached as the exact reasons for comprehension difficulties. However, some of the more common factors that are generally accepted as contributing to comprehension or miscomprehension of information are discussed in the following pages.

Intelligence is a critical factor in every area of learning but especially in comprehension. Recalling simple details from a story, while considered by some to be a lower-level comprehension skill, requires a rather complex thinking process. Inferential and analytical understanding often call for more intelligence. A student must use deductive and inductive reasoning capabilities for comprehending at all levels; therefore, intelligence plays a key role in the comprehension process.

Environmental factors include sociocultural awareness, background of experience, oral language, and interests in reading. Sociocultural factors are extremely important to comprehension. Often students from lower socioeconomic backgrounds have had very little opportunity to familiarize themselves with printed material. Generally, verbal rather than written stimuli are used for communication, making it difficult for these students to comprehend printed materials with any depth of understanding. Another unfortunate aspect is that comprehending the printed page may have little or no status in some neighborhoods where little reading is done. An important aspect of the sociocultural factor is dialectical differences. Many linguists have voiced concern that students using nonstandard American-English orthography, also called "divergent speakers," experience so much difficulty in reading materials written in standard American English that comprehending the printed material is virtually impossible. However, Gemake found that the dialect pattern of nonstandard black English did not interfere in the reading comprehension process of third-grade

African American students. It did however, interfere with oral reading. Gemake further found that comprehension of complex sentence patterns was more difficult for students speaking nonstandard black English.[3]

Oral language is crucial to comprehension. In order for written words to be understood, they must be a part of the student's oral and listening vocabulary. This is, of course, the premise upon which the language-experience approach is built. In a review of research, Christie found that students have difficulty comprehending written materials that contain syntactic structures not found in their oral language.[4] This factor is significant when instructing those who speak English as a second language, those whose dialect differs substantially from standard English, as well as language-delayed children who have been mainstreamed into the regular classroom. The language experience approach, along with an intensive language development program, is necessary to develop oral language to the point that it is not a major obstacle to reading comprehension.

A broad foundation of experiences is important for children entering school, since comprehending the reading material is often contingent on having had experiences like those described. For example, an inner-city student might be asked to read a story about a vacation at the beach, an experience of which the student has no prior knowledge. This lack of experience increases the difficulty level of the material and decreases the student's chances for success in reading. Stevens found that prior knowledge was a significant factor in comprehension of information read among ninth graders of all abilities.[5] Stahl, Jacobson, Davis, and Davis conducted a series of three studies that suggested that the ability of sixth graders to comprehend certain social studies materials was affected by prior knowledge and vocabulary difficulty.[6] Therefore, providing a variety of experiences is essential in aiding comprehension. Information for which students have an established schema or extensive prior knowledge can usually be read more rapidly than material filled with new concepts.

Another essential factor in comprehension is the student's interest in the material. Assuming that the level of the material is appropriate, comprehension is better when a student is interested in the subject. Research suggests that passages of high prior knowledge and passages of high topic interest in relation to the reader's experiences have a positive effect on comprehension.[7]

Some materials are difficult for students to comprehend because of specific features such as vocabulary, the presentation of complex ideas, and the rate at which they occur.[8] Thus, related to the interest of the material, the written message itself must be considered a critical factor in comprehension. Sentence structure and text structure, as well as the organization of ideas, can enhance or impede a student's comprehension of information.

Purpose setting, either by the teacher or the student, is another factor that facilitates comprehension. When students are aware of why they are reading, they derive more information and enjoyment from the selection.[9] Although this has been a common assumption about reading instruction, schema theory research underscores the need to have students recall what they know about a topic before they begin to read about it. The idea of establishing readiness for reading is further supported by many studies investigating the use of advance organizers and graphic organizers in content reading.[10] Research has established the value of having students relate their present knowledge to what they are expected to learn from new materials.

Another factor affecting comprehension is reading rate. Teaching students to adjust their reading rate to the type of material and to their purpose for reading will improve comprehension. Difficult material will require slower reading for better comprehension, while easier material can be read more quickly without impairing comprehension.[11]

A study conducted by Zabrucky and Ratner suggests that reading ability affects students' evaluation and regulation of comprehension.[12] Cognitive monitoring by students is crucial to comprehension.

Many factors affecting comprehension also influence other areas of reading. When students do not read well because of one or more of these factors, frustration and hostility result. Thus, consideration of these factors will help to ensure effective reading instruction.

RELATING TAXONOMIES AND COMPREHENSION

Comprehension is a thinking process, as such, it is difficult to define, it is not easily quantified, it is not precisely observable, and it begets other processes.[13] For many years comprehension has been viewed as a process that depends on the development and application of a variety of subskills. These subskills are arranged in some systematic sequence according to various taxonomies of learning. The hierarchies progress from lower levels of thinking to higher levels. Frequently, elementary-grade teachers and materials are criticized because students are not given the opportunity to develop their cognitive abilities as highly as possible. This is due, in part, to the questioning strategies used by some teachers. Often elementary students are asked low-level, literal questions that require only basic knowledge and result in one- or two-word answers. These literal-level questions force students to read strictly for main ideas, specific details, and other concrete information. In too many classes, students are rarely asked to synthesize and evaluate the information they read. As a result, their thinking abilities are not developed to process more complex ideas.

Taba found that teachers tend to pour out information to students and then using low-level questions, encourage them to recite this material back almost word for word. She states that thinking is incorrectly perceived "as a global process which seemingly encompassed anything that goes on in the head, from daydreaming to constructing a concept of relativity."[14]

A later study by Guszak further substantiated the theory that questions used in the elementary grades are primarily of the literal type.[15] He found that recognition and recall or memory questions formed 78.8% of all questions in the second grade, 64.7% in the fourth grade, and 57.8% in the sixth grade. Questions at higher levels such as translation and evaluation were used only 20% of the time and in many cases required only a yes or no response. As a result of these and other studies, publishers of reading materials and many teachers have become more aware of the need to enhance students' development in cognition by improving questioning strategies.

While criticism has been voiced about the tendency to use more literal-type questions than higher-level questions, research has shown that asking higher-level questions is not the more effective procedure for mastering factual or higher-level learning.[16] Experimental studies found that asking recall questions resulted in better student performance on recall tests and that all classes, regardless of the number of higher-level questions asked, did equally well on tests that contained higher-level questions.[17] With the confusion existing in this area, we suggest that teachers attempt to include all levels of questions in their instructional programs and assist students in understanding the processes involved in answering various types of questions. Indeed, Wixson found that student learning was related to the level of questions used during their instructional time.[18]

In an effort to help teachers improve learning, several important taxonomies indicating how the learner progresses from the lowest levels of thinking to the highest, have been developed. The primary purpose of these taxonomies is to enable the teacher to examine the learning process and develop more appropriate questioning strategies for students.

Three of the more widely used taxonomies and how they correlate with the three levels of comprehension skills suggested by the authors are presented in Table 9.1. The taxonomies listed were developed by Bloom, Sanders, and Barrett.[19]

Table 9.1 Relating Taxonomies to Levels of Comprehension

Level of Comprehension	**Taxonomy**		
	Bloom	*Sanders*	*Barrett*
Literal	Knowledge Comprehension	Memory Translation	Recognition Recall
Interpretive (inferential)	Application Analysis Synthesis	Interpretation Application Analysis Synthesis	Inference
Critical	Evaluation	Evaluation	Evaluation Appreciation

However, current research is questioning whether these taxonomies do indeed reflect actual level of question difficulty for students. Pearson and Johnson propose another classification of questions. Questions whose answers are exclusively text based are called textually explicit, while those that depend primarily on the text with some prior knowledge are called textually implicit. The third category of questions is scriptually implicit. Scriptually implicit questions rely more on prior knowledge with some input from the text.[20] Moreover concern is being voiced about the teaching of subskills as a means of improving comprehension. Discussions about the levels of thinking as well as the teaching of subskills have divided reading researchers into three groups who debate whether the reading process is best described using a top-down, bottom-up, or interactive model.

Those who believe that reading is a top-down process suggest that the student brings more information to the page than the page brings to him. This prior knowledge is used to make good guesses about the nature of the text. The student reads to confirm or modify a hypothesis as well as to appreciate the style and ideas of the author. In the top-down model, the student starts with a hypothesis and attempts to verify it by reading. Theorists who support this model maintain that students use this hypothesis-testing procedure even in recognizing words; they observe a few features of the word and confirm its identity. In this model, the higher levels of thinking in the taxonomies are used by students to unlock new information at the critical inferential and literal levels.[21]

Another model of thinking is the bottom-up model. Researchers who adhere to this position believe that the page brings more information to the student than the student brings to the page. This position is also referred to as text driven, because the student begins with little information about the text but sequentially processes the printed message until it is understood. The bottom-up model was the first to depict information as a series of discrete stages that correspond to a great extent with the levels in the learning taxonomies,[22] suggesting that learning begins at the literal level and moves up through the inferential level to the critical level.

Because many researchers have concluded that neither of these models accurately describes the reading process, particularly the comprehension phase, a third theory has emerged: the interactive model. In this theory, based on the work of Rummelhart, the reader and text work in concert to reveal a meaning. Strange contends that the interactive model begins as the student first attends to print. Prior knowledge is used to make decoding and comprehension decisions. This knowledge plus other sources such as past experiences, help the student derive a unique meaning from the printed text. This idea that readers combine past experiences (concepts) with new information from the text has led to further research in reading comprehension under the label of "schema theory," which attempts to describe how old information is combined with new ideas to enhance comprehension.[23]

Schema theory is not a new idea; it is an old idea that has been expanded. Schema theory, as discussed by Mason,

> has two key components: (1) that skilled readers draw simultaneously on several different sources of knowledge as they peruse text sources ranging from letter information and words to high-level concepts and from interpreting facts to constructing strategies and planning how to read; and (2) that skilled readers construct progressively refined hypotheses about a text in order to understand, learn, or remember it.[24]

However, schema theory research offers more to aid in developing comprehension. According to schema theory research, the ability to infer and the nature of the inference depend on the reader's knowledge; even explicit text is interpreted in different ways when the student constructs meaning from the text as well as from his previous knowledge. Schema theory supports our common sense about reading: "The more we know before we read, the more we learn when we read."[25]

The concepts of taxonomy, levels of questions, and specific subskills in comprehension acquire a different meaning as these new research areas become better understood. Mason, Osborn, and Rosenshine suggest, "General reading comprehension cannot be reliably subdivided into subskills, not even into the skill of deriving implicit meaning and the skill of deriving explicit meaning."[26] Sheridan argues that schema theory provides evidence that comprehension is a holistic process. Comprehension skills instruction is necessary but in relation to schemata rather than to isolated skills.[27] The way students organize information in their minds is an aid as they organize new information.

Different researchers have investigated the organization of text materials, using a procedure known as discourse analysis. By identifying the text structure of materials, students can be taught to identify various organizational patterns of text in order to better understand new information. Meyer identified five basic patterns: response, comparison, antecedent-consequent, description, and collections.[28] Although these organizational patterns have been identified from an analysis of students' writing, the concept of identifying the organizational patterns in text is not new. As early as 1917, Thorndike reported that one reason for failure in reading is the student's inability to organize and to understand organizational relationships in written materials.[29] In 1964, Smith and McCallister maintained that different patterns of writing exist in various content areas and serve as aids to understanding.[30] However, here too, schema theory research has provided additional insight into the use of organizational patterns to aid comprehension. Cheek and Cheek analyzed content textbooks and identified four organizational patterns commonly used in content writing. These patterns are enumeration, relationship, problem-solving, and persuasion.[31] Further, Collins found that by teaching those organizational patterns to middle-school students comprehension was significantly improved.[32]

Schema theorists suggest that if students were taught to recognize the organization of materials and if materials were written so as to follow the logical patterns that students understand, then comprehension would be a natural process of understanding. Rosenshine goes further to suggest that there is no clear evidence for distinct reading skills or for a skills hierarchy.[33] Readance and Harris have more cautiously considered those skills that seem essential to comprehension. They studied nine comprehension subskills: identifying main ideas, identifying outcomes, drawing conclusions, determining sequence, identifying pronoun referents, deriving meaning from context, using punctuation clues, understanding syntax, and affixes. One skill, affixes, was determined to be a false prerequisite for comprehension. Identifying outcomes, using punctuation clues, and understanding syntax were found to be necessary but insufficient in themselves to assure comprehension. The five remaining skills were deemed to be associated with competency.[34]

Much of the current research in comprehension questions the teaching of comprehension skills and proposes various strategies for developing comprehension. Many of these strategies offer classroom teachers excellent alternatives for teaching comprehension to students with different needs. Teachers cannot ignore the fact that comprehension is the goal of reading instruction and an integral part of the language process. However, neither can teachers escape the real world of state and local tests that focus on isolated comprehension skills and reading tests that continue to measure comprehension according to specific skill areas. Thus, the remainder of this chapter discusses various strategies that can be used to develop comprehension as well as activities for teaching the specific comprehension skills.

STRATEGIES FOR TEACHING COMPREHENSION

Comprehension Development

Comprehension skills are divided into three basic areas: literal, interpretive (inferential), and critical. The specific skills within these areas are listed later in this chapter and summarized in Appendix A. This section provides a discussion of each of the basic areas and its importance according to research findings.

Literal Skills

Developing literal comprehension skills is an integral part of the total reading process. Some teachers believe that students must develop proficiency in using these basic, low-level comprehension skills in order to progress to more difficult interpretive and critical skills. Such subskills as finding the main idea, recalling details, contrasting and comparing, interpreting abbreviations, symbols and acronyms, and several others are classified as literal skills.[35]

Subskills of particular importance in literal comprehension are identifying the main idea and reading for details. Dechant and Smith state that the ability to identify the main idea is essential to understanding what is written. Dawson and Bamman suggest that students must look for a definite sequence of details when learning to follow directions.[36] Without an understanding of these skills, comprehension is very difficult. Organizing words into meaningful units such as phrases, clauses, and sentences further assists in the comprehension process.[37] The overall organization of skills into some meaningful order is valuable for teacher direction and to assure that students are taught the comprehension skills in all areas: literal, interpretive and critical.

Interpretive (Inferential) Skills

Interpretive skills are believed by some to require a higher level of cognition and perception than literal skills. Drawing inferences and interpreting the language and mood of the writer become vitally important in comprehending the deeper meaning of the reading material. Interpretation goes beyond examining more than the superficial aspects of a selection; it involves drawing conclusions, making generalizations, predicting outcomes, and synthesizing ideas, as well as using other inferential skills.

In order to facilitate comprehension at a higher cognitive level, the reader must delve further into the meaning of the material. Understanding language patterns and syntax contributes to successful comprehension. A closer examination of language patterns will enhance the perception of the deep structure of a sentence.[38] Deese reinforced this concept by describing the syntax of a language as the bridge between the sound system and the semantic or meaning system in the language.[39]

The use of context clues to grasp the meaning of a selection is an essential interpretive comprehension skill. Reading teachers once felt that the student's use of context clues was beneficial only to comprehension. However, Burmeister found that understanding word meaning was aided by the use of context clues, while Allen stated that a student's experiential background plays a major role in gaining information from material through the use of context. Emans found that context clues could help students identify words they had forgotten, check the accuracy of words identified through the use of other clues, anticipate words (thus increasing the rate of recognition), and identify totally unfamiliar words.[40]

Another skill that promotes interpretive comprehension is proper use of signal words. These conjunctions enable students to determine the meaning of sentences and passages.[41] Teaching students to interpret figurative language and punctuation are two additional skills that assist students in acquiring meaning from materials. Figurative language is most helpful to elementary students, enriching their vocabulary and improving their ability to gain meaning from materials they encounter.[42] Punctuation is frequently used to replace the intonation pattern in speech, so this skill needs to be understood as quickly as possible.[43] Teaching the proper use of punctuation as an aid in comprehension, while seemingly an easy skill to learn, certainly becomes an instructional challenge with some students.

As with literal skills, many factors interact to influence interpretation of printed material. However, every student needs the opportunity to develop these skills in order to achieve a deeper understanding of the meaning of that material.

Critical Reading Skills

Just as interpretive skills sometimes are more difficult for students to master than literal skills, critical reading skills are believed to require an even higher level of cognition. When using critical reading skills, the reader uses her reasoning abilities to evaluate or make judgments about the material.

Numerous efforts have been made to reach a comprehensive, yet specific, definition of critical reading skills. Durkin views critical reading as both reading and reacting to printed material. Ives defines critical readers as those who, in addition to identifying facts and ideas accurately as they read, engage in interpretive and evaluative thinking. Burns and Roe state that critical reading is the evaluation of written material.[44] There seems to be little doubt that critical reading is the application of specific criteria such as validity, accuracy, and truthfulness in evaluating material.[45]

Reading is a process used to gain information.

Photo courtesy of Edward B. Lasher.

Teaching students to read critically is essential because of the various types of printed material that they will deal with in school and throughout their adult life. Perceiving bias, identifying relevant and irrelevant information, differentiating between fact and opinion, understanding fallacies in reasoning, and dealing with other situations that require critical evaluations of printed material form the basis for mature decision making. To enhance the learning of these skills, teachers should condition their students to read critically by expanding their knowledge, showing them how to question and use sound judgment in applying logic to all situations, and then instruct them to reach a decision based on the analysis of all the data.[46]

Simpson suggests that in order to teach children to become critical readers teachers must assist them in asking questions and accepting that many of these questions will not produce the type of critical understanding that both the teacher and the children are seeking.[47]

Unfortunately, critical reading has not been emphasized as much in the lower elementary grades as it should be,[48] even though research has shown that students at this level can read critically when given the opportunity and the appropriate instruction.[49] When including critical reading skills in the instructional program, good questioning techniques, discussion, analysis of propaganda, and sound reasoning must be included to provide for a broad range of expression and ideas in the classroom. These techniques have been quite successful in improving critical reading skills.[50]

Perhaps the skill most widely used in teaching critical reading is that of analyzing propaganda. Since the Institute of Propaganda Analysis released its list of techniques for influencing opinion in 1937, teachers have taught these techniques extensively. Those techniques identified by the institute are (a) name calling, (b) glittering generalities, (c) transfer, (d) plain folks, (e) testimonials, (f) bandwagon, and (g) card stacking. Although instruction about these techniques has been effective,[51] the perception of propaganda does not ensure that students will always be able to resist its more insidious aspects.[52]

As the research clearly indicates, developing the ability to read critically is an essential part of comprehension. Unless this ability is developed to its fullest, students will be unable to distinguish between important and unimportant information or to detect bias; they may fall prey to a fast-talking salesperson or to others who do not have their best interests at heart. Good evaluative judgments are based on good critical thinking.

Tips on Teaching Comprehension

Providing appropriate instruction in the various comprehension skill areas is based on evaluating students' strengths and weaknesses. Several methods of evaluation are presented in Table 9.2.

As in other chapters, assessment procedures for evaluating each area are presented. In using Table 9.2, note that several of the instruments listed do not separate comprehension into various skill subtests; therefore, it is necessary that the teacher evaluate data from these tests more carefully, using an item analysis technique, if you wish to deal with specific skills. The instruments or procedures that fall into this category are listed under each skill area to which they apply, with no subtest specified. The appropriateness of the informal procedures listed, as well as the *Reading Miscue Inventory,* depends on the teacher's questioning techniques for assessing the three categories of comprehension; thus, they are listed under all three skill areas.

Table 9.2 Assessment Techniques for Evaluating Comprehension Skill Areas

Skill Areas	Procedures
Literal and Interpretive	Cloze test
	Criterion-referenced tests
	Diagnostic Reading Scales (instructional level, independent level)
	Durrell Analysis of Reading Difficulty (oral reading, silent reading)
	Formal Reading Inventory
	Gates-MacGinitie Reading Test (comprehension)
	Gilmore Oral Reading Test (comprehension)
	Gray Oral Reading Test (comprehension)
	Group Reading Inventory
	Informal Reading Inventory
	Iowa Silent Reading Test (reading comprehension)
	Observation checklist
	Reading Miscue Inventory
	Stanford Diagnostic Reading Test Red Level (comprehension),
	Green, Brown, Blue, Levels (literal and inferential comprehension)
	Test of Reading Comprehension
	Woodcock Reading Mastery Tests (word comprehension test, passage comprehension test)
Critical	Criterion-referenced tests
	Group Reading Inventory
	Informal Reading Inventory
	Observation checklist
	Reading Miscue Inventory

In using various instruments to assess comprehension, great caution should be taken to avoid making decisions about the students' strengths and weaknesses in comprehension, especially on the basis of too limited information. Niles and Harris recommend that teachers consider the following when conducting reading assessment is conducted in comprehension:

- *Method of measurement.* Are the questions oral or written? Is a recall or multiple-choice format used? What is the level of the question? Is the question a quality question?
- *Instructional environment.* Does the environment provide a quality setting for reading? Is reading done orally or silently? What is the teacher's attitude toward reading?
- *Text.* What is the content and style of presentation?
- *Reader.* What does the reader bring to the situation in terms of interests, experiences, and intelligence?[53]

Each of these factors will affect the results of assessment in comprehension. For example, Wilson found that average readers in the sixth and seventh grades scored significantly higher than below-average readers on inferential and multiple-choice questions on the California Achievement Test, but there was no difference between the two groups on responses to factual questions.[54] Thus, test scores, especially in comprehension, should be analyzed to determine the validity of the information.

In providing prescriptive instruction in comprehension, teachers must be sure that they are instructing and modeling the behavior that is desired. Durkin has characterized the state of instruction in reading comprehension as basically no instruction.[55]

While there is not one way of teaching comprehension skills, there are some basic guidelines that should be followed:

1. The teacher should introduce the skill by modeling examples of the skill as used in the reading situation.
2. The teacher should model to the students how to use the skill in their reading.
3. Opportunities should be provided for the students, working together, to demonstrate their understanding of the skill.
4. Once the students demonstrate an understanding as they work with the teacher and peers, their individual knowledge can be evaluated through individual activities.

For instructors who continue to be troubled by the teaching of isolated comprehension skills and who view the current research on comprehension, emphasizing language process, as a glimmer of hope. Strange offers seven uses of schema theory that will aid in providing appropriate instruction. These newer ideas can be implemented immediately along with existing skills instruction.

1. *Prereading instruction.* Continue to motivate and provide purposes for reading. Add to your prereading instruction the notion of schema theory by helping students organize their related past experiences and make predictions about what will be learned from the new information.
2. *Vocabulary instruction.* Provide more instruction in vocabulary by helping students learn specific labels for their schemata.
3. *Analyze question-answer relationships.* Consider the lower and higher levels of questioning as outlined in the taxonomies, but also consider the text material to determine if, indeed, the question responses require literal, inferential, or critical thinking skills.
4. *Recall important details.* Noting details or recalling factual information is only valuable in helping students add to or change their existing schemata. Thus, minimal time should be spent on recalling details, and more time spent on helping students infer new ideas
5. *Compare stories.* Help students learn to compare stories by looking at the plots, characters, setting, and events. Story grammar research indicates that stories should not be dealt with as isolated units but should be interrelated to note similarities and differences.

6. *Model and stimulate.* Modeling is an important instructional element in teaching comprehension. Teachers can stimulate students to think of the stories they read by talking about the story, comparing it to another, or predicting what will happen. This modeling of the comprehension process helps students realize that understanding a selection goes beyond the answering of isolated questions. According to Gavelek and Raphael, it is particularly important to encourage students to build and deepen their response to literature through extensive discussion.[56] One very effective technique for accomplishing this is read-alouds. Barrentine discusses the effectiveness of engaging children through interactive read-alouds.[57] During these read-alouds, children have the opportunity to respond personally and interpersonally to the story.
7. *Understand miscomprehension.* There are many reasons for incorrect or different answers to comprehension questions. Answers are not merely right or wrong; some answers that differ from those given in the teacher's manual may actually be more correct when the students' schemata is considered. Possible explanations that can help the teacher better understand miscomprehension include

    - No existing schemata when students lack background in an area
    - Naive schemata when the students have only limited experiences to relate to the topic
    - No new information when a story adds nothing to the students existing knowledge, thus causing them to ignore the details because they are predictable and well understood
    - Poor story that does not assist the students in integrating or relating the new ideas to their schemata
    - Many appropriate schemata in some stories, which allows for different interpretations
    - Schematic intrusion, in which a response to a question comes to the student's mind with no plausible line of reasoning
    - Textual intrusion, in which a response to a question is based on information from the text but the response is unrelated to the question

The idea of miscomprehension provides another way of looking at answers to comprehension questions, just as miscues have added a dimension to the analysis of word identification errors.[58] Both kinds of evaluation consider the student, his background of experience, and the impact of the error on the reading process.

These ideas regarding comprehension instruction should be considered when classroom teachers are planning their instruction. Instruction by means of modeling is essential; teaching separate comprehension skills must be related to practical situations in order for students to view reading as a helpful process that may be used to gain new information or for enjoyment. Table 9.3 presents ideas for reinforcing instruction in each of the comprehension skills.

Table 9.3 Instructional Techniques for Comprehension Skills

Skill	Instructional Techniques
Literal Skills	
Understand concrete words, phrases, clauses, and sentence patterns	Give students pictures of objects or situations and words or sentences that correspond. Ask them to match the picture to the word or sentence it represents. List several words from a book, magazine, or newspaper for which students may not know the meaning. Begin a word chain that contains the word and a sentence on one side of the strip of paper and the dictionary definition on the other side. Each student may have a paper chain or a group may develop one to hang in the classroom.
Identify stated main idea	Ask students to read a paragraph and circle in red the sentence that tells what the paragraph is about. Let each student in a group read one sentence from a paragraph containing a stated main idea. The student who reads the main idea sentence and identifies it as the main idea is crowned "Mr. or Ms. M. I."
Recall details	Give students a paragraph to read. Ask them to circle the details that answer who, what, when, where, and how in green ink. Use a newspaper article and ask students to underline details that tell more about the title of the article.
Remember stated sequence of events	Give students a short story to read that contains a sequence of events. Ask them to retell the events in the proper sequence. If an event is skipped, the group must begin the sequence again. Ask students to read a story that has a sequence of events. Cut the story into sentence strips, giving each student one or more strips. Let them reconstruct the story in sequence. This is especially fun with a language experience story and big sentence strips that can be taped to the floor.
Select stated cause-effect relationships	Give students a story with a stated cause-effect relationship. Ask them why the effect occurred or what caused something to happen. For example, "Why was the store owner angry?" or "What caused the bike tire to go flat?" After reading a story containing cause-effect relationships, ask students to identify each cause-effect situation. Help them relate these to real-life situations.
Contrast and compare information	Use two or more ideas in a story and ask students to tell how each is like or unlike the other. For example, compare a bear and a dog in the story. Give students two sentences in which ideas or objects are being compared. Ask them to underline the things that are being compared.
Identify character traits and actions	After reading a selection containing characters, ask students to act out designated characters, noting specific habits, behaviors, or actions. Ask students to read a story about a famous person. Then list the traits of the person that they think helped make him or her famous.
Interpret abbreviations, symbols, and acronyms	Ask students to list abbreviations or acronyms from a selection. Then write the meaning of each. Make a list of abbreviations, symbols, and acronyms that students find as they read. Develop a class dictionary or card file.
Follow written directions	Give students sets of written directions. As they follow the directions, a picture of some object will be formed. Ask students to read directions for playing a game, tell the directions to another student, and follow the directions in playing the game.

. . . Continued

Table 9.3 Instructional Techniques for Comprehension Skills

Classify information	Give students lists of items and ask them to classify or group them according to some appropriate title or heading. Ask students to take sentences from various stories and group them according to some topic. They may use some as topic sentences and others as supporting sentences.
Interpretive Skills	
Predict outcomes	Tell students to read a story to a designated point. They should stop and predict what will happen next or how the story will end. This may be done orally, as a written paper, or through illustrations. Give students a comic strip with the last frame missing. Ask them to predict how the comic ends.
Interpret character traits	After reading a story that contains different characters, ask students to describe how they think a character would act in a given situation. Use puppets and let students write a script for them based on the characters they have read about in another story.
Draw conclusions	Give students several sentences that could be the beginning of a story. Ask them to develop a conclusion for the story from the given information. After reading a story, ask students questions that require them to reach some conclusions from the information.
Make generalizations	Let students read a story and ask them to respond to questions that require them to make generalizations such as these: Do the people in the story like each other? Which ones? Why do you think so? Could this story have happened in our city? Why? After reading a story, ask students to decide when the story took place and to say why they think it happened at that certain time. They may also make generalizations about the story setting and characters.
Perceive relationships	Give students a selection that shows a relationship between two ideas. Ask them to identify the relationship such as the way a little girl acted at a party and the way her mother acted. Using several selections, ask students to identify the relationships of some similar ideas such as the time at which the various ideas occurred, or the different ways the characters responded to problems.
Understand implied causes and effects	Give students a story that contains the cause of a situation and ask students to decide the possible effects. For example, the law says that dogs cannot be loose in the city, but Mr. Jones refuses to put his dogs in a pen. What may happen? Why will these things happen? Give students a list of effects of situations and ask them to identify the possible causes. For example: the ship spilled oil; the house burned down; the boy got a new bike. Tell why these things may have happened.
Identify implied main ideas	Ask students to read a selection in which the main idea is not stated. Have them relate the main idea. After reading a story, have students decide on a good title for the story.
Interpret figurative language	Develop a class file of figurative expressions found while reading. Use these expressions to create a booklet that depicts the expression in a literal manner and in its intended way. Have students read a selection containing figurative language. Each expression should be underlined, and groups of students asked to discuss them to interpret the meaning.
Interpret meaning of capitalization and punctuation in a selection	Give students some sentences without capitalization or punctuation and ask them to read the sentences. As a group, add the correct capital letters and marks. See how much easier the sentences are to read. Give students two sentences that are alike except for punctuation. Discuss the differences in meaning. For example: "Vicki," said her mother, "is nice." Vicki said her mother is nice.

. . . *Continued*

Table 9.3 Instructional Techniques for Comprehension Skills

Understand mood and emotional reactions	After reading a story, ask students to identify the emotions expressed through the actions of the characters and the words used by the author.
	Ask students to read a poem containing emotion. Let some students act out the various lines, while others guess which line is being dramatized.
Interpret pronouns and antecedents	Give students several sentences containing pronouns and antecedents. Ask them to identify the appropriate antecedents for each pronoun.
	Select a passage containing pronouns and antecedents. Delete the pronouns and have students try to interpret the ideas and add the correct pronouns.
Understand author's purpose and point of view	Have students read letters from the editorial page of the newspaper and decide the writer's point of view.
	After reading a story, ask students to decide why the author wrote the story and how she felt about the topic.
Construe meaning by signal words	Give students a selection containing signal words, such as *first, last, in summary, therefore.* Ask them to underline each signal word and tell what the word is signaling in this selection.
	Play a game giving clues about signal words. Ask students to identify the appropriate signal word from a given selection. For example, which word in the last paragraph tells you the story is almost finished?
Understand meaning of abstract words	Ask students to circle all words in a paragraph that cannot be defined through concrete objects or actions. Then discuss the meanings of these abstract words.
	Make a list of abstract words such as *democracy, freedom, love,* and identify concepts that help define these words. See how many ideas students can list to assist a person from outer space in understanding the words.
Summarize information	Give students a story and ask them to summarize it in an e-mail message to a friend. Tell them the message must be short but complete.
	Ask students to take a newspaper article and underline the key parts. They should summarize the article in several sentences to share with the class.
Recognize implied sequence	Use information from various sources and ask students to organize the ideas into a logical sequence.
	Give students a story that uses a flashback technique and ask them to identify the actual sequence of events.
Use context clues to determine meaning	Use sentences containing comparisons, antonyms, or synonyms that can aid in determining the meanings of other words in the sentence. Ask the students to underline the context clue word and circle the word it defines.
	Select a list of multiple-meaning words and use them in sentences. Ask students to read the sentences and tell how the meanings are different.
Synthesize data	Use the summary statements from various sources and ask students to synthesize all of them to formulate their own statement.
	Give students some information regarding a topic and ask them to synthesize it to form their own story.
Critical Reading Skills	
Identify relevant and irrelevant information	Give students a passage that contains some information that does not belong. Ask them to mark through the irrelevant information.
	Ask students to organize some information from materials that you give them. In order to complete the task, they must discard some material that does not belong and use only the relevant information.

. . . *Continued*

Table 9.3 Instructional Techniques for Comprehension Skills

Interpret propaganda techniques	Show students samples of literature from various groups who promote their beliefs through propaganda. Identify specific parts of the material and discuss the ideas or possible reasons for the statements.
	Give students some statements that are fact and others that are propaganda. Discuss how they differ.
Perceive bias	Give students selections to read that contain bias regarding local or national events. Ask them to identify the bias and to debate the issue with another student of a different opinion.
	Use the editorial page of the newspaper or magazine and ask students to locate articles or letters that reflect a bias.
Identify adequacy of materials	Ask students to review several materials and determine which is adequate to answer a list of questions that have been provided.
	Assign topics to the students. Give each four books and ask them to select two that provide the most information on the topic.
Understand reliability of author	Look at the information provided on the author and the topic of the material. Ask students to evaluate the qualifications of the author in terms of the topic.
	Give students a list of book titles and a list of authors with information on each. Ask them to match the title with the most appropriate author.
Differentiate facts and opinions	Give students a list of facts and opinions. Ask them to circle each opinion statement and tell why it is an opinion.
	Ask students to read several short selections on a topic and determine which is factual and which is opinion.
Separate real and unreal information	Give students a list of ideas. Ask them to identify the ideas that are real and to tell why they are real.
	Read passages to the students and ask them to stand up or clap when the information is unreal or cannot happen.
Understand fallacies in reasoning	Give students paragraphs that contain fallacies in reasoning, such as name calling, the bandwagon technique, and stereotypes. Ask them to underline the sentences that show these fallacies and to explain them.
	Use the advertisements in a newspaper to identify the fallacies in reasoning that attempt to lure people into buying merchandise.

Developing Vocabulary

Vocabulary is an essential element in the comprehension process. While this fact has been recognized for many years, its importance has been reinforced with a wealth of research in the last 20 years. As Johnson suggests, "The decade of the 1980s could be characterized as the period of rediscovery of the importance of vocabulary instruction to reading comprehension."[59] Students with adequate vocabularies find that understanding the meaning of material is generally less difficult than do students with inadequate vocabularies. Vineyard and Massey found this to be true even when intelligence was held constant; they support continuing teaching strategies designed to improve comprehension through the improvement of vocabulary.[60] Although the importance of vocabulary to comprehension has not been questioned, there has been debate as to the impact of various types of vocabulary instruction on comprehension. Robert Ruddell and Carr and Wixson provide guidelines to assist teachers in selecting vocabulary development strategies that will increase vocabulary knowledge as well as improve reading comprehension.[61] The guidelines proposed by Carr and Wixson are as follows:

1. Instruction should help students relate new vocabulary to their background knowledge. This helps vocabulary to develop a personal meaning that aids in remembering and improves comprehension.
2. Instruction should help students develop elaborate word knowledge. Strategies that help students develop more than a single definition of a word in one context serve to enhance vocabulary knowledge and comprehension by providing a broader knowledge base for more extensive learning.
3. Instruction should provide for active student involvement in learning new vocabulary. The age old strategy of locating the meaning of a word in the dictionary has not worked. Students remember what they are actively involved in learning—creating definitions of words from context is a more active process than copying a definition. Student-directed rather than teacher-centered instruction is important in vocabulary learning.
4. Instruction should develop students' strategies for acquiring new vocabulary independently. Effective vocabulary strategies help students become independent learners or strategic readers who monitor their reading.[62]

In teaching vocabulary to enhance comprehension, the understanding of concepts cannot be ignored. Sometimes concepts and the vocabulary to be learned are the same or the understanding of the vocabulary is crucial to acquiring new information. In any case, concepts, vocabulary, and comprehension do not operate in isolation, they represent an interwoven process that results in learning. When vocabulary instruction is related to the concepts to be learned and the students' knowledge and past experiences are incorporated, active learning occurs. Two similar strategies used to relate concepts and vocabulary are the advance organizer and graphic organizer. Ausubel suggests using an advance organizer to help students mentally anticipate the information they will read.[63] To establish this readiness for learning new information, teachers can use short reading selections, verbal introductions, or graphic displays; all provide a point of reference for the reader to begin to associate prior knowledge with new information. They serve to activate prior knowledge. Graves, Cooke, and LaBerge suggest using an advance organizer as a preview procedure for reading difficult selections.[64]

The graphic organizer is also used to help students relate old information to new information or concepts. The information is usually presented as a chart that shows the relationships among the vocabulary and concepts. While the teacher may provide a complete chart to introduce the new vocabulary, greater learning occurs when a chart with limited information is presented along with the new words or concepts to be learned; through discussion the students are involved in completing the diagram. Figure 9.1 provides an example of a completed graphic organizer and sample questions that could be used to guide the students in understanding the information.

Figure 9.1 Graphic Organizer in Science

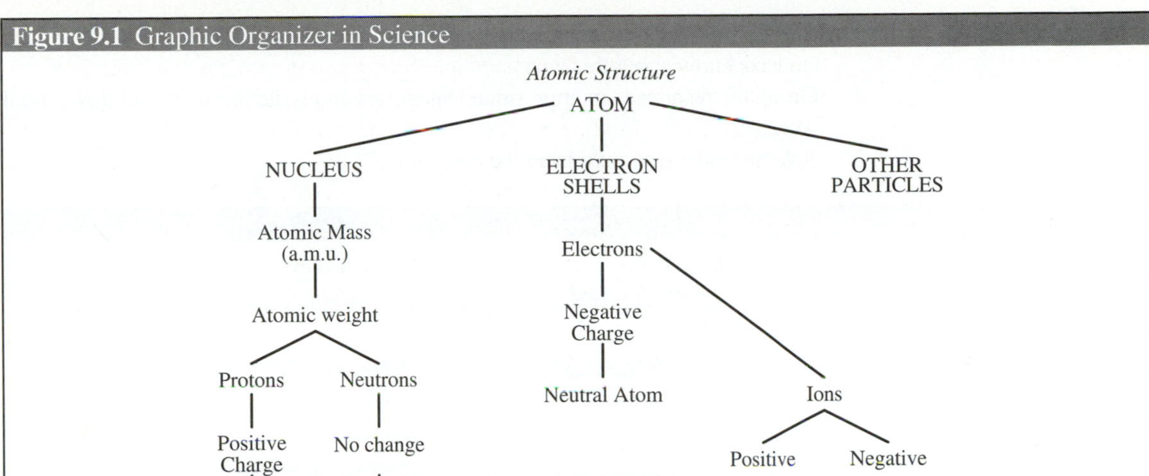

The following questions can be used to guide students in using the structured overview.

1. Of what basic components is an atom composed?
2. How were electrons discussed?
3. What type of charge do electrons possess?
4. What is a neutral atom?
5. How are ions related to electrons?
6. Of what basic components is the nucleus of an atom composed?
7. What is the relationship between protons and neutrons?
8. Why does mass play a significant role in atomic theory?

Developed by Mary Hamilton, East Baton Rouge Parish School System, Louisiana.

To further interrelate the learning of concepts and vocabulary, Gillet and Temple suggest the use of a concept ladder. A concept ladder is designed to show how the word is related to other words and concepts that are already known. Using several basic questions, the students complete the concept ladder as a small group to pool their knowledge or individually as they read.[65] An example of a concept ladder is given in Figure 9.2.

Semantic mapping, or webbing, is another strategy for involving students as concepts and vocabulary are presented. This strategy visually displays the relationship among words and helps to categorize words. Smith and Johnson suggest following basic steps in using this strategy.

1. Select a word that is central to what is to be learned.
2. Write the word in the center of the board.

3. Through class discussion, ask appropriate questions to elicit information that students know about this word.
4. Group the responses in appropriate categories and write them around this central word.
5. Ask the students to help label the categories.[66]

Figure 9.2 Concept Ladder for "The Shoe"

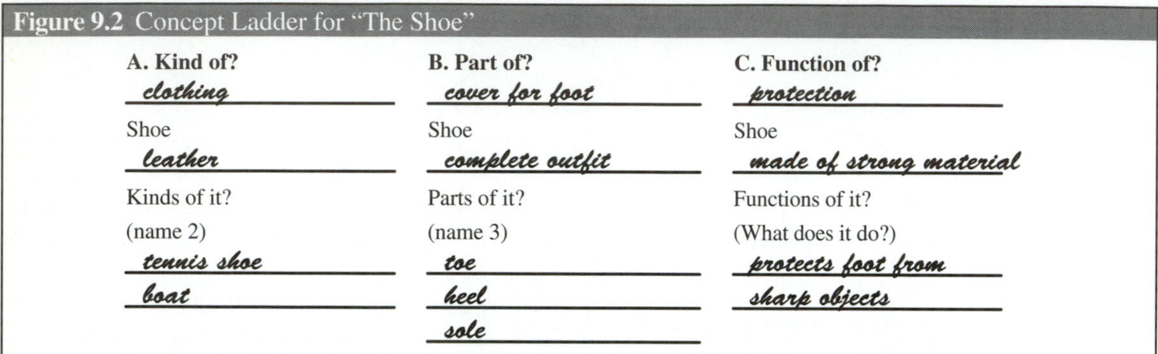

An example of a completed semantic map is given in Figure 9.3. This strategy, which is similar to some graphic organizers, makes use of the students' prior knowledge while developing new vocabulary and concepts.

Figure 9.3 A Semantic Map

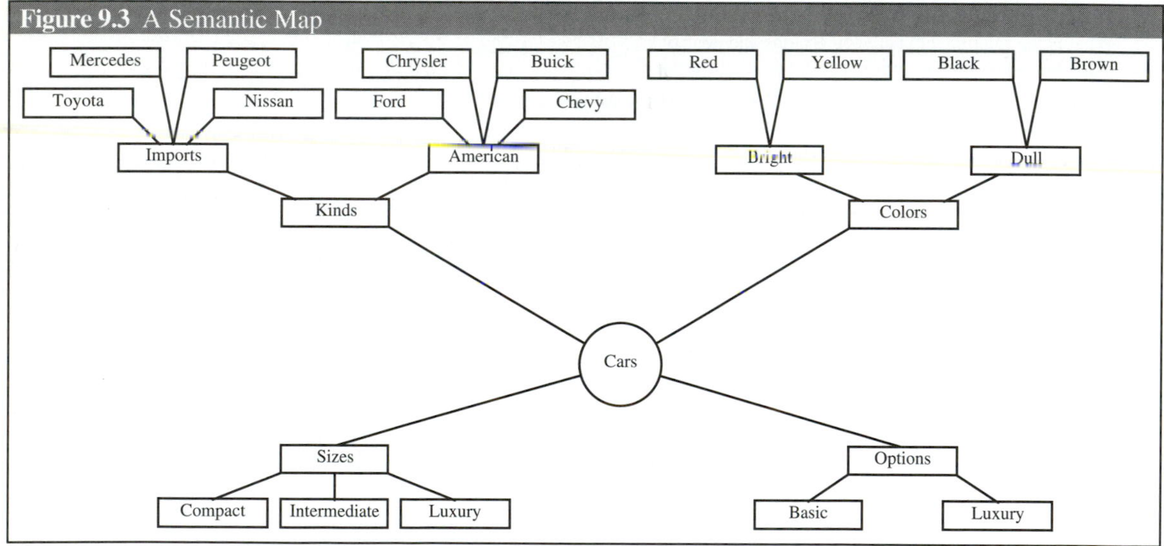

Another strategy that notes the semantic aspects of material for teaching vocabulary and concepts is semantic feature analysis (SFA). Anders and Bos propose this strategy to help students "to learn the relationships between and among the conceptual vocabulary and the major ideas in the text."[67] Based on schema theory, which uses students' prior knowledge for learning new information, the SFA can be developed and used in the following way:

1. The teacher thoroughly reads the assignment to be given to the student to determine the major ideas in the assignment.
2. List (using a phrase or single word) the vocabulary that the students need to know.
3. List the words that represent the major ideas (superordinate concepts) and then those that represent details related to these major ideas (subordinate concepts).
4. Organize the vocabulary into a relationship chart with the superordinate concepts as headings across the top and the related vocabulary down the side. This relationship chart becomes the instructional tool.
5. Give each student a copy of the chart. As the topic of the assignment is given, provide a definition of each superordinate word, encouraging students to add information that involves their personal experiences or understandings.
6. Then introduce each subordinate term and discuss how it is related to the superordinate concept.
7. If there is a positive relationship, use a plus (+), a negative relationship, use a minus (–). A zero (0) indicates that there is no relationship between the superordinate and subordinate idea.[68]

Again, this strategy involves the student in the learning experience and relates new learning to what is already known.

Many strategies exist for developing vocabulary. Hadaway and Young have identified specific strategies for building vocabulary that are especially effective with students from diverse language learning backgrounds.[69] These include the use of timelines, Venn diagrams, H-maps (comparison-contrast maps), and flowcharts. Don't forget the importance of using context; this simple strategy is most frequently used by mature readers and requires no teacher assistance. Teacher reinforcement of this technique is done using modified cloze passages that omit selected words. Teachers are only limited by time and their creativity. However, as we move from listing words on the board for students to locate in the dictionary or giving students a guide to complete as they read, remember the criteria for developing vocabulary: involve the students, use their prior knowledge, and help them become independent learners who use a variety of ways to discover the meaning of words.

Building Schemata

Students' past experiences can be used to activate their knowledge of an area in order to build vocabulary. But what about the student with very limited or no knowledge of an area? How are schemata activated? Spiro and Myers suggest that one major problem, which has been overlooked in the research on schema theory, is that "one cannot have a prepackaged knowledge structure for everything!" They suggest that "the best approach for such a situation is to tentatively encode as much information as possible in as many ways as possible."[70] In other words, students should be told that when they have no knowledge of an area and have no way of obtaining this knowledge, they should remember everything. Acknowledging that this may not be possible, however, they propose some new research questions.

In the meantime, what can the classroom teacher do to help students with few background experiences to build schemata? Barnes, Ginther, and Cochran suggest that students taught schemata and given a specific purpose for reading were able to learn new vocabulary from context significantly better than those students not receiving such instruction.[71]

Obviously, the best way to build these experiences is via first-hand visits or activities. Given that this is not always possible, how then do we realistically develop this knowledge that is so vital to comprehension? For some situations the use of an advance organizer, graphic organizer, or semantic map can help students learn from other students and visualize relationships. These tools can also be designed to delve into the existing knowledge of the student to find something that remotely relates to the concepts and to build on this limited knowledge. Such probing requires teacher skill in questioning and leading a discussion, as well as patience combined with much positive reinforcement.

Student questioning is a good way of eliciting information from students to help them determine what they know and don't know about a word or idea. Through such strategies as active comprehension and reciprocal questioning, students learn to ask questions to gain more information. Active comprehension, according to Singer, requires that the teacher ask questions that elicit questions in return. Asking the students what they would like to know about a picture or an introductory paragraph that you read serves to arouse curiosity and involve the student in what is being taught.[72] Reciprocal questioning, or "ReQuest," designed by Manzo, is a similar procedure that encourages students to ask questions about their reading material. To use this strategy, the teacher may follow this procedure:

1. The teacher and students read silently the first sentence of the passage to be studied.
2. The students then ask as many questions about the sentence as they can think of, and the teacher answers the questions clearly and completely.
3. The teacher then asks questions about the same sentence, and the students answer as completely as possible. In this way, the teacher is modeling good questioning strategies.
4. When these questioning sessions are complete, the students and teacher read the next sentence and proceed as before.
5. When the teacher feels that the students have a basic understanding of the information in the text and can understand the passage, they are asked to read the remainder of the passage.[73]

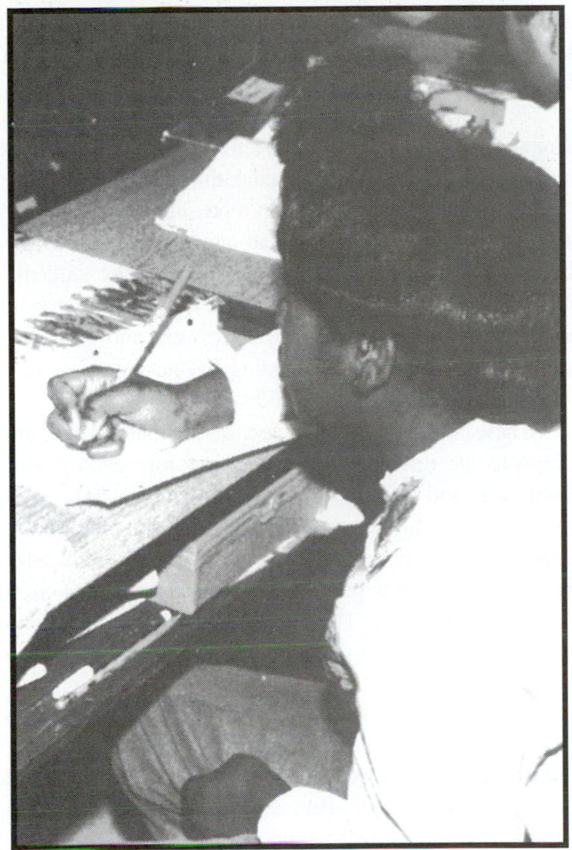

Organizing information is a study procedure which needs to be taught.

Photo courtesy of Edward B. Lasher.

This procedure can be modified to use with an individual student or a small group, and the teacher may use paragraphs instead of sentences for each reading.

Another student-centered strategy that aids in building schema is reciprocal teaching. Reciprocal teaching is based on teaching students to use four activities to improve their comprehension: question generating, summarizing, predicting, and clarifying. The teacher provides explicit instruction, modeling, and corrective feedback for each of the activities. In this strategy, the question generating is similar to the reciprocal questioning procedure outlined previously. Summarizing involves allowing students to monitor their own comprehension by telling the basic information gained from reading the material. Following this summary, the students are then asked to predict what they believe will happen in the passage (text-based prediction) or what they believe will be discussed (content-based prediction). The students then read to prove or disprove their hypotheses. In the last activity, the students seek to clarify information in the text by discussing the information, the text presentation, unclear sentences or vocabulary, and any other points of confusion.[74] This strategy encourages continuous dialogue that allows teachers to diagnose difficulties students are having with concepts and vocabulary due to inadequate schemata and allows students to learn from their peers and the teacher as questions are answered.

Teacher-student interaction with text seems to be crucial to building schema. The Directed Reading-Thinking Activity (DRTA) involves students in predicting, verifying, judging, and extending thinking as teachers pose open-ended questions. Using logical stopping points in a passage, the teacher poses questions for which the student provides a hypothetical answer based on his general knowledge. Class discussion extends or limits these ideas as the students read to verify information. Reading is halted at the next logical stopping point to allow students to address the correctness of their hypothetical answers and raise further questions and possible answers to be verified by reading the next portion of the passage. This process is continued through the passage.

These strategies, which use continuous teacher-student interaction, help build schemata by developing a readiness for reading short portions of information, discussing and clarifying the information, and providing additional prereading information for further reading. Presenting smaller units of information allows for the continuous development of schemata through discussing and reading, as compared to the more traditional procedure of giving students information on a larger unit of material at one time. These small steps help students process new information and relate their understandings as they build the schemata!

Using Text

Research on comprehension has introduced concepts such as considerate and inconsiderate text, text organization, story structure, and story grammar. Prior to this research, few considered the extent to which text could help or deter comprehension; if comprehension difficulties existed, the student was the problem. However, with the wealth of new information and a better understanding of the comprehension process, teachers, parents, and researchers are accepting what students have long known: some texts are easier to read than others. This accessibility has little to do with readability level or student interest in the passage (although this is a consideration to be discussed later), but rather is due to the way the text is put together.

Considerate text is organized to aid the reader in understanding the information. Sentences and paragraphs are put together for ease of communication, typographical aids are used, ideas flow in a logical order, that is, the writer is considerate of the reader and communicates ideas as directly as possible. Inconsiderate text, on the other hand, is unorganized and does not have a clear purpose. This type of text seems to be put together in haste without regard to the reader. As teachers preread materials that students are expected to study, they can readily identify considerate and inconsiderate text and plan instruction accordingly.

Various ways of approaching text analysis have been identified; however, one must remember that the structure of the text differs from one reader to another due to the individual's background experiences. Complex text analysis procedures have been outlined by Meyer, Kintsch, and Frederiksen, while Mandler and Johnson, Rummelhart, Stein and Glenn, and Thorndyke have developed systems for narrative prose or story analysis.[75]

Beginning reading materials usually are presented in a narrative style; thus, students need a knowledge of story structure, or story grammar. Teachers cannot use the complex story analysis procedures due to time limitations, yet they need to know how to evaluate the basic framework of stories to determine the extent to which stories follow a regular format and to prepare to help students deal with stories that deviate.[76] In order to assist students' understanding of the story's framework, Marshall further suggests that teachers draw from the structure of the story for their comprehension questions.[77] Story grammar refers to the basic elements of the story. Questions that can help students understand story grammar include the following:

- *Theme*. What is the major point? What is the moral point? What did X learn at the end?
- *Setting*. Where does the story happen? When did it happen?
- *Character*. Who is the main character? What is he/she like?
- *Initiating events*. What is X's problem? What does X have to try to do?
- *Attempts*. What did X do to resolve the problem? What did X not do to resolve the problem?
- *Resolution*. How did X solve the problem? What would you do to solve X's problem?
- *Reactions*. How did X feel about the problem? Why did X choose this particular solution? How did X feel at the end? Why did X feel that way? How did you feel about the resolution?[78]

As teachers increase their understanding of story grammar and use their knowledge to guide their instruction, students will become more aware of the importance of story grammar.

Strategies for developing story grammar have been used successfully to improve reading comprehension of narrative information.[79] Smith and Bean suggest several specific strategies that teachers can use to improve student awareness of story grammar.[80] One strategy is the story pattern. The teacher draws scenes from the top to the bottom of the page to represent major events in the story and uses these pictures to show students how to create a story. The students then make up a story to go with a new set of illustrations, using the structure just demonstrated by the teacher. Another strategy is the visual diagram, in which illustrations are provided in a circular format to represent the adventures of the main characters or events in the story. The student uses this information to write a story that represents the key elements of the story's structure. A third strategy is the tree diagram. Students are provided with a tree diagram containing questions such as Who? Where? Doing what? Story begins? Does what? and How does it end? Using these questions as the story frame, the students write their own story.

Story mapping is another strategy that has been used successfully to develop story grammar.[81] A story map uses a chart format to help students understand the relationships among the major events in the story. Once students understand the information in their general framework, broader, and more in-depth questions can be addressed. An incomplete framework for a story map is presented in Figure 9.4.

Figure 9.4 A Story Map Frame

Theme

Major Point:

Moral Point:

Setting

Time:

Place:

Character

Main Character:

Other Characters:

Sequence of Events

Initiating Events:

Attempts:

Resolution:

Reaction

Emery suggests extending story maps to explore the characters' motives and reactions in more complex stories.[82] These could help students understand why things happen, consider why the motives and reactions of characters may be different from theirs, and examine the perspectives of all important characters.

Another variation of story mapping involves the use of the cloze. Oja suggests developing story frames using a cloze format to help increase the understanding of text for students.[83]

Understanding story grammar seems to be automatic for some students; they learn to put story elements together just as they learn to put words together to form a sentence. Other students do not possess this natural ability and must be shown how to use story structure to improve their understanding of narrative information. However, story grammar should not be taught in isolation. Just as reading skills should not be taught as isolated components of the reading process, story structure instruction needs to be taught in the context of reading narratives.

As students move out of the primary grades, more of their reading materials are presented in an expository style. To understand the text structure of these materials, students need to be aware of the various organizational patterns of text. Expository text is written according to several basic patterns. Meyer has identified five patterns:

1. Enumeration
2. Time order
3. Comparison-contrast
4. Cause-effect
5. Problem-solution.[84]

Units and chapters within a text may contain several different patterns. Students need to be taught how to use clues or signal words to follow the author's presentation. Vacca, Vacca, and Gove have identified words that signal each of these different organization patterns (see Figure 9.5).[85]

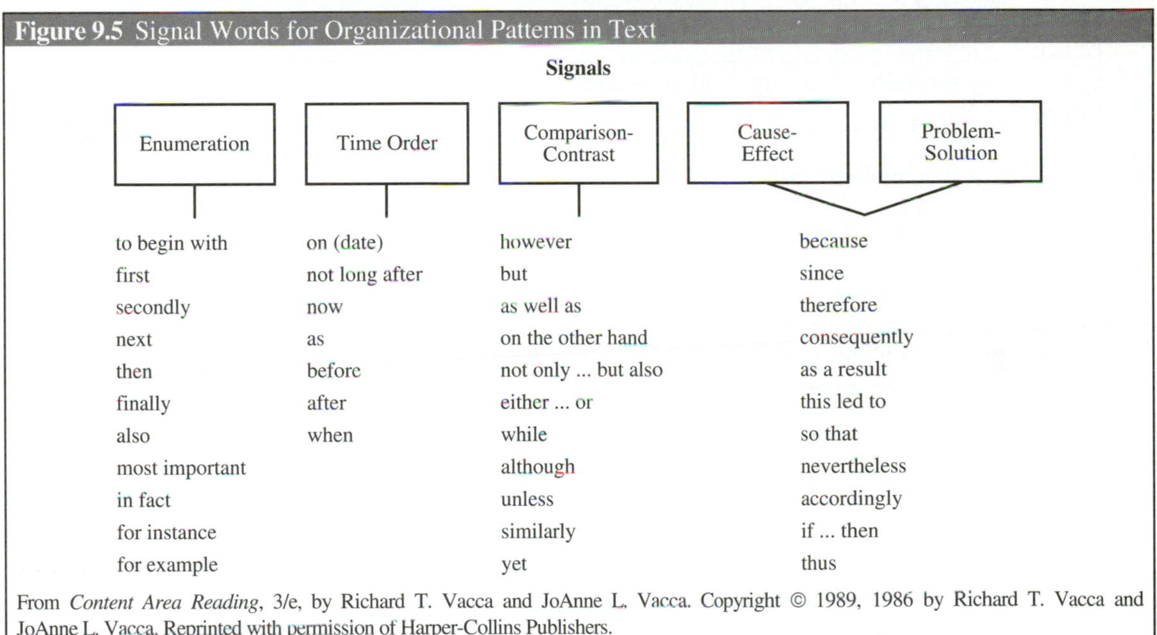

Figure 9.5 Signal Words for Organizational Patterns in Text

From *Content Area Reading*, 3/e, by Richard T. Vacca and JoAnne L. Vacca. Copyright © 1989, 1986 by Richard T. Vacca and JoAnne L. Vacca. Reprinted with permission of Harper-Collins Publishers.

The pattern guide is a useful strategy for helping students understand text structure. The pattern guide is designed by the teacher to help students identify the organizational pattern used in a selection and to remember the significant information. An example of a pattern guide is given in Figure 9.6.

Figure 9.6 A Pattern Guide for Cause and Effect Relationships

Topic: Development of Communities

Part I: Cause-Effect Relationships
In the chapter "Development of Communities," find the effects of the following causes. Write your answer in the space provided.

1. Cause: Communities with the same life forms
   Effect: ______________________________
2. Cause: Geography and climate
   Effect: ______________________________
3. Cause: Low average temperature and low annual precipitation
   Effect: ______________________________
4. Cause: Moderate rainfall, damp and acidic soil with no permafrost
   Effect: ______________________________
5. Cause: Above average rainfall and temperature climate
   Effect: ______________________________
6. Cause: Heavy rainfall and high temperature
   Effect: ______________________________
7. Cause: Very low rainfall and hot, cold, or temperate climates
   Effect: ______________________________

Part II: What do you think the author was trying to say? Write your answer in the space below each question.

1. Why should we be concerned about the development of communities?

2. How does the development of communities affect our quality of life?

3. Why has the future of our world's forests become a major concern to us?

From Earl H. Cheek, Jr., and Martha Collins-Cheek, *Reading Instruction through Content Teaching* (Columbus, Ohio, Merrill Publishing Co., 1983), p. 223.

Using these various strategies, students will become more aware of the organization of text, both narrative and expository. As their knowledge of organization improves, comprehension will improve as well.

Questioning

The traditional way of developing comprehension is by asking questions. However, there has been much criticism of questioning strategies used in elementary and middle-school classes. This criticism ranges from Durkin's statement that comprehension is continuously assessed, via questioning, rather than taught,[86] to a concern with how teacher-generated questions compare to student-generated questions.

Many alternative ideas have been proposed through the years to improve questioning. Because questioning is frequently developed via individual skills, information and examples of different types of questions were given in the previous section on developing comprehension skills. Teacher direction is the primary strategy considered in that section. However, consideration should be given to using student-generated questions to provide direction to reading and as a follow-up after reading. As teachers model effective questioning patterns through teacher-directed questions or reciprocal questioning, students learn how to pose their own questions prior to reading, as they read, and following reading. Thus, teachers will find that learning is greatly enhanced as students become more involved in the question-developing process.

Guides such as the three-level study guide and concept guide also offer students a framework for responding as they read. Using either questions or statements, these guides help students note important information when reading. While these guides tend to be more teacher directed than student directed, they may be effective with some students who need continuous direction as they read. An example of a concept guide is given in Figure 9.7.

Questioning will always be a primary strategy for developing comprehension. Teachers should use questions to monitor comprehension, making sure to use a variety of questions at different levels. Teacher questioning forms the basis for what students learn in a class.

AFFECT AND COMPREHENSION

Though many strategies exist for developing the cognitive facets of comprehension, sometimes comprehension remains poor. Why? The one component that has frequently been ignored in assessing comprehension is the affective domain. Teachers and parents, however, have long recognized that interests, attitudes, feelings, and overall motivation are essential ingredients in the learning process. When students read information that interests them, their comprehension is better than when they are directed to read a story simply because it comes next in the book. In fact, many times students can read material that is written at a higher level when the topic is of interest to them. One of the authors had an experience with an older student who was reading at a very low level yet took an interest in a particular magazine article when he saw his basketball hero pictured on the cover of *Sports Illustrated*. The student asked if he could take the magazine and read the story. Of course, the response was affirmative. This student labored through the article for a week, stopping his peers and teachers in the hallway to ask about specific words. At the end of the week, he brought the magazine back and said, "Now, let me tell you about this story!" He understood every detail, had learned many basic sight words that teachers had struggled to teach for the last seven years, and came to school every Monday morning looking for the new issue of the magazine. Had this student's reading level suddenly jumped about six years? Absolutely not, but he had found something to read that related to his interests and he now viewed reading with a new attitude.

Figure 9.7 A Concept Guide for Social Studies

Topic: The Historical Development of Canada

Part I: As you preview pages 422–435, complete these statements.

1. Energy produced by water power is __________ .
2. A __________ is a group of nations that includes Great Britain and many former British colonies.
3. Because both French and English are official languages in Canada, the country is referred to as being __________ .

Part II: Put the words in the list below into their proper group based on their relationship to the concept.

Jacques Cartier	Quebec	Hudson Bay
Samuel de Champlain	New France	Newfoundland
John Cabot	Roman Catholic	Protestant
Henry Hudson	Montreal	New Brunswick

	French Canada	British Canada
1.	__________	__________
2.	__________	__________
3.	__________	__________
4.	__________	__________
5.	__________	__________
6.	__________	__________
7.	__________	__________
8.	__________	__________
9.	__________	__________
10.	__________	__________
11.	__________	__________
12.	__________	__________

From Earl H. Cheek, Jr., and Martha Collins-Cheek, *Reading Instruction through Content Teaching* (Columbus, Ohio: Merrill Publishing Co., 1983), p. 392.

Chapter 11 deals with developing the personal aspect of reading, and Chapter 2 presented ways of assessing attitudes and interests. However, the focus of this section is on how the affective domain influences comprehension. Higher-level comprehension skills are best developed when students are asked to compare the feelings of the main character in the story to their feelings about a particular situation. Additionally, students can learn to deal with emotions through reading comprehension. Encouraging students to try to feel what a character is feeling, to put themselves in Hannah's shoes in *One Hundred Dresses*, for example, will help students comprehend what the author is trying to say. The comprehension process is a communication process between the author and reader; it is not completed when students simply recall the information printed on the page. Feelings, attitudes, emotions, and beliefs must be communicated for students to truly experience the full meaning of reading. For many students, this emotional relationship with reading first occurs when their teacher reads *Charlotte's Web* and they experience Fern's feelings about Wilbur, and later Wilbur's feelings when Charlotte dies. Why do students love this story and seem to never tire of it? Feelings, emotions, and beliefs form the basis of the story and the details only add more meaning. Most narrative stories evoke some reaction from students, be it positive or negative. Teachers cannot overlook this aspect of comprehension; use questioning strategies to get students involved in this affective part of the comprehension process.

The wealth of information on comprehension becomes more voluminous each day. Spache and Spache have provided an excellent summary of what works in comprehension instruction based on the research.[87] This information is presented in Table 9.4.

SUMMARY

Comprehending printed material is the purpose and goal of reading. For a student to be a successful reader, comprehension must occur. However, comprehension occurs at various levels. For example, some students may comprehend well at the literal level but experience great difficulty in interpreting information or evaluating material. Thus, it is essential that students be taught to understand all three comprehension levels: literal, interpretive, and critical.

Why some students comprehend well at all levels of reading and others do not has always puzzled teachers. Some of the reasons include experiences, language capabilities, intelligence, motivation, interests, attitudes, dialect, and purposes for reading. Difficulty in one or more of these areas may prevent students from realizing their potential.

Another important factor in teaching students to comprehend materials is related to cognitive development. Many teachers do not assist students in reaching their highest level of cognition because of the types of questions they use. It is essential to question students at the interpretive and critical levels, not just at the literal level. Taxonomies have been developed to assist teachers in achieving this goal. Three of the best-known taxonomies were developed by Bloom, Sanders, and Barrett.

Table 9.4 Comprehension Instruction

What Works	What Does Not Work
Providing direct instruction on meanings of words in the reading[88]	Chalkboard prereading presentation of new words
Learning multiplicity of word meanings by categorizing words	Teaching most common meanings of words
Asking pupils to attempt to define new words, eliminating study of those already known[88]	Previewing all new words in the selection
Teaching meaning and effect of signal words	Teaching connectives and signal words as sight words
Using cloze to promote development of contextual analysis; following with discussion of choices and training in hypothesis testing	Teaching contextual analysis as a group of terms
Teaching interpretation of paragraph types above fourth grade[89]	Assuming that author's style is not significant
Beginning assessment with factual questions—who, what, when, where[89]	Following only basal manual in questioning
Moving from factual to explanatory questions—how, why[90]	Mixing questions to test thoroughly
Moving then to higher-level questions—generalization, evaluation, and inferences[90]	Covering facts read as completely as possible
Confining imagery questions to grades above primary, expecting that some pupils cannot use them[91]	Teaching children to use imagery
Discussing pictures in the text to help recall[91]	Failing to discuss and react to pictures
Spending time relating pupil knowledge to content of selection by discussion, pretests, spelling out purposes, and previewing[92]	Getting into the reading as soon as possible
Reinforcing recall by writing pupil concepts on chalkboard, reorganizing this with aid of pupils[93]	Testing comprehension by questioning only
Teaching post-primary children to write a summary sentence after each paragraph in content material[91, 94]	Using teacher questioning and printed exercises for assessment
Recognizing that main ideas include most important idea, ideas related to theme, and what could be expressed in a new title[94]	Teaching main ideas as central thought
Realizing that a comprehension difficulty may require indirect treatments, as vocabulary, informational background, word analysis, etc.[94]	Curing comprehension difficulty by direct teaching of comprehension strategies
Using tests and discussion of correct answers, information feedback, and reviews[94]	Giving tests to measure comprehension
Direct teaching of comprehension strategies[95]	Using printed exercises to practice main ideas, details, etc.
Using children's prior experiences as related to selection as a basis for predicting probable ideas in the selection[96]	Talking with children about their experiences as they might be related to the title of the selection
If children answer a question correctly, they may ask one of the teachers or other children[97]	Having all questions come from the teacher
Teaching pupils how to summarize, outline, raise questions to be answered in the reading; providing practice in these skills[97]	Reserving study skills instruction only for subject matter lessons

. . . Continued

Table 9.4 Comprehension Instruction

Recognizing that comprehension is not really promoted by oral reading	Expecting oral readers to show more than bare, literal recall
Using inferential prereading questions that require a good deal of reading before answering, above primary grades	Using factual prereading questions
Supplying glosses or marginal headings on ditto sheets before reading to guide students	Assuming pupils can use present headings
If content of selection is beyond pupil informational background, helping them by prereading preparation with explanation and discussion[94]	Using an audiovisual aid to prepare students for new, difficult materials
Allowing at least five seconds after each question for think time[98]	Continuing to expect rapid responses to your questions
Recognizing that there may not be correct answers to some questions because they are a matter of opinion or judgment[99]	Expecting and demanding correct answers
Giving feedback by asking for elaboration or explanation or by pointing out why answer is correct[100]	
Recognizing answer is correct by saying so	

Current research in comprehension questions the teaching of specific subskills and encourages comprehension development using the student's knowledge structures or schemata. Although new ideas are provided in this research, much of the information confirms and amplifies on many of the present classroom practices.

To assist classroom teachers in applying these new research findings as well as cope with current requirements for instruction in comprehension, strategies for developing vocabulary, building schemata, dealing with text, and developing the affective area were also presented.

Applying What You Read

1. You have been transferred to a new school to teach the second grade. Your students have had very limited experiences and have poor oral language skills. How important are these impediments to the development of comprehension? How can these factors be partially nullified or reversed?
2. Using the taxonomies presented in this chapter as a model, develop your own taxonomy for teaching comprehension. Discuss the role of taxonomies in developing reading comprehension.
3. Design a program for assessing comprehension. Apply this assessment program to your classroom by selecting those procedures best suited to your students' needs.
4. After obtaining accurate assessment information about your students' strengths and weaknesses in comprehension skills, design appropriate instructional techniques for each student. Implement this instructional plan as early as possible.

NOTES

1. Dolores Durkin, *Teaching Them to Read*, 3rd ed., pp. 393–395.
2. Larry A. Harris and Carl B. Smith, *Reading Instruction: Diagnostic Teaching in the Classroom*, 4th ed., p. 256.
3. Josephine Gemake, "Interference of Certain Dialect Elements with Reading Comprehension for Third Graders," *Reading Improvement.*
4. James F. Christie, "Syntax: A Key to Reading Comprehension," *Reading Improvement.*
5. Kathleen C. Stevens, "The Effect of Background Knowledge on the Reading Comprehension of Ninth Graders," *Journal of Reading Behavior.*
6. Steven A. Stahl, Michael G. Jacobson, Charlotte E. Davis, and Robin L. Davis, "Prior Knowledge and Difficult Vocabulary in the Comprehension of Unfamiliar Text," *Reading Research Quarterly*.
7. R. Scott Baldwin, Ziva Peleg-Bruckner, and Ann H. McClintock, "Effects of Topic Interest and Prior Knowledge on Reading Comprehension," *Reading Research Quarterly.*
8. Durkin, *Teaching Them to Read,* pp. 394–395.
9. Harris and Smith, *Reading Instruction,* pp. 87–89.
10. Dolores Durkin, "What Is the Value of the New Interest in Reading Comprehension?" *Language Arts.*
11. George D. Spache and Evelyn B. Spache, *Reading in the Elementary School,* 4th ed., pp. 450–451.
12. Karen Zabrucky and Hilary Horn Ratner, "Effects of Reading Ability on Children's Comprehension Evaluation and Regulation," *Journal of Reading Behavior.*
13. Robert F. Carey, "Toward a More Cognitive Definition of Reading Comprehension," *Reading Horizons.*
14. Hilda Taba, "The Teaching of Thinking," *Elementary English.*
15. Frank J. Guszak, "Teacher Questioning and Reading," *The Reading Teacher.*
16. J. A. Stallings and D. Kaskowitz, *Follow-Through Classroom Observation Evaluation.*
17. M. D. Gall, B. A. Ward, D. C. Berliner, L. S. Cahen, K. A. Crown, J. D. Elashoff, G. C. Stanton, and P. H. Winne, *The Effects of Teacher Use of Questioning Techniques on Student Achievement and Attitude: Stanford Program on Teacher Effectiveness, A Factorially Designed Experiment on Teacher Structuring, Soliciting, and Reacting*.
18. Karen K. Wixson, "Level of Importance of Postquestions and Children's Learning from Text," *American Educational Research Journal.*
19. Benjamin Bloom et al., *Taxonomy of Educational Objectives, Handbook I: The Cognitive Domain,* pp. 168–172; Norris M. Sanders, *Classroom Questions: What Kinds?* p. 3; Thomas C. Barrett and R. Smith, *Teaching Reading in the Middle Grades.*
20. P. David Pearson and Dale D. Johnson, *Teaching Reading Comprehension.*
21. Michael Strange, "Instructional Implications of a Conceptual Theory of Reading Comprehension," *The Reading Teacher;* Keith E. Stanovich, "Toward an Interactive-Compensatory Model of Individual Differences in the Development of Reading Fluency," *Reading Research Quarterly;* H. Levin and E. L. Kaplan, "Grammatical Structure and Reading," in *Basic Studies in Reading,* edited by H. Levin and J. Williams; Kenneth S. Goodman, "Unity in Reading," in *Theoretical Models and Processes of Reading,* 3rd ed., edited by Harry Singer and Robert Ruddell.
22. Michael Strange, "Instructional Implications," p. 392; K. Stanovich, "Toward an Interactive-Compensatory Model," p. 33–34; D. LaBerge and S. Jay Samuels, "Toward a Theory of Automatic Information Processing in Reading," *Cognitive Psychology.*
23. Michael Strange, "Instructional Implications," p. 393; David Rummelhart, *Toward an Interactive Model of Reading;* Richard Rystrom, "Reflections of Meaning," *Journal of Reading Behavior;* Richard Anderson, Rand Spiro, and Mark Anderson, *Schemata as Scaffolding for the Representation of Information in Connected Discourse.*
24. Jana M. Mason," A Schema-Theoretic View of the Reading Process as a Basis for Comprehension Instruction," in *Comprehension Instruction: Perspectives and Suggestions,* edited by Gerald G. Duffy, Laura R. Roehler, and Jana Mason, p.28.
25. Durkin, "What Is the Value?" p. 27.
26. Jana M. Mason, J. H. Osborn, and B. V. Rosenshine, *A Consideration of Skill Hierarchy Approaches to the Teaching of Reading.*

27. E. Marcia Sheridan, *A Review of Research on Schema Theory and Its Implications for Reading Instruction in Secondary Reading*.
28. Bonnie J. F. Meyer, *Structure of Prose: Implications for Teachers of Reading*.
29. Edward Thorndike, "Reading and Reasoning: A Story of Mistakes in Paragraph Reading," *Journal of Educational Psychology*.
30. Nila Banton Smith, "Patterns of Writing in Different Subject Areas," *Journal of Reading;* James M. McCallister, "Using Paragraph Clues as Aids to Understanding," *Journal of Reading*.
31. Earl H. Cheek and Martha Collins-Cheek, "Organizational Patterns: Untapped Sources for Better Reading," *Reading World.*
32. Martha D. Collins-Cheek, *Organizational Patterns: An Aid to Comprehension*, American Reading Forum Conference Proceedings.
33. Barak V. Rosenshine, "Skill Hierarchies in Reading Comprehension," in *Theoretical Issues in Reading Comprehension,* edited by Rand J. Spiro, Bertram C. Bruce, William F. Brewer.
34. John E. Readance and Mary McDonnell Harris, "False Prerequisites in the Teaching of Comprehension," *Reading Improvement.*
35. Miles V Zintz, *The Reading Process*, pp. 231–232; Frank B. May, *Reading as Communication*, pp. 127–144, 160–173; John N. Mangieri, Lois A. Bader, and James E. Walker, *Elementary Reading,* pp. 66–74.
36. Emerald V. Dechant and Henry P. Smith, *Psychology in Teaching Reading,* 2nd ed., p. 254; Mildred A. Dawson and Henry A. Bamman, *Fundamentals of Basic Reading Instruction*, p. 182.
37. Robert Oakan, Morton Wierner, and Ward Cormer, "Identification, Organization, and Reading Comprehension for Good and Poor Readers," *Journal of Educational Psychology.*
38. Herbert D. Simons, "Linguistic Skills and Reading Comprehension," in *The Quest for Competency in Reading*, edited by Howard A. Klein, p. 165; F. A. Briggs, "Grammatical Sense as a Factor in Reading Comprehension," in *The Psychology of Reading Behavior*, edited by G. B. Schick, pp. 145–149; Mary Anne Hall and Christopher J. Ramig, *Linguistic Foundations for Reading*, pp. 61–79.
39. James Deese, *Psycholinguistics*, p. 1.
40. Lou E. Burmeister, *From Print to Meaning,* pp. 112–113; Roach Van Allen, *Language Experiences in Communication,* pp. 370–371; Robert Emans, "Use of Context Clues," in *Teaching Word Recognition Skills,* compiled by Mildred A Dawson, pp. 181–187.
41. Barbara D. Stoodt, "The Relationship between Understanding Grammatical Conjunctions and Reading Comprehension," *Elementary English.*
42. Harris and Smith, *Reading Instruction*, p. 225.
43. Edna L. Furness, "Pupils, Pedagogues, and Punctuation," *Elementary English*.
44. Durkin, *Teaching Them to Read*, p. 431; Josephine Piekarz Ives, "The Improvement of Critical Reading Skills," in *Problem Areas in Reading: Some Observations and Recommendations*, edited by Coleman Morrison, p. 5; Paul C. Burns and Betty D. Roe, *Teaching Reading in Today's Elementary Schools*, p. 218.
45. Helen M. Robinson, "Developing Critical Readers," in *Dimensions of Critical Reading,* edited by Russell G. Stauffer; William Eller and Judith G. Wolf, "Developing Critical Reading Abilities," *Journal of Reading*.
46. David H. Russell, *Children's Thinking*, Chapter 5.
47. Ann Simpson, "Critical Questions: Whose Questions?" *The Reading Teacher*.
48. Mary Austin and Coleman Morrison, *The First R: The Harvard Report on Reading in Elementary Schools*, Chapter 12.
49. Constance McCullough, "Responses of Elementary School Children to Common Types of Reading Comprehension Questions," *Journal of Educational Research.*
50. Charlotte Agrast, "Teach Them to Read Between the Lines," *Grade Teacher*; Alan R. Harrison, "Critical Reading for Elementary Pupils," *The Reading Teacher*.
51. Agrast, "Teach Them to Read"; Evelyn Wolfe, "Advertising and the Elementary Language Arts," *Elementary English*.
52. Robert R. Nardelli; "Some Aspects of Creative Reading," *Journal of Educational Research.*

53. Jerome A. Niles and Larry A. Harris, "The Context of Comprehension," *Reading Horizons.*
54. Molly M. Wilson, "The Effect of Question Types in Varying Placements on the Reading Comprehension of Upper Elementary Students," *Reading Psychology.*
55. Dolores Durkin, "What Classroom Observations Reveal about Reading Comprehension Instruction," *Reading Research Quarterly;* Dolores Durkin, "Reading Comprehension Instruction in Five Basal Reader Series," *Reading Research Quarterly.*
56. James R. Gavelek and Taffy E. Raphael, "Changing Talk about Text: New Rules for Teachers and Students," *Language Arts.*
57. Shelby J. Barrentine, "Engaging with Reading through Interactive Read-Alouds," *The Reading Teacher.*
58. Michael Strange, "Instructional Implications," pp. 394–397.
59. Dale D. Johnson, "A Themed Issue on Vocabulary Instruction," *Journal of Reading*, p. 580.
60. Edwin E. Vinyard and Harold W. Massey, "The Interrelationship of Certain Linguistic Skills and Their Relationship with Scholastic Achievement When Intelligence Is Ruled Constant," *Journal of Educational Psychology.*
61. Robert B. Ruddell, "Vocabulary Learning: A Process Model and Criteria for Evaluating Instructional Strategies," *Journal of Reading*; Eileen Carr and Karen K. Wixson, "Guidelines for Evaluating Vocabulary Instruction," *Journal of Reading.*
62. Carr and Wixson, "Guidelines," *Journal of Reading.*
63. David P. Ausubel, "The Use of Advance Organizers in the Learning and Retention of Meaningful Verbal Material," *Journal of Educational Psychology.*
64. M. F. Graves, C. L. Cooke, and M. J. LaBerge, "Effects of Previewing Difficult Short Stories on Low Ability Junior High School Students' Comprehension, Recall, and Attitudes," *Reading Research Quarterly.*
65. Jean Wallace Gillet and Charles Temple, *Understanding Reading Problems: Assessment and Instruction*, p. 227.
66. R. J. Smith and D. D. Johnson, *Teaching Children to Read.*
67. Patricia L. Anders and Candace S. Bos, "Semantic Feature Analysis: An Interactive Strategy for Vocabulary Development and Text Comprehension," *Journal of Reading.*
68. Anders and Bos, "Semantic Feature Analysis."
69. Nancy L. Hadaway and Terrell A. Young, "Content Literacy and Language Learning: Instructional Decisions," *The Reading Teacher.*
70. Rand J. Spiro and Ann Myers, "Individual Differences and Underlying Cognitive Processes in Reading," in *Handbook of Reading Research*, edited by P. David Pearson, p. 491.
71. Judy A. Barnes, Dean W. Ginther, and Samuel W. Cochran, "Schema and Purpose in Reading Comprehension and Learning Vocabulary from Context," *Reading Research and Instruction.*
72. Harry Singer, "Active Comprehension: From Answering to Asking Questions," *The Reading Teacher.*
73. Anthony V. Manzo, "ReQuest Procedure," *Journal of Reading.*
74. Annemarie Sullivan Palincsar, "The Quest for Meaning from Expository Text: A Teacher-Guided Journey," Gerald G. Duffy, Laura R. Roehler, and Jana Mason, eds., *Comprehension Instruction: Perspectives and Suggestions,* pp. 251–264.
75. B. J. F. Meyer, *The Organization of Prose and Its Effects on Memory*; W. Kintsch, *The Representation of Meaning in Memory*; C. H. Frederiksen, "Effects of Task-Inducted Cognitive Operations on Comprehension and Memory Processes," edited by J. B. Carroll and R. O. Freedle, in *Language Comprehension and the Acquisition of Knowledge*; J. M. Mandler and M. S. Johnson, Remembrance of Things Passed: Story Structure and Recall," *Cognitive Psychology;* D. E. Rummelhart, "Notes on a Schema for Stories," in *Representation and Understanding,* edited by D. G. Bobrow and A. M. Collins; N. L. Stein and C. G. Glenn, "An Analysis of Story Comprehension in Elementary School Children," in *New Directions in Discourse Processing*, edited by R. O. Freedle; P. W. Thorndyke, "Cognitive Structures in Comprehension and Memory of Narrative Discourse," *Cognitive Psychology.*

76. Robert J. Tierney, James Mosenthal, and Robert M. Kantor, "Classroom Applications of Text Analysis: Toward Improving Text Analysis," in *Promoting Reading Comprehension,* edited by James Flood.
77. Nancy Marshall, "Using the Story Grammar to Assess Reading Comprehension," *The Reading Teacher.*
78. Marshall, "Using Story Grammar," *The Reading Teacher.*
79. M. A. Bowman, *The Effect of Story Structure Questioning upon the Comprehension and Metacognitive Awareness of Sixth Grade Students* (doctoral dissertation, University of Maryland); Gloria M. McDonell, *Effects of Instruction in the Use of an Abstract Structural Schema as an Aid to Comprehension and Recall of Written Discourse*, (doctoral dissertation, Virginia Polytechnic Institute and State University); J. Fitzgerald and D. L. Spiegel, "Enhancing Children's Reading Comprehension through Instruction in Narrative Structure," *Journal of Reading Behavior.*
80. Marilyn Smith and Thomas W. Bean, "Four Strategies That Develop Children's Story Comprehension and Writing," *The Reading Teacher.*
81. D. Ray Reutzel, "Story Mapping: An Alternative Approach to Comprehension," *Reading World*; I. L. Beck, M. G. McKeown, E. S. McCaslin, and A. M. Burkes, *Instructional Dimensions That May Affect Reading Comprehension: Examples from Two Commercial Reading Programs.*
82. Donna W. Emery, "Helping Readers Comprehend Stories from the Characters' Perspectives," *The Reading Teacher.*
83. Leslie Ann Oja, "Using Story Frames to Develop Reading Comprehension," *Journal of Adolescent and Adult Literacy.*
84. Meyer, *The Organization of Prose.*
85. Jo Anne L. Vacca, Richard T. Vacca, and Mary K. Gove, *Reading and Learning to Read,* p. 218.
86. Durkin, "What Classroom Observations Reveal," *Reading Research Quarterly.*
87. George D. Spache and Evelyn B. Spache, *Reading in the Elementary School*, 5th ed., pp. 557–559.
88. Maryann Eeds, "What to Do When They Don't Understand What They Read: Research-Based Strategies for Teaching Reading Comprehension," *The Reading Teacher.*
89. David E. Rummelhart, "Schemata: The Building Blocks of Cognition," in *Theoretical Issues in Reading Comprehension*, edited by Rand J. Spiro, Bertram C. Bruce, and William F. Brewer.
90. Taba, "The Teaching of Thinking."
91. Joseph R. Jenkins and Darlene Pany, "Instructional Variables in Reading Comprehension," in *Comprehension and Reading: Research Review*, edited by John T. Guthrie.
92. Dale D. Johnson and Thomas G. Barrett, "Prose Comprehension: A Descriptive Analysis of Instructional Practices," in *Children's Prose Comprehension: Research and Practice,* edited by Carol M. Santa and Bernard I. Hayes.
93. Penny Baum Moldofsky, "Teaching Students to Determine the Central Story Problem: A Practical Application of Schema Theory," *The Reading Teacher.*
94. Joel R. Levin and Michael Pressley, "Improving Children's Prose Comprehension: Selected Strategies That Seem to Succeed," in *Children's Prose Comprehension: Research and Practice*, edited by Carol M. Santa and Bernard I. Hayes.
95. Ruth J. Kurth and M. Jean Greenlaw, "Research and Practice in Comprehension Instruction in Elementary Classrooms," in *Comprehension: Process and Product,* edited by George H. McNinch.
96. Jane Hansen, "An Inferential Comprehension Strategy for Use with Primary Grade Children," *The Reading Teacher.*
97. Ann L. Brown, J. C. Campione, and J. A. Day, "Learning to Learn: On Training Students to Learn From Texts," *Educational Researcher.*
98. Linda E. Gambrell, "Think-Time: Implications for Reading Instruction," *The Reading Teacher.*
99. Roscoe Davidson, "Teacher Influence and Children's Levels of Thinking," *The Reading Teacher.*
100. Elaine Schwartz and Alice Sheff, "Student Involvement in Questioning for Comprehension," *The Reading Teacher.*

CHAPTER 10

Study Skills and Strategies

The faculty at Twin Lakes School realizes that just as early language skills provide a foundation for reading, word identification skills assist word analysis, and comprehension skills improve thinking abilities, so study skills and strategies foster independence in reading. Ms. Lang sees daily the importance of study skills and strategies as students attempt to use reading skills in their activities in the content areas. For example, skills such as how to organize information, use reference skills, read maps and tables, and use the parts of a book are essential to becoming an independent reader. Thus, learning the proper use of study skills and strategies becomes another important task in the reading process.

This chapter discusses the various study skills and the research relevant to each area. This information assists Ms. Lang and her coworkers as they provide appropriate instruction in the content areas. In addition, there is a section on selected study strategies that can be effective in helping students become more efficient learners. Ideas for teaching are included along with specific procedures for assessing study skills. These specific questions are addressed.

- Why are study skills and strategies important?
- What are the study skills?
- What information does research provide about the development of study skills?
- What are some effective study strategies that students can use to become more efficient learners?
- Which assessment procedures are most effective in this area?
- What are some effective teaching ideas that can be used to develop study skills?

Vocabulary to Know

- K-W-L
- Organizational skills
- PARS
- PORPE
- PQRST
- RAM
- REAP
- Reference skills
- RIPS
- SIP
- Specialized study skills
- SQRQCQ
- SQ3R
- Study skills
- Study strategies

THE IMPORTANCE OF STUDY SKILLS AND STRATEGIES

The development of study skills is extremely important because of the high correlation between knowing how to use the skills and success in learning from and enjoying content materials. One of the first procedures that students must learn when reading content materials is which skills to use to understand the material. Although there is some emphasis on the development of study skills in some readers, these skills are not fully developed until students become more involved in reading science, literature, social studies, and other content materials.

Study skills are generally not used so much in pleasure reading as they are in learning situations involving content reading assignments. Quite often, completing these assignments is a task that few students enjoy. Smith summarizes the special situation that exemplifies the use of study skills: assignments are made by another person, materials are chosen by someone else, and testing will be conducted by this other person.[1] The other person, of course, is the teacher; however, practically speaking, the one who will benefit from the assignments is the student. The result of these assignments should be the development of specific study skills that become automatic responses that can be used as needed.

Much of the responsibility for learning to use study skills rests with the student; however, it is incumbent on the teacher to provide the necessary instruction if the learning of these skills is to occur. Unfortunately, instruction in this area often does not occur as frequently or with as much emphasis as is required. If students are to learn the effective use of study skills, they must receive carefully planned instruction in a variety of situations in the different content areas and be provided appropriate assignments to sharpen these skills. Dreher's research suggests that after students have been taught study skills, they should be given systematic guided practice in a meaningful context.[2] Research skills, for example, are understood best when a teacher incorporates research-related minilessons in social studies units. Without routine practice, many children are unlikely to transfer their knowledge to new situations.

Although material with which these skills must be used becomes more complex as the grade level increases, the basic application of the study skills remains unchanged. Thus, application in each of the content areas is the key to efficient use of the study skills.

There are various techniques for teaching the study skills. Perhaps the most effective way to instruct students is to demonstrate the skills, although many teachers use inductive approaches such as inquiry, discovery, and problem solving.[3] Using content materials for this purpose is generally the most efficient approach.

Study skills are important because they represent a structure of knowledge that can be transferred from one set of materials to another. The structure can be adapted to the specific content area and to various types of content materials. As students learn to apply these skills with some degree of consistency, they become more independent readers.

Four major influences on studying have been identified:

1. The nature of the criterion task or goal for which the student is preparing
2. The nature of the material the student is studying
3. The cognitive and affective characteristics of the student
4. The strategies the student uses to learn the material[4]

The interaction of these factors in many different ways compounds the difficult task of teaching students how to study.

The student should not only be given a purpose for reading by the teacher initially but should also learn to establish personal reasons or goals for studying. Students can best acquire this skill through the use of study strategies such as SQ3R, which is discussed later in this chapter.

The second factor affecting studying is the materials used by students. Effective content instruction requires the use of textbooks as well as supplementary materials. Because of the special relationship between the use of study skills and the acquisition of knowledge in the various content areas, it is essential that materials be carefully selected and that students understand how the information in the materials is organized. Difficulties frequently arise in studying content materials because students are unable to determine which comprehension skills to apply when reading the material. This difficulty results primarily from a lack of understanding of the organizational pattern used by the author (see Chapter 9).

Teachers and researchers often discuss whether one study strategy is more effective than others in helping students learn the material. Although note taking, outlining, summarizing, using book parts, and map reading are all useful in the study process, research has failed to substantiate the superiority of one technique over another. What it does indicate is that using the appropriate study strategy with the right material will enable the student to understand the information better and that students must be taught to use a strategy appropriately.[5] Furthermore, research confirms that introducing students who already study effectively to a new strategy may be harmful rather than helpful.[6] Thus, teachers must know the strengths and weaknesses of their students, so that appropriate instruction in the study skills can be provided.

Other factors that contribute to the difficult task of teaching students how to study effectively have been identified by Graham and Robinson.[7] These include attitudes, cultural background, general knowledge, general health, linguistic knowledge and flexibility, and readiness for study tasks.

- *Attitudes.* Attitudes play an important role in how well students learn. This is particularly true with study skills. Students with positive attitudes typically are more willing to try new or different study strategies. Students with less positive attitudes are usually the ones who experience difficulty in reading and understanding the various content materials assigned by the teacher.

  The teacher's attitude about the effective use of study skills is just as important as the students'. In order for students to read content materials successfully, they must understand what is expected of them. If the teacher's primary objective in a lesson is for students to understand the author's purpose, then this should be indicated to them before they begin to read. Discussion is an effective means of assisting students having difficulty understanding the author's purpose. Active communication between teachers and students is essential to success in learning to use study skills effectively.
- *Cultural Background.* Another important step in helping students become more adept at studying is to identify and use cultural attributes. A primary strength of this country is the diverse background of its people. Teachers should use this strength as it exists in their classroom to facilitate learning and help students use study skills more appropriately. Teachers should be aware of the cultural forces that have already influenced their students' development outside of the classroom. Students' multicultural backgrounds can be used to enrich the classroom environment and instructional procedures. Also, demonstrating a knowledge of the students' backgrounds will strengthen the rapport between students and teachers.
- *General Knowledge.* Another important factor that influences students' ability to apply study skills in learning content materials is general knowledge. This prior knowledge consists of ideas and information that students possess as a result of their experiences. Students differ in their cognitive development; thus, it is important for teachers to be aware of these differences. Typically, students will retain information, perceive relationships, and make inferences at various levels primarily because of their different experiences and their varying cultural and socioeconomic backgrounds.
- *General Health.* An important factor in developing effective study skills is the general health of students in the teacher's classroom. It is especially important to be aware of any physical problems that students exhibit, since physically ill students will not be able to achieve at their normal level.
- *Linguistic Knowledge and Flexibility.* Linguistic knowledge and flexibility influences the development of study skills. Fluent readers demonstrate flexibility in their use of language, which enhances their ability to apply study skills and

learn content materials. However, inexperienced readers have less flexible linguistic strategies and are thus less able to apply study skills. Both types of students require assistance from the teacher in either developing new study skills or expanding already learned strategies.

- *Study Skills Readiness.* Readiness for completing content assignments is another factor to consider when teaching students how to use study skills effectively. To acquire information students must be ready for the task. Appropriate instruction and supervision at school ensures that students are ready to undertake various content assignments; however, a problem may develop when assignments are to be completed at home. Assignments at home require more intrinsic motivation that some students may have. Students experiencing trouble with homework may exhibit these behavioral characteristics: (a) forgetting to complete their homework assignments, (b) inability to use time wisely in which to fit every subject, (c) rarely finishing the assignments they start, or (d) finding it generally difficult to complete schoolwork at home. These students need help in improving their readiness in applying study skills. It is also advisable to contact these students' parents so that appropriate supervision can be provided at home. Parents can help students construct and use assignment sheets, prepare a study schedule for recording their daily and weekly activities, and organize their study time. Coordination between parents and teachers is essential in developing effective study habits.

IDENTIFYING STUDY SKILLS

Study skills are divided into three basic categories: reference skills, organizational skills, and specialized study skills (see Figure 10.1). Each of these skill areas is discussed in more detail along with the relevant research findings.

Figure 10.1 Categories of Study Skills

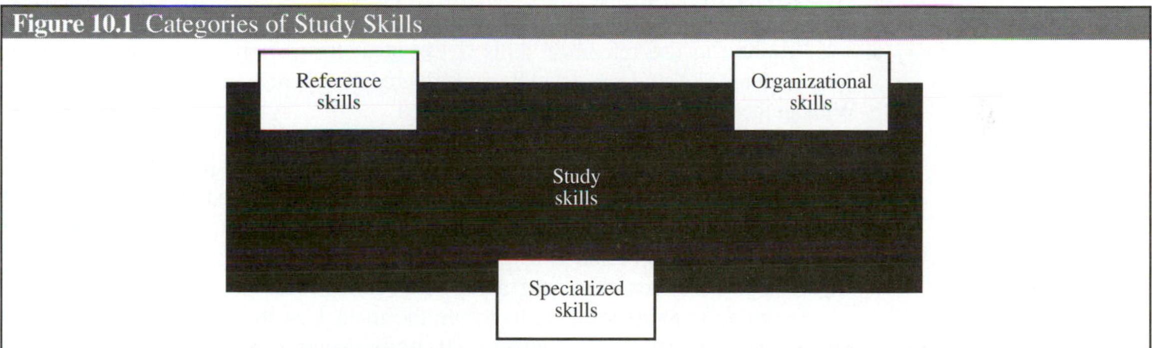

Reference Skills

Reference skills are primarily concerned with locating information in various sources. Skills in this category include learning to use the dictionary and related subskills, using encyclopedias, using specialized reference materials such as the atlas and the almanac, and using the library card or computer catalog.

Obviously, students need to understand the proper use of all the reference skills in order to gain information in the content areas. As students become more involved in the content areas in upper-elementary school, middle school, and high school, these skills become more and more important. Students are frequently given assignments requiring them to locate information that can only be found in reference materials. Thus, these skills are an indispensable tool for acquiring knowledge.

Unfortunately, many students from the upper-elementary through high-school grades lack proficiency in using reference skills. Although a summary of British research studies indicated that a majority of students with access to an atlas at home were able to use it to some extent at school,[8] many students do not have an atlas in their home. When these deficiencies occur, little is gained from criticizing prior instruction in the lower grades, and it becomes the responsibility of teachers at these upper levels to improve the students' skills.

Even with appropriate instruction, many students will still experience difficulty in using reference materials effectively because of the readability level of the material. When students read on lower instructional levels than their grade placement, reference materials written on an even higher level represent a serious obstacle to acquiring information. Thus, teachers must assist students in using reference materials that most closely match their students' reading levels.

Bond and Wagner suggest that skill in locating information in reference materials is dependent on certain abilities: (a) appraisal of the problem, (b) knowledge of appropriate sources, (c) locating a desired source, (d) using the index and table of contents, and (e) skimming.[9]

Learning to use reference materials is vital to the learning process and one of the primary objectives of the upper elementary grades.[10] For this reason, Nelson recommends closer cooperation between the media specialist and the teacher. She also recommends that games, films, and periodicals, such as *Sports Illustrated* and *Hot Rod,* should be used more in teaching reference skills.[11]

A suggestion for improving students' skill in using the dictionary is the use of word games featuring limericks and synonyms.[12]

Learning to use reference skills is essential. Instruction in the various content areas requires that students develop some degree of expertise in using reference skills. Without these skills, success will be hampered.

Organizational Skills

For some students an even more difficult task than learning to use reference skills is developing organizational skills. Organizing information requires the ability to synthesize and evaluate the material read. These tasks call for a high level of cognition. The skills included in this area include developing outlines, underlining important points or key ideas, and taking notes during reading.

Outlining requires students to locate the main idea in a passage and whatever details are essential to its development. The primary purpose of the outline technique is to help students locate the relevant information in a passage or series of materials. It is often suggested as a technique for studying for exams or preparing material for a research paper. Harris recommends teaching the use of outlines prior to teaching note-taking skills,[13] while Hansell found that appropriate training improves the ability to outline.[14]

Harris and Sipay suggest that students should be taught the effective use of outlining by

1. Discussing the importance of outlining with students
2. Demonstrating how to outline using previously read material
3. Giving students a series of graded exercises in outlining and providing assistance in completing this task[15]

The skill of underlining is another valuable tool for organizing data and gathering information for research papers. An interesting aspect of underlining is that research has clearly indicated its superiority to outlining in gathering information.[16] It is also clear that underlining key words in a passage increases the likelihood that the information will be remembered.[17]

Poostay has recommended that the following instructional sequence be used to assist students to develop and expand their underlining capabilities.

1. Copy a selection of 100–150 words.
2. Preview the selection, then underline key concepts. Include 5–7 key concepts per 100 words.
3. Make copies of the underlined selection for your students.
4. As you read a portion of the selection, have the students point to each underlined concept.
5. Demonstrate and discuss how and why each concept was selected.
6. Read the selection again and ask students to predict the content of the selection using only the underlined concepts.
7. Collect the underlined selection and give out the original source, and ask the students to read it.
8. Use unaided and aided recall strategies to check the students' comprehension of the selection.
9. Allow students to practice on other selections, and then encourage them to use this technique on their own.[18]

Note taking is the third important skill involved in organizing material. It is helpful when listening to a class discussion or a guest speaker. The primary task involved in taking notes is to distinguish relevant from irrelevant information. For taking notes, Hafner suggests the following procedures:

1. List the main points with necessary clarifying statements.
2. List illustrations (graphic and verbal) and experiments useful for clarifying points.
3. List key terms and their definitions.
4. List terms or concepts that need further clarification.[19]

Students must have opportunities to use library resources.

Photo courtesy of Edward B. Lasher.

Stahl, King, and Henk found that students' note taking could be enhanced through training and evaluation.[20] They suggest a four-step process that includes modeling, practicing, evaluating, and reinforcing.

According to various research studies, note taking appears to be a useful skill for students to develop as a technique for acquiring important information in both reading and listening situations.[21]

The importance of all three organizational skills cannot be overemphasized. They play a major role in successful reading. Research clearly indicates that training in these skills improves success in content reading, and that many students in the content areas are deficient in these skills.[22]

Specialized Study Skills

Specialized study skills are used to obtain as much information as possible from a book or other materials. In this particular skill area, all parts of a book or materials are analyzed to determine what information can be obtained from them and how best to understand the information presented. Some skills included in this area are previewing, scanning and skimming, materials, reading maps, tables, graphs, and diagrams, adjusting reading rate according to material and purpose, and using appropriate study strategies such as SQ3R.

Previewing, scanning, and skimming content materials are valuable tools for learning about the organizational structure of materials, determining whether or not the information is useful, locating details, and determining the main ideas. Research indicates that previewing is especially valuable as an initial step in reading, and that instruction in how to read and interpret subheadings when previewing is essential.[23]

Another very important skill, especially in social studies, science, and math, is reading maps, tables, graphs, and diagrams. Unfortunately, research does not indicate clearly the order in which these subskills should be presented; however, no one disputes their usefulness.[24]

Adjusting reading rate according to the difficulty of the material and one's purpose for reading is a valuable skill that students must learn. For example, students should realize that they do not read a comic book in the same manner or at the same rate as they read their social studies book. Hafner and Jolly suggest that an appropriate rate is the maximum comfortable speed at which one can read and still understand the passage.[25]

Another useful skill in reading content material is using appropriate study strategies such as SQ3R. Research suggests these strategies are being used more widely and successfully by teachers.[26] Study strategies are, in essence, learning strategies that students should activate when interacting with expository text. The ability to use study strategies effectively can be the determining factor in whether or not students understand the content materials that they are required to read. For students to gain the greatest benefit from these strategies, it is essential that teachers demonstrate their use. Also, students should be given ample time to learn how to use these strategies effectively through practice, teacher feedback, and evaluation. When properly used, study strategies should enhance the student's ability to understand expository material. Selected strategies are presented below.

SQ3R

One of the most widely used study strategies is SQ3R, developed by Robinson. It is especially beneficial when used as a teacher-guided activity to introduce a new chapter or a new textbook. It can be used in groups or with the class as a whole. SQ3R follows five steps:

1. *Survey.* The student surveys the material, giving careful attention to the title, introductory pages, heading, organization of the material, and summary. Following this survey, the student should try to recall as much information as possible before going on to the next step.
2. *Question.* As the student reviews what she remembers from the survey, she formulates specific questions to be answered as the material is read. These questions assist the student in establishing purposes for reading.
3. *Read.* With specific questions in mind, and given a purpose by the teacher, the student reads the material to locate answers. It is possible that answers to all of

the questions will not be found, and in that case other resources must be sought. In addition, the student should be encouraged to use these unanswered questions to stimulate class discussion.

4. *Recite.* After reading the material, the student should recite the answers to the questions formulated prior to reading. This assists in remembering and leads the reader to summarize the ideas presented. Recitation will help the reader to become more critical in analyzing the information and possibly question the logic of some of the author's ideas. This recitation is private and not a recitation to the class.
5. *Review.* At this point, the student reviews the ideas presented in the entire selection and may outline them mentally or on paper. She should attempt to fill in the specific details from what was read. If the student cannot review the material in this manner, then assistance is needed in developing the higher-level comprehension skills of interpretive and critical reading.[27]

There are variations of SQ3R for various content areas. The PQRST technique is recommended by Spache for studying science materials, and Fay has proposed the SQRQCQ technique for use in reading mathematics.

Science: PQRST

1. *Preview.* Rapidly skim the total selection.
2. *Question.* Raise questions to guide the careful reading that will follow.
3. *Read.* Read the selection, keeping the questions in mind.
4. *Summarize.* Organize and summarize the information gained from reading.
5. *Test.* Check your summary against the selection to determine if the summary was accurate.[28]

Mathematics: SQRQCQ

1. *Survey.* Read the problem rapidly to determine its nature.
2. *Question.* Decide what is being asked, what the problem is.
3. *Read.* Read for details and interrelationships.
4. *Question.* Decide what processes should be used.
5. *Compute.* Carry out the computation.
6. *Question.* Ask if the answer seems correct, check the computation against the problem facts and the basic arithmetic facts.[29]

Another variation of the SQ3R proposed by Walker is SRQ2R (survey, review, question, read, recite) which, when integrated with instruction in text structure, can be highly effective.[30]

PARS

This modified and simplified study strategy was developed by Smith and Elliot primarily for use with younger students who have limited experience in using study strategies.

1. *Preview* the material to get a general sense of movement and organization (i.e., check for important headings or concepts).
2. *Ask questions* before reading to make sure that you, as a student, are setting a purpose or purposes that satisfy you and your perception of what the teacher will emphasize.
3. *Read* with those purpose-setting questions in mind.
4. *Summarize* the reading by checking information gained against the preestablished questions.[31]

REAP

This study strategy was developed by Eanet and Manzo to be used in reading and content area classrooms. It is intended to develop independence in reading while strengthening thinking and writing skills. In this strategy, students are not required to preview the material or establish questions to guide reading. Since there is no preparation for reading, the emphasis is on reading the material and remembering what the author has said. It is helpful if the student has some previously developed ability to summarize and take notes.

1. *Read.* The student reads to find out what the writer is saying.
2. *Encode.* The student translates the writer's message into his own words.
3. *Annotate.* The student writes the message in notes for his own use using any one of several forms of annotation such as heuristic, summary, thesis, question, critical, intention, or motivation.
4. *Ponder.* The student thinks about the author's message and may wish to discuss his findings with others.[32]

K-W-L

This study strategy was developed by Ogle to enable teachers to assist students in activating prior knowledge when interacting with expository text and to heighten their interest in reading this material.

1. *What I Know.* Students brainstorm in response to a concept presented by the teacher before they read the selection. Teachers should write down these ideas on the chalkboard, poster board, or any convenient place to use them as a beginning point for discussion. After this, teachers should generate categories from the brainstorming session that will enable students to better understand what they will be reading.
2. *What Do I Want to Learn?* Students develop questions that highlight their area of interest as a result of the activities in the first step. Students then read the selection.

3. *What I Learned.* After completing their reading selection, students write down what they have learned, check this against their questions, and finish answering any remaining questions.[33]

Sippola recommends using a fourth step in the K-W-L strategy.[34] By adding the step "What I still need to learn" (K-W-L-S), students attend to what remains unanswered and is worthy of further inquiry after reading.

PORPE

This writing-study strategy was developed by Simpson primarily for students to use in learning how to study for essay questions. As students encounter more expository text material, especially in upper elementary and middle school, they also encounter an increased emphasis on the use of essay questions to assess knowledge. Additionally, the current emphasis on qualitative assessment to measure students' knowledge, particularly in the elementary grades, is heavily dependent on children's writing activities. Thus, it is likely that the use of essay questions for assessment purposes in the elementary grades will increase.

1. *Predicting* potential essay questions that may be asked.
2. *Organizing* key ideas for possible answers.
3. *Rehearsing* the key ideas for possible answers.
4. *Practicing* the recall of key ideas in self-assigned reading tasks.
5. *Evaluating* the completeness, accuracy, and appropriateness of their answers to essay questions as compared to key ideas and possible answers that were studied.[35]

RAM

This study strategy, developed by Dana, helps poor readers prepare for reading and sets the stage for the content.

1. *Relax* before beginning to read.
2. *Activate* purpose, attention, and prior knowledge.
3. *Motivate* yourself, as a student, for the reading task.[36]

SIP

This strategy, also developed by Dana, is designed to help poor readers focus their attention on content while reading. It is effective with both narrative and expository text.

1. *Summarize* the content of each page or section of the text.
2. *Image* the content. Students form an internal visual image of the content of the page or section. This step adds no time to the reading task and provides a second imprint of the text's content.
3. *Predict* while reading. Students should stop after each page or section in the text and predict what might happen next. This step usually piques the reader's interest to read more to verify their prediction.[37]

RIPS

This strategy was designed by Dana to help disabled readers repair comprehension problems while reading. It is especially effective in converting a negative experience with the text into a constructive one.

1. *Read on* and then *reread* when necessary. If comprehension breaks down during reading, then students should stop and reread until comprehension improves.
2. *Image* the content to create help imprint the material. Visual images that do not make sense will cue the readers that comprehension difficulties are continuing.
3. *Paraphrase* the problem section and restate the information in your own words.
4. *Speed up, slow down, or seek help.* This step reminds students that during the reading-on and rereading of text, they may need to speed up or slow down their reading rate. If all else fails, the readers should seek help.[38]

Learning the proper use of study skills is essential to the reading process. These skills are particularly vital to comprehension of content materials. Without the ability to organize materials, use the dictionary, outline, understand specialized vocabulary, use parts of a book, read maps and charts, and use the other specialized study skills, learning to read content-related material is a difficult task.

PROVIDING APPROPRIATE INSTRUCTION IN STUDY SKILLS

The last section of this chapter summarizes assessment procedures for evaluating study skills and offers appropriate instructional techniques for each skill. Appropriate assessment procedures are presented in Table 10.1. Unfortunately, there is a lack of formal assessment procedures for study skills; however, using informal assessment procedures can yield much specific information of value to the teacher. Since so few assessment procedures are available compared to the other skill areas, all of the study skills are grouped together.

Table 10.1 Assessment Procedures for Evaluating Study Skill Areas

Skill Areas	Procedures
Reference, Organizational, and Specialized Study Skills	Criterion-referenced tests Content Reading Inventory *MAT6 Reading Diagnostic Tests* (skimming, scanning) Observation checklist Test of Reading Comprehension

Once the teacher has assessed students' strengths and weaknesses in study skills, the next step is to implement an appropriate instructional program. Suggested activities are presented in Table 10.2.

Table 10.2 Study Skills

Skill	Activities
Reference Skills	
Use dictionary	Divide the group into teams. Call out a word and see which group can locate the word first. They must give the guide words in order to score a point.
	Give students a pronunciation key from the dictionary and a list of words spelled using the symbols from the pronunciation key. Take turns pronouncing the words using the appropriate accent.
Use encyclopedia	Put various topics on slips of paper and let students select one. Ask them to find the appropriate encyclopedia to locate information on the topic. Then identify five important facts about the topic.
	Play a game with the students taking turns being the librarian. The other students select prepared questions or make up questions to ask the librarian. When the librarian locates the answer in the encyclopedia, another student becomes the librarian.
Use specialized reference materials	Give students cards that tell about a trip they have won. Use an atlas to determine the roads they should take to get to their destination.
	Use student-prepared questions that can be answered with an almanac. Let a student ask a question and see who can locate the information first. The winner gets to ask the next question.
Use library card catalog or computer	Give assignments that can be answered from the catalog. Let students work in teams to locate the information requested.
	Ask students to prepare questions that other students may answer using the catalog. Different classes may exchange their questions and have contests.
Organizational Skills	
Develop outlines	Prepare a large model of an outline, omitting the words. Tape it to the floor or the wall. Give students the information that could complete the outline. Let them fill in the blanks.
	Give students sentence strips containing information that could be put together to form an outline. Ask them to develop the outline. Two groups may compete to see who can finish first. They may then write a story from the outline.
Underline important points or key ideas	Give each team a short selection and a red pen. Get them to discuss and agree upon the important points that should be remembered and underlined.
	Use several copies of a selection and ask students to underline the key ideas. Then compare what each student marked. For any points that differ, ask the student to explain why they were underlined.

. . . Continued

Table 10.2 Study Skills

Take notes during reading	Ask students to take notes as they read by listing important points. Then ask them to use their notes to report what they read to another student. Let them check one another to be sure all important points were covered.
	Let students read different sections of a chapter and take notes. Then combine the notes to see if the most important information is included as they use the notes to answer questions.
Specialized Study Skills	
Use title page	Give students several title pages and a list of questions that can be answered using the title page. Keep score as to who can answer the most questions.
	Ask each student to develop one question that can be answered from the title page. Let them ask the question of the class. When all the questions are answered, ask students to work in pairs and design their own title page.
Use table of contents and lists of charts	Play a game in which students give clues to locate information in the table of contents. For example, "I'm looking for the page number for the story "The Gray Fox."
	Give students a book without a table of contents and ask them to make one to go with the book.
Locate introduction, preface, and foreword	Have a treasure hunt in the classroom to locate books containing an introduction, preface, or foreword. Award one point for each one with an introduction, two points for each preface, three points for each foreword, and four bonus points for a book with all three components.
	Go through a book containing two or three of these components and develop questions from the information provided. To answer the questions, students must read the information in the book.
Use appendix	Give students materials that refer them to the appendixes in the material. Ask them to locate specific information in the designated appendix.
	Play I Am Looking For by telling the students things that you are looking for. All the information should be located in one of the appendixes in a book that they have.
Identify bibliography and list of suggested readings	After reading material in a book containing a list of suggested readings, refer the students to this list and ask them to select the two readings that seem most interesting to them and tell why they seem interesting.
	Ask students to look at the bibliography in a book and find one or more of the materials listed in the bibliography. Then look at the material and determine what the author used from this source in writing the material.

. . . Continued

Table 10.2 Study Skills

Use glossary and index	Give students a crossword puzzle using words from the glossary in the book. In order to complete the puzzle, the student must use the glossary. Ask students questions that can be answered from a book. However, to answer the questions they must locate the information in the index of the book.
Use study questions	Direct students to use the study questions to help establish their purposes for reading something. They may try to answer the questions prior to reading the material and then confirm their answers after they read. Let students read material and develop study questions that would aid other students as they read the material.
Read maps, tables, graphs, and diagrams	Draw a map to be followed as students go on a treasure hunt around the classroom or school. As they reach certain points, other maps are given until they find the one that directs them to the hidden treasure. Have one group in the class make a graph or table about the class, the weather, or some topic of interest to the students. Then let this group explain to the others in the class how to get information from the graph or table.
Use footnotes, typographical aids, and marginal notes	Give students material containing footnotes and ask them to answer a question from the information in a footnote. For example, "What is the first page of the information that the author used in this reference?" Ask students to make an outline of a chapter using only the words in bold and italic type. Then ask them to read the chapter to see if these were actually the most important ideas.
Preview, skim, or scan materials	Give students a short selection and two questions that can be answered from the selection. Allow them a very short time to skim the material to locate the answers. Ask students to preview a chapter before they read it and list at least two questions that they want to answer as they read the material.
Adjust rate according to material and purpose	Give students two selections to read, one technical expository and one light narrative. Ask them to choose a selection and tell how quickly they will read it by placing a "slow" or "fast" sign on their desk. Prior to each reading activity, ask students why they are reading the material and at what rate the material should be read according to their purpose. Let them keep a log for several days to note the material, the purpose for reading it, and the rate.
Understand general and specialized vocabulary	Develop a vocabulary bank that contains all new words learned in each class. Each card in the bank should contain the word, the definition, and a sentence. If the word is general or relates to every content area, a red line should be placed across the card; if it relates to math, a blue line, and so on for each subject area. Words relating to several areas would have the various definitions and colors on the card.

. . . Continued

Table 10.2 Study Skills

	Identify all vocabulary words in each lesson that may cause problems in reading the material. Discuss these words and their meanings as used in the context of the material. Use the newspaper to search for the words to see if they can be used to mean other things.
Use appropriate study strategies such as SQ3R	Make a large sign to hang as a mobile in the classroom to remind students to use the appropriate study technique as they read. Periodically review the study technique with the students to encourage them to use the procedure correctly.
	As students are introduced to the different study procedures appropriate to particular content areas, tell them they will have their own codes, or formulas, that other classes in the school will not know. Knowing these formulas, such as SQ3R, will help them read the content material more easily. Then use the ''code'' language frequently to refer to those techniques to encourage their use.

SUMMARY

Study skills provide the essential structure for the acquisition of knowledge from the printed page. The development of these skills is crucial to becoming an independent reader who can comprehend specific information, especially in various content materials.

The three primary categories of study skills are reference, organizational, and specialized study skills. Various techniques for teaching these skills include demonstration, inquiry, discovery, and problem solving.

Reference skills include such skills as using the dictionary, encyclopedias, and library catalog, while organizational skills include outlining, underlining, and note taking. The third category, specialized study skills, refers to learning skills such as how to use the parts of a book, previewing, skimming, scanning, and study strategies.

Study strategies are learning strategies that students should activate when interacting with expository text. The ability of students to use these strategies may be the determining factor in whether or not they understand the content materials that they are required to read in school.

Assessment procedures and activities were presented in table form.

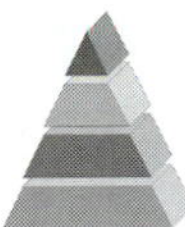

Applying What You Read

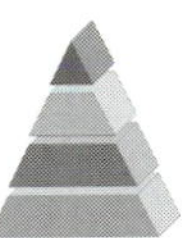

1. You are the language arts teacher for the sixth grade. The students have difficulty in using materials in the library. Which skills would you need to develop, and how would you go about it?
2. Study strategies are used most often in the content areas. How can the content teacher develop these strategies? Select one content area and some specific study strategies to use as an example.
3. Design a study skills program that would involve all the content teachers in your school. Decide how assessment data will be obtained and which content areas will be used to develop and review the specific skills.

NOTES

1. Carl B. Smith, *Teaching in Secondary School Content Subjects*, p. 252.
2. Miriam Jean Dreyer, "How Well Can Students Read to Find Information?" *Reading Today*.
3. Larry A. Harris and Carl B. Smith, *Reading Instruction: Diagnostic Teaching in the Classroom*, p. 334.
4. Bonnie B. Armbruster and Thomas H. Anderson, "Research Synthesis on Study Skills," *Educational Leadership*, p. 154.
5. Armbruster and Anderson, "Research Synthesis on Study Skills," p. 155.
6. B. Y. L. Wong and W. Jones, *Increasing Metacomprehension in Learning Disabled and Normally-Achieving Students through Self-Questioning Training*.
7. Kenneth G. Graham and H. Alan Robinson, *Study Skills Handbook: A Guide for All Teachers*.
8. Herbert A. Sandford, "Directed and Free Search of the School Atlas Map," *The Cartographic Journal*.
9. Guy L. Bond and Eva B. Wagner, *Teaching the Child to Read*, 4th ed., Chapters 10–11.
10. Ryland W. Crary, *Humanizing the School: Curriculum Development and Theory*, p. 195.
11. Raedeane M. Nelson, "Getting Children into Reference Books," *Elementary English*, pp. 884–887.
12. Mary Louise Labe, "Improve the Dictionary's Image," *Elementary English*.
13. Albert J. Harris and Edward R. Sipay, *How to Increase Reading Ability*, 6th ed., p. 491.
14. T. Stevenson Hansell, "Stepping up to Outlining," *Journal of Reading*.
15. Albert J. Harris and Edward R. Sipay, *How to Increase Reading Ability: A Guide to Developmental and Remedial Methods,* 8th ed., p. 521.
16. James Crewe and Dayton Hullgren, "What Does Research Really Say about Study Skills?" in *The Psychology of Reading Behavior,* pp. 75–78.
17. James Hartley, Sally Bartlett, and Alan Branthwaite, "Underlining Can Make a Difference—Sometimes," *Journal of Educational Research*.
18. Edward J. Poostay, "Show Me Your Underlines: A Strategy to Teach Comprehension," *The Reading Teacher*, pp. 828–829.
19. Lawrence E. Hafner, *Developmental Reading in Middle and Secondary Schools: Foundations, Strategies, and Skills for Teaching*, p. 176.
20. Norman A. Stahl, James R. King, and William A. Henk, "Enhancing Students' Notetaking through Training and Evaluation," *Journal of Reading*, pp. 614–623.
21. James W. Dyer, James Riley, and Frank Yekovich, "An Analysis of Three Study Skills: Notetaking, Summarizing, and Rereading," *Journal of Educational Research*; Vincent P. Orlando, "Notetaking vs. Notesaving: A Comparison While Studying From Text," in *Reading Research: Studies and Applications,* edited by Michael L. Kamil and Alden J. Moe, pp. 177–181; Carol A. Carrier and Amy Titus, "Effects of Notetaking Pretraining and Test Mode Expectations on Learning from Lectures," *American Educational Research Journal*.
22. George D. Spache and Evelyn B. Spache, *Reading in the Elementary School*, 4th ed., p. 291.
23. Spache and Spache, *Reading in the Elementary School*, p. 278; J. K. Hirstendahl, "The Effect of Subheads on Reader Comprehension," *Journalism Quarterly*.
24. Spache and Spache, *Reading in the Elementary School*, p. 282.
25. Lawrence E. Hafner and Hayden B. Jolly, *Patterns of Teaching Reading in the Elementary School*, p. 176.
26. Abby Adams, Douglas Carnine, and Russell Gersten, "Instructional Strategies for Studying Content Area Texts in the Intermediate Grades," *Reading Research Quarterly*.
27. Francis P. Robinson, *Effective Study*, 4th ed.
28. George D. Spache, *Toward Better Reading*.
29. Leo Pay, "Reading Skills: Math and Science," in *Reading and Inquiry*, edited by J. Allen Figurel.
30. Michael L. Walker, "Help for the 'Fourth Grade Slump': SRQ2R Plus Instruction in Text Structure and Main Idea," *Reading Horizons*.
31. Carl B. Smith and Peggy G. Elliot, *Reading Activities for Middle and Secondary Schools,* pp. 194–195.
32. Marilyn G. Eanet and Anthony V. Manzo, "REAP: A Strategy for Improving Reading/Writing/Study Skills," *Journal of Reading*.

33. Donna M. Ogle, "K-W-L: A Teaching Model That Develops Active Reading of Expository Text," *The Reading Teacher*.
34. Arne E. Sippola, "K-W-L-S," *The Reading Teacher*.
35. Michele L. Simpson, "PORPE: A Writing Strategy for Studying and Learning in the Content Areas," *Journal of Reading*.
36. Carol Dana, "Strategy Families for Disabled Readers," *Journal of Reading*.
37. Ibid.
38. Ibid.

important
of touch?

CHAPTER

11 Personal Reading

Up to this point, some teachers at Twin Lakes School continue to perceive reading instruction as involving strictly the teaching of individual cognitive skills. This is definitely not true in an effective reading program! Ms. Cunningham, the librarian, along with Ms. Bearfield, Ms. Blakely, and Mr. Dwyer, has formed a special study group to look at better ways of developing personal reading skills. They believe that until students have the opportunity to use reading skills in a personal reading situation and choose to read on their own, the instructional program has not fulfilled all of its objectives.

Personal reading development must be included in all classes at all levels. In a school that was failing to accomplish this goal, one of the students eagerly told a class visitor that she was working on compound words in reading. When asked how she used these skills, the student replied, "I don't know, but I get a check mark when I finish the game!" Without personal reading, teachers at Twin Lakes School are realizing that the word identification, comprehension, and study skills remain fragmented parts that do not contribute to the development of a mature reader.

This chapter provides ideas on how to incorporate personal reading into an effective program and addresses the following questions.

- What is personal reading?
- Why is personal reading important in an effective reading program?
- How is personal reading developed?
- How does personal reading relate to other reading instruction?
- How can students be motivated to read?
- What are some techniques for developing personal reading habits?

Vocabulary to Know

- ➢ **Affective domain**
- ➢ **Bibliotherapy**
- ➢ **Creative reading**
- ➢ **Personal reading**
- ➢ **Recreational reading**
- ➢ **Sustained silent reading**

THE IMPORTANCE OF PERSONAL READING

Recreational reading, reading for enjoyment, and application of reading skills are all ways of referring to personal reading. In personal reading, students apply all their knowledge to decode words and interpret printed symbols to increase their enjoyment and knowledge.

The importance of personal reading in the reading curriculum is reinforced in the recommendations of the Commission on Reading in *Becoming a Nation of Readers*. Five of the 17 recommendations given in the report relate to the importance of personal reading:

- Parents should read to preschool children and informally teach them about reading and writing.
- Parents should support school-aged childrens' continued growth as readers.
- Children should spend more time in independent reading.
- Schools should cultivate an ethos that supports reading.
- Schools should maintain well-stocked and managed libraries.[1]

These recommendations not only point to the importance of developing personal reading habits but also say explicitly that the development of such abilities requires effort on the part of parents, teachers, students, and entire school faculties.

Students who have developed the emergent literacy, word identification, comprehension, and study skills yet do not read to enrich their lives need effective instruction in personal reading, just as do students who have difficulty in understanding cause-effect relationships. Unless students perceive the learning of reading skills as an aid in reading materials they choose and developing a lifetime habit of reading, then their knowledge is of little benefit. Therefore, teachers should constantly remind themselves that skill knowledge in reading is not an end in itself but a means for pursuing personal reading goals.

In some reading programs, teachers and students become so involved with skills that applying their knowledge to personal reading becomes secondary. Teachers and administrators who make personal reading the major goal of the school reading program demonstrate to students that reading is more than skill development. This point cannot be overemphasized. The authors once worked with approximately 60 second and third graders. When asked to draw a picture of what reading meant to them, two drew a picture of the teacher reading to a class, five drew themselves reading books on their own, and the remainder showed skill development activities ranging from the basal reader groups to doing worksheets! Thus, effective reading instruction includes reading experiences that are meaningful and that help students want to read.

Read—Read—Read anywhere, anytime.

Photo courtesy of Martha D. Collins.

The following five "skill" areas of personal reading should be addressed in an effective reading program (see Figure 11.1).

- *Enjoy and respond to stories and poems read by others.* Personal reading habits begin at a very young age, prior to entering school, as parents read to their children. This reading is a pleasant experience that initiates enjoyment of the rhythm of language as well as the information from the story. Teachers continue to read to students to broaden their experience and motivate them to read on their own.
- *Read materials for enjoyment.* These materials include books, comic books, and any other materials that give the student pleasure. They are usually written at the student's independent reading level.

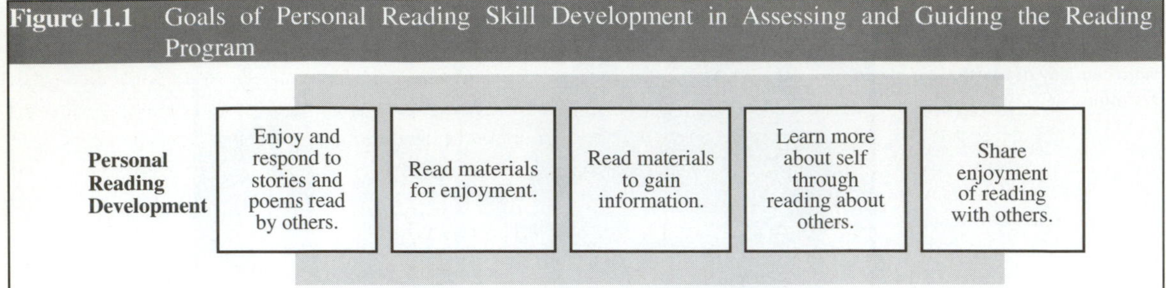

Figure 11.1 Goals of Personal Reading Skill Development in Assessing and Guiding the Reading Program

- *Read materials to gain information.* These materials include reference materials, books and magazines, brochures, and any other printed material.
- *Learn more about self through reading about others.* As students read, they learn about other people, their joys and sorrows as well as how they cope in life situations. This knowledge of others not only teaches the students about life but also helps them learn more about themselves as they face daily life. Books that present situations a student can identify with often help in dealing with problems or experiences the student is facing.
- *Share enjoyment of reading with others.* The student who has fully developed personal reading habits not only reads but shares with others the ideas gained from the materials.

Personal reading involves reading skills in the affective domain. Reading skills in the other areas emphasize the cognitive aspect of learning. In order for students to succeed with the cognitive skills, development of skills in the affective domain is vital. These skills include not only learning to enjoy reading but also developing a positive self-image. Pryor suggests that "changing a poor reader's self-concept by bolstering his feeling about himself is perhaps the first step toward improving the academic problem."[2] Additional ideas regarding the interrelationship of self-concept and reading are presented by Quandt.[3] The affective component of reading instruction aids in the development of personal interests, values, a positive attitude, and the ability to read for both information and enjoyment. To know how to develop personal reading with individual students, teachers use informal assessment measures along with their own knowledge of the children.

MOTIVATING STUDENTS TO READ

Motivating students to read is often a greater challenge to teachers than teaching the cognitive skills in reading. Motivation to learn involves two basic components: interests and attitudes. Motivation, interest, and attitude are closely related to reading achievement. Den Heyer found this relationship to be significant and that the relationship between motivation and reading achievement increases consistently with age, with the relationship being well established in the higher primary grades.[4]

Walberg and Tsai suggest that the strongest correlates of reading achievement are attitude towards reading, kindergarten attendance, use of English in the home, and stimulating materials in the home environment.[5] Further research has indicated a strong relation between liking or not liking reading and liking or not liking school.[6] With the increasing concern about school dropouts and illiteracy, teachers and administrators in the school reading programs must acknowledge the importance of motivation.

There is no simple way to motivate students, but much can be done to interest them in reading. Gambrell offers six research-based factors that are related to increased motivation to read:

1. A teacher who values reading and is enthusiastic about reading
2. A book-rich classroom environment
3. Opportunities for choice
4. Opportunities to interact socially with others
5. Opportunities to become familiar with many books
6. Appropriate reading-related incentives (e.g., bookmarks, books, reading with a partner)[7]

Attitudes can be improved by providing appropriate instruction in an exciting manner, rewarding the student with words of praise, using appropriate techniques, and providing materials that are interesting and written at the appropriate level.

Much research has been conducted regarding students' reading interests.[8] Teachers often attempt to select materials based on the age level of the students. Weintraub, however, concludes that no single category of books will give all children of the same age what they want to read. He suggests that each teacher identify the unique reading interests of the students in the classroom and select books with this knowledge in mind.

Moray reviewed the research in the area of reading interests. She concludes that

- Gender is a more important factor than intelligence, race, grade, or economic level in determining reading preferences at each age and grade level.
- At the age of 9 or 10, girls will read books that interest boys, but boys will not read books that interest girls.
- Teachers must be aware of individual student interests, rather than rely on broad generalizations.
- Materials other than textbooks must be included in the reading program, as basals do not contain the variety of stories necessary to meet the identified interests of students.[9]

Although reading interests vary from student to student, in a review of research relating to student's reading interests, Huus found several patterns that may be helpful in motivating students to read. She notes that primary-level students like animals, home and family, make-believe, and cowboys as topics, but they also express interests in history and science informational materials. Through the middle years of elementary school, although gender differences in interests appear, both boys and girls like mystery, animals, adventure, comics, and humor. Huus also observes that interests in reading appear to have changed little over the years, and that the factors that affect reading interest are gender, age, literary quality, and the reading program.[10]

Each year the International Reading Association and Children's Book Council conduct a joint project that evaluates children's books published during the year. From this evaluation, a list of children's favorites are identified and published in the October issue of *The Reading Teacher.* Sebasta evaluated the books selected for "Children's Choices" to determine if they had characteristics that differed from other books not selected by children. He found that

- Plots of the "Children's Choices" are faster paced than those found in books not chosen as favorites.
- Young children enjoy reading about nearly any topic if the information is presented in a specific way. The topic may be less important than interest studies have indicated, as specifics rather than topics seem to underlie the preferences.
- Children like detailed descriptions of settings. They want to know exactly how the place looks and feels before the main action occurs.
- One type of plot structure does not dominate these favorite books. Some stories have a central focus with a carefully arranged cause-and-effect plot, while others have plots that meander with episodes showing no connection.
- Children do not like sad books.
- Many books explicitly teach a lesson.
- Warmth was the most outstanding quality found in the books. Children enjoy books where the characters like each other, express their feelings in things they say and do, and sometimes act selflessly.[11]

If teachers expect students to develop personal reading skills, students need to have interesting materials. These include not only library books but also magazines, newspapers, and comic books. These materials sometimes interest students in reading; they seem to be more fun to read because they differ from the traditional school reading materials.[12] Helping a student develop an interest in some material and allowing the student to complete the material successfully is a motivating experience that will begin to change negative attitudes towards reading. Appendix F contains a selected bibliography of children's books.

Alexander and Filler identified several variables that seem to be associated with attitudes toward reading. These are achievement, self-concept, parents and the home environment, the teacher and classroom environment, instructional practices and special programs, gender, test intelligence, socioeconomic status, and interests.[13] As teachers attempt to improve students' attitudes toward reading, they should keep these ideas in mind:

- In order to have a positive feeling toward themselves and what they are doing, students need to be successful and commended for their efforts. Reading is no exception. Materials that are appropriate for the students' reading levels assist in developing this positive feeling.
- Teachers' awareness of students' attitudes toward reading is essential. This can be learned from observation, supplemented with the use of an attitude inventory. Some questions relating to attitude toward reading are included in the interest inventory instrument in Appendix C.
- A student's attitude toward reading material affects comprehension of the material. For example, the student who does not like social studies but enjoys science will probably read science material with greater understanding than social studies material.
- Initial attitudes toward reading are formed by parents and the home environment. This factor must be accepted and an effort made to help parents realize the effect of their attitude on the student's progress in reading.

In a study of the effect of home and school on early interest in literature, Morrow found that high-interest children preferred crayon and paper activities, looked at books more frequently, had more library cards, were read to more often, and watched less television than low-interest children. More parents of children in the high-interest group held college or graduate degrees and voluntarily read as a leisure-time activity. Parents of children in the high-interest group read more novels and magazines than did parents of children in the low-interest groups.[14] Parental cooperation is extremely important in overcoming negative attitudes toward reading.

Schools can communicate either positive or negative feelings about reading. Teachers who are enthusiastic about reading, classrooms that invite students to read, and a program that stresses reading as an exciting part of the school greatly assist in the development of positive attitudes toward reading. Flexible grouping and varied instruction are more conducive to improving attitudes toward reading than rigid ability groups.[15]

Teachers must be cautious about making generalizations regarding students' attitudes toward reading. Girls do not necessarily have better attitudes toward reading than boys,[16] just as brighter students do not always have a better attitude than less intelligent students.[17] Moreover, teachers should not assume that students from lower socioeconomic backgrounds are more likely to have negative attitudes toward reading.[18]

Roettger found that high-attitude, low-performance students viewed reading as important to life survival while low-attitude, high-performance students perceived reading as a means of personal improvement and academic success. Both groups felt, however, that too little time and concern was given to personal reading in their classrooms.[19]

To develop cognitive reading skills in a meaningful way, students must be motivated to read. This means meeting the interests and improving attitudes toward reading. The following section presents more ideas that can be used in the prescriptive teaching of personal reading.

TECHNIQUES FOR DEVELOPING PERSONAL READING

Motivate students to read, persuade students to be excited about reading, improve their attitudes toward reading. How many times have teachers heard these requests! In the area of personal reading, specific skills are not identifiable and assessing specific strengths or weaknesses is very subjective; likewise, ways to develop this area are less definite. This is because the behaviors are not easily identifiable, and students respond differently. Teachers find, as they review activity books, that most suggestions are directed toward the development of cognitive skills and few ideas are presented for the personal reading area. Yet personal reading is basic to developing good readers.

To assist teachers in developing personal reading, this section presents ideas that can be used in improving classroom atmosphere through the use of activities, bibliotherapy, and creative reading. Remember to share ideas with parents in order to derive maximum benefit from the school activities.

Classroom Atmosphere

On the first day of school as students go into their classroom, they notice that it is clean and colorful. The bulletin boards invite them into the room and give clues that learning will be fun this year. Book jackets and words indicating that reading is important are displayed throughout the room. In a back corner is a rug with bright cushions scattered around. Several shelves of books, magazines, comic books, and even a newspaper arouse the curiosity of the students. How soon can they go to the corner and stretch out on the floor to read a magazine?

The atmosphere in this room is conducive to the development of personal reading. However, teachers must plan for the students to obtain maximum benefit from these resources. Each student needs time to look at books every day, to expand interests in reading and to apply the reading skills that are being taught. Reading as a pleasurable activity does not just happen; the teacher pursues this objective through careful planning, structuring both opportunities and instruction, while making this learning appear to be unstructured.

Books are fascinating.

Photo courtesy of Edward B. Lasher.

To provide students with opportunities to read and to see others read, many teachers are using USSR (uninterrupted sustained silent reading), SSR (substantial, or sustained, silent reading), SQRT (sustained quiet reading time) in their classrooms. This procedure may be used with an entire classroom or the whole school so as to involve everyone in reading. In attaining this objective, the key to the success is that everyone be involved. If the idea is used throughout the school, all of the students, teachers, administrators, and staff must read some material silently for a designated time each day or at least twice a week. This brief time for silent reading is not a break for the teacher to plan or grade papers, or for the principal to check to see who is following directions. It is a time for teachers, as well as students, to read or look at printed material. This procedure serves as a motivational tool for many students when it is introduced in a positive manner and allows everyone to participate. The principal may want to read with various classes so students have another adult reading model. After the designated time for reading, the students proceed with their other work unless someone wants to share what was read. This is not a requirement and is done only if initiated by the student and for only a brief period of time.

A classroom teacher may wish to begin silent reading for 5 minutes one day a week to begin motivating students to read on their own. The time can be increased to a maximum of 15 minutes as students become more familiar with the procedure, and it may be expanded to include the entire school. This uninterrupted silent reading time is provided to allow students time to experience the joys of silent reading and to begin to develop good reading habits.

A modification of SSR may be used with beginning readers. "Book time" should be held at the same time each day, beginning with 1 to 5 minutes per group and progressing to 10 to 15 minutes. The teacher works with five to seven students at a time and places books, which have been introduced by the teacher as stories are read to the class, into a reading center. Just as in SSR, the teacher reads while the students read, but she may also answer questions and pronounce words at the students' requests. During book time the students may read in pairs and talk quietly about the books.[20]

Another good way to motivate students to read in their extra time is through the use of a reading area in the classroom. This classroom library needs a variety of books displayed in an interesting manner. The center may have some paperbacks in a book rack along with books borrowed from the school library. The teacher may add a rug and some large pillows to make the area more inviting. The authors have seen many motivating reading centers in classrooms at all levels. Some teachers add old bathtubs or sofas to encourage students to relax as they read. Another idea is to add a tree house or bunk bed in one corner of the room. The tree house may consist of a large tree limb planted in a container with paper leaves on which new words are written. More elaborate tree houses may be made by painting a large tree on the wall and ceiling, then building a small platform where students can sit while they read. Some teachers may build a "reading shack" in their reading area. This is a wooden, house-shaped frame covered with chicken wire. Cushions on the floor allow students to sit comfortably as they read in a more isolated environment.

In addition to providing an appealing reading area, teachers can enhance the classroom atmosphere by using colorful bulletin boards that encourage students to read. These displays are changed frequently and may be done by students as a way of sharing what they read. Beers recommends that to promote interest in unmotivated students teachers allow students to choose their own books to read, compare books to a movie, or develop book-related art activities.[21] Other ideas for motivating students to read are presented by Fennimore, Roeder and Lee, and Johns and Lunt.[22]

The importance of creating an atmosphere that is conducive to reading is crucial to the success of an effective reading program. Students must be motivated and want to read. Gambrell, Palmer, Codling, and Mazzoni have developed an assessment tool that examines children's self-concepts as readers and the value they see in reading.[23] This *Motivation to Read Profile* is designed to assess, monitor, and document student responses to innovations in the classroom that are intended to promote reading motivation.

The physical classroom atmosphere has a marked effect on student interest in reading. Desk arrangement, grouping procedures, reading centers, and displays can work to encourage or deter reading progress. Remember that the classroom atmosphere also includes teacher-student relationships, the teacher's attitude toward reading, and the overall attitude of the teacher toward the school and the students. An attractive room will not overcome a negative teacher attitude. Thus, the classroom teacher who is positive about learning and shows concern about meeting the individual reading needs of each student will have students with positive attitudes about reading. When both students and teachers feel good about where they are, the atmosphere is more conducive to learning.

Bibliotherapy

Bibliotherapy is defined as "getting the right book to the right child at the right time."[24] This procedure is used to help students acquire insight into areas of interest or problems that they may be facing. Bibliotherapy is a way of providing therapy through books. For example, the student whose parents are getting a divorce may get some help in dealing with the problem by reading *It's Not the End of the World* by Judy Blume (Bantam Press, 1972), *The Boys and Girls Book about Divorce* by Richard A. Gardner, M.D. (Bantam Press, 1970), or *Chloris and the Creeps* by Kin Platt (Dell, 1973). Huck and Kuhn suggest that the three processes in bibliotherapy correspond to the three phases of psychotherapy: identification, catharsis, and insight. In the identification phase, the student associates herself with another person. Catharsis is the release of the emotion in some manner. Insight is the emotional awareness to deal with the problem.[25]

The classroom teacher can use bibliotherapy to interest students in reading by guiding them to materials that relate to their particular needs. This motivates them to read more on their own to find out about others in similar situations. Thus, bibliotherapy is another way to assist students in developing personal reading.

Studies conducted using bibliotherapy in the classroom tend to be short-term. Tillman found that 14 weeks seemed to be the maximum length of treatment.[26] Such short-term studies have raised questions as to the usefulness of this strategy in changing student attitudes.[27] However, teachers are encouraged to consider this a helpful strategy for select students who are experiencing problems with self and are avoiding reading. In using the strategy, there needs to be a long-term commitment to student development over a period of time, since attitudes and personalities do not change quickly. When this strategy is used at school, teachers may find that results occur more quickly when parents are included. Edwards and Simpson found that the use of bibliotherapy with parents and children resulted in opening lines of communication, stimulating parents' interest in their child's reading, increasing the child's interest in recreational reading, and helping the parent and child appreciate the value of reading.[28]

Creative Reading

As the cognitive reading skills are developed, students should be encouraged to react to the printed word by expressing their own ideas about what they have read. This expression of feeling can be accomplished through dramatics, writing, art, music, or thought. Creative reading involves an expansion of the cognitive comprehension skills into the affective areas of individual reaction and expression.

Many students expand their personal reading because they enjoy expressing their interpretation of what the author has said. Language arts activities, including creative thinking, are often used to enhance the development of creative reading. Turner and Alexander suggest,

> A classroom environment in which reading is perceived by the teacher as a creative activity will be more likely to develop in children a view that reading is a fascinating and wonderful adventure. This concept of reading will not easily be lost in later years. But if it is not instilled early in school experiences, it will be even more difficult to gain in upper grades.[29]

Turner and Alexander identify four areas that need to be considered in developing creative reading:

1. The types of reading materials that provide the best stimulus for creative thinking
2. Ways of structuring oral questions and discussions to help students think creatively about reading
3. Reading tasks that open rather than close doors to productive, creative thoughts
4. Environments that encourage creative behavior

Teachers must provide opportunities for students to read creatively as another means of developing personal reading. Although creative reading is sometimes viewed as the highest-level cognitive skill, beginning readers enjoy expressing their reaction to the printed word. Activities such as role playing, dramatics, puppetry, composition, pantomime, and dance are used to enhance the development of creative reading skills and to motivate students to read.

Creative dramatics provides an excellent way for teachers to develop reading and language abilities. Creative drama includes dramatic play, pantomime, story dramatization, and sensitivity exercises along with other activities to encourage students to relate new learning to existing knowledge. However, teachers know that creative dramatics does not just happen in the classroom; careful planning is needed. As Prentice and Tabbert emphasize, creative drama is not an unstructured free-for-all but a structured undertaking in which the teacher sets limits, establishes guidelines, and intervenes when necessary to change the direction of the activity or make suggestions. They further suggest that students be introduced to creative drama slowly and that they be free to proceed at their own pace. Evaluation is an essential part of each activity with teachers asking questions as the process progresses.[30] Research has shown that creative drama enhances reading readiness, vocabulary development, oral reading, comprehension, and self-concept. Miller and Mason suggest that it also can be used to develop comprehension when exercises are given to help students improvise from a storyline by adding characteristics and actions that can be inferred from given information. This process develops comprehension by bringing plot, character, and setting from the written page into the mind of the student.[31]

Another important way of developing an atmosphere of creativity in the classroom is to read aloud to students. Trelease suggests that reading aloud to children is essential to promoting their literacy abilities.[32] He further believes that teachers should read to their students every day.[33] He points out that it is not only fun but simple and cheap. One of the primary benefits of reading aloud is that children are exposed to good books, which in turn serves to enhance independent reading. Other benefits of successful read-aloud programs in school districts are that parents become more involved, guest readings are used, and the community as a whole develops a more positive attitude toward reading.

Robb suggests that schools can create partnerships with parents that support personal reading by sponsoring monthly "Family Reading Nights."[34] These evenings offer children and adults uninterrupted time to read and talk in small family groups and with other families. The school provides an abundance of books and a relaxed environment where parents, siblings, grandparents, relatives, and family friends come to school to read with their children.

Fostering creativity in the classroom through storytelling is enjoying a rebirth and further enhances children's language acquisition and development. Peck believes that storytelling in the classroom promotes expressive language development in both speech and written composition.[35] She further states that it also promotes receptive language development in both reading and listening comprehension. Storytelling is an important tool for learning: when the teacher is the storyteller, students develop the skills of effective and critical listening; when the students are the storytellers, there is great opportunity for developing oral and written language.

Strickland and Morrow found that when children act as storytellers, according to the research, they are active participants in their learning of language through social contexts; they interact with other children and adults and actually construct language as they learn.[36] The authors also found that storytelling in the early grades is an excellent technique for fostering growth in language. They suggest that to encourage children to retell stories it is crucial for the teacher to model storytelling. When children are given the opportunity to tell stories, their language development is greatly enhanced. They also become active participants in the creation of language, learn to associate oral language with print, and improve socially through more contact with their peers.

A creative and unique way of encouraging independent reading in the elementary school is suggested by O'Masta and Wolf.[37] The "reading millionaires project" was initiated to enhance literacy in a small elementary school. The primary objective of the program was to reach a schoolwide goal of reading a million minutes at home, with all students participating in and contributing to the project. Other objectives included increasing the amount of independent reading by students, fostering a positive attitude toward reading in both students and parents, helping students see that reading occurs both at home and school, and providing parents with opportunities to interact in a positive manner with their child about reading. The project was monitored through the use of banking methods involving a "savings book." The results of the project were encouraging and demonstrated that the amount of reading children engage in at home can be readily increased.

In fostering independent reading, most of the emphasis is placed on using story-based literature. Glazer and Lamme suggest that picture books that feature a single poem can be used to help children appreciate poetry and artwork and to expand their language arts and content area capabilities.[38] In sharing poetry with children, they suggest using oral reading and chanting, adding music or sound effects, highlighting the poet, studying and comparing artwork, creating illustrations, and integrating poetry with content areas.

Personal reading is the application of reading knowledge. Teachers use many techniques to interest students in reading as a personal habit rather than just an assigned task. Materials such as paperback books seem to improve students' attitudes toward reading.[39] Bissett as well as Burger, Cohen, and Bisgaler found that by making books available and encouraging students to read them, the amount of personal reading triples.[40] Bamberger has pointed out that in areas throughout the world where personal reading habits have remained highly developed, the school library is the hub of the curriculum.[41] Thus, teachers who realize the importance of using many strategies and use these strategies to encourage personal reading develop students who enjoy reading. Strickler summarizes personal reading ideas as follows:

- Use the students' interests in planning instruction.
- Assure the students' success in the mastery of reading skills and strategies.
- Help students discover their own purposes for reading.
- Read often to the students.
- Carefully select books for the literature program, using children's literature to supplement the curriculum.
- Be an enthusiastic model of reading habits.
- Fill bookshelves in the classroom.
- Provide time for independent reading.
- Encourage students to read and share what they have read.
- Develop a literature program to help students realize the potential literature has for widening their world.[42]

SUMMARY

Personal reading is an integral part of an effective instructional program. Too much stress on skill development without adequate opportunities for application of these skills makes learning a boring process for students. Personal reading is especially desirable, since one of the primary goals of reading instruction is to enable students to read for pleasure as well as to gain information.

Fostering personal reading in the classroom enables the teacher to develop the affective domain in addition to the skills-oriented cognitive domain. The affective domain is important in developing a student's self-concept and awareness. It also plays a major role in motivating students by using high-interest books and a variety of other materials.

Developing personal reading habits is not an easy task, the key is motivation. You can develop students who are excited about reading by building on their interests. Some techniques for achieving this goal are enhancing the classroom atmosphere, using bibliotherapy, and encouraging creative reading.

The successful development of personal reading in the classroom provides much needed pleasure for students and certainly increases the effectiveness of the reading program. A bibliography of high-interest children's books is found in Appendix F.

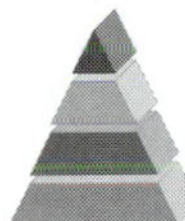

Applying What You Read

1. You have a group of students who seem to be developing their word identification and comprehension skills adequately; however, they are somewhat unenthusiastic about learning to read. Outline a program to develop their personal reading habits.
2. The atmosphere in a classroom frequently affects learning in either a positive or negative manner. Give some specific examples of how your classroom could be changed to promote a more positive attitude toward reading.
3. Using bibliotherapy in your classroom can exert a positive influence on the students. To implement this idea, go to the library, check out some books, and categorize them according to areas of need so that they are available.
4. Creative reading allows students to express their own ideas and to interpret what they read. Identify five activities you could do in your classroom to enhance creative reading.

NOTES

1. *Becoming a Nation of Readers: The Report of the Commission on Reading.*
2. Frances Pryor, "Poor Reading—Lack of Self-Esteem?" *The Reading Teacher.*
3. Ivan Quandt, *Self-Concept and Reading.*
4. Ken den Heyer, "Reading and Motivation," in *Language and Literacy: The Social Psychology of Reading,* edited by John R. Edwards, pp. 51–65.
5. Herbert J. Walberg and Shiow-Ling Tsai, "Correlates of Reading Achievement and Attitude: A National Assessment Study," *Journal of Educational Research.*
6. Lian-Hwang Chiu, "Children's Attitudes toward Reading and Reading Interests," *Perceptual and Motor Skills.*
7. Linda B. Gambrell, "Creating Classroom Cultures that Foster Reading Motivation," *The Reading Teacher.*

8. Helen M. Robinson and Samuel Weintraub, "Research Related to Children's Interests and to Developmental Values of Reading," *Library Trends*; Stephen Meisal and Gerald G. Glass, "Voluntary Reading Interests and the Interest Content of Basal Readers," *The Reading Teacher*; Samuel Weintraub, "Children's Reading Interests," *The Reading Teacher*; Beta Upsilon Chapter, Pi Lambda Theta, "Children's Interests Classified by Age Level," *The Reading Teacher*.
9. Geraldine Moray, "What Does Research Say about the Reading Interests of Children in the Intermediate Grades?" *The Reading Teacher*.
10. Helen Huus, "A New Look at Children's Interests," in *Using Literature and Poetry Affectively*, edited by Jon E. Shapiro, pp. 37–45.
11. Sam Leaton Sebasta, "What Do Young People Think About the Literature They Read?" *Reading Newsletter*.
12. Constance V. Alongi, "Response to Kay Haugaard: Comic Books Revisited," *The Reading Teacher*.
13. J. Estell Alexander and Ronald Claude Filler, *Attitudes and Reading*, p. 3.
14. Lesley Mandel Morrow, "Home and School Correlates of Early Interest in Literature," *Journal of Educational Research*.
15. Ann Kirtland Healy, "Effects of Changing Children's Attitudes toward Reading," *Elementary English*.
16. Terry Denny and Samuel Weintraub, "First Graders' Responses to Three Questions about Reading," *Elementary School Journal*.
17. Harlan S. Hansen, "The Impact of the Home Literacy Environment on Reading Attitude," *Elementary English*.
18. M. J. Heimberger, *Sartain Reading Attitudes Inventory*.
19. Doris Roettger, "Elementary Students' Attitudes toward Reading," *The Reading Teacher*.
20. Laraine K. Hong, "Modifying SSR for Beginning Readers," *The Reading Teacher*; Jim Kaisen, "SSR Booktime: Kindergarten and First Grade Sustained Silent Reading," *The Reading Teacher*.
21. G. Kylene Beers, "No Time, No Interest, No Way! Part II of the Three Voices of Literacy," *School Library Journal*.
22. Flora Fennimore, "Projective Book Reports," *Language Arts*; Harold H. Roeder and Nancy Lee, "Twenty-Five Teacher Tested Ways to Encourage Voluntary Reading," *The Reading Teacher*, Jerry L. Johns and Linda Lunt, "Motivating Reading: Professional Ideas," *The Reading Teacher*.
23. Linda B. Gambrell, Barbara M. Palmer, Rose M. Codling, and Susan A. Mazzoni, "Assessing Motivation To Read," *The Reading Teacher*.
24. Sara W. Lundsteen, *Children Learn to Communicate*, p. 216.
25. Charlotte S. Huck and Doris Young Kuhn, *Children's Literature in the Elementary School*, 2nd ed., p. 264.
26. Chester E. Tillman, "Bibliotherapy for Adolescents: An Annotated Research Review," *Journal of Reading*.
27. Frederick A. Schrank and Dennis W. Engels, "Bibliotherapy as a Counseling Adjunct: Research Findings," *Personnel and Guidance Journal*.
28. Patricia A. Edwards and Linda Simpson, "Bibliotherapy: A Strategy for Communication between Parents and Their Children," *Journal of Reading*.
29. Thomas N. Turner and J. Estill Alexander, "Fostering Early Creative Reading," *Language Arts*.
30. Walter C. Prentice and Jon Charles Tabbert, *Creative Dramatics and Reading: A Question of Basics*.
31. G. Michael Miller and George E. Mason, "Dramatic Improvisation: Risk-Free Role Playing for Improving Reading Performance," *The Reading Teacher*.
32. Jim Trelease, *The Read-Aloud Handbook*, 4th ed.
33. Jim Trelease, "Have You Read to Your Kids Today?" *Instructor*.
34. Laura Robb, "Read-Aloud Partnerships," *Reading Today*.
35. Jackie Peck, "Using Storytelling to Promote Language and Literacy Development," *The Reading Teacher*.
36. Dorothy S. Strickland and Lesley Mandel Morrow, "Oral Language Development: Children as Storytellers," *The Reading Teacher*.

37. Gail A. O'Masta and James M. Wolf, "Encouraging Independent Reading through the Reading Millionaires Project," *The Reading Teacher*.
38. Joan I. Glazer and Linda Leonard Lamme, "Poem Picture Books and Their Uses in the Classroom," *The Reading Teacher*.
39. Lawrence F. Lowrey and William Grafft, "Paperback and Reading Attitudes," *The Reading Teacher*.
40. Donald J. Bissett, "The Amount and Effect of Recreational Reading in Selected Fifth Grade Classrooms," in *Bringing Children and Books Together*, edited by Victor Burger, T. A. Cohen, and P. Bisgaler.
41. Richard Bamberger, *Promoting the Reading Habit*.
42. Darryl J. Strickler, "Planning the Affective Component," in *Classroom Practice in Reading*, edited by Richard A. Earle, p. 6.

CHAPTER 12

Teaching Students with Special Needs

As the faculty at Twin Lakes School gather to review their current reading program, Ms. Floyd and Ms. Knight express concern about how the students with special needs can best be accommodated. Mr. Blakely wants to address the needs of several new students who speak little or no English, and Ms. Menendez asks numerous questions about at-risk students, who have language deficits due to a limited background of experiences.

Because of their concern about students with special needs in their classrooms, the teachers decide to investigate several areas in greater detail so they can better accommodate the individual needs of these learners. While students with special needs have always been a concern for the classroom teacher, for many years these students were taught primarily in a special setting away from the regular classroom, or received special teaching assistance; thus, the classroom teacher did not have a major responsibility for meeting specialized needs. With the passage of P.L. 94-142 in 1975 and its reauthorization in 1990 as P.L. 101-476 (the Individuals with Disabilities Education Act, or IDEA) and the influx of students speaking a primary language other than English, the classroom teacher has become the facilitator of instruction for a very diverse population. To help teachers fulfill this role, this chapter presents some ideas on how to provide appropriate reading instruction to students with special needs. The following questions will be addressed.

- Who are the students with special needs?
- What effect have the concepts of mainstreaming and full inclusion had on reading instruction for classroom teachers?
- How are non-English-speaking students accommodated in reading instruction?
- How are at-risk or at-promise students involved in an effective reading program?

Vocabulary to Know

- **At-risk**
- **Bilingual**
- **Educationally different**
- **Emotional and behavioral disorders**
- **Full inclusion**
- **Gifted and talented**
- **Hearing-challenged**
- **Learning-disabled**
- **Mainstreaming**
- **Mildly challenged**
- **Multicultural**
- **Non-English speaker**
- **Physically challenged**
- **Psychologically challenged**
- **Visually challenged**

AN OVERVIEW

Many students in our schools have special needs that must be accommodated. These needs range from physical challenges to gifted and talented. It is imperative for the classroom teacher to be aware of ways to deal with these differences so that students with special needs are integrated into the classroom reading program. Here we identify specific categories of needs that the classroom teacher may encounter.

Students with special needs can be divided into three broad categories: educationally different, psychologically challenged, and physically challenged. Each of these groups is defined and general suggestions for appropriate teaching strategies are provided.

Students with special needs have become more numerous in the classroom with the adoption of mainstreaming and full-inclusion models as mandated by P. L. 94-142 in 1975 and P.L. 101-476 (the Individuals with Disabilities Education Act, or IDEA) in 1990. Birch defines mainstreaming as an amalgamation of regular and special education into one system to provide a spectrum of services for all children according to their learning needs.[1] Wang interprets mainstreaming as the integration of regular and exceptional children in a school setting where all children share the same resources and opportunities for learning on a full-time basis.[2] In its simplest form, Howard describes mainstreaming as "the process of integrating children with disabilities into regular classrooms."[3] In fact, it represents an effort to provide the most equitable educational opportunity for all students, including those with special needs. It is further intended to create an environment for students with special needs to associate with other students of their age. The implications for the classroom teacher are clear. Opportunities for all students to improve their reading capabilities must be provided. The law mandates significant changes regarding the education of children with special needs. The most significant change is the requirement that challenged children be educated with their nonchallenged peers as much as possible.

One of the primary keys to effective mainstreaming is the collaboration between the special education teacher and the regular classroom teacher. This cooperation is not only essential in planning but during the instructional process. Also crucial is the collaboration of the principal, students, and especially parents with the teachers in providing a supportive and nurturing environment for appropriate and effective instruction. Idol, Nevin, and Paolucci-Whitcomb[4] believe that the collaboration process requires that (a) group members view each other as unique individuals possessing needed expertise, (b) interaction among group members is frequent and supportive, (c) leadership responsibility is equally distributed, (d) reciprocity is emphasized, and (e) consensus building is stressed.

More recently, another model for educating challenged students in our classrooms has forcefully emerged, the full-inclusion model. The primary purpose of this model is to eliminate the separateness that occurs in schools through the use of resource (pull-out) and other types of exclusive programs that proponents believe are not in the best interests of students. According to Stainback and Stainback, two of the movement's strongest advocates, an inclusive classroom is "a place where everyone belongs, is accepted, supports, and is supported by his or her peers and other members of the school community in the course of having his or her educational needs met."[5] Giangreco, Cloninger, Dennis, and Edelman maintain that five specific components must be present in a teacher's daily plan in order for full inclusion to be in effect in a classroom setting: (a) heterogeneous grouping, (b) a sense of belonging to a group, (c) shared activities with individualized outcomes, (d) use of environments frequented by persons without disabilities, and (e) a balanced educational experience.[6]

There is considerable debate among special educators and others regarding the implementation of the full-inclusion model. In fact, the Council for Exceptional Children supports inclusion as a meaningful goal but believes that other current programs that provide specific services to meet the individual needs of both children and adults should be maintained.[7]

In order for challenged students to become more fully included in regular education classrooms, Stainback, Stainback, and Stefanich recommend three strategies for implementing an effective inclusive program.[8] These include (a) using flexible learning objectives, (b) adapting activities to encourage student participation, and (c) using multiple adaptations to accommodate the diverse needs and abilities of students in the classroom.

EDUCATIONAL DIFFERENCES

Five groups of students comprise an area of special needs arising from educational differences: learning-disabled students, at-risk students, non-English-speaking students, mildly disabled or challenged students, and gifted and talented students.

Learning-Disabled Students (LD, ADD-ADHD)

In the context of this chapter, learning-disabled refers to students with specific learning disabilities. More and more students are being placed in this category for the purpose of receiving special instruction in the regular classroom as well as in special resource programs. However, often, when an early and intensive intervention program is implemented, between 50 and 75% of the students who were identified as learning disabled no longer need special services after the program.[9] In fact, a child's learning problem may stem from inadequate or untimely instructional intervention.

Several definitions of specific learning disabilities have been offered; however, the most widely accepted definition is that proposed by the National Advisory Committee on Challenged Children in 1968.

> Children with special (specific) learning disabilities exhibit a disorder in one or more of the basic psychological processes involved in understanding or in using spoken or written language. These may be manifested in disorders of listening, thinking, talking, reading, writing, spelling, or arithmetic. They include conditions which have been referred to as perceptual handicaps, brain injury, minimal brain dysfunction, dyslexia, developmental aphasia, etc. They do not include learning problems which are due primarily to visual, hearing, or motor handicaps, to mental retardation, emotional disturbance, or to environmental disadvantage.[10]

Although their definition is widely accepted, the U.S. National Joint Committee on Learning Disabilities is urging that it be revised to better facilitate the identification and treatment of the individual.[11] The committee suggests that the revised definition has several advantages over the earlier definition because (a) it is not concerned exclusively with children, (b) it avoids the controversial phrase "basic psychological processes," (c) spelling is not included since it is more logically subsumed under writing, (d) it avoids the use of confusing terms such as perceptual handicaps, dyslexia, and minimal brain dysfunction, and (e) it clearly states that learning disabilities may occur in conjunction with other types of handicaps.[12]

Hallahan and Kauffman have grouped the causes of learning disabilities into three primary areas: organic and biological factors, which are manifested primarily in the central nervous system dysfunction, genetic factors, and environmental factors.[13]

Gilliland enumerates some characteristics of the learning-disabled student that should provide the classroom teacher with insight into how to meet better their learning needs.

- Students are usually much better in mathematics than reading.
- Word identification skills are poorly developed in comparison to other reading skills.
- Many students are hyperactive, experiencing difficulty in sitting still while working on a task.
- Concentration on interesting tasks is interrupted because of sounds or movement around them.
- There are difficulties in recognizing likenesses and differences in similar spoken or printed words.
- Students have difficulty in drawing simple shapes.
- Reversals of letters or changes of the order of sounds in a word are symptoms of specific learning disabilities.
- There is some lack of coordination in writing or walking.
- The student tends to repeat the same errors over and over.

- Many students have great difficulty in following directions.
- There is quite a lot of variance in performance in different areas. Mathematics may be very high and reading very low.
- Students experience difficulty in organizing their work.
- Many students are very slow in finishing their work.[14]

Since students with specific learning disabilities are difficult to assess and even more difficult to teach, it is imperative that classroom teachers use all their skills to identify these students as soon as possible. However, some educators believe that because faulty assumptions have been made, students identified as learning disabled have not really benefited as much as they could have from the increased emphasis on early identification and intervention. They point out the readiness of trained professionals to identify a student as learning disabled, vagueness in defining the area of learning disability, and the fact that intervention naturally follows identification.[15]

In discussing learning disabilities related to reading, Johnson and Myklebust describe two main types of reading disorders: visual processing and auditory processing.[16] Disorders in visual processing are recognized through

- Visual discrimination difficulties and confusion of similar letters and words
- Slow rate of perception
- Letter and word reversals and inversions
- Difficulty in following and retaining visual sequences
- Associated visual memory problems
- Inferior drawings
- Difficulty in visual analysis and synthesis
- Marked inferiority of visual skills in relation to auditory skills on diagnostic tests

In instructing students with this type of disorder, the teacher should use the auditory skills by teaching sounds and words through association. Auditory processing disorders are characterized by

- Associated auditory discrimination and perceptual problems that hinder the use of phonetic analysis
- Difficulty in separating words into their component phonemes and syllables or in blending them into whole words
- Difficulty in spontaneous recall of the sounds associated with letters or words
- Disturbances in auditory sequencing
- A general preference for visual activities over auditory tasks

Students with this type of disorder should be taught using strategies that emphasize the visual recognition of whole words while the auditory skills are being developed.

Another, perhaps more debilitating, disorder exhibited by many learning-disabled students is short attention span. Students with attention deficits are easily distracted; they lose "attention contact" regardless of the degree of stimulation of the activity in progress.[17] This can be very frustrating to students as well as teachers. Unfortunately, a number of students with learning disabilities experience this problem. Shaywitz and Shaywitz estimate that the frequency of occurrence of attention deficits in learning-disabled children range from as low as 33% to as high as 80%.[18]

The American Psychiatric Association refers to students having severe difficulty with inattention, hyperactivity, and impulsivity as having an attention deficit hyperactivity disorder (ADHD).[19] A variation of attention deficit hyperactivity disorder (ADHD) in which hyperactivity is less prevalent is known as attention deficit disorder (ADD). For children to be diagnosed as having attention deficit hyperactivity disorder (ADHD), they must exhibit six or more of these behaviors more frequently than normal for children of the same mental age, exhibit these behaviors before 7 years of age, and have exhibited these behaviors for at least six months.

In implementing instruction for learning-disabled students, it is essential to increase the amount of on-task reading, increase the amount of direct, supervised instruction the student receives, and be more aware of those students who are falling behind their classmates.[20]

Although teachers may note that learning-disabled students seem to have more difficulty in one modality than another, there is no one method of reading instruction that will work for learning-disabled students. Many techniques must be used to meet the special needs of these students. Some specific suggestions for teaching learning disabled students are to

1. Have students participate in plays, dramatizations, and role playing. These types of activities will help develop better language skills.
2. Provide immediate feedback to students after they have completed an assigned task or activity and reinforce correct responses.
3. Assign tasks in which students will experience success.
4. Use systematic and sequential instruction by carefully planning each reading lesson. It is also important to establish a specific routine with a minimum of changes.
5. Limit the number of concepts and vocabulary introduced.
6. Use process writing, which emphasizes the three stages of planning, drafting, and evaluating and revising.[21]
7. Introduce dialogue journals, which involve a written conversation between two writers, usually teacher and student, over a sustained period of time. The student writes in her journal, the teacher reads and writes a response to the student's journal, and the teacher and the student discuss the journal.[22]

Mainstreaming students encourages interaction with age appropriate peers and requires that classroom teachers use a diagnostic-prescriptive process within the class.

Photo courtesy of Edward B. Lasher.

At-Risk Students

The term "at-risk" is often used to describe a particular segment of the population of the United States that is thought of as underfed, undereducated, and underprivileged. This group is also often referred to as culturally deprived, culturally disadvantaged, or educationally disadvantaged. An equally descriptive term, "societally neglected," is defined by Swanson and Willis to refer to children and youth who experience environmental, cultural, and economic societal conditions that consistently prevent them from realizing their potential within the dominant educational, vocational, and social structures of society.[23]

At-risk students usually experience great difficulty in reading and communicating orally in the school setting. Part of the problem can be ascribed to environmental and experiential factors; however, much of the difficulty is with language acquisition. The language of the at-risk student is typically nonstandard American English, and usually dialectical in nature; this language difference creates many problems when students enter school. Teachers are often unaccustomed to divergent speaking patterns, and students are unaccustomed to the speaking pattern and cultural background of many teachers. Moreover, these students may receive most of their reading instruction from a basal reader or trade books written in standard American English and depicting a way of life that is unfamiliar to the at-risk student. As a result of these and other factors, such students lag behind others who have wider experience and are better able to cope with the language of the materials and the teacher. This situation creates frustration for the at-risk student and begins a cycle that may perpetuate a lifetime of failure.

To better meet the needs of these students, the teacher must first recognize the characteristics of these students:

- Most are from families below the poverty level.
- Many suffer from malnutrition and diseases such as severe anemia, rickets, and vitamin and protein deficiencies.
- Often these students suffer from retarded physical growth.[24]

In addition to these characteristics, many at-risk students will be poorly housed, not properly fed, subject to the effects of others' drug abuses, and provided with few (if any) positive adult role models.[25] The limiting factors for at-risk students as they develop their reading skills are poor language development, low self-concept, improper nutrition, and lack of motivation. Each of these factors affects the development of any learning capability.

Language development is limited because these students often come from homes where there is little verbal interaction and few, if any, reading materials. Verbal communication lacks content and is given primarily in brief commands. This language background does not provide the type of stimulation that the student needs for developing good expressive or receptive language skills.

Students from at-risk homes may also have a poor self-concept because of a lack of a clear identity in the home and lack of recognition of feelings or interests that are important to them. These feelings are more prevalent in students from lower socioeconomic levels, where positive feelings are often not expressed in the home. When the child with a poor self-concept enters school and is confronted with frustrating language experiences, reading difficulties begin.

An added impediment to learning for at-risk students is nutritional deprivation or malnutrition. Malnutrition has an effect on both physical and mental development prior to entering school and continues to retard learning by leaving the student with a physiological need. Until this basic need is fulfilled, maximum learning cannot occur.

All the above factors contribute to a lack of motivation to learn to read. The constant feelings of frustration and failure are reflected in an apathetic reaction to learning. Classroom teachers must attempt to deal with this problem by improving the students' language skills and self-concept, while the school provides nutritious meals. Language skills may be improved through the use of oral language activities throughout the school day. Self-concept can be improved as the student is given learning activities at which he can succeed. At-risk students also need much positive reinforcement. Thus, classroom teachers must make every effort to help these students succeed by

- *Carefully introducing vocabulary as well as concepts.* Because of these students' limited background experiences, they need more preparation for learning to increase the likelihood of success.
- *Being patient with their language usage.* Never ridicule a person's language. Language is essential for expressing emotions and ideas.
- *Providing an atmosphere conducive to class discussions that involve everyone.* Involving each student in the learning process improves self-concept, and the students begin to feel that they are an integral part of the class.

- *Being enthusiastic and receptive in dealing with the students.* Enthusiasm is contagious. If the teacher enjoys teaching, the student will enjoy learning.

At-risk children experience a number of problems in the literary learning process which adversely affect their ability to experience success in reading and writing. Two of the more critical factors are engagement and time. Engagement refers to the actual time children spend on reading and writing; time refers to the amount of time available to learners in the instructional setting. Greenwood found that when at-risk students are given more instructional time to complete tasks and academic engagement is increased, their ability to achieve at higher levels is enhanced.[26] Another study found that engagement and community were major factors in developing successful literary learning in at-risk students.[27] Here again, engaging in actual reading and writing and developing the belief that they were an integral part of the literate classroom community were the keys to unlocking learning for at-risk students.

Developing the at-risk student's language base should be a major focus of any instructional program. Roser, Hoffman, and Farest found that literature units were especially effective in developing literacy in at-risk students.[28] These units consist of groups of books that have a similar topic, theme, author or illustrator, or genre. The objectives of these literature units are to (a) offer exposure to a variety of children's books, (b) contribute to a rich literary environment, (c) motivate responsive reading, (d) encourage voluntary reading, (e) expand reading interest, (f) help children grow in language, reading, writing, and thinking, and (g) help children discover their own connections with literature.

Here are some other specific suggestions for teaching at-risk students.

1. Emphasize language-based activities, especially in the early reading stages, so that students become more aware of the relationship between oral language and print. The language experience approach is particularly effective with this population.
2. Use reading materials that focus on the cultural heritage of the students, and be sure to emphasize the positive aspects of the various cultures in this country. Reading materials that stress cultural diversity should be used.
3. Ignore dialectical differences that occur in oral reading situations when the meaning of the selection is not changed.[29]
4. Motivate students by emphasizing their positive attributes. Use their existing language base to develop more sophisticated language skills.
5. Encourage students to communicate their ideas by emphasizing writing activities that enable them to better understand the relationship between oral language and written language.
6. Encourage parents or caregivers of these children to engage in meaningful literacy events at home such as shared reading, games, making grocery lists, and reading from comic books.

In a study conducted by Purcell-Gates, L'Allier, and Smith, a wide variation in the degree to which print permeates the lives of poor inner-city children was found.[30] In some homes, family members used and engaged in print-embedded activities much more than others. The primary implication for teachers is that even in inner-city homes there is a wide variation in the use and development of literacy; thus, teachers must be careful to ensure that each at-risk student is provided appropriate instruction based on individual needs.

Non-English-Speaking Students

This segment of the school population comprises students who do not use American English as their primary language. This group may include Hispanics (Mexican Americans, Cubans, Puerto Ricans), Vietnamese, Europeans, Asians, and any other individuals who do not speak American English or who use American English as a secondary language. Obviously, such speakers will face difficulties in communicating orally and learning to read.

Students who speak English as a second language may be referred to as bilingual. Those who speak only their native language are monolingual. Lacking English as a primary language, many students who are very capable of learning are unable to do so because of the language barrier. Justin, for example, indicates that almost 1 million Spanish-speaking students in the Southwest will be unable to go beyond the eighth grade because of the language factor. Cordasco also found similar problems among Puerto Rican students on the East Coast.[31]

Another serious concern of some in the non-English-speaking population is the erosion or weakening of their cultural identity. Until recent decades, American schools were perceived as a "melting pot" where various cultural and language differences were dissolved as students adopted American standards, mores, and language and became assimilated into the mainstream. Although most cultural groups want to participate in the American way of life, they also wish to maintain their cultural heritage. Fortunately, educators are now providing better educational services to our non-English-speaking population. In addition, multicultural activities are being emphasized.

In an effort to ensure the right of students to an appropriate education, the U.S. Department of Health, Education, and Welfare has issued guidelines to prevent any type of language discrimination.[32] The National Education Association has set up a task force on bilingual/multicultural education, which defines bilingual education as "a process which uses a pupil's primary language as the principal medium of instruction while teaching the language of the predominant culture in a well-organized program, encompassing a multicultural curriculum."[33]

As classroom teachers attempt to teach reading to second-language learners, they should remember that instruction must be adapted to individual needs. However, the same sequence in learning words is used for the non-English speaker as for the English speaker. Students learn first through listening, add the word to the speaking vocabulary, then use it in reading, and finally learn to write the word. Employing this procedure, students can learn words more quickly. E. Perez found that extending practice in oral language skills through the elementary grades appears to increase the likelihood of reading success.[34] Gonzales suggests that using literature-based programs with interesting texts are also effective in helping second language learners improve their reading skills and their knowledge of English.[35] B. Perez found that using child-relevant instructional conversations that focused on concepts and content rather than conversational drills increased English language acquisition among culturally and linguistically diverse students.[36]

Some other suggestions that the teacher of the non-English speaker should remember are listed below.

- Become familiar with the student's culture.
- Teach the student some survival words in English (e.g., name, address, restroom).
- Teach sentence formation by speaking in simple sentences.
- Use resources from within the community to help the student. Adults or other students who speak the language can be valuable in teaching English to the student.
- Identify concepts, such as numbers, letters, time, and colors, that the student needs to learn. Provide systematic instruction.
- Do not automatically place these students in the low reading group. They should be placed in several groups to gain more experience with the language.
- Team the student with another student who assists in helping the foreign speaker become acquainted with the school.

Most importantly, use variety in teaching and do not drill the student in phonics. English has sounds that do not exist in other languages; thus, the teacher should not expect Spanish-speaking students to learn immediately the *j* sound, as in *jump*, for example, because this sound does not exist in their native language.

Mildly Challenged Students

For many years, IQ scores were used exclusively to identify students with mild disabilities (challenges). Recently, the debate over the accuracy of IQ scores, especially with regard to students from culturally and linguistically diverse backgrounds, has resulted in the use of other criteria along with IQ scores. Mildly challenged students exhibit several characteristics highlighted by Kirk, that the classroom teacher should consider in providing appropriate reading instruction.

- Such areas as auditory and visual memory, language use, conceptual and perceptual abilities, and imaginative and creative abilities may develop slowly.
- Academically, these students experience great difficulty with reading, writing, and spelling activities on entering school. These skills are often not acquired until the student is eight or even eleven years old.

- Progress in school is at one-half to three-quarters the rate of the average student, which is comparable to the student's mental development.
- Mildly disabled/challenged students often exhibit short attention spans and are easily frustrated; however, this situation improves when instruction is geared to meet the student's needs.
- Mildly disabled/challenged students often create more behavior problems in school than other students; however, much of this can be alleviated through the use of appropriate instructional techniques. Despite this reputation for disruptive behavior, evidence indicates that there is no significant difference between these students' behavior in the classroom and that of educationally challenged students.[37]

As teachers plan for providing appropriate reading instruction to mildly disabled students, they must recognize that these students need the same basic reading skills presented at a slower rate. Kolstoe has some additional recommendations for presenting learning tasks to the mildly challenged student:

1. The tasks should be uncomplicated. The new tasks should contain the fewest possible elements, and most of the elements should be familiar, so [the student] has few unknowns to learn.
2. The task should be brief. This assures that [the student] will attend to the most important aspect of the task and not get lost in a sequence of interrelated events.
3. The task should be sequentially presented so the learner proceeds in a sequence of small steps, each one built upon previously learned tasks.
4. Each learning task should be the kind in which success is possible.
5. Overlearning must be built into lessons. Drills in game form seem to lessen the disinterest inherent in unimaginative drill.
6. Learning tasks should be applied to objects, problems, and situations in the learner's life environment. Unless the tasks are relevant, the learner has great difficulty in seeing their possible importance.[38]

More specifically, mildly challenged students may benefit from using self-paced modules[39] and computer-assisted instruction in learning sight words,[40] and by learning how to compare unknown words that they already have in their sight vocabulary.[41]

Erickson and Koppenhaver found that the combined use of technology and child-centered instruction resulted in more active participation in reading and writing activities.[42] Nelson, Cummings, and Boltman suggest some general guidelines for teaching basic concepts to mildly challenged students.[43] For example, in presenting concepts at a concrete level, simple objects such as toys and clothing, as well as the children themselves, should be used so that the children are not distracted by a need to learn about unfamiliar objects. At more abstract levels, children should reverse concepts, such as holding a ball above a table and then below a table or by classifying objects according to color and size. Remember that these basic concepts should be taught in conjunction with instruction in reading and writing.

Mildly challenged students may also benefit from cooperative learning opportunities. Stevens and Slavin found evidence to suggest that cooperative learning can have a positive impact on the academic performance of students with mild disabilities.[44]

Knowledge of these procedures should assist the classroom teacher in providing appropriate instruction for the mildly challenged student.

Gifted and Talented Students

Just as in the other areas of special needs, it is important to identify at an early age those students exhibiting superior talent in one or more areas and to promote opportunities for developing their potential. The most widely accepted definition of the gifted and talented student was proposed by Marland in 1972. Noting that perhaps as many as 3 to 5% of the school-age population are gifted, he defined this group in the following way:

> Gifted and talented children are those identified by professionally qualified persons who, by virtue of outstanding abilities, are capable of high performance. These are children who require differentiated educational programs and services beyond those normally provided by the regular program in order to realize their contribution to self and society.[45]

Renzulli, on the other hand, believes that this estimate is needlessly restrictive and suggests that 15 to 25% of all children may have the ability, motivation, and creativity to exhibit gifted behavior at some time during their school career.[46] Furthermore, Renzulli and Purcell believe that when students are no longer labeled, more students, and perhaps all students, will be afforded a wide range of opportunities, resources, and encouragement.[47]

Children capable of high performance include those with demonstrated achievement or potential ability in any of the following areas:

- General intellectual ability
- Specific academic aptitude
- Creative or productive thinking
- Leadership ability
- Visual and performing arts
- Psychomotor ability

This rather broad definition encompasses a larger population and recognizes students exhibiting talent in areas other than intelligence, as determined by IQ scores. This interpretation also allows for some affective assessment of what constitutes giftedness and talented.

Classroom teachers may wish to note the following characteristics of giftedness, as suggested by Terman and Oden, to facilitate more individualized learning experiences for such students.

- Gifted students exhibit above-average health and physical characteristics.
- Gifted students are two to four years beyond the average level in school work.
- Mental health problems are rare in the gifted population.
- Contrary to some belief, gifted students interact well with peers.
- Wide ranges of interests are enjoyed by gifted students.
- Gifted students tend to be very successful adults.[48]

In the past, the classroom teacher has been totally responsible for providing instruction to this group of students with educational differences. However, with the renewed interest in gifted and talented students, school systems are developing programs that help in meeting their special needs. These programs include ability grouping, acceleration to provide more advanced content, enrichment programs to supplement the regular school offerings, and special classes within a school, or perhaps even Saturday sessions.

In an effective reading program, the gifted and talented student receives appropriate instruction at an accelerated rate with an emphasis on critical and creative thinking. Bynum has proposed that activities provide opportunities for students to do some of the following:

- Add breadth and depth to present knowledge.
- Use many instructional media, especially those that free the student from limited content restrictions.
- Develop efficient reading and study skills.
- Raise the conceptual level on which they function and think.
- Use problem-solving techniques.
- Develop and use critical thinking skills.
- Develop and use creative abilities.
- Do independent work.
- Explore many fields of interest, under guidance and independently.
- Deal with high-level abstractions.
- Converse with students of like abilities.
- Participate in planning learning experiences.
- Apply theory and principles to solving life problems.
- Develop leadership abilities or become effective followers.
- Develop a personal set of values.
- Set and reach immediate and ultimate goals.
- Develop self-discipline and a sense of social responsibility.[49]

Olenchak and Renzulli developed a schoolwide enrichment model for gifted students that is comprised of five components:

1. *Curriculum compacting*. Modifying the regular curriculum in order to eliminate repetition of previously mastered material, upgrade the challenge level of the regular curriculum, and provide time for appropriate enrichment and/or acceleration activities while ensuring mastery of basic skills.
2. *Assessment of student strengths*. Develop systematic procedures for gathering and recording information about students' abilities, interests, and learning styles.
3. *Type I enrichment: general exploratory experiences*. Design experiences and activities that expose students to a wide variety of disciplines, visual and performing arts, and any information not ordinarily covered in the regular curriculum.
4. *Type II enrichment: group training activities*. Use instructional methods and materials that are intentionally designed to promote the development of thinking and feeling processes.
5. *Type III enrichment: individual and small group investigations of real problems*. Develop investigative activities and artistic productions in which the learner assumes the role of a firsthand inquirer. In this stage, students think, feel, and act like a practicing professional.[50]

Teachers should remember that the gifted and talented need planned reading instruction to assist in expanding their vocabulary and in using the many ideas these students learn so quickly. They also need opportunities to interact with other students at all levels in order to become well-adjusted citizens in the school and community.

Riddle recommends providing quality literature in the classroom to stimulate and provoke more curiosity and meaning making for the gifted and talented student.[51] Literature circles can be used to discuss ideas and opinions and allow students to verbalize their critical thinking. Literature that uses words in unusual ways and nonfiction books in a variety of content areas should be emphasized.

PSYCHOLOGICALLY CHALLENGED STUDENTS

Teaching emotionally or behaviorally disordered students is a cause of great concern to educators. Many of these students are quite capable of performing school tasks; however, they are often unable to do so because of psychological problems manifested in deviant or disruptive behavior in the classroom. These students may show great enthusiasm for completing an assigned task, only to suddenly explode into disruptive behavior, creating many problems for the classroom teacher. They may also totally withdraw from classroom activities.

Bower has identified some specific behavior patterns of emotionally disturbed students. While the presence of these problems does not always mean that the student has a psychological impairment, their incidence over a long period of time deserves attention.

- Absence of knowledge and skill acquisition in academic and social behaviors not attributable to intellectual capability, hearing and visual status, or physical health anomalies.
- Absence of positive, satisfying interpersonal relationships with adults and peers.
- Frequent instances of inappropriate behavior episodes that are surprising or unexpected for the conditions in which they occur.
- Observable periods of diminished verbal and other motor activity (e.g., moods of depression or unhappiness).
- Frequent complaints of a physical nature, such as stomachaches, soreness in the arm, and general fatigue.[52]

When classroom teachers identify students with these characteristics and refer them for further evaluation, or when they have a student who has already been formally identified as having emotional or behavioral problems, they must have strategies for dealing with these students in the classroom. Such students can follow the same basic procedures in an effective reading program that other students do; however, the teacher must adjust his teaching strategies to meet the personal needs of students who may sometimes have unpredictable reactions.

The Peacock Hill Working Group, a group of nationally known leaders in the field of emotional and behavioral disorders, suggests that the following strategies when used in combination are likely to result in successful instructional outcomes.

1. Systematic, data-based interventions
2. Continuous assessment and monitoring of progress
3. Provision for practice of new skills
4. Treatment matched with the problem
5. Multicomponent treatment
6. Programming for transfer and maintenance
7. Commitment to sustained intervention[53]

As classroom teachers work with an emotionally and behaviorally disordered student in the reading program, the basic guidelines below will prove helpful.

- Be sure that instruction is based on the student's needs and interests, and that learning experiences are successful for the student.
- Offer options for learning a specified skill and allow the student to choose.
- Work with other resource persons in the community, such as social workers and psychiatrists, to meet the student's social and academic needs.
- Establish a positive relationship with the student. Teachers must sometimes have a high degree of tolerance for hateful or aggressive reactions.
- Provide guidance to help students realize the seriousness of their actions and to take steps toward self-control.

- Learn to read the student; try to determine why certain actions or reactions occur. Then try to be empathetic and help the student work out dilemmas.

In the instructional setting, do not restrict yourself to just one approach or just one type of reading material, such as basal readers. Instead, vary your approaches; use an integrated reading and writing program with language-based activities and literature to enhance the child's experience base and build on prior knowledge. D'Alessandro[54] found that using a literature-based reading program with emotionally and behaviorally disordered children had a very positive impact on the children's self-concept and attitude toward books.

PHYSICALLY CHALLENGED STUDENTS

Students with physical challenges include those with disorders of the nervous or musculoskeletal system, the visually disabled, and the hearing impaired. Because this book is limited to addressing the reading needs of students, the authors include under this category only those physical challenges that affect reading performance, namely the visual and hearing disorders. Students with such challenges experience difficulties in performing tasks because of a loss of acuity in either the visual or auditory mode. As a result of these losses, they must receive special assistance from the teacher in performing certain learning tasks.

Visually Challenged Students

Teachers should recognize that visually challenged students are equal to the sighted in reading comprehension when provided more time to read the tests. Bateman found that partially sighted students in grades 1 to 4

- Were similar to the reading achievement level of sighted students,
- Scored highest on a silent reading test and lowest on a timed oral reading test, and
- Made more reversal errors than the sighted group but either did not differ or made fewer errors in other areas than the sighted[55]

With this research information, teachers should recognize that educational objectives for the visually challenged are the same as for the sighted student; only the methods and materials must be changed. Lowenfeld suggests three basic ideas for the teacher to consider in teaching the visually impaired:

- *Concreteness.* Students must be provided with objects that can be manipulated and touched in order to learn about their size, shape, weight, etc.
- *Unifying experiences.* Systematic stimulation is necessary in order for the visually challenged to learn how parts relate to the total picture. For example, in order to learn how one part of the neighborhood connects to another the student must be taken to the places and provided explanations. Without adequate vision it is difficult for a person to unify parts into a meaningful whole.

- *Learning by doing.* The visually challenged student must be stimulated by sight, touch, or hearing to become involved with an activity. Thus, visually challenged students must be invited and shown how to become involved in a learning task because they cannot see the learning activity to automatically involve themselves.[56]

Classroom teachers can greatly assist visually challenged students by providing instruction in listening skills. Because so much of their education comes through listening to information, this area must be strengthened through direct instruction. Additionally, classroom teachers should be aware of special materials and equipment that can assist in providing appropriate instruction in reading.

For the visually challenged student, lighting is one of the most important considerations. Glare and direct sunlight limit vision, while evenly distributed light and appropriate artificial illumination assist the visually impaired reader. These students may also need adjustable desks to ensure the right angle of light, gray-green chalkboards that reflect more light, typewriters, dictaphones, tape players, magnifying lenses, large-type books, three-dimensional maps, and other specially designed teaching-learning aids.[57]

Classroom teachers should realize that visually challenged students fit into the effective reading program just as much as other students with specific reading needs. The only difference is that specialized materials and techniques are needed to further assist them.

Hearing-Challenged Students

The hearing-challenged student has deficits in many developmental areas, with language and related areas such as reading being most severely affected. Gentile has found that hearing-challenged students at age 8 scored at about grade 2 in reading and math computation, and at age 17 the children scored at about grade 4 in reading and grade 6 in math computation. These findings are substantiated by similar results in a study by Trybus and Karchmer.[58] Pflaster indicates that the factors that appear to most directly affect the academic performance of hearing-challenged students are oral communication, personality, and linguistic competence.[59]

Although hearing-challenged students seem to do poorly in language-related areas, their intelligence range is similar to that for normal children on nonverbal intelligence measures.[60] Larson and Miller provide the following list of suggestions for the classroom teacher to consider in teaching the hearing-challenged student.

1. Give the child favorable seating in the classroom and allow him to move to the source of speech within the room; let the child turn around or have speakers turn toward the child, to allow visual contact with anyone who is speaking.
2. Encourage the student to look at the speaker's lips, mouth, and face. Speech-reading should help clarify many of the sounds the child cannot hear.
3. Speak naturally–neither mumbling nor overarticulating. Speak neither too fast nor too slow, too loud nor too soft.

4. Keep hands away from the mouth when speaking, and make sure that books, papers, glasses, pencils, and other objects do not obstruct the visual contact
5. Take note of the light within the room so that the overhead light or window light is not at the speaker's back. Speech-reading is difficult when light shines in the speechreader's eyes. Try to prevent shadows from falling on the speaker's mouth.
6. Stand in one place while dictating spelling words or arithmetic problems to the group, allowing the hard-of-hearing child to see better, as well as to give a sense of security that the teacher will be there when she looks up.
7. Speak in complete sentences. Single words are more difficult to speech-read than are complete thoughts. Approximately 50 percent of the words in the English language look alike on the lips. Such groups of words are termed *homophenous*. (Examples: *man*, *pan*, *ban*, *band*, *mat*, *pat*, *bat*, *mad*, *pad*, *bad*.) Phrases and sentences placing the word in context help promote visual differentiation among homophenous words.
8. Give the student assignments in advance or give the topic that will be discussed. A list of new vocabulary to be used in an assignment also assists the student. Familiarity may help the child understand the word in context and help promote visual differentiation among homophenous words.
9. Occasionally have the hearing-challenged child repeat the assignment to some other child so you are sure the assignment has been understood.
10. Remember at all times that this is a normal child with a hearing problem; never single out a hearing-challenged child in front of the group or in any other manner encourage an attitude of being "different."
11. Understand that the child with a hearing loss may tire faster than a child with normal hearing.
12. Take into consideration that many children hear better on some days than they do on others. Also, children may suffer from tinnitus (hearing noises within the head), which may make them nervous and irritable.
13. Restate a sentence, using other words that have the same meaning, when the hearing-challenged student does not understand what has been said. The reworded sentence might be more visible. (Example: Change "Close your book" to "Shut the book" or "Please put your book away now." Look in a mirror and observe the difference.)
14. Encourage the hearing-challenged child to participate in all school and community activities.
15. Encourage an understanding of and interest in the hearing-challenged child by the entire group.[61]

In the classroom reading program, hearing-challenged students must develop the same basic skills as normal students. These students may learn them more slowly and in different ways because of their difficulty with language, but they can, with the guidance of patient teachers, become effective readers.

SUMMARY

In the effective reading program, the classroom teacher must be aware of the special needs of some students. The goal of this chapter was to help classroom teachers acquire some knowledge of these special needs and ideas on how to address them in the reading program.

Students with special needs fall into three basic categories:

- Students with educational differences, including learning-disabled, at-risk, non-English-speaking, mildly disabled or challenged, and gifted and talented students
- Students with psychological handicaps, including emotionally and behaviorally disordered students
- Students with physical handicaps, including visually challenged and hearing-challenged students.

In addition to defining and describing the characteristics of each group, ideas for developing appropriate reading strategies were presented. The classroom teacher must assume the primary responsibility for educating all students and must acquire the skills necessary for accommodating those students and their special needs in the school reading program.

Applying What You Read

1. In your classroom, you have several students who fit into the special needs category as defined in this chapter. How can they be accommodated in the effective reading program?
2. Some parents have just been told that their visually challenged children will become an integral part of your classroom. How would you explain to them how the children will function in the regular classroom?
3. You have just been assigned two new students who speak only Vietnamese. What should you do to help them learn English?

NOTES

1. J. W. Birch, *Mainstreaming: Educable Mentally Retarded Children in Regular Classes.*
2. Margaret C. Wang, "Mainstreaming Exceptional Children: Some Instructional Design and Implementation Considerations," *The Elementary School Journal.*
3. William L. Heward, *Exceptional Children*, 5th ed., p. 63.
4. L. Idol, A. Nevin, and P. Paolucci-Whitcomb, *Collaborative Consultation*, 2nd ed.
5. Susan Stainback and William Stainback, eds., *Curricular Considerations in Inclusive Classrooms: Facilitating Learning for All Students*, p. 3.
6. M. F. Giangreco, C. J. Cloninger, R. E. Dennis, and S. W. Edelman, "Problem-Solving Methods To Facilitate Inclusive Education, in *Creativity and Collaborative Learning: A Practical Guide to Empowering Students and Teachers*, edited by J. S. Thousand, R. A. Villa, and A. I. Nevin, p. 322.
7. Council for Exceptional Children Delegate Assembly, *Policy on Inclusive Schools.*
8. William Stainback, Susan Stainback, and Gregory Stefanich, "Learning Together in Inclusive Classrooms: What about the Curriculum?" *Teaching Exceptional Children.*
9. Richard Long, "Education Issues Part of Busy Fall Schedule," *Reading Today.*

10. National Advisory Committee on Handicapped Children, *First Annual Report, Subcommittee on Education of the Committee on Labor and Public Welfare, U.S. Senate*, p. 14.
11. U.S. National Joint Committee on Learning Disabilities, "Revised Definitions of LD," *The Reading Teacher*.
12. U.S. National Joint Committee on Learning Disabilities, "Revised Definitions of LD," *The Reading Teacher*.
13. Daniel P. Hallahan and James M. Kauffman, *Exceptional Children: Introduction to Special Education*, pp. 121–167.
14. Hap Gilliland, *A Practical Guide to Remedial Reading*, pp. 282–283.
15. Carol Strickland Beers and James Wheelock Beers, "Early Identification of Learning Disabilities: Facts and Fallacies," *The Elementary School Journal*.
16. Donald J. Johnson and Helmer R. Myklebust, *Learning Disabilities: Educational Principles and Practices*.
17. Earl H. Cheek, Rona F. Flippo, and Jimmy D. Lindsey, *Reading for Success in Elementary Schools*.
18. S. E. Shaywitz and B. A. Shaywitz, *Attention Deficit Disorder: Current Perspectives*, paper presented at National Conference on Learning Disabilities.
19. American Psychiatric Association, *Diagnostic and Statistical Manual of Mental Disorders (DSM-III-R)*, 3rd ed.
20. Gaea Leinhardt, Naomi Zigmond, and William W. Cooley, "Reading Instruction and Its Effects," *American Educational Research Journal*.
21. Ada L. Vallecorsa, Rita Rice Ledford, and Ginger G. Parnell, "Strategies for Teaching Composition Skills to Students with Learning Disabilities," *Teaching Exceptional Children*.
22. Martha Gonter Gaustad and Trinka Messenheimer-Young, "Dialogue Journals for Students with Learning Disabilities," *Teaching Exceptional Children*.
23. B. Marion Swanson and Diane J. Willis, *Understanding Exceptional Children and Youth*, p. 133.
24. Swanson and Willis, *Understanding Exceptional Children and Youth*, p. 133.
25. Robert Rossi and Samuel Stringfield, "What We Must Do for Students Placed at Risk," *Phi Delta Kappan*.
26. Charles R. Greenwood, "Longitudinal Analysis of Time, Engagement, and Achievement in At-Risk versus Non-Risk Students," *Exceptional Children*.
27. JoBeth Allen, Barbara Michalove, Betty Shockley, and Marsha West, "I'm Really Worried about Joseph: Reducing the Risks of Literacy Learning," *The Reading Teacher*.
28. Nancy L. Roser, James V. Hoffman, and Cynthia Farest, "Language, Literature, and At-Risk Children," *The Reading Teacher*.
29. Donald J. Leu, Jr. and Charles K. Kinzer, *Effective Reading Instruction in the Elementary Grades*, pp. 463–464.
30. Victoria Purcell-Gates, Susan L'Allier, and Dorothy Smith, "Literacy at the Harts' and the Larsons': Diversity among Poor Inner City Families," *The Reading Teacher*.
31. Neal Justin, "Culture Conflict and Mexican-American Achievement," *School and Society*; F. Cordasco, "Puerto Rican Pupils and American Education," in *Education and the Many Faces of the Disadvantaged: Cultural and Historical Perspectives*, edited by W. W. Brickman and S. Lehrer, pp. 126–131.
32. Swanson and Willis, *Understanding Exceptional Children and Youth*, p. 154.
33. National Education Association, "America's Other Children—Bilingual Multicultural Education: Hope for the Culturally Alienated," *NEA Reporter*.
34. Eustolia Perez, "Oral Language Competence Improves Reading Skills of Mexican American Third Graders," *The Reading Teacher*.
35. Phillip C. Gonzales, "Literature-Based ESL Program Works," *Reading Today*.
36. Bertha Perez, "Instructional Conversations as Opportunities for English Language Acquisition for Culturally and Linguistically Diverse Students," *Language Arts*.
37. S. A. Kirk and J. W. Gallagher, *Educating Exceptional Children*, 3rd ed.
38. Oliver P. Kolstoe, *Teaching Educable Mentally Retarded Children*, 2nd ed., p. 27.

39. David C. Gardner and Margaret Kurtz, "Teaching Technical Vocabulary to Challenged Student," *Reading Improvement*.
40. M. Lally, "Computer-Assisted Teaching of Sight-word Recognition for Mentally Retarded School Children," *American Journal of Mental Deficiency*.
41. Frances M. Guthrie and Patricia M. Cunningham, "Teaching Decoding Skills to Educable Mentally Challenged Children," *The Reading Teacher*.
42. Karen A. Erickson and David A. Koppenhauer, "Developing a Literacy Program for Children with Severe Disabilities," *The Reading Teacher*.
43. R. Brett Nelson, Jack A. Cummings, and Heidi Boltman, "Teaching Basic Concepts to Students Who Are Educable Mentally Challenged," *Teaching Exceptional Children*.
44. Robert J. Stevens and Robert E. Slavin, "When Cooperative Learning Improves the Achievement of Students with Mild Disabilities: A Response to Tateyama-Sniezek," *Exceptional Children*.
45. Sidney P. Marland, *Education of the Gifted and Talented*, p. 10.
46. J. S. Renzulli, "Dear Mr. and Mrs. Copernicus: We Regret to Inform You . . . ," *Gifted Child Quarterly*.
47. J. S. Renzulli and J. H. Purcell, *Roeper Review*.
48. Lewis M. Terman and Melita H. Oden, *The Gifted Group and Midlife: Thirty-Five Years' Follow-Up of the Superior Child*.
49. Margaret Bynum, *Curriculum for Gifted Students*.
50. F. R. Olenchak and J. S. Renzulli, "The Effectiveness of the Schoolwide Enrichment Model on Selected Aspects of Elementary School Change," *Gifted Child Quarterly*.
51. Sharla Riddle, "Is Your Classroom a Literature Oasis?" *Gifted Child Today*.
52. Eli M. Bower, *Early Identification of Emotionally Challenged Children in School*, 2nd ed.
53. Peacock Hill Working Group, "Problems and Promises in Special Education and Related Services for Children and Youth with Emotional or Behavioral Disorders," *Behavioral Disorders*.
54. Marilyn D'Alessandro, "Accommodating Emotionally Handicapped Children through a Literature-based Reading Program," *The Reading Teacher*.
55. Bateman, *Reading the Psycholinguistic Process of Partially Seeing Children*.
56. Berthold Lowenfeld, ed. *The Visually Challenged Child in School*.
57. Kirk and Gallagher, *Educating Exceptional Children*, 3rd ed., p. 268.
58. A. Gentile, *Further Studies in Achievement Testing, Hearing Impaired Students*; Raymond J. Trybus and Michael A. Karchmer, "School Achievement Scores of Hearing Impaired Children: National Data on Achievement Status and Growth Patterns," *American Annals of the Deaf*.
59. Gail Pflaster, "A Factor Analysis of Variables Related to Academic Performance of Hearing-Impaired Children in Regular Classes," *The Volta Review*.
60. Richard G. Brill, "The Relationship of Wechsler IQ's to Academic Achievement among Deaf Students," *Exceptional Children*.
61. Alfred D. Larson and June B. Miller, "The Hearing Impaired," in *Exceptional Children and Youth: An Introduction*, edited by Edward L. Meyen, pp. 463–465.

STEP 5

FITTING THE PARTS TOGETHER

As the teachers at Twin Lakes School consider assessing and guiding reading instruction, the importance of the various steps in the process became very apparent. Teacher, parent, and student involvement is essential for the overall effectiveness of the program. As the steps are implemented, careful evaluation is necessary to determine how the parts are blending to form an effective program that meets the individual learning needs of each student.

CHAPTER 13

Making It Work

As the teachers and administrators at Twin Lakes School initially assessed and guided their reading program, there was a tendency to follow a step-by-step procedure without looking at the total program. This chapter reviews the essential components of an effective reading program and shows how they fit together to make a total program. This review may serve as a standard for evaluating any reading program.

Vocabulary to Know

- **Approaches**
- **Appropriate instruction**
- **Assessment**
- **Basal instruction**
- **Collaborative learning**
- **Comprehension**
- **Coordination**
- **Direct instruction**
- **Effective instruction**
- **Emergent literacy**
- **Grouping**
- **Guided instruction**
- **Indirect instruction**
- **Individualization**
- **Language-based instruction**
- **Parental involvement**
- **Personal reading**
- **Record-keeping procedures**
- **Scope and sequence**

THE EFFECTIVE READING PROGRAM

In reviewing an effective reading program, it is necessary to examine the component parts of the program. A weakness in any one of them results in a program that may not provide maximum learning opportunities for students. Therefore, faculties continuously evaluate their programs and strive to improve. The essential components of an effective reading program are outlined in the following pages and summarized in Table 13.1.

Table 13.1 Essential Components of an Effective Reading Program

Continuum of Skills	Basis for assessing and instruction
Initial Assessment	Identify strengths and weakness
	Use variety of instruments
Instruction	Based on assessment
	Use variety of approaches and materials
Planned Lessons	Provides format for reading lessons
	May be adapted as necessary
Record-Keeping Procedure	Based on continuum of skills
	Record strengths and weaknesses of students
Commitment	Encourage students to read
	Meet individual student needs
Ongoing Assessment	Work together to diagnose
	Plan together for instruction
Personal Reading	Develop leisure-time reading habits
	Learn to read for information
	Use SSR and RIF
	Motivate students to read
Grouping	Use variety of groups
	Aids in organizing and managing the class
	Have flexible groups
Parental Involvement	Invite parents into school
	Tell them about program
	Train them to assist

Familiarity with a hierarchy of skills (scope and sequence) in language and knowledge expectations in listening, speaking, and writing guides the teacher

As discussed in Chapter 1, teacher knowledge of a hierarchy of skills and an understanding of language development are necessary components of the program. Effective instruction is predicated on the assumption that each student will make continuous progress. The students' strengths and weaknesses in various areas are determined so that the teacher can provide appropriate instruction. Even though a basal reading series is developed around a planned scope and sequence of skills, teachers may be unaware of this structure or use it only as outlined in the teacher's manual. Teachers who do not use basal materials or have a district curriculum have to be knowledgeable of reading and language development to guide their instruction. Based on student need, instruction is adjusted by omitting skills that the student knows, reteaching those that appear to be causing difficulty, and revamping lessons to met the reading/language needs of the student.

Assessment determines the reading needs of each student

Assessing the strengths and needs of each student in the classroom is vital to the success of an effective reading program. Determining instructional, independent, and frustration reading levels, interests, and specific strengths and weaknesses in reading and language is the first step that enables the teacher to locate appropriate materials and to develop instructional plans to meet the needs of the students. These data are obtained through the use of informal and formal assessment procedures. Testing procedures represent only one way of obtaining information about students. Kid watching, or observing students during various reading activities, provides excellent assessment information. Furthermore, teachers can not allow test scores to influence their judgments more than their observation. The observational data gained is much more informative for guiding instruction than the three scores given for the various reading levels of the student on an IRI.

A variety of materials and teaching techniques should be used

As teachers learn about student needs in reading and language through the different assessment procedures, they soon realize that there is no one type of material, approach, or strategy that is appropriate for all students. Various approaches, using basal and language-based instruction in conjunction with the other approaches described in Chapter 6, are essential in providing appropriate instruction.

Schools implementing an effective reading program need a variety of materials that accommodate not only the skill needs but also the interests and learning styles of the students. Using an assortment of approaches and materials, the teacher matches the instructional strategies with the assessed student needs. Thus, in an effective reading program, the teacher facilitates the instructional program.

Planned lesson procedures include both direct and indirect teaching strategies

Teachers organize the reading lessons used for effective instruction. The guided or directed reading lesson format helps teachers to organize their instruction using a step-by-step procedure that incorporates the areas important to the development and application of reading skills. By following this process, the teacher is able to provide direct instruction, interrelate learning for the lesson, and show students how learning is applied. This procedure, presented in Chapter 6, includes these steps:

- *Readiness.* Developing background for the material to be read together with the concepts and vocabulary needed for reading it is the essential first step.
- *Skill development.* The teacher introduces or reviews the skills that students need in order to read the material.
- *Review.* The concepts, vocabulary, and skills should be reviewed to help students relate these to the material to be read. In addition, the teacher and students should establish purposes for reading the material to guide their silent reading.
- *Guided reading.* With purposes for reading the materials clearly established, the student is asked to read the material silently. Following the silent reading, the material is discussed. At this time, the teacher may ask students to read portions aloud as they locate specific information or to identify character attitudes by verbalizing their statements with appropriate expression. However, direct instruction is not needed for each student every day. Indirect teaching strategies, which encourage students to learn independently and explore through reading and language activities, are important in developing lifelong learners.
- *Follow-up.* After the students have read the material and discussed it with others to summarize the ideas of the author, some follow-up activities may be done. These may include more skill development in areas of need or activities to encourage students to extend the information given by the author. Activities such as reading other materials related to the topic or interpreting what has been read through artwork or creative writing are possibilities. Personal reading habits can be greatly enhanced at this time.

Teachers may deviate from this structured format to give more variety to their reading lessons, to adjust their instruction to different materials or approaches, and to better meet student needs. However, keep this procedure in mind for every lesson so that the necessary elements of a good reading lesson are always present.

A systematic record-keeping procedure helps monitor the progress of the students

The effective reading program is based on the idea that the teacher knows the reading needs of the students and provides appropriate instruction based on those needs. Thus, the teacher must have a systematic way of recording the strengths and weaknesses of the entire class as well as individual students.

Teachers sometimes get so involved in record keeping that they lose sight of teaching. This must not happen. Record-keeping procedures should help in the instructional program, not interfere with teaching. Schools that have an effective reading program usually have a record-keeping procedure that is used throughout the school. This procedure provides continuity as students progress from grade to grade. Record-keeping procedures are crucial in an effective reading program. Teachers cannot remember the specific needs of every student without having some systematic way of noting the information; record keeping will help the teacher guide instruction, confer with parents, and evaluate progress.

Teachers and administrators must commit themselves to meeting the individual reading needs of each student in the school

In an effective reading program, the school staff believes that every student can learn to read and communicates this belief to the students. The staff provides various types of learning experiences to help students overcome weaknesses and reach their reading potential. In this type of reading program, the teachers realize that students read at many different levels and have varying needs. Thus, they use various approaches, strategies, and materials.

The school atmosphere encourages students to read because the adults in the school think reading is important and they demonstrate this by reading to and with the students and talking about what they read. The teachers motivate the students to read and help them understand how the skills are applied. In a school where the entire school staff is committed to reading improvement and individual reading needs are considered, students feel good about learning; therefore, they tend to learn more.

Teachers work together to develop good reading habits for each student in all classes

As teachers assess specific reading/language needs and record this information for use in providing appropriate instruction, the information is shared with all teachers who work with the student. This means that assessment information obtained by the classroom teacher, the special reading teacher, and the content teacher are combined, so that each teacher can provide the most appropriate instruction for each student.

Coordination is an essential ingredient in an effective program. As outlined in Chapter 1, many people must work together to implement the program. This involves working together to share assessment information and to plan for appropriate instruction. The classroom teacher and the special reading teacher, such as the Title I teacher, coordinate the instructional program for the students that they share. This is essential because without such coordination, the two teachers may end up working against one another by using different approaches and materials to develop the needed skills. Additionally, time is wasted repeating assessment procedures when the information could be shared.

Content teachers are also a part of this coordinated effort. All teachers in a departmentalized situation have responsibilities regarding the development of reading in their content area. This includes determining their students' strengths and weaknesses and incorporating reading development into their instructional program. The assessment data collected by the language arts teacher should be shared with all of the other content teachers. Conversely, the assessment information from the various content teachers is shared with the language arts teacher, who may keep the up-to-date assessment records on the students. The exchange of information enhances the coordination and planning of joint units and activities. Planning with the media specialist and guidance counselor greatly assists in the development of personal reading habits. Their encouragement and leadership will guide students into areas of reading that they have not explored.

Students spend time reading for leisure and to gain knowledge

One of the major weaknesses of many reading programs is the overemphasis on isolated skill development to the virtual exclusion of language application and personal reading. In an effective program, students are encouraged to read materials on their own during their extra time and during planned free reading times. Moreover, students are shown how to read materials to gain information as a variety of different materials are used for instruction.

To enhance reading as a leisure-time activity, many schools have incorporated sustained silent reading periods as described in Chapter 11. Through community efforts, other schools have initiated community sponsored reading programs. There are many ways to encourage students to read. Teachers must continuously try to motivate students to develop their personal reading habits; otherwise, reading has no purpose.

The use of collaborative learning and various grouping procedures helps to meet the needs of the students

In some classrooms, students spend most of their time with the students in their group. If this is the "low" group, these students are immediately labeled and tend to associate primarily with others in their group. Their performance seldom improves because they are expected to be in the low group. The same is true for the other groups when only achievement grouping is used for instruction. Thus, teachers must use a variety of grouping patterns to enhance learning as well as social development. Groups should never become permanent.

Interest groups and skill groups provide some opportunities to vary the composition of groups. At some point instruction must be individualized, and occasionally the entire class may work together on a task. Various grouping procedures are used in an effective program to meet student needs, and students move from group to group as instruction is provided to aid their reading development. Grouping should always be flexible and fluid.

Parents are involved in the program

No reading program is fully effective until parents are involved. Parents assist in reading development in many ways. They serve as reading models in the home environment. This modeling has consistently been identified as a significant factor in reading development.

Parents can also assist in reinforcing concepts introduced at school. Teachers involve parents in the development of necessary reading skills when this seems feasible for the student, and when the parents are willing to work with the teacher. Some parents may pressure students to such an extent that more harm than good results. Other parents may use their own instructional procedures, which may confuse the student. These situations exist and teachers must consider them when involving parents. Nevertheless, parents should be included in the reading program; they are crucial in helping their child realize the importance of reading. Some parents may prefer to work in the school as volunteers to tutor students or perform clerical tasks for the teacher. They are all welcome additions.

When including parents in the reading program, the school faculty needs to consider developing a training course to help parents understand the program as well as activities they can use to help their children. Some schools present information regarding child growth and development and ideas on getting along with children. These programs help parents to feel like they're a part of the school, meet other parents with similar concerns, and learn how they can help their children. The total reading program is not functioning properly until parents are welcomed as a part of the school team.

SUMMARY

The different components of an effective reading program have been summarized in this chapter and in Table 13.1. As schools implement a balanced reading program that meets the needs of all students, they must consider all of these elements. These constituents may serve as evaluative criteria as the program is reviewed and revised.

Faculty commitment and administrative leadership are required to develop a reading program that meets the needs of the students. This is not an easy assignment, but the rewards of seeing students who enjoy learning because they can read and the feeling of satisfaction that comes from guiding students in their reading make teaching and learning a joyous experience for all.

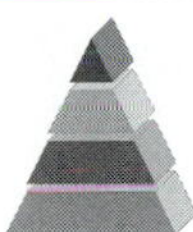

Applying What You Read

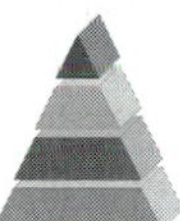

1. As a reading teacher in a middle school, you are asked to help evaluate the school's reading program. What would you look for?
2. Ten components of an effective reading program have been identified. Which component do you feel is the most important and why? How would you rank the others?

APPENDIX A

READING SKILLS LIST

PREREADING SKILLS

A. Oral Language Skills

1. Recognize word boundaries.
2. Use adequate vocabulary.
3. Understand basic concepts such as colors, shapes, size, direction.
4. Tell about a picture or object.
5. Express ideas in complete sentences.
6. Relate story in sequence.
7. Participate in discussions.

B. Visual-Motor Skills

1. Coordinate eye-hand movements.
2. Execute directionality in coordinated eye-hand movements.
3. Draw specified designs such as circles and lines.
4. Reproduce designated designs, numerals, letters, or words.
5. Reproduce own name in manuscript.

C. Visual Discrimination and Visual Memory Skills

1. Match shapes, objects, and pictures.
2. Recognize likenesses and differences in objects and designs.
3. Recognize likenesses and differences in numerals, letters, and words.
4. Match uppercase and lowercase letters.
5. Identify from memory objects, pictures, or designs briefly presented.
6. Classify objects or pictures.
7. Recognize own name in manuscript.
8. Recognize designated designs, numerals, letters, or words.
9. Match colors.
10. Follow picture, design, letter, or word in sequence.
11. Identify uppercase and lowercase letter symbols.

D. Visual Comprehension Skills
1. Identify details in pictures.
2. Identify missing parts in picture or symbol.
3. Identify sequence of pictures or story from pictures.
4. Identify common characteristics of objects.

E. Auditory Discrimination and Auditory Memory Skills
1. Discriminate among various environmental sounds.
2. Discriminate among different sounds of letters and words.
3. Identify simple everyday sounds.
4. Recognize rhyming words.
5. Follow simple one- and two-step directions.
6. Identify sounds in words.
7. Reproduce simple sounds, letters, and words.
8. Identify beginning sounds in words.
9. Identify ending sounds in words.
10. Identify medial sounds in words.
11. Use rhyming words to complete sentences.
12. Identify syllables in words.

F. Auditory (Listening) Comprehension Skills
1. Follow directions.
2. Associate object or picture with oral description.
3. Identify main idea.
4. Identify main character.
5. Identify details in sentence and story.
6. Identify sequence of events.
7. Identify relationships such as cause and effect and comparisons.
8. Interpret descriptive language.
9. Recognize emotions of characters and story.
10. Draw conclusions.
11. Anticipate outcomes.

WORD IDENTIFICATION SKILLS

A. Sight Vocabulary
1. Identify familiar words (e.g., nouns, verbs)
2. Identify basic sight words in context.

B. Phoneme-Grapheme Correspondences (Phonics)
1. Reproduce from memory uppercase and lowercase letter symbols.
2. Associate concept of consonants with appropriate letters.
3. Associate concept of vowels with appropriate letters.

4. Associate sounds and symbols for initial, medial, and final consonant sounds.
5. Recognize sounds and symbols of variant consonant patterns.
6. Associate sounds and symbols for initial, medial, and final long- and short-vowel patterns.
7. Recognize sounds and symbols of variant vowel patterns.
8. Blend sounds to form words.
9. Substitute initial, medial, and final sounds to form new words.

C. Structural Analysis
   1. Recognize compound words.
   2. Recognize contractions and original word forms.
   3. Analyze affixes (suffixes and prefixes) in words.
   4. Recognize inflectional endings.
   5. Divide unknown words into syllables.
      a. Divide between two consonants
      b. Divide between single consonants
      c. Divide with *le* endings
      d. Divide words with prefixes and suffixes
      e. Divide words with common endings
   6. Accent appropriate syllables in words.
      a. Accent first syllable
      b. Accent compound words
      c. Accent base word with prefix or suffix
      d. Use primary and secondary accents

D. Contextual Analysis
   1. Use picture clues to determine unknown words.
   2. Use context clues to determine unknown words.
      a. Sentence sense (missing word) clue
      b. Synonym, antonym, and homonym clue
      c. Familiar expression clue
      d. Comparison and contrast clue
      e. Words and multiple-meaning clue
      f. Summary clue

COMPREHENSION SKILLS

A. Literal Skills
   1. Understand concrete words, phrases, clauses, and sentence patterns.
   2. Identify stated main ideas.
   3. Recall details (who, what, when, where, how).
   4. Remember stated sequence of events.
   5. Select stated cause and effect relationships.

6. Compare and contrast information.
7. Identify character traits and actions.
8. Interpret abbreviations, symbols, and acronyms.
9. Follow written directions.
10. Classify information.

B. Interpretive (Inferential) Skills
   1. Predict outcomes.
   2. Interpret character traits.
   3. Draw conclusions.
   4. Make generalizations.
   5. Perceive relationships.
   6. Understand implied causes and effects.
   7. Identify implied main ideas.
   8. Interpret figurative language.
   9. Interpret meaning of capitalization and punctuation in a selection.
   10. Understand mood and emotional reactions.
   11. Interpret pronouns and antecedents.
   12. Understand author's purpose and point of view.
   13. Construe meaning by signal words.
   14. Understand meaning of abstract words.
   15. Summarize information.
   16. Recognize implied sequence.
   17. Use context clues to determine meaning.
       a. Synonym, antonym, and homonym clues
       b. Familiar expression clues
       c. Comparison and contrast clues
       d. Words and multiple meaning clues
       e. Summary clues
   18. Synthesize data.

C. Critical Reading Skills
   1. Distinguish relevant and irrelevant information.
   2. Interpret propaganda techniques.
   3. Perceive bias.
   4. Identify adequacy of materials.
   5. Understand reliability of author.
   6. Differentiate facts and opinions.
   7. Separate real and unreal information.
   8. Understand fallacies in reasoning.

STUDY SKILLS

A. Reference Skills
   1. Use dictionary.
      a. Alphabetical order and guide words
      b. Pronunciation symbols
      c. Accent marks
      d. Syllabication
   2. Use encyclopedias.
   3. Use specialized reference materials such as the atlas and almanac.
   4. Use library card catalog.

B. Organizational Skills
   1. Develop outlines.
   2. Underline important points or key ideas.
   3. Take notes during reading.

C. Specialized Study Skills
   1. Use title page.
   2. Use table of contents and lists of charts.
   3. Locate introduction, preface, and foreword.
   4. Use appendix.
   5. Identify bibliography and lists of suggested readings.
   6. Use glossary and index.
   7. Use study questions.
   8. Read maps, tables, graphs, and diagrams.
   9. Use footnotes, typographical aids, and marginal notes.
   10. Preview, skim, or scan materials.
   11. Adjust reading rate according to material and purpose.
   12. Understand general and specialized vocabulary.
   13. Use appropriate study strategies such as SQ3R.

PUBLISHED INFORMAL READING INVENTORIES

Analytical Reading Inventory
- Mary Lynn Woods and Alden J. Moe
- Charles E. Merrill, 1995
- Grade range: 1–9
- Forms: 3

Basic Reading Inventory
- Jerry Johns
- Kendall/Hunt, 1998
- Grade range: PP–8
- Forms: 3

Classroom Reading Inventory
- Nicholas J. Silvarali
- William C. Brown, 1998
- Grade range: PP–8
- Forms: 4

Ekwall/Shanker Reading Inventory
- Ed Ekwall
- Allyn and Bacon, 1999
- Grade range: PP–9
- Forms: 4

Informal Reading Inventory
- Paul Burns and Betty Roe
- Houghton Mifflin, 1999

- Grade range: PP–12
- Forms: 4

Flynt-Cooter Reading Inventory
- E. Sutton Flynt and Robert B. Cooter, Jr.
- Gorsuch Scarisbrick, 1995
- Grade range: PP–12

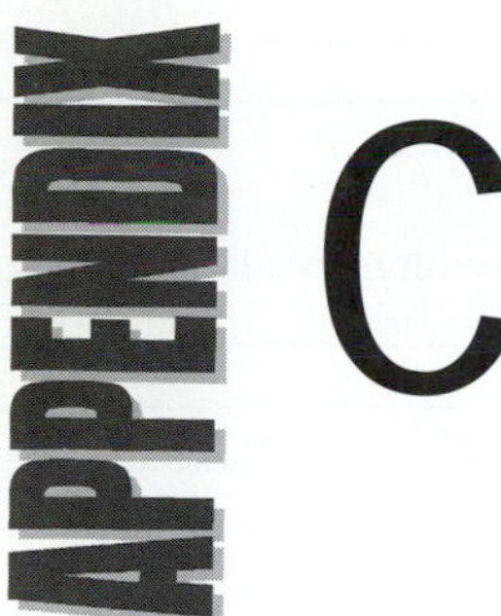

INTEREST AND ATTITUDE INVENTORY

Name: ____________ Date: ____________

Grade in School: ____________ Age: ____________
Teacher: ____________

A. Family
   1. Do you have brothers or sisters? _____ brothers _____ sisters
      Are they older or younger? _____ older _____ younger _____
      What kinds of activities do you like to do with them? ____________________
   2. Who lives in your home with you? ____________________
   3. What do you like to do with your family? ____________________
   4. Do you help with chores at home? _____
      What do you do to help? ____________________
   5. When you have time at home to spend just like you want, what do you like to do? ____________________

B. Self
   1. What would you like to be when you grow up? ____________________
   2. Why do you want to be that? ____________________
   3. What do you like most about yourself? ____________________
   4. If you could change anything about yourself, what would it be? ____________________
   5. What do you like best about your home or family? ____________________
      What do you like least about your home or family? ____________________
   6. Do you have an area at home to go and be alone? _____
      Where? ____________________
   7. I am happy when ____________________
   8. I really get excited when ____________________

9. My greatest worry is ______________________________
10. The best thing that ever happened to me was ______________________
11. When I was younger ______________________________
12. I am really afraid when ______________________________

C. Reading/Language
1. Given a choice, which do you like the best: writing, reading, talking, listening to stories, or drawing? ______________________
   Why? ______________________________
2. Do you have any books of your own to read at home? ______________
   What are the names of some of them? ______________________
3. What is the name of your favorite book? ______________________
   Why is it your favorite? ______________________________
4. Does someone read to you at home? _____ What kinds of stories do you like for them to read? ________ Why? ______________________
5. Do you read to someone at home? _____ Who? ______________________
   What do you like to read to them? ______________________
6. Given a choice of the following, which would you prefer to do?
   _____ watch television   _____ go to the mall
   _____ play with Nintendo games   _____ visit the zoo
   _____ watch videos   _____ go to the library
   _____ read a book   _____ play with a friend
7. Do you ever read the following?
   _____ magazines   _____ comics   _____ newspapers
8. How important do you think it is to learn to read?
   _____ very important   _____ a little   _____ not at all
9. I would love to read if ______________________________
   OR
   I love to read when ______________________________
10. Reading is ______________________________

D. School
1. Do you like school? ______________________________
   What is your favorite subject? ______________________
   Why? ______________________________
   What is your least favorite subject? ______________________
   Why? ______________________________
2. What did you enjoy most about school during the past year? ____________
3. Do you ever get into trouble at school? ______________________
   If so, what kind? ______________________________
4. When do you do your homework? ______________________
   Where do you do it? ______________________________

Is anyone available to help you with your homework? __________________
Who? __________________

5. Do you have a set time to go to bed on school days? __________________
6. School would be better if only __________________

E. Friends

1. Do you have a best friend? __________________
   Why is this person your best friend? __________________
2. What do you enjoy doing most with your friends? __________________
3. Would you rather play with a friend or be by yourself? Why? __________
4. I wish that __________ was my friend because __________________
5. I wish that my friends __________________

F. Interests

1. What are your favorite indoor games or activities? __________________
2. What are your favorite outdoor games or activities? __________________
3. Do you like sports? _____ What sports do you like best? ______________
4. Do you have any after-school activities such as team practice, music lessons, tutoring? _____
   What do you think about these activities? __________________
5. Do you have any hobbies or collections? _____ What are they? __________
6. Do you have any pets at home? __________________
   What kind? __________________
   What do you do to help care for it/them? __________________
   OR
   If you don't have any pets, what kind of pet would you like to have? _____
   Why? __________________
7. If you could have three wishes and they might all come true, what would you wish for? __________________
8. What do you usually like to do after school? __________________
   when it rains? __________________
   on Saturdays? __________________
   in the summer? __________________
9. Who do you admire the most? __________________
   Why? __________________
10. What are your favorite TV programs? __________________
11. Do you like to go to the movies? _____
    What is your favorite movie? __________________
12. Do you like videos? _____ How often do you watch one? ______________

G. First-Hand Experiences

1. Have you been to any of the following places?

_____ to the zoo	_____ to a farm
_____ to the circus	_____ to summer camp
_____ on an airplane	_____ to a swimming pool
_____ on a train	_____ to the grocery store
_____ to the beach	_____ to a shopping center or mall
_____ to the mountains	_____ on a long vacation trip
_____ on a boat	_____ to a restaurant

H. Now that you have answered these questions, is there anything else you would like to tell me about yourself? ____

Appendix D: Observation Checklist for Reading

Name: ___________ Grade: _____ Age: _____
Teacher: ___________ Date: ___________

A. General Skills

_______ 1. Reads in spare time
_______ 2. Shares with others
_______ 3. Works well independently and in groups
_______ 4. Seeks help when needed
_______ 5. Has varied interests
_______ 6. Assumes leadership role when appropriate
_______ 7. Has good rapport with teacher
_______ 8. Accepts responsibility
_______ 9. Organizes time efficiently
_______ 10. Other ___________________________

B. Oral Reading Skills

_______ 1. Pronounces words accurately
_______ 2. Enunciates words in a natural speaking voice
_______ 3. Uses pleasing voice skills (rate, pitch, expression)
_______ 4. Uses correct phrasing
_______ 5. Reads fluently
_______ 6. Holds book correctly
_______ 7. Reads without pointing to words
_______ 8. Does not lose place while reading
_______ 9. Recognizes and uses appropriate punctuation
_______ 10. Reads without repeated words or phrases
_______ 11. Reads without making omissions or additions of words
_______ 12. Other ___________________________

C. Silent Reading Skills

_______ 1. Holds book correctly
_______ 2. Reads without moving head
_______ 3. Reads without pointing to words
_______ 4. Does not vocalize
_______ 5. Uses no lip movement
_______ 6. Reads at a steady rate
_______ 7. Other ______________________________

D. Listening Skills

_______ 1. Listens to follow directions
_______ 2. Listens for different purposes
_______ 3. Listens to remember sequence of ideas
_______ 4. Listens to answer questions
_______ 5. Listens to understand main ideas
_______ 6. Listens to predict outcomes
_______ 7. Listens to summarize
_______ 8. Listens when someone reads or speaks
_______ 9. Other ______________________________

E. Prereading Skills

Oral Language Skills

_______ 1. Participates freely and easily in discussions
_______ 2. Speaks in complete sentences
_______ 3. Expresses experiences
_______ 4. Uses an adequate vocabulary
_______ 5. Develops sequence of ideas in conversation
_______ 6. Uses descriptive words and phrases
_______ 7. Describes simple objects
_______ 8. Relates words and pictures
_______ 9. Other ______________________________

Visual Perception Skills

_______ 1. Notes similarities in objects and words
_______ 2. Classifies objects into appropriate categories
_______ 3. Identifies from memory what is seen briefly
_______ 4. Recalls items in sequence
_______ 5. Recognizes likenesses and differences in objects and words
_______ 6. Matches picture parts
_______ 7. Matches numbers
_______ 8. Recognizes upper and lowercase letters

_______ 9. Matches words
_______ 10. Recognizes geometric shapes
_______ 11. Recognizes colors
_______ 12. Recognizes own name
_______ 13. Reproduces numerals, letters, and words
_______ 14. Other _______________________________

Auditory Perception Skills

_______ 1. Identifies and differentiates between common sounds
_______ 2. Differentiates sounds of loudness, pitch, and sequence
_______ 3. Identifies rhyming words
_______ 4. Hears differences in environmental, letter, and word sounds
_______ 5. Imitates sound sequences
_______ 6. Repeats words and sentences in sequence
_______ 7. Hears beginning, medial, and final sounds
_______ 8. Other _______________________________

Visual-Motor Skills

_______ 1. Develops left-to-right eye movement
_______ 2. Coordinates hand-eye movement
_______ 3. Other _______________________________

F. Word Identification Skills

Sight Vocabulary

_______ 1. Recognizes words in isolation
_______ 2. Recognizes words in context

Phonetic Analysis

_______ 1. Identifies initial consonant sounds in words
_______ 2. Identifies medial consonant sounds in words
_______ 3. Identifies final consonant sounds in words
_______ 4. Substitutes initial consonant sounds to form new words
_______ 5. Substitutes medial consonant sounds to form new words
_______ 6. Substitutes final consonant sounds to form new words
_______ 7. Identifies vowel sounds in initial position
_______ 8. Identifies vowel sounds in medial position
_______ 9. Identifies vowel sounds in final position
_______ 10. Substitutes vowel sounds in initial position to form new words
_______ 11. Substitutes vowel sounds in medial position to form new words
_______ 12. Substitutes vowel sounds in final position to form new words

Structural Analysis

_______ 1. Recognizes compound words
_______ 2. Recognizes contractions
_______ 3. Recognizes base (root) words
_______ 4. Recognizes suffixes
_______ 5. Recognizes prefixes
_______ 6. Identifies common word endings
_______ 7. Divides words into syllables
_______ 8. Accents appropriate syllables when sounding out words
_______ 9. Recognizes possessive forms of nouns
_______ 10. Knows common rules for forming the plural of nouns
_______ 11. Other

Contextual Analysis Skills

_______ 1. Uses context to read unfamiliar words and to gain meaning
_______ 2. Other _______________________________

G. Comprehension Skills

Literal Skills

_______ 1. Reads for detail (who, what, when, where, why)
_______ 2. Reads for the main idea
_______ 3. Reads for a purpose
_______ 4. Reads to follow directions
_______ 5. Reads to follow sequence of events
_______ 6. Understands cause and effect in stories
_______ 7. Identifies meanings of words, phrases, and sentences
_______ 8. Identifies character traits
_______ 9. Understands the sense of the sentence
_______ 10. Other _______________________________

Interpretive Skills

_______ 1. Reads to interpret illustrations
_______ 2. Reads to draw conclusions
_______ 3. Reads to make generalizations
_______ 4. Reads to get implied meaning
_______ 5. Reads to understand author's purpose
_______ 6. Interprets and appreciates figurative language
_______ 7. Understands writing style and literary quality of material
_______ 8. Makes inferences
_______ 9. Predicts outcomes
_______ 10. Recognizes mood of the story

________ 11. Identifies characters' feelings and actions
________ 12. Uses punctuation to interpret author's message
________ 13. Other ____

Critical Skills

________ 1. Differentiates between real and unreal
________ 2. Identifies propaganda in material
________ 3. Identifies relevant and irrelevant information
________ 4. Notes qualifications of the author
________ 5. Reads to evaluate and judge
________ 6. Distinguishes between fact and opinion
________ 7. Discerns the attitudes of the writer
________ 8. Other ____

H. Study Skills

________ 1. Alphabetizes words by one, two, three, four, and five letters
________ 2. Finds words in dictionary using guidewords
________ 3. Locates main entry in a dictionary for a word containing an inflectional ending or suffix
________ 4. Uses the key in a dictionary to pronounce words
________ 5. Outlines a paragraph
________ 6. Outlines a chapter
________ 7. Develops an outline using several sources
________ 8. Summarizes a paragraph
________ 9. Summarizes a chapter
________ 10. Synthesizes information from several sources
________ 11. Skims or scans material when appropriate
________ 12. Locates information using an encyclopedia
________ 13. Locates information using the library catalog
________ 14. Locates information using the table of contents
________ 15. Locates information using an index
________ 16. Locates information using an appendix
________ 17. Locates information using a glossary
________ 18. Locates information using an atlas
________ 19. Interprets diagrams
________ 20. Interprets charts and tables
________ 21. Interprets maps
________ 22. Adjusts rate of reading according to material and purpose for reading
________ 23. Other ____

I. Other Observations

INTERPRETIVE REPORT

I. STUDENT DATA

Student's Name: Kim
Date of Birth: August 2, 1990
Sex: Female
Nationality: Asian American
Age: 8 years and 4 months (100 months)
School: Flowing River Elementary
School District: East Baton Rouge
Parents: Mr. and Mrs. Tran
Address: Baton Rouge, Louisiana
Examiner: Walter Johnson

II. BACKGROUND INFORMATION

Family, Birth, and Developmental History

Kim is an 8-year-old Asian American female. She lives at home with her parents, an older sister and brother, and a younger brother. Kim is one of four children; she is third in birth order. The two older children are adults. Kim's older brother, James, now appears to be the family spokesperson. He attends parent conferences for both Kim and her younger brother, Paul.

Kim's mother and father, Mr. and Mrs. Tran, both work in their family-owned printing shop. They and the two oldest children immigrated to the United States after the Vietnam War. Both parents completed high school in Vietnam, and they have limited English proficiency. Vietnamese is the language spoken in the home. The Tran family lives in an inner-city environment; their home is attached to their business. They would be considered to be in the low socioeconomic class.

According to James, Kim was a full-term baby with no reported complications during pregnancy or delivery. He felt that she had accomplished all developmental tasks at the appropriate age. James reported that Kim has had no serious illnesses or accidents that would impact her educational performance. She rarely is absent from school.

Social History
Kim is a shy and very soft-spoken child with many indicators of low self-esteem. She has a close relationship with her older brother, James, and with her two other siblings, Jane and Paul. From her journal entries it appears that Kim would like to spend more time with her mother:

> "I Was so mad because my mom don't let me go to shopping with her."
> "my mom makes me so happy When she play with me sometimes and We cook cakes and We had a fun time."

Kim's teacher, Mrs. Smith, reported that Kim has three close friends at school (Sally, Martha, and Courtney). During work time, Kim works with these three children or with two younger children, Randy and Lee. Kim frequently chooses to work alone. During recess she also chooses to play with these children. Kim has no playmates in her neighborhood. Her mother does not allow Kim to play outdoors; their home does not have a yard and the neighborhood is noted as being one of the most dangerous in the city. Kim said that she spends much of her time in her room watching television, listening to the radio, playing indoor games, and reading.

Kim appears to have a very limited experiential background. She reported that she has never been on a train or boat and has never flown in an airplane. She has never been to a farm, the mountains or a summer camp. Kim has never taken a long vacation. She has been to a zoo, a circus, a beach, a mall, and a restaurant.

Educational History
Kim is a third-grade student in the Montessori Magnet Program at Flowing River Elementary School in Baton Rouge, Louisiana. Prior to enrolling at Flowing River in 1998, Kim attended two other public schools. She attended kindergarten and the first half of first grade in Orleans Parish. When her family moved to Baton Rouge, Kim began attending the Montessori Magnet Program at Smith Elementary. She attended this school for the remainder of first grade and all of second grade.

Physical Factors
Kim has no limiting physical conditions that would interfere with her educational functioning. She has good visual acuity and no vision problems.

General Behavior during Testing

Kim was familiar with the examiner; in his role as Montessori Coordinator, he has frequently observed in Kim's class at Smith Elementary. During these visits the examiner worked with Kim on various tasks; each time rapport was easily reestablished. Kim appeared enthusiastic about going to his classroom "to do some reading work." Frequently, when passing the examiner in the hallway or seeing him on the playground, Kim would give him a hug and ask, "Are you coming to get me today, Mr. Johnson?" Kim remained attentive during all tests. She appeared to lack self-confidence. Kim had difficulty making eye contact with the examiner. She spoke in an almost inaudible voice and frequently looked at the examiner in an attempt to determine the correctness of her answers. When Kim could not answer the question, she responded with a shrug.

Kim's performance during the testing sessions was hindered by her lack of English proficiency and her limited experiential background. It is the examiner's opinion that the test results are representative of Kim's level of functioning but not of her abilities.

III. ASSESSMENT

Test Data

Slosson Intelligence Test (SIT)
Date administered: November 19, 1998
Chronological age: 8–4
Mental age: 7–10
Intelligence quotient: 89

Slosson Oral Reading Test (SORT)
Date administered: November 13, 1998
Present grade: 3.4
Raw score: 48
Reading level: 2.4

Silvaroli Classroom Reading Inventory
Date administered: November 1, 1998

Graded Word Lists

PP 90%
P 100%
1 95%
2 70%

Graded Paragraphs

	Word Recognition	*Comprehension*
PP	Independent	Independent
P	Independent	Instructional
1	Instructional	Instructional
2	Frustration	Instructional

Reader Response

Level 1
Prediction: 3, Retelling: 2, Problem: 1, Outcomes: 1, Total: 7

Comprehension needs assistance
Comfortable reading level: Below grade level

Durrell Analysis of Reading Difficulty
Date administered: November 1, 1998; November 4, 1998

Oral Reading

1A. Time 30 seconds, Errors: 0, Comprehension: 100%
1B. Time 55 seconds, Errors: 4, Comprehension: 100%

Approximate level: 1M

Silent Reading

1A. Time: 30 seconds, Memories: 5, Level: 1M
1B. Time: 59 seconds, Memories: 1, Level: lL–lM

Approximate level: lL–lM

Listening Comprehension

Grade 1	6 out of 7 correct
Grade 2	7 out of 7 correct

Grade 3	6 out of 7 correct
Grade 4	1 out of 7 correct

Approximate level: 3

Spelling

List 1	10 out of 20 correct

Approximate level: 3

Analysis and Interpretation of Data

Elementary Interest Inventory

Kim was given the Elementary Interest Inventory on November 7, 1998. This instrument, developed by Martha Collins and Earl Cheek, is a questionnaire arranged in seven parts: Family, Self, Reading and Language, School, Friends, Interests, and First-hand Experiences. It provides the examiner with information about the student's home and school relationships, interests, and first-hand experiences.

Family. Kim indicated that she spends a lot of time with James, her older brother. He takes her to the movies, the zoo, Celebration Station, and to New Orleans to visit relatives. Kim reported that she sometimes plays Nintendo with Jane, her older sister. Kim also enjoys playing with Paul, her younger brother. They play with his toys and Kim reads to him. Based on the interview with Kim, it appears that she spends more time with her mother than with her father. She enjoys helping her mom with household tasks, such as cleaning and cooking. Kim said that she is really happy when she helps her mom bake cakes and cookies.

Self. Kim stated that she wants to be a nurse because she likes "helping people." Kim said the thing she most likes about herself is that she is a good math student. Kim reported that she has her own bedroom with a radio and television. She said that she is really happy when she is alone. Kim said she really gets excited when it's Christmas. "I love Christmas!" she exclaimed. Her greatest fear is when her mom leaves her at home alone.

Reading and Language. Kim prefers drawing over writing, reading, talking, and listening to stories. Kim indicated that she has limited access to books. Two of the books she has are *The Night Before Christmas* and *Cinderella. Aladdin* is her favorite book because "sometimes he is funny." Her sister, Jane, reads to her at home. Two of her favorite books are *101 Dalmatians* and *Goosebumps.* Kim reads to her younger brother; some of the books she has read to him are: *Mr. Brown Can Moo, Can You?*, *The Cat in the Hat*, and *Green Eggs and Ham.* When given a choice of activities, Kim selected three as being her favorites: going to the mall, reading a book, and playing Nintendo. Kim views reading as a very important activity. She enjoys reading when she is alone. Kim thinks reading is fun.

School. Kim reported that she likes school. Art is her favorite subject because she likes to paint. Kim's teacher reported that she draws well. Kim said that she never gets in trouble at school. She does her homework when she gets home from school. Kim's bedroom has a desk where she can do her homework. Her sister, Jane, helps Kim with her homework.

Friends. Kim reported having three friends at school: Sally, Martha, and Courtney. She also likes Randy and Lee. Kim said that she has no friends at home because she does not go outside. Kim does not participate in any after-school activities and has no hobbies or collections. She indicated that she would rather play with friends than be by herself.

Interests. Kim's favorite activity is helping her mom and dad. She also enjoys playing basketball with her brother. Basketball is Kim's favorite sport. Kim expressed a desire to take piano lessons. She reported that she has no hobbies or collections. Kim has no pets; she expressed a desire to have a pet—"a puppy, a baby cat, a rat or maybe a rabbit." Kim's favorite TV programs are cartoons and her favorite movie is *Major Payne*.

First-hand Experiences. Kim has been to a zoo, a circus, a beach, a mall, and a restaurant. She has never been on a train or boat and has never flown in an airplane. Kim has also never been to the mountains, to a farm, to summer camp or on a long vacation.

Attitudes and Interests Survey (Reading and Writing)

Kim was given the attitudes and interests survey for reading and writing, published by Harcourt Brace and Company, on November 8, 1998. This questionnaire is designed to elicit the student's feelings with regard to reading and writing. It also yields information about how the student perceives herself as a reader or writer. Kim is happy when she reads a story or someone reads a story to her. She indicated that she likes to read books about science. Kim perceives herself to be a poor reader but a good writer. She likes to write about the pictures she draws.

Slosson Intelligence Test (SIT)

The SIT was administered to Kim on November 19, 1998, and yielded an intelligence quotient of 89, which places her in the low-average range. The Slosson Intelligence Test is an individually administered screening tool that yields an intelligence quotient. This examiner feels that Kim's score of 89 is not an accurate reflection of her intelligence or her potential. It appears that the score was greatly influenced by Kim's limited English proficiency.

Kim's major areas of weakness were auditory memory, vocabulary, and general concepts. Kim was unable to repeat a series of numbers (7 3 6 4 1). She was also unable to repeat a sentence: "The train carrying people and bags of mail goes fast on the track." Kim did not know the meaning of *infection*, *hero*, *vacant*, and *submarine*. She did not know who Christopher Columbus was, where ham comes from, and what paper is made of. Kim's strength appeared to be judgment reasoning. She was able to tell how a crayon and pencil are alike and different. Kim was also able to tell how a cat and a dog are alike and different. When asked how a fish and a submarine are alike and different, Kim was unable to discuss their similarities and differences. Upon further questioning it was determined that Kim did not know the meaning of the word *submarine*. The SIT indicates that Kim needs instruction in the areas of auditory memory, vocabulary, and general concepts.

Slosson Oral Reading Test (SORT)

The SORT was administered to Kim on November 13, 1998, and yielded a reading level of 2.4. The Slosson Oral Reading Test is an individually administered reading test composed of 10 word lists ranging in difficulty from the primer level through the high school level. Each word list has 20 words for a total of 200 items. The score obtained on this test is representative of median school achievement. Kim was able to read all words on the primer list. She read 17 of 20 words on list 1 and 11 of 20 words on list 2. The majority of the words that Kim was able to identify were one-syllable words. She encountered problems with words of two or more syllables. Kim's most common errors were vowel substitution (*was* for *wish* and *dump* for *damp*) and vowel omission (*rod* for *road* and *hid* for *hide*). When Kim encountered a word she did not know, she usually made a guess based on the beginning sound of the word (*breakfast* for *basket* and *beautiful* for *better*). Kim also had difficulty with words that contain phonograms (e.g., *station*).

Classroom Reading Inventory (Silvaroli)

The Classroom Reading Inventory is an individually administered informal reading inventory; it is not norm referenced. It has three subtests: Graded Word Lists, Graded Paragraphs, and Reader Response Test. The Classroom Reading Inventory yields a functional reading level. The words and passages begin with the preprimer level and go through the eighth-grade level. The graded word lists are administered first. The list on which the student makes six or more errors is a good indicator of where to start the graded paragraphs. This examiner usually goes back one or two levels to begin the graded paragraphs. Doing this gives the student the opportunity to experience initial success. The Reader Response Test focuses on predicting and retelling stories and allows the examiner more flexibility in questioning. It yields a comfortable reading level.

Kim was given the Classroom Reading Inventory on November 1, 1998. On the Graded Word Lists Kim missed two words on the PP list, no words on the P list, one word on the first-grade list, and six words on the second-grade list. Errors were of the same type as noted on the Slosson (*jub* for *job*, *hill* for *hall*, and *low* for *law*).

Graded paragraphs were begun at level 1. At this level, Kim made two significant word recognition errors and two comprehension errors. At level 2 Kim made ten significant word recognition errors (frustration level) and two comprehension errors (instructional level). Most of Kim's word identification errors centered around vowel substitution and vowel omission errors. Comprehension errors were on questions that required making inferences. Testing was stopped at this point because Kim was having a great deal of difficulty decoding the text. It appears that Kim uses context to aid comprehension (high comprehension/low word recognition).

On the Reader Response Test, Kim was able to read the first story, "It's My Ball." On this passage her word identification errors were of the same type. She was able to make predictions and retell the story but was unable to identify the problem or determine the solution.

Durrell Analysis of Reading Difficulty

The Durell Analysis of Reading Difficulty is an individually administered norm-referenced reading test. It is composed of a number of subtests that evaluate numerous aspects of the student's reading ability.

The Oral Reading subtest is composed of timed passages. After reading the passages the student is asked to answer several comprehension questions. Kim took 30 seconds to read passage 1A. She had no word identification errors and her comprehension was 100%. Kim took 55 seconds to read passage 1B. She had four word identification errors and her comprehension was 100%. Kim's approximate reading level was determined to be mid 1. Kim's word recognition errors were of the same type as those on other tests that were administered. Although she had four word identification errors on passage 1B, Kim had 100% comprehension. This verifies that Kim uses context as an aid to comprehension.

The Silent Reading subtest is similar to the Oral Reading subtest; the student is asked to silently read timed passages and is asked to recall story details or memories. The student's reading level is determined by the amount of time it takes the student to read the passage and the number of memories the student has about the passages. Kim took 30 seconds to read passage 1A and had 5 memories from this passage (mid 1). She took 59 seconds to read passage 1B and had 1 memory (low 1). Kim's approximate reading level was determined to be low to mid 1.

Kim obtained a grade equivalent of 3.0 on the Listening Comprehension subtest. This subtest requires the student to listen to a passage read by the examiner and to immediately answer a series of comprehension questions about the passage. At grade level 3.0 Kim was able to answer six of the seven questions. At grade level 4.0 she was able to only answer one out of seven. Kim is performing slightly below grade placement in this area. Listening Comprehension was the only strength Kim exhibited on the Durrell Analysis of Reading Difficulty.

The Spelling subtest consists of two lists of words to be called out to the student by the teacher. The student then spells the words on a blank word-list form. On list 1 Kim was able to spell 10 of the 20 words. Her performances on this subtest translates to third-grade level. As with Listening Comprehension, Kim is performing slightly below grade placement. Kim easily spells three- or four-letter phonetic words. She has more difficulty with words of more than one syllable and words that contain phonograms.

Synthesis

In summary, Kim is functioning two years below grade placement in reading. Kim shows no indication of a modality preference (visual, auditory, kinesthetic, or tactile). The major strength noted was Kim's use of context to aid in comprehension. This should be considered when planning an instructional program for Kim. Kim's phonetic analysis and structural analysis skills are weak. She possesses almost no decoding strategies; guessing appears to be Kim's only strategy when encountering new words. Kim also evidenced weaknesses in both oral and written vocabulary and in general knowledge. It is this examiner's view that Kim's lack of proficiency in English and her limited experiential background have contributed greatly to creating this reading disability. ESL classes should be a major part of her educational instructional plan.

IV. Instructional Plan

Kim's needs in reading can best be met through an eclectic approach. ESL classes in conjunction with a wide variety of instructional methods and materials should be considered when developing an educational plan for Kim. The combination of a basal reader at the first-grade level, many tradebooks, an SRA kit, and specific skills series books at the first-grade level would provide a good core of materials for Kim's reading instruction. Since Kim is now in third grade, an intense phonics program is not recommended. Syllabication should be taught and the use of context modeled. Good reading strategies should also be modeled. Vocabulary building and language development (oral and written) should be strongly emphasized. Vocabulary can be increased by teaching homonyms and synonyms for words that she already knows. Prefixes, suffixes, and compound words should also be taught to Kim. Language development can be encouraged by providing Kim with a wide variety of experiences she has never had (field trips to museums, art galleries, historical landmarks, an airport, and so on). Since Kim likes art and enjoys drawing and painting, this could be useful as a stimulus for writing and reading.

Kim enjoys watching television and listening to the radio. Videos and audiotapes may be another way to stimulate vocabulary development. Getting Kim involved in some after school activities with other children her age would help her oral language development and her overall general knowledge. It would also give Kim the opportunity to practice her English in a nonthreatening environment. Kim needs a print-rich environment both at home and at school. One way of getting Kim to read and write at home is to provide a reading-writing suitcase, an old briefcase that contains books, tapes, a tape player, paper, pencils, crayons, and markers. This can be taken home on a daily basis. Kim can listen to the books being read on tape. She can draw pictures and respond to the book through writing. If a blank tape is provided, she can record her own reading of the text. Buddy reading should also be considered. Kim and another child could read to each other or Kim could read to a younger child. Becoming a library worker might stimulate her to read more and would allow her time to choose quality books with the assistance of the librarian.

With the appropriate instructional plan, Kim's level of reading can be increased. Progress should always be monitored and modifications made to the plan as needed. Pre- and post-testing should be used to monitor progress toward objectives.

CHILDREN'S FAVORITE BOOKS

Each year the International Reading Association and Children's Book Council publishes a list of "children's choices" in *The Reading Teacher*. The titles below are some of the selections chosen for 1993–97. For additional titles, see the October issues of *The Reading Teacher*.

All Ages

- *Belly's Deli*, by R. L. Shafner and Eric Jon Weisberg. Illustrated by Nancy Bauer.
- *The Best School Year Ever*, by Barbara Robinson.
- *Chicken Sunday*, by Patricia Polacco. Illustrated by the author.
- *Gonna Sing My Head Off!* collected and arranged by Kathleen Krull. Illustrated by Allen Garns.
- *I Am Really a Princess*, by Carol Diggory Shields. Illustrated by Paul Meisel.
- *Making Books: A Step-By-Step Guide to Your Own Publishing*, by Gillian Chapman and Pam Robson. Illustrated with photographs.
- *Martha Speaks*, by Susan Meddaugh. Illustrated by the author.
- *Mrs. Bretsky's Bakery*, by R. L. Shafner and Eric Jon Weisberg. Illustrated by Nancy Bauer.
- *Somebody Catch My Homework*, by David L. Harrison. Illustrated by Betsy Lewin.
- *The Stinky Cheese Man and Other Fairly Stupid Tales*, by Jon Scieszka. Illustrated by Lane Smith.
- *That Terrible Baby*, by Jennifer Armstrong. Illustrated by Susan Meddaugh.

Beginning Independent Reading

- *The Cajun Gingerbread Boy,* Retold by Berthe Amoss. Illustrated by the author.
- *The Cut-Ups Crack Up*, by James Marshall. Illustrated by the author.
- *Dinosaur Stomp! A Monster Pop-Up*, by Paul Strickland. Illustrated by the author.
- *Do Pigs Have Stripes?*, by Melanie Walsh. Illustrated by the author.

- *Draw Me a Star*, by Eric Carle. Illustrated by the author.
- *Easy to See Why*, by Fred Gwynne. Illustrated by the author.
- *The Giant Zucchini*, by Catherine Siracusa. Illustrated by the author.
- *The Great Snake Escape*, by Molly Coxe. Illustrated by the author.
- *How Do You Say It Today, Jesse Bear?*, by Nancy White Carlstrom. Illustrated by Bruce Degen.
- *Let's Go, Froggy!*, by Jonathan London. Illustrated by Frank Remkiewicz.
- *The Letters Are Lost*, by Lisa Campbell Ernst. Illustrated by the author.
- *Look Once, Look Twice*, by Janet Marshall. Illustrated by the author.
- *Monkey Soup*, by Louis Sachar. Illustrated by Cat Bowman.
- *Monster Math*, by Grace Maccarone. Illustrated by Marge Hartelius.
- *My Little Sister Ate One Hare*, by Bill Grossman. Illustrated by Kevin Hawkes.
- *My Tooth Is About to Fall Out*, by Grace Maccarone. Illustrated by Betsy Lewin.
- *Sheep Out to Eat*, by Nancy Shaw. Illustrated by Margot Apple.
- *Ten Tiny Turtles: A Crazy Counting Book*, by Paul Cherril. Illustrated by the author.
- *Trade-In Mother*, by Marisabina Russo. Illustrated by the author.
- *Uglypuss*, by Caroline Gregoire. Translated by George Wen. Illustrated by the author.
- *What Goes Around Comes Around*, by Richard McGuire. Illustrated by the author.
- *When I Was Five*, by Arthur Howard. Illustrated by the author.
- *When I Was Little: A Four-Year-Old's Memoir of Her Youth*, by Jamie Lee Curtis. Illustrated by Laura Cornell.

Younger Readers

- *Alexander, Who's Not (Do You Hear Me? I Mean It!) Going to Move*, by Judith Viorst. Illustrated by Robin Preiss Glasser.
- *Andrew Wants a Dog*, by Steven Kroll. Illustrated by Molly Delaney.
- *Annie and Cousin Precious*, by Kay Charao. Illustrated by the author.
- *Art Dog*, by Thacher Hurd. Illustrated by the author.
- *Aunt Elaine Does the Dance from Spain*, by Leah Komaiko. Illustrated by Petra Mathers.
- *The Bear That Heard Crying*, by Natalie Kinsey-Warnock and Helen Kinsey. Illustrated by Ted Rand.
- *The Bear Santa Claus Forgot*, by Diana Kimpton. Illustrated by Anna Kiernan.
- *A Beautiful Feast for a Big King Cat*, by John Archarmbault and Bill Martin, Jr. Illustrated by Bruce Degen.
- *Bright and Early Thursday Evening: A Tangled Tale*, by Audrey Wood. Illustrated by Don Wood.
- *Calico Cows*, by Arlene Dubanevich. Illustrated by the author.
- *Courtney*, by John Burningham. Illustrated by the author.
- *Cousin Ruth's Tooth*, by Amy McDonald. Illustrated by Marjorie Priceman.

- *Diane Goode Book of Silly Stories and Songs*, by and illustrated by Diane Goode.
- *Discovering Friendship*, by Sharona Kadish. Illustrated by Dee deRosa.
- *Dogs Don't Wear Sneakers*, by Laura Numeroff. Illustrated by Joe Mathieu.
- *Don't Wake Up Mama! Another Five Little Monkeys Story*, by Eileen Christelow. Illustrated by the author.
- *Earthquake in the Third Grade*, by Laurie Myers. Illustrated by Karen Ritz.
- *Every Monday in the Mailbox*, by Louisa Fox. Illustrated by Jan Naimo Jones.
- *The Flamingos Are Tickled Pink: A Book of Idioms* by Chip Lovitt. Illustrated by Marshall Toomey.
- *Granny Greenteeth and the Noise in the Night*, by Kenn and Joanne Compton. Illustrated by Kenn Compton.
- *Grown-Ups Get to Do All the Driving*, by William Steig. Illustrated by the author.
- *If I Had a Robot*, by Dan Yaccarino. Illustrated by the author.
- *Kashtanka*, by Anton Chekhov. Illustrated by Gennady Spirin.
- *Lilly's Purple Plastic Purse*, by Kevin Henkes. Illustrated by the author.
- *Lunch Money and Other Poems about School*, by Carol Diggory Shields. Illustrated by Paul Meisel.
- *Mommy's Briefcase*, by Alice Low. Illustrated by Aliki.
- *Mona the Brilliant*, by Sonia Holleyman. Illustrated by the author.
- *Mud*, by Mary Lyn Ray. Illustrated by Lauren Stringer.
- *My Grandmother's Patchwork Quilt: A Book and Pocketful of Patchwork Pieces*, by Janet Bolton. Illustrated with patchwork by the author.
- *My Working Mom*, by Peter Glassman. Illustrated by Ted Arnold.
- *Never Ride Your Elephant to School*, by Doug Johnson. Illustrated by Abby Carter.
- *Nine Candles*, by Maria Testa. Illustrated by Amanda Schaffer.
- *Now Everybody Really Hates Me*, by Jane Read Martin and Patricia Marx. Illustrated by Roz Chast.
- *The Rainbow Fish*, by Marcus Pfister. Translated by J. Alison James. Illustrated by the author.
- *Rats on the Range and Other Stories*, by James Marshall. Illustrated by the author.
- *A Regular Flood of Mishap*, by Tom Birdseye. Illustrated by Megan Lloyd.
- *Roses Are Pink, Your Feet Really Stink*, by Diane deGroat. Illustrated by the author.
- *Today Is Monday*, retold by Eric Carle. Illustrated by Eric Carle.
- *Tops and Bottoms*, adapted and illustrated by Janet Stevens.
- *True Blue*, by Joan Elste. Illustrated by DyAnne DiSalvo-Ryan.
- *The Turtle Who Lost His Shell*, based on a script by Paul Levy. Illustrated by Rick Grayson.

- *The Very Lonely Firefly*, by Eric Carle. Illustrated by the author.
- *Wagons West!*, by Roy Gerrard. Illustrated by the author.
- *Way Out West Lives a Coyote Named Frank*, by Julian Lund. Illustrated by the author.
- *When Cows Come Home*, by David L. Harrison. Illustrated by Chris L. Demarest.
- *Pets of the President*, by Janet Caulkins. Illustrated with photographs.

Middle Grades

- *Being Bad for the Baby-Sitter*, by Richard Tulloch. Illustrated by Coral Tulloch.
- *Best Friends*, by Elisabeth Reuter. Illustrated by Antoinette Becker.
- *The Boy Who Sailed with Columbus*, by Michael Foreman. Illustrated by author.
- *Call Waiting*, by R. L. Stine.
- *Custer*, by Deborah King. Illustrated by the author.
- *Doesn't Fall Off His Horse*, by Virginia A. Stroud. Illustrated by the author.
- *Don't Read This Book, Whatever You Do! More Poems about School*, by Kalli Dakos. Illustrated by G. Brian Karals.
- *Goodbye, Vietnam*, by Gloria Whelan.
- *Home Is Where Your Family Is*, by Katie Kavanagh. Illustrated by Gregg Fitzhugh.
- *How to Be Cool in the Third Grade*, by Betsy Duffey. Illustrated by Janet Wilson.
- *I Saw You That Night!*, by R. L. Stine.
- *Jesse Owens: Olympic Star*, by Patricia and Frederick McKissack. Illustrated by Michael David Biegel; with photographs.
- *Mummies and Their Mysteries*, by Charlotte Wilcox. Illustrated with photographs.
- *Riddle City, USA! A Book of Geography Riddles*, by Marco Maestro and Giulio Maestro. Illustrated by Giulio Maestro.
- *Summer Wheels*, by Eve Bunting. Illustrated by Thomas B. Allen.
- *Three Terrible Trins*, by Dick King-Smith. Illustrated by Mark Teague.
- *What's on the Menu? Food Poems*, selected by Bobby Goldstein. Illustrated by Chris L. Demarest.

Intermediate Readers

- *Abby's Wish*, by Liza St. John. Illustrated by Michael Krone.
- *Class Act: Riddles for School*, by John Jansen. Illustrated by Susan Slattery Burke.
- *Falling Up*, by Shel Silverstein. Illustrated by the author.
- *Fly Traps! Plants That Bite Back*, by Martin Jenkins. Illustrated by David Parkins.
- *Give Me Bach My Schubert*, by Brian P. Cleary. Illustrated by Rick Dupré.
- *The Goof Who Invented Homework: And Other School Poems*, by Kalli Dakos. Illustrated by Denise Brunkus.

- *Harvey's Wish*, by Matthew Fitzgerald. Illustrated by Jean Pidgeon.
- *I Spy a Freight Train: Transportation in Art*, devised and selected by Lucy Micklethwait.
- *The Magic School Bus Blows Its Top: A Book about Volcanoes,* based on the series by Joanna Cole. Illustrated by Bruce Degen.
- *Math Curse*, by Jon Scieszka. Illustrated by Lane Smith.
- *My Heart Is Full of Wishes*, by Joshua Grishaw. Illustrated by Lane Yerkes.
- *The Sea of Tranquility*, by Mark Haddon. Illustrated by Christian Birmingham.
- *See You Around, Sam!*, by Lois Lowry. Illustrated by Diane de Groat.
- *She's Wearing a Dead Bird on Her Head!*, by Kathryn Lasky. Illustrated by David Catrow.
- *Teach Us, Amelia Bedelia*, by Peggy Parish. Illustrated by Lynn Sweat.
- *When Someone in the Family Drinks Too Much*, by Richard C. Langsen. Illustrated by Nicole Rubel.
- *You Can't Eat Your Chicken Pox*, by Amber Brown and Paula Danziger. Illustrated by Tony Ross.

Advanced Readers

- *Arthur Ashe: Breaking the Color Barrier in Tennis*, by David K. Wright. Illustrated with photographs.
- *Crash*, by Jerry Spinelli.
- *Danger at the Fair*, by Peg Kehret.
- *A Fate Totally Worse Than Death*, by Paul Fleischman.
- *The Humane Societies: A Voice for the Animals*, by Shelley Swanson Sateren. Illustrated with photographs.
- *53 1/2 Things That Changed the World: And Some That Didn't!*, by Steve Parker. Illustrated by David West.
- *Skin Deep and Other Teenage Reflections*, by Angela Shelf Medearis. Illustrated by Michael Bryant.
- *Slam Dunk: Poems*, compiled by Lillian Morrison. Illustrated by Bill James.
- *Something Very Sorry*, written and translated by Arnold Bohlmeijer.
- *True Fright: Trapped beneath the Ice! and Other True Stories Scarier Than Fiction*, by Ted Pedersen.
- *Who Killed Mr. Chippendale? A Mystery in Poems*, by Mel Glenn.

Older Readers

- *All But Alice*, by Phyllis Reynolds Naylor.
- *The Blizzard (Survive!)*, by Jim O'Connor.
- *Crosstown*, by Kathryn Makris.
- *Did You Hear Bout Amber? Surviving 16 #1*, by Cherie Bennett.
- *Flip-Flop Girl*, by Katherine Paterson.
- *Help! I'm Trapped in My Teacher's Body*, by Todd Strasser.
- *It Happened in America: True Stories from the Fifty States*, by Lila Perl. Illustrated by Ib Ohlsson.

- *Just One Tear*, by K. L. Mahon.
- *Kriss Kross Krazy!*, by Anne Raso.
- *Letting Swift River Go*, by Jane Yolen. Illustrated by Barbara Cooney.
- *The Los Angeles Riots: America's Cities in Crisis*, by John Salak. Illustrated with photographs.
- *Moonshiner's Son*, by Carolyn Reeder.
- *Rosa Parks: My Story*, by Rosa Parks with Jim Haskins. Illustrated with photographs.
- *Stephen Biesty's Cross-Sections: Castle*, by Richard Platt. Illustrated by Stephen Biesty.

CONSTRUCTION OF AN INFORMAL READING INVENTORY

An IRI consists of a series of graded passages of approximately 100 to 200 words. Passages at the lower levels, such as preprimer, may have fewer than 100 words, while passages at the upper levels, such as senior high, may have more than 200 words. These passages may be selected from graded basal reading series that are unfamiliar to the student, from children's books whose readability level has been determined by the publisher or by the teacher, or from any other graded materials the teacher wishes to use.

Task 1

Select a list of words that can be used to assess the student's sight vocabulary level (optional). This first step assists in determining an approximate level at which to begin to administer the graded reading selections. A teacher may use word lists that are already developed and leveled, such as the Dolch Basic Sight Word List or the Slosson Oral Reading Test. The teacher may prefer to prepare a word list using words from the basal reader or a graded word list such as the Harris-Jacobson Basic Reading Vocabularies.

To develop a word list from a basal or another more extensive list of words, select at random about 20 words from each level of the basal (preprimer through the highest available level) or from each grade indicated on the word list. These words should be typed by level on a sheet for teacher use and placed individually on index cards for student use. Remember, such a list only measures sight vocabulary. It does *not* measure the most important area of reading, comprehension.

Task 2

Obtain two passages of *approximately 100 to 200 words for each readability level (preprimer through senior high school).* One of the passages will be used to assess oral reading skills, and the second will be used to measure silent reading proficiency.

It is essential to select passages that will interest students, regardless of their age. Remember that you may have a 7-year-old who reads at an eighth-grade level or a 14-year-old who reads at a second-grade level. Obviously, if a student's interest in the content of the material is high, a more accurate and complete diagnosis is likely. High-interest content has a greater effect on increasing comprehension instructional level than on increasing word recognition instructional level. High-interest materials have a greater effect on boys than on girls, and a greater effect on average and below-average readers than on above-average readers. Therefore, examine the material being used for the IRI to be sure that the passages are as interesting as possible; you will obtain better results from the inventory.

Task 3

Develop comprehension questions for each of the passages. After the series of graded passages has been chosen and the readability level of each passage determined, the next step is to develop a series of comprehension questions for each passage. It is strongly suggested that a minimum of 5 and a maximum of 10 questions be used. Although using 10 questions requires more teacher time, the greater number ensures a more precise evaluation of the students' comprehension.

Questions should measure the three levels of understanding: literal, interpretive, and critical. In developing questions for the IRI, there are certain guidelines to keep in mind. After reading the passages, prepare as many questions as possible; then classify each question in the light of the skill being measured. Following this classification, select the best questions to sample adequately the students' performance at each of the three levels of comprehension, as well as their proficiency in the specific skills. The questions can then be tested with selected students to determine their quality. Poor questions should be replaced with others from the list.

Task 4

Develop response sheets to use when administering the inventory. The teacher needs response sheets on which to record student errors made during administration of the IRI. These sheets have various formats, ranging from a one-page sheet with blanks for recording errors to copies of each page of the inventory, on which the teacher marks oral reading errors and other responses. Combining the latter with a single-page response sheet used as a summary is preferable.

The single-page response sheet should provide spaces to record information such as the following:

- Student's name
- Name of person administering the inventory
- Date of administration
- Levels of the IRI passages used during oral reading
- Responses to the comprehension questions following oral reading; the simplest procedure to use is a plus and minus for right and wrong responses
- Words asked during silent reading
- Responses to the comprehension questions following silent reading
- A summary of word errors during oral and silent reading
- A summary of responses to comprehension questions

- Special notes and comments
- The independent, instructional, and frustration level of the student

Multiple response sheets should include a copy of the passage that the student is reading followed by the comprehension questions for the passage. As the student reads, the teacher makes appropriate marks and comments on the sheet. This information is then transferred to the one-page summary sheet if both are being used.

Task 5

Type the passages that the student will read. If the passages are written by the teacher or taken from materials that may be inconvenient to use, each should be typed on a separate sheet or a large index card. Type and spacing should be appropriate to the student; for example, a primary-level type and double-spaced line are used for the younger student.

GLOSSARY

Accent. The part of a word that receives stress when it is spoken.

Achievement groups. A system in which students are divided into several groups based on their demonstrated ability and aptitude.

Acronyms. Abbreviations that consist of the first letter (or letters) of each word in a phrase (e.g., Nabisco, for the National Biscuit Company).

Advance organizer. A type of outline that is written at a higher level of abstraction than a normal summary; it forms a framework to aid text reading.

Affective domain. That part of the taxonomic hierarchy that involves the feelings, emotions, and attitudes of a student.

Affix. A prefix or suffix added to a word to change its meaning.

Analysis. The evaluation of data for decision making.

Analytic phonics. A method of reading instruction that begins with teaching an entire word and then teaching the sounds within a word.

Approaches. Different techniques used to provide reading instruction.

Appropriate instruction. Instruction that meets the needs of each student in the classroom.

Assessment. The procedures and methods used to evaluate the progress that a student makes in skill development.

Assessments. Informal and formal evaluations of performance in an identified area.

At-risk. Referring to children and youth whose environmental, cultural, and socioeconomic conditions prevent them from realizing their potential within the current educational, vocational, and societal structures.

Attitude inventory. A rating form used to assess a student's feelings toward reading.

Auditory discrimination. The ability to differentiate a variety of sounds.

Auditory memory. The ability to recall sounds.

Authentic assessment. The use of assessment techniques to learn more about students' reading capabilities in fair and nonjudgmental ways that are representative of the actual reading activities that students encounter in the classroom.

Automaticity. Reaction to print without conscious attention to the behavior. In word identification, this means providing the correct pronunciation of a word without consciously decoding the word.

Basal instruction. Reading instruction that uses the basal and the specific procedure outlined in the accompanying teacher's manual.

Basal reader approach. An approach to reading instruction that uses the basal and follows basal instruction. This approach includes the development of specific reading skills in a specified order and uses books, workbooks, and other materials designed by the publisher.

Basals. Textbooks used in the elementary grades with the primary purpose of introducing students to reading skills in a sequential order.

Bibliotherapy. Encouraging a student to read a particular book that will help him gain insight about interests he has or problems he may be facing.

Bilingual. Students who speak two or more languages, with English often being the second language.

Book handling. A strategy for helping students learn about a book by teaching them to identify the front and back, author and illustrator, table of contents, index, and other parts so they can obtain the most information.

Book sharing. A strategy that encourages students to share books they have read with peers. The sharing can take the form of character plays, dress-ups, interviews, and so on.

Cause-and-effect relationships. A comprehension skill that requires the reader to determine what event was precipitated by another event in the story.

Classroom community. The atmosphere that exists in a classroom in which students work together to learn.

Cloze procedure. An informal assessment technique consisting of a 250- to 300-word passage in which every fifth word has been deleted. Its primary purpose is to determine the students' instructional and independent reading levels, as well as their ability to use context when reading.

Cognitive development. The growth of the intellect.

Collaborative learning. A type of intraclass grouping that stresses shared learning experiences and group interaction and cooperation to reach a common goal or solve a common problem.

Comparisons. The ability to determine which ideas are alike and in what way they are alike.

Compound words. Words that are composed of two or more shorter words that have independent meanings.

Comprehension. Understanding the meaning of printed text in relation to personal experiences and the context of the information.

Computer-assisted instruction. Reading instruction that uses computer software to provide learning experiences.

Concepts. Abstract ideas generalized from several pieces of related specific information. They include also theories, views, and goals.

Concept-based instruction. Teaching focused on the specific ideas or concepts presented in a lesson.

Concept density. The complexity or difficulty of the specific concept being presented. For example, a basic concept such as "colors" is more easily understood than the concept of "freedom," even by a group of students who have always lived in a democracy.

Consonant cluster. The occurrence of two or more consonant sounds that represent one or more sounds. Also called *consonant blends* or *digraphs*.

Consonants. The letters *b*, *c*, *d*, *f*, *g*, *h*, *j*, *k*, *l*, *m*, *n*, *p*, *q*, *r*, *s*, *t*, *v*, *w*, *x*, *y*, and *z*.

Content reading inventory. An informal assessment procedure that uses content materials such as textbooks to assess the student's skill in reading content information.

Context clue. Words other than the word being read that aid in obtaining the meaning or recognizing an unknown word.

Contextual analysis. The use of the meaning of a phrase, sentence, or passage, in conjunction with other word identification skills to decode an unknown word or to derive meaning from a word or passage.

Continuous assessment. The ongoing process of continuously updating previous assessment data.

Contractions. A combination of two words from which one or more letters have been replaced by an apostrophe.

Contrasts. The ability to determine which ideas are different and in what ways they differ from each other.

Cooperative learning. Learning activities organized so that each participant in a group has a specific role and the success of each role is essential to accomplishing a common goal.

Coordination. The cooperation of classroom teachers, reading specialists, and content teachers to ensure the success of the total school reading program.

Correlation. The degree of relationships between two variables expressed by the coefficient of correlation, which extends along a scale from 1.00 (a perfect positive relationship) through 00.00 (no relationship) to –1.00 (a perfect negative relationship).

Creative reading. A type of reading in which the reader reacts to the printed word by expressing her own ideas about what has been read.

Criterion-referenced tests. Tests based on objectives that contain the specific conditions, outcomes, and criteria that are expected for satisfactory completion of the task.

Critical reading. The process of analyzing and evaluating what is read.

Critical skills. Comprehension skills that require the reader to make an evaluation or judgment of the material read.

Cross-age tutoring. An instructional format in which an older student works with a younger student in an effort to improve the reading skills of the younger student.

Data. Information that has been gathered about a specific subject from a variety of sources.

Dictation. The process whereby a person (usually a student when using language experience) tells information to the teacher to write in order to transfer information from speech to print.

Direct instruction. The conscious interaction between the teacher and student in which new information is presented via teacher demonstration and teacher-student discussion.

Directed learning activity. An instructional plan for use in content instruction that includes these basic steps: identifying learning skills, determining concepts, assessing students, and outlining teaching strategies, which includes introducing concepts and vocabulary and purposes for reading, reading information, discussion, and reteaching.

Directed reading activity. An instructional plan based on these five basic steps: readiness, skill development, review, guided reading, and follow-up.

Discourse analysis. The analysis of syntax in text materials to enhance reader comprehension.

Eclectic approach. A method of teaching reading that stresses a variety of approaches based on individual students needs, learning styles, and interests.

Educationally different. A term that refers to mildly disabled or challenged students, learning disabled students, at-risk students, non-English-speaking-students, and gifted and talented students.

Effective instruction. Instruction that is appropriate for each student in the class.

Effective teaching. Teaching characterized by clear and respectful communication between the teacher and students and the use of an explicit teaching model that emphasizes student interests and makes language literacy instruction a team effort of parents, students, and teachers.

Emergent literacy. The development of the language process for success in the school environment, especially informal language instruction in the home before formal school instruction begins.

Emotional and behavioral disorders. Students who are socially maladjusted, manifest inappropriate behavior, suffer periods of diminished verbal and motor activity, or have frequent complaints of a physical nature, including general fatigue, which interfere with their success in learning situations.

Environment. The home and school climate which affects learning both positively and negatively.

Environmental print. Familiar symbols within the environment that prompt children to associate labels and words (e.g., McDonald's golden arches, a tooth-paste tube, a red six-sided sign saying "STOP").

Facilities. The materials, physical features, and physical arrangement of the classroom.

Figurative language. Language that is rich in comparisons, similes, and metaphors.

Formal assessment procedures. The standardized techniques used by teachers and reading specialists to learn more about students' strengths and weaknesses in reading.

Frustration level. The level at which a student has extreme difficulty in pronouncing words and comprehending the material.

Full inclusion. A philosophy of accommodating students with special needs in a classroom where everyone belongs, is accepted, and supports and is supported by his peers and other members of the school community in the course of having his educational needs met.

Gifted and talented. Referring to students who exhibit superior talent in one or more areas.

Graded basal series. A group of readers published by a specific company and intended for sequential use during the elementary years.

Grade equivalent. A score derived from the raw score on a standardized test, usually expressed in terms of a grade level divided into tenths.

Grade level. The actual grade in which a student is enrolled.

Grade placement. The level at which a student is placed for instruction.

Group achievement tests. Tests administered to a large number of students simultaneously that measure the depth of a student's knowledge in various broad areas of the curriculum.

Group-administered formal tests. Assessment procedures that include assessment reading tests, achievement tests, and intelligence tests that are designed to be administered to a large number of students simultaneously and that have been standardized with populations of students.

Group assessment tests. Assessment instruments that are administered to many students simultaneously and provide the teacher with in-depth information.

Grouping. Any of a variety of methods by which a classroom of students is subdivided for appropriate reading instruction.

Grouping procedures. The methods and criteria used to combine students for instruction. These include achievement grouping, skills grouping, interest grouping, and cross-age, or peer, grouping.

Group survey tests. Assessment instruments that are administered to many students simultaneously, providing scores for vocabulary, comprehension, and sometimes the rate of reading for each student.

Guided instruction. Teacher-directed instruction that is based on established goals and uses planned materials and procedures.

Hearing challenged. Students who have auditory processing impediments that make it difficult for them to function in the classroom.

Hesitations. Pauses of more than five seconds between words during the administration of an Informal Reading Inventory.

Heterogeneous. A word taken from the Greek term meaning different. Used in reading instruction to describe a randomly formed group.

Homogeneous. A word taken from the Greek term meaning same. Usually used in reading instruction to define a group formed on the basis of similarities of knowledge.

Independent level. The level at which students read for recreational purposes. The material is easy enough to read quickly with maximum comprehension.

Indirect instruction. The interaction between the student and learning resources (other students or materials) to further extend or review information gained via direct instruction.

Individual assessment reading tests. Instruments that provide the most thorough assessment of a student's reading problems by incorporating various subtests that aid the teacher in identifying specific reading strengths and weaknesses.

Individual auditory discrimination tests. A test that is given to one person at the time to measure her skill is determining likenesses and differences in sounds.

Individual intelligence tests. Tests given to a single student in order to predict the level of proficiency that may be expected from his performance of a specific activity.

Individualization. Giving students assignments based on their own instructional level and engaging them in tasks that meet their specific needs.

Individualized instruction. Instruction that is geared to the instructional level of each student, so that every student is working on an assignment to meet his specific needs.

Individualized reading approach. A teaching technique based on Olson's philosophy of child development, which promotes the concepts of seeking, self-selection, and pacing.

Individually administered formal tests. Assessment instruments designed for use with a single student. These tests can be categorized as oral reading tests, assessment reading tests, auditory discrimination tests, auditory and visual screening tests, and intelligence tests.

Individual oral reading tests. Instruments administered to a student by asking her to read aloud so the teacher can note errors and difficulties such as mispronunciations, omissions, repetitions, substitutions, unknown words, and sometimes hesitations.

Inflectional ending. A word ending that, when added to a root word, denotes tense, number, degree, gender, or possession.

Informal assessment. The use of nonstandardized techniques by teachers to determine their students' strengths and weaknesses in reading.

Informal reading inventory. A compilation of graded reading selections with comprehension questions accompanying each selection. This inventory is individually administered to determine the student's strengths and weaknesses in word recognition and comprehension.

Insertions. Words that do not appear on the printed page but are added by the reader during the administration of an informal reading inventory.

Instructional level. The reading level at which a student can read the material but has some difficulty with recognition of words and comprehension, such that a teacher is required to assist him.

Instructional teaching into practice. An instructional model developed by Madeline Hunter that includes seven steps: anticipatory set, stating objectives, information input, modeling, checking for understanding, guided and independent practice, and closure.

Integrated instruction. A crucial component of the effective reading program that involves the simultaneous implementation of reading, writing, expressive and receptive language, studying, researching, and using content strategies in the classroom.

Interactive model. A theory of the reading process, developed by Rummelhart, that postulates that the reader and the text work in concert to reveal the meaning of the passage.

Interest groups. An organizational plan in which students with similar interests are allowed to work together to explore their mutual interests in greater depth.

Interest inventory. An inventory used to measure a student's likes, dislikes, and areas of enjoyment.

Interpretation. An in-depth evaluation of data in which the strengths and weaknesses of each student are examined and the underlying causes for poor test results are explored.

Interpretive comprehension. The process of assimilating information in an effort to infer the author's meaning.

Interpretive skills. Comprehension skills that involve comprehending the deeper meaning of the material read.

Invented spelling. Children's use of their sound-symbol knowledge to write words representing the message they wish to communicate (e.g., "I lv u" for "I love you").

K-W-L. A study strategy developed by Ogle to enable teachers to assist students in activating prior knowledge when interacting with expository text and to heighten their interest in reading this material.

Language-based instruction. The development of listening, speaking, reading, and writing through learning activities that involve several of these areas and encourage the use of children's literature, invented spelling, and group discussions.

Language development. The increase in quantity, range, and complexity of language production as children grow.

Language experience approach. An instructional method that makes use of reading materials created from the spoken language of the student; initially the teacher writes down exactly what the student says.

Learning-disabled. Referring to students who exhibit a disorder in one or more of the basic neurological or psychological processes involved in understanding or in using spoken or written language.

Listening comprehension. The recall, recognition, and understanding of ideas after hearing information.

Literal skills. Basic comprehension skills such as recalling details, finding the main idea, and interpreting symbols and acronyms. This area of comprehension involves the recognition or recall of text information.

Literature-based reading. The use of children's books as the primary classroom reading material for the development of the reading/language process.

Mainstreaming. The practice of integrating students with special needs into a regular classroom.

Management. The total process of selecting, organizing, and presenting classroom materials to the students.

Mean. The average of a set of numbers derived by taking the sum of the set of measurements and dividing it by the number of measurements in the set.

Median. The central number in a set, above and below which an equal number of scores fall.

Mildly challenged. Referring to students who have slower auditory and visual memory, conceptual and perceptual ability, or imaginative and creative ability.

Miscomprehension. Performance in which students frequently misunderstand questions and give inappropriate answers.

Miscues. Any responses during oral reading that deviate from those anticipated.

Mispronunciations. Words that are called incorrectly in the oral reading process or during an informal reading inventory.

Multicultural. A school or classroom population that shows cultural and ethnic diversity.

Multisensory approach. A teaching technique that involves the senses of touch and muscle movement as well as vision and hearing.

Non-English speaker. The segment of the school population who do not use English as their primary language.

Normal curve. A distribution graphed as a bell curve that has more scores at the mean or median and a decreasing number in equal proportions to the left and right of the center.

Naturalistic assessment. Informal testing procedures that use the daily work within the instructional environment to evaluate students' strengths and needs in instruction.

Objective-based tests. Tests based on specific objectives but for which no predetermined criteria for achievement are provided.

Observations. Teacher analysis of a student's knowledge, traits, behaviors, attitudes, and interactions as part of an ongoing assessment program.

Omissions. Words that are left out by the reader during the administration of an informal reading inventory.

Oral language. An area of emergent literacy that emphasizes speaking skills, including vocabulary and syntactical ability.

Organization. The instructional design used to manage groups in a classroom situation effectively.

Organization patterns. The manner in which textual material is written. In content writing, enumeration, relationship, problem solving, and persuasion are common patterns.

Organizational skills. A category of study skills that involves the ability to synthesize and evaluate material read so that it can be arranged into a workable format.

Parental involvement. A facet of the total school reading program wherein parents act as reading models and are actively involved in their child's learning.

PARS. A modified study strategy developed by Smith and Elliot primarily for use with younger students. The steps are preview, ask questions, read, and summarize.

Peer groups. Students organized in a way in which they are working with age-similar colleagues to accomplish a common goal.

Peer tutoring. An instructional format that involves students who are in the same grade level working together. These students do not have the same reading level or mastery of the same reading skills.

Percentile. The percentage score that rates a student relative to the percentage of others in a group who are below his score. Percentiles cannot be averaged, added together, subtracted, or treated arithmetically in any manner.

Personal reading. The use of all reading skills by the student when pursuing reading as a leisure-time activity. Personal reading combines all the cognitive skills with a positive attitude towards reading.

Phoneme-grapheme correspondences. The association of specific sounds with specific symbols in beginning reading.

Phonemic awareness. The awareness of sounds as important units of words.

Phonic analysis. The process of using letter sounds to pronounce an unknown word.

Physically challenged. Students with disorders of the nervous system, the musculoskeletal system, vision, or hearing.

Picture clue. A clue to an unknown word that appears in the form of a picture in the text.

PORPE. A writing-study strategy developed by Simpson primarily for students to use in learning how to study for essay questions. The steps are predicting, organizing, rehearsing, practicing, and evaluating.

Portfolios. The systematic collection of student work for use in evaluating changes in student performance in reading and language.

PQRST. A study strategy developed by Spache for studying science materials. The steps are preview, question, read, summarize, and test.

Prefix. A word component that is attached to the beginning of the root word to change its meaning.

Prereading. The stage of language development in which children are aware of the importance of print in the reading process, are beginning to associate sounds with letters, and are experimenting with language to change meanings. These are the emergent literacy activities that precede formal instruction in reading.

Prereading skills. The basic skills necessary for developing a foundation that will enable a student to master higher-level reading skills and learn to read. These skills include oral language development, visual perception, listening comprehension, and visual-motor development.

Prior knowledge. The knowledge structures that readers bring to a written text.

Psychologically challenged. Referring to students who suffer from an emotional or behavioral disorder.

Questioning. A primary strategy for developing student comprehension of reading materials. Ideally questions of many types are employed, including those generated by the student.

RAM. A study strategy developed by Dana to prepare disabled readers for reading. The three steps are relax, activate, and motivate.

Range. The distance between the largest and smallest numbers in a set.

Raw score. An untreated test score usually obtained by counting the number of items correct. It is the basis for determining all the derived scores.

Readability. The determination of the approximate grade level at which various materials are written.

Reading/language process. The processes used to communicate information via speaking, listening, reading, and writing. In the reading process, students learn to identify printed symbols and associate meaning with those symbols in order to understand ideas conveyed by the writer. This is also part of the language process.

REAP. A study strategy developed by Eanet and Manzo for use in reading and content area classrooms. The steps are read, encode, annotate, and ponder.

Reciprocal questioning. A procedure in which teacher and student take turns asking each other questions about a passage they have both read.

Reciprocal teaching. A form of reading instruction in which students engage in an interactive dialogue.

Instruction includes generating questions, summarizing, predicting, and clarifying, all of which are modeled by the teacher.

Record-keeping procedures. A system by which a teacher keeps track of the reading needs of the student in order to provide the appropriate ongoing instruction.

Recreational reading. Reading done by a student for enjoyment and personal satisfaction.

Reference skills. Skills that are concerned with locating information in various sources.

Relevant and irrelevant information. A critical reading skill that requires the reader to determine whether the author's evidence or examples are germane to the point she is making.

Reliability. The consistency with which the test agrees with itself or produces similar scores when readministered over a period of time by the same individual.

Repetitions. Words that are reread during the administration of an informal reading inventory.

Retelling. A strategy used to determine a student's understanding of information read without the use of questions. This strategy asks students to orally relate what they have read in their words; this retelling is then followed by probes (questions) to gain additional information.

RIPS. A study strategy developed by Dana to help disabled readers repair comprehension problems while reading. The steps are reading on and then rereading, imaging, paraphrasing, and speeding up, slowing down, or seeking help.

Schema. A theory of comprehension that states that to understand information the reader uses knowledge and structures that are in his mind and fits new information into these structures.

Scope and sequence. The identification and orderly presentation of reading skills to be taught at each level from kindergarten to the highest level. A scope and sequence chart is used to present this information.

Semantic mapping. A strategy that visually displays the relationships among words and helps to categorize them.

Sight words. The words that students see most frequently in reading and recognize instantly without using decoding skills.

Signal words. Connectors such as conjunctions that help the reader to understand the meaning of a passage(e.g., *therefore*, *however*, *in addition*, *and*).

Skill development. The process of teaching reading through instruction of individual skills in some systematic sequence.

Skills groups. The use of reading skills to place students into learning groups.

SIP. A study strategy developed by Dana to help disabled readers focus their attention on content while reading. The steps are summarizing, imaging, and predicting.

Specialized study skills. Study skills that involve analyzing all parts of a book or other material to determine what information can be obtained from it and how best to understand the information presented.

SQRQCQ. A study strategy developed by Fay for use in reading mathematics. The steps are survey, question, read, question, compute, and question.

SQ3R. A study strategy developed by Robinson that involves these five steps: survey, question, read, recite, and review.

Standard deviation. The variation of scores from the mean, a condition that varies with the range in a set of scores.

Standard score. A raw score expressed in some form of standard deviation unit. Standard scores can be dealt with arithmetically and are easier to interpret than raw scores.

Stanine. A type of standard score that is based on a nine-point scale with a mean of five and a standard deviation of about two.

Story grammar. A framework for specifying the organizational structure of a narrative; sometimes called *story structure*.

Story structure. The components of a story including the plot, setting, characters, and main events, which can be identified to aid in comprehension.

Structural analysis. The word identification skill that stresses the analysis of word parts to aid in pronunciation as well as comprehension.

Structured overview. A way of representing the conceptual vocabulary of written material as a visual pattern to show how concepts are related. It may be used to initiate or review a lesson.

Study skills. The higher-level reading skills that require the application of many other reading skills.

Study strategies. Essential learning strategies that students should activate when interacting with expository text.

Substitutions. Words that the student gives as replacements for the actual printed word during the administration of an informal reading inventory.

Suffix. A word part that is attached to the end of the root word to change its meaning.

Summarizing. Organizing interpreted data into a compact format that makes it easily accessible for classroom use.

Sustained silent reading. A classroom activity wherein everyone is required to read some material silently for a designated period of time.

Syllables. Parts of a word that are combined to form the entire word. Each syllable has one vowel sound.

Synthesis. The ability to form a point of view after reading several sources of information.

Synthetic phonics. A method that presents the isolated sounds in a word, then blends them to form the entire word.

Taxonomy. A hierarchy of the learning processes, classified from lowest to highest or a categorizing of the learning process.

Teacher effectiveness. Quality of teachers who are effective in helping students learn and achieve success in the classroom.

Text structure. A framework for specifying the organizational structure of expository texts.

Time on task. The time that students spend directly engaged in a given activity.

Use of material. The matching of available classroom teaching instruments to assessed student needs.

Validity. The extent to which a test measures what it is designed to measure.

Variant patterns. Vowel combinations in words that represent a unique sound or do not follow rules typically taught for decoding different sounds in unknown words.

Visual comprehension. A prereading skill that requires the interpretation of visual stimuli in reading materials.

Visual discrimination. The ability to differentiate among printed symbols.

Visually challenged. Referring to a student who is blind, has limited vision, or has low vision that prevents him from functioning normally in a classroom situation.

Visual memory. The ability to recall printed symbols.

Visual-motor skills. A prereading skill that includes eye-hand coordination, direction, and drawing specific designs using circles and lines.

Vowels. The letters *a*, *e*, *i*, *o*, *u*, and sometimes *y*.

Whole-language assessment. The evaluation of language performance through student work in language activities such as story retelling, invented spelling, discussions, and book handling.

Word boundaries. A prereading subskill that involves recognizing the spacing between words in oral language.

Word identification. The use of prior memory or a decoding process by the reader to assist in identifying words and associating meaning with the identified symbols.

Word identification inventories. Graded lists of words pronounced by a student so a teacher can learn more about the student's word recognition skills.

Writing. The communication of a message using symbols to represent ideas. The writing process involves several stages including the initiation of an idea, the development of the idea using words and sentences, editing this product, and presenting the finalized written product.

BIBLIOGRAPHY

Acheson, K., & Gall, M. (1997). *Techniques in the clinical supervision of teachers: Preservice and inservice applications* (4th ed.). New York: Longman.

Adams, A., Carmine, D., & Gersten, R. (1982). Instructional strategies for studying content area texts in the intermediate grades. *Reading Research Quarterly, 18*, 27–55.

Adams, M. J. (1990). *Beginning to read: Thinking and learning about print.* Urbana-Champaign, IL: University of Illinois.

Adams, M. J., & Huggins, A. W. F. (1985). The growth of children's sight vocabulary: A quick test with educational and theoretical implications. *Reading Research Quarterly, 20*, 262–281.

Agrast, C. (1967). Teach them to read between the lines. *Grade Teacher, 85*, 72–74.

Ahead Designs. (1987). *Create with Garfield.* Allen, TX: Developmental Learning Materials.

Alexander, J. E., & Filler, R. C. (1976). *Attitudes and reading.* Newark, DE: International Reading Association.

Allen, J., Michalove, B., Shockley, B., & West, M. (1991). I'm really worried about Joseph: Reducing the risks of literacy learning. *The Reading Teacher, 44*, 458–472.

Allen, R. V. (1973). The language-experience approach. In R. Karlin (Ed.), *Perspectives on elementary reading* (pp. 158–166). New York: Harcourt Brace Jovanovich.

Allen, R. V. (1976). *Language experiences in communication.* Boston: Houghton Mifflin.

Allington, R. L. (1994). The schools we have. The schools we need. *The Reading Teacher, 48*, 14–29.

Allington, R. L., & McGill-Franzen, A. (1980). Word identification errors in isolation and in context: Apples vs. oranges. *The Reading Teacher, 33*, 795–800.

Alongi, C. V. (1974). Response to Kay Haugaard: Comic books revisited. *The Reading Teacher, 27*, 801–803.

Altwerger, E., Edelsky, C., & Flores, B. (1987). Whole language: What's new? *The Reading Teacher, 41*, 141–154.

Amanda Stories. (1989). Los Angeles: Voyager.

American Psychiatric Association. (1994). *Diagnostic and statistical manual of mental disorders* (4th ed.). Washington, DC: Author.

Ames, W. S. (1966). The development of a classification schema of contextual aids. *Reading Research Quarterly, 2,* 57–82.

Anders, P. L., & Bos, C. S. (1986). Semantic feature analysis: An interactive strategy for vocabulary development and text comprehension. *Journal of Reading, 29,* 610–616.

Anderson, R. C., Hiebert, E. H., Scott, J. A., Wilkinson, I. A. G., & Members of the Commission on Reading. (1985). *Becoming a nation of readers: The report of the commission on reading.* Washington, DC: National Institute of Education.

Anderson, R. C., Spiro, R., & Anderson, M. (1977). *Schemata as scaffolding for the representation of information in connected discourse* (Technical Report No. 24). Urbana-Champaign, IL: University of Illinois, Center for the Study of Reading.

Armbruster, B. B., & Anderson, T. H. (1981). Research synthesis of study skills. *Educational Leadership, 39,* 154.

Armstrong, R. J., & Mooney, R. F. (1971). The Slosson intelligence test: Implications for reading specialists. *The Reading Teacher, 24,* 336–40.

Ashby-Davis, C. (1985). Cloze and comprehension: A qualitative analysis and critique. *Journal of Reading, 28,* 585–589.

Asher, S. (1980). Topic interest and children's reading comprehension. In R. Spiro, B. C. Bruce, & W. F. Brewer (Eds.), *Theoretical issues in reading comprehension.* Hillsdale, NJ: Erlbaum.

Athey, I. (1985). Reading research in the affective domain. In H. Singer and R. B. Ruddell (Eds.), *Theoretical models and processes of reading* (3rd ed., pp. 527–557). Newark, DE: International Reading Association.

Aukerman, R. D. (1984). *Approaches to beginning reading* (2nd ed.). New York: John Wiley.

Austin, M., & Morrison, C. (1963). *The first R.: The Harvard report on reading in elementary schools.* New York: Macmillan.

Ausubel, D. P. (1960). The use of advance organizers in the learning and retention of meaningful verbal material. *Journal of Educational Psychology, 51,* 267–272.

Baghban, M. (1984). *Our daughter learns to read and write: A case study from birth to three.* Newark, DE: International Reading Association.

Bailey, M. H. (1967). The utility of phonic generalizations in grades one through six. *The Reading Teacher, 20,* 413–418.

Baldwin, R. S., Peleg-Bruckner, Z., & McClintock, A. H. (1985). Effects of topic interest and prior knowledge on reading comprehension. *Reading Research Quarterly, 20,* 497–504.

Balsam, M., & Hammer, C. (1985). *Success with reading.* New York: Scholastic.

Bamberger, R. (1975). *Promoting the reading habit.* Paris: UNESCO Press.

Banks, J. (1989). Integrating the curriculum with ethnic content: Approaches and guidelines. In J. Banks, & C. McGee-Banks (Eds.), *Multicultural education: Issues and perspectives* (pp. 189–207). Boston: Allyn & Bacon.

Barnes, J., Ginther, D. W., & Cochran, S. W. (1989). Schema and purpose in reading comprehension and learning vocabulary from context. *Reading Research and Instruction, 28*, 16–28.

Barrentine, S. J. (1996). Engaging with reading through interactive read-alouds. *The Reading Teacher, 50*, 36–43.

Barrett, T. C. (1965). The relationship between the measures of pre-reading visual discrimination and first-grade achievement: A review of the literature. *Reading Research Quarterly, 1*, 51–76.

Barrett, T. C., & Smith, R. (1976). *Teaching reading in the middle grades.* Reading, MA: Addison-Wesley-Longman.

Bateman, B. (1963). *Reading and the psycholinguistic process of partially seeing children.* Arlington, VA: Council for Exceptional Children.

Baumann, J. F. (1986). Teaching third-grade students to comprehend anaphoric relationships: The application of a direct instruction model. *Reading Research Quarterly, 21*, 70–90.

Beck, J., & Juel, C. (1995). The role of decoding in learning to read. *American Educator, 19*(2), 8, 21–25, 39–42.

Beck, I. L., McKeown, M. G., McCaslin, E. S., & Burkes, A. M. (1979). *Instructional dimensions that may affect reading comprehension: Examples from two commercial reading programs.* Pittsburgh, PA: University of Pittsburgh, Learning Research and Development Center.

Beers, C. S., & Beers, J. W. (1980). Early identification of leaning disabilities: Facts and fallacies. *The Elementary School Journal, 81*, 67–76.

Beers, G. K. (1996). No time, no interest, no way! Part II of the 3 voices of literacy. *School Library Journal, 42*(3), 110–113.

Berger, E. H. (1991). *Parents as partners in education: The school and home working together* (3rd ed.). New York: Macmillan.

Bergeron, B. S. (1990, Summer). What does the term whole language mean? Constructing a definition from the literature. *Journal of Reading Behavior, 21*, 301–329.

Beta Upsilon Chapter, Pi Lambda Theta (1974). Children's interests classified by age level. *The Reading Teacher, 27*, 694–700.

Birch, J. W. (1974). *Mainstreaming educable mentally retarded children in regular classes.* Reston, VA: Council for Exceptional Children.

Bissett, D. J. (1969). *The amount and effect of recreational reading in selected fifth-grade classrooms.* Unpublished doctoral dissertation, Syracuse University.

Blanchard, J. S. (1985). *Computer-based reading assessment instrument.* Dubuque, IA: Kendall/Hunt.

Blanchard, J. S., & Rottenberg, C. J. (1990). Hypertext and hypermedia: Discovering and creating meaningful learning environments. *The Reading Teacher, 43*, 656–661.

Bloom, B. (Ed.). (1956). *Taxonomy of educational objectives: Handbook I. The cognitive domain.* New York: Longman.

Bloomfield, L., & Barnhart, C. L. (1961). *Let's read: A linguistic approach.* Detroit, MI: Wayne State University Press.

Boehm, A. E. (1986). *Examiner's manual: Boehm test of basic concepts–revised* San Antonio, TX: Psychological Corporation, Harcourt Brace Jovanovich.

Bond, G., & Dykstra, R. (1967). *Final report, project no. X–001*. Washington, DC: U.S. Department of Health, Education, and Welfare, Bureau of Research, Office of Education.

Bond, G., & Wagner, E. B. (1966). *Teaching the child to read* (4th ed.). New York: Macmillan.

Borg, W. (1980). Time and school learning. In C. Denham & A. Lieberman (Eds.), *Time to learn* (pp. 33–72). Washington, DC: U.S. Department of Education.

Bormuth, J. (1968). The Cloze readability procedure. *Elementary English, 45*, 429–436.

Bower, E. M. (1969). *Early identification of emotionally handicapped children in school* (2nd ed.). Springfield, IL: Charles C Thomas.

Bowman, M. A. (1980). *The effect of story structure questioning upon the comprehension and metacognitive awareness of sixth grade students.* Unpublished doctoral dissertation, University of Maryland.

Boyd, R. D. (1969). Growth of phonic skills in reading. In H. M. Robinson (Ed.), *Clinical studies in reading III* (Supplementary Educational Monographs No. 97, pp. 68–87). Chicago: University of Chicago Press.

Brackett, G. (1989). *Super story tree.* New York: Scholastic.

Braun, Carl. (1969). Interest-loading and modality effects on textual response acquisition. *Reading Research Quarterly, 4*, 428–444.

Briggs, F. A. (1969). "Grammatical sense" as a factor in reading comprehension. In G. B. Schick (Ed.), *The psychology of reading behavior* (pp. 8–16). Milwaukee, WI: National Reading Conference.

Brill, R. G. (1962). The relationship of Wechsler IQs to academic achievement among deaf students. *Exceptional Children, 28*, 315–321.

Bristow, P. S., Pikulski, J. J., & Pelosi, P. L. (1973). A comparison of five estimates of instructional level. *The Reading Teacher, 37*, 273–279.

Britton, J. (1970). *Language and learning.* Miami, FL: University of Miami Press.

Bromley, K. D. (1989). Buddy journals make the reading-writing connection. *The Reading Teacher, 43*, 122–129.

Brophy, J. (1991). Teacher praise: A functional analysis. *Review of Educational Research, 51*, 5–32.

Brountas, M. (1987, November–December). Whole language really works. *Teaching Pre-K–8, 18*, 57–60.

Brown, A. L., Campione, J. C., & Day, J. A. (1981). Learning to learn: On training students to learn from texts. *Educational Researcher, 10*, 14–21.

Brown, L. L., & Sherbenou, R. J. (1981). A comparison of teacher perceptions of student reading ability, reading performance, and classroom behavior. *The Reading Teacher, 34*, 557–560.

Bruckerhoff, C. (1977). What do students say about reading instruction? *The Clearing House, 51*, 104–107.

Burger, V., Cohen, T. A., & Bisgaler, P. (1956). *Bringing children and books together.* New York: Literary Club of America.

Burmeister, L. E. (1975). *From print to meaning.* Reading, MA: Addison-Wesley-Longman.

Burns, J. M. (1986). *A study of experiences provided in the home environment associated with accelerated reading abilities as reported by parents of intellectually superior preschoolers.* Unpublished doctoral dissertation, Louisiana State University.

Burns, J. M., & Collins, M. D. (1987). Parent perceptions of factors affecting the reading development of intellectually superior accelerated readers and intellectually superior nonreaders. *Reading Research and Instruction, 26*, 239–246.

Burns, P. C., & Roe, B. D. (1980). *Teaching reading in today's elementary schools* (2nd ed.). Chicago: Rand McNally.

Bussis, A. M., & Chittenden, E. A. (1987). Research currents: What the reading tests neglect. *Language Arts, 64*, 302–308.

Bynum, M. (1976). *Curriculum for gifted students.* Atlanta, GA: State Department of Education.

California achievement test. (1987). Monterey, CA: CTB/McGraw-Hill.

Cambourne, B. (1995). Toward an educationally relevant theory of literary learning: Twenty years of inquiry. *The Reading Teacher*, *49*, 182–190.

Canney, G., & Schreiner, R. (1976). A study of the effectiveness of selected syllabication rules and phonogram patterns for word attack. *Reading Research Quarterly, 12*, 102–124.

Carey, R. F. (1980). Toward a more cognitive definition of reading comprehension. *Reading Horizons, 20*, 293.

Carr, E., & Wixson, K. K. (1986). Guidelines for evaluating vocabulary instruction. *Journal of Reading, 29*, 588–595.

Carrier, C. A., & Titus, A. (1981). Effects of notetaking, pretraining and test mode expectations on learning from lectures. *American Educational Research Journal, 18*, 385–397.

Carroll, J. B., Davies, P., & Richman, B. (1971). *Word frequency book.* New York: American Heritage.

Cassidy, J. (1977). Cross-age tutoring and the sacrosanct reading period. *Reading Horizons, 17*, 178–180.

Cazden, C. B. (1982). Contexts for literacy: In the mind and in the classroom. *Journal of Reading Behavior, 14*, 413–427.

Chall, J. (1967). *Learning to read. The great debate.* New York McGraw-Hill.

Cheek, E. H., Jr., & Collins, M. D. (1983). *Reading instruction through content teaching.* Columbus, OH: Merrill/Prentice Hall.

Cheek, E. H., & Collins-Cheek, M. D. (1983). Organizational patterns: Untapped sources for better reading. *Reading World, 22*, 278–283.

Cheek, E. H., Flippo, R. F., & Lindsey, J. D. (1997). *Reading for success in elementary schools.* Madison, WI: McGraw-Hill.

Child Study Committee on the International Kindergarten Union. (1928). *A study of the vocabulary of children before entering first grade.* Washington, DC: International Kindergarten Union.

Chiu, L.-H. (1984). Children's attitudes toward reading and reading interests. *Perceptual and Motor Skills, 58*, 960–962.

Chomsky, C. (1969). *The acquisition of syntax in children from 5 to 10.* Cambridge, MA: MIT Press.

Chomsky, C. (1972, February). Stages in language development and reading exposure. *Harvard Educational Review*, 1–33.

Chomsky, C. (1979). Approaching reading through invented spelling. In L. B. Resnick & P. A. Weaver (Eds.), *Theory and practice of early reading* (pp. 43–65). Hillsdale, NJ: Erlbaum.

Chomsky, N. (1972). *Language and mind* (enlarged ed.) New York: Harcourt Brace Jovanovich.

Christie, J. F. (1980). Syntax: A key to reading comprehension. *Reading Improvement, 17*, 313–317.

Clark, A. D., & Richards, C. J. (1966). Auditory discrimination among economically disadvantaged and nondisadvantaged preschool children. *Exceptional Children, 33*, 259–262.

Clark, M. (1978). *Young fluent readers.* London: Heinemann.

Clarke, B. K. (1977). *A study of the relationship between eighth grade students' reading ability and their social studies and science textbooks.* Unpublished doctoral dissertation, Florida State University.

Clarke, L. K. (1988). Invented versus traditional spelling in first graders' writing: Effects on learning to spell and read. *Research in the Teaching of English, 22*, 281–309.

Clay, M. (1972). *The early detection of reading difficulties: A diagnostic survey.* Auckland, New Zealand: Heinemann.

Clay, M. (1993). *An observational survey or early literacy achievement.* Portsmouth, NH: Heinemann.

Climo, S. (1989). *The Egyptian Cinderella.* New York: Harper Collins.

Clymer, T. (1963). The utility of phonic generalizations in the primary grades. *The Reading Teacher, 16*, 252–258.

Cohen, E. G. (1982). Expectation states and interracial interaction in school settings. In R. H. Turner & J. F. Short (Eds.), *Annual Review of Sociology, 8*, 209–235.

Cole, N. (1990). Conceptions of educational achievement. *Educational Researcher, 3*, 2–7.

Collins, M. D. (1986). Evaluating basals: Do they teach phonics generalizations. In D. Lumpkin, M. Harshberger, & P. Ransom (Eds.), *Evaluation in reading-learning-teaching-administering. The 6th yearbook of the American Reading Forum.* Muncie, IN: Ball State University Press.

Collins, M. D. (1988). *Lecture supplement.* Baton Rouge, LA: Louisiana State University.

Collins, M. D. (1989, October). *How do three-year olds select favorite books?* Paper presented at the meeting of the College Reading Association, Philadelphia, PA.

Collins, M. D. (1993). *Reading interests of five-year olds: Effects of language development.* Paper presented at the meeting of the College Reading Association, Boston, MA.

Collins, M. D., & Cheek, E., Jr. (1993). *Diagnostic-prescriptive reading instruction: A guide for classroom teachers* (4th ed.). Dubuque, IA: McGraw-Hill.

Collins-Cheek, M. D. (1982). *Organizational patterns: An aid to comprehension.* American Reading Forum conference proceedings.

Cordasco, F. (1962). Puerto Rican pupils and American education. In W. W. Brickman & S. Lehrer (Eds.), *Education and the many faces of the disadvantaged. Cultural and historical perspectives.* New York: Wiley.

Cosmic Osmo. (1990). Menlo Park, CA: Activision, Cyna Software.

Cothern, N., & Lyman, B. G. (1993). ". . . So I write it out": Seizing the power of personal journal writing in affirming African-American student identities. In T. V. Rasinski & N. Padak (Eds.), *Inquiries in literacy learning and instruction. The 15th yearbook of the College Reading Association* (pp. 97–106). Pittsburgh, PA: College Reading Association.

Council for Exceptional Children Delegate Assembly. (1993). *Policy on inclusive schools.* San Antonio, TX.

Courtney, B. L. (1960). Methods and materials for teaching word perception in grades 10–14. In H. M. Robinson (Ed.), *Sequential development of reading abilities* (Supplementary Educational Monographs No. 90, pp. 42–46). Chicago: University of Chicago Press.

Crafton, L. K. (1996, April). *Standards in practice: Grades K–12.* Urbana, IL: National Council for Teachers of English.

Crary, R. W. (1969). *Humanizing the school: Curriculum development and theory.* New York: Alfred Knopf.

Crewe, J., & Hullgren, D. (1969). What does research really say about study skills? *The psychology of reading. The 18th yearbook of the National Reading Conference.* Austin, TX: National Reading Conference.

Cunningham, P. M. (1990). The names test: A quick assessment of decoding ability. *The Reading Teacher, 44*, 124–129.

Cunningham, P. M. (1992). Reasonable rimes. *The Reading Teacher, 46*, 282.

D'Alessandro, M. (1990). Accommodating emotionally handicapped children through a literature-based reading program. *The Reading Teacher, 44*, 288–293.

Dallmann, M., Rouch, R. L., Chang, L., & DeBoer, J. J. (1974). *The teaching of reading* (4th ed.). New York: Holt, Rinehart & Winston.

Dana, C. (1989). Strategy families for disabled readers. *Journal of Reading, 33*, 31–32.

Davidson, R. (1969). Teacher influence and children's levels of thinking. *The Reading Teacher, 22*, 702–704.

Dawson, M. A., & Bamman, H. A. (1959). *Fundamentals of basic reading instruction.* New York: David McKay.

Dechant, E. V., & Smith, H. P. (1977). *Psychology in teaching reading* (2nd ed.) Upper Saddle River, NJ: Prentice Hall.

Deese, J. (1970). *Psycholinguistics.* Boston: Allyn & Bacon.

DeGrella, J. B. (1989). *Creating a literate classroom environment.* (ERIC Document Reproduction Service No. ED 312 610). Las Vegas, NV: U.S. Department of Education.

den Heyer, K. (1981). Reading and motivation. In J. R. Edwards (Ed.), *Language and literacy: The social psychology of reading, Vol. 1,* (pp. 381–396). Silver Spring, MD: Institute of Modern Languages.

Denny, T., & Weintraub, S. (1966). First graders' responses to three questions about reading. *Elementary School Journal, 66*, 441–448.

DeSanti, R. J. (1989). Concurrent and predictive validity of a semantically and syntactically sensitive Cloze scoring system. *Reading Research and Instruction, 28*, 29–40.

Deutsch, M. (1964). *Communication of information in the elementary school classroom.* New York: New York Medical College: Institute for Developmental Studies.

Dickerson, D. P. (1982, October). A study of use of games to reinforce sight vocabulary. *The Reading Teacher, 36*, 46–49.

Doyle, C. (1988). Creative applications of computer-assisted reading and writing instruction. *Journal of Reading, 32*, 236–239.

Doyle, W. (1986). Classroom organization and management. In M. Wittrock (Ed.), *Handbook of research on teaching* (3rd ed., pp. 392–431). New York: Macmillan.

Dreikurs, R., Grunwald, B., & Pepper, F. (1971). *Maintaining sanity in the classroom. Illustrating reading techniques.* New York: Harper & Row.

Dreyer, M. J. (1995). How well can students read to find information? *Reading Today, 12*(5), 40.

Duffelmeyer, F. A., & Duffelmeyer, B. B. (1989). Are IRI passages suitable for assessing main idea comprehension? *The Reading Teacher, 42*, 358–363.

Duffelmeyer, F. A., Kruse, A. E., Merkley, D. J., & Fyfe, S. A. (1994). Further validation and enhancement of the names test. *The Reading Teacher, 48*, 118–128.

Duffelmeyer, F. A., Robinson, S. S., & Squire, S. E. (1989). Vocabulary questions on informal reading inventories. *The Reading Teacher, 43*, 142–148.

Duffy, G. G., & Roehler, L. R. (1986). *Improving classroom reading instruction: A decision-making approach* (2nd ed.). New York: Random House.

Dunn, N. E. (1981). Children's achievement at school-entry as a function of mother's and father's teaching sets. *Elementary School Journal, 81*, 245–253.

Durkin, D. (1966). *Children who read early: Two longitudinal studies.* New York: Teacher's College Press.

Durkin, D. (1978a). An earlier start in reading. *Elementary School Journal, 6*, 92–116.

Durkin, D. (1978b). *Teaching them to read* (3rd ed.). Boston: Allyn & Bacon.

Durkin, D. (1978c). What classroom observations reveal about reading comprehension instruction. *Reading Research Quarterly, 15*, 481–533.

Durkin, D. (1981). Reading comprehension instruction in five basal reader series. *Reading Research Quarterly, 16*, 515–544.

Durkin, D. (1981). What is the value of the new interest in reading comprehension? *Language Arts, 58*, 27.

Durkin, D. (1987). *Teaching young children to read* (4th ed.) Boston: Allyn & Bacon.

Durkin, D. (1990). Dolores Durkin speaks on instruction. *The Reading Teacher, 43*, 472–476.

Durrell, D., & Catterson, J. (1980). *Durrell analysis of reading difficulty* (3rd ed.). San Antonio, TX: Psychological Corporation.

Dyer, J. W., Riley, J., & Yekovich, F. P. (1979). An analysis of three study skills: Notetaking, summarizing, and rereading. *Journal of Educational Research, 73*, 3–7.

Dykstra, R. (1968, Fall). Summary of the second phase of the cooperative research program in primary reading instruction. *Reading Research Quarterly, 4*, 49–70.

Dyson, A. H. (1984). N spell my grandmama: Fostering early thinking about print. *The Reading Teacher, 38*, 262–271.

Eanet, M. G., & Manzo, A. V. (1976). REAP: A strategy for improving reading/writing/study skills. *Journal of Reading, 19*, 647–652.

Edlesky, C., Draper, K., & Smith, K. (1983, Winter). Hookin 'em in at the start of school in a "whole language" classroom. *Anthropology and Education Quarterly, 4*, 257–281.

Educational Products Information Exchange. (1977). *Report of a national study of the quality of instructional materials most used by teachers and learners* (Technical Report No. 76). New York: EPIE Institute.

Edwards, P. A., & Simpson, L. (1986). Bibliotherapy: A strategy for communication between parents and their children. *Journal of Reading, 30*, 110–118.

Eeds, M. (1981). What to do when they don't understand what they read: Research-based strategies for teaching reading comprehension. *The Reading Teacher, 8*, 565–575.

Eeds, M. (1985). Bookwords: Using a beginning word list of high frequency words from children's literature K–3. *The Reading Teacher, 38*, 418–423.

Ekwall, E. E. (1974). Should repetitions be counted as errors? *The Reading Teacher, 27*, 365–367.

Ekwall, E. E. (1976). Informal reading inventories: The instructional level. *The Reading Teacher, 29*, 662–665.

Ekwall, E. E., & Shanker, J. L. (1983). *Diagnosis and remediation of the disabled reader* (2nd ed.). Boston: Allyn & Bacon.

Elam, S. (1989). The second Gallup/Phi Delta Kappa poll of teachers' attitudes toward the public schools. *Phi Delta Kappan, 70*, 785–798.

Eller, W., & Wolf, J. G. (1966). Developing critical reading abilities. *Journal of Reading, 10*, 192–198.

Emans, R. (1967). The usefulness of phonic generalizations above the primary grades. *The Reading Teacher, 20*, 410–425.

Emans, R. (1969). Use of context clues. In J. A. Figurel (Ed.), *Reading and realism* (pp. 36–43). Newark, DE: International Reading Association.

Emans, R. (1971). Use of context clues. In M. A. Dawson, (Ed.), *Teaching word recognition skills* (pp. 57–62). Newark, DE: International Reading Association.

Emans, R., & Fisher, G. M. (1967). Teaching the use of context clues. *Elementary English, 44*, 243–246.

Emery, D. W. (1996). Helping readers comprehend stories from the characters' perspectives. *The Reading Teacher, 49*, 534–541.

Erickson, K. A., & Koppenhauer, D. A. (1995). Developing a literacy program for children with severe disabilities. *The Reading Teacher, 48*, 676–684.

Erickson, L. (1995). *Supervision of literacy programs: Teachers as grass-roots change agents.* Boston: Allyn & Bacon.

Evans, M. A., & Carr, T. H. (1985, Spring). Cognitive abilities, conditions of learning, and early development of reading skill. *Reading Research Quarterly,* 20, 327–350.

Evertson, C. (1987). Managing classrooms: A framework for teachers. In D. Berliner, & B. Rosenshine (Eds.), *Talks to teachers* (pp. 52–74). New York: Random House.

Evertson, C. M., & Anderson, L. M. (1979). Beginning school. *Educational Horizons, 57*, 164–168.

Farr, M. (Ed.). (1985). *Advances in writing research: Vol. 1. Children's early writing development.* Norwood, NJ: Albex.

Farr, R. (1988). Trends: A place for basal readers under the whole language umbrella. *Educational Leadership, 46*, 86.

Farr, R. C., Prescott, G. A., Balow, I. H., & Hogan, T. P. (1986). *MAT6 reading diagnostic tests. Teacher's manual.* San Antonio, TX: Psychological Corporation, Harcourt Brace Jovanovich.

Farr, R. & Tone, B. (1994). *Portfolio and performance assessment: Helping students evaluate their progress as readers and writers*. Fort Worth, TX: Harcourt Brace, 1–19. (ERIC Document Reproduction Service No. ED 363 864).

Farris, P. J., & Kaczmarski, D. (1988). Whole language, a closer look. *Contemporary Education, 59*, 77–81.

Fay, L. (1965). Reading study skills: Math and science. In J. A. Figurel (Ed.), *Reading and inquiry* (pp. 72–79). Newark, DE: International Reading Association.

Fennimore, F. (1977). Projective book reports. *Language Arts, 54*, 176–179.

Fernald, G. M. (1943). *Remedial techniques in basic school subjects.* New York: McGraw-Hill.

Fidell, R., & Fidell, E. A. (Eds.). (1976). *Children's catalog* (13th ed.). Bronx, NY: H. W. Wilson.

Fisher, C. W., Filby, N. N., Marliave, R., Cahen, L. S., Dishaw, M. M., Moore, J. E., & Berliner, D. C. (1978). *Teaching behaviors, academic learning time, and student achievement: Final report of Phase III-B, beginning teacher evaluation study.* San Francisco: Far West Educational Laboratory for Educational Research and Development.

Fitzgerald, J., Spiegel, D. L. (1983). Enhancing children's reading comprehension through instruction in narrative structure. *Journal of Reading Behavior, 15*, 1–17.

Fitzgerald, J., Spiegel, D. L., & Cunningham, J. W. (1991). The relationship between parental literacy level and perceptions of emergent literacy. *Journal of Reading Behavior, 23*, 191–213.

Flesch, R. F. (1965). *Why Johnny can't read and what you can do about it.* New York: Harper.

Fogarty, J. L., & Wang, M. C. (1982). An investigation of the cross-age peer tutoring process: Some implications for instructional design and motivation. *The Elementary School Journal, 82*, 451.

Frederiksen, C. H. (1972). Effects of task-induced cognitive operation on comprehension and memory processes. In J. B. Carroll & R. O. Freedle (Eds.), *Language comprehension and the acquisition of knowledge* (pp. 123–147). New York: Halsted Press.

Fry, E. B. (1968). A readability formula that saves time. *Journal of Reading, 11*, 587.

Fry, E. B. (1977a). *Elementary reading instruction.* New York: McGraw-Hill.

Fry, E. B. (1977b). Fry's readability graph: Clarifications, validity, and extension to level 17. *Journal of Reading, 21*, 242–252.

Fry, E. B. (1980). The new instant word list. *The Reading Teacher, 34*, 284–289.

Furness, E. L. (1960). Pupil, pedagogues, and punctuation. *Elementary English, 37*, 184–189.

Gall, M., & Gall, J. (1990). Outcomes of the discussion method. In W. Wilen (Ed.), *Teaching and learning through discussion* (pp. 32–46). Springfield, IL: Charles C Thomas.

Gall, M. D., Ward, B. A., Berliner, D. C., Cahen, L. S., Crown, K. A., Elasholf, J. D., Stanton, G. C., & Winne, P. H. (1975). *The effects of teacher use of questioning techniques on student achievement and attitude: Stanford program on teacher effectiveness, a factorially designed experiment on teacher structuring, soliciting, and reading.* San Francisco: Far West Laboratory for Educational Research and Development.

Gambrell, L. E. (1981). Think-time: Implications for reading instruction. *The Reading Teacher, 34*, 143.

Gambrell, L. E. (1996). Creating classroom cultures that foster reading motivation. *The Reading Teacher, 50*, 14–25.

Gambrell, L., Palmer, B. M., Codling, R. M., & Mazzoni, S. A. (1996). Assessing motivation to read. *The Reading Teacher, 49*, 518–533.

Gardner, D. C., & Kurtz, M. (1979). Teaching technical vocabulary to handicapped students. *Reading Improvement, 16*, 252–257.

Gates, A. I. (1926). *A reading vocabulary for the primary grades.* New York: Columbia University, Teachers College.

Gaustad, M. G., & Messenheimer-Young, T. (1991). Dialogue journals for students with learning disabilities. *Teaching Exceptional Children, 23*, 28–32.

Gavelek, J. R., & Raphael, T. E. (1996). Changing talk about text: New roles for teachers and students. *Language Arts, 73*, 182–192.

Gemake, J. (1981). Interference of certain dialect elements with reading comprehension for third graders. *Reading Improvement, 18*, 183–189.

Gentile, A. (1973). *Further studies in achievement testing, hearing impaired students: Annual survey of hearing impaired children and youth.* Washington, DC: Gallaudet College.

Giangreco, M. F., Cloninger, C. J., Dennis, R. E., & Edelman, S. W. (1994). Problem-solving methods to facilitate inclusive education. In J. S. Thousand, R. A. Villa, and A. I. Nevin (Eds.), *Creativity and collaborative learning: A practical guide to empowering students and teachers* (ERIC Document Reproduction Service No. ED 369 547, pp. 322–333). Baltimore: Paul H. Brookes.

Gibbs, J., & Huang, L. (Eds.). (1985). *Children of color: Psychological interventions with minority youth.* San Francisco: Jossey-Bass.

Gillet, J. W., & Temple, C. (1982). *Understanding reading problems: Assessment and instruction.* Boston: Little, Brown.

Gilliland, H. (1978). *A practical guide to remedial reading.* Columbus, OH: Merrill/Prentice Hall.

Glass, G. G., & Burton, E. H. (1973). How do they decode? Verbalizations and observed behaviors of successful decoders. *The Reading Teacher, 26*, 645.

Glasser, W. (1986). *Control theory in the classroom.* New York: Harper & Row.

Glazer, J. I., & Lamme, L. L. (1990). Poem picture books and their uses in the classroom. *The Reading Teacher, 44*, 102–109.

Gleitman, L. R., & Rozin, P. (1973). Teaching reading by use of syllabary. *Reading Research Quarterly, 8*, 447–483.

Gonzales, P. C. (1996). Literature-based ESL program works. *Reading Today, 13*(4), 27.

Good, T. (1987). Two decades of research on teacher expectations: Findings and future directions. *Journal of Teacher Education, 38*, 32–47.

Goodman, K. S. (1965). A linguistic study of cues and miscues in reading. *Elementary English, 42*, 639–643.

Goodman, K. S. (1969). Let's dump the up-tight model in English. *Elementary School Journal, 69*, 1–13.

Goodman, K. S. (1973). The 13th easy way to make learning to read difficult: A reaction to Gleitman and Rosin. *Reading Research Quarterly, 8*, 484–493.

Goodman, K. S. (1976). Behind the eye: What happens in reading. In H. Singer & R. Russell (Eds.), *Theoretical models and processes in reading* (2nd ed., pp. 5–17). Newark, DE: International Reading Association.

Goodman, K. S. (1985). Unity in reading. In H. Singer & R. Russell (Eds.), *Theoretical models and processes in reading* (3rd ed.) (pp. 179–196). Newark, DE: International Reading Association.

Goodman, K. S. (1988). Look what they've done to Judy Blume! The "basalization" of children's literature. *The New Advocate, 1*, 29–41.

Goodman, K. S., & Buck, C. (1973). Dialect barriers to comprehension revisited. *The Reading Teacher, 25*, 6–12.

Goodman, Y. M. (1978). Kid watching: An alternative to testing. *National Elementary School Principal, 57*, 41–45.

Goodman, Y. M., & Burke, C. L. (1982). *Reading miscue inventory.* New York: Richard Owen.

Goodman, Y. M., & Goodman, K. S. (1963). Spelling ability of a self taught reader. *The Elementary School Journal, 64*, 149–151.

Gordon, T. (1974). *Teacher effectiveness training.* New York: David Mackay.

Graham, K. G., & Robinson, H. A. (1984). *Study skills handbook: A guide for all teachers.* Newark, DE: International Reading Association.

Grant, L., & Rothenberg, J. (1981). *Charting educational futures: Interaction patterns in first and second grade reading groups.* Washington, DC: National Institute of Education.

Graves, D. H. (1983). *Writing: Teachers and children at work.* Exeter, NH: Heinemann.

Graves, M. F., Cooke, C. L., & LaBerge, M. J. (1983). Effects of previewing difficult short stories on low ability junior high school students' comprehension, recall, attitudes. *Reading Research Quarterly, 18*, 262–276.

Gray, W. S. (1960a). *On their own in reading: How to give children independence in analyzing new words* (rev. ed.). Chicago: Scott, Foresman.

Gray, W. S. (1960b). Physiology and psychology of reading. In C. W. Harris, (Ed.), *Encyclopedia of educational research* (3rd ed., pp. 1096–1114). New York: Macmillan.

Greenwood, C. R. (1991). Longitudinal analysis of time, engagement, and achievement in at risk versus non-risk students. *Exceptional Children, 57*, 521–535.

Gundach, J. B., McLane, F. M. S., & McNamee, G. D. (1985). The social foundations of children's early writing development. In M. Farr (Ed.), *Advances in writing research: Vol. 1. Children's early writing development* (pp. 1–5). Norwood, NJ: Albex.

Gunning, T. G. (1995). Word building: A strategic approach to the teaching of phonics. *The Reading Teacher, 48*, 484–488.

Guszak, F. J. (1967). Teacher questioning and reading. *The Reading Teacher, 21*, 227–234.

Guthrie, F. M., & Cunningham, P. M. (1982). Teaching decoding skills to educable mentally handicapped children. *The Reading Teacher, 35*, 54–59.

Guthrie, J. J. (1982). Effective teaching practices. *The Reading Teacher, 35*, 766–768.

Guthrie, J. T. (1996). Educational contexts for engagement in literacy. *The Reading Teacher, 49*, 432–445.

Guzzetti, B. J., & Marzano, R. J. (1984). Correlates of effective reading instruction. *The Reading Teacher, 37*, 754–759.

Hadaway, N. L., & Young, T. A. (1994). Content literacy and language learning: Instructional decisions. *The Reading Teacher, 47*, 522–527.

Hafner, L. (1977). *Developmental reading in middle and secondary schools: Foundations, strategies, and skills for teaching.* New York: Macmillan.

Hafner, L. E., & Jolly, H. B. (1972). *Patterns of teaching reading in the elementary school.* New York: Macmillan.

Hajek, E. (1984). Whole language: Sensible answers to the old problems. *Momentum, 15*, 39–40.

Hall, M. A. (1978). *The language experience approach for reaching reading* (2nd ed.). Newark, DE: International Reading Association.

Hall, M. A. (1989). *Teaching reading as a language experience* (3rd ed.). Columbus, OH: Merrill/Prentice Hall.

Hall, M. A., & Ramig, C. J. (1978). *Linguistic foundations for reading.* Columbus, OH: Merrill/Prentice Hall.

Hallahan, D. P., & Kauffman, J. M. (1991). *Exceptional children: Introduction to special education.* Upper Saddle River, NJ: Prentice Hall.

Haller, E. J., & Davis, S. A. (1980, Winter). Does socioeconomic status bias the assignment of elementary school students to reading groups?

American Educational Research Journal, 17, 409–418.

Halliday, M. A. K. (1975). *Learning how to mean: Exploration in the development of language.* London: Edward Arnold.

Hancock, J. (1989). Learning with databases. *Journal of Reading, 32*, 582–589.

Hanna, P. R., & Moore, J. I. (1953). Spelling: From spoken word to written symbol. *Elementary School Journal, 53*, 329–337.

Hansell, T. S. (1978). Stepping up to outlining. *Journal of Reading, 22*, 248–252.

Hansen, H. S. (1969). The impact of the home literacy environment on reading attitude. *Elementary English, 46*, 17–24.

Hansen, J. (1981). An inferential comprehension strategy for use with primary grade children. *The Reading Teacher, 34*, 665–669.

Hargis, C. H., & Gickling, E. F. (1978). The function of imagery in word recognition development. *The Reading Teacher, 31*, 870–873.

Harlin, R., & Lippa, S. (1990). Emergent literacy: A comparison of formal and informal assessment methods. *Reading Horizons, 30*, 209–223.

Harris, A. J. (1976). Practical applications of reading research. *The Reading Teacher, 29*, 559–565.

Harris, A. J., & Jacobson, M. D. (1972). *Basic elementary reading vocabularies.* New York: Macmillan.

Harris, A. J., Serwer, B., & Gold, L. (1967). Comparing approaches in first grade teaching with disadvantaged children extended into second grade. *The Reading Teacher, 20*, 698–703.

Harris, A. J., & Sipay, E. R. (1975). *How to increase reading ability* (6th ed.). New York: David McKay.

Harris, A. J., & Sipay, E. R. (1985). *How to increase reading ability: A guide to developmental and remedial methods* (8th ed.). New York: Addison-Wesley-Longman.

Harris, A. J., & Sipay, E. R. (1990). *How to increase reading ability* (9th ed.). New York: Addison-Wesley-Longman.

Harris, L. A. (1969). Interest and the initial acquisition of words. *The Reading Teacher, 22*, 312–314, 362.

Harris, L. A., & Smith, C. B. (1980). *Reading instruction: Diagnostic teaching in the classroom* (3rd ed.). New York: Holt, Rinehart, & Winston.

Harrison, A. R. (1967). Critical reading for elementary pupils. *The Reading Teacher, 21*, 244–252.

Harste, J. C., Burke, C. I., & Woodward, V. A. (1981). *Children, their language and world: Initial encounters with print.* Bloomington, IN: Indiana University.

Hartley, J., Bartlett, S., & Branthwaite, A. (1980). Underlining can make a difference—Sometimes. *Journal of Educational Research, 74*, 218–224.

Hays, W. S. (1975). *Criteria for the instructional level of reading* (ERIC Document Reproduction Service No. ED 117 665). Tucson, AZ: University of Arizona.

Healey, A. K. (1963). Effects of changing children's attitudes toward reading. *Elementary English, 40*, 255–257, 279.

Heath, S. B. (1983). *Ways with words: Language, life, and work in communities and classrooms.* New York: Cambridge University Press.

Heath, S. B., & Thomas, C. (1984). The achievement of preschool literacy for mother and child. In H. Goelman, A. A. Oberg, & F. Smith (Eds.), *Awakening to literature* (pp. 51–72). Exeter, NH: Heinemann.

Hebert, E., & Schultz, L. (1996). The power of portfolios. *Educational Leadership, 53*(7), 70.

Heimberger, M. J. (1970). *Sartain reading attitudes inventory* (ERIC Document Reproduction Service No. ED 117 665). Pittsburgh, PA.

Helgren-Lempesis, V. A., & Mangrum, C. T., II. (1986, Spring). An analysis of alternate-form reliability of three commercially prepared informal reading inventories. *Reading Research Quarterly, 21*, 209–215.

Henk, W. A. (1987). Reading assessments of the future: Toward precision diagnosis. *The Reading Teacher, 40*, 860–870.

Henk, W. A., & Melnick, S. A. (1995). The reader self-perception scale (RSPS): A new tool for measuring how children feel about themselves as readers. *The Reading Teacher, 48*, 470–482.

Heward, W. L. (1996). *Exceptional children* (5th ed.). Upper Saddle River, NJ: Merrill/Prentice Hall.

Hiebert, E. H. (1983). An examination of ability grouping for reading instruction. *Reading Research Quarterly, 18*, 232–255.

Hiebert, E. H., & Adams, C. (1987). Fathers' and mothers' perceptions of their preschool children's emergent literacy. *Journal of Experimental Child Psychology, 44*, 25–37.

Hiebert, E. H., & Colt, J. (1990). Patterns of literature-based reading instruction. *The Reading Teacher, 43*, 14–20.

Hillerich, R. L. (1967). Vowel generalizations and first grade reading achievement. *Elementary School Journal, 67*, 246–250.

Hillerich, R. L. (1974). Word lists: Getting it all together. *The Reading Teacher, 27*, 353–360.

Hillerich, R. L. (1976). The truth about vowels. In R. Williams (Ed.), *Insights into why and how to read* (pp. 63–73). Newark, DE: International Reading Association.

Hirstendahl, J. K. (1968). The effect of subheads on reader comprehension. *Journalism Quarterly, 45*, 123–125.

Hodgkinson, H. (1985). Guess who's coming to college? *Academe, 69*, 13–20.

Hoffman, J. L. (1995). The family portfolio: Using authentic assessment in family literacy programs. *The Reading Teacher, 48*, 594–597.

Hong, L. K. (1981). Modifying SSR for beginning readers. *The Reading Teacher, 34*, 888–891.

Huck, C. S., & Kuhn, D. Y. (1968). *Children's literature in the elementary school* (2nd ed.). New York: Holt, Rinehart, & Winston.

Hudson, J., & Haworth, J. (1983). Dimensions of word recognition. *Reading, 17*, 87–94.

Huey, E. B. (1908). *The psychology and pedagogy of reading.* New York: Macmillan.

Hunter, M. (1984). Knowing, teaching, and supervising. In P. Hosford (Ed.), *Using what we know about teaching* (pp. 169–192). Alexandria, VA: Association for Supervision and Curriculum Development.

Huus, H. (1979). A new look at children's interests. In J. E. Shapiro (Ed.), *Using literature and poetry affectively* (pp. 37–45). Newark, DE: International Reading Association.

Idol, L., Nevin, A., & Paolucci-Whitcomb, P. (1994). *Collaborative consultation* (2nd ed.). Austin, TX: Pro-Ed.

Irwin-DeVitis, L. Literacy portfolios: The myth and the reality. In M. D. Collins & B. G. Moss (Eds.), *Literacy assessment for today's schools.* Akron, OH: College Reading Association.

Ives, J. P. (1966). The improvement of critical reading skills. In C. Morrison (Ed.), *Problem areas in reading: Some observations and recommendations* (pp. 72–80). Providence, RI: Oxford Press.

Jagger, A. (1985). On observing the language learner: Introduction and overview. In A. Jagger & M. R. Smith-Burke (Eds.), *Observing the language learner* (pp. 216–229). Newark, DE: International Reading Association.

Jastak, J., Bijou, S., & Jastak, S. (1976). *Wide range achievement test.* New York: Psychological Corporation.

Jenkins, J. R., & Pany, D. (1981). Instructional variables in reading comprehension. In J. T. Guthrie (Ed.), *Comprehension and teaching: Research reviews* (pp. 163–202). Newark, DE: International Reading Association.

Johns, J. L. (1988). *Computer-based graded-word lists.* Dekalb, IL: Northern Illinois University.

Johns, J. L., Edmond, R. M., & Mavrogenes, N. A. (1977). The Dolch basic sight vocabulary: A replication and validation study. *The Elementary School Journal, 78*, 31–37.

Johns, J. L., & Lunt, L. (1975). Motivating reading: Professional ideas. *The Reading Teacher, 28*, 617–619.

Johns, J. L., & Magliari; A. M. (1989). Informal reading inventories: Are the Betts criteria the best criteria? *Reading Improvement, 26*, 124–132.

Johnson, D. D. (1971). The Dolch list re-examined. *The Reading Teacher, 24*, 449–457.

Johnson, D. D. (1986). Journal of Reading: A themed issue on vocabulary instruction. *Journal of Reading, 29*, 580.

Johnson, D. D., & Barrett, T. G. (1981). Prose comprehension: A descriptive analysis of instructional practices. In C. M. Santa & B. I. Hayes (Eds.), *Children's prose comprehension: Research and practice* (pp. 72–102). Newark, DE: International Reading Association.

Johnson, D. D., Smith, R. J., & Jensen, K. L. (1972). Primary children's recognition of high frequency words. *The Elementary School Journal, 73*, 162–167.

Johnson, D., & Moe, A. (with Bauman, J.). (1983). *The Ginn word book for teachers.* Lexington, MA: Ginn.

Johnson, D. J., & Myklebust, H. R. (1967). *Learning disabilities: Educational principles and practices.* New York: Gruen & Stratton.

Johnson, R. T., & Johnson, D. W. (1986). Action research: Cooperative learning in the science classroom. *Science and Children, 24*, 31–32.

Jongsma, E. R. (1971). *The Cloze procedure: A survey of the research.* Bloomington, IN: Indiana University.

Jongsma, K. S., & Jongsma, E. A. (1981). Test review: Commercial informal reading inventories. *The Reading Teacher, 34*, 697–705.

Jonz, J. (1990, Spring). Another turn in the conversation: What does Cloze measure? *TESOL Quarterly, 24*, 61–83.

Jorm, A. F. (1977). Effect of word imagery on reading performance as a function of reading ability. *Journal of Educational Psychology, 69*, 46–54.

Juel, C. (1980). Comparison of word identification strategies with varying context, word type and reader skill. *Reading Research Quarterly, 15*, 358–376.

Juel, C., & Holmes, B. (1981). Oral and silent reading of sentences. *Reading Research Quarterly, 16*, 545–568.

Justin, N. (1970). Culture conflict and Mexican-American achievement. *School and Society, 98*, 27–28.

Kalmbach, J. R. (1986). Getting at the point of retellings. *Journal of Reading, 29*, 326–333.

Karlsen, B., & Gardner, E. (1984). *Stanford diagnostic reading test.* San Antonio, TX: Psychological Corporation.

Kaster, L. A., Roser, N. L., & Hoffman, J. V. (1987). Understandings of the forms and functions of written language: Insights from children and parents. In J. E. Readance & R. S. Baldwin (Eds.), *Research in literacy: Merging perspective. The 36th Yearbook of the National Reading Conference* (pp. 85–92). Rochester, NY: National Reading Conference.

Kean, M., Summers, M. R., Ravietz, M., & Farber, I. (1979). *What works in reading.* Philadelphia, PA: School District of Philadelphia.

Keegan, S., & Shrake, K. (1991). Literature study groups: An alternative to ability grouping. *The Reading Teacher, 44*, 542–547.

King, E. L., & Siegmar, M. (1965). Different sensory cues as aids in beginning reading. *The Reading Teacher, 19*, 163–168.

Kirk, S. A., & Gallagher, J. J. (1979). *Educating exceptional children* (3rd ed.). Boston: Houghton Mifflin.

Knapp, M. I., & Turnbull, B. J. (1991). Better schooling for the children of poverty: Alternatives to conventional wisdom. In M. S. Knapp (Ed.), *Study of academic instruction for disadvantaged students: What is taught, and how, to the children of poverty. Interim report from a two-year investigation: Vol. 1.* Washington, DC: U.S. Department of Education; Office of Planning, Budget, and Evaluation.

Kolker, B., & Terwilliger, P. N. (1981). Sight vocabulary learning of first and second graders. *Reading World, 20,* 251–258.

Kolstoe, O. P. (1976). *Teaching educable mentally retarded children* (2nd ed.). New York: Holt, Rinehart, & Winston.

Kucera, H., & Nelson, F. W. (1967). *Computational analysis for present-day American English.* Providence, RI: Brown University Press.

Kuchinskas, G., & Radenchich, M. C. (1986). *The semantic mapper.* Gainesville, FL: Teacher Support Software.

Kuchinskas, G., & Radenchich, M. C. (1990). *The literary mapper.* Gainesville, FL: Teacher Support Software.

Kulik, C. C., & Kulik, J. A. (1982). Effects of ability grouping on secondary school students: A meta-analysis of evaluation findings. *American Educational Research Journal, 19,* 415–428.

Kurth, R. J., & Greenlaw, M. J. (1981). Research and practice in comprehension instruction in elementary classrooms. In G. H. McNinch (Ed.), *Comprehension: Process and product. First yearbook of the American Reading Forum* (pp. 51–56). Athens, GA: American Reading Forum.

Labbo, L. D., & Teale, W. H. (1990). Cross-age reading: A strategy for helping poor readers. *The Reading Teacher, 44*, 362–369.

Labe, M. L. (1971). Improve the dictionary's image. *Elementary English, 48*, 363–365.

LaBerge, D., & Samuels, S. J. (1974). Toward a theory of automatic information processing in reading. *Cognitive Psychology, 6*, 293–323.

Lahey, B., & Drabman, R. (1974). Facilitation of the acquisition and retention of sight word vocabulary through token reinforcement. *Journal of Applied Behavior Analysis, 7*, 307–312.

Lally, M. (1981). Computer-assisted teaching of sight-word recognition for mentally retarded school children. *American Journal of Mental Deficiency, 85*, 383–388.

Larkins, G., McKinney, C., Oldham-Buss, S., & Gilmore, A. (1985). *Teacher enthusiasm: A critical review.* Hattiesburg, MS: University of Southern Mississippi.

Larson, A. D., & Miller, J. B. (1978). The hearing impaired. In E. L. Meyen (Ed.), *Exceptional children and youth: An introduction* (pp. 223–251). Denver, CO: Love.

Learning Company. (1989). *The children's writing and publishing center.* Fremont, CA: Author.

Learning Company. (1993). *Storybook weaver.* Fremont, CA: Author.

Lehr, F. (1986). Direct instruction in reading. *The Reading Teacher, 39*, 706–709.

Leichter, H. J. (1984). Families as environments for literacy. In H. Goelman, Oberg, A. A. & Smith, F. (Eds.), *Awakening to literacy* (pp. 38–50). Exeter, NH: Heinemann.

Leinhardt, G., Zigmond, N., & Cooley, W. W. (1981). Reading instruction and its effects. *American Educational Research Journal, 18,* 356–358.

Leu, D. J., Jr., & Kinzer, C. K. (1987). *Effective reading instruction in the elementary grades.* Columbus, OH: Merrill/Prentice Hall.

Levin, H., & Kaplin, E. L. (1970). Grammatical structure and reading. In H. Levin & J. Williams (Eds.), *Basic studies in reading* (pp. 67–78). New York: Basic Books.

Levin, H., & Watson, J. (1963). The learning of variable grapheme-to-phoneme correspondences: Variations in the initial consonant position. In *A basic research program on reading* (U.S. Office of Education Cooperative Research Project No. 639, pp. 1–79). Ithaca, NY: Cornell University.

Levin, J. R., & Pressley, M. (1981). Improving children's prose comprehension: Selected strategies that seem to succeed. In C. M. Santa & B. I. Hayes (Eds.), *Children's prose comprehension: Research and practice* (pp. 68–81). Newark, DE: International Reading Association.

Liebert, R. E., & Sherk, J. K. (1970). Three Frostig visual perception sub-tests and specific reading tasks for kindergarten, first, and second grade children. *The Reading Teacher, 24*, 130–137.

Lipa, S. (1985). Test review: Diagnostic reading scales. *The Reading Teacher, 38*, 664–667.

Loban, W. (1963). *The language of elementary school children.* Urbana, IL: National Council of Teachers of English.

Long, R. (1995). Education issues part of busy fall schedule. *Reading Today, 13*(2), 8.

Lowenfield, B. (Ed.). (1973). *The visually handicapped child in school.* New York: John Day.

Lowrey, L. F., & Grafft, W. (1968). Paperback and reading attitudes. *The Reading Teacher, 21*, 618–623.

Lundgren, L., Lapp, D., & Flood, J. (1995). Strategies for gaining access to the information superhighway: Off the side street and on to the main road. *The Reading Teacher, 48*, 432–436.

Lundsteen, S. W. (1976). *Children learn to communicate.* Upper Saddle River, NJ: Prentice Hall.

MacGinitie, W. H., & MacGinitie, R. K. (1989). *Gates-MacGinitie reading tests: Teacher's manuals.* Chicago: Riverside.

Magic slate. (1985). Pleasantville, NY: Sunburst Communications.

Mandler, J. M., & Johnson, M. S. (1977). Remembrance of things passed: Story structure and recall. *Cognitive Psychology, 9*, 111–151.

Mangieri, J. N., Bader, L. A., & Walker, J. E. (1982). *Elementary reading.* New York: McGraw-Hill.

Mangieri, J. N., & Kahn, M. S. (1977). Is the Dolch list of 220 basic sight words irrelevant? *The Reading Teacher, 30*, 649–651.

The manhole. (1990). Menlo Park, CA: Activision, Mediagenic.

Manning, M. M., & Manning, G. L. (1984). Early readers and nonreaders from low socioeconomic environments: What their parents report. *The Reading Teacher, 38*, 32–34.

Many, J. (1988). *Lecture supplement.* Baton Rouge, LA: Louisiana State University.

Manzo, A. V. (1969). ReQuest Procedure. *Journal of Reading, 13*, 123–126.

Marland, S. P. (1972). *Education of the gifted and talented.* Washington, DC: U.S. Office of Education.

Marshall, N. (1983). Using story grammar to assess reading comprehension. *The Reading Teacher, 36*, 616–620.

Martin, J., & Evertson, C. M. (1980). *Teachers' interactions with reading groups of differing ability levels.* Washington, DC: National Institute of Education.

Marzano, R. J., Case, N., DeBooy, A., & Prochoruk, K. (1976). Are syllabication and reading ability related? *Journal of Reading, 19*, 545–547.

Mason, G. E. (1987). *Language experience recorder plus.* Gainesville, FL: Teacher Support Service.

Mason, J. M. (1984). A schema-theoretic view of the reading process as a basis for comprehension instruction. In G. G. Duffy, L. R. Roehler, & J. Mason (Eds.), *Comprehension instruction: Perspectives and suggestions* (pp. 62–81). New York: Addson-Wesley-Longman.

Mason, J. M., & Allen, J. (1986). A review of emergent literacy with implications for research and practice in reading. In E. Z. Rothkopf (Ed.), *Review of research in education* (pp. 52–69). Washington, DC: American Educational Research Association.

Mason, J. M., Osborn, J. H., & Rosenshine, B. V. (1977). *A consideration of skill hierarchy approaches to the teaching of reading* (Technical Report No. 42). Champaign, IL: University of Illinois.

Mavrogenes, N. A., Hanson, E. F., & Winkley, C. K. (1976). A guide to tests of factors that inhibit learning to read. *The Reading Teacher, 19*, 343–358.

May, F. B. (1982). *Reading as communication.* Columbus, OH: Merrill/Prentice Hall.

McBroom, M., Sparrow, J., & Eckstein, C. (1944). *Scale for determining a child's reader level.* Iowa City, IA: State University of Iowa, Bureau of Publications, Extension Division.

McCallister, J. M. (1965). Using paragraph clues as aids to understanding. *Journal of Reading, 8*, 11–16.

McCarthey, S. J., & Hoffman, J. V. (1995). The new basals: How are they different? *The Reading Teacher, 49*, 72–74.

McCullough, C. (1957). Responses of elementary school children to common types of reading comprehension questions. *Journal of Educational Research, 51*, 65–70.

McDonell, G. M. (1983). *Effects of instruction in the use of an abstract structural schema as an aid to comprehension and recall of written discourse.* Unpublished doctoral dissertation, Virginia Polytechnic Institute and State University.

McFeely, D. C. (1974). Syllabication usefulness in a basal and social studies vocabulary. *The Reading Teacher, 27*, 809–814.

McGee, L. M., & Richgels, D. J. (1990). *Learning how to mean: Exploration in the development of language.* Boston: Allyn & Bacon.

McGee, L. M., & Tompkins, G. E. (1995). Literature-based reading instruction: What's guiding the instruction? *Language Arts, 72*, 405–414.

McKeachie, W., & Kulik, J. (1975). Effective college teaching. In W. Wilen (Ed.), *Teaching and learning through discussion* (pp. 165–209). Springfield, IL: Charles C Thomas.

McKeever, K. (1992). *A place for owls.* Buffalo, NY: Firefly Books.

McKenna, M. C. (1990). *Computer-assisted reading achievement.* Burlington, NC: Southern Micro Systems.

McKenna, M. C., & Kear, D. J. (1990). Measuring attitude toward reading: A new tool for teachers. *The Reading Teacher, 37*, 629–639.

McKenna, M. C., & Kear, D. J. (1990). Measuring attitude toward reading: A new tool for teachers. *The Reading Teacher, 43*, 626–639.

McKenna, M. C., & Layton, K. (1990). Concurrent validity of Cloze as a measure of intersentential comprehension. *Journal of Educational Psychology, 82*, 372–377.

McNeil, J. D., & Keislar, E. R. (1963). Value of the oral response in beginning reading: An experimental study using programmed instruction. *British Journal of Educational Psychology, 33*, 162–168.

Meek, A. (1988). On teaching as a profession: A conversation with Linda Darling-Hammond. *Educational Leadership, 46*, 11–17.

Meisal, S., & Glass, G. G. (1970). Voluntary reading interests and the interest content of basal readers. *The Reading Teacher, 23*, 655–659.

Merserau, Y., Glover, M., & Cherland, M. (1989). Dancing on the edge. *Language Arts, 66*, 109–118.

Meyer, B. J. F. (1974). *Structure of prose: Implications for teachers of reading* (Research Report No. 3.) Tempe, AZ: Arizona State University, Department of Educational Psychology.

Meyer, B. J. F. (1975). *The organization of prose and its effect on memory.* Amsterdam: North Holland.

Miller, G. M., & Mason, G. E. (1983). Dramatic improvisation: Risk-free role playing for improving reading performance. *The Reading Teacher, 37*, 128–131.

Miller, J. W., & McKenna, M. (1989). *Teaching reading in the elementary classroom.* Scottsdale, AZ: Gorsuch Scarisbrick.

Milone, M. N., Jr. (1995, October). Electronic portfolios: Who's doing them and how? *Technology and Learning, 16*, 28–29, 32, 34, 36.

Moacdieh, C. (1981, April). *Grouping for reading in the primary grades: Evidence on the revisionist argument.* Paper presented at the meeting of the American Educational Research Association, Los Angeles, CA.

Moldofsky, P. B. (1983). Teaching students to determine the central story problem: A practical application of schema theory. *The Reading Teacher, 36*, 740–745.

Montessori, M. (1966). *The secret of childhood.* New York: Ballantine.

Moray, G. (1978). What does research say about the reading interests of children in the intermediate grades? *The Reading Teacher, 31*, 763–768.

Morrice, C., & Simmons, M. (1991). Beyond reading buddies: A whole language cross-age program. *The Reading Teacher, 44*, 572–579.

Morrow, L. M. (1982, July–August). Relationships between literature programs, library corner designs, and children's use of literature. *Journal of Educational Research, 75*, 339–344.

Morrow, L. M. (1983). Home and school correlates of early interest in literature. *Journal of Educational Research, 76*, 221–230.

Morrow, L. M. (1989). *Literacy development in the early years.* Upper Saddle River, NJ: Prentice Hall.

Mosenthal, P. B. (1989). The whole language approach: Teachers between a rock and a hard place. *The Reading Teacher, 42*, 628–629.

Mullis, I. V. S., & Jenkins, L. B. (1990, January). *The reading report card, 1971–1988: Trends from the nation's report card.* Princeton, NJ: National Assessment of Educational Progress.

Nardelli, R. R. (1957). Some aspects of creative reading. *Journal of Educational Research, 50*, 495–508.

National Advisory Committee on Handicapped Children. (1986). *First annual report, subcommittee on education of the committee on labor and public welfare, U.S. Senate.* Washington, DC: U.S. Government Printing Office.

National Education Association. (1976). America's other children—Bilingual multicultural education: Hope for the culturally alienated. *NEA Reporter, 15*, 13.

National Education Association. (1992). *Status of American public school teachers, 1991.* Washington, DC: Author.

Nelson, R. B., Cummings, J. A., & Boltman, H. (1991). Teaching basic concepts to students who are educable mentally handicapped. *Teaching Exceptional Children, 23*, 12–15.

Nelson, R. M. (1973). Getting children into reference books. *Elementary English, 50*, 884–887.

Niles, J. A., & Harris, L. A. (1981). The context of comprehension. *Reading Horizons, 22*, 33–42.

Ninio, A. (1980). Picture book reading in mother infant dyads belonging to two subgroups in Israel. *Child Development, 51*, 587–590.

Noll, E., & Goodman, K. (1995). "Using a howitzer to kill a butterfly": Teaching literature with basals. *The New Advocate, 4*, 113–123.

O'Masta, G. A., & Wolf, J. M. (1991). Encouraging independent reading through the reading millionaires project. *The Reading Teacher, 44*, 656–662.

Oakan, R., Wierner, M., & Conner, W. (1971). Identification, organization, and reading comprehension for good and poor readers. *Journal of Educational Psychology, 62*, 71–78.

Ogbu, J. (1990). Minority education in comparative perspective. *Journal of Negro Education, 59*, 45–57.

Ogle, D. M. (1986). K-W-L: A teaching model that develops active reading of expository text. *The Reading Teacher, 39*, 564–570.

Ohnmacht, D. C. (1983). The effects of letter knowledge on achievement in reading in the first grade. In L. M. Gentile, M. L. Kamil, & J. S. Blanchard (Eds.), *Reading research revisited* (pp. 141–142). Columbus, OH: Merrill/Prentice Hall.

Oja, L. A. (1996). Using story frames to develop reading comprehension. *Journal of Adolescent and Adult Literacy, 40*(2), 129–130.

Olenchak, F. R., & Renzulli, J. S. (1989). The effectiveness of the schoolwide enrichment model on selected aspects of elementary school change. *Gifted Child Quarterly, 33*, 36–46.

Ollila, L. (1976). Reading: Preparing the child. In P. Lamb & R. Arnold (Eds.), *Reading: Foundations and instructional strategies* (pp. 57–72). Belmont, CA: Wadsworth.

Olson, A. V., & Johnson, C. L. (1970). Structure and predictive validity of the Frostig developmental test of visual perception in grades one and three. *Journal of Special Education, 4*, 49–52.

Olson, W. C. (1949). *Child development.* Boston: D. C. Heath.

Orlando, V. P. (1979). Notetaking vs. notehaving: A comparison while studying from text. In M. L. Kamil & A. J. Moe (Eds.), *Reading research: Studies and applications. The 28th yearbook of the National Reading Conference* (pp. 177–181). Clemson, SC: National Reading Conference.

Otto, W. (1973). Evaluating instruments for assessing needs and growth in reading. In W. H. MacGinitie (Ed.), *Assessment problems in reading* (pp. 126–151). Newark, DE: International Reading Association.

Otto, W., & Chester, R. (1971). Sight words for beginning readers. *The Journal of Educational Research, 65*, 425–443.

Palincsar, A. S. (1984). The quest for meaning from expository text: A teacher guided journey. In G. G. Duffy, L. R. Roehler, & J. Mason (Eds.), *Comprehension instruction: Perspectives and suggestions* (pp. 251–264). New York: Addison-Wesley-Longman.

Paradis, E. (1974). The appropriateness of visual discrimination exercise in reading readiness materials. *Journal of Educational Research, 67*, 276–278.

Parker, F. W. (1894). *Talks on pedagogics: An outline of the theory of concentration* [Microform]. Chicago: Kellogg.

Peacock Hill Working Group. (1991). Problems and promises in special education and related services for children and youth with emotional or behavioral disorders. *Behavioral Disorders, 16*, 299–313.

Pearson, P. D., & Fielding, L. (1982). Research update: Listening comprehension. *Language Arts, 59*, 617–629.

Pearson, P. D., & Johnson, D. (1978). *Teaching reading comprehension.* New York: Holt, Rinehart, & Winston.

Peck, J. (1989). Using storytelling to promote language and literacy development. *The Reading Teacher, 43*, 138–141.

Pennema, E., & Peterson P. (1987). Effective teaching for boys and girls: The same or different? In D. Berliner & B. Rosenshine (Eds.), *Talks to teachers* (pp. 111–125). Hillsdale, NJ: Erlbaum.

Persell, C. (1977). *Education and inequality: The roots and results of stratification in American schools.* New York: Free Press.

Perez, B. (1996). Instructional conversations as opportunities for English language acquisition for culturally and linguistically diverse students. *Language Arts, 73*, 173–181.

Perez, E. (1981). Oral language competence improves reading skills of Mexican American third graders. *The Reading Teacher, 35*, 24–29.

Peterson, P., Wilkinson, L., & Hallinan, M. (1984). *The social context of instruction: Group organization and group processes.* New York: Academic Press.

Pflaster, G. (1980). A factor analysis of variables related to academic performance of hearing impaired children in regular classes. *The Volta Review, 82*, 71.

Piaget, J. (1969). *The psychology of intelligence.* Paterson, NJ: Littlefield, Adams.

Pikulski, J. (1973). The validity of three brief measures of intelligence for disabled readers. *Journal of Educational Research, 67,* 67–68, 80.

Pikulski, J. (1990). Informal reading inventories (assessments). *The Reading Teacher, 43*, 514–516.

Pikulski, J., & Kiroch, I. S. (1979). Organization for instruction. In R. C. Calfee & P. A. Drum (Eds.), *Teaching reading in compensatory classes* (pp. 72–86, 187–191). Newark, DE: International Reading Association.

Pikulski, J. J., & Shanahan, T. (1982). Informal reading inventories: A critical analysis. In J. Pikulski & T. Shanahan (Eds.), *Approaches to the informal evaluation of reading* (pp. 94–116). Newark, DE: International Reading Association.

Plattor, E. E., & Woestehoff, E. S. (1970). Specific reading disabilities of disadvantaged children. In W. Durr (Ed.), *Reading difficulties: Diagnosis, correction and remediation* (pp. 55–60). Newark, DE: International Reading Association.

Plessas, G., & Oakes, C. R. (1964). Prereading experiences of selected early readers. *The Reading Teacher, 18*, 241–245.

Poostay, E. J. (1984). Show me your underlines: A strategy to teach comprehension. *The Reading Teacher, 37*, 828–829.

Prentice, W. C., & Tabbert, J. C. (1978). *Creative dramatics and reading: A question of basics.* Grand Forks, ND: University of North Dakota, Center for Teaching and Learning.

Price, L. (1976). How thirty-seven gifted children learned to read. *The Reading Teacher, 30*, 44–49.

Pryor, F. (1975). Poor reading: Lack of self-esteem? *The Reading Teacher, 28*, 359.

Purcell-Gates, V., L'Allier, S., & Smith, D. (1995). Literacy at the Harts' and the Larsons': Diversity among poor innercity families. *The Reading Teacher, 48*, 572–578.

Purcell-Gates, V., McIntyre, E., & Freppon, P. A. (1995). Learning written storybook language in school: A comparison of low SES children in skill-based and whole language classrooms. *American Educational Research Journal, 32*, 659–685.

Purves, A. C., & Beach, R. (1972). *Literature and the reader: Research in response to literature, reading interests, and the teaching of literature.* Urbana, IL: National Council of Teachers of English.

Pusch, M. (1981). *Multicultural education: A cross-cultural training approach.* Chicago: Intercultural Network.

Quandt, I. (1972). *Self-concept and reading.* Newark, DE: International Reading Association.

Radencich, M. C. (1986). Test review: Gray oral reading tests-revised and formal reading inventory. *Journal of Reading, 30*, 136–139.

Rankin, E. F., & Overholzer, B. M. (1969). Reaction of intermediate grade children to contextual clues. *Journal of Reading Behavior, 1*, 50–73.

Rasinski, T., & Padak, N. (1990). Multicultural learning through children's literature. *Language Arts, 67*, 576–580.

Readance, J. E., & Harris, M. M. (1980). False prerequisites in the teaching of comprehension. *Reading Improvement, 17*, 18–21.

Reid, D. K., Hresko, W. P., & Hammill, D. D. (1989). *Manual: The tests of early reading ability* (2nd ed.) Austin, TX: Pro-Ed.

Reinking, D. (1987). *The comprehension connection.* St. Louis, MO: Milliken.

Renzulli, J. S. (1982). Dear Mr. and Mrs. Copernicus: We regret to inform you . . . . *Gifted Child Quarterly, 26*, 11–14.

Renzulli, J. S., & Purcell, J. H. (1996). Gifted education: A look around and a look ahead. *Roeper Review, 18*(3), 173–178.

Reutzel, D. R. (1984). Story mapping: An alternative approach to comprehension. *Reading World, 24*, 18–25.

Reutzel, D. R., & Cooter, R. B., Jr. (1991). Organizing for effective instruction: The reading workshop. *The Reading Teacher, 44*, 548–555.

Reutzel, D. R., & Hollingsworth, P. M. (1988). Whole language and the practitioner. *Academic Therapy, 23*, 405–416.

Reutzel, D. R., & Larson, N. S. (1995). Look what they've done to real children's books in the new basal readers! *Language Arts, 72*, 495–507.

Rich, S. J. (1985). Restoring power to teachers: The impact of "whole language." *Language Arts, 62*, 717–724.

Richards, J. C., Gipe, J. P., & Thompson, B. (1987). Teachers' beliefs about good reading instruction. *Reading Psychology, 1*, 1–6.

Richgels, D., Poremba, K. J., & McGee, L. M. (1996). Kindergartners talk about print: Phonemic awareness in meaningful contexts. *The Reading Teacher, 49*, 632–642.

Rickelman, R. J., & Henk, W. A. (1990). Telecommunications in the reading classroom. *The Reading Teacher, 43*, 418–419.

Riddle, S. (1996). Is your classroom a literature oasis? *Gifted Child Today, 19*(5), 30–33.

Ridley, L. (1990). Enacting change in elementary school programs: Implementing a whole language perspective. *The Reading Teacher, 43*, 640–646.

Robb, L. (1994, December–1995, January). Read-aloud partnerships. *Reading Today, 12*(3), 26.

Robinson, F. P. (1970). *Effective study* (4th ed.). New York, Harper & Row.

Robinson, H. (1964). Developing critical readers. In R. G. Stauffer (Ed.), *Dimensions of critical reading* (pp. 72–76). Proceedings of the Annual Education and Reading Conference. Newark, DE: University of Delaware.

Robinson, H., & Weintraub, S. (1973). Research related to children's interests and to developmental values of reading. *Library Trends, 22*, 81–108.

Roeder, H. H., & Lee, N. (1973). Twenty-five teacher tested ways to encourage voluntary reading. *The Reading Teacher, 27*, 48–50.

Roettger, D. (1980). Elementary students' attitudes toward reading. *The Reading Teacher, 33*, 451–453.

Roney, R. C. (1984). Background experience is the foundation of success in learning to read. *The Reading Teacher, 38*, 196–199.

Rosenblatt, L. M. (1969). Towards a transactional theory of reading. *Journal of Reading Behavior, 1*, 31–49.

Rosenholtz, S. J. (1984). Modifying a status-organizing process of the traditional classroom. In J. Berger and M. Zelditch, Jr., (Eds.), *Pure and applied studies in expectation states theory* (pp. 126–137). San Francisco: Jossey-Bass.

Rosenshine, B. V. (1980). Skill hierarchies in reading comprehension. In R. J. Spiro, B. C. Bruce, & W. F. Brewer (Eds.), *Theoretical issues in reading comprehension* (pp. 221–246). Hillsdale, NJ: Erlbaum.

Rosenshine, B. V., & Berliner, D. C. (1978). Academic engaged time. *British Journal of Teacher Education, 4*, 3–16.

Rosenshine, B. V., & Furst. (1997). In K. A. Acheson & M. D. Gall (Eds.), *Techniques in the clinical supervision of teachers: Preservice and inservice applications* (4th ed.). New York: Addison-Wesley-Longman.

Rosenshine, B. V., & Stevens, R. (1984). Classroom instruction in reading. In D. Pearson (with R. Barr), M. L. Kamil, & P. Mosenthal (Eds.), *Handbook of reading research* (pp. 560–618). New York: Addison-Wesley-Longman.

Roser, N. L., Holfman, J. V., & Farest, C. (1990). Language, literature, and at-risk children. *The Reading Teacher, 43*, 554–561.

Ross, R. (1964). A look at listeners. *Elementary School Journal, 64*, 369–372.

Rossi, R., & Stringfield, S. (1995). What we must do for students placed at risk. *Phi Delta Kappan, 77*, 73–76.

Rothman, R. (1990, March 14). NEAP board adopts blueprint for 1992 reading test. *Education Week*, p. 40.

Routman, R. (1996). *Literacy at the crossroads: Crucial talk about reading, writing, and other teaching dilemmas.* Portsmouth, NH: Heinemann.

Routman, R., & Butler, A. (1995). Phonics fuss: Facts, fiction, phonemes, and fun. *School Talk, 1*(2), 6–8.

Routman, R., & Maxim, D. (1996). Invented spelling: What it is and what it isn't. *School Talk, 1(4)*, 15–19.

Ruck, L. V. (1974). Some questions about the teaching of syllabication rules. *The Reading Teacher, 27*, 583–588.

Ruddell, R. B. (1974). *Reading-language instruction: Innovative practices.* Upper Saddle River, NJ: Prentice Hall.

Ruddell, R. B. (1986). Vocabulary learning: A process model and criteria for evaluating instructional strategies. *Journal of Reading Behavior, 29*, 581–587.

Rummelhart, D. E. (1976). *Toward an interactive model of reading center for human information services?* (Technical Report No. 56). San Diego, CA: University of California.

Rummelhart, D. E. (1980). Schemata: The building blocks of cognition. In R. J. Spiro, B. C. Bruce, & W. F. Brewer (Eds.), *Theoretical issues in reading comprehension* (pp. 372–396). Hillsdale, NJ: Erlbaum.

Rummelhart, D. E. (1984). Understanding understanding. In J. Flood (Ed.), *Understanding reading comprehension* (pp. 1–20). Newark, DE: International Reading Association, 1984.

Rupley, W. H., & Blair, T. R. (1981). Specification of reading instructional practices associated with pupil achievement gains. *Educational and Psychological Research, 1*, 161–169.

Russavage, M., Lorton, L., & Millham, R. (1985). Making responsible instructional decisions about reading: What teachers think and do about reading. *The Reading Teacher, 39,* 314–317.

Russell, D. H. (1956). *Children's Thinking.* Boston: Ginn.

Rystrom, R. (1977). Reflections of meaning. *Journal of Reading Behavior, 9*, 193–200.

Samuels, S. J. (1976). Automatic decoding and reading comprehension. *Language Arts, 53*, 323–325.

Sanders, N. M. (1966). *Classroom questions: What kinds?* New York: Harper & Row.

Sandford, H. A. (1980). Directed and free search of the school atlas map. *The Cartographic Journal, 71*, 83–92.

Schell, L. M. (1968). Teaching structural analysis. *The Reading Teacher, 21*, 133–137.

Schell, L. M. (1982). The validity of the potential level via listening comprehension: A cautionary note. *Reading Psychology, 3*, 271–276.

Schell, L. M., & Jennings, R. E. (1981). Test review: Durrell analysis of reading difficulty (3rd ed.). *The Reading Teacher, 35*, 204–210.

Schickedanz, J. A., & Sullivan, M. (1984). Mom, what does U-F-F spell? *Language Arts, 61*, 7–17.

Schieffelin, B. B., & Cochran-Smith, M. (1984). Learning to read culturally. Literacy before schooling. In H. Goelman, A. A. Oberg, & F. Smith (Eds.), *Awakening literacy* (pp. 210–234). NH: Heinemann.

Schrank, F. A., & Engels, D. W. (1981). Bibliotherapy as a counseling adjunct: Research findings. *Personnel and Guidance Journal, 60*, 143–147.

Schwartz, E., & Sheff, A. (1975). Student involvement in questioning for comprehension. *The Reading Teacher, 29*, 150–154.

Schwartz, R. M., & Stanovich, K. E. (1981). Flexibility in the use of graphic and contextual information by good and poor readers. *Journal of Reading Behavior, 13*, 263–269.

Sebasta, S. L. (1979). What do young people think about the literature they read? *Reading Newsletter, 8.* Rockleigh, NJ: Allyn & Bacon.

Shannon, T. (1989). *Broken promises: Reading instruction in twentieth century America.* New York: Bergin & Garvey.

Shaywitz, S. E., & Shaywitz, B. A. (1987, April). *Attention deficit disorder: Current perspectives.* Paper presented at the National Conference on Learning Disabilities, Bethesda, MD.

Sheridan, E. M. (1978). A *review of research on schema theory and its implications for reading: Instruction in secondary reading.* (ERIC Document Reproduction Service No. ED 167 947).

Simons, H. D. (1972). Linguistic skills and reading comprehension. In H. A. Klein (Ed.), *The quest for competency in reading* (pp. 69–81). Newark, DE: International Reading Association.

Simpson, A. (1996). Critical questions: Whose questions? *The Reading Teacher, 50*, 118–127.

Simpson, M. L. (1986). PORPE: A writing strategy for studying and learning in the content areas. *Journal of Reading, 29*, 407–414.

Singer, H. (1969). Theoretical models of reading. *Journal of Communications, 19*, 134–156.

Singer, H. (1971). Teaching word recognition skills. In M. A. Dawson (Ed.), *Teaching word recognition skills.* Newark, DE: International Reading Association.

Singer, H. (1978). Active comprehension: From answering to asking questions. *The Reading Teacher, 3l*, 901–908.

Singer, H. S., & Ruddell. R. (Eds.). (1985). *Theoretical models and processes of reading* (3rd ed.) Newark, DE: International Reading Association.

Singer, H. S., Samuels, J., & Spiroff, J. (1973). The effect of pictures and contextual condition on learning responses to printed words. *Reading Research Quarterly, 9*, 555–567.

Sippola, A. E. (1995). K-W-L-S. *The Reading Teacher, 40*, 542–543.

Slater, M. (1973). Individualized language arts in the middle grades. *The Reading Teacher, 27*, 253–256.

Slaughter, H. B. (1988). Indirect and direct instruction in a whole language classroom. *The Reading Teacher, 42*, 30–34.

Slavin, R. (1983). *Cooperative learning.* New York: Longman.

Slavin, R. (1989/1990). Research on cooperative learning: Consensus and controversy. *Educational Leadership, 47*, 52–54.

Slosson, R. L. (1990). *Slosson oral reading test.* East Aurora, NY: Slosson Educational.

Smith, C. B. (1978). *Teaching in secondary school content subjects.* New York: Holt, Rinehart, & Winston.

Smith, C. B., & Elliot, P. G. (1979). *Reading activities for middle and secondary schools.* New York: Holt, Rinehart, & Winston.

Smith, F. (1988). *Understanding reading: A psycholinguistic analysis of reading and learning to read* (4th ed.). Hillsdale, NJ: Erlbaum.

Smith, H. P., & Dechant, E. V. (1961). *Psychology in teaching reading.* Upper Saddle River, NJ: Prentice Hall.

Smith, M. C. (1990). A longitudinal investigation of reading attitude development from childhood to adulthood. *Journal of Educational Research, 83*, 215–229.

Smith, M. C., & Bean, T. W. (1983). Four strategies that develop children's story comprehension and writing. *The Reading Teacher, 37*, 295–301.

Smith, N. B. (1965). Patterns of writing in different subject areas. *Journal of Reading, 8*, 31–37.

Smith, N. B. (1974). *American reading instruction* (3rd ed.). Newark, DE: International Reading Association.

Smith, R. J., & Johnson, D. D. (1980). *Teaching children to read.* Reading, MA: Addison-Wesley-Longman.

Smith-Burke, M. T. (1987). Classroom practices and classroom interaction during reading instruction: What's going on? In J. R. Squire (Ed.), *The dynamics of language learning: Research in reading and English* (pp. 226–265). Urbana, IL: National Conference on Research in English. ERIC Clearinghouse on Reading and Communication Skills. (ERIC Document Reproduction No. ED 280 080).

Snow, C. E. (1983). Literacy and language: Relationships during the preschool years. *Harvard Educational Review, 53*, 165–189.

Spache, G. D. (1963). *Toward better reading.* Champaign, IL: Garrard Press.

Spache, G. D. (1972). *Diagnostic reading scales* (rev. ed.). Monterey, CA: CTB/McGraw- Hill.

Spache, G. D. (1973). *Diagnostic reading scales* (Technical Bulletin). Monterey, CA: CTB/McGraw-Hill.

Spache, G. D. (1976). *Diagnosing and correcting reading disabilities.* Boston: Allyn & Bacon.

Spache, G. D., & Spache, E. B. (1977). *Reading in the elementary school* (4th ed.). Boston: Allyn & Bacon.

Spache, G. D., & Spache, E. B. (1986). *Reading in the elementary school* (5th ed.). Boston: Allyn & Bacon.

Spiro, R. J., & Myers, A. (1984). Individual differences and underlying cognitive processes in reading. In P. D. Pearson (Ed.), *Handbook of reading research* (pp. 471–501). New York: Addison-Wesley-Longman.

Squire, J. R. (1987). Introduction: A special issue on the state of assessment in reading. *The Reading Teacher, 40*, 724–725.

Stahl, N. A., King, J. R., & Henk, W. A. (1991). Enhancing students' notetaking through training and evaluation. *Journal of Reading, 34*, 614–623.

Stahl, S. A., Jacobson, M. G., Davis, C. E., & Davis, R. L. (1989, Winter). Prior knowledge and difficult vocabulary in the comprehension of unfamiliar text. *Reading Research Quarterly, 24*, 27–43.

Stainback, S., & Stainback, W. (Eds.). (1992). *Curricular considerations in inclusive classrooms: Facilitating learning for all students.* Baltimore, MD: Paul H. Brookes.

Stainback, W., Stainback, S., & Stefanich, G. (1996). Learning together in inclusive classrooms: What about the curriculum? *Teaching Exceptional Children, 28*(3), 14–19.

Stallings, J. A., & Kaskowitz, D. (1974). *Follow-through classroom observation evaluation, 1972–1973.* Menlo Park, CA: Stanford Research Institute.

Standards for English language arts. (1996). Newark, DE: International Reading Association; Urbana, IL: National Council of Teachers of English.

Stanovich, K. E. (1980). Toward an inter-active compensatory model of individual differences in the development of reading fluency. *Reading Research Quarterly, 16*, 34–35, 42–45.

Stanovich, K. E. (1990). A call for an end to the paradigm wars in reading research. *Journal of Reading Behavior, 3*, 221–231.

Stanovich, K. E. (1994). Are we overselling literacy? In J. Gillet & C. Temple (Eds.), *Understanding reading problems: Assessment and instruction* (pp. 90–99). New York: HarperCollins.

Stauffer, R. G. (1970). *The language-experience approach to the teaching of reading.* New York: Harper & Row.

Stein, N. L., & Glenn, C. G. (1979). An analysis of story comprehension in elementary school children. In R. O. Freedle (Ed.), *New directions in discourse processing* (pp. 192–206). Norwood, NJ: Ablex.

Steptoe, J. (1987). *Mufaro's beautiful daughters: An African tale.* New York: Lothrop, Lee & Shepard.

Stern, P. R., & Shavelson, R. (1981, April). *The relationship between teachers' grouping decisions and instructional behavior: An ethnographic study of reading instruction.* Paper presented at the meeting of the American Educational Research Association, Los Angeles, CA.

Stevens, K. C. (1980). The effect of background knowledge on the reading comprehension of ninth graders. *Journal of Reading Behavior, 12*, 451–454.

Stevens, R. J., & Slavin, R. E. (1991). When cooperative learning improves the achievement of students with mild disabilities: A response to Tateyama-Sniezek. *Exceptional Children, 57*, 276–280.

Sticht, T. G., Beck, L. J., Hanke, R. N., Kleiman, G. M., & James, J. H. (1974). *Auding and reading: A developmental model.* Alexandria, VA: Human Resource Research Organization.

Stoodt, B. D. (1972). The relationship between understanding grammatical conjunctions and reading comprehension. *Elementary English, 49*, 502–504.

Strange, M. (1980). Instructional implications of a conceptual theory of reading comprehension. *The Reading Teacher, 33*, 392.

Strickland, D. S. (1972). Black is beautiful vs. white is right. *Elementary English, 49*, 220–224.

Strickland, D. S. (1994/1995). Reinventing our literacy programs: Books, basics, balance. *The Reading Teacher, 48*, 294–301.

Strickland, D. S. (1996). In search of balance: Restructuring our literacy programs. *Reading Today, 14*(2), 32.

Strickland, D. S., & Morrow, L. M. (1988). New perspectives on young children learning to read and write. *The Reading Teacher, 42*, 70–71.

Strickland, D. S., & Morrow, L. M. (1988). Reading, writing, and oral language. *The Reading Teacher, 42*, 240–241.

Strickland, D. S., & Morrow, L. M. (1989a). Assessment and early literacy. *The Reading Teacher, 42*, 634–635.

Strickland, D. S., & Morrow, L. M. (1989b). Oral language development: Children as storytellers. *The Reading Teacher, 43*, 260–261.

Strickland, D. S., & Morrow, L. M. (1990). Emerging readers and writers: Sharing big books. *The Reading Teacher, 43*, 342–343.

Strickler, D. J. (1977). Planning the affective component. In R. A. Earle, (Ed.), *Classroom practice in reading* (pp. 3–9). Newark, DE: International Reading Association.

Success with writing. (1988). New York: Scholastic.

Sulzby, E. (1985). Children's emergent reading of favorite storybooks: A developmental study. *Reading Research Quarterly, 22*, 458–481.

Swanson, B. M., & Willis, D. J. (1979). *Understanding exceptional children and youth.* Chicago: Rand McNally.

Taba, H. (1976). The teaching of thinking. *Elementary English, 42*, 534.

Tauber, R. (1990). *Classroom management from a–z.* Fort Worth: Holt, Rinehart & Winston.

Taylor, D. (1983). *Family literacy.* Exeter, NH: Heinemann.

Taylor, S. E., Frackenpohl, H., & White, C. (1969). *A revised core vocabulary: A basic vocabulary for grades 1–8, An advanced vocabulary for grades 9–13.* Huntington, NY: Educational Development Laboratories.

Taylor, W. L. (1953). Cloze procedure: A new tool for measuring readability. *Journalism Quarterly, 30*, 415–433.

Teale, W. H. (1978). Positive environments for learning to read: What studies of early readers tell us. *Language Arts, 55*, 922–932.

Teale, W. H. (1987). Home background and young children's literacy development. In W. H. Teale &

E. Sulzby (Eds.), *Emergent literacy: Writing and reading* (pp. 173–206). Norwood, NJ: Ablex.

Teale, W., Hiebert, E., & Chittenden, E. (1987). Assessing young children's literacy development. *The Reading Teacher, 40*, 772–777.

Teale, W., & Sulzby, E. (1987). *Emergent literacy: Writing and reading*. Norwood, NJ: Ablex.

Terman, L. M., & Oden, M. H. (1959). *The gifted group on midlife: Thirty-five years' follow-up of the superior child. Genetic studies of genius: Vol. 5.* Stanford, CA: Stanford University Press.

Thome, R. (1996). The fourth R is research. *Electronic Learning, 16*(2), 58.

Thorndike, E. (1971). Reading and reasoning: A study of mistakes in paragraph reading. *Journal of Educational Psychology, 8*, 323–332.

Thorndyke, P. W. (1977). Cognitive structures in comprehension and memory of narrative discourse. *Cognitive Psychology, 9*, 77–110.

Tierney, R. J., Carter, M. A., & DeSai, L. E. (1991). *Portfolio assessment in the reading-writing classroom.* Norwood, MA: Christopher-Gordon.

Tierney, R. J., Mosenthal, J., & Kantor, R. M. (1984). Classroom applications of text analysis: Toward improving text selection and use. In J. Flood (Ed.), *Promoting reading comprehension* (pp. 139–160). Newark, DE: International Reading Association.

Tillman, C. E. (1984). Bibliotherapy for adolescents: An annotated research review. *Journal of Reading, 27*, 713–719.

Tomkins, G. (1997). *Literacy for the twenty-first century: A balanced approach.* Upper Saddle River, NJ: Prentice Hall.

Trelease, J. (1995). *The read-aloud handbook* (4th ed.). New York: Penguin.

Trelease, J. (1996). Have you read to your kids today? *Instructor, 105*(8), 56–59.

Trybus, R. J., & Karchmer, M. A. (1977). School achievement scores of hearing impaired children: National data on achievement status and growth patterns. *American Annals of the Deaf, 122*, 62–69.

Turner, J., & Paris, S. G. (1995). How literacy tasks influence children's motivation for literacy. *The Reading Teacher, 48*, 662–673.

Turner, T. N., & Alexander, J. E. (1975). Fostering early creative reading. *Language Arts, 52*, 786.

U.S. National Joint Committee on Learning Disabilities. (1981). Revised definition of LD. *The Reading Teacher, 35*, 134–135.

Vacca, J. A. L., Vacca, R. T., & Gove, M. K. (1987). *Reading and learning to read.* Boston: Little, Brown.

Vacca, R. (1996). The reading wars: Who will be the winners? Who will be the losers? *Reading Today, 14*(2), 3.

Valencia, S. W. (1990a). A portfolio approach to classroom reading assessment: The whys, whats, and hows. *The Reading Teacher, 43*, 338–340.

Valencia, S. W. (1990b). Alternative assessment: Separating the wheat from the chaff. *The Reading Teacher, 44*, 60–61.

Vallecorsa, A. L., Ledford, R. R., & Parnell, G. G. (1991). Strategies for teaching composition skills to students with learning disabilities. *Teaching Exceptional Children, 23*, 52–55.

Veatch, J. (1959). *Individualizing your reading program.* New York: Putnam.

Veatch, J. (1996). From the vantage of retirement. *The Reading Teacher, 49*, 510–516.

Vinyard, E. E., & Massey, H. W. (1957). The interrelationship of certain linguistic skills and their relationship with scholastic achievement when intelligence is ruled constant. *Journal of Educational Psychology, 48*, 279–286.

Wade, S. E. (1990). Using think-alouds to assess comprehension. *The Reading Teacher, 43*, 442–451.

Walberg, H. J., & Tsai, S.-L. (1985). Correlates of reading achievement and attitude: A national assessment study. *Journal of Educational Research, 78*, 159–167.

Walker, M. L. (1995). Help for the "Fourth grade slump": SRQ2R plus instruction in text structure and main idea. *Reading Horizons, 36*(1), 38–57.

Wang, M. C. (1981). Mainstreaming exceptional children: Some instructional design and implementation considerations. *The Elementary School Journal, 81*, 195–221.

Wardhaugh, R. (1966). Syl-lab-i-ca-tion. *Elementary English, 43*, 785–788.

Watson, D. J. (1989). Defining and describing whole language. *The Elementary School Journal, 90*, 129–141.

Waugh, R. F., & Howell, K. W. (1975). Teaching modem syllabication. *The Reading Teacher, 29*, 20–25.

Wepman, J. (1973). *Auditory discrimination test.* Chicago: Language Research and Associates.

Wepner, S. B. (1990). Holistic computer applications in literature-based classrooms. *The Reading Teacher, 44*, 12–19.

Wheeler, H. E., & Howell, E. A. (1930). A first grade vocabulary study. *Elementary School Journal, 31*, 52–60.

Whitehurst, F. F., Lonigan, C. J., Fischal, J. E., DeBaryshe, B. D., Valdez-Manchaca, M. C., & Culfield, M. (1988). Accelerating language development through picturebook reading. *Developmental Psychology, 24*, 552–559.

Wiederholt, J. L. (1985). *Formal reading inventory.* Austin, TX: Pro-Ed.

Wiederholt, J. L., & Bryant, B. R. (1986). *Gray oral reading tests—Revised Manual.* Austin, TX: Pro-Ed.

Wiederholt, J. L., & Bryant, B. R. (1992). *Gray oral reading tests—Revised Manual.* Austin, TX: Pro-Ed.

Williams, J. P. (1968). Successive vs. concurrent presentations of multiple grapheme-phoneme correspondences. *Journal of Educational Psychology, 59*, 309–314.

Williams, P., Reese, C., Campbell, J., Mazzeo, J., & Phillips, G. (1994). *1994 NAEP reading: A first look. Findings from the National Assessment of Educational Progress.* Washington, DC: U.S. Department of Education, Office of Educational Research and Improvement.

Wilson, M. M. (1980). The effect of question types in varying placements on the reading comprehension of upper elementary students. *Reading Psychology, 1*, 93–102.

Winkley, C. (1966). Which accent generalizations are worth teaching? *The Reading Teacher, 20,* 219–224, 253.

Wixson, K. K. (1984). Level of importance of post-questions and children's learning from text. *American Educational Research Journal, 21,* 419–433.

Wolfe, E. (1965). Advertising and the elementary language arts. *Elementary English, 42,* 42–44.

Wong, B. Y. L., & Jones, W. (1981). *Increasing metacomprehension in learning disabled and normally achieving students through self-questioning training* [Mimeograph]. Burnaby, BC, Canada: Simon Fraser University.

Wood, K. D. (1985). Free associational assessment: An alternative to traditional testing. *Journal of Reading, 29,* 106–111.

Wood, M., & Brown, M. (1979). Beginning readers' recognition of taught words in various contextual settings. In M. L. Kamil & A. J. Moe (Eds.), *Reading research studies and applications. The 28th yearbook of the National Reading Conference* (pp. 55–61). Clemson, SC: National Reading Conference.

Yaden, D. B., Jr., & McGee, L. M. (1984). Reading as a meaning seeking activity: What children's questions reveal. In J. Niles (Ed.), *The 33rd yearbook of the National Reading Conference* (pp. 101–109). Rochester, NY: National Reading Conference.

Yopp, H. K. (1995a). A test for assessing phonemic awareness in young children. *The Reading Teacher, 49,* 20–29.

Yopp, H. K. (1995b). Read-aloud books for developing phonemic awareness. *The Reading Teacher, 48,* 538–542.

Zabrucky, K., & Ratner, H. H. (1989). Effects of reading ability on children's comprehension evaluation and regulation. *Journal of Reading Behavior, 21,* 69–83.

Zintz, M. V. (1980). *The reading process.* Dubuque, IA: McGraw-Hill.

Zutell, J. (1995). The directed spelling thinking activity (DSTA): Providing an effective balance in word study instruction. *The Reading Teacher, 48,* 538–542.

INDEX

Note: Page references in *italics* refer to illustrations; page references followed by *t* refer to tables.

—A—

—B—

—C—

—D—

—E—

—F—

—G—

—H—

—I—

—J—

—K—

—L—

—M—

—N—

—O—

—P—

—Q—

—R—

—S—

—T—

—U—

—V—

—W—

—Y—

—Z—